BITS AND PIECES OF ALASKAN HISTORY

PUBLISHED OVER THE YEARS IN
FROM KETCHIKAN TO BARROW®
A DEPARTMENT IN THE ALASKA SPORTSMAN® AND ALASKA® magazine

VOLUME TWO
•1960~1974•
Includes Index for Volume One and Volume Two

ALASKA NORTHWEST PUBLISHING COMPANY

The Publisher has made a conscientious effort to contact all of the sources individually credited herein as contributors of the photos and other material reprinted from the pages of The ALASKA SPORTSMAN®, ALASKA SPORTSMAN® *and* ALASKA® *magazine.*

Copyright 1982 by Alaska Northwest Publishing Company. All rights reserved. No part of this book may be reproduced or transmitted in any form or by any means, electronic or mechanical, including photocopying, recording, or by any information storage and retrieval system, without written permission of Alaska Northwest Publishing Company.

Library of Congress cataloging in publication data:
Main entry under title:
Bits and pieces of Alaskan history.
   Vol. 2- has imprint: Edmonds, Wash.
   Includes index.
   Contents: v. 1. 1935-1959 — v. 2. 1960-1974
   1. Alaska—History—Miscellanea. I. Alaska
Northwest Publishing Company. II. Alaska sportsman.
III. Alaska magazine.
F904.5.B57   979.8   81-3618
ISBN 0-88240-156-4 (v. 1)   AACR2
ISBN 0-88240-228-5 (v. 2)

Printed in the United States of America

Alaska Northwest Publishing Company
Box 4-EEE, Anchorage, Alaska 99509

FOREWORD

Welcome to the pages of Volume Two of "Bits and Pieces of Alaskan History" out of our From Ketchikan to Barrow® pages in *ALASKA*® magazine (nee *The ALASKA SPORTSMAN*®). Correction... from pages of *ALASKA SPORTSMAN*® ... UNTIL it became *ALASKA*® magazine in October 1969.

Volume One, beginning in 1935 when the little magazine began in Ketchikan, was replete with "early recent" history of Alaska before World War II, before fish traps were legislated out of business, before Statehood... back when white and Native population was roughly evenly divided at around some thirty-plus thousand each... before Prudhoe and when the oil contractors and the unions jacked up Alaska wages and prices clear out of sight... the whole bit from when it was all nice "back of beyond" country right up to the Indian Claims Settlement Act and a mad rush of Federal bureaucracies and State bureaucracy to get bigger and get more. It's all here... the bear stories, the big headlines, the story of modern Alaska on the move. Volume One is the early quiet pioneering years from 1935 through 1959; Volume Two is MODERN ALASKA. The two volumes together comprise a large portion of what essentially is Alaska history of the modern time... when the land began to awaken from the deep forgetting period after World War I to the no-turning-back times of World War II, Prudhoe Bay, and Indian-Eskimo-Aleut Emancipation in the claims settlement.

And... please note, librarians... an index to both volumes is included in Volume Two.

If you like Volume One you can't be without Volume Two. If you like Volume Two and haven't yet found a copy of Volume One... get it. This is Alaska... in "Bits and Pieces"... the most beautiful, wonderful, exciting, unbelievable corner of North America.

And another kudo to veteran and now retired Alaska newspaperman Roy Anderson, who pulled these odds and ends together. Anderson, as owner of the old *Ketchikan Chronicle*, printed the first few issues of *The ALASKA SPORTSMAN*® back in 1935.

"I still don't believe it!" he says. And that's the way we feel about all those wonderful years from then until now... unbelievable... but somehow the essence is preserved in these wonderful pickups out of those old *ALASKA SPORTSMAN*® and *ALASKA*® magazine pages.

Robert A. Henning
Publisher

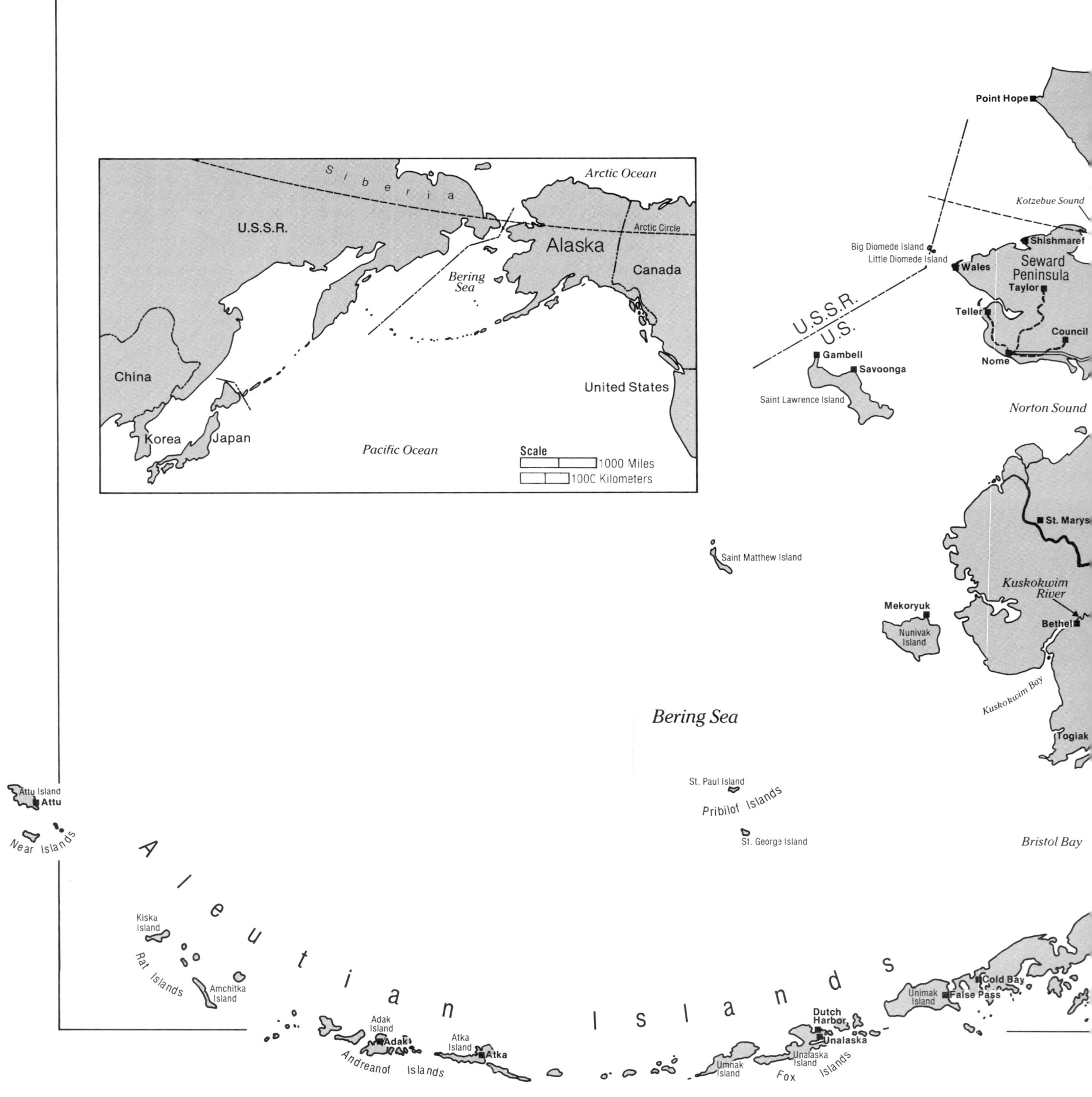

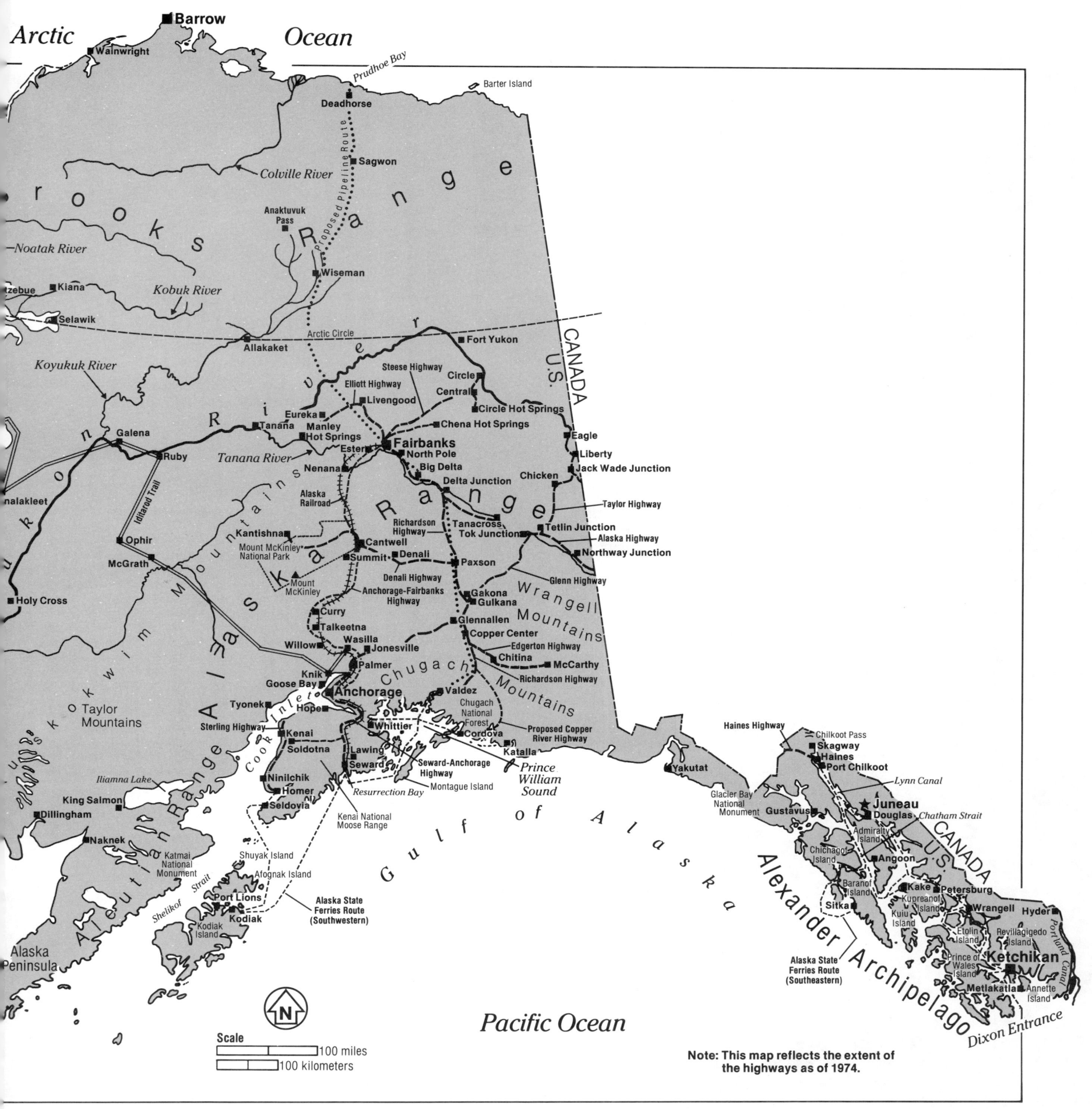

1960

FROM KETCHIKAN TO BARROW

Each month these pages carry items of current or historic interest about Alaska or Alaskans.

Distant Kinfolk from the Other Side
January 1960

● John Angalook of Gambell on St. Lawrence Island, correspondent for the *Fairbanks Daily News-Miner,* describes a recent visit from distant kinfolk from the Siberian side of the Bering Sea:

"The people on Other Side do not clothed like Gambell people. Men wears dyed seal-skin short boots with very fancy laces which the decoration were reindeer hair sewed. And their pants are reindeer skin with long hair. And their parkas are also heavy skin, but where is the hood? I do not know except there is long hair dog roughs right around the neck, nothing on the outside. The women brings dyed reindeer skins, reindeer sinews, deer legs and other stuff and trade them for wooden wares and other stuff.

"During their visit there were many entertainments such like ball games, singing, dancing and all sorts of things held with them. After they left, everything seems to be quiet."

Angalook adds some observations about the life of his own people:

"First snowfall came and an old lady keep watch for her young daughter in case she took fresh snow and ate some, for else she will get fat.

"Papa says, you better mix that reindeer fat while we have snow. But don't you touch that other fat which is for the moon ceremony.

"Mom will have to cut some grass for boot insole and if grass is long she may cut enough for our bed."

And one last observation which may sound like an echo of a universal complaint: "According to the time, obedience of older folks was more important than anything else. All grandparents and parents are honored. But now, who is honoring who? Nobody!"

Happy Hunting Grounds... Sealskins and Seaweed... Beaded Moccasins for the Tourists

January 1960

● Minnie Johnson of Yakutat is seventy-six, but she still spends part of each summer with her husband, Frank W. Johnson, at his hair-seal hunting camp on Icy Bay, seventy-five miles west of their home village. Here, floating ice from Malaspina and Guyot Glaciers creates boating hazards, but also the sort of conditions under which hair-seals thrive.

Seal hunting is part of the Johnsons' livelihood. The state pays a small bounty on hair seals, which prey on salmon; the meat is edible, and the skins are the raw material for Mrs. Johnson's winter occupation. For sixty years and more she has made hair-seal moccasins, lined and trimmed and decorated with fine beadwork in Alaskan Indian designs. She sells her moccasins wholesale to curio shops and retail to tourists. A growing part of her production goes to fill re-orders from people in various parts of the country, and even in Europe, who have bought from her when they visited Yakutat.

The Johnsons take some time from their seal-hunting and skin-drying to gather and cure seaweed, "very tasty and much praised as a health food."

Mrs. Johnson, herself a grandmother, can't resist "mothering" baby seals orphaned by the hunters. The pups are easy to take, as they stay on the ice beside the bodies of their mothers and show no fear of their captors. Soon they become loving, playful pets. The three-week-old pup Mrs. Johnson holds in the photo at left was not yet born when its mother was killed last April. Minne, though she knew its chances were slim, tried her best to save it. When it died, three days after the photo was taken, she asked the hunters to bring her another one.

A product of Minnie Johnson's skillful hands is this Thlingit dance costume with totem symbols intricately beaded on hair-seal skin.

Kunert, a neighbor's dog, comes over often to play with Minnie's pet seal.

Photos by Frank W. Johnson

Frank and Minnie Johnson stretch the hair-seal skins at their Icy Bay camp. This summer harvest is raw material for Minnie's fine beaded moccasins.

1960

Hot Day on the Ice
January 1960

● At Station A, also known as T-3 and Alpha II, the scientific camp on a fifty-square-mile chunk of floating ice somewhere up northwest of Barrow, everything is on ice, but it got hot for a few minutes one day last fall.

The excitement began when Colonel E. D. Feathers, then commander of Station A, emerged from the mess hall and a Polar bear emerged from the wild white yonder. The colonel ran. The bear ran after him and, being much better adapted to foot-racing on ice, gained fast. Tramp, one of the camp's sled-dog pets, attacked the bear and got a vicious blow in the midsection that broke several ribs and knocked him unconscious. Then Tramp's mate, Red, took up the fight. The bear grabbed her and started squeezing.

Among them they made enough commotion to attract Bert Reynolds, weather observer, from his comfortable quarters. He wounded the bear with a Colt .45, just as Red was sure she was gasping her last. The shot brought men from every hut, shooting rifles, pistols and what-not.

When the volley was over the colonel was safe in his quarters, Tramp lay unconscious, Red was in bad shape and the bear was dead. Both dogs got first-class medical attention and both recovered. In fact, two weeks later Red added seven pups to Station A's canine population.

Reindeer Meat
January 1960

● About 110,000 pounds of reindeer meat was shipped from Mekoryuk, on Nunivak Island, to southern markets last fall aboard the SS North Star. Part of the meat was destined for Anchorage, the rest for buyers in the other states from New York to Hawaii.

The Nunivak Island herd, about fourteen thousand, is the increase from two hundred reindeer transplanted there between 1920 and 1928. By 1940 they had multiplied so satisfactorily that seventeen thousand animals were slaughtered and sold. The current kill is about two thousand annually.

The reindeer share the Nunivak Island range with Alaska's only musk-ox herd, also transplanted.

Century's Smallest Pack
January 1960

● Alaska's canned salmon pack for 1959 the first year of statehood, was the smallest since 1900, when the canned salmon industry was still in its infancy.

The 1959 pack was 1,770,795 cases—1,216,098 cases below the pack of the previous year. The 1900 pack was 1,548,-139 cases.

The decline was not unexpected, as 1959 was a low-cycle year for all three salmon species customarily canned. Bad weather in the central area during the peak of the season's run crippled fishing efforts and contributed further to the decline. In the western area (Kodiak and Bristol Bay) the pack was slightly larger than in 1958.

■ A Christmas greeting card from the "Liard and Lady" of Upper Russian Lake shows an artist's sketch of the lodge they hewed out of the wilderness.

'Liard and Lady' Retire from the Wilderness
January 1960

● Mr. and Mrs. Luke Elwell, for twenty years "Liard and Lady" of Upper Russian Lake Lodge on the Kenai, have announced the sale last October of their hunting and fishing lodge to Alaskan Safaris, Incorporated, of which the well-known pilot, guide and outfitter, Ward Gay, is vice-president.

Luke, a big game guide for thirty of his forty years in Alaska, and Mamie, known in publishing circles as Niska Elwell, the outdoor writer, hewed their lodge and guest cabins log by log out of a wilderness even now accessible only by bush plane—and bush planes can't always land—where the only neighbors for many miles are moose and bears. They "stayed in" winters, often seeing no other human faces for weeks at a time, trapping, operating a weather station and "loving every minute of it."

"We wouldn't have considered leaving," said Niska, "but for Luke's doctor's verdict that he must never so much as look at a snow shovel again."

"Even so," added Luke, "we wouldn't have sold to anyone but a real veteran —like Ward Gay."

The Elwells are spending the winter "struggling with the intricacies of civilization" in Washington and Oregon.

"Forty years in the bush have ruined me for this rat-race," said Niska. "I totter around on high heels like a cow moose on glare ice, root into my handbag like a wolverine digging a den." (Truth is, she looks more like a fashion model than a lady trapper.)

Come spring the Elwells plan to take their fly rods and, after visiting Hawaii, investigate rumors that the rainbow trout in New Zealand are even bigger than those on the Kenai. Later they will "settle down somewhere in Alaska."

Angry Moose Rescued ... Enmeshed in a Tow Cable
February 1960

● While some men were out last fall looking for a bull moose to bag, others were out setting one free.

Lt. Donald R. Massey of the Army's Yukon Command, flying a small plane, was coming in for a landing at Ladd Air Force Base late last October when he noted a young bull moose apparently fast to a tree two miles east of North Pole. He reported the animal's plight and position and Harry Pinkham, FWS agent in Fairbanks, Sgt. S. J. Taylor, conservation officer at Ladd, Dr. Jack D. Douglas of the Aero-Medical Laboratory and S 4 Jim Doyle, Yukon Command photographer, went to the rescue in a helicopter piloted by Captain J. R. Luttinger.

They found that the moose had run afoul of an aerial towing cable which had been lost in flight, and was hopelessly entangled. One foreleg was drawn up almost to his snout and his head was snubbed up to a tree. He had been snared for two days at least and he was hungry, thirsty and weary of struggling. Even so, he was still vigorous enough to injure anyone who tried to approach him.

The rescuers fired two charges of succinylcholine chloride from a compressed air gun at the angry bull. They failed to take effect. Believing the drug was freezing before contact, Dr. Douglas warmed a drug-loaded dart against his face, then, while the others distracted the bull's attention, Captain Luttinger crept up as close as he dared and scored a direct hit in the rump. The moose kicked furiously, then sank to the ground and went to sleep. Dr. Douglas gave him another shot as a precaution while Pinkham and Taylor went to work with wire cutters.

When the animal, evidently uninjured and in no need of further aid, began to revive, the rescuers took to the helicopter and watched from safety aloft. The moose got to his feet, tested his legs, then without so much as a grateful glance toward the men who had saved his life, began eating his way toward a herd of some two dozen moose grazing nearby.

Fatal Native Delicacies
January 1960

● Fish-egg cheese brought death last September to Ben Nathan of Hydaburg. Also in September, Aloysius Smith of Hooper Bay died after eating whale flipper in seal oil. Nathan died shortly after being flown to the hospital in Ketchikan; Smith, while en route by air to a hospital in Anchorage.

The cause of death in both cases was botulism, a diagnosis confirmed by Ralph B. Williams, director of State Health Laboratories, and Dr. C. E. Dolman, head of the University of British Columbia bacteriology and immunology department.

Fish-egg cheese, prepared by ripening salmon eggs in a warm place, is a traditional delicacy among Southeastern Alaska Indians. Whale flipper preserved in seal oil has delighted the palates of generations of Eskimos. These and other uncooked foods traditional with native peoples have caused nine agonized deaths in Alaska since 1947, Williams said. Though cooking would alter the cherished flavor of such foods, Williams added, adequate cooking before and after storage would destroy the death-dealing organism.

Open-air Court
April 1960

● Two former Siberians of St. Lawrence Island became citizens of the United States last November in a two-part court session believed to be unique.

Cora Iya of Gambell and her sister, Doris Uglowook of Savoonga, who came from Siberia as young girls about thirty-five years ago, wished to become citizens of their adopted country. Federal Judge Vernon D. Forbes of Fairbanks, temporarily in Nome, made the 175-mile flight to Gambell on November 9 to conduct a naturalization hearing. Bad weather delayed Mrs. Uglowook, who had to come sixty miles from Savoonga by dogsled. Standing under the wing of the plane on the snow-covered airport runway, before parka-clad spectators, Judge Forbes convened court. Mrs. Iya passed her examination and became a citizen.

Next day the weather cleared, the other applicant reached Gambell, Judge Forbes returned and re-convened his open-air court, and Mrs. Uglowook won citizenship.

Another Oil Well
January 1960

● Existence of a fourth producing oil well in the Swanson River unit on Kenai Peninsula, this one known as SRU-32-15, was announced last October by the Standard Oil Company of California. Preliminary tests indicate its maximum flow is 1,300 barrels a day.

About 700 barrels of oil a day were being trucked from Swanson River to Seward for shipment by tanker to West Coast refineries.

Sustained production of 3,000 barrels a day would justify construction of a pipeline from the Swanson River wells to Cook Inlet, according to Board Chairman R. G. Follis.

At left, Nome ski club in 1901.
Above, the same on race day two or three years later.
Below, ski-jumpers on Anvil Mountain course, 1906.

Alaska's First Ski Club Enriched Life in Nome

● The people of early Nome, believed to have run the world's longest sled-dog races, had other outdoor sports to help fill the long winter months while their isolation was complete and gold mining impossible. One of them, skiing, was probably stimulated by the presence of the three young Seppala brothers from Norway—Asle, Sigurd and Leonhard, the latter to become known in both hemispheres as the greatest dog musher of them all. The photos are from his collection.

Nome's first ski club, almost certainly the first in Alaska, was organized in 1901. As in dog racing, there was strenuous competition. The ski area was the slope of Anvil Mountain, which offered a natural ski jump on the course of Dry Creek. On this jump, in 1906, both Asle and Leonhard Seppala accomplished 103-foot jumps. That year, on April 5, Leonhard Seppala won first prize in Nome ski competition—a gold-encrusted medal in the shape of skis and ski poles, which he still has.

Faces in the bottom photo, which Seppala believes was taken in 1903, will have changed, of course, but some of the names he remembers will be familiar to many readers. Of the skiers, 8 is Albert Rapp; 7, George Kaasen; 11, Leonhard Seppala; 4, Mr. Beldo; 6, Asle Seppala; 2, John Kaasen; 5, Sigurd Seppala; 12, Ole Rapp; 9, Peter Burg. Of those not on skis, the man with the prominent watch chain is Lieutenant Pedersen, a Dane, and to his left, with dark mustaches, is Paul Kjeksted. At 11's right is Alfred Lomen, then about fifteen, youngest of the three Lomen Commercial Company brothers.

After twenty-three years on the Seward Peninsula and more than that in the Fairbanks area, Leonhard and Mrs. Seppala retired to Seattle where they celebrated their golden wedding anniversary last October 29. He, at eighty-two, doesn't hear so well, but both are hale, active and as much interested in what happens tomorrow as in what happened sixty years ago.

Nome ski club on race day, about 1903.

Three-Antler Spread on Moose Felled by Kenai Hunter
February 1960

● Fred A. House of Kenai got a good deal when he was moose-hunting last fall on Drift River across Cook Inlet, with Bud Lofstedt, also of Kenai, as pilot. Most hunters are glad to settle for a moose with a pair of antlers. House bagged one with three. The antlers were thick and heavy, and though their spread was nothing to brag about —fifty-one inches—the moose beneath them was. He dressed out at more than eight hundred pounds.

Two years earlier, in the same area, House spotted what he believes was the same bull moose. That year he was sporting a crown—a single antler growing from both sides of his head to meet

Donnis Thompson

without a break in the middle, with tips all the way around it. Bull moose shed their antlers and grow new ones annually, and it is said that freak antlers are "habitual" with some bulls.

House came to Alaska in 1948 to set up and operate a sawmill, got "homestead fever," and now operates his sawmill on his homestead north of Kenai.

Two Polar Bear Hunters Die; Others Barely Escape
May 1960

● Pilot-guide Ward Carroll of Spenard and Stanley Gordon of Anchorage, hunting Polar bears on the ice pack west of Kotzebue last February 19, were killed when their PA18 plane struck a pressure ridge while attempting a landing. The plane was demolished.

George Kitchen of Anchorage, piloting a companion plane, witnessed the crash. He marked the spot before flying back to report the accident, but when planes flew out to recover the bodies the floe had apparently broken loose and drifted across the International Dateline into Siberian waters. Search for the wreckage was finally abandoned.

Eight days later, on February 27, two other planes also hunting Polar bears were forced to land on the ice when they overshot Point Hope and ran low on fuel.

An Air Force helicopter picked up the men from one of the planes, Warren Johnson of Anchorage and Gordon Eastman of Omak, Washington, two days later.

The other hunters, George Baumann of Nevada, Missouri, and Lee Holen of Anchorage, waited for two days but bad weather prevented their rescue. Then they fashioned a raft from the plane's gas tanks and made their way across about thirty miles of disintegrating ice to the shore. They had sleeping bags and some food. They melted snow for water and built igloos for shelter. They hiked down the coast for four days until they met a party of Eskimos with dog teams, who took them to Kivalina.

"We weren't lost and we weren't discouraged," Holen said later, "but we sure were glad to see those Eskimos!"

Undaunted by Flood
February 1960

● When the Little Susitna River got more run-off than it could handle late last August, it kicked up a rampage such as only old-timers of 1931 vintage, or earlier, could remember. About seventy comparative new-comers on the north bank of the river found themselves with no way to get across.

This predicament taxed the ingenuity of all, and especially of homesteaders like Mr. and Mrs. Dewey Welsh (1953-ers), who own nineteen or twenty fine milch cows. They couldn't get their milk to market, and they couldn't well afford to lose it.

Mrs. Welsh solved the problem by scouring out the family washing machine, using it for a churn, and converting the daily output of the herd into butter until the "Little Sue" settled down and her husband could build a bridge across its new channel.

Armories for 48 Native Villages... They'll Double As Community Centers
April 1960

● When the spring construction season begins, work will be resumed on the construction of forty-eight Alaska National Guard armories in Indian and Eskimo villages from Dillingham, on Bristol Bay, around the west and north coasts to Barter Island and down to Fort Yukon. The $1,050,600 project, about eighty per cent completed when the freeze came last fall, is being built by the Manson-Osberg Company under contract to the U.S. Army Engineer District, Alaska.

One of the new armories looks like another—steel-sheeted buildings twenty feet wide, sixty feet long, each equipped with two space heaters and a small power generator.

Most of them, however, present special problems, mainly in transportation. Some are as widely separated as Chicago and Boston or New Orleans; all are far from sources of supply; almost none have cargo-handling facilities. At some, Eskimos loaded supplies from barges to oomiaks and paddled them ashore. At others, dog teams pulled cartloads of supplies from beach to building site. At still others, where native ingenuity could not devise an easier way, materials were carried piece by piece over tide flats and rocky beaches. Women as well as men carried materials on their backs and shoulders.

The local people, who are doing most of the labor under contractors' foremen, will be allowed to use the armories as community centers when they are not needed by the First and Second Scout Battalions. The primary purpose of the buildings is not likely to be forgotten, however, as these people are well aware of their proximity to the Iron Curtain. From Wales, on a clear day, they can see Siberia. On Little Diomede, where the armory is still to be built, they can see through binoculars some of the activities on Russian-owned Big Diomede. From King Island, Teller, Teller Mission, Wales, Shishmaref, the trails of Soviet jets are sometimes visible in the western sky.

U.S. Army Photos

Ice Lotteries Legalized
May 1960

● The Nenana and Chena River ice break-up lotteries and certain other nonprofit gambling activities were made legal in Alaska last March 8 by a law which passed a joint session of the Legislature over the governor's veto.

According to the new law, civic, religious and service organizations and other nonprofit groups may continue such games of chance as they have carried on during the previous five years. The Nenana Ice Classic began in 1917 and involves up to $160,000. The Chena pool, dating from 1904, involves some $15,000.

Opposition to the law, by Governor Egan and the seventeen senators and representatives who voted to sustain his veto, was not based upon a desire to kill these traditional activities, but upon the belief that the law as written could open the door to other gambling.

Gas for Anchorage
January 1960

● The Union Oil Company of California and the Ohio Oil Company, working in partnership, drilled for oil near the town of Kenai and got natural gas instead—enough, company officials estimated, to supply the needs of Anchorage, 165 pipeline miles away, for the next 20 years.

One of the new armories looks like another. Shaktoolik's stands beside a driftwood pyramid built to shelter the remains of a long-dead hunter and his earthly treasures, of which only the metal parts of a rifle, badly rusted, are still distinguishable.

Like youngsters anywhere, those at Kivalina gathered to watch as the new National Guard armory went up, and posed willingly for pictures. In this tiny far-North village, as in most of those that got new armories, a construction job is a rarity.

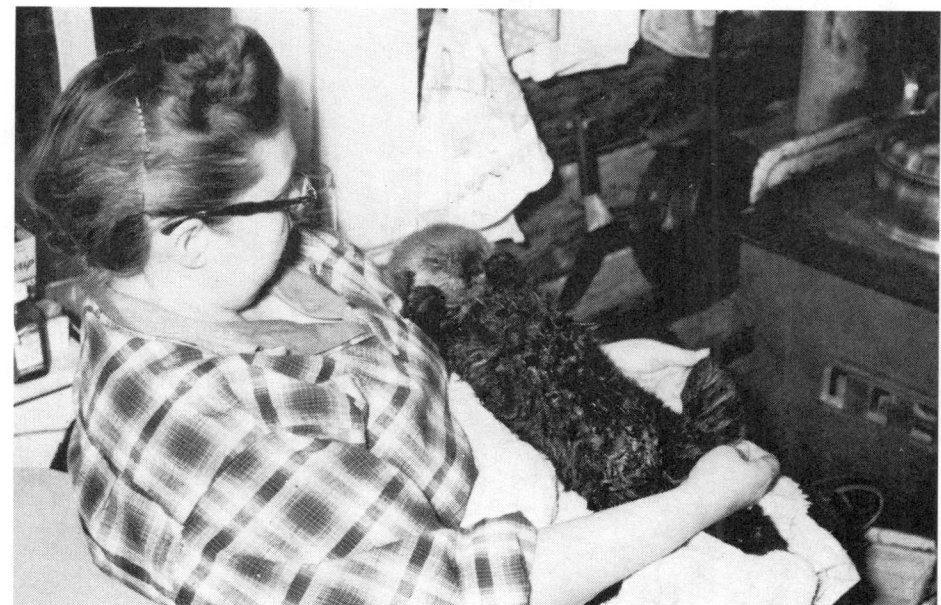

Photos by Robert Glud

Otto, the baby sea otter of Strawberry Point, was happy in Bertha Glud's arms or in the family's collapsible bathtub.

Friendly Sea Otter Pup... Sad Ending to Rescue from Eagle's Grasp
May 1960

● Bob Glud of Strawberry Point, on Hinchinbrook Island, was gathering driftwood on the beach last December when he saw an eagle swoop down to attack something. He drove the eagle away and found that its intended victim was a sea otter pup. There was no sign of other otters, and the tiny creature was obviously weak from hunger and exhaustion.

Rather than leave it to the eagle, Glud took it home and radioed the Fish and Wildlife Service office in nearby Cordova for instructions. The reply was to keep the pup alive if possible until a plane could come for it, and if it died, freeze the body for a specimen. A later message gave information about the habits and food preferences of sea otters.

Bob's wife, Bertha, patiently spoon-fed milk to the five-pound infant until its shrieks of fright and indignation turned to gurgles of content. It snuggled in her arms and went to sleep. Bob set up the canvas bathtub in the middle of their tiny cabin and filled it with cold sea water, for Otto, as they named the baby otter, was a creature of the sea. Then, although one of the winter's worst storms was raging, he went gallantly out to the beach and dug clams and cockles for his small guest.

Otto quickly regained his strength and for five days splashed happily in the tub, scooted around the cabin, faced flashbulbs without much flinching as the Gluds and their neighbors aimed cameras, and allowed himself to be cuddled. In fact, one night he refused to go to sleep—or let anyone else—until Bertha took him into her bed.

Then, suddenly, Otto died, and his frozen remains were sent to Cordova on the next mail plane. If FWS biologists can discover the cause of his death, after his apparent recovery, Otto may yet make a valuable contribution to the still-scant knowledge about his once-vanishing species.

As it is, he convinced Strawberry Pointers that sea otters would be as desirable for pets as for furs. Everyone loved Otto—everyone except the Gluds' two dogs, who found themselves literally out in the cold while he was there.

Migrant Steelhead
June 1960

● Steelhead trout, the sea-going rainbows, apparently go a lot farther to sea than anyone suspected. One of them, released from the Oregon Game Commission's Alsea hatchery in April, 1958, came back last March wearing a University of Washington Fisheries Research Institute tag placed on it about seventy-five miles southwest of Kodiak Island in September, 1958.

The tag proved that, though steelheads were thought to stay close to the coast from Washington to the northern part of the Alaskan panhandle, this one had traveled at least three thousand miles in two years of fattening at sea.

It is now indicated that steelheads mingle with Pacific salmon on the high seas, and possibly with Japanese and Russian salmon in the areas where vessels of these nations are fishing.

The Fisheries Research Institute will have two tagging vessels working in the Kodiak and Aleutian Island areas from April to September, according to Director William Royce.

Curry – Town That Was
May 1960

● Curry, at Mile 248.5 on the Alaska Railroad, has become a town that was.

In earlier years, when it was a two-day trip by rail from Seward to Fairbanks, trains stopped overnight at Curry and passengers dined, slept and breakfasted in the big railroad-operated Curry Hotel. It had accommodations for a hundred and fifty, meals were sumptuous, and the murmur of the nearby Susitna River lulled guests to sleep. There was little else for them to do.

Modern locomotives speeded up the rail trip, and for several years there were few guests at the big hotel. Then in 1955 it burned, with the loss of one life, and all the ninety or so inhabitants who were not involved with railroad or Alaska Communications System operations moved away. The post office, housed in a corner of the hotel (see photo), was not reactivated.

Meanwhile Talkeetna, Mile 226.7, has

Couch Alaska Archives

become increasingly active, what with homesteaders moving into the area.

Last December 26, the last of Curry was moved down the line to Talkeetna.

Distinguished Juneauite – She's 107
January 1960

● Mrs. Mary Johnson of Juneau has several distinctions. At the age of 107 years she is the oldest person in Juneau, older than the town itself; she is the oldest social security beneficiary and possibly the oldest resident in Alaska; she is one of 28 social security beneficiaries older than 103 years in the entire nation.

Mrs. Johnson was born in Auke Village on August 10, 1852, long before the town of Juneau was established nearby. At that time, of course, Alaska was Russian-owned and Sitka was its capital. She lived with her son, Charles, until he entered Mt. Edgecumbe Hospital a year ago. Now she and her cat, Snowball, live alone, though neighbors come in occasionally and help her.

She worked in salmon canneries for years, then in a Juneau market until she retired at the age of one hundred.

1960

Cue Bifelt (above) and Wilbur Sampson (right) swept first and second places in the major 1960 sled-dog races.

All photos from Couch Alaska Archives

The Championship Races... Working Dogs and Mushers Sweep the Field

June 1960

● Working dogs and working mushers swept the field in 1960 sled-dog racing last February and March, with Indian or Eskimo contenders taking first, second and third in both the All-Alaska and North American Championships, and taking some thousands of dollars in prize money home to their small villages. That has happened before, but never before have two mushers taken the same honors in both major races.

Cue Bifelt, Huslia Indian, ran the seventy-five-mile Alaska Championship in Anchorage in a total elapsed time of 5 hours, 40 minutes, 29 seconds, then three weeks later in Fairbanks ran the seventy-mile North American in 307 minutes flat. Bifelt, forty-three and a former tuberculosis patient, had never entered a major race before.

Wilbur Sampson, Noorvik Eskimo, finished second in Anchorage, second in Fairbanks, and after 145 miles of racing his total elapsed time was just thirty-seven seconds more than Bifelt's. Sampson, only twenty-four, won the North American Championship five years ago. His winnings in Anchorage were $1,350; in Fairbanks, $1,500. Bifelt won $1,700 and $1,900.

Leo Kriska, Allakaket Indian, took third and $1,400 in Anchorage, but in Fairbanks fell to sixth in total time and won $600.

In Anchorage, 1959 Alaska Champion Jimmy Malemute from Galena took fourth place, but he finished out of the money in Fairbanks.

Warner Vent, another "Huslia Hustler," who did not race in Anchorage, took third place and $1,400 in Fairbanks, and David David, another Allakaket Indian, took fourth for $700.

Dr. Roland Lombard from Weyland, Massachusetts, popular 1959 North American Champion, fell to ninth place in Anchorage and finished out of the money in Fairbanks. Two other outsiders, New England champion Keith Bryar from Laconia, New Hampshire, and Dr. Charles Belford from Deerfield, Massachusetts, were among the twenty-nine North American contenders. Neither placed, but Bryar later won the Nenana championship.

Women's Races: The North American Championship...
June 1960

● North American Women's Champion of 1960 is Libby Wescott, who ran the three-heat, thirty-four-mile race in 130 minutes and 5 seconds—4 minutes and 32 seconds ahead of Mrs. MacInnes. Mrs. Wescott, who was finishing her year as first woman president of the Alaska Dog Mushers' Association, and her husband, Bob, operate Wescotts' Alaska Husky Kennels, where many winning-team dogs have been bred.

Mrs. Jean Bryar, well-known mushing champion from Laconia, New Hampshire, was a close third. Effie Kokrine of Fairbanks, Women's Champion of 1952, '53 and '54, took fourth. Only three-time winner to date, the "mushing grandmother" said this was her last year of racing.

...and the All-Alaska
June 1960

● Petite Kit MacInnes, wife and mother of the dog-mushing MacInneses of Anchorage, sped to the All-Alaska Women's Championship last February 14, driving eleven dogs around the twelve-mile course in 51 minutes and 41 seconds, with defending champion Natalie Norris coming in six minutes and four seconds behind her.

That same day Ray Redington of Flat Horn Lake won the Anchorage Junior Mushers' three-dog championship, and Kit MacInnes's daughter Ann came in only fifteen seconds behind him for next-to-top place.

Also that same day, the distaff champion's small son Scotty won first place in the Anchorage Junior one-dog race.

Mrs. MacInnes then entered the All-Alaska Championship races a week later, the only woman who did, and finished thirteenth from the top, fourteenth from the bottom. It was her second time to enter the "big" race.

The following week she was in Fairbanks, taking second place in the Women's North American Championship.

Three-Team Finish for the Junior Mushers

June 1960

● Junior mushers also staged a rare performance during the 1960 racing season—a three-team finish. The race was the final heat of the three-day, twenty-five-mile North American Junior Dog Mushers' five-dog championship in late February, when Alfred Mayo and Janice Lundgren of Fairbanks and Bruce Pettit of Anchorage finished in that order. Pettit had taken second in the Anchorage five-dog junior race. Young Mayo had to drop one dog after the second heat. Hence the four-dog hitch in the photo (left).

Bob Stoecker, fifteen, driving huskies from the Wescott Kennels, won the five-dog championship with a total elapsed time of 108 minutes and 54 seconds. He is president of the Junior Mushers.

Anchorage winner Wade Charles from Eagle River took second place in this race, in 110 minutes and 40 seconds.

Cranberry Lode for Cleary Hill Miner
April 1960

● Aminotriazole, which inadvertently brought economic distress to commercial cranberry growers last fall, just as inadvertently brought good fortune to an old-time gold-miner near Fairbanks.

Fred Wackowitz, who mines on Cleary Hill some thirty miles north of Fairbanks, found himself facing the long, cold winter with a slender grubstake. Gold-mining doesn't pay so well any more, what with the price of gold pegged to the value of yesteryear's dollar, and Wackowitz, at seventy-seven, can't work hard enough now to wrest a living from his long-worked claim.

He looked at the wilderness surrounding his lone cabin and saw one other possible source of income—wild lingenberries, or lowbush cranberries. They grow profusely in his area, and keep well without processing. He picked lingenberries, jar after jar of them, and before the first snowfall he had a hundred cases of lingenberries ready for sale. He took them to town. The kindly manager of a local supermarket took the lot of them, doubting whether they would sell in competition to national brands, but wanting to help the old man.

Then came the aminotriazole scare. Commercial cranberries were taken off most grocers' shelves, and Fred Wackowitz' unsprayed lowbush cranberries had the Fairbanks market almost to themselves.

Oil! Biggest Well Yet
June 1960

● A new producing oil well described as the biggest yet in Alaska was tested briefly last March 14 and flowed at a rate of 1,870 barrels a day, according to a joint announcement by the Standard Oil Company of California, Western Operations, and Richfield Oil.

The wildcat well, known as Soldatna Creek Unit 41-4, is several miles south of the Swanson River oil field on the Kenai Peninsula. It was said to produce 260 cubic feet of gas per barrel of 35-degree gravity oil.

"This new well confirms the commercial oil producing promise of Alaska," said Standard's Western Operations president, H. G. Vesper, "but we must continue drilling activities to confirm the extent of the field."

$4 Million Oil Leases
April 1960

● The State of Alaska received a little more than four million dollars from its first competitive lease sale of offshore oil lands last December 10. Largest single bid was $1,001,123 from the Union Oil Company of California jointly with the Ohio Oil Company, for a parcel of 2,026 acres.

29 Die on Highways
May 1960

● Twenty-nine persons were killed on Alaska's highways during 1959. Football, coincidentally, caused the same number of deaths in the older states.

Escapeproof 'Jail' for Kenai Burglar
June 1960

● The transition from Territorial to State law-enforcement and judicial systems in Alaska caused a dilemma in Kenai last February when Jerry Hobart, Pacific Northern Airlines employee, apprehended two men in the act of burglarizing his office at two o'clock one morning. He captured them single-handed, but keeping them wasn't so easy. Kenai has no marshal and the state patrolman, who must cover all the western side of the Kenai Peninsula, was in Anchorage. Hobart called on Stan Thompson, last incumbent under the U.S. Commissioner system, for help. While he was calling, one of the prisoners broke away and fled in the cold and darkness.

Donnis Thompson

The escape of half the prisoners didn't solve half the detention problem. Kenai's jail since time immemorial was closed last year on the theory that "whatever problems arose could be handled through Anchorage," at least four hours away by road. Wildwood, the nearby military establishment, could not handle civilians. It looked as if Citizen Hobart and Commissioner Thompson were in for guard duty.

Then Thompson remembered the cribbed fifteen-foot well hole under his office (see photo). They removed the floorboards over the well, gave the prisoner a chair and sent him down to share the six-by-six-foot space at the bottom with the electric pump. Then they nailed the floorboards down and went back to bed.

At seven-thirty they invited the prisoner up and served him coffee. Eventually the state patrolman arrived to take him into custody, and the other burglar was caught in a roadblock.

The gentleman shown at the bottom of the well, incidentally, is not the prisoner. This one, who prefers not to be identified, went down to oblige the photographer and lend perspective.

The 'Iron Dog'... A Threat to Alaska's Historic Dog Team
June 1960

● While sled-dogs were holding the sport spotlight in Fairbanks last March, three "iron dogs" were making a demonstration trek that may push flesh-and-blood dogs even further into the background as freighters in the bush.

The "iron dogs," known commercially as Snow-Travelers, left Bethel on the lower Kuskokwim March 4, traveled fifteen hundred miles up the frozen Kuskokwim, Yukon and Tanana Rivers and, with one-day stopovers at Galena and Manley Hot Springs, reached Fairbanks March 24. They averaged seventy miles a day, at least twice the speed of a dog-team on such a journey, and made twenty miles to the gallon of gasoline.

The drivers were (left to right in the photo) Erling Falk and Edgar Hetten of Roseau, Minnesota, and Mrs. Bessie Billberg and her husband, Rudy, of Fairbanks. Falk and Hetten are connected with Polaris Industries, Incorporated, manufacturers of the sled. The Billbergs, he a bush pilot, lived in Bethel and Lake Minchumina before homesteading near Fairbanks. She was full-time cook and part-time driver.

The Snow-Traveler is a ski-equipped sled powered by a one-cylinder, air-cooled Kohler engine driving endless cleated track. Two of the three used have nine and one-half horsepower engines and carried eight hundred pounds apiece. The third, with seven horsepower, served as trail-breaker and trail scout (there were no roads to follow). The only bad going encountered was on the portage between the Kuskokwim and the Yukon, where gales had blown the frozen ground free of snow. The temperature never got up to zero but the sledders camped out except when they were lucky enough to reach a settlement at the end of a day's trek.

Couch Alaska Archives

Whaling Fleet Idled by Market Slump
July 1960

● The whaling plant of British Columbia Packers, Ltd., on Vancouver Island, only still-active whaling operation north of San Francisco, will remain closed this summer and its fleet will stay in port. The sixty men of the fleet and ninety who worked in the plant have found other jobs or are unemployed.

The reason is the slump in the world market for whale oil and meal. Eight or nine years ago, according to President J. M. Buchanan of B. C. Packers, whale oil sold for 17 cents a pound and meal for $2.10 a unit. The current price is eight cents for oil, $1.20 for meal.

Mystery Solved... Why Deer Thrive
July 1960

● Writes Old-timer Ed Sande of Ketchikan, "After nearly forty years in Alaska I have at last discovered the reason for our small population of human beings and our long population of deer. Recently our neighbor's dog (who had pups) ran out and bit a lady who was walking by on the highway. The police were called and, after duly considering the matter, decided they could do nothing.

"A few days later the same dog chased a deer down the road. Again the proper authorities were called, and promptly shot the dog."

Nest of Plover Eggs – Rare Wildlife Picture
July 1960

● A semipalmated plover (Charadrius semipalmatus to the ornithologist), nesting on a gravel bar along the Tanana River, would have saved a lot of bother if she'd been discretely quiet when Jim Couch and his wife came along, and they'd have missed a rare wildlife picture.

The bird's broken-wing act and other tactics intended to divert Jim and Ione's attention from her nest diverted them instead from their grayling fishing on nearby Shaw Creek. After two hours of heel-to-toe inspection of a plot of gravel some fifty feet in diameter, they found the bird's newly laid black-and-brown-mottled gray eggs. The plover usually has a four-egg clutch. This one's was three.

One week later, mama plover was still incubating her eggs. Two more weeks later the nest, a shallow depression in the gravel, lined more or less with tiny bits of driftwood, was empty. Not even a scrap of shell remained to indicate whether the fledglings had hatched and flown or had fallen victim to some predator.

July 1960

Subscription and newsstand prices for Alaska Sportsman going up!

Dear Reader:

For us this is like pulling teeth. We have tried to fight off the inevitable, but like a lot of other businesses, rising costs give us little choice.

Paper and labor have gone up several times in recent years and so have postal rates. For us, it is simply a choice of getting more income, or sacrificing quality. The latter is something we refuse to do. We're proud of Alaska Sportsman. Our paper and engraving work is better than most. To cut corners in these items would be neither fair to the product nor to you.

So—"up she goes"—to 50c a copy for the newsstands, and to $5 a year for basic subscription price.

Again, we hate to be forced to do this, but we do want to keep on putting out a magazine of which we can be proud. We can only hope that you will (1) stay with us, and (2) that we can soon bring you an even bigger and better magazine to help take the sting out of this necessary increase.

Sincerely,

Robert A. Henning
Editor & Publisher

Order Now at Current Prices and Save!
Until September 1, 1960 . . .
  First year, **$3.50**   Each additional year **$3**

After September 1, 1960 . . .
  1 year **$5**   2 years **$9**   3 years **$12**   5 years **$20**

Whisky Jack... An Awkward but Brazen Bird
July 1960

● The Canada jay has the Latin name of Perisoreus canadensis, plus various descriptive nicknames. Anyone who has spent much time in Alaska's Interior has seen this brazen bird demonstrating the aptness of one nickname, camp robber. He's also called whisky jack because of his alleged eagerness for scraps of food soaked in whisky and his antics after he's had a few.

The bird in this photo, taken beside the Chatanika River north of Fairbanks, is busily camp-robbing but ignores the newspapers beverage ads beside him.

Cold sober, the Canada jay has an awkward gait and confidential approach that might suggest he's had too many, but his calculating eye is on any food within reach and he'll get it. His audacity and unstudied clownishness add amusement value to the wilderness scene.

1960

Award for Courage
October 1960

RAYMOND H. TREMBLAY, USFWS game management agent at McGrath, received the Department of the Interior's Valor Award last April for an act of courage and daring performed almost a year earlier.

Tremblay knew that a prospector on the headwaters of Big River had planned to come downstream by raft shortly after the breakup. Several weeks after the breakup the prospector had not appeared, so Tremblay took off in his float plane to investigate. Flying low, he saw the prospector waving frantically from a sand bar in the middle of Big River, shortly above its confluence with the Kuskokwim.

After ten passes over the sand bar, Tremblay managed to put his plane down and take the prospector aboard. To take off, he had to keep the plane on the step around three bends of the meandering river before it could gather speed to break the suction of the floats and climb above the trees on the bank.

According to the citation accompanying the award, "By foresight, follow-up and skillful execution without regard for his own personal safety, Mr. Tremblay undoubtedly saved a life."

Bear vs. Bear
August 1960

● Fred Bear of the Bear Archery Company in Grayling, Michigan, took his bow and arrows to Kodiak Island last May looking for brown bears. He found some, but they weren't big enough, so he went on to the Alaska Peninsula with guides Ed Bilderback and Harley King of Cordova.

On the beach in Wide Bay, Bear saw a bear that suited him. He shot an arrow from fifty feet, striking a vital spot. Bear headed for Bear and his companions. Bear shot again from twenty-five feet, but bear kept coming and almost got there before he veered off, went into the brush a few hundred feet, and died.

Bear's bear squared nine feet ten inches and his green skull measured 27¾ inches—any good trophy for any hunter, a triumph for an archer, but no great surprise to Fred Bear. His company is said to make more than half the bows and arrows produced, and he has used some of them to take more than eighty big game trophies to date.

Two Jurists Honored
July 1960

● Two names, Mount Wickersham and Mount Dimond, will take their places on the map of Alaska in honor of two prominent Alaskan statesmen and jurists, the Board of Geographic Names has announced.

Mount Wickersham, about 7,000 feet high, on the west edge of Matanuska Glacier, will honor James Wickersham, attorney, district judge and long-time delegate to the United States Congress, who died in 1939.

Mount Dimond, also about 7,000 feet, south of the Tsina River, will honor Anthony Dimond, Territorial senator, delegate to Congress and district judge. He died in 1953.

Up the Yukon From Whitehorse ... a New Adventure
September 1960

FOR the first time since 1955, visitors to Whitehorse, Yukon Territory, can embark on a comfortable passenger vessel for a trip on the Yukon River. And, for the first time ever, their trip will take them upstream rather than down. They pass over the formerly treacherous Whitehorse and Squaw Rapids, through Miles Canyon where Jack London made a stake as a river pilot and many an inexperienced Klondiker lost his life during gold-rush days, and along some of the most beautiful parts of the historic river.

A big power dam, recently completed, has backed up the Yukon, quieted the seething rapids of former years, and made the present cruise possible. Vehicle for this three-hour river cruise is the brand new and completely modern steel river vessel *Schwatka*, appropriately named for Lieut. Frederick Schwatka, U.S. Army, who made a military reconnaissance of the river by rafting down it from source to mouth in 1883.

Built early this year at Vancouver, B.C., the forty-eight-foot *Schwatka* has a flat bottom with tunnel stern and is powered by a pair of ninety-horsepower diesel engines which drive her at better than twelve miles an hour. Her equipment includes hydraulic steering gear, electric light plant, heating plant, public address system, complete plumbing and a galley. She is licensed to carry thirty-eight passengers.

It's a thousand miles from Vancouver to Whitehorse, and the *Schwatka* made most of it on deck of the freighter *Clifford J. Rogers*. Too big to go through the tunnels of the White Pass Railroad between Skagway and Whitehorse, she was lowered into the water for what may be the only salt water voyage of her career, a dozen miles down Lynn Canal to Haines and Port Chilkoot. There she was lifted onto a large truck and carried over the Haines Cutoff and the Alaska Highway to her home port.

Owner of the *Schwatka*, now the only commercial vessel on the Yukon south of Dawson, is John D. Scott, a mining engineer who first came to the North in 1916 and to Whitehorse in 1922. Her skipper is Captain George Ross, another long-time resident of Yukon Territory. He spent many seasons on the river steamboats of years past. Captain Ross is assisted by two deckhands and a hostess during the cruise season—about one hundred days, from June into September. The enterprise is operated under the name Yukon River Industries, Ltd., and provides another "must" for Northland visitors.

Bill Horback

The "Schwatka" passes easily through Miles Canyon, where some gold-seekers lost their lives. Dangerous rapids here are submerged by backwaters of a new power dam.

Memorial to a Flyer... The Humble Start of Elmendorf Air Base
October 1960

A MEMORIAL to the late Captain Hugh M. Elmendorf now stands one block from the main gate to the Air Force base near Anchorage which bears his name. The monument was unveiled June 8 at a ceremony marking the base's twentieth anniversary, and Captain Elmendorf's only daughter, Mrs. Ray Johnston, was a guest of honor.

Captain Elmendorf, a pioneer military pilot, was killed January 13, 1933, at Wright Field in Dayton, Ohio, while flight-testing a new type of pursuit plane.

On June 8, 1940, a crew of twenty-five Anchorage workmen began construction of Elmendorf AFB. They were equipped with one tractor, a carryall, a cement mixer and four dump trucks. Nineteen days later the initial Alaska defense force arrived. It consisted of 30 officers and 744 enlisted men, who pitched tents for living quarters and laid pipe to Ship Creek for water.

Today Elmendorf AFB, one of the largest in the United States, has more than seven thousand military personnel and fifteen hundred permanent civilian employees. Some twenty-eight hundred passengers and half a million pounds of cargo are landed on its two runways in an average month.

Banks Forge a Chain
July 1960

● Six pioneer banking institutions in Alaska joined forces and began operation last April 1 as the National Bank of Alaska, with main offices in Anchorage. The merging banks are, National Bank of Alaska, Anchorage; Miners and Merchants, Ketchikan; First Bank of Sitka, and the Banks of Wrangell, Kodiak and Homer.

Death of a Dog-musher
July 1960

● Hortense Parker Landru, better known as Jackie, accomplished dog-musher and writer, died in Fairbanks March 14 after a long illness. Fairbanks-born, daughter of Mr. and Mrs. Fred B. Parker who came north during the Klondike gold rush and later operated a placer mine thirty miles north of Fairbanks, she won the North American Women's Championship sled-dog races when she was fourteen. She continued racing until her health failed, then turned to writing about dog-mushing. H. C. "Buck" Landru was her husband and collaborator. She is also survived by a son, Fred.

40-Mile Hike, Age 113
July 1960

● Peter Bobby Sr., Stony Pass Eskimo, believes himself to be 113 years old, but he can still walk when he wants to get somewhere.

Last March he wanted to get to Anchorage for some dental work, so he walked the forty miles down to Sparrevohn and hitched a ride on an Air Force cargo plane bound from Bethel to Anchorage.

Military personnel in Sparrevohn confirmed the fact that Bobby walked the forty miles, using two canes, but declared he "doesn't look a day over 112." The troublesome teeth were those nature gave him.

Haines House
* * *
Historic Mission Closes Its Doors

October 1960

HAINES House, historic Presbyterian mission at Haines, closed its doors and ceased operation on July 1. It was one of the oldest missions in Alaska. Staff members have been assigned to other places but no decision has been announced as to the disposition of the mission buildings.

Haines Mission, as it was long known, resulted from a canoe trip by Dr. S. Hall Young, Presbyterian missionary, and John Muir, the famed naturalist, to Lynn Canal in 1879. Dr. Young asked the Chilkat Indians, who lived at several villages near the present town of Haines, to pick a site for a school and a new Christian town. They selected a spot on Portage Bay on the west side of Lynn Canal.

Mrs. George Dickinson, wife of a trader, opened a school the following year, and the mission became fully established in July, 1881, with the arrival of Dr. Sheldon Jackson and the Rev. and Mrs. Eugene S. Willard and their small daughter. A dwelling for the Willards was quickly erected, while a small building purchased from the trading company served as a schoolhouse. The site was named Haines for Mrs. F.E.H. Haines, secretary of the Women's Executive Committee for Home Missions. The post office of Haines was established July 24, 1882.

A boarding house for children was started in connection with the school in 1883 and was gradually enlarged during the following decade. Before long a town began to grow up around the mission and the growth was accelerated first by the Klondike gold rush, then by the discovery of gold on tributaries to the nearby Chilkat River.

The original mission buildings burned in 1896. One of the present three-story structures was erected the following year and served as a boarding school until 1907, then as a hospital and sanitarium and as a nurses' training school. A new manse and a church were built in 1904. About the same time, when the Army decided to build Fort William H. Seward at Haines, a hundred acres of the mission grounds were donated for that purpose.

Haines House returned to its original status as a boarding home for children in 1921 and a second three-story building was put up in 1927. Since then from twenty-five to forty-seven children, most of them orphans or from broken homes, have been housed and cared for at the mission while they attended government or public schools in Haines.

The Presbyterian Board of National Missions has announced that it will continue to provide child care in Alaska, utilizing other facilities it owns or operates at various places in the state.

A sketch of the original Haines Mission buildings which appeared in "Frank Leslie's Illustrated Newspaper" two years after the school was founded in 1880.

Unexpected Oil Riches Add to State Surplus
October 1960

ALASKA's general fund balance as of June 30 was $15,152,137.98, a gain of $9,814,654.46 during the first fiscal year of statehood and more than $6 million above the estimate made when the year's budget was planned last fall.

The unexpected gain, according to Revenue Commissioner Peter Gatz, is "for the most part the result of increased revenue over budget estimates in oil and mineral leases, taxes and licenses, and interest income."

It is, said Governor William A. Egan, "vivid evidence that Alaska's economy is a growing economy which warrants looking to the future with optimism."

118 Rural Schools
November 1960

THE state of Alaska is operating 118 schools outside of incorporated areas this year, including eight on military bases. Total enrollment in the 110 schools not on military bases was estimated at 6,500 at the beginning of the present school year. They range in size from the Gildersleeve school near Ketchikan with nine pupils to the Chugiak school near Anchorage with an enrollment of 576. Other large schools supported entirely by state funds include Homer with 403 pupils; Wasilla, 400; Bethel, 357; Metlakatla, 286; Fort Yukon, 229; Dillingham, 208, and Anchor Point, 185. New school buildings are being occupied this year for the first time at Soldotna, Delta Junction, Mentasta, Nelson Lagoon and Bethel.

A Tenderfoot
October 1960

A MEMBER of a Bureau of Land Management fire crew, combating a blaze on the Russian River last May, came out with a foot injury that had nothing to do with the fire.

Douglas Olson of Anchorage and a friend, Richard Smith, were alone in camp. Olson was dressing, Smith was still asleep, when a yearling black bear came to call. Olson threw scraps of food to the visitor and, not wanting Smith to miss such an interesting experience, woke him with a warning to be quiet lest he frighten the animal. Smith took one look and remembered he had business elsewhere.

The bear finished the scraps, looked around for more, found none, so began to chew on Olson's bare foot. Olson's reaction, sudden and loud, sent the bear scurrying off to return no more and brought Smith back to the rescue. Olson was taken to Kenai for medical treatment.

Fierce Gales, Mountainous Seas... Boats Lost... Three Sailors Missing
November 1960

FALL gales, beginning to sweep across the Gulf of Alaska and into the bays and narrow channels along the coast before summer had officially ended, took a heavy toll of Alaska shipping during the early days of September.

The 85-foot towboat *Amelie*, owned by Parker Tug and Barge Co. of Juneau and bound from Juneau for Whittier with a barge of lumber, battled for hours against mountainous seas and 90-mile winds off Yakutat Bay. The tow line eventually parted and the barge drifted ashore, where it was quickly holed by the boulders and became a total loss. It was hoped that the lumber, to be used in rebuilding the Columbia Lumber Co. sawmill in Whittier, could be salvaged. The *Amelie* and her battered crew of five finally found shelter in Yakutat Bay.

The same gale caught the fish packer *Theo E.* heavily loaded with 13,000 salmon and bound from Yakutat for Excursion Inlet. The vessel, owned by Norman Holm of Bellingham, Wash., began to take water faster than her pumps could get rid of it and was beginning to sink when her skipper beached her in the breakers a few miles south of Dry Bay. The three men aboard escaped but the *Theo E.* was done for.

Out to the west, north of Kodiak Island, the seiner *Thrasher*, owned by Emil Gunderson of Sand Point, was in Shelikof Strait in tow of the *Jim B.* when a storm struck. Winds reached more than 70 miles an hour and the *Thrasher* soon headed for the bottom. Gunderson, his wife Marina, and crew member Alex Olsen jumped into the waves and were picked up by the *Jim B.*

South of Juneau, in Stephens Passage, Sam Cesar was homeward bound for Juneau in his fishing boat, the *It*, running before heavy seas. When a tiller line parted, the vessel broached, rolled over and sank. Cesar swam clear and was quickly picked up by a Coast Guard patrol boat which happened by on its way to the aid of another fishing vessel.

Near the same spot, the 55-foot steel dredge-tender *Tom*, with a barge in tow, was apparently overwhelmed by the seas during a black, wind-torn night. The following morning the 120-foot barge was discovered in the channel with the tow cable leading directly to the bottom. It was assumed, as salvage operations began, that the *Tom* was still on the other end of the cable. No trace was found of the crew of three. The *Tom*, built last year at a cost of $100,000, was owned by Puget Sound Dredge Company of Seattle.

Perils of the Hunt... Walrus Attacks Boat
September 1960

THE perils of walrus hunting, as reported in the *Diomede Island Midnight Sun*, published by island school children: "Frank Elasanga and Walter Menadelook plugged two holes in Frank's skin boat with their feet on the way home from hunting. A crippled bull walrus had run his two tusks through the boat from underneath it. He was mad!"

1960

New Life for Skagway's Golden North Hotel

September 1960

THE conspicuous dome of Skagway's Golden North Hotel now glitters with three coats of fresh gilt paint. The historic hotel, vacant off and on since the death in 1936 of its original owner's widow, has been restored, redecorated, refurnished, and re-opened under new ownership last June 1.

Mr. and Mrs. Hans Soldin, the new owners, are not newcomers. They have grandchildren who are the third Alaskan-born generation. Mrs. Soldin's parents, David and Catherine Hukill, came to Skagway in January, 1899. Mrs. Hukill and three of her six children still live there.

The story of the hotel began in 1898, when George R. Dedman reached Skagway and formed a partnership with Ed Foreman. They built the Golden North Hotel on Fourth Avenue. In ten years Skagway's business center had shifted to the lower end of Broadway. The partners bought the Sylvester Building, a large two-story store, and Dedman and Al Parker (now of Gustavus), with wooden rollers, a horse and a capstan winch, moved the building one block and turned it around to face Broadway. This building then succeeded the original Golden North Hotel. Later the third story and conspicuous dome were added. Still later, Dedman bought out Foreman's interest.

George Dedman, better known outside of Skagway as owner of Dedman's Photo Service, died in 1925. Mrs. Dedman and their son, Henry, operated the hotel until her death in 1936. Henry Dedman died in 1954, but his wife and their daughter, Barbara Kalen, still operate the Photo Service.

In the "new" Golden North, only the mattresses are "modern." Antique furniture, early-day photographs (many of them on loan from the famed Pullen House) and turn-of-the-century interior decorating style have been used, with the accent on gold throughout.

The Soldins held open house June 3 and various rooms on the second floor were dedicated to pre-1900 pioneers whose descendants still live and work in Skagway. Pioneers so honored were Mr. and Mrs. George R. Dedman, "Ma" Rapuzzi, Ferdinand De Gruyter, Herman D. Kirmse, Mr. and Mrs. H. D. Clark, Mr. and Mrs. Peter N. Crepeau, Mr. and Mrs. Winfield Scott Sparks, Mr. and Mrs. E. J. Liddicoat, Peter Lunde, Alfred McCann, George Dillon, Mr. and Mrs. John E. Feero and "Ma" Pullen.

Pre-1900 Skagway pioneers who left no heirs will be honored in a later ceremony. They include Frank Fowler, Joseph J. Ward and Martin Itjen.

Photos from Dedman's Photo Service

Above: George and Clara Dedman in marigolds beside the Golden North in 1923. She, famed for her green thumb, gardened outside and in. Left: Golden North's "new look."

Members of Skagway's "old families" were photographed June 3 in hotel rooms dedicated to their forebears. Among them:

Right: Francis Liddicoat Richter, longest-term resident, arrived with her parents, Mr. and Mrs. E. J. Liddicoat, February 12, 1898. She owns and operates Richters Jewelry Store.

Lower right: Barbara Dedman Kalen, granddaughter of Golden North's co-founder, and her daughter, Barbie.

Below: Mr. and Mrs. George Rapuzzi, he the son of "Ma" Rapuzzi who ran the Washington Fruit Store.

Left below: Artist Vic Sparks' parents were Mr. and Mrs. Winfield Scott Sparks; his wife, Abbie, is daughter of Mr. and Mrs. Peter N. Crepeau. Fathers of both arrived in 1897, Crepeau went to Dawson, Sparks to Atlin, both returned to Skagway.

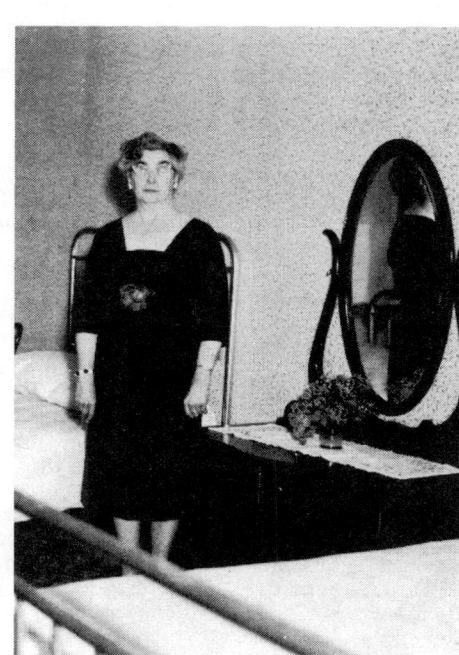

1960

Old Katmai Erupts
* * * *
Alarmed Old-timers Recall Disaster of '12

November 1960

W. A. Nove

VOLCANIC activity beginning Monday, August 22, made major alterations for the second time in half a century in the landscape of Mount Katmai National Monument on the Alaska Peninsula. The extent of the alterations may not be determined for months, or even years, and in fact there may be more to come.

First hint of goings-on in the unpeopled Katmai area came when a huge black cloud of smoke and ash changed a beautiful morning into a gloomy day on Kodiak Island. The photo at right shows the ash cloud as seen from the Kodiak Naval Air Station, ten miles southwest of the town of Kodiak and about a hundred miles east-southeast of Katmai. Ash fall on the air base was about half an inch, lighter on the town, heavier on Port Bailey about thirty miles closer to the eruption, before a shift of wind diverted the cloud.

Gil Jarvela, Kodiak Airways pilot on a routine flight to Larsen Bay on Monday, reported visibility obscured and a cloud of ash and smoke rising at least thirty thousand feet from one of the mountains in the Katmai area. He could not determine which one, nor could the crew of a Coast Guard plane which made an observation flight over the area later that day.

Alf Madsen, Kodiak big-game guide, flew over the following Wednesday and reported Old Katmai, a lesser peak in the Valley of Ten Thousand Smokes, still in eruption. A river of purple-black lava three hundred yards wide was gushing from Old Katmai, meandering down the sides of a smaller mountain that rises about four thousand feet above the valley floor, then flowing toward Shelikof Strait. Huge black sulphur-smelling clouds were still issuing from the mountain, and blowing southwestward down the Alaska Peninsula. At intervals of about fifteen minutes, Old Katmai would hiss and belch forth a "huge white cloud like an atomic blast." Vegetation in the area was devastated.

The real old-timers of Kodiak had reason to be alarmed when they saw a black cloud coming their way from the Alaska Peninsula. When Mount Katmai erupted on June 6, 1912, Kodiak was blacked out completely for two days and nights. So dense was the ash fall that a twenty-room log building burned to the ground and people two hundred feet away didn't know there was a fire. Five hundred people, in terror lest they be buried alive, crowded aboard the Revenue Cutter *Manning*, which groped her way out to the open sea. When the skies finally cleared the people returned, to find their town and the entire island buried under eighteen inches to three feet of volcanic ash.

That eruption, one of the major volcanic disturbances in the earth's history, displaced about two cubic miles of solid material, which fell over a radius of fifteen hundred miles, and created the phenomenal Valley of Ten Thousand Smokes which, in turn, led to creation of the Mount Katmai National Monument.

Prelude to the August 22 eruption was one in the night of August 10, reported by the crew of a Coast Guard plane. A mountain in the vicinity, possibly Old Katmai, was said to be hurling molten lava three to four thousand feet into the air and blowing smoke and ash to thirty thousand feet.

8,000th Arrival
October 1960

DWIGHT LONG, infant son of Chief Warrant Officer and Mrs. Robert F. Long, was the eight-thousandth baby born at the 5040th USAF Hospital at Elmendorf Air Force Base, near Anchorage, since its dedication in 1955. Little Dwight arrived last June 1. The thousand youngest babies of Elmendorf's bumper crop were born in the previous nine and one-half months.

Guide Disappears, Empty Boat Found
October 1960

HENRY GLEASON, one of the best known guides in the Telegraph Creek area of northern British Columbia, disappeared in May and is believed to have drowned in the Iskut River, tributary to the Stikine. Gleason had been beaver trapping about fifteen miles up the Iskut with Mike Williams and had gone to visit another trapper near the river's mouth. When he failed to return to camp, Williams made a canvas boat and started a search. Word was sent upriver to Telegraph Creek where the RCMP organized a boat and plane search. The gas tank from Gleason's boat was discovered near the mouth of the Stikine and later his empty boat was located in a drift-jam.

It is assumed that Gleason fell overboard as he started his motor, but efforts to find the body have been fruitless. Gleason, 55, had been employed for many years as a guide at the Ball Ranch near Telegraph Creek.

New Highway Bridges
November 1960

TWO new bridges, scheduled for opening late this fall, will eliminate two ferry crossings for the Whitehorse-Dawson road and make it an all-weather route. The ferries now transport cars across the Stewart River and the Pelly River, both tributaries to the Yukon.

Both bridges are of steel truss construction. The Pelly River bridge is 865 feet long; the one across the Stewart River, 692 feet.

The ferry *Campbell*, one of two used for the Stewart crossing, will be moved down to Dawson to help with traffic across the Yukon, now carried by the ferry *McQuesten*. The other Stewart ferry, the *Carmacks*, will be dismantled and moved to the Francis River in the Watson Lake area. The Pelly ferry boat, the *Generc*, is to be taken out of service and offered for sale.

Gunfire in Oyster Piracy
December 1960

GUNFIRE rattled in the darkness of the early hours of a Sunday morning and two rubber boats were sunk and another was scuttled as guards battled oyster pirates in the Tsimpsean Peninsula area, a short distance north of Prince Rupert, B.C.

Tipped off by a conversation overheard in a cafe, the guards were ready and waiting for an expected raid. The pirates were equipped with modern gear, including the inflatable rubber boats, frogman suits and underwater breathing apparatus.

In the dim light of dawn, the guards spotted a swimming frogman who was towing a rubber boat loaded with oysters at the end of a twenty-foot line. The guards opened fire and quickly sank the boat. The frogman submerged and got away under water.

T. A. Retallack

Tourist Plans Charted in Historic Wheelhouse
December 1960

REMINISCENT of the colorful era of river steamers on the Yukon is the wheelhouse of the old *Nasutlin*, perched high and dry in Dawson and serving as an information booth for tourists who now come by road or air.

The *Nasutlin*, 405 tons, was built in Whitehorse by the British Navigation Company in 1912. For three decades she carried Dawson-bound freight and passengers, and once, in 1914, during the Shushanna stampede, she left the big river for a hazardous excursion up the shallow, silt-laden White River as far as the mouth of the Donjek. The Yukon River ice claimed her at Dawson in 1932. Present owner of her wheelhouse is George Shaw, who lent it to the Klondike Visitors' Association.

Colorful Hydrants Yield to Progress
December 1960

TRIAL and error, necessary but sometimes costly pioneering methods, have finally eliminated the red metal hoods long worn in winter by Fairbanks fire hydrants. The city's present circulating water system and the use of antifreeze in hydrant caps have solved the problem of getting water where and when it is needed, according to Fairbanks Fire Chief Franklin Jensen.

Better than no protection, the fireplug hoods were not the best solution to the problem. Property worth many thousands of dollars, and some of Fairbanks' most colorful pioneer structures, went up in smoke while firemen with frost-numbed fingers struggled to remove metal fire-plug covers. All too frequently the cover had not done its job, and firemen's efforts were frustrated by a frozen hydrant.

Author Lectures on Sitka's Historic Role
December 1960

TWO lectures on Sitka's place in history were delivered by author Hector Chevigny during the city's Alaska Day celebration which this year marked the ninety-third anniversary of the raising of the American flag over Alaska.

Chevigny is the author of two historical novels based on early Russian days in Alaska—*Lord of Alaska* and *Lost Empire*. His subjects for the two lectures in Sitka were "Sitka's Role in Colonial America" and "Sitka's Role in American History."

A native of Missoula, Montana, where he was born June 28, 1904, Chevigny graduated from Gonzaga University in Spokane and did graduate work at the University of Washington. For several years he was a staff writer for Station KOMO in Seattle, then went to Hollywood with CBS and Station KNX.

Loss of his eyesight in 1944 did not stop his career, and he has written many short stories and a total of five books. In recent years he lived in New York, with Mrs. Chevigny and their two children. Following his visit to Sitka, however, he is planning to stay in the Pacific Northwest.

Harry Conner

The Sternwheeler Keno leaves Whitehorse for her voyage down to Dawson. Her wheelhouse has been moved to the upper deck and her tall smokestack hinged so it can be dropped back while she passes under the bridge at Carmacks.

Last Voyage on the River... Old Paddleboat Steams to a New Career
December 1960

IN what may well be the last steamboat voyage ever on the upper Yukon, the 613-ton *Keno* steamed out of Whitehorse August 25 with her bright orange paddlewheel churning the river. Four days later she arrived at Dawson City, more than four hundred miles downstream and a thousand feet lower in elevation. At Dawson she will remain, to be fitted out as a museum which will recall the glorious days of river navigation when dozens of paddle steamboats plied the Yukon.

Smallest of the old White Pass paddleboat fleet, the *Keno* was built at the Whitehorse shipyards in 1923 and launched in July of that year. In 1937 she was rebuilt at the same yards and lengthened ten feet to a total of 140. Designed primarily as a freighter, the *Keno* accommodated only twenty passengers.

In the early spring of the year, when the water was too low for the larger vessels, the *Keno* sometimes relayed freight from Whitehorse to Lake Laberge and made the run to Dawson only when the volume of cargo warranted. She was used a good deal on the Stewart River, carrying supplies up to Mayo for the mines and returning with ore concentrates.

In 1953 the *Keno* was taken out of service and placed on the ways at Whitehorse. Two years later when the *Klondike* was scheduled for several tour trips in a joint White Pass-Canadian Pacific venture, the *Keno* was returned to the water as a standby vessel but was not used.

Recently the White Pass and Yukon Railroad donated the *Keno* and its other vessels laid up at Whitehorse to the Canadian government with the hope that some of them might be preserved for their historic interest. The Department of Northern Affairs of the federal government in Ottawa decided this year to put the *Keno* in shape for a last river voyage to Dawson City and convert her to a museum at the historic Klondike port.

Captain Frank S. Blakely, 71, a waterways veteran of the Mackenzie and Columbia Rivers, was in command of the *Keno* on her final voyage. H. J. Breaden of Whitehorse signed on as mate. Emil Forrest, also of Whitehorse, who began a long career on the river in 1910, was to have acted as pilot for the downriver trip but collapsed and died on August 20 while helping to move the vessel from the ways. His place was taken by Frank Slim, 62-year-old Yukon Indian who also had spent many years on riverboats.

Aboard the *Keno* for the trip to Dawson City were twelve radio, television and newspaper people. The Canadian Broadcasting Corporation's television crew made a film for nationwide showing, while the CBC radio staff from station CFWH at Whitehorse made a series of five "Roving Reporter" tapes during the voyage.

Engine Fails... Three Hunters Adrift at Sea for 14 Days... For Sale: One 18-foot Whaleboat
December 1960

WHAT started as a week's elk hunting trip on Afognak Island turned into an undesired fourteen-day ocean voyage for three sailors from Kodiak Naval Station.

Louis R. Sparks, Robert L. Hoylman and Gary S. Crawford left Kodiak on September 1 in an eighteen-foot converted whaleboat and headed northward for Afognak. The boat was powered by a forty-horsepower engine and they carried a ten-horsepower outboard as an auxiliary. They also had a ten-day supply of food, some water, and camping gear.

The engine broke down when they were about an hour out of Kodiak, the outboard refused to start, and the boat drifted as they worked on the engine. When they realized they could not repair it, they began to ration the food supply.

Drifting erratically, at the mercy of tide and wind, they were never out of sight of land but could do little about getting closer to it. Water was something of a problem, but they managed to catch some rain and secured additional water from rain pools on some isolated offshore rocks.

When the hunters failed to return home on September 8, as planned, an air-sea search began. The Coast Guard vessels *Storis* and *Bittersweet*, a Navy crash boat, Coast Guard and Navy planes, a State Fish and Game Department plane and local commercial aircraft joined the search and fishing boats in the area were alerted.

More than 16,000 square miles of sea and shoreline were covered by the searchers, who failed to sight the tiny craft. The men in the whaleboat saw both aircraft and boats and tried to attract attention by waving a small yellow flag, the only signaling device they had aboard.

Finally, on September 14, their boat drifted ashore near Cape Chiniak, to the southward of Kodiak. They made their way to a Naval radio station nearby and were soon picked up and taken first to the base hospital for a check-up, then home to their anxious wives.

Sparks is from Baltimore, Maryland; Hoylman is from Murphy, Oregon, and Crawford from Vista, California.

The next issue of the weekly *Kodiak Mirror* carried a notice, signed by the three men, thanking all those who had assisted in the search effort. The notice also carried a brief postscript:

"For Sale: One converted 18-foot whaleboat. Sleeps two."

1961

Pilotless Takeoff
March 1961

AN ALASKA bush pilot, knocked down by his own plane, picked himself up off the ground to see the plane take off by itself toward the center of the town of Bethel. The pilot, Stan Smith, was starting the Cessna 180 owned by King Charter Service when it got away from him. It taxied along the frozen Kuskokwim River, climbed a steep bank under its own power, narrowly missed a service station, and finally crashed in the middle of Bethel's main street. Damage to the plane was estimated at $1,000. Smith was not injured.

Historic First... Alaskans Vote for President
February 1961

FOR thousands of Alaskans, November 8, 1960, was a very special day. It was the day on which they cast their first ballots for a president of the United States, a privilege they gained two years ago with statehood.

A total of 62,177 Alaskans went to the polls or cast absentee ballots in the election. Many of them had reached voting age, which in Alaska is nineteen years, since the last election. But a majority of those who were voting for a presidential candidate for the first time were either born in Alaska or had lived here since statehood.

One of the latter was Robert Steel, Fairbanks hotelman, now 81. He delayed a visit to a son in Florida so he could cast his first presidential ballot in person. Born in California, Steel came to Alaska in 1898 at the age of nineteen.

But this year another long-time Alaskan marked a presidential ballot for the second time in his life. It was a long while between. Frank Hart, now a resident of Tenakee Springs, near Juneau, first voted in Philadelphia the year he became twenty-one. That year he voted for James A. Garfield, who became the twentieth president. The year was 1880. Yes, that's right, Frank Hart is now 101, and he is looking forward to a third chance in a presidential election.

Alaskan voters upset most pre-election forecasts by awarding the state's three electoral votes to Richard Nixon by a margin of 30,953 to 29,809 for John F. Kennedy. On the other hand, they returned Senator E. L. "Bob" Bartlett and Congressman Ralph J. Rivers, both Democrats, to office by substantial majorities.

Sensational 'Starter'
January 1961

SOURDOUGH "starter," a potent rising agent for hotcakes, rolls and bread, is almost as common in Alaska as fried chicken in Dixie, and ordinarily it creates no excitement whatever. One small batch of the stuff, however, caused a great deal of commotion around the Fairbanks International Airport one morning recently.

A passenger boarded a southbound Pan American plane, carrying with her a small jar of starter.

"I hope it doesn't blow up," she commented as she carefully set the jar under her seat.

A bomb-conscious stewardess overheard the remark and things began to happen at once. All passengers were unloaded. Airport security officers, state police and agents of the Federal Bureau of Investigation swarmed over the plane. Every nook was scrutinized. Baggage was unloaded and examined.

When the plane finally took off, two hours late, the passenger was again aboard. So was her precious sourdough, but if she was having any thoughts about what might happen to it, she was keeping them to herself.

Ed Ferrell

Ketchikan's Chief Johnson Totem Pole
* * * * *
84-Year-old Indian Carves a Replica for Mount Edgecumbe School

April 1961

A NEW eleven-foot replica of Ketchikan's cherished Kadjuk totem pole, carved by Casper Mather, eighty-four-year-old Indian carver of Ketchikan, has a place of honor outside the auditorium of the Mount Edgecumbe School on Japonski Island, just out of Sitka.

The original, also known as the Chief Johnson pole, at the intersection of Mission and Stedman Streets in Ketchikan, belongs to the Kadjuk House of the Tlingit Ravens, and was erected in 1901 when the late Chief Johnson was the Kadjuk chief. At one time a community house stood behind the pole, on the bank of Ketchikan Creek. In earlier years, Kadjuk and related houses owned the land at the mouth of Ketchikan Creek, and there each summer they caught and smoked salmon.

The figure at the top of the pole is Kadjuk, fabled bird of the high mountains and special crest of the Kadjuk chief. Its position far above the other figures symbolizes both the bird's lofty habitat and the high esteem in which the crest is held.

The lower figures are Gitsanuk and Gitsaqeq, slaves of Raven, then Raven, and between his outstretched wings, his wife, also known as Daughter of Fog over Salmon, or Fog Woman. In her hands she holds two salmon, the first in the world, with faces above their tails to represent wealth.

These lower figures illustrate the myth of the creation of the first salmon, which Fog Woman accomplished by dipping her finger into a basket of spring water. Raven demanded more salmon. She created many by washing her hair in a basket of water, which was then poured into the creek. The salmon made Raven so wealthy he began to treat his wife badly, so she left, and all the salmon followed her. But, because they were created in fresh water, the salmon come back each year, in midsummer when the fog lies low over the mouths of the streams. Fog Woman's daughter, Creek Woman, directs their return.

John the Turk – of Nome
January 1961

FOR more than half a century he was known around Nome as "John the Turk," although he was born in Greece and his name was John Karametros.

For many years he roamed the streets, clad in ragged cast-offs. He picked over the contents of garbage cans, swamped out saloons, shoveled snow and did other menial tasks. Nome storekeepers let him make off with an occasional potato or onion, and many others aided him in small ways.

John the Turk died at Nome last spring. In his pocket was an airplane ticket for Greece, more than ten years old and expired. Its refund value was believed to have been his only asset.

Just recently it was disclosed that he had a bank balance of more than $16,000 in Nome. Other assets were discovered in a safety deposit box in Seattle, along with a will.

The will directed that his estate be divided among three sisters in northern Greece. It also disclosed the existence of a wife, also in Greece, to whom he left one dollar.

Exactly when John Karametros arrived in Nome is not certain, but it was in early gold-rush days. He had often talked of making a trip back to Greece, but he never got around to using the ticket he had hoarded so long.

Volcanic Eruption
March 1961

MOUNT Trident, a 6,090-foot volcanic peak in Katmai National Monument on the Alaska Peninsula, erupted January 6, shooting a column of smoke and ash nearly 20,000 feet into the air. The eruption was reported by Captain Terry McDonald, a Northern Consolidated Airlines pilot who was flying in the vicinity. The volcano, which was also active last year, is in an uninhabited area.

Alaska Methodist... The State's Newest University

January 1961

ALASKA Methodist University, the state's newest institution of higher learning, was formally dedicated October 13 and is now in full operation. More than 150 students enrolled for the opening of courses at the beginning of October and it was anticipated that the number would reach 200 before the end of the year.

During an open house on October 16, nearly 5,000 persons inspected the first two buildings on the university's 505-acre campus near Goose Lake, on the outskirts of Anchorage. The two buildings were officially named during the dedication ceremonies.

The $1,600,000 academic building, containing laboratories, classrooms and a library, was named in honor of Bishop A. Raymond Grant, chairman of the school's board of trustees and bishop of Portland, Oregon, area, from which Methodist churches in Alaska receive direction.

The university's first dormitory, with quarters for 100 students, was named P. Gordon Gould Hall in honor of the Reverend Gould. He was born at Unga, Alaska, in 1901, and is at present with the Division of National Missions of the Methodist Church.

President of the university is the Rev. Frederick P. McGinnis, a resident of Alaska for the last ten years. He has served as pastor of Methodist churches in Juneau and Anchorage and at the time of his appointment as president was superintendent of all Methodist work in Alaska.

The idea of a Methodist university in Alaska began in the late 1940's when the Division of National Missions conducted a preliminary survey in the then territory. A number of possible locations were considered before the one near Anchorage was selected. Funds for the project have come from churches, other groups, and individuals in all parts of the nation.

Additional buildings are being planned and it is expected that the school will have an enrollment of 600 by the 1963-64 term.

Mac's Foto Service
Grant and Gould Halls form the nucleus of Alaska's new university.

Three New Wildlife Ranges
February 1961

THREE new national wildlife ranges were established in Alaska by Secretary of the Interior Fred A. Seaton on December 7. They total about 11.2 million acres in area.

At the same time, Secretary Seaton restored about 20 million acres, in reserve status since 1943, to the public domain. This is a portion of about 48.8 million acres withdrawn for defense purposes during World War II.

Included in the new reserves is the Arctic National Wildlife Range of about nine million acres in the extreme northeastern corner of the state. Legislation for the establishment of this range was before the last Congress and was approved by the House but was not acted upon in the Senate.

The other new reserves are the Kuskokwim National Wildlife Range of about 1.8 million acres on the Yukon-Kuskokwim delta, one of the most important waterfowl nesting grounds in North America, and the Izembek National Wildlife Range of about 415,000 acres on the north side of the Alaska Peninsula, which will be primarily a refuge for brown bear.

Grizzly Wrecks Plane
March 1961

AN angry grizzly bear may have been "getting even" when it completely demolished a small airplane at a camp near Watson Lake, British Columbia, last fall. The 700-pound bear was reported to have been hanging around Canada Tungsten's mining camp all summer and it had frequently been "buzzed" by pilots flying small planes.

After the camp had been closed for the winter, pilot Walter Forsberg of Watson Lake flew in for an inspection visit. His Super Cub plane flipped over on landing, but was not seriously damaged. Forsberg was uninjured and settled down in the camp to await rescue.

While he waited, the bear ambled out of the woods, surveyed the plane carefully, then methodically ripped it to pieces. The wings, tail assembly, fuselage, instrument panel and motor were smashed and ruined.

The bear then headed toward Forsberg, who was unarmed. He barricaded himself in the camp kitchen and vigorously rattled and banged the pots and pans, keeping the bear at bay. It turned its attention to a bunkhouse and tore it to bits.

Forsberg was picked up by another pilot three days later. The camp is in a game reserve and special permission was secured from Ottawa to shoot the bear. At last reports, however, it was still at large, perhaps looking for another wounded airplane.

11 Alaska Cities and How They Grew... 3 Others Lost Population

February 1961

Eleven Alaska cities gained in population between 1950 and 1960, while three cities showed a population loss during that period, according to a preliminary report by the U. S. Department of Commerce on the 1960 census of Alaska.

Major cities, with 1960 population, 1950 population and percentage of gain or loss, as reported by the Bureau of the Census, are shown below:

Anchorage—43,753; 11,254; up 288.8%.
Bethel—1,274; 651; up 95.7%.
Cordova—1,107; 1,165; down 5%.
Douglas—1,039; 699; up 48.6%.
Fairbanks—13,061; 5,771; up 128.3%.
Juneau—6,344; 5,956; up 6.5%.
Ketchikan—6,317; 5,305; up 19.1%.
Kodiak—2,585; 1,710; up 51.2%
Nome—2,296; 1,876; up 22.4%.
Palmer—1,182; 890; up 32.6%.
Petersburg—1,452; 1,619; down 10.2%.
Seward—1,845; 2,114; down 12.7%.
Sitka—3,226; 1,985; up 62.5%.
Wrangell—1,311; 1,263; up 3.8%.

Preliminary 1960 census report, by election districts.*
1. Prince of Wales: 1,750.
2. Ketchikan: 9,842.
3. Wrangell-Petersburg: 4,083.
4. Sitka: 6,744.
5. Juneau: 9,646.
6. Lynn Canal-Icy Strait: 2,929.
7. Cordova-McCarthy: 1,729.
8. Valdez-Chitina-Whittier: 2,899.
9. Palmer-Wasilla-Talkeetna: 5,189.
10. Anchorage: 82,321.
11. Seward: 2,910.
12. Kenai-Cook Inlet: 6,085.
13. Kodiak: 7,080.
14. Aleutian Islands: 5,745.
15. Bristol Bay: 3,996.
16. Bethel: 5,546.
17. Kuskokwim: 2,317.
18. Yukon-Koyukuk: 4,182.
19. Fairbanks: 43,870.
20. Upper Yukon: 1,630.
21. Barrow: 1,974.
22. Kobuk: 3,563.
23. Nome: 5,959.
24. Wade-Hampton: 3,125.

TOTAL: 224,094.

* No comparison with 1950 census is possible because areas in that census were entirely different.

The above figures include all military personnel, which are especially heavy in districts 10, 13 and 19.

More Musk-ox
January 1961

THE musk-ox population of Nunivak Island in the Bering Sea was 256 last fall, according to David L. Spencer, regional refuge supervisor of the U.S. Fish and Wildlife Service, who made the annual herd census. This total indicates that the transplanted herd has doubled its size in the last four years.

Path to Canine Fame
* * *
A Pet Portrait by Josephine Crumrine

March 1961

BUTTONS, pet Pomeranian of Mr. and Mrs. Jim Hawkins, Fairbanks, inspects the finished Crumrine portrait of herself and her offspring, Alexander, to be exhibited in Juneau's 17th Annual Arts and Crafts Show.

Buttons seems overwhelmed, and no wonder. The shortest road to canine fame in Alaska, for aristocrat or mongrel, is to sit for Artist Josephine Crumrine, now Mrs. Robert Liddell of Fairbanks, whose animal portraits are especially renowned.

Amos Burg

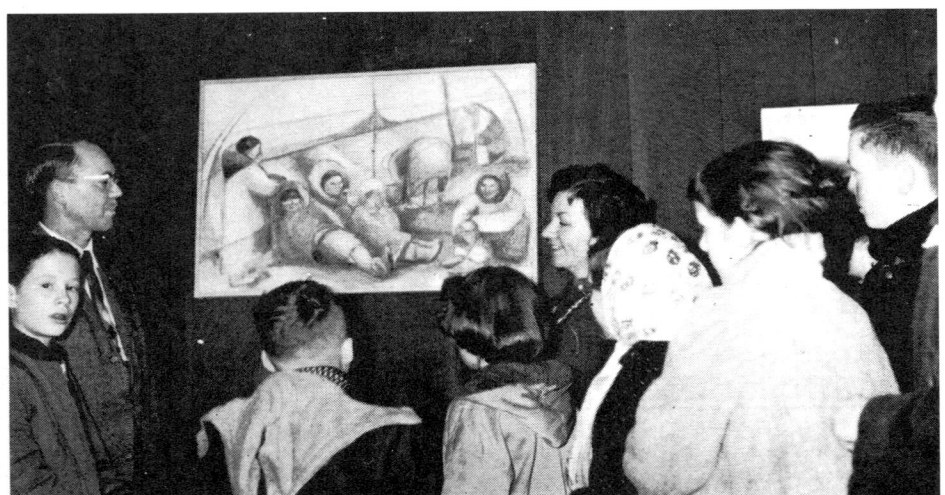

Couch Alaska Archives

Fairbanks Artist Portrays Whale Feast
March 1961

ANOTHER Fairbanks woman of increasing stature as an artist, Claire Fejes specializes in Eskimo life. Painting in the photo, taken at a one-man show in Fairbanks last winter, is her portrayal of Nulakatuk, the spring whale feast, which she (right of painting) describes to John Poling's seventh-grade class.

A Fairbanks resident for sixteen years, Mrs. Fejes has spent much time among the Alaskan Eskimos, studying and sketching them at work and play. Her oils and watercolors have been shown in various "outside" galleries.

The Lady Known as Diamond Lil ... Her Klondike Fortune Is Gone ... At 90 She Lives on Charity
June 1961

PROBABLY few sourdoughs ever knew the name of Honora Ornstein, but few have forgotten the glittering "Diamond Lil," Dawson dance-hall queen with the diamond-studded front tooth, who skillfully dug gold from the pokes of miners who had dug it out of the frozen Klondike earth.

Nor does anyone know just how big a fortune Diamond Lil brought out of the Klondike, but it's all gone now. Since November of 1935, Honora Ornstein has been a patient at the Western State Hospital for the mentally ill, at Steilacoom, Washington. She has had a series of guardians, most of whom she has outlived, who dutifully doled out her money under supervision of the court to pay for her care—first at $20 a month, gradually increasing with inflation to $120—and sold her jewels when the cash was gone.

There was the spectacular white-gold "snake," studded with 125 diamonds, Lil used to wear twined around her arm from shoulder to wrist. There were other diamonds, including the one she wore in her front tooth. They didn't "sell like hotcakes," as some women didn't want diamonds once worn by "that woman," but all are sold now and the money they brought is exhausted. The one-time queen is now a charity patient.

She has no known relative. Her age is unknown, but believed to be about ninety years. Physically she is in good health, but her mind is elsewhere—perhaps in a hilariously gay Klondike dance hall of sixty-some years ago, where lonely prospectors would gladly exchange gold nuggets for the favors of Diamond Lil.

Oldest Jail, Courthouse ... Soon It May be Given to the Town of Eagle
March 1961

THE oldest courthouse and jail in Interior Alaska, together with the ground on which it stands, may soon be turned over to the town of Eagle. On November 9, 1900, District Judge James Wickersham signed an order reserving the ground for courthouse purposes. Exactly sixty years later, on November 9, 1960, Judge Walter H. Hodge, the present U. S. District Judge for Alaska, granted a motion vacating the earlier order. Actually, the building was officially abandoned in 1924 and was declared surplus by the United States Attorney General in 1946. The motion granted by Judge Hodge provided that the land be turned over to the Bureau of Land Management, which is expected to transfer title to the town.

First Try: Eskimo Is New North American Champion
June 1961

BEATTUS MOSES, a 22-year-old Eskimo from Allakaket, won the three-day North American championship sled dog races at Fairbanks this year with a total elapsed time of 4 hours, 54 minutes, 33 seconds for the 70-mile event. It was his first try in the big annual race and he carried away $4,300 in cash as well as other prizes. The race was run in two 20-mile and one 30-mile heats.

Henry Beatus of Hughes took second place, only a minute and a half behind Moses, while Warner Vent of Huslia finished third. Dr. Roland Lombard of Wayland, Mass., won the third heat of the race, covering the 30 miles in 2 hours, 8 minutes, 57 seconds. He placed fourth in the over-all event.

In the 34-mile women's championship race at Fairbanks, Kit MacInnes of Anchorage placed first with an elapsed time of 2 hours, 20 minutes, 27 seconds. Jeri Best and Rosie Losonsky, both of Fairbanks, placed second and third.

Joe Reddington of Flat Horn Lake took first place in the five-dog junior race. Carol Lundgren of Fairbanks was winner of the three-dog event, and Chuck Dagley of Fairbanks, defending champion, placed first in the one-dog race.

Joe Reddington: Junior Champ
June 1961

JUNIOR champion of the year, and a young man with a promising future in racing, is Joe Reddington of Flat Horn Lake. Joe took the seven-dog junior event in Anchorage in February, then the five-dog junior event in Fairbanks, where he ran the 3-heat, 24-mile race in 94.48 minutes. Among the competitors were Wade Charles of Eagle River, who had placed first in Anchorage, second in Fairbanks, in 1960, and Bob Stoeker of Fairbanks, NA junior champ last year. Wade placed second, Stoeker third, this year.

Joe's father is a homesteader and dog-sled freighter at Flat Horn Lake, about a hundred miles north of Anchorage. There's no school there, but Joe has finished the eighth grade under the Calvert correspondence system with his mother's supervision.

The Women's Champion Does Better Than Ever in '61 Dog Mushing
June 1961

KIT MacInnes of Anchorage, accustomed to sled-dog racing triumphs, did better than ever during the 1961 season.

Last January, in Anchorage, she took the David Dial Memorial over nine other contenders, all of them men and one her husband, Chuck MacInnes, who placed third. (Orville Lake, well-known breeder and musher, placed second.)

Last February, also in Anchorage, she took the All-Alaska women's championship for the third consecutive year.

Last March, in Fairbanks, she took the North American women's championship to become the second three-time winner in the history of that competition. (Previous wins were in 1955 and '56, with a second place in '60; other three-time winner, Effie Kokrines, the "mushing grandmother" of Fairbanks.)

Facing all-male competition in January was no new experience for Kit. In 1955, for example, she placed second in the All-Alaska championship and seventh in the North American, the "big" ones, which women may enter but never have won. There's more competition coming up at home, too. Daughter Ann and Son Scott, junior class champions, make four "mushing MacInneses."

Charlie the Hair-seal Pup Finds a Good Living
June 1961

CHARLIE was a hair-seal pup who got tangled in a salmon net in Chignik Lagoon last summer, was rescued by operators of the Alaska Department of Fish and Game weir on the Chignik River, and became rival to Chignik, the dog pup, as camp mascot. The two pups called a truce at mugup time (below), finding there was milk enough for both, and lapped eagerly from the same pan.

Charlie, marine mammal though he was, evidently thought he had a good thing at the weir camp, or maybe he didn't want to take any more chances with salmon nets. He refused to swim or even go near the water unless thrown in. His favorite pastime was lying in someone's arms (Marv Stenberg obliges at left) and having his neck scratched.

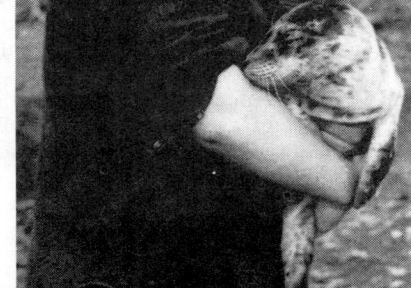

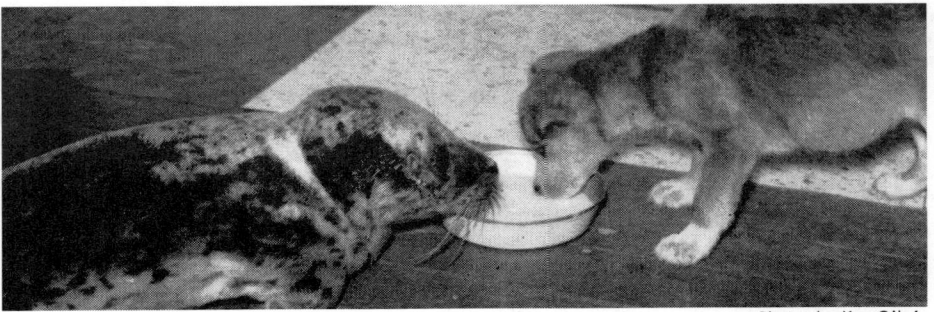

Photos by Ken Gilpin

'Million Dollar Bridge'
March 1961

CONVERSION of the "Million Dollar Bridge" on the old Copper River and Northwestern Railroad to highway use is expected to begin early this summer. The bridge was considered a major engineering feat when it was built half a century ago as part of the railroad made famous by Rex Beach as the "Iron Trail." The railroad carried copper ore from the Kennecott Mine to the docks at Cordova and ceased operation more than twenty years ago. The bridge is at Mile 49 out of Cordova on the Copper River Highway which follows the old rail line. The Juneau firm of Cole and Paddock submitted the low bid of $299,933 for the job of converting the bridge.

Frontier Pests Invade New Lawn
* * *
Playfield for Moose

June 1961

MR. AND Mrs. Vern Stall have a 110-acre property which covers the site of the gold-rush ghost town of Sunrise on the north shore of the Kenai Peninsula. Ghosts don't haunt them, but they have neighbors who do. Writes Mrs. Stall:

"I often see articles about the problems of raising a lawn in the 'lower '48,' but I have never seen one on my problem. Last summer I tried to start a back-yard lawn. My husband helped me prepare the ground and plant the seed. Then one evening shortly afterward, I looked out the window and saw a young bull moose cavorting around on the tender new grass, showing off to his girl friend, who was watching from my flower garden. He seemed to enjoy the nice, soft ground and every evening he came back just at dusk, to kick up his heels and shadowbox with the bushes

"We finally gave up on the flower garden, and built a high fence around the vegetables to save what were left. Then late in the summer the moose stopped coming. We raked the lawn smooth and replanted.

"Early in the fall the young bull came back and brought more friends. We looked out one morning and saw three bull moose on the new lawn. They had dug deep holes in the soft earth, and one bull was just daring the others to come closer—shaking his head and snorting and dancing to show how he could fight if they did. It was much too early in the morning for good pictures, but we wasted a lot of film trying.

"We also had a spruce hen who brought her chicks to the lawn every day, but they ate the weed seeds, so they were welcome."

Barbara Stall

White Alice Network
March 1961

THE dedication of the new Radio Corporation of America Service Co. building in Anchorage November 19 marked the company's formal acceptance of responsibility for operating and maintaining the extensive White Alice communications system which now stretches from Cape Lisburne on the Arctic coast to Middleton Island in the Gulf of Alaska.

The White Alice network, consisting of 33 sites, is owned by the Air Force, which contracts for its operation and maintenance. It was placed in full operation in March 1958 and the Federal Electric Corporation held the operating contract until last fall.

The network is an ultra-modern radio relay communications system with stations that amplify both telephone and telegraph signals and send them from one station to another. It ties together 30 aircraft control and warning stations which are part of the DEW Line and also serves the Army, Navy, Federal Aviation Agency and other government agencies.

Moose Attacks Boy, 5
May 1961

A CHARGING cow moose broke Michael Garrett's leg last January, but the boy fortunately escaped other injuries. The five-year-old son of Mr. and Mrs. Ralph Garrett was playing behind his home on the outskirts of Anchorage when the cow appeared with her calf. She immediately charged and knocked Michael down. The incident was witnessed by Wayne Lofgren from his furniture store near by, but he did not have time to warn Michael. "He didn't do anything to provoke the cow and I don't know that he even saw the animal before it was upon him," Lofgren said.

Anchorage Women Find New Mushroom Species
April 1961

THREE new species of mushrooms have been discovered by a trio of Anchorage women who make a hobby of mycology—the scientific study of fungus growths. The three are Mrs. Ward W. Wells, Mrs. U. M. Culver and Mrs. G. O. Kempton, and one of the new species has been named *Galerina wellseae* for Mrs. Wells who initiated the hobby group. The *wellseae* species was discovered on a cottonwood log near Palmer. Another, which has been named *Galerina subarctica*, was located south of Anchorage. Both are quite small. The third discovery grows under hemlock trees and is bright red in color but turns blue when touched. It was found near Anchorage. Confirmation that the species are new came from Dr. Walter Snell of Brown University and Dr. A. H. Smith of the University of Michigan.

New Ice Island
January 1961

THE United States Navy, undaunted by the disintegration of two Arctic ice islands upon which successive research stations were located, has established a new station, known as Arlis One, on a slab of ice 420 miles northeast of Point Barrow and 180 miles inside the Polar Ice pack.

The site was selected after aerial reconnaissance and the icebreaker USS Burton Island moved in materials and equipment about mid-September. Forty hours and forty-five minutes after the first piece of cargo was landed on the bare ice, ten buildings complete with electric lights, water and oil heaters were ready for occupancy. Food and equipment were stored, radios and machinery were in operation, even the bunks were made up.

After a brief flag-raising ceremony, the Burton Island, captained by Commander Griffith C. Evans of Hollister, California, sailed southward and left the isolated camp to the seven scientists stationed there. Dr. Kenneth Bennington of the University of Washington, a specialist in petrofabrics of sea ice, is in charge of the station. Some half a dozen non-scientific personnel arrived by air in October.

Working closely with the Arlis One station is the Arctic Research Laboratory in Barrow, directed by Dr. Max Brewer, who assisted in selecting the ice-island site and establishing the new station.

The Army's Northernmost Major Installation
March 1961

FORT Jonathan M. Wainwright near Fairbanks, now the United States Army's northernmost major installation was dedicated on January 2 by Secretary of the Army Wilber. The dedication ceremony followed the formal transfer of the post, formerly Ladd Air Force Base, to the Army.

The new name honors the memory of General Wainwright, whose resistance to the Japanese invasion of the Philippines won him the nation's highest military decoration, the Medal of Honor.

On hand for the ceremony were more than twenty veterans of Bataan and Corregidor who are now stationed or retired in Alaska.

Back in 1935 Congress authorized construction of an Alaskan air base, and appropriated $4 million. The first Army Air Corps detachment arrived there in 1940 and it was named Ladd Field for Major Arthur K. Ladd, a Texan who earned his wings during World War I and who was killed in an airplane crash in South Carolina in 1935.

During World War II, Ladd Field became the northern anchor of a chain of air fields that stretched along the Alaska Highway. Later, as Ladd Air Force Base, it has been the home of jet fighters assigned defense responsibilities north of the Alaska Range. The Air Force has now consolidated its facilities at Eielson Air Force Base, twenty-six miles southeast of Fort Wainwright.

Fort Wainwright will be headquarters for the Army's Yukon Command and a major cold weather testing center.

Air Field for Isolated Island? ... Volcanic Ash May Be the Key
May 1961

THE extreme isolation of St. George Island, in Bering Sea, may be partially alleviated by the construction of an air field on the island within the coming year. Mail for residents of the island is now dropped from a plane en route to St. Paul Island to the north, or brought in by occasional vessels of the U. S. Fish and Wildlife Service. Mail leaves the island only by boat.

Lack of suitable construction material on the island and a shortage of funds have prevented construction of an air strip in the past. Now, however, a mountain of volcanic ash has been discovered on the island and it will provide the necessary material. The Fish and Wildlife Service has offered to build the strip if the state Division of Aviation will do the engineering work, and plans for the job are now being completed.

There are about 275 people on St. George, one of the Pribilof Group and one of the main rookeries of the eastern Pacific fur seal herd.

New Explosive Harpoon
July 1961

GUY SELMAN, registered guide of Anchorage, was busy last winter turning out a new type of explosive harpoon head for use by Alaska Eskimos in whale hunting. Whales loom large in the Eskimo economy and in the past have been hunted with harpoons charged with crude black powder time bombs. These frequently did not explode at all, but some of them exploded prematurely and a number of hunters have been killed in such accidents. Selman's new harpoon heads feature a modern and much safer explosive and fuse system. The harpoon heads are attached to shafts which fit snugly into rebored Mauser rifles for firing. Selman is delivering a number of the weapons to the villages of Point Hope, Kivalina and Barrow for use in this year's whale hunts. He will also instruct local people in the technique of reloading the harpoon heads.

Oil Line Dedication
January 1961

ALASKA'S first crude oil pipeline and a marine shipping terminal at Nikiski, on Cook Inlet, were dedicated on October 10 and began operating at once.

Oil, at the rate of 5,000 barrels a day, began flowing through the 19-mile pipeline and into storage tanks at Nikiski. The two tanks, each capable of holding 132,000 barrels of oil, provide for rapid loading of tankers at the dock. Oil from Kenai Peninsula wells had previously been carried by tanker truck from the wells nearly a hundred miles to Seward, at the rate of about 750 barrels a day.

The $5 million pipeline and terminal are a joint venture of Standard Oil Company of California and Richfield Oil Company and will initially handle the production of wells drilled by the two firms on the Swanson River and Soldotna Creek drilling units. Other production from the upper Kenai Peninsula may utilize the line later.

In November, Standard's big tanker, the *W. H. Berg*, after delivering fuel oil at Anchorage, moved down the inlet to the Nikiski terminal to take aboard approximately 100,000 barrels of crude oil for delivery to a refinery at Richmond, California.

Skookum Jim's Legacy
April 1961

ACCRUED interest in the estate of Skookum Jim, one of the discoverers of gold in the Klondike, will finance the construction of a meeting house for the Indian people of Whitehorse, Yukon Territory. Construction is to start in May. The building will include a fully equipped kitchen, dining room, conference room, children's activity room, caretaker's suite, and possibly a nursery. Skookum Jim was one of two Tagish Indians who accompanied George Carmack when the famed gold discovery was made on August 17, 1896. He died many years ago and the Royal Trust Company was made executor of his estate, with the Bishop of the Yukon and Commissioner of Yukon Territory as administrators.

Nenana's Old-timers Learn to Cope with Recurring Floods
November 1961

CANOES and kicker boats were the mode of travel on Nenana streets early last July, when the flooding Tanana River flowed about four feet deep in parts of the little town. Nenanans, old hands at dealing with floods, simply put their possessions out of the water's reach and enjoyed the brief version of Venice, Alaskan style. Above: kids with assorted craft make like early-day voyageurs exploring unknown passages. Below: old-timers sprawl at ease on a kicker boat drawn up at the post office steps and talk of floods of other years. This one, they concluded, didn't compare with the flood of '48, when they could run an outboard right into the bar.

Photos by Mike Bradner

She Recalls First Whites to Visit Her People
December 1961

MRS. John Sheldon of Shungnak looks back upon ninety years and more in the Arctic—how many more, she does not know. There are no records except her own memories, and few recorded events by which to date them. She does know she was past childhood when she saw both Lt. G. M. Stoney and Lt. John C. Cantwell, who explored the Kobuk River between 1883 and 1886 and were probably the first white men to penetrate her inland-Arctic home area.

Mrs. Sheldon was born at the mouth of the Pah River, a few miles up the Kobuk from her present home, where there once was a village known as Pahmeet. Her people, on the undefined border between Eskimo and Athabascan Indian culture, considered themselves Indian-Eskimos. Her native name, Nahtahnuk, is Eskimo, but her mother took her as an infant to live with Indians on the Koyukuk River and she learned their language first. After a trip to the Arctic Coast she returned to the Kobuk River, learned the Eskimo language, eventually forgot the other, and now regards herself as an Eskimo.

Her husband, now dead, was born in the old village of Sulukpoaktukmeet at the mouth of the Selby River, just

Dorothy Jean Ray

upstream from the Pah, to people of the same Indian-Eskimo culture.

Nahtahnuk now lives with her son, Charles A. Sheldon, a Baptist missionary. Though she is mentally alert, the years have taken their physical toll and she doesn't get out much any more. Last summer, to oblige a guest, she wrapped herself against the wind and stepped outside to have her picture taken.

Fracas with Bears
September 1961

■ Olaf Erickson of Haines suffered a broken leg during a fracas with two bears near Haines Junction, where he was visiting. While hiking in to a remote location to visit a friend, in the Kathleen Lake region, Erickson met the two bears on the trail and attempted to circle them. One of the bears charged and Erickson shot it, but at such close range that it fell on him, breaking his leg in two places. The other bear then attacked him and he killed it. Erickson crawled several miles and swam a stream before reaching his car, then drove the car to Haines Junction, using an axe handle to operate the accelerator pedal. He was hospitalized at Whitehorse.

First Cargo for Dock
July 1961

■ The barge *Kev Alaska*, owned by Pacific Western Lines, was the first vessel to discharge cargo at the new Port of Anchorage dock. Arriving from Portland, Oregon, in tow of the tug *Mary Foss*, the barge carried 4,900 tons of general cargo, lumber, mobile homes and bulk cement. After unloading part of its cargo at the new port facilities, the barge shifted to the Alaska Aggregate Corporation dock to complete its discharge.

Picture Puzzle
December 1961

Photo by Harold R. Smith

WHAT is it? Chances are some who saw it daily, though from a different perspective, won't recognize this portion of Juneau's waterfront as seen some eighteen years ago from the side of Mount Roberts. The "fingers" are composed of rock which, once deep inside the mountain, yielded some millions of dollars in gold on its way through the mills of the Alaska-Juneau Mine and came out as waste rock or mill tailings.

The story of the A-J Mine is older than the town itself, as the last area mined covered all the lode claims first staked by Joe Juneau and Dick Harris in October, 1880—ground that had been worked by one party or another since the spring of 1881. The mining company was organized in 1897, built a ten-stamp mill, and operated on a small scale. The original mill was finally discarded as unsuited to the ore, and the pilot mill of the present A-J was constructed in 1914, after owners of the famous Treadwell property on Douglas Island had bought control.

How many tons of ore went through the A-J mill, and how much gold it yielded, no one really knows, but the ore reserve was tremendous and the cost of recovery relatively low, and in its heyday the A-J was said to be the biggest producer of gold from low-grade ore on earth.

Nor is the reserve exhausted. According to calculations based on diamond-drilled samples, there's gold worth many millions of dollars in Mount Roberts still. But war, labor troubles and sharply rising costs, with no compensating change in the fixed price of gold, conspired against the A-J. The mill shut down for the last time at midnight April 8, 1944. Maintenance was eventually discontinued and much of the machinery has been scrapped or sold. Since then, too, the "fingers" of the rock dump have been leveled and a barge landing, oil tanks and other structures have been added to the scene.

Survives Dizzying Fall
August 1961

"THE next time I empty the garbage, I'll wear a parachute," quipped Willard A. Watson as he rested in Providence Hospital at Anchorage after falling at least 500 feet and riding an avalanche another 3,000 feet down the steep slope of Mount Susitna. Watson is site foreman at a telephone relay station atop the 4,320-foot peak and lives there with his wife, Clarice. When he left the house to empty a garbage can over the edge of a snow and ice cornice, the cornice broke, dropping him 500 feet or more and touching off a slide of snow and rocks. Fortunately, most of the avalanche was ahead of Watson and he rode its back down the mountain.

He then made two attempts to climb back up the mountain but was thwarted by a heavy snow squall and then by steep and rocky terrain, although he did get to within 150 feet of the top. Thomas was getting cold and numb when he was picked up by a helicopter which had been sent to search for him. A stiff back and a sore heel were his only injuries and after an overnight stay in the hospital he returned to the mountain. It wasn't quite finished with him, though. He had to snowshoe the last three miles as the helicopter ran into a sleet storm.

'Wild West' Gunfire
July 1961

AFTER what was described as a "regular wild west gun battle" between poachers and agents of the U. S. Fish and Wildlife Service, the FBI arrested seven residents of the Bethel area on charges of assault. On May 1, while checking on migratory waterfowl from a plane, the wildlife agents spotted the poachers killing birds. They landed their plane and approached the seven hunters, who fired on them and on two other agents in another plane. When the wildlife agents returned the fire, the seven fled. The agents picked up more than 70 dead birds in the area and the poachers were arrested the following day and convicted before the magistrate at Bethel on a charge of illegally taking migratory waterfowl. They were then taken to Anchorage for arraignment on the assault charge.

A Short, Stormy Season ... Rugged Test for Man and Vessel
May 1961

EVERY year, in late April, vessels of the Canadian and American halibut fleet converge at Sand Point to take on food, water, fuel and bait before the last leg of their long voyage through Unimak Pass to the halibut grounds of the Bering Sea. As these photos show, Sand Point's weather can be calm, as it can be on the grounds but usually is not.

These long-line fishermen have no time to wait out storms. The entire year's catch must be made in a season only weeks long. They work around the clock, sometimes with frost-bitten hands and frozen gear, with an hour's sleep now and then and a hot meal when seas are calm enough to permit a fire in the galley. A man overboard is usually a man lost at sea, as the icy water takes his life in mere minutes.

When the fleet returns to Sand Point, holds heavy with halibut, rigging often heavy with ice, the crews have once again stood one of the world's most rigorous tests of seamanship and endurance. Yet the price of halibut, and thus the fisherman's annual wage, is about the same now as twenty years ago.

Photos by Ken Gilpin

Red Dragon's Birthday
October 1961

■ The 53rd anniversary of the opening of the Red Dragon was observed in Cordova on July 16. The Red Dragon is the parish hall of St. George's Episcopal Church and was established by the Rt. Rev. Peter T. Rowe, then Bishop of Alaska. M. J. Heney, builder of the Copper River and Northwestern Railroad, contributed $10,000 so Bishop Rowe could build a club for the railroad construction workers and the building was painted a warm railroad red, giving it the distinctive name. The opening in 1908 was marked by a three-day celebration in which Chief Joseph of the Eyak Indians and twenty-four of his people took part. In the years since then the Red Dragon has served at various times as headquarters of the American Red Cross in Cordova and as a public library as well as a parish hall.

Bear Wrecks Cabins, Burns Warehouse
July 1961

AN "educated" bear not only shredded supposedly bear-proof doors and wrecked several cabins but also burned down a warehouse at Camp Denali, according to evidence on the scene. Miss Celia Hunter, one of the operators of the wilderness camp near McKinley National Park, and Alison Smith flew to the camp early in May and discovered the damage. Miss Hunter, who surmised that the depredation took place last fall, said there was no evidence of human vandalism. She believes the bear ignited some matches while tearing up the contents of the warehouse.

Busy Year on the Rivers
July 1961

WITH a busy season ahead on the Tanana, Yukon and Koyukuk Rivers, all vessels of the Yutana Barge Lines were in operation by the first of June. The *Yukon,* under Capt. William Mackie and with Teddy Dietrick as pilot, left Nenana on June 1 for the lower Yukon. The *Tanana,* Capt. Allen Brown, with Jim Neary as pilot, sailed about the same time for Fort Yukon and other points on the upper Yukon. The *Taku Chief,* Capt. Al Demientieff, with Don Clark as pilot, made her first trip of the 1961 season to points on the Koyukuk River.

A Queen Rises to the Occasion
June 1961

A QUEEN photo with a difference is this one of Judith Onstad, Miss Alaska of 1961, trying the Eskimo blanket-toss during Winter Carnival activities in Fairbanks last March. Miss Onstad, an Alaska Airlines stewardess, succeeds Miss Evelyn Bly as Miss Alaska and will represent the state in the Miss Universe contest this summer.

'Copters Rescue Motorists from Flooded Highway
July 1961

TWO helicopters from Eielson Air Force Base worked all night on May 7–8 to rescue 69 marooned motorists from the Steese Highway north of Fairbanks. An ice jamb in the Chatanika River backed up the water and flooded the highway at Mile 39 to a depth of three feet. The two helicopters made a total of 15 trips to airlift the motorists from the flooded highway to Fort Wainwright.

Search for Copper Ore in Stikine Area
November 1961

■ Four mining companies were doing exploratory work last summer in the Stikine River area, searching for copper ore, according to Captain Al Ritchie, operator of the Ritchie Transportation Company on the river. One company went so far as to stake out a townsite about 75 miles up the river from Wrangell as a result of its test drilling, which indicated a 13-year supply of copper ore, Ritchie said. If further drilling reveals an additional nine-year supply of the ore, Ritchie was told by company officials, a mill will be built with a daily capacity of 8,000 tons of ore. The ore would be concentrated to about 1,000 tons a day and the concentrates shipped to smelters in other parts of Canada.

Lost for 10 Weeks: 'Prepared to Die'
November 1961

■ "I prepared to die," said William C. Waters of Erlander, Kentucky, as he was recovering in a Fairbanks hospital after the ordeal of being lost in the Alaska wilderness for ten weeks. It was on June 20 that Waters, a postal employee in Cincinnati, Ohio, who was vacationing in Alaska, left his car at the end of the Steese Highway and hiked a few miles to Big Lake. He became lost when he attempted to take another route back to the highway. A widespread search failed to find him and it was not until August 27 that two moose hunters saw him on the bank of a stream some 70 or 80 miles from where he had left his car. Waters said he kept alive by eating wild cranberries, raspberries and rose hips, but he had lost 90 of his 190 pounds and was barely able to stand when found. In the continuous daylight of the northern latitude, he had lost all track of time and believed that he had been lost for only two or three weeks.

New Ferry System Closer to Reality
July 1961

■ Alaska's two proposed ferry systems, one in Southeastern Alaska and another to operate between Kodiak Island and the mainland, moved several steps closer to actuality during the early months of 1961. The Alaska Legislature provided for the sale of general obligation bonds which had been approved by the voters last November and which will furnish funds for the construction of vessels and other facilities. And in May the appointment of Rear Admiral Bafford E. Lewellen, U. S. Navy, retired, as director and general manager of the ferry systems was announced by Richard A. Downing, Alaska Commissioner of Public Works. A 1931 graduate of the Naval Academy, Admiral Lewellen was on active duty with the submarine forces during World War II and later served as director of the Transportation Branch in the office of the Chief of Naval Operations. He assumed his duties with the Alaska ferry system on May 15.

The Bush Circuit: Seals, Wolves . . . and Millions of King Eider

News from Alaska's outlying areas as reported by correspondents of the *Fairbanks News-Miner:*

ALAKANUK, by Segundo Llorente, S.J. Sept. 18. This is the seal season. Hardly a day goes by without some seal popping her head out of the water in front of the village. In less time than it takes to say it, one dozen or more kickers will take after the seal. Then the usual pattern follows. With one hand the man handles the kicker, with the other he brandishes menacingly a long arrow while with his two eyes about to come out of their sockets he searches the water all around. The seal must come out to breathe; that's for sure.

At first she does it innocently and exposes herself dangerously till, as the battle closes on her, her instinct tells her to be more cautious and she shows just the tip of her nose, and fast, thus making it harder and harder for the men to spot her. At the same time she gains ground gradually towards the wide open depths in the Yukon where she has a fighting chance. More boats arrive with their motors roaring madly. A man on the bank watches the whole operation as if it were a three-ring circus.

It could be that the seal gets harpooned right away, or she may run the men out of gas and force them to go home in shame. It has been estimated that the average seal persecuted by the villagers costs the village in gasoline $78. If she runs away, the money is a total loss. If she is captured, she brings, at the most, $24. So any way you look at it, the appearance of a seal in these fluvial waters is a middle-size disaster, to put it mildly. The men call it sport, fun, excitement. They would sell their shirts to buy gasoline to pursue a seal. Certainly, added to the enormous consumption of liquor and tobacco, seal hunting contributes greatly to keep these people eternally poor.

The church was full of people and Mass was about to start in what looked like routine. But when Curtis Augline and Margaret O'Malley stood up and walked to the altar flanked by the two witnesses, it was certainly news. Rubbernecking in the pews was so uninhibited that I had a hard time looking dignified. To think that a boy and a girl could keep it so secret was too much for the village folks. But they did it. Papa Augline is making himself a brand new cabin so his eldest son, Curtis, may use the old family house to get started comfortably. As for the O'Malleys, don't think that it has any connection whatever with the Irish. It was adopted simply because it was easier to pronounce than Piyuatchoar.

NUNIVAK ISLAND, by Henry Shavings. April 28. The seal hunters ready their boats and outboard motors for spring. Day before yesterday Edward Shavings and Walter Amos went down to the ocean, catch one mukluk seal. Also same day Carl Amos got one too. Some men went out this morning to kill reindeers before they get skinny. People of the island living on reindeer meat, seal meat, dried fish, fresh fish once in a while. Our native store run out some food what we like, that's why we do order sometimes from Bethel.

ANAKTUVUK PASS, by Homer Mekiana. March 11. Two boys went over to Wild River to see their wolf traps, and one of them brought two wolves and one fellow lose three traps running away by wolves. And one of the boys who went toward west brought three wolves home and also one man brought one wolf, too.

KOTZEBUE, by Alfred G. Francis. March 25. The Kotzebue Library Association has been formed with James Hayes as its elected president. Both individuals and organizations have offered books. It is hoped that we can establish a reading room as well as a lending library. The Bureau of Indian Affairs has allowed us to use an old building of theirs as the library.

WALES. April 29. Thousand of millions of king eider migrating north along the shore. And people here ever since the village is set usually live on the birds while walrus and ogrooks is not migrating, and seem it hurts lot of residents that birds are not allowed to be killed this time of year for food what the Eskimos used to get. No tomcods here, no caribou to get, and this time seals are hard to find while there is lots of floating ice.

1962

'Mrs. Alaska'
* * *
A Queenly Way with Broiled Salmon

Ketchikan Daily News Photos

March 1962

HER way with broiled king salmon helped the current Mrs. Alaska—Fern Kubley of Ketchikan—win her title and a "wonderful" trip last November to Fort Lauderdale, Florida. Here's what she does:

Cut king salmon steaks an inch to an inch and a half thick; spread with a sauce of mayonnaise, garlic, salt and pepper and one tablespoon of fresh lemon juice; broil for about five minutes on each side—a little longer if steaks are more than an inch thick, but don't overcook. Serve immediately.

Of course the fresher the salmon, the better, but not everyone can use her way of insuring fresh fish: she catches them. She and her husband, Wally, love to fish, and each of their three children—Larry, Karen and Donnie, ages fifteen, fourteen and nine—began fishing at age four. If the others are too busy, Fern sometimes takes the family cruiser out alone—and sometimes, as shown at left, she has a little trouble carrying home her catch. (That king weighed forty pounds.) She's also an expert at trapshooting, and she hunts ducks, geese and deer.

Wallace Kubley, Ketchikan-born, was in the Coast Guard when he met Fern Bellamy in Prince Rupert, where her father was stationed with the Army Transportation Corps, in August, 1945. She was a sixteen-year-old with pigtails, but she and Wally were married the following October. She found Ketchikan quite different from her native Minneapolis, but she "wouldn't think of living anywhere else."

Through Wally's membership in the Pioneers of Alaska, she is a member of Auxiliary 7, and an active member of several civic organizations. She coaches a girls' softball team, works in Girl Scouts, has taken a turn as Den Mother. She bakes her own bread, pastries and cookies by the hundreds for her own children and their friends who come to play in the huge downstairs recreation room. She mows the lawn occasionally and does the "fixing" around the house. "Wally's too busy," she said. (He's a businessman, active too in civic organizations, and a member of the State House of Representatives.) Last summer Fern leveled off a space in their front yard, hand-sawed log blocks, and laid a patio. For relaxation, when the weather is too bad for fishing, she knits.

Bulldog a Moose? No!
March 1962

■ "Don't try to bulldog a cow moose. It can't be done." That is the advice of a former rodeo performer who tried it.

Bob Pool tackled the moose in an effort to save his dogs from injury or possible death from the flailing feet of the moose. It happened while Pool was taking his eleven-dog team for a run near his home on the outskirts of Anchorage. They had gone only half a mile when the cow moose jumped out of the underbrush and into the middle of the team. In the tangle of dogs, sled, harness and moose that resulted, the dogs were clearly getting the worst of it. Pool jumped into the melee, grabbed the moose around the neck and tried to wrestle her to the ground. It was, he said afterward, like trying to throw a house.

Finally, after a great deal of scrambling and with the dogs barking and Pool shouting, the moose untangled herself and trotted off into the woods. By then five dogs had broken loose and scattered, three were down, and three were still fast to the harness and able to travel.

"I don't think I'll lose any dogs, although some of them got kicked pretty hard," Pool said, "but three of them, including my leader, aren't going to be much use this racing season."

There Goes $150!
January 1962

■ Three wolves, worth $150 in bounties, sank to the bottom of Behm Canal, to the distress of Clyde Wardlow of Ketchikan and his wife, Suzie. But the Wardlows, who were on a deer hunting trip, did secure one wolf for a $50 bounty. While out in a small boat during their trip, the couple saw six wolves swimming across the channel and gave chase. Wardlow shot three of them before he ran out of ammunition, but all three sank before he could reach them. Two of the wolves reached shore and escaped, but Wardlow managed to overtake the sixth and last one, wear it down and club it to death with an oar. And, in addition to losing the three wolves, the Wardlows failed to get a deer.

Man-eating Sharks Invade Southeast Alaska
January 1962

THE waters off the west coast of Prince of Wales Island were invaded last summer by white or man-eating sharks, *Carcharodon carcharias,* a species seldom seen north of California. Many fishermen reported seeing them singly in various bays and inlets during the summer and fall fishing, and one saw a school of seven twenty miles off Cape Addington. Some old-timers had seen an occasional straggler before, but the concensus was that their appearance in such numbers was most unusual—and undesirable.

When the specimen in the photo was washed up on the beach at Craig, unwanted though quite dead, L. R. Hall sent photographs and two upper teeth to the Fisheries Research Institute of the University of Washington. Dr. William F. Royce, director, made the identification and replied that, to his knowledge, this is the first actual record of a man-eating shark's occurrence in Alaskan waters.

The dead shark was fifteen feet and four inches long, nine feet and one inch in girth, and "mighty heavy," according to the men who got rid of the carcass. The recorded weight of one specimen only two inches shorter was 1,720 pounds.

L. R. Hall

Comeback for Sea Otter

March 1962

■ The sea otter, the marine mammal with the valuable fur which greatly influenced Alaska's early history, is making a comeback from near extinction. There has been a sizeable increase in the sea otter population in Western Alaska in recent years, particularly around the Aleutian Islands, and a sea otter was seen near Ketchikan late last fall. Mrs. Richard Olmstead reported a strange animal near her home at Point Higgins, a few miles north of Ketchikan, and Loren Croxton of the Alaska Department of Fish and Game positively identified it as a sea otter. This is said to have been the first one sighted in that vicinity in fifty years, although a few have been reported from time to time among the outer islands of the Alexander Archipelago. The animal was described as about five feet long from nose to tip of tail and was estimated to weigh about sixty pounds.

Possessing one of the world's most beautiful and valuable pelts, the sea otter was prevalent along the Pacific rim from Lower California to the islands of Japan in 1741 when Vitus Bering discovered Alaska, but at that time very few of the skins had been placed on the market. Survivors of Bering's ill-fated expedition carried some nine hundred sea otter skins back to Siberia with them and these eventually reached Kyakhta on the Russian-Chinese border, then one of the world's great fur markets. They brought high prices and a demand for more, with the result that Russian traders and fur hunters moved into what is now Alaska. The hunting of the sea otter soon became a large-scale business and traders from the United States, England and other nations began to take a part in it.

There is no record of the total sea otter catch during the early years, but Russian traders were reported to have taken nearly 110,000 pelts from Alaska between 1745 and 1797, when the Russian-American Company secured a monopoly in Alaska. Between 1798 and 1821 the Russian-American Company took 86,644 sea otter pelts, or an average of 3,938 per year, while traders and hunters from other countries probably took at least as many along the coast from Lower California north through Southeastern Alaska. By 1821 the sea otter herds had been depleted almost to extinction along the lower coast and had seriously dwindled in the waters of northern and western Alaska. The Russian-American Company then instituted some stringent conservation measures. The Alaska coast was divided into districts and hunting was rotated among the districts. The catch was also curtailed. Between 1821 and 1862 the company took 51,315 sea otter pelts, or an average of only about 1,250 a year. These measures restored the herds to a considerable degree and during its last five years in Alaska the company averaged 2,227 sea otter skins a year, about the number, it was calculated, that could be taken on a sustained yield basis.

No census of the sea otter population was made when Russia turned Alaska over to the United States in 1867, but some estimates have placed it as high as 100,000. It may have been even higher, but it again dwindled rapidly. Fur trading companies in Alaska purchased 100,000 sea otter pelts between 1867 and 1890, and thousands more were taken by vessels, both American and foreign, which hunted offshore and sold their catches elsewhere.

Some conservation measures were attempted by the government. The use of firearms in taking sea otter was prohibited and hunting of them was limited to native aboriginals. The latter regulation brought a loud protest from Alaska. The federal government in Washington, it was asserted, was stifling progress and hampering business enterprise in the new territory. So the regulation was modified to extend otter hunting privileges to white men married to native women. This did nothing for the sea otter, but it did keep the priests in the Russian Orthodox churches in Alaska villages busy performing weddings.

The sea otter catch climbed to nearly 5,000 a year by 1890, then began to drop rapidly and in 1910, the last year in which otter hunting was legal, only 24 pelts were shipped from Alaska. In 1911 the protection was extended to international waters under terms of a treaty between the United States, Canada, Japan and Russia.

A Precious Pelt, a Childlike Charm

Alaska Department of Fish and Game

U. S. Fish and Wildlife Service

THE sea otter, mammal with the precious pelt, is also endowed with exceptional charm and the unselfconscious cuteness of a small child. It is said that when sea otters first came in contact with human beings, they were friendly, unafraid, and so curious that a man with a club could kill them by the dozens (and did) as they came to investigate him.

Learning that murder was man's intent, the sea otters became exceedingly shy and wary, which may have saved them from complete extermination, and remained so for decades after the taking of the species became illegal.

The specimen shown at left, taken with others for transplanting to an area which had formerly supported the species, appears to know he is in no danger. The one above was photographed in a characteristic pose in its Aleutian Island home, probably unaware that it was not alone.

Alaska Day at Expo 21
April 1962

■ July 7 is to be Alaska Day at Seattle's Century 21 Exposition, the date having been chosen to coincide with a scheduled visit of a group of King Island Eskimo dancers. Alaska will also have an exhibit, open through the duration of the exposition.

Free Farm Land for the Asking? It's a Myth
July 1962

■ The myth of Alaska as a vast source of free farm land, to be had for the asking, is gradually fading, and a report now being completed by the Bureau of Land Management should finally dispel the fable. The survey shows that only 3,137 homestead patents have been issued since the program began in Alaska about 1900. The homesteads averaged 120.7 acres each. Another 6,857 people applied for homesteads but gave up without meeting patent requirements after doing varying amounts of work on the land. And although the 3,137 tracts were homesteaded as farm land, only about five per cent of the total acreage is presently being farmed to any extent.

Alaska's Oil Reserves
October 1962

■ Alaska's recoverable oil reserves were 350 million barrels at the beginning of this year, according to a report of the Interstate Oil Compact Commission. This is slightly more than one per cent of the nation's total oil reserves which are estimated by the commission at 31,758 million barrels.

Screams Scatter Bears
January 1962

■ Dick Gordon, civilian employee at Elmendorf Air Force Base, and his wife say that a lusty two-part scream will scare off the average bear, and they speak from experience.

Last summer the Gordons set out from Eagle intending to canoe up the Yukon River to Dawson. On the second night out they pitched camp on a small island about fifty feet offshore. Not five minutes after they had sacked out, the garbage, which they had neglected to burn, began to rustle. Seconds later they heard what Gordon described as "sniffs, accompanied by the kind of deep breathing that comes from a tuba," the tent collapsed, and a great weight descended upon Gordon.

Mrs. Gordon, from somewhere in the folds of the tent, but not under the bear, whispered to her husband, "Let's scream."

They did. The great weight was no longer on Gordon. After a few minutes they got the tent flap opened and peeped out timidly. The bear was no longer in camp. Nonetheless, they moved to an isolated sand bar for the rest of the night. In the morning Mrs. Gordon suggested, "Let's go back to Eagle and drive to Dawson." They did.

The Gordons, from Mt. Vernon, New York, had been in Alaska only a year, but they'd had previous experience with a bear—in Yellowstone Park, in 1959. That bear—it, too, breathed like a tuba—sat down on Gordon's sleeping bag just after they'd sacked out, causing the tent to collapse. That time, too, a lusty scream drove the bear away.

Winter Ice for Summer Homes... No Easy Task!
February 1962

THE iceman doesn't come as far as Harding Lake, forty-five miles south of Fairbanks, and mechanical means aren't yet ready to take over the job of cooling the lemonade and keeping food fresh. As many of the summer homes on the lake are far from the road, getting ice in summer is a real problem.

Some of the home-owners solve this summer problem on a winter outing. Station wagons loaded with shovels, a chain saw, sacked sawdust, peavey, king-size ice tongs and a boy's ice sled, they drive to their cabins on a trail bulldozed out of the snow on the frozen lake.

First step in the ice-storing project is to shovel some three feet of snow out of the way. Then, as Neal Johnson (with saw) and Roger Butler demonstrate at upper left, the ice is cut to the length of the chain saw blade and a chunk is pried out with the peavey. After that first chunk is out (note their smiles of triumph at upper right) the cutting is easy.

It isn't so easy to lash a two-hundred-pound chunk of slippery ice onto a sled and coax it up the steep bank, as Butler and John Bowman are discovering in the photo at right, but they can cut enough ice in one day, and store it in sawdust insulation, to last four families through the summer.

Photos by Margilee Watts

Owl Comes for Visit, Decides to Stay
March 1962

SOME people keep parakeets, or canaries, or mynas. The Jack Bovees of College kept Tweedy, a short-eared owl.

Maybe Tweedy knew the Fairbanks area was going to have its coldest winter on record. Maybe he just wanted to live with people. Anyway, he flew into the Bovee house one day last November, when the mercury was moving down and pickings were slim outdoors, and simply settled down.

His hosts—Jack, Joan, four-year-old Jeffrey and two-year-old Crystal—were flabbergasted, then fascinated.

How does one entertain an owl? Tweedy made it easier than his nocturnal nature and three-foot wing-spread would suggest. Jack sawed off a tree branch and made a perch in the living room, with appropriate protection for the floor, and after the first two or three nights Tweedy sat on it, sleeping quietly while the family slept. During the day he was free to fly around the general living quarters, and he always took wing when some sudden noise startled him. Usually he would land on a curtain rod. Once he landed on a freshly frosted cake, but, surprisingly enough, that was the only thing he damaged during his stay. When anyone, even a casual visitor, would say, "Back to your perch, Tweedy!" he would promptly obey.

The Bovees fed him regularly, a mixture of raw meat, bird seed and gravel, which he would pick gently from their fingertips. His personal habits were described as "clean, regular and precise."

The accompanying photos undoubtedly represent Tweedy's first experience with cameras and strobe lights. In his first portrait, at left, he is wide-eyed, not expecting the flash. By the time the photo at right was snapped he had acquired some sitting savvy. Just before the flash he drew the nictating membrane over his nearer eye to protect it from the unpleasant glare. Hence the blind look of the left eye.

"All birds have this thin membrane, like a third eyelid," said Photographer Jim Couch. "I had hoped for years to capture the evidence on film, and Tweedy cooperated wonderfully."

The Bovees would gladly have kept Tweedy as long as he cared to stay, and though he had frequent chances to leave as he had come, he wasn't interested. But an owl is wildlife, and Alaska has laws against keeping wildlife in captivity. After two months there came a letter saying that Tweedy must be released.

Reluctantly the Bovees gathered at the door, and waved an equally reluctant wild bird out into the winter cold.

Photos by Jim Couch

Klondike Locomotive
Historic No. 673 Comes Back to Dawson

February 1962

AFTER almost half a century of waiting for something to happen to it, No. 673, the little diamond-stacker locomotive that once ran between Skagway and Whitehorse and later served the Klondike Mines route, has come back to Dawson to stay.

This little wood-burning locomotive was first brought north for use on the narrow-gauge White Pass and Yukon Railway, then in 1906 was purchased by the Klondike Mines Railway to haul passengers and freight on its thirty-two miles of track from Dawson's Front Street station to Sulphur Springs on the Bonanza.

One Dawsonite, Mrs. Harry McDonnell, who came north in 1899, was in Grand Forks that day in 1906 when the first KMR train arrived, gaily decked with flags and bunting, and the whole population of about five thousand turned out to greet it. Mrs. McDonnell recalls the steep grades and trestle bridges high over deep ravines along the route, and the ease and speed of traveling by train in comparison to horse and wagon or foot travel.

The KMR had three locomotives—the 73,350-pound diamond-stacker, built in 1881; No. 55, 100,000 pounds, built in 1885, and No. 57, 159,000 pounds, built in 1899. Their biggest freight load by far was cordwood, rafted down the rivers to Dawson then loaded onto flatcars and hauled to the placer operators along the creeks, who thawed their ground with wood fires.

No More Payload

As the pay grew thin the individual miners sold out one by one to dredge operators, who used cold-water thawing. The population on the creeks dwindled, and in 1912 the KMR closed down. Its roundhouse and shops at Klondike City disappeared and the weeds grew tall around the three little engines.

Then, when Dawson began to gather mementos of its fantastic past in preparation for next summer's Yukon Gold Festival, the little engines again attracted attention. Last winter, through the efforts of the Klondike Visitors Association and the Museum Society, the eighty-year-old diamond-stacker and its larger partners were moved across the ice of the Klondike River and set up on narrow-gauge tracks in Minto Park, where they are being restored as museum pieces.

T.A. Retallack

Editor's note – There's more to the story of the Klondike Mines Railway, as the following letter testifies. It appeared in the May, 1962 Alaska Sportsman®, correcting and amplifying the history of the old diamond-stacker and its younger companions.

I note with considerable interest your picture on page 38 of the February issue, showing the diamond-stacker locomotive of the Klondike Mines Railway, and I have a few corrections and additions to make to the item.

The locomotive is KMRy #1, formerly White Pass & Yukon #63, sold to KMRy in 1902. I noticed last summer that the old WP&Y numbers were showing through, and were more prominent than the newer KMRy numbers.

The following is the correct roster of the four KMRy locomotives:

KMRy #1, built in 1881, weight 73,350 pounds, ex-WP&Y #63, sold to KMRy in 1902.

KMRy #2, built in 1885, weight 100,000 pounds, ex-WP&Y #55 (formerly Columbia and Puget Sound #8), sold to KMRy in 1904.

KMRy #3, built in 1899, weight 159,000 pounds, ex-WP&Y #57, sold to KMRy in 1906.

KMRy #4, built in 1912, weight 120,000 pounds, purchased new and used for two years, stored until 1942, when purchased by WP&Y, retired in 1952 and sold to the Oak Creek Central (Oakwood, Wisconsin) in 1955.

CARL E. MULVIHILL
Skagway, Alaska

Bear Prowls Smokehouse... So Chilkat Dancers Have a New Bearskin

May 1962

THE Chilkat Dancers of Port Chilkoot and Haines got a new bear costume recently, but not before its original owner had caused some excitement.

Sam Johnson, a fisherman who lives near Port Chilkoot, came home for lunch one day during the canning season last summer and mentioned to his wife, Helen, that a big brown bear had been seen on the beach near her brother's cabin, and people were wondering whether it was the same bear as one seen swimming Lynn Canal a day or two earlier. Mrs. Johnson, busy preparing the meal, remarked that she hoped no bear came prowling around there, and stepped onto the back porch to get something. There was the bear, a "great big one," right beside the back-yard smokehouse where they were smoking seal meat!

Johnson went out to chase it away. It did not choose to leave. He grabbed his .257 and called to his wife for some shells. She brought a whole boxful. He shot once and hit the bear in the rear.

The bear now chose to leave, but too late. A second shot caught it behind the right ear. It got a short way up the hillside, tearing up the brush in its way, then stumbled over a log and got no farther.

Johnson and a couple of neighboring fishermen, Walt Rigsby and Chris Tagg, tied a rope around the bear's neck and pulled it down the hill. Quite dead, it no longer looked so big—it measured six feet and weighed about five hundred pounds—but it was still too much bear to have around the place. The problem of what to do with it was solved when someone thought of Carl Heinmiller, manager of the Chilkat Dancers.

Yes, Heinmiller could use the pelt, so he and Walter Porter, one of the dancers, loaded the carcass onto a jeep and took it to Port Chilkoot. There, in a reversal of rolls, the white man from "down south" showed the Chilkat Indian how to skin a bear.

The pelt, properly tanned and with Porter inside and a hand-carved, hand-painted bear mask on top, now takes the leading part in the ancient Bear and Raven dance of the Chilkats.

Photos from Mimi Gregg

1962

Refinery for Cook Inlet
April 1962

■ A contract for the construction of an oil refinery on Kenai Peninsula has been awarded to Ralph M. Parsons Construction Co. of Los Angeles by Standard Oil Company of California. The refinery, which will have a capacity of 20,000 barrels a day, will be built on a 482-acre tract near the present marine terminal on Cook Inlet. Standard purchased the tract from the State of Alaska last October for $250,000. The cost of the project has not been announced but estimates place it close to $10 million. Work is expected to start immediately after the spring break-up.

Floods Close Mines
April 1962

■ Two mines in the Hyder area, in the extreme southeastern corner of Alaska, were closed after the flooding Salmon River washed out sections of the road there. The Riverside Mine, about seven miles from Hyder, owned by Carl Wickstrom and his wife, and the Silbak Premier Mines, fourteen miles from Hyder and on the Canadian side of the border were both closed. The flood was caused by a midwinter thaw which sent a torrent of water from Summit Lake into the Salmon River. Normally the river is about thirty feet wide and two feet deep, but it swelled to a width of 1,000 feet with a depth of six feet during the height of the flood, according to Wickstrom. Several sections of the road were washed away entirely and others were heavily damaged.

Gold Prospects Sought
May 1962

■ Shell Oil Company and a number of individuals have applied to the State of Alaska for permits to prospect the bottom of Norton Sound, off Nome, for gold. It is estimated that $80 to $100 million in gold was taken from the three Nome beach lines in early years, and large quantities of gold are believed to be mixed with the sand and gravel of the ocean floor in that area. Prospecting permits are something new in mining regulations and are a feature found in no other state. The permit protects the prospector's rights in an exploratory area if he finds workable deposits there. After the discovery has been made, the prospector may stake a claim if the discovery is on land or may lease the area from the state if it is submerged.

Matanuska Maid
November 1962

■ Members of the Matanuska Valley Farmers Cooperative Association have voted to change the name of the organization to Matanuska Maid, Inc. The former name has been in use since the cooperative was organized on October 28, 1936, but the members have considered it too long and unwieldy. The trade name, Matanuska Maid, has also been in use since the founding of the cooperative, which has grown to be the largest distributor of locally grown produce in Alaska.

Wolf at the Door... Money for Food, and Shoes for Little Feet
August 1962

A WOLF at the door was a modest bonanza for the Paul Tony family, now of Kodiak, who spent the winter of 1960-'61 in a Fairbanks Exploration Company cabin on the Steese Highway out of Fairbanks.

"That winter," Mrs. Tony wrote, "a pack of eight wolves used to come down the highway, detour around the cabin, and continue toward Chatanika. Sometimes they howled from a ridge back of the cabin at night. When spring came, only a large female [see photo] and her mate remained to serenade us. Her high, mournful voice was a sharp contrast to the magnificent depth of his. He always sounded as though he howled for the sheer joy of hearing himself, while she seemed impelled to voice an ancient, endless grief.

"The children [Karen, pulling wolf's ears in photo, Paul Junior at the other side of dad, and Peter] had played out late the evening of April 30, shouting and laughing as they watched the full moon rise, and were just as noisy inside the cabin as they prepared for bed.

"Suddenly Paul said urgently, 'Put out the light!' I leaped to obey, and the children leaped to the window as he opened it, raised his rifle, and fired. A dark form fell in the moonlight. We rushed outside in time to see it disappear in the black spruce shadows. Rifle ready, Paul went cautiously toward the spot as the scantily clad youngsters shivered on the doorstep. I snatched a jacket for each child and was trying to get Peter into his when their dad returned, dragging the female wolf.

"Groceries, a car battery, summer shoes for little feet—the 'wolf money' bought them all. Now, when the dogs of Kodiak howl at night, the children waken and ask, 'Are the wolves here?' More often they ask, 'When are we going back to the Steese?'"

How to Catch a Fish – A Really Big One –
January 1962

MOST stories about the catching of a "soaker" king salmon involve long and patient effort to invite the strike, followed by long, exciting battles of perseverance and skillful manipulation of tackle on the one side, agility, stamina and desperation on the other, with the outcome uncertain to the end.

Robert George of Klawock, who caught the 68-pound king shown in the photo, dispensed with all that. He used sudden surprise tactics.

George, a member of the *Cindy Sue's* crew seining off the west coast of Prince of Wales Island last summer, was in the act of coiling the lead line when the big king cruised up outside the seine. He simply reached down and caught the fish in his arms, one under its head, one under its tail, and scooped it out of the water. By the time the fish knew something was happening, he had it safe in the seine skiff.

It happened last August 10, and Larry Demmert, owner and skipper of the *Cindy Sue,* saw it all. The snapshot was taken minutes later aboard the seiner.

A Record Season for Ferry 'Chilkat'
February 1962

■ The state-owned ferry *Chilkat* went into winter moorings at Juneau late in November after setting a new record for carrying vehicles and passengers on its run between Tee Harbor, Port Chilkoot and Skagway. Captain G. David Gitkov reported that the season's traffic totaled 7,554 passengers and 2,080 vehicles. This was an increase of 26 per cent in passengers and 13 per cent in vehicles over last season. California motorists again led all other out-of-staters in use of the ferry, with 116 of the cars carried bearing California registrations. There were 61 from Washington, 56 from Oregon, 30 from Michigan, 29 from Montana and 25 from Texas. All other states except North Carolina, Rhode Island, Tennessee, Vermont and Hawaii were represented during the 1961 season.

No Drinking, No Gambling, No Fighting...
September 1962

■ Six rules have been adopted by the Village Council of the village of Togiak, in Western Alaska, to make the village a better place in which to live. The rules, according to the *Bristol Bay Digest,* published at Naknek, are as follows:

1. All school children shall be home by 9 p.m. from Sunday evening through Thursday evening. All school kids shall be home on holidays by 10 p.m. and on Friday and Saturday.
2. There shall be no gambling in this village.
3. There shall be no drinking or making anything to make a person drunk. PLEASE DO NOT DO THIS. Also no person shall come into this village drunk from another village. Drunk persons coming from other villages will be fined $25. If he can't pay his fine, he shall work off the fine. Pilots will be fined $250 for bringing in drunk people.
4. There shall be no stealing in this village. If you borrow something, return it as soon as you can or let the owner know what you borrowed.
5. Watch your dogs. Dogs shall be tied. Skinny dogs will be killed. After three days of running loose, dogs will be killed. Puppies six months old or older will be tied.
6. There will be no fighting in this village between people.

Hal Tye, Alaska Division of Agriculture

Dairies Produce Most of State's Farm Income
October 1962

A HERD of dairy cattle grazing placidly in the shadow of Pioneer Peak, in Matanuska Valley, makes a striking picture, and also a contribution to Alaska's largest agricultural industry. There are about 367 farms in Alaska, of which only 80 are grade A dairy farms, yet their total production in 1961 (23,570,000 pounds or 10,912,037 quarts of milk —an increase of 17 per cent over 1960) accounted for $2,318,000 or 53 per cent of total cash receipts for farm products.

There's another side to the coin, however. The 3,200 head of milk cows on those 80 dairy farms on January 1, 1962, represent an inventory value of $1,376,000. Counting the cleared land, machinery, buildings and stock, an Alaskan dairy farm represents an average investment of $65,000. Further, as Acting Director of Agriculture George Crowther points out, dairying demands long hours of work every day of the week and every week of the year, as well as greater versatility, foresight and managerial skill than most farming requires.

The Matanuska and Susitna Valleys and the Anchorage area have 67 or all but 13 of the state's dairies, three-quarters of its milk cows. Milk sales in these areas totaled $1,904,000 last year, and sale of other farm products brought the year's grand total up to $3,052,400.

Once She Was the Queen of the Stikine...
September 1962

THOSE who knew the *Hazel B.* when she was queen of the Stikine River run would be sad to see her now, listing dejectedly where receding floodwaters left her, on the bank of the Tanana near the railroad bridge at Nenana.

In the days of the Barrington Transportation Company the *Hazel B.* carried Cassiar-bound prospectors, vacationers and trophy hunters up the Stikine from Wrangell to Telegraph Creek. Later she went farther north to become a veteran of other great rivers—the Kuskokwim, Iditarod, Koyukuk, Tanana and Yukon —where she was one of the earliest and largest screw-type vessels in service. Now she seems doomed to neglect and eventual destruction in the swirling, silt-laden Tanana.

Michael Bradner

Mauled by a Grizzly
* * * *
Loses His Sight, But Not His Nerve

October 1962

IN July, 1959, Lee Hagmeier, 17, of Auke Bay, near Juneau, Alaska, was badly mauled by a brown grizzly while he and a companion were on a fishing trip near his home.

Lee lost his sight in that accident, but has never lost the nerve he displayed at the time. When the tragic accident took place, sportsmen and sympathetic friends contributed from literally all corners of the earth to help Lee get needed plastic surgery and the best care possible. We refrained from reporting Lee's progress, for the experience of publicity can sometimes be as terrifying and as damaging as any woods tragedy, and for Lee's saddened parents, Mr. and Mrs. John Hagmeier, continuing publicity likewise presented its problems.

Now we can report that three years later, Lee is getting a Seeing Eye Dog, has gone successfully through school at Perkins School for the Blind, near Boston, graduating with college course honors and is planning college this fall.

Under the care of Dr. Bradford Cannon of the Massachusetts General Hospital in Boston, Lee went through a two year program of surgery to erase as much as possible the damage done by the attacking bear. Graduating with high school seniors in 1960, he went back for post graduate work and underwent another shattering experience, falling ill with meningitis and losing the hearing in his right ear.

Lee's illness forced his return home to Auke Bay, in the spring of 1961, but he weathered this new storm and returned once more to post graduate work at Perkins in the fall, completing his studies and further surgery. This past spring, before graduation, Lee also found time to show his abilities in track, running a two mile race in company with another lad, partially blind, in the time of 11 minutes and 31 seconds, a record for the Eastern Athletic Association for the Blind.

We don't know how Lee has come out with his Seeing Eye Dog, or just what his college plans are this fall, but we're sure Lee will continue to be an inspiration to all of us.

Lee will not see again, with both optic nerves severed, and then, too, there is that loss of hearing in one ear, but we think this picture of Lee taken last spring speaks for itself—when a boy really loves his hunting and fishing and the great outdoors, he gains a spiritual strength that will carry him through. May his courageous facing of really tough odds be a beacon in the night for others who will face physical and spiritual odds and may the knowledge that his love of the outdoors has helped him over the roughest spots remind us all that to give other youngsters love and understanding of the things of the wild can help to build more strong young men, a better America, and a better world.—*The editors.*

Although blinded as a result of an encounter with a bear, Lee Hagmeier hasn't given up his fishing. Here Lee proudly displays a 32 pound king salmon he caught with his father near his Auke Bay home in the spring of last year.

New Bridges Lack Romantic Charm of Old River Ferries

June 1962

BRIDGES may be handy and even handsome, but for romantic and photographic appeal they will never rival the old river ferries which they are rapidly replacing. Three ferries are still in use on the Whitehorse-Dawson-Tetlin Junction highways—an alternate route of both scenic and historic interest often taken by travelers either to or from Alaska, and actually only 136 miles farther than the direct route by way of the Alaska Highway. A bridle ferry takes cars across the Pelly River, but those crossing the Stewart and the Yukon at Dawson (shown here) are drive-on, back-off ferries. Wrote the photographer, Mrs. H. W. Barker of Reseda, California, "They bump into the bank and hold while the Indian deckhand jumps ashore, shovel in hand, to smooth off your exit with dirt, old lumber, rocks, logs, anything handy." Small ferries, they don't carry many cars and the motorist may have to wait a while when traffic is heavy, but it's always pleasant to find that passage is free.

Mrs. H. W. Barker

Shemya Plane Base Outdated by Jets
April 1962

■ Northwest Orient Airlines has closed its operating base on Shemya Island near the western end of the Aleutian chain, but for the next few months the company will maintain radio and ground control approach facilities there for the Air Force. Shemya was a vital base on Northwest's great circle route between Seattle and Japan when piston-engine aircraft were used. With the coming of long-range jets, however, Shemya has become useful only as a weather, radio and, occasionally, a refueling station. The company's facilities on the island are being turned over to the Air Force.

Where's Alaska?
October 1962

■ Alaska's admission to statehood did a good deal to educate the American public about their northern domain, but misconceptions still exist, particularly in the eastern states. A man in Anchorage is still shaking his head over the reply he received from a New York City firm. Interested in buying a boat, the man wrote to Seafarer Fiberglass Yachts, Inc., in New York for information. The company replied:

"Thanks for your inquiry regarding Seafarer Yachts. Please be advised that all sales outside the North American continent are handled by our office at Rotterdam, Holland. Your inquiry has been forwarded to our Rotterdam office and no doubt they will reply to you soon."

The Halibut Capital
April 1962

■ Prince Rupert, B.C., has kept her title as Halibut Capital of the World with total halibut landings of 16,973,000 pounds during the year 1961. Landings on the Pacific Coast totaled 69,637,000 pounds during the year, and of this total, 29,613,000 pounds were caught by Canadian vessels, 40,024,000 pounds by American vessels. Seattle was second high as a port of landing, with 13,168,000 pounds, while landings at all ports in Alaska amounted to 25,926,000 pounds.

Pioneer Firm Returns
October 1962

■ The first trading company in Yukon Territory, Canada, is returning there after an absence of many years. It was in 1843 that the Hudson's Bay Company sent Robert Campbell to the Yukon country. He established several trading posts, including Fort Selkirk at the junction of the Yukon and Pelly Rivers, which was burned by the coast Indians because it interfered with their trade routes. Today the Hudson's Bay Company and a subsidiary operate 40 department stores and 190 other stores and posts in Canada. October 1 the company is opening its newest department store, in Whitehorse, capital of Yukon Territory.

Snow for Frostbite? No
April 1962

■ "Don't rub a frostbite with snow, even though an ancient adage prescribes that treatment." That is the advice of Dr. Henry G. Storrs of Fairbanks who has completed a two-year study of frostbite cases at St. Joseph's Hospital in Fairbanks. "Rubbing a frostbite with snow actually causes more injury," according to Dr. Storrs and other doctors. The proper first-aid for frostbite, according to the doctors, is to place the frostbitten area in warm water. The frostbitten area will first become red; then it may become white and blister. If the frostbite is deep enough, the area will later become black. Carelessness and alcoholism are the major causes of frostbite, according to Dr. Storrs.

State Gets Old Building
April 1962

■ The largest office building in Seward, built in 1904 as offices for the Alaska Central Railroad and later taken over by the federal government, has now been acquired by the State of Alaska. In addition to various state offices, the building is now occupied by offices of the Seward city government on a lease arrangement. The city offices were moved to the building from the Seward Fire Hall, where they had been located since that building was constructed in the late 1940s.

Log Exports Approved
October 1962

■ Applications for the export of 1,800,000 board feet of cottonwood logs from Southeastern Alaska to Japan have been approved by the Alaska Department of Natural Resources. To date, some 500,000 board feet of cottonwood logs have been shipped from the Haines area, at a dockside price of around $32.50 per thousand board feet. Most of the logs shipped thus far have been used for wooden soles for sandals.

New Tower for Anchorage's Merrill Field
September 1962

THERE'S a fine new control tower building at Anchorage's Merrill Field, a four-floor steel and concrete structure (lower photo) built at a cost of $177,000 and dedicated last July 14. The new structure replaces a wooden tower built twenty years ago to replace, in turn, a steel beacon-tower erected in 1931.

But the memorial plaque, shown with Airport Manager William Morgan II, is the one presented thirty years ago by the Anchorage Women's Club (who also presented the field's original beacon-tower), moved now to a new place of honor beside the new structure. The plaque reads: "To that dauntless pioneer of the air, Russel Hyde Merrill, whose life's aim was the development of aviation in Alaska."

Merrill, born in Des Moines, Iowa, in 1894, came to Alaska in 1925 after serving as a Naval aviator and pioneered in air cargo service out of Anchorage. He was a member of the chamber of commerce committee which, in June, 1929, petitioned for the establishment of a landing field in Anchorage. The following September 16 he took off in a Whirlwind Travel Air with freight, and was never seen again. The initial clearing for Anchorage's "aviation field" had already begun, and it was officially named Merrill Field.

City of Anchorage photographs

Kodiak Cold Storage
August 1962

■ Kodiak's long-awaited cold storage plant went into operation at the end of May when 110 tons of frozen halibut bait, including 70 tons of octupus from Japan, arrived on the Alaska Steamship Company freighter *Tanana*. The bait was the first fish to be stored in the new plant, owned by Alaska Ice and Cold Storage, Inc., and located in Kodiak City Dock area. Wrangell-born Howard Wakefield, who has been associated with Alaska's fisheries most of his life, is manager of the plant. L. C. Berg, fish buyer at Sitka for the past 30 years, is production foreman. Present daily freezing capacity of the plant is 80,000 pounds, with storage capacity of around 1,750,000 pounds. Another million pounds of storage capacity is to be added during the coming winter.

Mount Kathryn
April 1962

■ A 4,305-foot mountain some 125 miles northeast of Fairbanks has been named Mount Kathryn in honor of the late Mrs. Kathryn Stanton Patty. Mrs. Patty, the wife of the President Emeritus of the University of Alaska, died last year. The peak is located between Woodchopper Creek and Coal Creek in an area where Mrs. Patty spent many years while her husband, Dr. Ernest N. Patty, was engaged in mining there. The name has been officially approved by the U. S. Board of Geographic Names in Washington, D.C.

Millions for State
May 1962

■ The State of Alaska received $2,050,060.36 from the Bureau of Land Management last February 23, representing payment under the Mineral Leasing Act of the state's share of bonuses, royalties and rentals received by the federal government on public domain lands in Alaska during the second six months of 1961.

The Bush Circuit: Too Much Drinking ... A Good Shepherd ... Reindeer Fat and Seal Oil

Happening in far corners of the 49th State, as reported by correspondents of the *Fairbanks News-Miner*:

POINT BARROW, by Guy Okakok. February 24. A wolverine was caught by Winiford Akvokana. Winiford said he would have caught two, but the other wolverine got away. This wolverine has been caught in a trap before, because two toes were loose. He and his father, Floyd Akvakana, were away trapping. Floyd said on up their lines there are hardly any wolves at all, only wolverine tracks. And most of the wolverines are amongst the caribou herds.

March 1. Something fishy going on here. Week ago four or five flashlight codes have been going on from different posts. These signals had planned by the young people. People here wondered, why this situation, have been going during the night. They said, this must be stopped right away, before anything happens.

March 3. Our village is getting worser every year. People who drink know that they go too far sometimes, and don't know what they are doing. Yesterday one fellow pointed his shotgun at his wife; lucky he didn't pulled the trigger.

TUNUNAK by Paul Albert. All the sorrow when Rev. Paul C. Deschout, S.J. left for good after staying over 30 years and we won't see him again, only in Heaven if we win our religion. Rev. Deschout was young and full of skill when he came here. He had three villages 20 to 60 miles apart where he spent winter months at two other villages and summer at Tununak. So he divides his time in three parts during the year: Nightmute and Chifornak during winter and Tununak during summer as Tununak his home headquarters.

Later he realizes that only dog team was used to travel in winter and boat in summer. He raised his own dog team and ordered a dory and a kicker that he can travel on his own risk, for so many trips he had to make such as sick calls from here and there. He travels by dog teams for quite a number of years; like sick calls he travels from few miles to 60 miles, yet he always smiles with kindness to everyone he meets on trails. About 10 years ago he had a stroke of paralysis that struck one whole side of his body, but still he did not gave up, but remain staying with his people. He is a shepherd that watches his flock with great love. We owe him many thanks and only way to pay him back is by our prayers.

NUNIVAK ISLAND, by Henry J. Shavings. Nov. 1. Beginning today, Northern Consolidated F-27 is coming to Mekoryuk taking reindeer meat to Hooper Bay. There is at least 7500 pounds of meat to go there.

The up-river is starting to freeze. Some people are beginning to fish through the ice. They get quite a bit of tom cods by hooks.

Some families have moved to the other village. They are netting for seals. They use nets to catch seals—small seals. I hope they will be lucky.

Our weather has been very poor lately. We have fog, snow, blowing snow and high winds. We never have mail for quite awhile because of the weather.

There seems to be only fat women at Nunivak Island. I don't know why. Maybe they eat too much reindeer fat and seal oil.

In the Land of Gold
* * * *
Rich Silver Ores Barged Out in '20s

August 1962

THE story of Yukon gold is so glamorous that little is heard about Yukon silver, yet the territory has been producing substantial quantities of silver for some four decades. The road to Dawson, the "golden city," is in fact a spur of the Mayo Highway built in 1953 for year-round transport of silver-lead-zinc concentrates from the Mayo district, about 125 miles almost due east of Dawson, to Whitehorse for transshipment by rail and ocean steamer to a smelter in Trail, B.C. In pre-road years, cencentrates were shipped from Mayo Landing by way of the Stewart and Yukon Rivers.

The accompanying photos are from the late L.C. Short of Hillsboro, Illinois, purser on Yukon River sternwheelers from 1913 to his retirement in 1946. Mr. Short wrote:

"Silver mining in Yukon Territory began in 1921 or '22. Ore was mined at Keno Hill and hauled into Mayo during the winter months to await the spring breakup of the Stewart River. At that time I was purser on the Str. *Alaska*, of American registry. Later she was changed to Canadian registry and renamed the *Aksala*.

"In 1923 we left Mayo towing the barge *Cannocko* with a load of silver ore. It was early summer and the water was quite swift. On rounding a bend the steamer was unable to handle the barge with its heavy load, and we hit a rock bluff some miles below Mayo, sinking the barge. When the water went down we were able to salvage most of the ore.

"At that time there was such a heavy tonnage of ore that it could not all be moved up the Yukon to Whitehorse, and for a couple of years we hauled a portion of it downriver, then up the Tanana to Nenana. We delivered it there to the Alaska Railroad, to go to Seward and be loaded on ocean steamers. It was smelted in Bradley, Idaho.

"Tranportation in the North surely has changed since my day up there!"

Barges of silver ore from Keno Hill at dock in Dawson. Sternwheelers are, left to right, Casco, Yukon and Whitehorse.
At this time (1923) part of the heavy tonnage was shipped down the Yukon, then up the Tanana for loading on the Alaska Railroad at Nenana, rather than upriver to Whitehorse and the White Pass-Yukon route.

Silver ore hauled from Keno Hill during the winter of 1922-23 awaits shipment from Mayo Landing. The longer steamer is the Alaska, the other, the Nasutlin.

During summer's low water, crew salvages ore from the sunken barge, Cannocko, in the Stewart River.

Photos from L. C. Short

1963

Photos from Emery F. Tobin

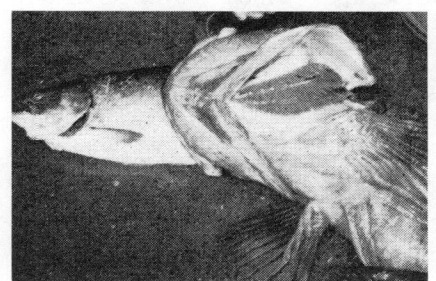

Surprised Sportsman Boats Two Big Fish on Single Lure
January 1963

KING salmon fishing was good in the Ketchikan area for those sportsmen who could brave the stormy, chilly weather of last November, and Darrell Edwards (at left), trolling off the south end of Pennock Island, was reeling in the twentieth king he had taken over a two-week period.

Suddenly, instead of the lively fight of an indignant king, Edwards felt the resistance of a heavy, dead weight on the end of his line. He got the weight to the surface and found he still had the king, a twenty-pounder, but its tail half was fast inside the gullet of a forty-pound ling cod. Evidently the ling had struck the king just after the king had struck the lure, and was unwilling or unable to let go, so Edwards caught both.

A retired Coast Guardsman, Edwards was stationed in Ketchikan during World War II. He returned recently for some more of Ketchikan's famous sport fishing, and is now employed in the post office.

Andy Simons... The Dean of the Big Game Guides
January 1963

■ A colorful guiding career which spanned half a century ended September 17 with the death of Andrew A. Simons, the "Dean of Alaska Big Game Guides" and holder of Guide License No. 1 for many years. He died in a Seward hospital at the age of 80.

Born in Finland, Simons came to Alaska in 1901, worked in Juneau, prospected near Nome, and finally settled down to stay on a homestead in the Kenai Lake area near what is now Mile 20 of the Seward Highway.

His guiding career began in 1910 with a chance encounter on the trail with some unsuccessful hunters from England. Andy joined the party and located game. When the homeward-bound hunters stopped off in Juneau with their beautiful trophies they sang Andy's praises to Territorial Governor Walter E. Clark. The governor followed through by presenting Andy with an honorary guide's license, and License No. 1 was his until the numbering system was discontinued.

Andy's fame grew in big game circles and he guided hunters from all over the world. He also served for 27 years on the old Territorial Game Commission.

Stumpage Prices Fall
March 1963

THE U. S. Forest Service has cut minimum stumpage prices from $3 to $2 per thousand feet for Sitka spruce and from $1.50 to $1 per thousand feet for all other species. Stumpage is the price charged for timber cutting rights on an "as is, where is" basis.

Survives Bear's Attack
January 1963

■ Some 250 stitches were required to close the wounds and punctures suffered by a moose hunter who was mauled by a grizzly bear in the Puritan Creek area near Mile 90 of the Glenn Highway. The attack occurred September 15 after the hunter, 45-year-old Harold Tuttle of Anchorage, had become separated from his hunting companions.

Tuttle said he came upon the bear in a small clearing and was able to get only one shot away from his .30-'06 rifle before the animal attacked him. Tuttle rolled himself into a ball on the ground to protect as much of his body as possible, but he suffered a crushed wrist and multiple lacerations and punctures. In the fracas, Tuttle's rifle was knocked into the shape of a boomerang.

When the bear finally left, Tuttle walked two miles to the highway where he flagged a passing motorist.

Leg Broken in Fall
February 1963

■ Don't try this on a freeway, it was tough enough on a lonely Shuyak Island road. Howard Anderson of Anchorage, 37-year-old mechanic for the Federal Aviation Agency on Shuyak, which is about sixty miles north of Kodiak, fell over a cliff onto the beach and broke his leg in three places. With his legs useless and the tide coming in, Anderson dragged himself three hundred yards back to his jeep. Then he lay on the floorboards of the jeep and drove for help, operating the foot pedals with one hand and the steering wheel with the other. It took him about two hours to cover half a mile.

Oldest Firm Quits
January 1963

■ Alaska's oldest continuous mercantile firm, started in 1796 by Alexander Baranof under the name of the Russian Trading Company, has gone out of business in Kodiak. Liquidation of the grocery, clothing and hardware departments of the firm, which now is known as Donnelley and Acheson, began in October. Robert Acheson, an official of the firm, said that only the automobile distributorship would continue. After Alaska was purchased by the United States, the firm was known as the Alaska Commercial Company. It was owned for many years by the Erskine family, who sold it to Donnelley and Acheson.

Uranium Quota
March 1963

ALASKA'S only producing uranium mine, the Baywest Company on Prince of Wales Island, completed its uranium allotment of 6,000 tons of ore for 1962 early in November and closed down mining operations for the year.

U.S. Coast Guard photo

The Last Lamplighter... Prey to Progress
January 1963

THE historic profession of the lamplighters has fallen prey to progress. As of November 15, the services of Raymond E. Burton, lamplighter of Kasilof Range Lights at Cohoe, on the Kenai Peninsula, and last lamplighter of the U. S. Coast Guard, were no longer required.

Since 1716, when the first lighthouse in America was built at the entrance to Boston Harbor, dedicated men have lighted and maintained lighted aids to navigation. These men have served under many federal departments, but since 1939 they have been employed by the Coast Guard.

Many of the lighted aids to navigation seen throughout Alaska were once illuminated by burning kerosene. It was the lamplighter's job to see that the lights remained burning, no matter what the hardship or weather.

In 1950 there were 32 lamplighters in Alaska. As late as 1958, there were 13 aids to navigation which burned fuel for illumination. Now, with the electrification of the range lights at Cohoe, all operate without lamplighters' services.

Captain Albert E. Harned, Chief of Staff for the 17th Coast Guard District, wrote to Burton:

"Your work has been completely satisfactory in every respect and your faithful service over the past years is appreciated. Since you are the last lamplighter remaining in the Coast Guard, it is with regret that we must terminate your service."

1963

Six Days Adrift on Ice
June 1963

AN Eskimo cries only when his world is coming to an end—or just beginning.

Two King Island Eskimos wept when the search plane high in the air flew on—then turned and circled the tiny ice floe upon which they had drifted for six days and nights in the Bering Sea.

Hours earlier their companion, 55-year-old Frank Kayvanuk, had died of exhaustion and exposure in the subzero weather. But the two who survived, John Angusac, 38, and Ignatiuous Annayoc, 42, were in surprisingly good condition when they were hospitalized at Nome after their rescue by an Air Force helicopter.

The nightmare of northern hunters, who must seek their winter livelihood on the ice, is the sight of a widening strip of water between themselves and the mainland. For the three King Island hunters, the nightmare began December 31. They had no boat and little gear because they planned only a short trip on the pack ice near their home. Three days later they shot a seal. It was their only food. When rescue finally came, their ice floe had drifted ninety miles southeast of King Island and was forty-four miles off Northeast Cape on St. Lawrence Island.

Pony for Orphans
March 1963

WHAT is the best thing to go with a cowboy outfit? Why, a pony, of course. So the forty-man crew of the Alaska Steamship Company freighter *Chena* delivered one, complete with saddle, bridle and stirrups, to the orphans of the Jesse Lee Home at Seward last Christmas. Along with the Shetland pony came individual gifts for each of the forty-three children in answer to their letters to Santa Claus. Each year for the last six years the crewmen of the *Chena* have drawn the children's Santa Claus letters out of a hat. Sometimes the children ask for the moon, but the sea-going Santas usually manage to come through. This year's gifts ranged from transistor radios to walking dolls—and ran heavily to cowboy outfits.

Frantic Fishing
March 1963

THERE was some rather frantic fishing along the banks of Ketchikan Creek recently after a combination high tide and seven-inch rainfall swept the pilings out from under the Arctic Bar. Customers left hastily when the floor began to tilt shortly after seven o'clock that damp December evening. Owner Mae Torgerson grabbed the contents of the till and fifteen minutes later the Stedman Street structure slid into the water. Townsfolk gathered at the river with landing nets as bottles of liquor and cases of beer bobbed downstream along with the debris from the two-story frame building. Loss of the bar and its contents was estimated at $36,000, but fishing was good with the catch running as high as 151 proof.

Photo by Dolores D. Roguszka

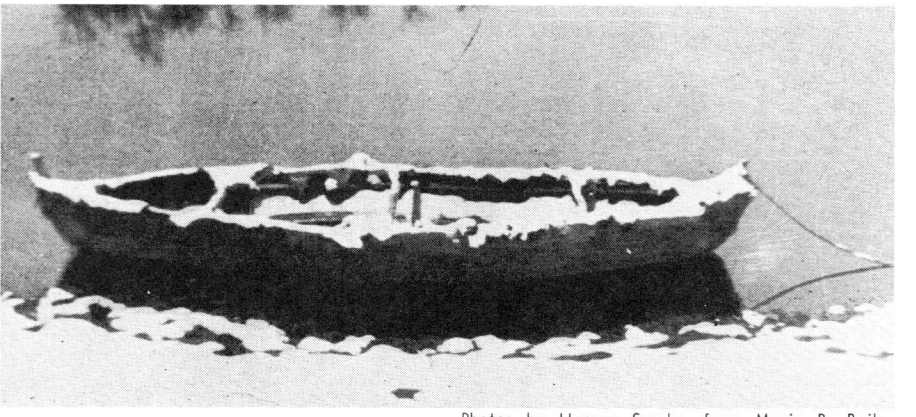

Photos by Horace Smoke, from Marie B. Bailey

A Moose Makes a Wreck out of an Airplane...
February 1963

"AND I've been out hunting for a moose!"

Steve McCutcheon of Anchorage, on his way to his own small plane one day last fall, stops to ponder the quirks of fate as he inspects the rudders and elevators of a Piper Super-Cub after a bull moose altered its tail section.

Tracks indicated that the moose had come during the night, passed by several other planes, and attacked this one whose owner had also been flying in search of good moose-hunting ground.

The planes are moored at the Lake Hood-Spenard Seaplane Basin at the Anchorage International Airport, a state-operated facility where more than one-tenth of all the seaplanes in the world are based. All types of seaplanes from Taylorcraft to Dehaviland Otter, owned and flown by businessmen, air taxi operators and John Q. Public, are moored at the basin.

...and a Man Makes a Canoe out of a Moose
February 1963

THE man who met the wolf at his door and made a robe from its hide had nothing on Harry Sam of Stevens Village, who shot a moose and brought home its meat in a canoe made of its hide.

Sam was alone on the Dall River, which empties into the Yukon just below Stevens Village, when he shot an exceptionally large moose. He couldn't face the prospect of packing out all that meat, nor did he care to leave any of it behind. With only his hunting knife as a tool he set out to build a canoe.

He skinned the moose, cut birch saplings, fashioned them into a frame, lashed the moose hide to it, loaded the meat aboard and paddled down the Dall.

Horace Smoke—the "Holy" Smoke of sled-dog racing fame—and his family lived on the Yukon at the mouth of the Dall, and Smoke snapped the accompanying photos of Sam's ingenious craft before taking him and the moose on upriver to the village. Said Marie Beemer Bailey, who sent the photos, "This happened in 1953, while I was teaching in Stevens Village. Horace gave me the negatives, but I mislaid them until recently."

Pioneer Physician
February 1963

Dr. Will H. Chase, pioneer physician who performed his first appendectomy in a tent along the gold-rush trail to Dawson, retired last fall after 65 years of practice in Alaska. He and his wife will live with a daughter in Seattle. Dr. Chase came to Alaska from New York in 1897, after only a few months' practice. He landed at Skagway and trekked in to Dawson, where he spent two years as a part-time prospector and part-time doctor, traveling by dog team to visit his patients. He moved on to Fairbanks, Valdez and Katalla, then in 1908 settled down to stay in the prosperous little coastal town of Cordova where, with another doctor, he set up a hospital in an abandoned cannery. Since that time he has served 24 terms as mayor of Cordova and delivered more than 3,000 babies.

An ardent sportsman as well as a civic leader, Dr. Chase was one of the original members and for six years head of the Alaska Game Commission. He was appointed Alaska's first health commissioner in 1909. Sixteen years later, when he aspired to become game commissioner instead of health commissioner because of his strong interest in preserving Alaska's wildlife, he was named to both positions. He also found time to write a number of articles and books on his big game hunting experiences including *Alaska's Mammoth Brown Bear*, a scientific treatise on a subject in which he is considered an authority.

Oil Search Approved
March 1963

THE Interior Department has approved an exploration contract with Sinclair Oil Company and British Petroleum Exploration Company (Alaska) for a search for gas and oil on a 611,725-acre tract in the Chandler River area east of Umiat. Under terms of the contract, the firms are required to drill at least three exploratory wells during the next five years and spend one and a half million dollars in exploration activities.

Isolated Drilling Site
May 1963

RICHFIELD Oil Corporation chalked up another first in Alaska oil exploration late last year when it began drilling an exploratory oil well from a platform connected to shore by a 2,300-foot causeway in Wide Bay. The work was complicated by the fact that the site lies 350 miles southwest of Anchorage, 100 miles south of King Salmon, 150 miles west of Kodiak, and close to absolutely nothing.

Supplies and materials were brought in by Foss Launch and Tug Company barge. Nine 52-foot trailers were set up for the Morrison Knudsen construction crews which built the causeway, and later to provide housing for the 44-man drilling crew.

The rig was erected at the far end of the long structure, and Wide Bay Unit No. 1 was spudded early on the morning of December 13th. By February 6th, drilling had reached a depth of 2,742 feet.

Woodworking Skill Eases Isolation in Bush Country
January 1963

HOW do dwellers in the isolated bush country spend the long, dark hours of the sub-Arctic winter?

Victor Hill of Ophir has spent many of those hours at woodworking. He has no power tools, just a handsaw, an ax, a jackknife, infinite patience, and pride in his workmanship. A pair of rocking chairs, in which he and Mrs. Hill are seated in the larger photo, speaks for his skill. The chairs are made with neither screw nor nail, every joint cemented with wood glue, and the exquisite carving (see smaller photo for detail) was done with the jackknife. They represent the work of three winters.

Ophir, in the Kuskokwim Mountains thirty air miles northwest of McGrath, was a booming mining town when the Hills came, in 1917. Other people moved away, one by one, as the ground was worked out, but the Hills stayed on. They have a neat little log home, bright in summer with flower gardens, about a mile outside the ghost town. They grow vegetables, gather wild berries and build up their woodpile during the long, warm summer daylight. In summer, too, they have an occasional neighbor, as a few mines still operate in the vicinity. A road goes to Takotna, about halfway to McGrath, where there is a post office, but the nearest trading post is in McGrath and accessible from Ophir only by bush plane.

Eugene C. Curtis Jr., from Sandy Jensen

The dramatic seasonal changes of the sub-Arctic were not new to the Hills even when they came to Ophir, as they were born and reared in Finland. Now, after close to half a century, they have no desire to pull up stakes and spend their twilight years in a strange place.

Asked for more information about his chairs, Hill replied in painstaking English, "I got Birch tree. Let it dry 2 years. I start to make chare. Mostly was in my head. Hand make. I med chare vit han saw. Come to Alaska, 1905. Come to Ophir, 1917. I be 80 year old, 1962."

He would be willing to sell the chairs, he said, but definitely not for the price of ordinary factory-built rockers.

Sandy Jensen

'Ice Broke Off – We Lost Our Ship' ... Tragic Exploration Recalled
February 1963

■ The death this year of Arctic explorer Vihljalmer Stefansson touched off reminiscences by 71-year-old Jimmy Killigivuk, Point Hope Eskimo, who was hired by Stefansson as a hunter during the 1913-18 expedition along the Arctic Coast. Killigivuk recalled, in a story told to *Fairbanks News-Miner* reporter Terry Brady, how the expedition's flag ship, the 250-ton steam whaler *Karluk*, was caught fast in the ice and vanished while he, Stefansson and some others were off hunting. Nearly half of the 25 men aboard the *Karluk* lost their lives as the vessel drifted, still trapped in the ice, some 1,100 miles westward.

Killigivuk recalled: "In 1913 I worked with Stefansson. He came to Point Hope in his boat *Karluk*. It was a big boat and burned coal. It was a steamer. One more man from Point Hope, Jerry Powyouruk, and me, we go with Stefansson to hunt for him.... We left Point Hope in August and go to Point Barrow. We get stuck in ice there.... After few days, Stefansson decided we should go ashore and hunt caribou. We way out and can't see shore. We take two sleds, each nine dogs, Stefansson and me and Jerry and some more. Six men altogether. We went towards shore but we couldn't make it inshore. We stay overnight on the ice and next morning go to an island and overnight there again.... The next morning Stefansson tell us 'Jimmy and Donald, you better go to *Karluk* tomorrow and get more groceries and ammunition.' When I get up next morning, ice broke off. Big lead. Open water and we cannot make it. We lost our ship.

"Every night we burn big driftwood fire. Burning driftwood hope our ship see us. Nobody see us.... We started out for Point Barrow. No food except a little tea, little sugar, and some dog pemmican.... In five days we make Point Barrow.... I rested in Point Barrow until 1914. Then left Point Barrow with three men and six dogs. I don't know how many days later we make Point Hope. I didn't stay with Stefansson three years. I never saw him again. I never saw Point Barrow again...."

Bob De Armond

A Rare Argillite House Model... Carved by a Haida Indian Craftsman

May 1963

A MODEL of a house made of carved slabs of argillite, one of three such models known to exist, was recently presented to the Alaska Historical Museum at Juneau by Mrs. Belle Simpson, also of Juneau. Mrs. Simpson is owner of the Nugget Shop, one of the largest dealers in Alaska paintings and aboriginal Alaskan handcraft work.

The house, which measures twelve and a half by fourteen and a quarter inches and is nine and three-quarters inches high at the gables, is entirely of argillite slabs pegged together except for the base, which is of red cedar. The whole weighs twenty-eight pounds nine ounces

It is believed to be the work of Charles Edenshaw, a famed Haida Indian craftsman who lived on the Queen Charlotte Islands of British Columbia where argillite, a black, clayey material which hardens after being exposed to the air, is mined. Edenshaw was a silversmith as well as a carver.

Two other argillite houses of similar type are presently in the Canadian National Museum at Ottawa and the American Museum of Natural History in New York City. The one in Ottawa is believed to have been displayed in the World's Columbian Exposition in Chicago in the summer of 1893.

The house in the Juneau museum is carved on all four sides and on both slopes of the roof. Figures on the front shown in the upper photograph include Wasgo, a mythical sea monster, and the face of the man who captured Wasgo. There are also four small heads, mounted under the gable, which represent Wasgo. The roof is decorated by two sea lions, one of which shows clearly in the lower picture. Below it are traditional eye, ear and claw designs.

One peculiarity of the house is the absence of a doorway. This is believed to be because, according to E. L. Keithahn, the museum curator, the Haidas did not usually make model houses either of argillite or wood. But they did make boxes, which were often carved and had lids. This piece was carved much as a box would have been, then the roof was added in place of the usual lid. The roof does have a large smokehole just as the early-day Haida houses did.

Mrs. Goldstein acquired the rare piece from her father, R. Goldstein, who came to Juneau in 1885 and traded with the Indians until his death in 1900.

Bears Raid Cattle Herds
March 1963

IT's been a bad year for bears and bulls—and we're not talking about the New York stock market. Cattlemen on Kodiak Island said that raids on their herds by the giant Kodiak bears there had been worse than usual. De-Witt Fields, who has a ranch in the Larsen Bay area, said that he lost forty-five of his cattle—about half of his herd —to the bears during the year and that other cattlemen suffered heavy losses, too. Three of his cows were killed during the first week of November in a single raid by seven bears, four of which were shot. The bear attacks were most frequent during the late fall months after the salmon had gone and just before the bears went into hibernation. Personnel of the Protection Division of the State Department of Fish and Game cooperate with the cattlemen in attempting to control the bears with the taste for beefsteak.

Discovery Well
April 1963

THE first certification of a discovery well on lands leased from the State of Alaska was approved January 10 by Commissioner of Natural Resources Phil R. Holdsworth. The well, known as Middle Grounds Shoal No. 1, is located offshore in Cook Inlet and was drilled by Pan American Petroleum Corporation and its associates in the venture. Certification is issued upon evidence of the first discovery of oil or gas in commercial quantities, and reduces the royalty rate that must be paid the state from twelve-and-a-half per cent to five per cent.

A Pioneer Returns
January 1963

Mrs. Mary Etoline Watt, who was born in Wrangell before the turn of the century, visited there in August after an absence of more than 60 years. Mrs. Watt's father was Duncan McKinnon, for whom McKinnon Street in Wrangell was named. He came from Scotland during the Civil War and joined the Union Army. By 1867 he was a sergeant, and he was sent to Sitka with the first contingent of American troops and took part in the raising of the United States flag on October 18, 1867. Following his discharge from the Army, Mr. McKinnon moved to what was then known at Fort Wrangle and opened a general store which was soon advertised as "The Most Complete Outfitting House in Alaska." In 1888 he returned to Scotland and married Mary McDougall. Two children were born to the couple in Wrangell—Mary Etoline and a younger brother, John Duncan. Mrs. McKinnon died in September, 1899, and her husband the following January. The orphaned children returned to Scotland and were reared by friends of the family. Mrs. Watt, now a grandmother, is proud of her middle name, Etoline, taken from Etolin Island near Wrangell. She christened her oldest daughter Margaret Etoline, and she in turn named her first daughter Marilyn Etoline.

Road for Talkeetna
April 1963

TALKEETNA finally has a road. The only trouble is that it doesn't go anywhere, and you can get to it only when the river is frozen. It starts at the bank of the Susitna River opposite Talkeetna, runs through virgin timber for twenty-seven miles, and then it stops. It's not as useless as it sounds, however. Financed by Shell Oil Company, it will be used to facilitate oil exploration in the wilderness area. Meanwhile, the homesteaders across the river can get into Talkeetna, and the Talkeetnans can enjoy Sunday spins in their Arctic Cats, Snow-Gos, tractors and trucks—as long as the river stays frozen.

Dial Phones – Color, Too
July 1963

THE old hoot 'n' holler radio communications system for isolated villages in Southeastern Alaska is rapidly becoming a thing of the past.

Regular telephone service, complete with dial telephones (available in the latest decorator colors), is scheduled for the towns of Kake and Angoon in July. Similar service was installed for the towns of Hoonah and Pelican late in 1961.

The service will be furnished by Southeastern Telephone Company, with Alaska Communications System providing the long distance lines.

All the equipment necessary, including ACS micro-wave equipment, is installed and tested in especially built vans in Seattle and shipped north by boat. Only the tower is built on location.

Southeastern Telephone Company is owned and operated by John Cushing, president; Martha Cushing, secretary-treasurer; and R. J. Cushing, vice president and general manager. The Cushings are old-timers in the Alaska telephone business, having placed the original Sitka and Kodiak telephone systems in service.

Another Oil Discovery
November 1963

MORE good news for Alaska's growing oil industry. Shell Oil Co. reported an initial oil discovery near the middle shoals area of Cook Inlet, the first strike on submerged lands in Alaska. Shell made the announcement as operator of the well, a joint venture among Shell, Richfield Oil Corp. and Standard Oil of California.

Alaska's Infinite Variety –

From Desert Sand...

Dolores D. Roguszka

June 1963

DESERT sands in Alaska? Yes, indeed! The vast area of the 49th state provides almost every imaginable type of terrain and much of the northern part of Alaska is arid. North of the Arctic Circle, on the Kobuk River, lie the Great Kobuk Sand Dunes and the Little Kobuk Sand Dunes. They are approximately a hundred miles upriver from the mouth and are near the northern limit of timbered country. The dunes cover an area from twelve to fifteen miles long and from three to six miles wide. A traveler coming upon the dunes unexpectedly might feel that he had wandered into the middle of the Sahara rather than the "frozen North."

...to Endless Swamp

Barbara Murray

June 1963

ALTHOUGH a few sections of Alaska show desert characteristics, as in the upper picture, a far greater part is so swampy that overland travel is a nightmare except in the winter when the ground and waterways are frozen solid. This aerial view of a part of the Tetlin-Northway basin of Central Alaska is typical of thousands of square miles of the state. Innumerable small lakes and ponds are separated from each other by narrow strips of soggy ground, a part of it covered with scrubby timber. This kind of country provides nesting grounds for ducks, geese and other waterfowl, and home for mink and muskrat, but few other uses have been found for it.

Historic Cutter 'Bear'
* * * *
A Grave at Sea Instead of a Lowly Role Ashore

June 1963

A VESSEL famed in the annals of Alaska and of both the Arctic and the Antarctic reached the end of her eighty-nine year career in March. The auxiliary barkentine *Bear* sank on March 20 about a hundred miles south of Halifax, Nova Scotia. She was being towed from Dartmouth, N.S., to Philadelphia where she was to have been fitted out as a museum and restaurant.

Built at Greenock, Scotland, in 1874 for the Newfoundland sealing trade, the *Bear* was heavily constructed to withstand the rigors of seal hunting in the ice packs. After eleven years as a sealer, she and another sealing vessel, the *Thetis*, were purchased by the U. S. Navy and sent in search of an American expedition to the Arctic which two previous searches had failed to find. The *Bear* rescued the seven survivors, including the Army officer who headed it, Lt. A. W. Greeley.

Following her return from that mission, the *Bear* was turned over to the U. S. Revenue Cutter Service, now a part of the Coast Guard, and brought to the Pacific. Her hull was further reinforced for work in Arctic ice and until she was retired in 1929 she was one of the principal units of the annual Bering Sea Patrol. On this assignment, she pushed through Bering Strait and into the Arctic each summer, performed countless rescue missions and carried medical aid to far northern villages.

On September 21, 1891, the *Bear* landed several head of reindeer at Unalaska, the start of the Alaska reindeer herds. During the next several years she made frequent visits to Siberia to pick up additional reindeer for transportation to Alaska.

After she was retired by the Coast Guard in 1929 the *Bear* was moored at Oakland, California, as part of a marine museum. Then in 1933 Admiral Byrd selected her as part of his expedition to the Antarctic and she made new history in that service. During World War II the *Bear* was on active duty as a patrol ship in the Atlantic. She then returned to her original trade as a sealing vessel out of Canadian ports. Since 1952 she had been laid up at Dartmouth, Nova Scotia.

Recently the old ship was purchased by Alfred M. Johnson of Villanova, Pennsylvania, who spent some $175,000 in restoration and reconversion work. She left Dartmouth for Philadelphia on March 17 in tow of the tug *Irving Birch* and ran into an Atlantic gale. The towline broke when thirty-foot waves rolled up and the two men aboard the *Bear* were taken off. Battered by wind and sea, the *Bear* sank before the tug could get a line on her again.

At his Seattle home, Rear Admiral F. A. Zeusler, U. S. Coast Guard, retired, who served aboard the *Bear* in 1914-1916, was advised of the sinking. Said he, "I'd much rather have her on the bottom than turned into a museum-restaurant. She was a fine vessel and that kind of service was beneath her."

Coast Guard Photo

Ice Box for Eskimos
September 1963

AN ice box for the Eskimos? Sure. The natives on Little Diomede Island can really use one. Most Eskimos can dig a hole in the perma-frost to keep their meat frozen during the summer months. But Little Diomede is on solid rock. The Rev. James A. Flynn, one of the few white people on the island which lies just across the International Dateline from Russia, explained that the people often must eat partially spoiled walrus, seal, whale and polar bear meat when it becomes warm in the summer. "We call it stink meat," he said. So four U. S. firms contributed a big 40-by-12-by-8 foot refrigerator and a portable generator to operate it, and sent it north last spring on the Bureau of Indian Affairs' supply ship, *North Star III*.

Lost Boy 'Not Scared'
July 1963

TWELVE-year-old Andy Lutz landed in the Whitehorse, Y. T., hospital with a couple of frostbitten toes after wandering for five days in the freezing bush near Upper Liard. He got lost on a Sunday while hunting rabbits. He had matches for only one fire which he built the first night, and the rest of the time he slept between his two dogs to keep warm. His only food was a squirrel which he shot Wednesday and ate raw ("It sure was funny to eat"). Rescue parties reached Andy on Thursday—but by that time he was on the right track out anyway.

"I wasn't scared," said the 12-year-old. "I've been hunting since I was a little kid."

Busy Bee Post Office
October 1963

THINGS were really buzzing around the Soldotna post office recently after a shipment of bees with a hole in the package arrived for a Clam Gulch resident. Petite Postmaster Mickey Faa was a little dubious, but the carrier assured her the bees would not leave the queen which was in a separate container at the top of the package. He advised her to put the bees in a warm place, and the package was placed in a storeroom.

The advice was dead wrong. The warmth brought the bees out of hibernation, and when someone opened the door—briefly—they were buzzing excitedly about the storeroom. Mickey contacted the offices of the Department of Fish and Game and the Fish and Wildlife Service, but personnel there disclaimed all knowledge of how to cope with the situation and indicated they wished to take no part in the procedure. Helpful friends suggested, from a distance, that she entice them with a container of syrup; lure them with a flashing mirror; or stupefy them by smoking a big black cigar.

Finally Mickey came up with a workable idea of her own. The heat in the storeroom was turned off and the fans turned on to cool things down. Then she put a clean bag on her vacuum cleaner and proceeded with mop-up operations on the subdued creatures. The bag was stapled shut and delivered, true to postal tradition.

Last Dog Sled Mail Carrier Misses Ceremony . . . His Plane Was Late
September 1963

A GRAND gesture towards the old and new in postal service was planned at ground-breaking ceremonies for the new post office annex at the Fairbanks International Airport last June. But it didn't quite come off.

Along with the usual formalities, William Hartigan, assistant postmaster general in charge of transportation, was on hand from Washington, D. C. to break the ground. And it was noted that Hartigan had ridden the first mail service truck to come up the Alaska Highway in 1961.

But the real kicker of the affair was supposed to be the presentation of a certificate to Chester Noongwook of Savoonga, the last dog sled mail carrier in the United States. Actually Chester made his last run over the 100-mile route from Gambell to Savoonga on St. Lawrence Island last January when airplanes took over the service. But the special award was planned to take proper note of the end of the dog sled mail route era.

Chester didn't make it. The very transportation which had displaced him —the airplane—got hung up some place and didn't get into Fairbanks until four hours after the ground-breaking ceremonies.

But postal officials regrouped upon his arrival and handed him his certificate when he got off the plane.

Collision in Laundry
December 1963

CHICKEN and Sandy-Andy collided in the Laundry. Feathers fly? Nope. Just a few cohos.

Translation: Clell Hodson on his troller *Chicken* and Roy Clements aboard his troller *Sandy-Andy* were fishing near Elfin Cove in a narrow channel called "The Laundry" because the water runs so rapidly. They were so busy hauling in coho salmon they didn't notice each other. No harm done to speak of, other than a broken pole, tangled gear, and a few loosed fish.

Longest Police Beat?
October 1963

THERE may be a bigger police beat in the world, but we bet there isn't a longer one. State Trooper C. E. "Jim" Hussey was transferred to Fairbanks recently after four years of "patrolling" the 1,200-mile long beat which stretches from Kodiak Island to Attu, the farthest west island on the Aleutian Chain. During the three months before his departure alone he logged 6,000 miles. His means of travel varied from fish boats to bush planes, and helicopters to automobiles. His replacement is State Trooper Donald Church.

Boys Wreck Ferry, Dock
November 1963

TWO small boys wandered into the empty wheelhouse of one of Alaska's new ferries, the *Taku*, as the vessel was tied up with engines idling at the Petersburg terminal. They wondered what would happen if they pushed a couple of shiny control levers. Plenty, they found out.

The vessel surged forward, twisting and breaking two 75-foot steel counter-balance towers, pulling out a portion of the dock, and dropping the 180-foot loading ramp into the water. Fortunately no one was on the ramp at the time. The boys flew out and a crew member flew in and got the ferry into reverse just short of shore.

The ferry sustained about $4,000-worth of damage, and the cost of rebuilding the dock was expected to run around $100,000. Ferry service to Petersburg was suspended for several months and out-of-state cars stranded there were taken off by barge. The parents of the boys, who were from San Diego, were fined $1,000—$500 for each boy, the maximum under state law.

The Ferry 'Chilkat's' Classy Cooks
October 1963

SOME pretty classy cooks were aboard the state ferry *Chilkat* when she left Juneau early last July to begin new passenger and auto service between Valdez and Cordova. The kitchen crew consisted of Alaska's first lady, Neva Egan (right), wife of Governor William A. Egan, and Hazel Downing (left), wife of Public Works Commissioner Richard A. Downing. In the center is Bob Smith, mate, approving the whole idea. The ladies had originally intended to make the trip partly for the fun of it and partly to put some feminine finishing touches on the passengers' lounge. But they suddenly found that there would be a little galley duty along with it when bids for a concession for crew and passenger food service aboard the *Chilkat* went a-begging. At the end of the two-day voyage from Juneau to Cordova, crewmen agreed that the cooking was great, and the ladies were given an honorable discharge after a chef was transferred to the *Chilkat* from one of the new Marine Highway System ferries. The 99-foot *Chilkat* was displaced on its run between Juneau, Haines and Skagway early this year by the state's sleek new ferry fleet. But she was given a rousing welcome by the citizens of Cordova and Valdez where she will provide three weekly round trips during the summer months, and twice weekly during the winter.

Juneau Landmark... Nugget Shop Changes Hands
October 1963

THE Nugget Shop, a Juneau landmark, was sold recently by Mrs. Belle Simpson, widow of Dr. Robert Simpson who started the store in 1921 in partnership with the late Charlie Ostrum. New owners of the shop are William Stiley of Auke Bay and James Nelson of Juneau. Mrs. Simpson is a member of the pioneer Goldstein family and was born in Juneau. Dr. Simpson, who came to Juneau from Iditarod, frequently traveled to the Indian villages of Southeastern Alaska, building up a collection of artifacts which he offered along with nugget jewelry, ivory carvings and the paintings of famous Alaska artists.

Gas Find Confirmed
July 1963

RUMORS of a natural gas field of enormous potential in the Beluga River Unit across Cook Inlet from Anchorage were confirmed in Richfield Oil Corporation's 1962 report to stockholders. The report said the discovery well, drilled to 16,429 feet, tested a gas sand at 4,800 feet at varying flows of 4.3 to 17 million cubic feet a day. Three additional wells also have been drilled, further outlining the productive area. The wells were drilled by Standard Oil Company of California, a partner with two other companies in the venture with Richfield.

Nunivak Herd Grows
December 1963

THEY counted the woolly humps on Nunivak Island again last fall and found that the musk ox herd is still increasing. U. S. Fish and Wildlife Service personnel said they observed a total of 406 musk oxen, including 73 calves. That's up from the 340 animals tallied a year ago. And the weather was bad during the count this year, so there may be more.

The musk ox once was a native resident of the Arctic slope of Alaska but was wiped out shortly after the introduction of firearms to the area in 1865. In 1930, 34 head were corraled in Greenland and transplanted to the College Experimental Farm near Fairbanks. They were moved to the predator-free Nunivak Island in the Bering Sea in 1935 and 1936. Prospects are now good for a carefully planned restoration of the animal to northern Alaska in areas not occupied by other big game animals. The musk ox yields a good grade of meat, similar to beef.

Killed by Bear
December 1963

THE two-year mystery over the disappearance of Sitka businessman Mark Rigling was cleared up last fall with the tragic discovery of bone fragments, a clawed plastic helmet, and a rifle on Chichagof Island. The evidence indicated that Rigling had been killed by a bear. The discovery was made by Jay Holmes, also of Sitka, and identification was confirmed by a local dentist after examination of a jaw bone found at the scene. Rigling disappeared while on a hunting trip two years ago and was the object of an intensive search.

Photo from Silas Trepus

Shooting the Moose Was Easy... Collecting the Meat Was the Problem
August 1963

SHOOTING this moose was no problem for Morley New of Fort St. John, British Columbia, but collecting the meat was something else again.

Morley and his dad, Howard New of Perdue, Saskatchewan had just finished their lunch while hunting off Mile 92 of the Alaska Highway when the big bull wandered out of the brush within 200 yards of them. Whamo—and that was that. They took the picture of Morley and the moose, dressed out the meat, and headed back to town for a jeep.

Upon their return, however, they found a sow bear and her two cubs chomping away on their winter meat supply. The mother bear cuffed the cubs up a tree and proceeded to give the hunters a real argument. "I didn't know a bear could make such a hideous noise," said Morley's dad. "She wouldn't back up from the meat and she wouldn't leave her cubs. We didn't want to shoot her since the cubs were too small to look after themselves."

Finally when the hunters were about fed up with the whole thing, the cubs came down the tree and departed with their snarling ma. They had ruined one front quarter, "but that still left a lot of meat for us," said Morley.

1963

Milestone for Oil
* * *
Major Refinery Opens at Nikiski

November 1963

ANOTHER major milestone in Alaska's growing petroleum might was the opening August 24 of Standard Oil's new ten million dollar refinery at Nikiski on the Kenai Peninsula. It is the first modern refinery to be built in the 49th State.

The refinery will process about 20,000 barrels of oil a day from the nearby Swanson River oil field into fuels ranging from heavy heating oil to jet fuel for Standard's Alaska customers. The facility also includes a 17-tank oil storage farm with a 800,000-barrel capacity—enough to load six tankers of the size that serve major Alaska ports.

Alaska's oil industry has developed rapidly over the past six years following the first major discovery by Richfield Oil Corp. in July of 1957 in the Swanson River field. Standard acquired half interest in the venture which has now grown to 52 producing wells that flow at an average of 28,500 barrels a day.

In October of 1960, construction was completed on a deep water tanker terminal, connected to the field by a 22-mile pipeline. Construction of the new refinery adjoining the terminal began in June of 1962.

Opening of the new plant touched off a gala celebration in nearby Kenai built around the theme "Whale Oil to Standard Oil," and featuring a full-fledged whale hunt for anyone who wanted to try it.

And as a real topper for the dedication ceremonies, H. G. Vesper, president of Standard's Western Operations, announced a one-cent-a-gallon cut in the Alaska price of gasoline and other petroleum products.

Photos by Delores D. Roguszka

Major Oil Find
December 1963

A MAJOR oil discovery under the waters of Cook Inlet was announced last September by Shell Oil Company, operator in a joint venture with Richfield Oil Company and Standard Oil of California. Shell said oil flowed at a rate of more than 600 barrels a day from an off-shore well drilled in the Middle Ground Shoals about 60 miles southwest of Anchorage. The oil was 35.5 gravity and came from a 550-foot productive interval between 7,480 and 8,177 feet. Shell's strike was the first confirmed oil producer outside of the Swanson River field, which lies about 22 miles to the east.

Bristol Bay Failure
October 1963

THE 1963 salmon season in Bristol Bay, normally one of the world's greatest red salmon areas, was a complete failure last summer. In the worst season on record, the Bristol Bay catch totaled only 2.5 million fish, well below the previous record low of 2.9 million fish in 1958. State fisheries experts, whose predictions have been highly accurate in recent years, had forecast a total return of some 15 million fish this year, including those caught on the high seas by Japanese fishermen. Last year the total return of Bristol Bay reds, including the Japanese high seas catch, was approximately 12 million fish. Despite the disastrous run, regional biologists say some 3.2 million fish escaped to spawning streams.

Food Relief for Bay
December 1963

SOME 125 tons of surplus food have been ordered by the State of Alaska for distribution to residents of the Bristol Bay area, hard hit by the disastrous red salmon run last summer. That order was in addition to some 19 tons of food sent to the area shortly after the normally rich salmon run went bust. An initial shipment of 190,000 pounds of food left Seattle early in September for distribution in the Dillingham area. It included flour, corn meal, dried eggs, dry milk, dry beans, rice, rolled wheat, lard, butter, processed cheese, canned meats and peanut butter, enough to meet the needs of 1,400 persons for three months.

'Pirates Return!' ... Angry Crab Fishermen Protest Russian Intrusion
December 1963

THE tempers of Alaska crab fishermen are wearing thin.

Two Kodiak fishermen were furious enough last September over Russian intrusion into their traditional fishing grounds to put in a ship-to-shore telephone call direct to Governor William A. Egan.

"What would happen if we blasted a few windows out of those Russian trawlers when they foul American gear?" asked Skippers Vic Hansen of the *Mercator* and Anton Isaaksen of the *Eileen*. They said that a fleet of Russian fishing vessels, operating in international waters west of Cape Low on the south end of Kodiak Island at the entrance of Shelikof Strait had deliberately fouled their crab pots. The two said they were driven off the grounds because they "couldn't afford to lose any more gear."

The Russian fleet left the area without incident after the arrival of a U. S. Coast Guard cutter, and the governor sent State Attorney General George Hayes to Kodiak to investigate.

After a marathon meeting with Kodiak fishermen which lasted for more than ten hours, Hayes said evidence showed the Russians deliberately destroyed thousands of dollars worth of American fishing gear.

"The Russians know that our people are familiar with the best crab grounds. So they went there. The Russians also must have decided that if they destroy our gear, our people would have to pull up their remaining gear and leave the area to the Russians. This is exactly what has happened. . . . Our crab pots actually became targets for the Russians, not merely gear to be avoided."

Hayes said that the United States, which has built up the king crab fishery by adhering closely to conservation practices, should declare the king crab a creature of the continental shelf, thereby reserving it to the United States.

In the past, the Russians have said they were only interested in bottom fishing in the area. But the fishermen who testified at the meeting and U. S. Coast Guard observers at the scene said they saw king crab in commercial quantities on the decks of the Russian vessels. In one instance, Russian crews attempted to cover the crab with tarpaulins.

The feeling was pretty much summed up by a two-inch headline in the weekly newspaper, the *Kodiak Mirror*: "Pirates Return!"

Dying Moose Falls on Hunter ... Five Broken Ribs
December 1963

HADDON Davis of Chena Hot Springs Road isn't likely to forget last fall's moose hunt. He and his wife, Orlena, were hunting south of the Tangle Lakes area off the Denali Highway when they spotted a couple of moose in a brushy area. Orlena picked out a bull with a good rack and downed it. As Haddon watched the animal through the scope of his rifle, he heard a rustling near his left elbow. Then his scope blacked out. Another moose was standing up right in front of him.

"Without even thinking," Haddon says, "I reached over with my left hand and put it on the moose's shoulder and pushed him away from me. Then I swung my rifle (in his right hand) over my left shoulder and fired. The bullet went through the moose's ear. His eyes popped out. And he fell down. Right on me!"

The Davises came out of the hunt with two-and-a-half freezers full of moose meat, one trophy moose rack (Orlena's) and five broken ribs (Haddon's).

Big King for Little Boy
August 1963

HOW would you like to have your first king salmon weigh just about 18 pounds less than you do? Seven-year-old Greg Johns Jr. of Craig had luck like that while fishing with his dad last spring. Greg weighs 54 pounds and his fish tipped the scales at 36 pounds 11 ounces—good enough for fourth place as of April 21 in the seasonal Craig-Klawock Salmon Derby. Young Greg's dad did all right that trip, too. He caught a king which weighed 37 pounds 8 ounces.

First Mental Hospital
January 1963

■ Alaska's first full-scale mental hospital, the $6.5 million Psychiatric Institute at Anchorage, was dedicated September 9. The 225-bed facility, financed by a federal grant to Alaska, is situated on a 70-acre tract in the Goose Lake area some four miles southeast of the city center, near the new Providence Hospital and the Alaska Methodist University.

Pioneer Birthday
September 1963

THE fiftieth anniversary of the establishment of the Alaska Pioneers' Home was celebrated at Sitka June 2. The date for the ceremonies was set to coincide with the 99th birthday of Emmett Koons, formerly of Juneau, who has lived at the home since 1935 and is its oldest guest. The home has grown from the cluster of U. S. Marine barracks which were turned over to the Territory of Alaska in 1913 to today's modern three-story building in the heart of downtown Sitka. Its first guest was Edward Ludecke, a member of the 9th Infantry color guard which raised the United States flag on Castle Hill in 1867 marking Alaska's transfer from Russia. One of today's 215 guests is E. B. Collins who was speaker of the Territorial House of Representatives in 1913 when the Pioneers' Home was established.

'Tustumena' Irks Kodiak
December 1963

RESIDENTS of Kodiak Island don't think much of the name Governor William A. Egan has picked for the new state ferry which will go into service next summer between Kodiak and the mainland. The governor, carrying out the theme of naming Alaska's new ferries after Alaska glaciers, says the vessel will be called the *Tustumena*.

"Sounds South African," commented one resident.

Just about everybody in Kodiak has been referring to the new ship as the *Kodiak Islander*. One unhappy resident said that when the ferry system was planned, state officials said the vessels would be named "for large land masses, including glaciers."

"Where can you find a bigger or more prominent land mass than Kodiak Island itself?" he grumbled.

The Tustumena Glacier, incidentally, lies about 45 miles southeast of Kenai and covers 154 square miles. The other ferries named after glaciers are the *Malaspina*, the *Taku*, and the *Matanuska*.

Last Regular Voyage for an Old Alaska Friend
April 1963

THE *Princess Louise*, shown here as she backed away from the wharf in Juneau last fall, southbound, may have made her last Alaska voyage. The picture was taken just forty years and a few months after the ship made her first call at Juneau. The popular steamer was built by the Wallace Shipbuilding and Engineering Company at North Vancouver, B.C., for the Canadian Pacific Steamship Company and has sailed under the house flag of that company since her launching. She had her first trial run on December 1, 1921. Measuring 4,200 tons gross and 330 feet long, her triple-compound four-cylinder engine drove her at 17.3 knots on trials.

The *Louise* first called at Juneau on May 22, 1922, on her maiden voyage north. She was in command of Captain A. Slater, who had moved to her from the popular *Princess Mary*. Captain James W. Troup, commodore of the line and a veteran of the northern channels, also made the voyage on her. Other well-known skippers who commanded her over the years included Captains Thomas Cliffe, Peter Leslie and Graham O. Hughes. Her last regular master was Captain Harry Murray.

During her forty years of service the *Princess Louise* carried thousands of passengers, a great many of them round-trip tourists, between Vancouver, B.C., and Skagway, Alaska, as well as between various British Columbia ports and other Alaska towns. Known as a comfortable ship and a lucky one, she had few accidents during her northern career and was never in serious trouble—an unusual circumstance for a vessel with so much mileage in these rock-studded and tide-swept channels.

Three More Disappear in the 'Headless Valley'
December 1963

THREE more persons have disappeared in the Yukon's sinister Nahanni Valley, sometimes known as the "Headless Valley." The story is told by Charles Hankins of Whitehorse, a helicopter mechanic and prospector who has spent the past two summers in the valley as a member of a group conducting a geological survey for the federal government.

Hankins says three young men, seeking tales of adventure for a Swiss publication, went into the valley last June and never came out. The three were identified as Fritz Weismann, 26; Wolfgang Mahmoke, 25; and Manfield Wutrich, 21.

"I saw them on Watson Lake in June," Hankins says. "They were dressed in buckskins from head to toe, and were obviously greenhorns." When he ran into them again a month later on the Little Nahanni River they had already swamped their canoe once because they didn't know how to load it. A body, believed to be that of Wutrich, was found August 6, along with the party's canoe and tent. "With those buckskins on," Hankins says, "they'd go down like rocks."

Hankins says there's nothing mysterious about the valley. "It is just a rugged, dangerous place where inexperienced people lose their lives. Legends have sprung up about it. It's full of hot springs and high mountains and glaciers. When you take all those things together, I guess it can seem a little eerie."

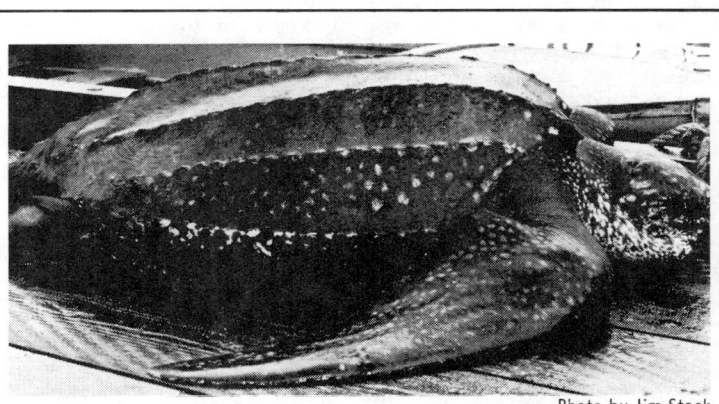

Alaska's Biggest, Ugliest... and only... Sea Turtle
December 1963

THE biggest, ugliest and—so far as is known—the only sea turtle ever landed in Alaska was hauled in last September by Cordova fisherman Dean Crammer. He was fishing at Egg Island Bar near the Copper River flats when the turtle got caught in his gillnet.

The turtle drew a lot of attention on the Cordova docks where it was identified by Fish and Game Department officials as a Leathery Turtle (the name of it). It was about six feet long, three feet wide, and two-and-a-half feet from the ridge of its shell to the bottom of its belly.

Sea turtles normally stick to warmer waters. But this wanderer gave a lot of Cordovans their first taste of fresh turtle soup.

Bush Flyers vs. Stork... One Loss, One Win
December 1963

THE truly exciting races with the stork in the Northland usually pit the bush plane against the big-winged bird. Last fall, for example, two planes were racing expectant mothers to the U. S. Public Health Service hospital at Tanana at the same time, but from opposite directions. One lost; one won.

The former was a Civil Air Patrol craft with a two-man Air Force crew and a medic aboard, along with the mother, Mrs. Eleanor Wholecheese. It became apparent shortly after their departure from Galena that they should have left earlier. The medic, however, had delivered babies before, and Mrs. Wholecheese, her 8-pound 10-ounce son, and the crew all came through fine. The birth certificate properly recorded the place of birth at 35 miles west of Tanana and 2,000 feet up.

The latter plane, flown by bush pilot Marc Stella, made it to Tanana a close ten minutes before Mrs. Nita Paneok of Fairbanks gave birth to her baby, also a boy. Pilot Stella, who keeps track of these things, said it was his 238th win in the race with the stork, against no losses. He specializes in flying expectant mothers to, and mothers and babies from, Public Health Service hospitals, and his Cessna 180 has been nick-named the "Baby Buggy." He even carries such emergency equipment as bottles and disposable diapers.

The margin of difference in this particular race was a strong easterly wind which helped Mrs. Paneok and hindered Mrs. Wholecheese.

No Lake, No Breakup
November 1963

THERE wasn't any Lake George breakup this year because there wasn't any Lake George. The spectacular annual phenomenon is caused by a seven-mile wide expanse of glacial ice which forms against the Chugach Mountain cliffs and plugs up the outlet. The glacier dam usually backs up water to form a 16-mile lake until the pressure becomes so great the ice falls away. This year, however, the runoff tunneled under the glacial ice and drained away down the gorge to the Knik River instead of backing up to form a lake. Alaska Railroad records, which date back to 1918, list breakups for every year since then.

Bush Circuit: Empty Meat Racks... Whaling
Frontier news from correspondents of the 'Fairbanks News-Miner':
June 1963

GAMBELL, by John Apangalook. The men have been out hunting various places and have had little luck, and as usual the meat has been very scarce. The racks are almost empty of dried meat, and what is worse the ducks are messing up the racks. All the natives are disappointed in the hunting situation and the restriction on ducks and geese. St. Lawrence Island isn't very suitable for raising pork chops and hamburger you know, but we CAN raise a few wild ducks and a goose or two. I wish those guys that make those laws would sit down and eat nothing but sea meat for awhile and then they'd know how good a duck can taste, and how silly it is for someone to fly in here and tell someone they can't eat ducks messing up their own meat racks.

The only way people can legally shoot ducks to feed their families is to drag boats across the ice to the water, then row out to international "dateline," and let the man at the bow of the skinboat shoot ducks where they cannot break the law. However this year looks like it will be very bad as the ice looks solid all around and extends way out making it difficult to get the boats to the water.

February 1963

BARROW, by Killitokti. Lloyd Nungak, one of the younger hunters from the village has been missing for several weeks. Lloyd went out with his dog team about the 18th of September to do some fishing. The next day four of his dogs returned home. An air search was made in the area south of Barrow. Several hunters were located on this search, but Lloyd was not found.

The fall whaling season is again under way, and many whales have been sighted and chased. As yet no kills have been made, but with all of the enthusiasm shown by the many hunters, muktuk and whale meat should be on all tables this winter. Whale muktuk and whale meat are the most prized of all sea mammals.

Saturday night we had a box social to raise money for street lights in Barrow. A large crowd was on hand and the evening was a success. Some of the boxes sold for over $50.00. One white man from the Site paid $33.00 for a box, when he got home that night what a surprise. This box had muktuk, frozen whale meat, dried caribou, and some dried salmon. Jerry Crow who sold all the boxes, said that he thought this box had fried chicken. What a joke.

Bonus Bids for State
October 1963

ALASKA'S tenth competitive petroleum lease sales May 8 netted the state a total of $4,137,027.12 in bonus bids on the total of 200 tracts offered. The highest bonus bid was $288,640 by Humble Oil and Refining Company for a 640 acre tract in the former Susitna Gunnery Range. Natural Resources Commissioner Phil Holdsworth said that the 158 tracts upon which bids were received sold for an average bonus price of $29.23 an acre. Bids ranged from $1.17 to $451 an acre. Alaska's nine sales to date have produced a total of $42,599,160 in bonuses.

1964

Alaska's Beloved Flag
* * * *
Orphaned Designer's Prize Watch Joins Flag in Museum

February 1964

THIRTY-SEVEN years ago, Bennie Benson, an orphaned schoolboy at the Jesse Lee Mission home in Seward, gave Alaska the design for its beloved flag, the golden Big Dipper and North Star on a field of blue. The American Legion, which sponsored the contest for the flag design, gave Bennie a white-gold watch.

Just recently, Bennie gave the State of Alaska his watch, too—for display in the state museum along with his original cut-out design. The watch is inscribed:

"Awarded in 1927 to Bennie Benson, Seward, Alaska, as first prize in the American Legion Alaska Flag Contest, whose design was adopted by Alaska as its official flag."

Beside the original flag design now in the museum is Bennie's explanation in 13-year-old schoolboy handwriting:

"The blue field is for the Alaskan sky and the forget-me-not, an Alaskan flower. The north star is for the future state of Alaska, the most northerly of the Union. The dipper is for the great bear, Symbolizing strenth (sic)."

Bennie, who has been ill and has undergone major surgery during the past year, made a special trip to Juneau from his home in Kodiak to present the watch, which was accepted by Governor William A. Egan and museum Curator E. L. Keithahn.

Alaska Pavilion for World's Fair in New York
January 1964

HERE is an artist's sketch of the Alaska pavilion at the New York World's Fair. The two-story building was constructed along the same general pattern as the Alaska exhibit at Seattle's Century 21 Exposition. It has an overall floor space of approximately 10,000 feet, and is designed to include two concession areas with a total floor space of 362 square feet. There's also room for additional concession space under cover in front if it is needed. The New York Fair will run from April through September in 1964 and 1965.

Bootleggers' Loss, Kotzebue's Gain
January 1964

KOTZEBUE is beginning to see some merit in the old motto: "If you can't beat 'em, join 'em." Nearly $65,000 profit, as a matter of fact. After years of trying to fight the bootlegging problem, the city began operating its own community-controlled liquor store. And after 16 months, it found that bootlegging had been practically eliminated, and the profits had paid for a new skating rink, a warmup shack, playground equipment, street maintenance vehicles, a garbage pickup program, and a city policeman.

After viewing the results at Kotzebue, the citizens of Bethel on the Kuskokwim River voted last fall to go "wet" with a community-controlled liquor store, too. The action came after Mayor David P. Swanson pointed out that Bethel could hardly have been considered "dry" since 340 out of 349 city court cases the previous year were linked to liquor consumption. And he asked: "Wouldn't it be better to bring liquor out where you can see it and have a better chance of controlling it, and let it pay for some of the costs it creates?"

Top Pay in Alaska
February 1964

FIGURES compiled by the Library of Congress rank Alaska state employes as the highest paid in the nation. The average weekly earnings of full-time Alaska state employes, not counting those in the State Department of Education, was $147.99 during the month of October. Second highest were California state employes with a weekly average of $124.69. Low on the totem pole were state employes in Tennessee with an average of $65.08 a week.

Blow for Whittier
January 1964

THE bubble burst for an infant Alaska industry last fall when the Koppers Company creosote treatment plant at Whittier closed down after just two years of operation. The closure came upon completion of a government contract calling for 50,000 railroad ties for the Alaska Railroad. Koppers was underbid by a Seattle firm on a new contract calling for delivery of 70,000 more ties.

The shutdown was a bitter blow to the dwindling community. All that is left is the vast abandoned Port of Whittier facility built by the Army during World War II, where about 30 servicemen are stationed on a maintenance basis, and the Union Oil Company's petroleum storage farm which has a payroll of five.

The Koppers Company employed only about ten men, but it purchased cut ties from small logging operations at Haines, Portage and Hope, Alaska, and utilized hemlock, a relatively hard wood not much used by other Alaska operators. It also manufactured creosoted ties for various spur lines and guard rails for highways. But without the Alaska Railroad job, that just wasn't enough.

'North to the Future'... Centennial in '67
March 1964

ALASKANS sharpened their wits and their pencils recently and came up with more than a thousand suggestions for emblems or slogans for use in Alaska's Centennial celebration in 1967.

Pictured here is the prize-winning emblem, submitted by Major Robert Vodicka of Elmendorf Air Force Base who has been in Alaska two-and-a-half years. His prize was $1,000.

The emblem features a totem pole depicting the transition of Alaska from a Russian colony to the 49th State. The onion-shaped dome of a Russian church forms the base. Above it, representing the ensuing periods of Alaska's history, are an American eagle, a miner panning for gold, a railroad locomotive, and the statehood star.

The slogan part of the contest was won by Richard Peter of Juneau, radio-television newsman for Station KINY, with the centennial slogan: "North to the Future." He got $300.

Oil Well in Cook Inlet Fuels 14-month Fire
January 1964

A BLAZING monument to the difficulties of oil exploration in Cook Inlet was extinguished late last October after burning out of control for more than a year. It was Pan American Petroleum Corporation's Cook Inlet State Well No. 1. The flames were snuffed out after a lengthy and expensive operation which included pumping some 40,000 barrels of sea water down a relief well. The sea water apparently caused the walls of the blowout to soften and slough off, forming a plug to block the flow of oil and gas.

The original well, located in mid-inlet about 35 miles south of Anchorage, had been drilled to the 12,500-foot level when, on August 21, 1962, unexpected pressures at the bottom of the hole caused oil and gas to blow out at the surface. Blowout preventor valves were closed, but failed to function properly. Finally the fuels were ignited to prevent contamination of the water, and the well burned continuously for the next 14 months.

Although the relief operation cost the oil companies millions of dollars, there is a bright side. The blowout was the first indication of commercial oil deposits in Cook Inlet, an indication subsequently confirmed by completion of a well by Shell Oil Company, Standard Oil of California and Richfield Oil Corporation.

Big Tonnage Gain for Port of Anchorage
January 1964

THE Port of Anchorage handled more than two-and-a-half times as much cargo during the first six months of 1963 as it did in the first half of the previous year. It added up to 53,374 tons against 19,947 tons in 1962, which isn't bad considering the fact that 1963 was just the third year of the port's operation. Another boost came recently with an offer by Standard Oil of California and Shell Oil Company to provide funds on a matching basis for a petroleum facility at the port. The city plans to match the offers of $136,000 and $66,000 respectively with monies from the federal Accelerated Public Works program.

1964

Back to Bootlegging?
February 1964

PROFITS or no profits, Kotzebue has decided to go "dry" again. The decision came in a 199–183 vote by the villagers to ban the sale of alcoholic beverages completely. For 18 months, Kotzebue had operated a community-controlled liquor store in an effort to beat the bootlegging problem. And they made enough money in the venture to pay for a number of community improvements, including street maintenance and a garbage pickup program, playground equipment, and the services of a city policeman. After viewing the results, the community of Bethel on the Kuskokwim River decided to try it, too. Now, with the vote, it will be back to bootlegging. Well, maybe that new city policeman will help.

Outhouses Out
March 1964

OUTHOUSES will be out at Whitehorse, Y. T., after July 31 of this year. The city council there has ruled that all residences must be connected to city water and sewer lines by that date.

Wien Propjets Take Over PAA's Whitehorse Route
March 1964

A COUPLE of veterans in Far North flying swapped a route recently to the benefit of all concerned. After 28 years on the route, Pan American World Airways turned over its Fairbanks-Whitehorse-Juneau run to Wien Alaska Airlines on December 20. With the transfer, Wien began three-times-weekly service between Fairbanks and Juneau with its F27 propjets replacing Pan Am's hard-working DC6B, the line's last propellor-driven aircraft left in Alaska service.

Both airlines sought the transfer. Pan American, which pioneered the route, explained: "With inadequate runways for jets, and insufficient travel to justify their use even with improved runway and airport facilities, Pan American has had to say farewell to Whitehorse." But the parting was not without a pang. For many years, Whitehorse had served as a vital link on the "mainline" to the north when the Juneau-Fairbanks hop was just too much for the range of smaller planes.

And for Wien, the oldest airline in Alaska with almost 40 years of service, the expansion southward was a logical move. With the addition of Juneau to its schedule, the airline now links 88 communities throughout the state. The new more frequent service not only brings Interior and Arctic Alaska in closer touch with the state capital, but provides an alternate route south with connections at Juneau for daily jet service.

Savage Arctic Storm Nearly Destroys Barrow
January 1964

SNOW and cold an Eskimo can handle. But it was wind and water that nearly wiped out the little village of Barrow on the Arctic Coast last fall. A savage gale with winds up to 80 miles an hour swept 15-ft. waves and chunks of ice right through the village streets.

Twenty houses were destroyed and many more were damaged. Four warehouses containing food which the last supply ship of the year had dropped off just weeks before were demolished. Small boats and planes were swept away. The winds toppled a 300-foot flight communications tower and the raging waters tore up portions of the landing mat on the airstrip, hampering rescue efforts. Sea water poured into the fresh water lake from which the villagers obtain their water supply.

Two big fuel storage tanks were ruptured, and the natural gas line which serves Barrow was cut, but miraculously there was no fire. Just as miraculously, no one was seriously hurt. Civilian property loss was estimated at $600,000.

Tales of heroism were numerous. One of them is of Carl Okpeaha, who battled his way through freezing winds and high water to reach the home of his grandparents seven miles from Barrow. He persuaded them to flee to higher ground just moments before their home was washed away. The grandfather was knocked unconscious by a large wave, but Carl managed to hold his head above water and drag him to safety. The grandfather, Clair Okeaha, was the Eskimo who many years ago ran 12 miles to bring word to the world of the deaths of Will Rogers and Wiley Post in the crash of their plane near Point Barrow.

Big Oil Platform
February 1964

PLANS for the construction of a $5.5 million production platform, designed to withstand the tremendous pressure of ice floes in Cook Inlet, have been announced by Shell Oil Company. The huge platform, which company officials say will be "as large as the 14-story Anchorage-Westward Hotel," will be erected over the site of the oil discovery at Middle Ground Shoal. It will be mounted on four legs 16 feet in diameter which will be sunk in the bed of the inlet. From the platform, 20 or more wells may be drilled directionally into the oil-bearing formation. S.F. Bowlby, senior vice president of Shell Oil Company, says it is hoped that the platform can be in place before the freeze-up next fall. Shell is the operator of the inlet venture, in partnership with the Richfield Oil Corporation and Standard Oil of California.

Saved from Ice Floe
April 1964

BRAVING high winds and freezing rain, a helicopter from Eielson Air Force Base snatched an Eskimo hunter from an ice floe in the Bering Sea after he had drifted alone for three days. The hunter, Ramauld "Romeo" Katexac of King Island, had been hunting for seals near his home when the portion of shore ice on which he was standing broke away. He had drifted nearly 26 miles in the general direction of Siberia by the time he was rescued. After he was whisked aboard the helicopter and given a steaming cup of coffee, Romeo thanked his rescuers and admitted, "I began to worry."

Fur Seal Treaty Renewed ... Dates Back to '11
January 1964

A SIX-YEAR extension of an agreement prohibiting fur seal hunting on the high seas of the North Pacific Ocean has been signed by the United States, the Soviet Union, Canada and Japan. The agreement, one of the oldest to have endured among the four nations, dates back to 1911 with a break only during World War II. Under terms of the treaty, hunting of fur seals is limited strictly to the Pribilof Islands, owned by the United States, and the Komandorsky and Roben islands, owned by Russia. The two nations give 15 per cent of their catch to both Canada and Japan. The treaty extension which was signed last October also provides for an investigation in 1968 to determine whether the herds are big enough to permit the resumption of sealing on the high seas.

Nome Recalls the Gold Rush of '98 ... Panful of Anvil Creek Nuggets Adds Glitter to Memories

February 1964

SYMBOLIC nuggets from Anvil Creek were featured last fall in an informal commemoration of the discovery of gold in the Nome area. Some 40 members and guests of the Nome Chamber of Commerce, each armed with a box lunch, traveled by Wien tour bus to Anvil Creek for their weekly luncheon meeting.

There, under a pale autumn sun, the group picnicked and listened to a review of the site's colorful history given by Carl Glavinovich, Nome manager of the U. S. Smelting, Refining and Mining Company. The $1,000 panful of gold nuggets taken from Anvil was brought along to add glitter to the memories.

A strike at Council, some 70 miles from Nome, brought rushers to the Seward Peninsula in 1898. According to the story, a young Eskimo lad named Tony Tony reported gold on Anvil Creek in September of that same year. White men from Council hurried to the new strike, and the first claim was taken by John Bryntson, Erik Lindblom and Jafet Lindeberg. In jig-time, 40 men had filed on 7,000 acres.

Springing from bare tundra near the diggings, the little town of Anvil City at one time boasted a post office, a saloon and several eateries. But today, no trace of Anvil City remains. Only a few isolated tailing piles tell of the riches once to be had there. Five million dollars in gold, at the rate of $20.67 an ounce, was taken from a two-mile stretch along the creek, which also yielded two of the largest nuggets ever found in Alaska—one weighing 298 ounces and the other 180 ounces.

It was a pleasant afternoon at that lonely unmarked site, and after it was over the group boarded the tour bus again—which promptly got lost among the trails through the tailing piles before returning to Nome.

Photo by Alice Osborne

Ferry Terminal Repaired
February 1964

PETERSBURG finally got regular ferry service back November 10 after it had been by-passed for nearly three months while its terminal was being rebuilt. The terminal was badly damaged late last summer when two youngsters took an unauthorized turn at the controls in the *Taku's* empty pilot house while the ferry was idling at the dock.

Residents were glad to see the ferries again—but there wasn't any great welcoming committee. The first two docked within an hour, southbound at one a.m. and northbound at two a.m. on Sunday morning.

New Crab Fishery
February 1964

NOT just King crab, but king-sized Dungeness crab are being found in commercial quantities in waters surrounding Kodiak Island. The fishing is still considered largely experimental, but was good enough last fall to keep five boats going and processing lines busy at Alaska Ice and Storage at Kodiak. Individual specimens measuring 11 inches across the back and 24 inches from leg tip to leg tip, and weighing up to six-and-a-half pounds have been hauled in. That compares with the average West Coast Dungeness which weighs from one-and-a-half to two pounds. If all goes well, it could be a great opportunity for owners of small boats not suitable for deep sea King crab fishing.

Boom in Oil Drilling
May 1964

THIS winter's exploratory oil drilling program was the largest in Alaska's history. Three new wildcat wells were spudded late in December, and three more were scheduled for January.

The three wells spudded in December were Standard Oil Company of California's Beluga River Unit No. 14-19; Mobile Oil Company's Salmon Berry Lake Unit No. 1, east of Lake Louise in the Copper River Basin; and Humble Oil and Refining Company's Susitna-State Unit No. 1, across Knik Arm from Anchorage.

New wells slated for drilling in January include Pure Oil Company's Pure-Kahiltan River State Unit No. 1, across the Susitna River from Talkeetna, operated by Union-Texas Petroleum Company; and two exploratory wells in the Umiat area on the Arctic slope by British Petroleum Exploration Company (Alaska).

First Bank Robbery
April 1964

ANCHORAGE is getting to be a big city with big city woes. Its first bank robbery went into Federal Bureau of Investigation records November 19 when a husky man described as "raunchy looking" made off with $6,000 in cash from the National Bank of Alaska's Fifth Avenue branch.

Mac's Foto Service

Fiery Death of Anchorage Landmark
April 1964

THE historic Hawver or Shonbeck Building, one of the oldest buildings in Anchorage, was completely destroyed in a spectacular fire on New Year's Day.

The structure, which had been used for offices in recent years, was built in 1919 to replace the original Anchorage Labor Temple which burned down at a different location in 1916. It had two stories with a dance floor upstairs, and oldtimers recall playing basketball there in the early 1920's. It was damaged by fire in 1922, and shortly thereafter was purchased and remodeled by the late A. A. Shonbeck, pioneer Alaska miner and Anchorage businessman. It became the Hawver Building during World War II.

Owners at the time of the fire were John Holmberg of the National Bank of Alaska and B. D. Hamilton, an Anchorage architect. They estimated the loss at $200,000. The building, located at Fourth Avenue and H Street, housed the Jade Room, The Pub, the Alaska Business College, several jewelry firms, an interior design firm, and the offices of the Community Chest and the Campfire Girls.

Bear Posse's Bad Luck
February 1964

A POSSE looking for a wounded bear wound up beached by a burned boat last fall. Didn't get the bear, either.

The bear, a brownie, started things off by jumping Fred Lewis, winner of the 1963 Sitka Salmon Derby, while Lewis was deer hunting in the Nakwasina Passage area near Sitka. Lewis got one shot away when the bear reared up about eight feet in front of him. When the animal attacked, Lewis covered his head with his hands, dove between two logs, and hollered for his hunting companions. But before the others could come to his aid, he was badly mauled on the right arm.

Nobody wants a wounded bear roaming around in the woods, so a posse consisting of three Fish and Game Department employes, two state troopers, and two hunters returned to the area to finish the job. While they searched unsuccessfully for the battered bruin, their 30-foot boat, the *Onerka*, burned to the water line, and they had to cool their heels on the beach until picked up by a passing purse seiner.

U.S. Pays an Old Debt
May 1964

Jimmy St. Clair, who came to Alaska around the turn of the century, got a nice surprise when the mail plane landed near his homestead at Alexander Creek early this year. On it was a check for $6,000 from the U. S. Treasury for civil service retirement benefits dating back to 1943, and notice that he'll be getting $33 a month from now on. The longtime Alaskan, now 81, said he'd contacted the Civil Service Commission five or six years ago to see if he had any retirement pay coming for the 15 years he worked on the Alaska Railroad and at Ft. Richardson. He never got a response. So last August he took another whack at it, and wrote of his problems to U. S. Senator Ernest Gruening of Alaska. Gruening followed through, and so did the commission. The oldtimer and his wife, Nellie, have been living at Alexander Creek for about 13 years. It is located about 40 miles east of Anchorage and 12 miles from the mouth of Susitna Creek, and can be reached in the wintertime only by plane.

Wilderness Survival
May 1964

ONCE in a while just about everything goes right in a wilderness survival situation. But it takes experience and preparation—along with a lot of luck. Pilot Martin Ott, 45, of Fairbanks had all three working for him when his light plane hit a downdraft and smacked nose-first into a large spruce tree last December 29. He was flying two sisters, Yvonne and Rita Coutu, both school teachers, from Rampart to Fairbanks when the accident occurred.

The plane flopped over, and then descended through the branches of neighboring trees at a perfectly level pitch, like an elevator. The three hung upside down in their seatbelts and suffered only minor bruises. Ott, who has been flying since 1951, broke out the survival gear he carried in the plane, including two sleeping bags, a couple of warm blankets, enough rations for two weeks, a canopy cover, and a rifle.

The trio slept comfortably on birch boughs, and kept busy gathering firewood. Two nights later, when help still had not arrived, they hailed the New Year in by sitting around the campfire, drinking hot cocoa, and listening to New Year's Eve festivities in Fairbanks over Ott's transistor radio. The next morning Ott cooked up a special New Year's Day breakfast of ham, potatoes and gravy. That afternoon he shot a rabbit, but rescue came before they had a chance to cook it.

About the only thing wrong with the whole show was that Ott, father of five children, had no insurance on his plane, which was completely demolished.

Eskimo Chiefs Convene
February 1964

IT wasn't a meeting for outsiders. Some 25 chiefs of Eskimo villages on the Bering Sea Coast, the lower Yukon and Kuskokwim rivers, and as far away as Mekoryuk on Nunivak Island, gathered at Bethel late last September to discuss mutual problems. The discussions were conducted in the Eskimo language. The meeting was limited to their own people, but District Attorney Herbert D. Soll, several officials of the Bureau of Indian Affairs, and two state troopers were on hand to answer questions at the invitation of the Eskimos. The main topics of discussion were village rules, land problems, financing the new organization, and migratory bird hunting.

The issue of taking migratory birds out of season was the hot one. "We can't see why we have to eat fish all of the time," the Eskimos said. The land they occupy is abundant with ducks and geese, which have gone south by the time hunting is permitted under international law. The delegates said they felt they had the right to take what they need, as long as they use what they take. They also discussed means of gaining title to the lands which the villages now occupy; drew up a set of model village rules to take back to their people for approval; and decided to finance their independent organization by assessing each house in each village 25 cents.

EARTHQUAKE!

Good Friday 5:37 P.M.

* * * *

Disaster Without Warning

Salvage operations, 300 block of Fourth Avenue, Anchorage, looking east. Buildings and part of the street here dropped eight to ten feet.

June 1964

It was 5:37 p.m., Alaska Standard Time, on Good Friday, March 27. Like millions of other people around the world, Alaskans were preparing for Easter. In addition, many Alaskans were looking forward to a holiday week-end that would include Monday. Monday, March 30, was Seward Day, a state holiday commemorating the signing of the treaty by which Alaska was purchased from Russia.

The earthquake appears to have centered somewhere beneath Prince William Sound. The area of greatest destruction and damage extends from somewhere east of Cordova to the westward of Kodiak and northward beyond the Matanuska Valley. Valdez, Seward, Kodiak and Anchorage were especially hard hit, as was the port of Whittier. Several small villages on Prince William Sound and Kodiak Island were obliterated.

The earthquake struck suddenly. If there was prior warning, it was not of a kind that was meaningful to a layman. It lasted for approximately five minutes. Property damage resulting from the quake itself and from the ocean waves it generated amounted to at least a hundred million dollars a minute. At least 114 lives were snuffed out in Alaska, others in distant places the waves reached.

It is far too early, as this is being written, to make an accurate summary of total damage. Some facts, however, are clear. The docks and industrial area of Seward were destroyed. On the other hand, the west side of Kenai Peninsula was touched relatively lightly. The important ports of Valdez and Whittier were also destroyed. The Port of Anchorage dock was damaged but remained usable and cargo was being discharged there within a few days after the quake. It appears that for some time to come waterborne cargo for interior Alaska and Anchorage will move through that port.

The fishing industry also sustained heavy losses. Processing plants were wiped out entirely or damaged beyond immediate repair. Fishing vessels were tossed ashore, sunk, or otherwise put out of commission, temporarily or permanently. Only time will tell what damage was done to clam beaches, crab grounds and salmon spawning streams.

On the other hand, the facilities of the state's tourist industry came through, on the whole, in very good shape. The tourist business may suffer this season but if it does the reason will be psychological rather than physical. How many potential visitors will "scare out" because of the earthquake remains to be seen, but operators for the most part are optimistic.

As in any great catastrophe, there were humorous incidents and there were many tales of heroism and sacrifice. There were some miracles, too, not the least of which was the fact that Anchorage had no major fires. And it is perhaps miraculous, considering the amount of damage, that there were not more fatalities.

The Government Hill Elementary School, about a mile north of Anchorage's main business district, is considered a total loss. West Anchorage High School was also heavily damaged. Ten days after the quake, half of the city's twenty elementary schools reopened, others were to follow as rapidly as relatively minor repairs could be completed. High school students were double-shifting at East Anchorage High.

1964

Turnagain Heights, approximately two miles southwest of the main business district of Anchorage, was an exclusive residential district on a bluff overlooking Knik Arm. The Good Friday earthquake wrought almost unbelievable havoc over an area of half a square mile or more, shattering dwellings and leaving nothing solid on which to rebuild them.

Unbelievable Havoc in Exclusive Residential Area

William Wakeland Photos

These three views show some of the devastation in the Turnagain Heights area. Many of the dwellings appeared sound but had hidden structural damage. Others, almost undamaged, were virtually isolated by fissures and chasms that had opened in the ground.

Widespread Devastation in Anchorage

At the intersection of M Street and Eighth Avenue. The leaning tower and heap of rubble at the left is what remains of the six story concrete Four Seasons Apartment which was still under construction when the quake struck.

Looking east on Fourth Avenue from the D Street intersection and showing the enormous damage to building on the north side of the avenue. The Mt. McKinley Apartments, in the far distance, although still standing, was badly damaged, may have to come down.

More quake pictures on next page.

1964

Anchorage

The Denali Theatre on Fourth Avenue dropped ten feet in the Good Friday quake.

Wide World Photo

Seward

Not only were the railroad tracks torn asunder at Seward, but the highway itself was demolished.

Wide World Photo

Valdez

Over the macabre scene drifted a pall of black smoke from burning oil tanks.

Fairbanks Daily News-Miner Photo

Aftermath of Earthquake and Tidal Wave
June 1964

Kodiak

When the great seas that followed the quake rose, rushing all before them, Kodiak's boat harbor and its great crab and salmon fishing fleet was largely wiped out along with a large segment of the Kodiak business district and cannery wharves.

Wide World Photo

Devastated Valdez Eyes Another Site
July 1964

After a lonely half-century, civilization may come to the old townsite of Hazeletville just northwest of Valdez. Once considered as a terminus for the Copper River and Northwestern Railroad, Hazeletville's deep natural harbor was a debarking point for vessels in the early 1900's. But the early day miners didn't like the hike over the mud flats en route to the mountain pass, and the townsite was bypassed while Valdez grew instead.

Since the Good Friday earthquake, the residents of Valdez have been taking another look at old Hazeletville and its high, well-drained, rocky terrain. Not only was Valdez devastated by the quake and subsequent seismic wave, but a massive submarine landslide along the face of Valdez Delta makes rebuilding on the same site risky business.

The original town of Hazeletville was platted by two gold rush prospectors, Andrew Johnson Meals and George C. Hazelet, and is now owned by their four sons, Owen Meals of Valdez, John Meals of Kirkland, Washington, Calvin Hazelet, also of Kirkland, and Craig Hazelet of Louisville, Kentucky, plus a few other part owners in California and Kentucky.

They got together recently and organized a corporation which is offering free land to all home or business owners who were in Valdez at the time of the quake —if they agree to rebuild. Newcomers would have to purchase sites.

Hazeletville already has one resident. He is oldtimer Nicholas Mishko, who moved out of Valdez four years ago after a tiff with a neighbor. The onetime miner and longshoreman who came to Valdez in 1914 now lives in lonely splendor in a snug little cabin on a five-acre parcel of land. Mishko, who apparently has cooled off, says he doesn't mind if the whole town follows him. "I won't move from here. I like it." And, as an after-thought, he added, "Nobody bothers me."

First the Quake, Now the Russians!
July 1964

As if the Good Friday earthquake and waves weren't enough for the hard-hit king crab fishermen of Kodiak, the Russians moved in again. A scant three weeks after the devasting quake, the 13,000-ton Russian factory ship *Chebotnyagin* and twelve 40 to 50-foot picker boats were sighted off Chirikof Island at the southwestern tip of Kodiak Island fishing for king crab. Worst of all, they were using tangle nets.

The use of tangle nets has been outlawed for American fishermen because of the indiscriminate damage they do to females and undersized crabs. In addition, if the nylon nets are lost, they remain a constant and irretrievable hazard on the ocean floor, snagging crabs for years to come.

While the area is a traditional crab fishing ground for American fishermen, present international law, the Russians have the right to fish there.

King Salmon Fishing Ban
April 1964

CLOSURE of the Cook Inlet to king salmon fishing, both commercial and sport, has been ordered by the State Board of Fish and Game. The action came in a move to build up the runs which have been decreasing steadily over the past ten years. Fish and Game Commissioner Walter Kirkness says the most obvious cause of the decline of the runs is overfishing as the population of the area increased. He said the commercial catch of king salmon reached a high of 187,000 fish in 1951, only to slide in a steady decline to 17,600 fish last year. Prior to the 1950's, the commercial catch held fairly steady at about 77,000 fish a year. Kirkness said that the many miles of spawning and rearing areas utilized by king salmon in Cook Inlet remain intact, and that the area still has the potential of producing fish as it has in years past if a greater number of fish get to the spawning grounds.

Vital Sign
February 1964

POINT Hope isn't exactly the kind of place you wander into, not knowing where you are. Nevertheless, a nice new sign has been erected near the new airstrip which carries all the vital information for the occasional newcomer. It reads:

Point Hope, Alaska, 130 Miles Above The Arctic Circle, Pop. 350, Estab. Date Unknown. "Polar Bear Hunters' Paradise" "Home of Bowhead Whale Hunters" Governed by Village Council—Dan Lisbourne, President.

Highest Teacher Pay
May 1964

ALASKA public school teachers receive the highest average annual salaries in the nation, according to figures released by the National Education Association. The average salary for teachers in the 49th State is $8,150 a year—but then the cost of living is a little higher up here. Next behind Alaska is California, where the average annual salary for teachers is $7,375. Alaska's expenditure of $634 per pupil per year is second only to New York's $705.

Fishway Opens Vast Spawning Area for Red Salmon
January 1964

ONE of the greatest potential red salmon producing areas in Western Alaska was opened recently with the completion of the Frazer Fishway on Kodiak Island. The fishway, constructed around the 33-foot Frazer Falls, opens up a 5,000-acre rearing area in the Frazer Lake watershed which covers 72 square miles, according to Walter Kirkness, Commissioner of the Alaska Department of Fish and Game.

Biologists of the department estimate that the once-barren waters could produce as many as three million red salmon a year if all optimum conditions were met.

The fishway itself is something new in construction, too. It utilizes portable aluminum steeppass troughs which can be pre-fabricated in a shop and flown to the required area. These were developed by Gil Ziemer, director of engineering for the department, and consist of ten-foot sections of laddering

Alaska Department of Fish and Game

trough weighing a total of 550 pounds each. The sections can be further broken down into a 150-pound bottom panel, two 190-pound side panels, and twenty pounds of spacers and bolts.

It is not intended that the steeppass will be a substitute for conventional fish ladders now in use in many areas. It will, however, make possible installations in many areas where conventional ladder construction would be both difficult and costly.

Skagway Scare... Railroad Closed in Dispute
January 1964

SKAGWAY got the scare of its historic life early last October when the White Pass & Yukon Railroad closed down for the first time since it began carrying gold seekers over the pass in 1900. Canadian officials suspended the line's operations "indefinitely" after wage negotiations with the American Teamsters' Union at Skagway stalled, and a strike threat was in the wind.

Trains stopped rolling on October 4, and the company's freighter *Clifford J. Rogers*, which provides the sea link between Vancouver, B. C., and the Skagway-Whitehorse rail line, was sent into drydock for overhaul. Freight operations to the north were shifted immediately to an overland route via the Pacific Great Eastern Railroad, from Vancouver to Fort St. John, and on by truck over the Alaska Highway to Whitehorse.

For awhile, all was gloom and doom in Skagway, whose population of some 750 is almost entirely dependent upon the year-round payroll of shop work for the railroad and longshoring for its freighter. Finally, however, a strike moratorium was signed by officials of White Pass and the non-operating employees' union to provide more time for wage negotiations. And after three weeks of idleness, the little White Pass & Yukon Railroad, one of the last of the narrow gauge railroads in the nation, was operating again.

The Skin-sewing Capital... Boosterism in an Isolated Eskimo Village
May 1964

DON'T speak of mid-winter doldrums in connection with the little Eskimo village of Noorvik, way up in the Kobuk country. Judging from the activity up there, the Honolulu Chamber of Commerce better look to its laurels.

Last winter the villagers organized the Noorvik Economic Development Committee, and got off to a fast start by setting out a four-point list of objectives. These were: (1) Promote Noorvik as the "Skin-sewing Capital of Alaska"; (2) promote its potential as a guide center for big game hunting and sports fishing; (3) encourage tourists to come to the village (Noorvik is about 50 miles east of Kotzebue—no roads); and (4) investigate the possibility of establishing small or light industry in the area "so the men can make a living at home without having to travel to other places to work."

And that wasn't all. The Noorvik Sports Club sponsored sled dog races in February complete with an impressive cash prize list. A four-team volleyball league went full tilt throughout the winter, and the Mothers Club met each week to do skin sewing. Noorvik's Boy Scout Troop 98 held its installation ceremony and 17 boys received their Tenderfoot badges. And the Village Council's first official act of 1964 was to petition the magistrate of the Second Judicial District for public hearings on incorporating the village into a fourth class city.

Cattle Rustling by Boat
April 1964

CATTLE rustling by fishing boat is an Alaska twist to an old Western problem. An Angus cow was stolen from the McCord Ranch on Sitkalidak Island off Kodiak Island, and evidence was found on the beach where the animal had been butchered. State troopers apprehended the rustlers at Old Harbor after turning up bits of flesh on their fishing boat. The two, who said they needed the food to feed their families (one of them has 13 children), agreed to pay for the stolen cow.

Gold Down, Oil Up
May 1964

PRELIMINARY reports on mineral production in Alaska during 1963 show that crude oil from the Swanson River field on the Kenai Peninsula provided nearly 50 per cent of the state's total valuation of mineral output. The U. S. Bureau of Mines says crude oil worth $32,700,000 was produced in Alaska last year. The total mineral production value for the year was $65,308,000.

On the other end of the stick, the state's output of gold for the year dropped to 99,000 ounces, the smallest quantity produced since 1894, not counting World War II years. The gold was valued at $3,465,000.

Sand and gravel ranked second behind crude oil in value, reflecting increased production for the state's stepped-up highway construction program. Sand and gravel production was valued at $19,634,000. In third place, in terms of valuation, was a group of minerals including coal, gem stones, peat, stone, and platinum-type metals with a total of $8,346,000.

Production values of other minerals included: natural gas, $1,072,000, mercury, $75,000, and silver, $16,000.

Kills Lynx, Saves Kits
May 1964

AN airman stationed at Unalakleet went black bear hunting last winter and wound up playing foster mother to three little kittens—little lynx kittens, that is. A. 2 C. Nicholas Kokoles of Oakmont, Pennsylvania, had gone only a few hundred yards from the Air Force base on the Bering Sea when he found he was being stalked by a big Canadian lynx. When he stopped to see what the lynx would do, the big cat bounded towards him with appropriately hair-raising high-pitched growls. Kokoles dropped it at 30 yards.

Back at the station while Kokoles and an Eskimo friend were skinning out the unexpected catch, they found that it was a female that had recently had kits. Off to the tundra they went and soon found three baby lynx, which explained their mom's belligerent behavior. Kokoles bedded the kits down in his footlocker until, through the combined efforts of the Alaska Air Command and the State Department of Fish and Game, they were given free transportation and a new home at the Portland, Oregon, zoo.

1964

Four-block Desolation
* * * *
Digging Out after the Quake

September 1964

LOOKING down from the top of the Anchorage Westward Hotel on the excavation left by the demolition of nearly four blocks of Fourth Avenue in Anchorage following the earthquake of March 27. A segment of the fault remains in the lower corner of the parking lot which was behind Fourth Avenue shops between C and E Streets.

Alice Puster Photo

Again: The Task of 'Refusing to Die' ... All-American City in Ruins
July 1964

CITIZENS of the little seaport city of Seward were jubilant last March when their community was one of 11 in the nation to receive the coveted title of All-American City. One of the smallest cities ever to earn the honor, Seward was specifically cited as "the community that refused to die."

In 1961 after the military, a tuberculosis sanitarium, two fish processing plants and a freight company pulled out, the residents determined to hold the town together. They voted to pave the streets, upgrade the water system, and place their entire capital improvement budget of $34,000 into improving the small boat harbor. Meanwhile, the Women's Club raised $27,000 to transform an old store into a 10,000-volume public library, and volunteers built a relay station on a nearby mountain to bring in a television channel.

The work paid off. Thanks to the boat harbor improvements, there was a 600 per cent increase in fish processing by one of the remaining plants. And business expansion planned by a barite processing plant and the halibut co-op was expected to add 120 new jobs.

Announcement of the honor was made on March 26. With the same enthusiasm that won them the All-American City title, Sewardites immediately began making plans for the biggest celebration ever. It was going to be a week-long party with parades, concerts, crab feeds, dedication of the new fire station and Civil Air Patrol headquarters, an art show, street dances and speeches. A special train to be run from Anchorage, and Navy vessels were to come from Kodiak with a Marine band.

But at 5:36 p.m. the next day, March 27, it was all off. The earthquake which struck Southcentral Alaska, the worst ever recorded in the Western Hemisphere, had left the little All-American City in ruins. And Sewardites were faced with the task of "refusing to die" all over again.

Alaska's First Budget $65,000 ... 'We Didn't Have the Money Then, Either'
July 1964

HENRY RODEN, the sole surviving member of Alaska's first Territorial Senate, made a sentimental journey back to Juneau last spring to address a joint session of the Alaska State Legislature. The veteran lawyer, who was elected to the Senate from Iditarod in 1913, now makes his home at the Savoy Hotel in Seattle and will be 90 years old this August.

But the years have effected neither his mind nor his wit. He talked for a solid hour-and-a-half without sitting down and entertained lawmakers with his tales of the early days and his own brand of advice for the future.

He made it down to the first Legislature, he said, by dog team from Iditarod to Ruby, by foot from Ruby to Fairbanks, by stage from Fairbanks to Valdez, and by steamer from Valdez to Juneau.

"We were paid $900 for a 60-day session—and it took us 30 days to get here and longer than that to get back.

"We got 15 cents a mile for travel expenses, and a total of $3 for stationary, stamps and miscellaneous expenses.

"That year we passed an appropriation bill of $65,000 to run the territory for two years—and we didn't have the money then, either."

As far as advice for the future was concerned, Mr. Roden shot just about every sacred cow in Alaska right out of the pasture. For example:

Pioneers' Home: "Never mind building a new branch of the Pioneers' Home. Give the old folks the money instead, and let them live where they want to."

Agriculture in Alaska: "It never will amount to anything."

Living Costs: "I live in Seattle because it's cheaper."

Alaska's Biggest Problem: "It's in the worng place."

E. B. Collins, the last surviving member of the First Territorial House of Representatives, also was invited to address the Legislature, but ill health prevented his coming. He now lives at the Pioneers' Home in Sitka.

Pulp Lost at Sea
April 1964

FIVE freight cars loaded with pulp toppled off a barge into the sea during heavy weather off Dixon Entrance late last November. The Ketchikan Pulp Company shipment was bound for Tacoma, Washington, and transshipment to stateside points and Mexico. It was the first water shipment loss sustained by the pulp company since it started operations ten years ago. Loss was estimated at $50,000, not counting the freight cars which were owned by various railroads.

Eyes Turn to North Slope
September 1964

THE eyes of Alaska's oil industry turned north last spring when Secretary of the Interior Udall signed an order opening 3.6 million acres on the north slope of the Brooks Range to mining and mineral leasing.

The lands involved are part of a 16 million acre parcel which was withdrawn by the federal government in 1943 for defense purposes. That order was modified in 1958 to permit mining and mineral leasing only after protraction diagrams and leasing maps have been prepared and filed. The protraction work has been completed, and leasing maps for the area are expected to be ready this July.

The area has been described by petroleum experts as the most attractive spot on the North American Continent for oil exploration.

The tract is bordered on the west by the Colville River, which is the boundary for Petroleum Reserve No. 4; on the north by state land selections along the 70th parallel; and on the east by the Sagavanirktot River. The southern end of the lease block is irregular.

Another Town Moves to Higher Ground
November 1964

ANOTHER Cook Inlet community is pulling up stakes and heading for high ground in the wake of land shifts and high tide problems following the March 27 earthquake. The town of Portage at the southeast tip of Turnagain Arm has decided to move about 25 miles down the Seward Highway to Indian Creek. The new site is on a sweeping turn in the highway with the mountains just behind it. Businesses which will relocate include a garage, a heavy equipment yard, a restaurant and a gift shop. Earlier, the town of Girdwood, with a similar problem, picked a new townsite nearer the Alyeska ski recreation area.

Paving for Skagway
November 1964

SKAGWAY residents were delighted last summer to get one good paved street, complete with paved sidewalks. State Street, through the center of town, was black-topped along with the new ferry parking area.

Gift to U: Four Years' Pay
September 1964

Dr. Terris Moore didn't stop thinking about the University of Alaska when he retired as its second president in 1953. Over the years he donated more than $30,000 in gifts and grants towards what he called his "sentimental objective" of repaying the entire salary he received during his four years as president. At commencement exercises last May, he made the final installment in the form of a check for $31,325. The check was presented by a member of the Board of Regents during Dr. Moore's tenure, Dr. C. Earl Albrecht, who received an honorary doctorate degree from the university. Dr. Moore, a licensed pilot and member of the Explorers' Club, was often referred to as "The Flying President" during his years at the university. He now lives in Cambridge, Massachusetts.

Cordova Rebuilds
September 1964

A block of new buildings in downtown Cordova reopened for business last June, just a little over a year after a $3 million fire swept through the heart of the city. Everything was bigger and better. The old Van Brocklin Apartments were replaced by the new Prince William Motel with 17 modern units, wall-to-wall carpeting, and an inter-com music system. The old Club Bar emerged as the new Club Bar with authentic Prince William Sound marine decorations in the cocktail lounge, and a banquet room, restaurant, barber shop, taxi stand and package liquor store. Jumping the gun on the official opening were Cordova Commercial hardware, Flynn's Menswear and Sporting Goods, Davis Super Foods, the First Bank of Cordova and the Variety Shop, all in bright new quarters. Rebuilding of the old *Cordova Times* structure has been delayed until a future date, but meanwhile the paper is publishing out of the second floor of the Davis Super Foods warehouse on Second Street. Only one little building in the entire city block came through the fire relatively unscathed. That was the bowling alley which was equipped with a sprinkler system. A word to the wise—now they all have sprinkler systems.

SOS in Snow: Two in Year
April 1964

Yukon bush pilot Chuck Hamilton is getting jumpy over SOS signals stamped in the snow. Last March he was the first to spot the SOS and directional arrow marked in the snow by Ralph Flores of San Bruno, California, who, with Helen Klaben of Brooklyn, was rescued after spending seven weeks in the wilderness without food following the crash of their light plane. Late last November, he spotted another SOS in the same general area south of Watson Lake. The latter rescue didn't have such a happy ending, however. He landed and was able to evacuate the pregnant wife of a trapper and two children suffering from malnutrition, but a third child had died of pneumonia.

A New Eskimo Artist
On the Icy Shores of Northern Seas

November 1964

A new Eskimo artist on the scene is Florence Melewotkuk of St. Lawrence Island. A visiting white woman, Kay Roberts, felt the Eskimo woman deserved attention and seeking new entree to the competitive art sales market reproduced a number of Florence Melewotkuk's black and white sketches on plastic.

Sled dogs, walrus, polar bear—all the ingredients of Eskimo life on the shores of the northern seas, are encased in place mats and coasters. Friend Kay Roberts hopes Florence's art, in its commercialized version, will catch on and bring greater rewards to this Eskimo woman who lives in Gambell on St. Lawrence Island with her husband and adopted son and daughter-in-law.

Eerie Lights of an Arctic Night ... The Strange Story of a Lost Flier
July 1964

The eerie lights that flicker in the midwinter darkness of Arctic Alaska have long been a mystery. But listen to this incident related by Carl Brady, owner of Era Helicopters, Incorporated:

One of Brady's pilots, Joe Nightingale, left camp at Chavio Lake on the Shavioviko River about 20 miles southwest of Flaxman Island on the Arctic Coast February 1 for a round trip flight to Umiat. On his way back to camp he ran into a whiteout about 40 miles from his destination and lost his bearings. He continued to fly around seeking camp until he got low on fuel. Then he radioed camp that he was landing at the confluence of two rivers, but he did not know which ones. There are a lot of rivers on the Arctic Slope.

A search began the next day of the area in which Nightingale was believed downed, but no trace was found. That night, however, a mechanic at a British Petroleum Exploration (Alaska) Incorporated drilling camp reported seeing three distress flares fired at about one minute intervals some 30 miles northwest of the drilling site. He immediately relayed the information to the Wien Airlines office at Umiat. The spot was about a hundred miles from where the helicopter was believed downed, but a check made made at daybreak and, sure enough, there was Nightingale and his craft.

Sounds like any other rescue in the Far North? Well, with one exception. Nightingale didn't have any flares with him. Even if he'd had some, he says he wouldn't have fired them because the night was too foggy for them to be seen at any distance.

Japanese Pilgrimage to the Battlefield on Attu
November 1964

The lonely island of Attu far out in the Aleutian Chain was the scene of a strange pilgrimage last summer. Eighteen Japanese citizens, including two Buddhist priests, relatives of slain Japanese soldiers, and one of the 29 survivors of the 2,350-man World War II Japanese garrison on the island, made up the party. The survivor, Kunio Sato, said no scars of the bloody battle could be found, and described Attu of 1954 as "beautiful." The pilgrims also expressed satisfaction over the manner in which the cemetery and Japanese memorial had been kept. It was the first time since the battle, which began on May 29, 1943, that a party of Japanese civilians had visited the site.

1964

Raw Porcupine – Tough!
July 1964

A 25-year-old hunter, Jeffery Gates of Anchorage, got pretty hungry while awaiting rescue in the Chakachamna River valley about 30 miles east of Tyonek. He and his companion, Ray Wells, 24, had been forced down in their light plane by bad weather, and Gates was left behind with most of the cargo so that the plane could lift off the slushy snow. Weather conditions delayed his rescue for three days.

Gates had two sandwiches and two apples for sustenance, and when that wore off he knocked a porcupine out of a tree and ate the two front legs raw. "It was pretty barky and tough," he says. "The more you chew, the bigger it gets."

Montana, 'Too Crowded'
September 1964

Rancher Rufus Choate, who moved his family out of Montana because it was getting "too crowded", is settling down nicely in a space about as wide open as things can get. Choate's new ranch is on Unalaska Island far out the Aleutian Chain on the slopes of an inactive volcano. He made the long voyage from Seattle aboard a 96-foot wooden vessel which was built in 1891 as a fire boat, then rebuilt into a small freighter for the Alaska trade. Choate, in turn, altered it again to accommodate 500 sheep, five saddle horses, five pigs, a banty rooster and a dog named Smokey, along with his wife and three children, aged 20, 19 and 10. The first trip north was made uneventfully in 11 days. And the intrepid 52-year-old rancher hopes to squeeze in a few more trips to haul in more sheep and cattle before the bad weather sets in. He sold his ranch near Miles City, Montana, because "when you can hear your neighbor's rooster crow, it's time to move."

Beaver Creeks Galore
May 1964

WHEN the newly activated State Geographic Board said one of its first problems would be dealing with duplication of names throughout Alaska, it wasn't kidding. Board Chairman E. L. Keithahn of Juneau reports that Alaska has at least 21 Beaver Creeks, 28 Black Creeks, 26 Boulder Creeks, 27 Eagle Creeks, 35 Fox Creeks and, in all likelihood, an unthinkable number of Icy Creeks.

Unimak Island Volcano Unleashes a Fiery Display
July 1964

Military personnel stationed on Unimak Island had their Fourth of July fireworks a little early this year when Mt. Pogromni boomed into fiery activity March 10. The volcano is situated only eight miles from the Coast Guard lighthouse at Scotch Cap, and only 23 miles from an Air Force radar site located on the northwest corner of the island. Great flaming chunks of debris were thrown up to 6,000 feet in the air, casting a red glow over the whole southeast corner of the island. A Coast Guard cutter was dispatched to remove the men from the island, but neither of the bases were threatened.

Historic False Fronts Damaged by Flames
August 1964

Two false-fronted relics of early construction in Juneau, both built around the turn of the century, were heavily damaged by fire May 19. The buildings, on Second Street between Seward and Main in the downtown district, housed the AFL Labor Hall, a furniture store, and several apartments. The blaze was reported shortly after two o'clock on one of the Capital City's truly beautiful afternoons last spring, and provided a welcome excuse for businessmen, office workers and school children to cut out, watch the excitement, and enjoy the sunshine. The gentleman on the left wasn't playing hookey, however. He is E. J. "Buck" Emery, general manager for Radio Station KINY, who was helping with the news coverage of the fire. By the time it was extinguished several hours later, about all that remained were the ornate facades of the two structures.

Closing the Open Door
April 1964

Some old nosey who thought he was being helpful reported the door to the Fairbanks Elks Club standing open over the Thanksgiving weekend and asked police to check for unauthorized persons on the premises. The police found something unauthorized, all right, but it wasn't a prowler. It was a room full of slot machines, illegal in Alaska. They were promptly confiscated.

The incident seemed to set other brotherhoods to thinking. Shortly thereafter, the Golden Eagle Bulletin of Eagles Lodge 1037 of Fairbanks carried the following notice: "Monty Montgomery, Worthy President of the Aerie, has announced some new rulings for the bar. The opening and closing hours will conform to the State laws from now on."

Big Mouth
September 1964

Big Mouth Honors: An 80-pound halibut, caught last winter off Kodiak Island, was found to have three whole mature female king crabs in its stomach. The discovery was made by state research biologist George W. Gray, who said each crab measured more than 24 inches from tip to tip. State fisheries experts said it was the first evidence that halibut prey on adult king crabs—and are capable of swallowing them.

First Roe to Japan
November 1964

A program for utilizing fisheries products which Alaskans don't need got off the ground last June with the first shipment of herring roe to Japan. The roe, about 10 tons of it, was shipped by Western Alaska Enterprises, Incorporated, a subsidiary of the Taiyo Gyogyo Company, Ltd., of Japan, said to be the world's largest private fishing company. The firm was established in Alaska last October with the objective of exporting fishery resources not normally utilized by Alaska. In the future, the company hopes to purchase such fishery products as sea urchins and sea cucumbers.

New Marine Highway Costs Less Than Roads
November 1964

The balance sheet for the first full year of operation of the three-ferry fleet of Southeast Alaska's new Maritime Highway System showed operating losses of $1.2 million. Operating expenditures during fiscal 1964 totaled $3.6 million while operating income amounted to $2.4 million. That averaged out to an annual cost to the state of approximately $1,785 per mile, which isn't bad when you view it as a highway, which it is. Maintenance costs for other Alaska highways run from $1,818 a mile per year on the Glacier Loop Road near Juneau to a top of $3,078 a mile per year on the Copper River Highway near Cordova.

Cushman Street It Is, Cushman It Remains
November 1964

Cushman Street it is, and Cushman Street it will stay. A proposal by the Fairbanks Chamber of Commerce Tourism Committee to give the old street "a more colorful name" was definitely quashed after protests from the Pioneers of Alaska and Fairbanks oldtimers.

Not quite so definite, however, was just whom Cushman Street was named after. Oldtimers say it was named by Judge James Wickersham after his friend, F. M. Cushman, who was serving in Congress in 1903 and helped with a lot of Alaska's problems. But during the name-change hassle, the Chamber received a letter from a Harriette Cushman who said the street was named after her uncle, Robert Cushman, an early-day Fairbanks businessman and miner. She said her uncle mined at Vault and Dome creeks in the gold rush days, and later built the first two-story building in the Fairbanks camp on the corner of what is now First Avenue and Cushman Street. It burned down in the big fire of 1906.

30 Miles by Snowshoe to Play Basketball
May 1964

Basketball players who are weary of bus or plane travel from game to game have it better than they realize. Consider the eight-man basketball squad from the little Interior Alaska village of Minto. One Friday night, when the temperature stood at 40 degrees below zero, they had a game scheduled with Nenana, 30 miles away. Seven members of the team left early in the afternoon and made the trip by dog team. But their star center, Arthur Charlie, didn't have a dog team, so he left early in the morning and made the trip on snowshoes. It took him about ten hours. He played the whole game and was his team's high scorer with eight points. Minto lost the game to Nenana 72-24. The boys admitted they were a little tired, but they didn't blame the loss on their trip. They were just off on their shooting.

Largest Timber Harvest
December 1964

The largest cut on record—a total of 194 million board feet of hemlock, spruce and cedar logs—was harvested in the North Tongass National Forest during the fiscal 1964. The Forest Service received $478,528.71 for the sale of the logs, and turned twenty-five per cent of that amount over to the state and borough governments for school and road financing.

Rundown on Oil... $300 Million Spent
December 1964

A pretty good rundown on exploration and production expenditures of the oil industry in Alaska to date was given recently by Rollin Eckis, president of the Richfield Oil Corporation. He told the Greater Anchorage Chamber of Commerce that the oil industry has spent more than $300 million in Alaska since January of 1957. In return, it has produced 34.5 million barrels of oil and 7.5 billion cubic feet of gas with a total value of about $100 million. He said the state's cash return from leases and royalties now totals $77.5 million, in addition to an annual payroll which has now reached about $6 or $7 million. Of the $77.5 million, some $27.5 million came from lease and royalty payments, and about $50 million from bonuses paid for leases on state lands—a one-shot affair. In view of that split, he said, the state must look primarily to the development of new oil fields and resultant increased production for continuing benefits and long-term payments.

Look What My Dad Caught
* * *
Big Koyukuk Sheefish

August 1964

"Oh yeah? Well, look what MY dad caught!" says three-year-old Fred Nelson Vent, Jr. after his father lifted this 40-pound sheefish from the waters of the Koyukuk River near their home at Huslia. The fish gave the elder Vent's family of five a good start on provisions while he was away for the summer working as a riverboat pilot for the Yutana Barge Lines of Nenana.

Food Airlifted for Eskimos' Starving Dogs
December 1964

Four-thousand pounds of dog food were airlifted on short order to the Eskimo villages of Gambell and Wales last fall when 600 dogs were threatened with starvation because of a miserable walrus hunting season. Pleas for help from Don Harry Uglowowook of Gambell and John Tokeina of Wales were relayed to Fannie L. Hoopes of Anchorage, who is chairman of the American Humane Association's animal relief program in Alaska. She wired the association's Denver office for funds, bought the dog food, arranged for its free airlift to the villages via Alaska Airlines, and within 48 hours the dogs were in groceries again. Earlier Eskimo hunters had reported Russian vessels off Gambell, and accused the Russians of slaughtering walrus for their hides, leaving the carcasses to rot on the ice.

The Bering Sea Patrol... Century-old Service Expands Its Role
December 1964

The historic "Bering Sea Patrol" is a thing of the past. After nearly a century of service, its name has been changed by the Coast Guard to the "Alaska Patrol" to conform with its widened arc of activity which now stretches from the Alaska-Canadian border in the south to the Arctic Ocean in the north.

The Bering Sea Patrol was born in 1867 when the revenue cutter *Lincoln* was sent north following Alaska's purchase from Russia. At that time there was only one lighthouse and scattered Russian settlements in the district. During its early years, the captains of the revenue cutters, and later the Coast Guard cutters, served as U. S. Commissioners and were almost the only law in wide areas of the territory. Notable among these figures was "Hell Roaring" Mike Healy, captain of the famed old cutter *Bear* which plied Alaska waters for 87 years. He commanded the *Bear* longer than any other skipper, and many a lawbreaker came to respect his swift effective frontier justice. Captain Healy also had a great deal to do with the introduction of reindeer from Siberia to provide food for famine-stricken native settlements.

Now the patrol works closely with Coast Guard planes to provide a combined air-surface operation in northern waters. One of its main functions is to enforce treaties with foreign nations in sealing and fishing activities. Figurative flagship of the patrol is the *Northwind*, with the *Klamath*, *Wachusett*, *Storis* and others helping out in the season's operation which usually runs from April to November.

U. S. Coast Guard Photo

Record Mineral Output, Thanks to Black Gold
December 1964

Alaska's mineral production hit an all-time record $67.8 million valuation last year, thanks to its "black gold" oil and gas resources which accounted for 50 per cent of the output. The $67.8 figure was 25 per cent above the previous year, 1962, according to figures compiled by the U. S. Bureau of Mines. Next highest production was in sand and gravel with a value of $22 million. Coal production was third at $5.9 million, and gold fourth at $3.5 million. The four made up 96 per cent of the value of mining output in the state.

While oil production increased seven per cent over the previous year, gold production dropped to the lowest quantity output since 1894.

Production of mercury from the Red Devil mine in the Kuskokwim fell, and the mine was reported closed in late August. Platinum mining continued at Goodnews Bay close to 1962 levels.

Significant beryllium deposits on the Seward Peninsula and on Prince of Wales Island in Southeast Alaska were reportedly in the exploration stage, and Kennecott's copper deposit on the upper Kobug River moved another step towards production this year.

Noel Wien: 40 Years of Alaska Flying 'Firsts'
December 1964

Fairbanks pulled out all the stops in marking pioneer aviator Noel Wien's 40th year of flying in Alaska. Some 400 guests, including many oldtime pilots and present-day airline executives, gathered at a testimonial dinner at the University of Alaska to pay tribute to the flier who chalked up so many Alaska firsts. These included: first air trip between Anchorage and Fairbanks in 1924; first to fly across the Arctic Circle; first to pilot a plane to Fort Yukon, Wiseman, Nome, and even to North Cape in the Siberian Arctic; and first commercial flight beaween Fairbanks and Seattle in 1935. Noel is now in semi-retirement from Wien Alaska Airlines, a firm he and his brothers, Sig and Fritz, built from a small bush flying enterprise.

Bristol Bay Run Fails Second Year in Row
October 1964

For the second year in a row, the Bristol Bay red salmon run was a bust. As the peak of the run passed, only 10.5 million of the predicted 17.4 million run had returned, and the most important fishing area in the bay, the Naknek-Kvichak district, was termed an "absolute failure." In that district alone, a run of 12.4 million fish had been predicted, while only 4.3 million turned up. Half were caught and half were permitted to go to the streams to spawn. Last year Bristol Bay red salmon run totaled only 6.9 million, and proved an economic disaster to the people of the area.

Island's Ups and Downs
October 1964

MONTAGUE Island in Prince William Sound certainly has its ups and downs. A U.S. Geological Survey team visited the island last summer and found that its south end had risen 33 feet as a result of the March 27 earthquake. One of the members of the team Dr. Dallas Hanna of the Academy of Science in San Francisco, who has been making scientific expeditions into Alaska ever since 1911. He said that while the island's recent rise was spectacular, scientific evidence shows that it has bounced around quite a bit in ages past. Several driftwood piles were discovered inland with mature trees growing through them, indicating an earlier rise of the land. On another portion of the island, tree trunks were found in four and five feet of sea water, indicating a depression. Samples of the submerged trunks were taken so that scientific dating tests could be made. The island is uninhabited by humans, but has a whopping population of brown bears who probably got a rude and early awakening last spring.

Accident Rate Soars!
December 1964

TWO-THIRDS of the vehicles in the little Southeast Alaska fishing village of Pelican were involved in a single traffic accident recently. Anywhere else that percentage would be sensational, but not in Pelican. It has—or had—three vehicles, a car, a truck and a motor bike. Its accident rate soared to 66 2/3rds per cent when Joe York was tooling down the village boardwalk on his motor bike and cracked into Billy Worrell's truck when his handlebars suddenly flipped down.

New Industry
December 1964

SALMON-EGG caviar for the Japanese has created a new industry in the Ketchikan vicinity. The Annette Islands Packing Company at Metlakatla put up nearly a quarter of a million pounds of salmon-egg caviar last season, while at Ketchikan, the Fidalgo Packing Company packed "general purpose eating eggs" known as sujiko. Both are considered a delicacy in Japan, but the caviar eggs must meet exacting requirements and be processed within two hours after the fish is caught. The finished goodies were sold to the Northern Whalig Company, a Japanese firm.

Nome's All-time High
December 1964

AFTER one of the coldest springs on record, Nome hit the other end of the thermometer late last summer with an all-time high of 81 degrees recorded August 12th. Dry, too. The .29 inch of rain that had fallen to that date made it the driest summer since 1907, when the weatherman started keeping records.

1965

The Odd Year
* * *
Japanese Freezer Ships Help Process Record Run of Pinks

Photos by Jerry Bowkett

January 1965

AN odd salmon fishing season in Alaska last year added up to the highest production season since 1949. The canned salmon pack of 3,509,400 cases was well over the 2,656,009 cases packed the year before, and that was supplemented by 18,837,900 pounds of salmon which were frozen or cured during the season. The frozen and cured figure included 16,050,400 pounds of salmon processed on Prince William Sound, the bulk of it by Japanese freezer ships which bought raw American-caught salmon.

There were strange goings-on in the Southcentral District from the very outset. Kenai fishermen, locked in an early season price dispute with packers, gave away free fish on the streets of Anchorage before coming to an agreement. When Prince William Sound packers and fishermen found themselves unable to reach a meeting of minds, Governor William A. Egan invited Japanese freezer ships (one of them pictured here) in to process what promised to be a record run of pinks. And for the second year in a row, the Bristol Bay red salmon run was a dismal failure.

However, when the waters calmed at the end of the season, the tally showed a Southcentral pack of 1,721,000 cases, a Southeastern District pack of 1,225,300 cases, and a Western Alaska pack of 563,100 cases. By area, Kodiak topped them all with 655,250 cases; Ketchikan was second with 580,050, and Bristol Bay third with 535,450. By species, pink salmon accounted for 1,903,000 cases, followed by reds with 720,300; chums, 689,000; cohos, 155,330; kings, 41,000.

Glad Tidings: Biggest Iron Ore Discovery ... Biggest Oil Well
January 1965

GLAD tidings in any number of departments came last fall from Pan American Petroleum Company, a subsidiary of Standard Oil of Indiana. In one power-packed news conference in Anchorage, Pan Am announced the biggest iron ore find on the North American continent and the biggest oil well producer in Alaska to date.

Pan Am President Randolph Yost said his firm held claims covering some 9,940 acres in the Aleutian Mountain range at the head of the Alaska Peninsula, some 200 miles southwest of Anchorage, containing "roughly a billion tons of recoverable ore." The ore contains 15 per cent iron, compared with 22 per cent contained in the Taconite reserves now mined in the Lower 48. However, Yost said, natural gas power could be used to reduce the ore to a concentrate of 95 per cent iron. He described the discovery as "one of the top seven or eight iron ore discoveries ever made." Only the famed ore deposits in Minnesota are known to exceed the new find in reserves in the United States.

For an encore after that bit of good news, Yost announced that Pan Am's Middle Ground Shoal Well No. 4 had increased its daily productive flow to 3,022 barrels, topping all producers thus far. He said the company plans to construct a $9 million all-weather drilling platform at the lease site in Cook Inlet from which 16 wells could be drilled, and a $12 million nine-mile pipeline from the site to the East Forelands area on the Kenai Peninsula.

The whole happy session had the headline writers in Alaska flipping coins, and pushed the parent company's stock 6-1/2 points higher before the close of business that day on the New York Stock Exchange.

New School for New Valdez
January 1965

"It is fitting that the first building constructed in the new Valdez is a school." So said Governor William A. Egan at the dedication of the first building to be completed at the city's new townsite, four miles from the present location which the city must abandon because of ground shifts since the March 27 earthquake. The new elementary school, which swung right into operation, is named Growden-Harrison School after two of the 31 Valdez residents who died in the quake and seismic waves. They were James Growden, a school teacher, and Robert Harrison, a businessman.

"I know it was not easy for many of you to accept the idea of abandoning good old Valdez," Egan said at the dedication ceremonies, "but it is to your credit that you have done so, recognizing that this historic community could be perpetuated only by relocating here on Mineral Creek..."

The governor did know, too. He was born and raised in Valdez, graduated from high school there, married a Valdez school teacher, and made it his home.

News from the Deep
February 1965

A couple of long-gone ladies of the Alaska Steamship Company line were back in the news recently. Divers retrieved the four bronze propeller blades and other metal fittings from the ill-fated steamship *Mariposa* which sank on a reef in Sumner Straits 40 miles west of Wrangell on November 18, 1917. The 265 passengers aboard were saved. The divers also salvaged the ship's whistle, which they intend to keep, and found dishes still stacked in the ship's sink. And out at Uyak Bay, oil slicks appearing on the surface of the water weren't another Alaska oil strike, but rather seepage from the tanks of the old luxury liner *Aleutian* which hit an uncharted rock off the southeast tip of Amook Island some 35 years ago. She sank within minutes, but the only loss of life was that of a Filipino galley boy who went back aboard to get his good luck charm.

Jets Replace Dog Teams
March 1965

Now the 400 residents of the little Eskimo village of Savoonga on far-off St. Lawrence Island have personalized jet service. With the completion of a new airfield there late last fall, a Wien Airlines F27 propjet touched down for the first time November 4 to provide passenger service for the village. In the past, villagers had to rely on dog team transportation in the winter and boats in summer to reach the air strip at Gambell across the island. The passengers heading out for Nome on the inaugural run were Mrs. Mary Seppilu and her three children, who got a big hand-waving send-off from the other 396 villagers.

Mac's Foto Service

April 1965
70th Anniversary
* * *
Historic Icons in Juneau Church

Tiny, onion-domed St. Nicholas Russian Orthodox Church of Juneau celebrated its 70th anniversary last December. It was built in 1891 by the sizeable Russian settlement then in the area, and consecrated December 19, 1894 on the day of its patron Saint Nicholas. Carrying the nominal coincidence one step further, the consecrating ceremonies were performed by Bishop Nicholas, who later became Archbishop of Warsaw. The church, located at 326 East Fifth, houses icons that are three centuries old. Its congregation now has shrunk to some 115 parishioners whose priest, Father Simeon Oskolkoff, was born in Anchorage and served as acting dean of the Pribilof and Aleutian Islands before coming to Juneau a year ago.

Population Grows... and Grows...
January 1965

Still they come. Alaska's population has reached the quarter-of-a-million mark, according to the U. S. Bureau of Census. Her 250,000 residents include a civilian population of 218,000 and armed forces personnel totaling 32,000. The new figures show an increase of 12.5 per cent since the 1960 census, which makes Alaska the fifth fastest growing state in the nation, behind Nevada, Arizona, California and Florida.

The quarter-of-a-million milestone looked big to Alaskans, but they still have a way to go. The population compares with that of Dayton, Ohio; El Paso, Texas; and Wichita, Kansas—only more spread out.

'Flying Fish'... Rugged Old '31 Plane
August 1965

Anyone who thinks "they don't build them like they used to any more" will get a vigorous second from bush pilot Chuck Kirk. He's flying salmon this summer in a plane that is only five years younger than Lindbergh's "Spirit of St. Louis." His plane is a single-engine Pilgrim, built in 1931, that can pack a payload of 2,500 pounds.

The plane has spent most of its life in Alaska and at one time was used by Alaska Airlines to fly passengers and mail on the Yukon run. For the past two years it has carried smoke jumpers from Wenatchee, Washington, to fight forest fires in the Cascade Mountains. This summer, however, it's under charter to the Bellingham Canning Company for picking up salmon at beach sites and other isolated areas and delivering them to the cannery at Yakutat. When the fishing season is over, Kirk plans to fly trappers, hunters and prospectors into remote areas.

"There isn't one made today that will do the job this one will do—if you don't have to go too fast," Kirk says. "She cruises at about 115 miles an hour." Other pilots agree the plane is in mint condition, despite 9,000 hours in the air and over a million travel miles.

New Wrangell Sawmill
September 1965

Alaska Pacific Lumber Company's new $4 million sawmill at Wrangell was dedicated late last May. The new mill and its related facilities are located at Shoemaker Bay, some seven miles south of town. The complex includes a power plant, bark chipper and deep water dock. It employes about 50 men per shift, not including woods crews.

First Coin-op Laundry North of Arctic Circle
January 1965

One of the most popular spots in Kotzebue this winter is Bonnie's Bubble Room—and it isn't what you might think. It's probably the first coin-operated laundromat north of the Arctic Circle. And it's not only efficient, it's entertaining. No longer do the Eskimo housewives have to melt snow and ice to get wash water in the winter. The laundry is especially popular with the children in town who like to watch the lights flash on and off and the clothes go round and round through the glass doors. "Their heads usually follow in a circular motion," says Bonnie who owns and operates the laundromat with her husband, bush pilot Lee Stajeli. The laundry is easily the most automation to have come to town in one lump. Along with the washers, driers and dry cleaning machines, it has soap powder, bleach, coke, candy and sandwich vending machines. The only other coin-operated machines in town are a couple of juke boxes.

The King Crab in Northern Waters:

Bob Karmatique with a big king crab aboard the M.V. AKUTAN at Port Wakefield.

Mac's Foto Service

Japan Agrees to Reduce Its Catch
March 1965

A MONTH-LONG high-level go-round on king crab fishing in northern waters has resulted in a compromise agreement between the United States and Japan. The Japanese agreed to cut their king crab take in the Eastern Bering Sea by 21 per cent during the next two years to a maximum of 185,000 cases, and to stay out of an area near Kodiak which is heavily fished with American crab pots. At the end of the two-year period, negotiations will be resumed on the basis of conservation studies of the king crab fishery resource. Alaska's private fishing interests had sought a ban on all foreign king crab fishing on the theory that the crab is a creature of the continental shelf. But at least the agreement, said Governor William A. Egan, was "a step in the right direction."

Big Gain in Alaska Production
April 1965

TOTAL king crab production in Alaska last year was in excess of 85 million pounds, as compared with 78 million pounds the year before. State Fish and Game Commissioner Walt Kirkness says that while last year's big quake and tidal waves brought a decrease in crab production at Kodiak, fishermen more than made up for it by shifting their efforts to the Alaska Peninsula-Aleutian-Bering Sea area. There, production amounted to 31.1 million pounds, up from the 13.7 million pounds from July 1 to December 10 of 1964, down 2 million pounds from production during the same period the previous year. The Cook Inlet area also showed a decrease, from 8.3 million pounds in 1963 to about 7 million pounds.

Kennecott Returns to Alaska... Kobuk Copper Development Work Begins
April 1965

BACK on the active mining scene in Alaska after an absence of about a quarter of a century, the Kennecott Copper Corporation is going right to work on its holdings in the upper Kobuk River country. Michael J. O'Shaughnessy, general manager of Kennecott's New Mines Division, says the firm expects to spend several million dollars in the next two years developing deposits on Ruby Creek 15 miles north of the village of Kobuk and 50 miles above the Arctic Circle. The mining company acquired the deposits a year ago January from prospectors Rhinehart Berg, Jack Bullock and others, for $3 million.

The first year's work was slowed by difficulty in getting supplies and equipment into the area. A late-breaking ice pack on the Bering Sea was followed by low water on the Kobuk River, up which everything must be transported by barge. As a result, supplies and equipment finally were freighted the last 30 miles overland by tractor train during the winter freeze-up. However, a camp employing 60 to 100 men, most of them natives of the Kobuk Valley, was established, along with a post office named "Bornite" after one of the minerals found in copper.

O'Shaughnessy says the company hopes to sink an 1,100-foot shaft this summer and set up an office in Fairbanks with teletype connections to the camp.

The project represents the corporation's first major return to Alaska since the closure of the fabulous Kennecott mines, 120 miles from Cordova, in 1938.

Doctor, Janitor, Mechanic... and Teacher, Too
May 1965

MR. and Mrs. Maurice Carmody took a break in Mexico last winter upon retirement from a 25-year teaching career in Alaska, but they'll be back in their cabin at Hope this summer. Their first northern post was at the Cook Inlet village of Tyonek where Mr. Carmody served as storekeeper, doctor, mechanic and janitor as well as teaching the Tyonek children. During his stay, he saw electric lights introduced at the village, and watched Art Woodley, now president of Pacific Northern Airlines, land the first plane on what was then Tyonek's new airstrip. The Carmody's were teaching on the tiny island of Afognak north of Kodiak when World War II broke out. While Mr. Carmody enlisted in the Army to serve in the Alaska and Aleutian campaigns, Mrs. Carmody continued the family tradition by teaching at Wrangell. Since then, they have lived relatively civilized lives in Anchorage, where Mr. Carmody served as principal of a number of schools.

Tailor-made Town
May 1965

THE ancient village of Afognak was abandoned last December as its residents moved—lock, stock and Christmas presents—up the coast to their new tailor-made town of Port Lion. They wanted to be in their new homes by Christmas and, after much last minute scrambling around, they were.

Almost every standing structure was destroyed in the old village of Afognak by last year's earthquake and tidal waves. Its fishing fleet was wiped out, and 47 families were left without homes or means of support. The drive to build a new town for the villagers was spearheaded by Lions Club organizations throughout the nation with the help of many other agencies. For example, the Salvation Army provided $8,500 for the rental of a barge to move the families and their possessions to the new town when it was found no funds were available for that last all-important item.

The new Port Lion now boasts 40 homes, a community hall, a school, water and sewer lines, and an airstrip, which add up to a $1.5 million development.

Arctic Slope Oil Leases Bring the Big Money
April 1965

Arctic Slope lands brought the big money last December in Alaska's 13th competitive oil and gas lease sale. More than three-fourths of the total of $5,614,773 received by the state in oil lease bonuses came from acreage lying in a block of land extending about 36 miles east of the Colville River and 24 miles south of the Arctic Ocean. Offshore lands in the Cook Inlet and Kodiak Island areas drew the rest of the bonus cash.

A major chunk of the Arctic Slope petroleum leases went to British Petroleum Exploration Company (Alaska) in joint venture with Sinclair Oil and Gas Company. Their total bonus payments amounted to $3,789,173 for 296,150 acres of land.

By area, Arctic Slope bonuses totaled $4,382,095 for 476,157 acres, or an average bonus of $9.20 per acre. Offshore acreage sales totaled $1,232,678 for 263,506 acres, with Cook Inlet lands bringing an average of $7.08 per acre and lands off the southern portion of Kodiak Island averaging only $1.55 per acre.

It was the largest land sale held by the State of Alaska thus far in terms of toal acreage offered. Overall, the 739,663 acres leased brought an average bonus of $7.59 an acre. With the sale, the state's bonus income rose to a total of about $55 million for some 1.8 million acres of potential oil and gas lands.

Full Accreditation for New University
March 1965

Full academic accreditation in record time has been won by the Alaska Methodist University at Anchorage. No school is eligible for accreditation until after it has completed four years of operation—and AMU got it on the dot. The university now has a student body of 421 full and part time students, a faculty of 40, and is headed by Dr. Fred P. McGinnis, president. The state's only other fully accredited institution of higher learning is the Univeristy of Alaska.

'Better than Beef'
* * * *
Boy, 15, Downs Big Bison
March 1965

Ernie Stolen, Jr., 15-year-old sophomore at West High School in Anchorage, and the bison he downed in a special hunt near Delta Junction last fall. The big animal took three shots from a .30.06 at 200 yards and still trotted for nearly half a mile before he dropped. Ernie and his father were nine and a half hours skinning, quartering and packing out the meat which totaled 837 pounds and was pronounced "better than beef" by members of the Stolen family.

Alaska Fisheries Suffer from the Big Quake
August 1965

Detailed accounts of the effects of last year's mighty earthquake on Alaska's salmon industry are contained in a newly published report by the Alaska Department of Fish and Game. The 72-page booklet, entitled "Post Earthquake Fisheries Evaluation," outlines damages to fishing grounds, spawning areas, processing facilities, fishing vessels and gear, and streams and harbors in the three major fishing areas affected, the Kodiak-Afognak Island complex, the Cook Inlet-Kenai Peninsula area and the Prince William Sound-Copper River area.

Kodiak Island counted a $6.4 million loss in processing and fishing facilities alone, and the total economic loss for the Kodiak-Afognak complex was estimated at $10 million. No total dollar loss was placed on damage in the Prince William Sound-Copper River area, but the fishing village of Chenega was destroyed and the land area at Valdez so severely affected that the city had to be relocated. In addition, extensive dredging was necessary in many areas to provide access to facilities left high and dry.

The Kenai Peninsula-Cook Inlet area suffered the least actual damage. But in the "interesting phenomenon" department in that area, the report notes that the Kasilof River was found to be bone dry shortly after the quake. Cause of the temporary stoppage of the flow of water was attributed to the tilting of Tustumena Lake towards its eastern end and away from its outlet.

Jury Assails Nome for Its Extended Tax Holiday
April 1965

Nome's Common Council has been prodded into collecting a few taxes this year after being strongly crititcized by a grand jury for not sending out 1963 tax statements to the city's 2,800 residents. The residents didn't pay any taxes in 1961 either.

Councilmen claimed they didn't collect the taxes because Nome didn't need the money. The grand jury asserted that Nome did too need the money, since none of the streets are paved, water is still delivered in trucks, and sewage is still collected in "honey buckets" (although a sewage system is now under construction). It added that the city has no parks, no recreation facilities, no library, and needs a new school.

After the grand jury report, the council hurriedly called a meeting; gave themselves, the mayor and the city clerk a vote of confidence; and declared a moratorium on 1963 personal and property taxes. They did agree, however, to collect property taxes for 1964.

One council member said he'd served on the council for 18 years and had been criticized on numerous occasions, but never for not collecting taxes. He said his feelings were hurt.

Blind, 82... and Rugged
August 1965

Last spring David Adams asked to be picked up at his Moose Island camp in Central Alaska and flown to his home at Stevens Village. But when the mail plane had to pass him by because it was loaded, he decided not to wait for the next flight and hiked the 25 miles for home. Nothing special for an Alaskan? Maybe not. But Adams is 82 years old and totally blind.

Land of the Young
March 1965

America's second newest state has the nation's youngest population. Figures released recently by the Census Bureau reveal that 84 per cent of the persons living in Alaska are not yet 45 years old, and only 2.6 per cent of Alaska's residents are 65 or older. The national average is 71 per cent and 9.3 per cent, respectively.

'Walking' Sweazey Retires...
Legendary Sportsman, Salesman
March 1965

Manley "Walking" Sweazey, who has sold insurance in Alaska for over a quarter of a century, retired last December and moved to Seattle. He got his nickname because of numerous walking sales trips along the ties of the Alaska Railroad between Anchorage and Fairbanks. Those trips weren't all work, however, as he is an ardent fisherman, a licensed hunting guide, and a capable craftsman in making jewelry of mammoth tusks, sheep horns and semi-precious stones. A Harvard graduate with a master's degree in business administration, he has represented Northern Life Insurance Company for the past 30 years.

1965

Hunters Die in Crash
July 1965

Two Anchorage area high school principals lost their lives last March when their light plane crashed in a snowy mountain pass while they were returning from a wolf hunt near Lake Iliamna. The victims were George Marsters, principal of East Anchorage High School, and Clifton Cline, principal of Chugiak High School.

Marsters, 39, came to Alaska in 1961 and had held the post at East Anchorage High since April of 1964. Cline, 37, was named principal of Chugiak High when it opened last fall. He came North in 1954, taught at Chignik, Pauloff Harbor and Kenai, and then served as principal of Eagle River Elementary School the year before his appointment to the Chugiak post.

Three weeks later, tragedy was piled upon tragedy when Eagle River pilot Chester C. Dee was killed in an ill-fated attempt to salvage parts from the wreckage of the plane in which the educators lost their lives. Dee's plane crashed just a short distance from the wreckage after he attempted a down-slope take-off from a glacier. A 19-year resident of Alaska, he was owner and operator of Dee's Flying Service and Dee's Service Station.

12,000 Aftershocks in Seven Months
February 1965

The big shake is over, but Alaska still has the shimmies. Approximately 12,000 earthquakes were recorded in the state during the seven-month period following the major March 27 quake. Most of the aftershocks were too mild to be noticed by the general public, but 200 to 300 of them were strong enough to have caused damage in densely populated areas. Since the big quake, the aftershocks have been coming at a steadily diminishing rate.

Fire Devastates Abandoned A-J Mine Mill
June 1965

A Juneau landmark for half a century, the mill of the Alaska Juneau Gold Mining Company on the mountainside just south of the city, was almost entirely destroyed by a fire that started on Saturday, March 20, and burned for nearly 48 hours. The first unit of the mill began operating on March 6, 1914, and the machinery was shut down for the last time at midnight on April 8, 1944. Most of the milling machinery had long since been removed from the buildings and in recent months hoists, ore cars and other equipment was salvaged from the mine itself. The property is owned by A. J. Industries, Inc.

Port Still 'On Ice'
February 1965

Visions of a seaport danced in the heads of land-locked Yukoners recently with word that Grand Pacific Glacier, which formerly lopped over the Southeast Alaska border, had retreated two miles, leaving a salt water arm extending through the Alaska Panhandle into Northern Canada. The new channel is located at the head of Tarr Inlet in Glacier Bay, only 90 miles from the Canadian portion of the Haines Cutoff highway. The Yukon's only outlet to the sea now is via the White Pass & Yukon Railroad to Skagway where, from the Canadian viewpoint, American longshoremen are occasionally crotchety. Closer inspection showed that the salt water arm existed, all right, but a study of the erratic history of advances and retreats of the Grand Pacific Glacier over the past 85 years put the project "on ice" for the time being anyway.

No Cash for Bounties
February 1965

Bounty hunters are going begging in Alaska this year. No money to pay them. The State Department of Fish and Game says that a $50,000 appropriation for bounty payments for all of fiscal 1965 was expended only 29 days after the fiscal year began last July 1. All but $905 of that amount went for hair seal bounties. And the unpaid bounty claim bills, for wolves, coyotes and wolverines, as well as hair seals, have been stacking up ever since.

A year ago, the legislature passed a bill which would have eliminated the bounty on hair seals, since their pelts are bringing good money on the open market. However, the bill was vetoed by Governor William A. Egan. Then the legislature couldn't muster the two-thirds vote necessary to override the governor's veto, so it just quietly didn't appropriate sufficient money to fund the program.

Proud to Be an Indian
May 1965

Of the many plaudits received by the late naturalist, John Muir, we doubt if any would please him more than this book review written recently by a student at Mt. Edgecumbe Indian School in Sitka:

"John Muir in 'Travels in Alaska' tells the story of an adventurer who likes to study glaciers and rivers and trees. He traveled in Alaska in 1879. . . .

"The part I really liked is where Muir and his companions came back to Hoonah from a long rainy and wet journey, the Chief Ka-hook-oo-shough put on wet clothes too because he was ashamed to think they were out in the cold wet weather while he was in a warm dry place. He said that he had done this because he wanted them to know that he loved them also, and he wanted to suffer with them.

"This makes me proud that I am an Indian because I wouldn't want to think that our friends were suffering while I am in a warm place either.

"John Muir is such a good writer . . . I didn't know how beautiful Alaska really is and how lucky we are to have such a country. (Illustration) He said, 'It shows that God was taking pride in Alaska'."

Eskimo Manager for New Barrow Airport
March 1965

One of the Eskimos who helped bring the bodies of Will Rogers and Wiley Post to the village of Barrow after their fateful plane crash 30 years ago has been named the manager of the new airport at Barrow. He is 52-year-old Rex Ahvakana, long-time mechanic for Wien Alaska Airlines who was familiar with the inner workings of airplanes long before he ever set eyes on an automobile. The modern 5,000-foot airfield is located about a half mile from Barrow.

Spectacular Addition
* * * *
New Federal Building in Juneau

Mac's Foto Service

October 1965

The M/V Taku of the Southeast Alaska Marine Highway System's three-ferry fleet glides by the new federal building, a spectacular addition to Juneau's waterfront. The federal office building is expected to be ready for occupancy early next year.

1965

Bar Doubles as Church
May 1965

"Cool temperatures kept most of us pretty close to our stoves but we managed to attend a very nice Christmas service," wrote Daisy Hetherington, Manley Hot Springs correspondent for the *Fairbanks News-Miner*. "When our Episcopal minister, Father Sarles, flew in overnight on the 28th of December, we warmed the bar up and converted it to a very respectable little church. It is amazing how Alaskans can improvise."

First Negro Elected
February 1965

With his election to the North Star Borough Assembly last fall, homesteader Pete Aiken became the first Negro to be elected to public office in Alaska. The 44-year-old father of three was elected from a predominantly white district on the Chena Hot Springs Road out of Fairbanks. He is a carpenter by trade, and the family's neat two-story log cabin is the third he's built since moving to Alaska permanently in 1951. He first came north with the U.S. Army in 1942. He doesn't have any particular feelings about being the first of his race to be elected to public office. "I feel the people elected me because I am just Pete Aiken. The people who voted for me would have voted for me no matter what color I was. Even if I were purple."

He Remembered when...
April 1965

Walter Stickman, one of the oldest native residents of Alaska who was born two years before its purchase from Russia, died in Anchorage last December 22 at the age of 98. He was born, fittingly enough, at Old Man Lake in the Mendeltna River area and lived the life of his Indian people until 1918 when he went to work in the Chickaloon coal fields. When that community faded into a ghost town, he moved to the Palmer area where he became well known for his handmade snowshoes, many of which are still in use. In later years, he lived in a cabin near Anchorage where a niece, Mrs. Katherine Wade, could look after him. He chopped his own wood for his cabin stove until just two years ago when the local supply of timber gave out. He claimed his decline in health began after his relatives bought him an oil stove.

Fairbanks Help-a-Dial
April 1965

Fairbanks' new outdoor telephone booths checked out fine last winter. The only problem was that the dials, like most moving parts in cold weather, got a little sluggish when the temperatures dipped to around 50 below. When you dialed a digit, sometimes you had to help the dial back to its starting position.

A Lonely Hydrant... Last Vestige of Abandoned Village

September 1965

This lonely hydrant is one of the last vestiges of the village of Chickaloon in the Matanuska Valley. Chickaloon was founded in 1918 as part of a government coal mining project to provide coal for the U. S. Navy, and was abandoned in 1922.

Mac's Foto Service

Five-Day Walk on Ice Just to Stay Even
March 1965

Imagine walking five days and most of five nights just to stay even. Two seal hunters, stranded on a massive drifting ice floe that broke away from the shore near Nome, did just that. And their Arctic know-how helped save their lives. When they realized they were drifting to the southwest, they started walking northeast to counteract the movement of the ice and stay as close as possible to their original position. The maneuver paid off when they were spotted by Eskimo hunters on shore and rescued by an Air Force helicopter. The hunters were John Burns, a biologist for the State Fish and Game Department, and Tony Koezuma, an Eskimo who serves as Burns' helper and assistant. They were hunting seal for Koezuma's family.

Diamond Jubilee... Home for Homeless Children Still Looks to Future
August 1965

The Jesse Lee Home, which has provided care for homeless and needy Alaskan children of all races since its tiny beginning in 1890, is marking its Diamond Jubilee this year. But it's not looking to the past, it's looking to the future.

The home began when Miss Agnes Soule came to Alaska from Maine 75 years ago to teach in a government school at Unalaska in the Aleutian Chain. She found many needy youngsters there, and shortly after assuming her teaching duties she took six of them into her own home. By the year's end the number had grown to 30. She sought financial aid from her friends at home and construction was started on a building to house them. She named the home for the Rev. Jesse Lee, a pioneer Methodist missionary and co-worker with her grandfather, Bishop Joshua Soule. In 1898, Miss Soule married the Rev. Albert Newhall who became teacher, physician and minister for the home and the village of Unalaska, and she was known as "Mama" Newhall at the home until her death in 1917.

In 1925 the Women's Missionary Society moved the home to Seward and consolidated its functions with those that had been performed at the children's home in Nome. It served the children from all of Alaska, Aleuts, Eskimos and Indians as well as white. The children attended the public school at Seward, but at the home they were taught cooking, sewing, music and handicrafts. They were particularly proud when one of their number, Bennie Benson, submitted the prize-winning design for Alaska's beautiful flag.

With combat too close, the home was closed during World War II, but during that period the buildings were renovated to provide new boys' and girls' dormitories, a gymnasium and the Albert Newhall Chapel, and the home reopened bigger and better. Then came last year's terrible earthquake which devasted much of the city of Seward. Damage to the home was so serious that one of its buildings had to be demolished.

So the decision was made to move again, this time to a site a few miles south of Anchorage on Abbott Loop Road, overlooking Turnagain Arm. There the new home will utilize cottage-type facilities, rather than the big old dormitories, to provide a more home-like atmosphere. The project is a huge one, requiring the efforts of many people, but while the appeal for funds is in progress so, with faith, is the construction.

Cooking with Gas
April 1965

Paul Kignak's home has a shiny new heating stove and a new gas cooking range—the first in the Eskimo village of Barrow on the Arctic Ocean. And he can use it. He has a family of ten, and has been paying $33 to $35 per 55-gallon drum of fuel oil ever since seal and whale oil went out of vogue. The Kignak family was the first to hook into the new natural gas mains which will supply the village from the wells on Naval Petroleum Reserve No. 4.

The use of natural gas was made available to villagers a year ago by special congressional action, and financing for construction of piping facilities was provided in a loan from the Bureau of Indian Affairs. It's all under the direction of Barrow Utilities, Inc., a cooperative headed by an all-Eskimo board of directors. The gas comes from three producing wells five miles from Barrow, the latest of which was drilled in April of last year. Until that time, the output of the other two wells was used solely by the U. S. Government installations at Barrow, the DEW line facility and a construction camp several miles north.

Naval Petroleum Reserve No. 4 was established in 1923 by executive order of President Harding. A total of 35 wells were drilled by the Navy between 1944 and 1953, when it ceased petroleum exploration.

The Big Silver Theft
March 1965

How do you swipe 70 tons of silver ore? Easy. Just steal two boxcars, too. Anthony Bobcik, a former employe of United Keno Silver Mines, was found guilty recently of the theft of $170,000 worth of silver ore in one of the longest trials ever held in the Yukon. Bobcik was accused after police in Helena, Montana, siezed two railroad boxcars at the American Smelting and Refining Company in July of 1963 containing ore which had been shipped from the vicinity of United Keno at Elsa, some 220 miles north of Whitehorse. The trial lasted six weeks.

Mac's Foto Service

September 1965

At Piamute on the Lower Yukon River, Jake Aloyisious, Jr., carries a pair of fat king salmon from the river to the fish house.

'Petticoat Gazette'
October 1965

SEWARD' only newspaper, the weekly *Petticoat Gazette,* completed its first decade of service to the community last June. Back in 1955 when there was no newspaper in Seward and little likelihood of a commercial paper starting up, the Business and Professional Women's Club decided it would be a good project to fatten up its treasury a bit and fill a community need. Today the paper has a circulation of 600 and has never missed an issue, not even during earthquake week a year ago last March. In addition, all proceeds from the paper have been funneled right back into community projects.

Socked in? Not for Long
April 1965

ESKIMOS snickered and airline pilots protested when the contractor for construction of the new airport at Barrow hung up a white wind sock as the finishing touch on the project. They pointed out that since everything else around the snowy place was white, nobody could see it. But the contractor said that the specifications called for a white wind sock, and that was that.

When complaints finally trickled down to the state capitol at Juneau, another wind sock was sent in an appropriate color. But that one was part plastic, and when the icy winds blew, as they do almost constantly at Barrow, it stiffened straight out and stayed that way. Still no good.

Finally airport Manager Rex Avhakena took matters into his own hands. He dug out the original white sock, dyed it orange, hung it up, and everybody (except perhaps the contractor) was happy.

Lost in 'White Out'... Saved after Six Days
July 1965

ONE can live in Alaska a lifetime and still not know the course of its elements. So said Father William McIntyre, a Roman Catholic missionary, who was lost for more than six days just a few miles from his home at Alakanuk. Furthermore, he knew the area well as he had served there for nearly a quarter of a century.

The incident occurred last March when Father McIntyre left Alakanuk shortly after noon on a Sunday and headed for Sheldon Point, just a few miles across the Yukon River, to offer mass. Less than a mile from Alakanuk he found himself in the midst of a "white out," with complete loss of horizon. He built himself a snow shelter, and then "walked and walked" around a circle-like path to keep moving as much as possible.

Five days later, when a visitor from Sheldon Point reported Father McIntyre had not appeared for mass, a search party was organized which found the priest, wet, cold and hungry, since he had taken no provisions nor survival gear with him for the "short" trip across the river.

Old R.R. Bridge Tumbles in Quake
January 1965

A HISTORIC bridge which took a dive after the March 27 earthquake was the old Copper River Railroad bridge which was built in 1909. The bridge, located about 27 miles from Cordova, has been used in recent years as a highway bridge, spanning the Copper River between Round Island and Long Island.

The Famed 'Million Dollar' Span is Doomed
February 1965

THE famed "Million Dollar Bridge," one of Alaska's best known manmade landmarks, apparently is doomed, a lingering victim of last year's devastating earthquake. Built in 1911, the span first served as a vital link on the Copper River and Northwestern Railroad from the Kennecott mines to tidewater at Cordova, and after the mines closed down in 1939, it was an important factor in Cordova's dreams for a highway tie-in with Alaska's road system. A recent report by state engineers, however, revealed that it would be more expensive to repair the old structure than build a new one.

The report to Governor William A. Egan said in part: "The northern pier is completely shattered and will collapse in the near future. The remaining spans are seriously displaced and distorted. Since the movements of all piers appear . . . a result of movements of the underlying foundation material, there is question of continuing stability of all substructure elements . . . It is most distressing, but we are obliged to advise you that damage to the bridge is such that it is apparently not economically salvable."

Construction of the bridge between the faces of Miles and Childs glaciers was hailed as a major engineering triumph, and was the subject of Rex Beach's novel, "The Iron Trail." The job was done under the direction of the young engineer, Michael Heney, who had made his reputation in the construction of the seemingly impossible White Pass & Yukon Railroad. Bridge crews worked through a bitterly cold winter to take advantage of the solid ice on the river, and completed construction with just minutes to spare before the spring break-up.

Busiest Airport?
August 1965

SOME say Anchorage's Merrill Field is the busiest airport in the country. Not so. According to Federal Aviation Agency statistics, it's the 78th busiest in the nation, with a total of 155,832 landings and takeoffs in 1964. The FAA figures also show that Alaska's capital city of Juneau has the dubious distinction of being the un-busiest of FAA controlled airfields in the nation.

Second Arctic Slope Sale: Bidders Choosy
August 1965

BIDDERS were pretty choosy at the second non-competitive oil lease sale of Arctic Slope lands which was held in Fairbanks last April. Only 264 of the 1,580 lease blocks available were filed upon, indicating that the 31,431 applicants were well informed as to which were the most favorable lands. The blocks, each containing about 2,560 acres of land, are located west of the Arctic National Wildlife Range and east of Naval Petroleum Reserve No. 4. All formerly were closed to oil and gas leasing. Successful applicants must pay 50 cents an acre annual rental, but most of them resell their holdings to oil companies. At the first sale, which was held a year ago June, bids were made on about 1,000 of the 1,400 tracts offered. After that drawing, many of the holdings were resold for $1.50 to $4 an acre. Rumor had it after the sale last April, however, that prime holdings might go for as much as $30 an acre. Dates have not yet been set for the two additional sales scheduled for the North Slope area.

Attacked by Bear
September 1965

A TIMBER cruiser was badly mauled by a bear which attacked him near Mile 25 on the Haines Cutoff last May. The victim, Elvin Hess, was checking a timber stand for the Schnabel Lumber Company when the bear appeared without warning about twenty feet away. Hess had a gun, but the bear charged so quickly he was unable to use it. Although severely mauled about the head, shoulder and thigh, Hess managed to crawl back to the highway where he was picked up by a passing motorist, Mrs. Ernest Lindquist of Haines. She drove him to the White Swan Roadhouse at Mile 10 where he was treated by a physician and then flown to Juneau for hospitalization. Hess, about 50 years old, previously had lived in Sitka and had worked in the Haines area for about two months before the attack.

Downed Flyer Safe; Lived on Boiled Grass
August 1965

BOILED grass and survival know-how brought Master Sergeant Kenneth Keen through eight days of sub-zero weather in the Canadian wilderness. The 40-year-old career airman was downed 58 miles west of Watson Lake when his plane ran out of gas as he was dodging a snowstorm. He was en route from Fort Nelson, B.C., to Fairbanks, Alaska, where he is stationed at Eielson Air Force Base.

Keen stamped out an SOS in the snow, outlined it with tree branches, and stayed near his plane until he was spotted by search planes. He had a three-day supply of survival rations, but used only a small portion of it, subsisting mainly on "about a gallon of boiled grass daily."

Said Keen, "I knew if it keeps moose alive, it would keep me alive."

He pulled in his belt four notches during the eight days, but when he was examined after his rescue, a Fort Nelson doctor observed that he was in better shape than many of the men who had been searching for him.

Tide Spares Seldovia
March 1965

SETTLING Seldovia breathed a sigh of relief when it weathered the highest tides of the year late last November without major damage. On the peak tide of 22.4 feet, water lapped eight to ten inches over the main street boardwalk of the little fishing village, which dropped several feet during the big earthquake last March. But the winds were calm and there was little surge to the water. While the pilings were somewhat weakened by the weight of 20,000 sandbags laid out to hold the boardwalk in place, the only damage reported was to a section that was lifted by the tide and plunked back in a tilted and twisted condition. Seldovians plan to replace the old boardwalk this year with a new raised paved street.

A Whale Hunting Club
October 1965

Whale hunting turned into a big thing on Cook Inlet last summer, both for the sportsmen and the Kenai Beluga Whale Hunt Club. A four-day package hunt offered a trip across Cook Inlet, a stay in a wilderness camp, and the excitement of hunting and harpooning the big mammals. The club also arranged for the custom canning of the whale meat at Kasilof under a deal wherein the canner, the customer, and the sponsoring Chamber of Commerce split the take. "You might say we are share-cropping whales," said John Hulien, chief whale wrangler.

Dall Sheep for Kodiak
September 1965

An experimental colony of 13 Dall Sheep was moved to Kodiak Island recently by the Alaska Department of Fish and Game. The sheep, including two young rams and eleven ewes, six of whom were pregnant, were captured in the Cooper Landing area of the Kenai Peninsula, tranquilized, checked for disease, and then flown to Kodiak. There they were released at Mink Point on the south arm of Uganik Bay.

"The last we saw of them," says game biologist Oliver Burris, "they were half way up the mountainside. They climbed a mountainous arm that connects with the main range on the island, so they now have access to all the higher alpine plateaus."

Burris emphasized that the transplant attempt would have to be classified as experimental for several years. Meanwhile, periodic aerial surveys will be made to determine whether the new residents "feel at home."

Low Tax, High Return
October 1965

Alaskans paid the lowest combined state and local taxes in the nation in fiscal 1964, which amounted to $80.78 for every $1,000 in personal income, according to Census Bureau figures. The national average was $103.52. But don't cry for City Hall. The Census Bureau says that if revenues state and local governments receive from the federal government are added, Alaska's $256.26 for each $1,000 of personal income leads the nation. The average for all states is $156.69.

Peril on the High Seas
August 1965

Talk about a blow! Skipper Kaare Novik of the halibut boat KAARE is still wondering how he made it back to Kodiak. Caught in a Bering Sea storm last spring with winds to 100 miles per hour, the vessel lay flat over in the water on one sea and Novik says he will never know how she came about. It left the KAARE and her eight-man crew without lights, radio, electronic equipment, and with four feet of water in the galley.

A Trapper Brings his Catch to Market

November 1965

Trapping has decreased in Alaska in recent years but is still important to the economy in many areas of the state. S. T. "Bud" Saario, Fairbanks furrier, right, measures a beaver pelt brought in by trapper Les Jacobson, left. Jacobson caught the beaver on the upper Chena River. It measures 75 inches, which is the sum of the two diameters--up and down and across.

Fire in Ketchikan
August 1965

One of the worst fires in Ketchikan's history wiped out the New England Fish Company's cannery and severely damaged its cold storage unit last spring. Loss was estimated at $1 million. Howard Lee, superintendent of the operation, said that the fire started from spontaneous combustion in the web loft where seines had been stored for the winter. The cannery site was left a twisted mass of charred timbers and warped metal, and the entire second story of the adjoining cold storage operation was destroyed. No early announcement was made as to plans for rebuilding, but the firm decided to use the Fidalgo Island plant, closed since fish traps were banned in 1958, to can fish during the summer. The damaged cold storage plant remained in operation during the season, supplying ice and bait, and buying fish.

First Russian Ship Boarded by Coast Guard
August 1965

The first boarding by the U. S. Coast Guard of a Russian vessel on the high seas took place off Kodiak last March. Commander R. A. Ritti, skipper of the cutter *Storis*, one of his officers and a member of the U. S. Fish and Wildlife Service climbed aboard the Russian factory ship *Pavel Chevatniagin* to point out that the Russians were illegally using tangle nets in waters restricted to the use of crab pots under a treay drafted a year ago. They said the Russian skipper was very polite, but professed to know nothing about the treaty. However, he ordered his twelve catcher boats to haul in their nets, and they moved off to unrestricted waters which *Storis* officers marked out in big bold outlines on the Russian skipper's charts.

Oil News Is Good News
October 1965

Alaska's oil news gets brighter and brighter. Discovery of a new field offshore in Trading Bay of Cook Inlet was anounced last June by Union Oil Company of California and Marathon Oil Company. A well, known as Trading Bay No. 1-A, showed a stabilized flow after casing was set of 1,670 barrels a day of 30 degree gravity crude oil from 5,600 to 5,700 feet. That is the shallowest depth of oil production discovered thus far in Cook Inlet. Company officials described it as "the largest oil well ever completed anywhere in Alaska."

Meanwhile, Mobil Oil Company reported another major oil discovery at its Granite Point Field in Cook Inlet where its Wildcat Granite Point No. 1 flowed at an average rate of more than 1,300 barrels per day from a depth of 8,700 feet.

1965

Jerry Bowkett

Three interested spectators watch varied activities which marked the celebration last July of the Diamond Jubilee of missionary work along the Arctic Coast of Alaska.

Jerry Bowkett

Standing in the doorway of the Episcopal Church's little St. Thomas Mission at Point Hope are the Rt. Rev. William J. Gordon, Bishop of Alaska; Governor William A. Egan; and the Rt. Rev. John A. Hines, Presiding Bishop of the Episcopal Church of the United States.

Diamond Jubilee:
Christian Missions on Alaska's Arctic Coast

November 1965

A **Wind-Swept** sandspit far above the Arctic Circle was the scene last July of ceremonies commemorating the Diamond Jubilee of Christian missionary work along the Arctic Coast of Alaska. Gathered at the Episcopal Church's St. Thomas Mission in the Eskimo village of Point Hope were dignitaries from throughout Alaska and the nation, including Presiding Bishop John E. Hines of the Episcopal Church of the United States and Alaska's Governor William A. Egan. Everybody packed sleeping bags along, which were rolled out in tents and dormitories, and the food was flown out in the form of box lunches from Fairbanks. Bishop Hines himself flew out in a bush plane piloted by Alaska's "Flying Bishop," the Rt. Rev. William J. Gordon.

The first missionary work in the Arctic began in 1890 simultaneously at Point Hope by the Episcopal Church, and at Wales by the Congregational Church. The missionaries of these churches also were commissioned by the Territory of Alaska to start schools. One of the guests attending the celebration was Tony Joule who taught at Point Hope for more than 30 years.

Area of Quake Damage Largest in History
November 1965

Geologists confirmed recently what a lot of Southcentral Alaska residents were pretty sure about in the first place. The March 27, 1964 earthquake caused the largest known surface movement of land from a single earthquake in recorded history. The land level was altered in a 65,000 to 77,000-square-mile area, and at least 23,000 square miles were uplifted. The famed New Madrid, Missouri, earthquake of 1811, believed to have been the strongest ever to shake the United States previously, altered only a 6,000-square-mile area.

Two Russ Defect to Alaska
December 1965

NO guards, no walls, no fences--only the open waters of the Bering Straits separate the United States and the Soviet Union off the northwestern coast of Alaska. But until last August, when two Siberian smelter workers touched shore in their small boat at the little Eskimo village of Wales, there had been no defectors to Alaska soil.

Actually, they were a strange pair of defectors. Gregory Sarapushkin, 29, and Peter Kalishenko, 35, from Laurentia said that the two outboard motors on their skin boat failed while they were on a mushroom-hunting expedition off their home shores, and that they drifted helplessly to the Alaska coast 70 miles to the west. First they asked to be returned to their homeland. But during the two-day wait for the Coast Guard cutter BALSAM to pick them up for the return trip, they changed their minds.

So the two were taken to Anchorage instead, and after lengthy conversations with Soviet Embassy and U. S. State Department officials, asylum was granted. No one quite knew what brought about the change of heart. But it was noted that while in the Eskimo village they spent much time pouring over, with excited gestures, that great old Alaska "wish book," the Sears Roebuck catalogue.

Now It's Official ...
November 1965

Any Kodiak Island cattleman could have told them the same thing, but State Fish and Game personnel have determined after a study that cattle and bears are not compatible on the same range. A total of 33 cattle were reported killed by the big Kodiak brown bears during a 14-month period ending last July, and about that many more were missing and listed as probable kills. The study showed that the cattle have the roughest time in late spring and early fall, the off-season for berries and fish when the bears are scrounging around for something else to eat. What's to be done about it? The study made no recommendations, but it did note that sport hunting on the island was not sufficient to eliminate predation.

Pedro Creek Stampeder Returns ... 'Many Changes' Since '02
November 1965

One of the few Indians to join the gold rush stampede to Pedro Creek, 82-year old Paul Solomon, moved back into Fairbanks last summer. Paul hit the trail from Circle City into the Fairbanks camp in the winter of 1902 when he was only 20 years old. "I thought I could get rich too," he recalls. Actually he did more moose hunting than mining since many of the "new pioneers" didn't know how to get food. "The store was empty and everybody was living on rabbit and flour. I thought I could make a little money selling moose meat. But each time I'd get one, somebody would come along who was poorer than me, so I'd just give it away." Paul tried mining, but since he didn't know how to do it and couldn't speak much English, he never found any gold. So he moved back to Circle City, turned to trapping, and taught himself to read and write. In recent years he has made his home at Fort Yukon. Now back in Fairbanks, he shakes his head as he looks around and says, "Many changes."

Alaska's Largest Highway Project

February 1965

SHOWN here is a portion of the Knik-Matanuska bridge complex which will cut eight curvy miles from the drive between Anchorage and Palmer. Work progressed nicely through the past construction season on the $6 million project, the largest single road building job yet undertaken by the state. It involves construction of four major steel girder bridges on the new route, which branches from the present Glenn Highway at Eklutna Flats and crosses the Knik and Matanuska rivers. Contractor for the work is the M-B Construction Company of Anchorage.

Mac's Foto Service

Another 'Biggest' Oil Find
November 1965

The latest largest oil well in a long parade of "the biggest one yet" was announced by Pan American Petroleum Corporation after tests on its new Cook Inlet wildcat, Tyonek State 18742 No. 1, located 48 air miles southwest of Anchorage. The well brought in 2,455 barrels of 41 degree gravity oil per day through a five-eighths inch choke from an interval of 8,180 to 8,300 feet. That was well over the previous record-holder, Trading Bay 1-A, which had tested only a month before at a rate of 1,670 barrels a day.

Meanwhile, the State of Alaska pulled in $6,145,472 in bonus money last July from a competitive oil and gas lease sale of Arctic Slope lands. Of the 297 tracts offered, 159 drew bids. Richfield Oil Company and Humble Oil & Refining Company, bidding jointly, offered high bids which amounted to $3,927,189, well over half the bonus money. The lands, covering 754,033 acres, extend eastward along the Arctic Slope about 150 miles west of Point Barrow.

Bristol Bay Boom Ends Years of Bust
November 1965

After four years of near-disaster, the red salmon came swarming back to Bristol Bay in record numbers last summer. In a wild four weeks' of activity, fishermen hauled in more than 22 million reds from a run estimated at well over 44 million, the largest in history. The catch figure was the greatest since the record 24.6 million taken in 1938, and the pack of nearly 1.5 million cases, with an estimated value of some $56 million, was the largest since the 1.9 million cases packed in 1937. All this despite the fact that only 11 shore canneries were operating in the bay this year, as compared to an average of 30 canneries that operated in the 1920's and 1930's.

From the very first day of the season, the salmon charged into the bay at a record rate. Canneries operating at capacity placed a limit of 1,000 fish per man per day. Tender boats, built for a 60,000-fish capacity, wallowed back to the canneries loaded with 75,000 and 80,000 fish. Canneries ran out of cans, and more had to be flown in. The Alaska Steamship Company pressed a seventh vessel into service to haul the mammoth pack to Seattle. The fishermen were jubilant. They made an average of $10,000 from the run, and some took in over $20,000.

Nobody could quite believe it, although a "good" run of some 27 million had been forecast. But on top of a spring highlighted by screams of protest over Japanese high seas fishing of the salmon and the seizure of a Japanese fishing boat for poaching on the wrong side of the salmon treaty abstention line, followed by threats of a boycott against Japan and/or the damming of Bristol Bay if such activities did not cease, the record return of the Bristol Bay salmon seemed almost an impertinence.

Growth in New Valdez
November 1965

July was a month of new beginnings for the town of Valdez, terribly hit by last year's Good Friday earthquake which washed the very land out from under it. Relocation of homes to a new townsite at Mineral Creek, four miles from its present location, began with the issuance of building permits for the construction of private residences. The first permit was granted July 20 to longtime Valdez resident Isaac Woodman, and at the same time offers were accepted on about 50 more residential lots. Property owners from the old town got first pick.

Earlier in the month, the Alaska Steamship Company resumed regular weekly service to the newly completed dock at new Valdez with the arrival of the COASTAL MONARCH. The old dock was destroyed with a heavy loss of life when the seismic waves struck while an Alaska Steam vessel was unloading cargo. Since the quake, the new townsite has been cleared, a water system and other utilities have been installed, and a new school completed. Work also is well under way on the first commercial construction in the new town, a bulk storage plant being built by Standard Oil of California.

All Traffic Stops for Skagway's Foolhardy Foolhen

August 1965

ONE of the names given to grouse in Alaska is "foolhen," but "foolhardy" would better apply to one who took on the functions of traffic cop at Skagway last spring. The grouse evidently had staked out a nesting site by an old spruce tree above the railroad track just south of the Standard Oil warehouse on Dock Road, and he deeply resented both highway and rail traffic. Each morning and at noon when the longshoremen normally were heading for work, he would appear in the middle of the road and stop traffic, clucking threateningly and pecking at tires and bumpers. Despite their reputation, longshoremen are a kind-hearted lot, and since the grumpy grouse refused to be "shooed," a line of 15 to 20 cars would often be backed up before he withdrew in his own good

Dedman's Photo Shop

Self-appointed traffic cop, this grouse at Skagway is now the pet of the town, as he comes boldly out to stop the cars on the road to Skagway wharf. No one wants to hit him, but he refuses to be "shooed" out of the way. He's caused the longshoremen to be nearly late to work quite a number of times, as he picks peak traffic hours to make his appearances.

time. In between peak traffic periods, he dive bombed the trains on the White Pass & Yukon Highway. iFnally, after holding forth for nearly two months, the grouse met his inevitable end.

Railroad Under Ice
September 1965

WHITE Pass & Yukon railroaders hope this winter won't be like the last one. They're used to battling too much snow on the 110-mile run between Skagway and Whitehorse, but last winter they were plagued with massive tongues of ice which spread out over the railroad tracks to a depth of two or more feet. The trouble started when a deep freeze came before the snow, forcing the water out of the top of the ground and over the railroad right-of-way. For 75 Arctic days, they fought the ice with dynamite, bulldozers equipped with "ripper teeth," drum fires and muscle, with men working 24 hours a day in some areas clearing the tracks. But through it all, the trains kept rolling and never missed a schedule.

Quake vs. Wildlife
August 1965

EVEN the moose and waterfowl are still trying to get themselves resettled following least year's big earthquake. State game personnel say that 2,000 acres of moose winter range in the Portage-Twenty Mile area and 2,500 acres in the Big and Little Indian drainage area were lost due to land-lowering and extensive flooding. In the Cordova area, just the opposite occurred. There the land mass rose, leaving once prime waterfowl nesting and resting areas high and dry.

Rush for Oil Leases
December 1965

A LAND rush of sorts developed late last summer in oil and gas lease filings on federal lands far removed from the present producing areas of Cook Inlet and the Kenai Peninsula. During one hectic week, the Bureau of Land Management office in Anchorage received filings on a total of 700,000 acres of land for ten-year leases, which will add up to more than $3.5 million in rental fees. Two major oil firms and several individuals filed for leases covering some 515,000 acres in the Pt. Heiden and Becharoff Lake areas on Bristol Bay. And another major oil firm filed on a 200,000 acre tract in the Copper River area. Company officials would make no comment on possible plans for development work.

'Mirror' Is Home Again
November 1965

The weekly KODIAK MIRROR finally went to press on its own home ground again, 15 months after quake-triggered seismic waves washed out its press and plant. Each week since the March, 1964 earthquake, its publishers, first Sig and Betha Digree and then Wayne and Nancy Kotula, flew with copy in hand over to Kenai on the mainland to print on the borrowed CHEECHAKO NEWS press. It added up to 130 flights, but they never missed an issue.

1966

A New Boat Harbor for Sitka
March 1966

U. S. Army Photo

A NEW million dollar small boat basin in Crescent Bay on Sitka's waterfront was completed last December after a year and a half of labor. The work was done under a U. S. Army Corps of Engineers contract with Manson-Osbert Company of Seattle. A 15-acre area was excavated to 10-foot depths below low tides, and 150,000 tons of rock was quarried, hauled and placed to form two breakwaters, one of which measures 1,145 feet and the other 200 feet. The breakwaters were especially designed to quell the action of waves which roll in from the open sea. Seventeen feet high, they are five feet across at the top and flare to thirty to form the outer barrier, leaving pockets to divert the surging. Fill from the excavation was made available to the City of Sitka for reclaiming about 20 acres of waterfront, which will be used for a park among other things, and to provide a right-of-way for a scenic harbor drive. The new facility will accomodate about 450 boats.

Boat Capsizes . . . 51 Hours Clinging to Pilings in Raging Glacial Stream
January 1966

Two Juneau area men figure they're lucky to be alive after clinging to pilings of an old bridge in the middle of the swift glacial waters of a tributary of the Taku River for 51 hours before their rescue. Harry Lupro, 38, and Sam Paul Jr., 49, became marooned when their 18-foot aluminum boat capsized while they were on a hunting trip, and wedged against the four pilings in the middle of the river. All of their equipment was cast adrift, but they were able to lash themselves to the pilings by using the bow rope of the boat. There they hung, hoping to heaven that someone downstream would spot their drifting gear and send up a search party.

Night came without aid, and the next day, a Saturday, the waters of the river began to rise. The two climbed to the top of the pilings and perched there on a single cross plank which joined three of them together. That afternoon a helicopter flew within several miles of the stranded men, but then turned away. They thought about trying to swim for shore, but feared they were too weak to make it.

Finally on Sunday another member of their hunting party, Sam Rengard of Douglas, became alarmed over their failure to return and set off upriver. When he came upon one of their gas cans lodged in a snag he contacted the helicopter pilot, John Watson, and the search began in earnest. Even then the stranded pair were nearly missed since searchers were concentrating on the riverbanks, hardly expecting to find anyone in the middle of the stream. But they were spotted at last and hoisted aboard the hovering helicopter on a rope. "Just in time, too," said Lupro. "It was beginning to get dark."

'That Settled That!' Bankrolled by Mayor
January 1966

At a recent Ketchikan City Council meeting, a dispute between Merritt Klepser and Mrs. Eden Odell over the ownership of a patch of tidelands property waxed long and loud. It seems Mr. Klepser's platform extended 2.57 feet over Mrs. Odell's property. Each wanted the other off, but both were hanging tough. Finally Mayor James G. Pinkerton had enough.

"Mrs. Odell, will you sell?" he interrupted.

"Yes," she replied.

"Mr. Klepser, will you buy?" the mayor demanded.

"Will you loan me the money?" Mr. Klepser countered.

"Yes," said the mayor and put $400 on the table. City Attorney Harris Bullerwell wrote out the receipt.

"That settled that," mumbled the mayor.

Operation Tin Snip . . . Bear Is out of the Can
January 1966

A yearling black bear who got himself in a terrible predicament is out of the can now. Literally. And he owes a heap of thanks to Doc Hall of Seward.

Doc was flying his plane from Anchorage to Seward when he spotted a bear in the Devil's Creek area near Mile 32 of the Seward Highway who was acting very strangely. Closer inspection showed that the bear was plodding around and around in small circles with a 20-pound coffee can on his head. Doc flew on to Seward, enlisted the aid of two policemen, and with a tranquilizer gun borrowed from the dog catcher, a length of rope and some tin snips, flew back to the scene.

The bear was still there, still canned, and still walking around in circles. "In fact," Doc reported, "there were five or six smooth circular paths worn in the mat of leaves that covered the ground. That bear must have walked 500 miles."

Three light dog loads of tranquilizers were shot into the bear cub but they didn't faze him. So the men got the rope around his neck and hind legs and went to work with the tin snips anyway. By the time they got the can off, the dope, fortunately, had taken effect and the bear just lay on the ground, snoozing it off. When he finally came to he looked his benefactors over with a rather dazed expression, then pulled himself together and made tracks for the timber--straight as an arrow.

Dog Team Then, Car Now
January 1966

Miss Juneau of 1936, who drove her dog team more than a thousand miles to Fairbanks in the dead of winter to enter the Miss Alaska contest that year, made the trip again late last summer by late model sedan. "I always wanted to see what the trip was like in a car," said Mary Joyce, now owner-operator of the Top Hat Bar in Juneau.

Mary Joyce came to Alaska in 1930 after quitting her job in a Hollywood hospital. She accompanied a family on a boating-hunting-fishing trip as their nurse, and liked the northland so much she just stayed. One of her main interests was dog mushing, so when she was asked to represent Juneau in the winter carnival at Fairbanks it seemed natural enough to hitch up her five-husky team and take off.

She left Juneau with an Indian guide December 22. Arriving at Tanacross after 52 days on the trail, she realized she wasn't going to make Fairbanks in time for the carnival so she flew the rest of the way with bush pilot Herman Lerdahl. She didn't win the queen contest, but Fairbanksans were so impressed that they made her an honorary member of the Pioneer Women of Alaska. And, for the record, when the contest was over she returned to Tanacross, retrieved her team and finished the trip over the trail to Fairbanks.

A Grand 'Grand Opening'
January 1966

It looked just like any other grand opening of an extra-nice department store, but to the people of Anchorage it was a lot more than that. When the pink ribbon was cut opening the new J. C. Penney Company store last September, the crowd of distinguished visitors and early shoppers were thinking back 522 days to the terrible Good Friday earthquake. The old store--which was really new at the time--was demolished along with much of the rest of Anchorage, but the Penney firm was one of the first to announce plans to rebuild on the same site.

Honored guest at the grand opening was Mrs. J. R. Lewis who was in the store at the time of the earthquake and credits one of Penney's employees, Dave Brown, for saving her life on that day. He shielded her with his body when the air around them became thick with crumbling concrete and flying glass. Mrs. Lewis cut the ribbon for the opening of the greatly expanded new store, and gave Mr. Brown a big kiss of thanks.

New Hospital
January 1966

A new $3.3 million Alaska state psychiatric hospital is going up at Valdez to replace the one destroyed by the great Alaska earthquake. The new structure will include a 144-bed wing for mentally retarded patients and a 15-bed wing for acute cases. Completion is scheduled for next October.

Juneau Artist Honored
Native Life-Figures for Alaska Museum

March 1966

Fred Belcher, Alaska Travel Division

ALASKA'S Governor William Egan, left, gives Karen Werner, young Juneau artist, a certificate of merit for her native life figures she created for the State of Alaska Museum now in new and temporary quarters in Juneau. Next to Egan is another Alaskan artist, totem carver Amos Wallace, who is also President of the Alaska Native Brotherhood. Watching approvingly are Mrs. Egan, center, and the new Museum Curator, Susan Barrow. One of the life-sized figures Miss Werner created is behind Governor Egan.

Miss Werner made eight native figures in old tribal dress for the exhibit, employing foamed plastic for support, carefully carved with a variety of tools to simulate lifelike poses. Faces she sculptured, cast molds and built up fiberglass overlays painted in proper tones.

A promising artist in a variety of mediums, Miss Werner, the daughter of Mr. and Mrs. Joseph Werner of Juneau, was born in Seward, attended Juneau schools and graduated in art from the University of Washington with a major in ceramics.

The State of Alaska Museum is now temporarily housed in the Masonic Temple across the street in Juneau from its old location in the capitol building. Efforts are under way to secure grants for construction of a new museum building in Juneau.

Lael Morgan photos

Eskimo woman and child, done in styrofoam and fiberglassed sculptured faces, executed by Juneau artist Karen Werner. At right, a Thlinget Indian woman figure decorated with dentalium and trade beads is another Karen Werner created figure now in the Alaska State Museum in Juneau.

Two-Minute Hunt Becomes Two-Week Ordeal
February 1966

WHAT WAS to be a "two-minute" goat turned into a two-week ordeal for two hunters and their guide-pilot last fall. The trouble began when big game guide Ralph Marshall of Anchorage landed his plane on a small glacial lake in a little valley near Cordova so that one of the hunters, Thomas E. Brawner of Houston, Texas, could collect a quick mountain goat. The wing strut collapsed and the trio, which also included Anchorage sportswoman Helen Burnett, was stranded.

Because of the rocky terrain and lack of fuel for a fire, the three made their way to a small island on Bering Glacier which opened out of the valley. They made up a camp of sorts, but the fuel wasn't much better there--just small bushes and grass. All they had was a plastic tarp for shelter, sleeping bags to go around, and a little salt.

"We built a fire about every other day and cooked as much goat meat as we could," Miss Burnett said. In between fires, they just ate the meat cold.

"I didn't know goat meat could taste so good with nothing but salt, washed down with glacier water," said Marshall.

"Sixteen days living on very, very rare goat meat is a pretty strenuous diet," commented Brawner.

When rescue finally came after an intensive two-week air search, the trio was picked up by helicopter and flown to Anchorage. Brawner, who is 62, went to the hospital for a few days for treatment for exhaustion. But when he got out he was good as new, and promised to come back this year after a polar bear.

At Last – Paved Streets
January 1966

After talking about it for nearly half a century, Seward finally got its streets paved last fall. Practically the whole town turned out to watch the start of the operation, and when the job was completed eight days later the dust was laid forever and Seward had four miles of brand new blacktop within its city limits. The paved area takes in all of the major thoroughfares running roughly four blocks north and south, and from Second to Seventh Avenues east and west. Oldtimer Sol Urie, who was among those cheering from the sidelines, said they were talking about paving the streets when he arrived in town 40 years ago and he's mighty glad they finally got around to it.

Homecoming
January 1966

Establishment of Loomis Armored Car service in Anchorage and Fairbanks recently was a homecoming of sorts to the firm's founder, Lee Loomis. He says he first got the idea for his whole thriving business when he packed out gold by dog team in the early days of the Fairbanks camp. Lee Loomis came north in 1898, and acted as "banker" and transportation agent for mining and mercantile interests, carrying much of the wealth that was mined in that area. Later he was branch manager for the Northern Commercial Company at McGrath. He left Alaska in 1925, and that same year built his first armored car and started service in Portland, Oregon. Later he expanded all over the West Coast.

Frontier 'Past Master'
February 1966

OLDTIMER Alex Bolam of Cooper Landing recently became the first member of the Seward Masonic Lodge ever to receive the title of "Honorary Past Master," and his life reads like a history of that Resurrection Bay community. In the early 1900's, Alex with his dog team was one of the mail carriers on the Seward to Iditarod trail, a trip of about 460 miles. In 1915 he won the Seward Marathon Race, setting a record that stood for many years. As a former Seward police chief, he served as one of the guards for the late President Warren G. Harding when he passed through Seward in 1923 after dedicating the Alaska Railroad. Just prior to World War II, Bolam received national recognition for the giant potatoes and strawberries he raised at his homestead on Kenai Lake, and he has guided big game hunters to trophies too numerous to name. In addition, he annually hosts the Seward Scottish Rite's "Cornbread and Bean" picnic at his homestead, where he proves over the campfire that he truly is a "past master."

A Few Errands... First Trip Outside in 45 Years
February 1966

THE FIVE-HOUR jet trip to Seattle was just about as exciting to Mrs. Emma Leach last fall as her three-week boat trip to Fort Yukon, Alaska, in 1920. It was her first trip Outside in 45 years. Mrs. Leach is the widow of Frank Leach who founded the Circle Hot Springs resort north of Fairbanks.

After serving as a Red Cross nurse during World War I, Mrs. Leach came north to work in the mission hospital at Fort Yukon. There she met her future husband, who had mined at Circle Hot Springs since 1907, when he came to the hospital for treatment of a broken leg. Following their marriage the two gradually built up the resort, with Mr. Leach doing most of the construction work himself and Mrs. Leach cooking for the guests that came in increasing numbers after the completion of the highway from Fairbanks in 1930. But with the closure of most of the gold camps in the area during World War II, the little community became quieter and quieter. Mr. Leach passed away in 1955, and five years later Mrs. Leach retired from the business.

She still lives at Circle Hot Springs, however, and she'll be back after visiting relatives in Wisconsin and tending to a few errands that have been piling up over the years, such as the purchase of some new glasses. "I'm near-sighted, you know, and the glasses I had when I came to this country don't fit like they used to."

If 'Copter Fails... the Good Old Dog Team
February 1966

WHEN the helicopter fails, there's still the good old dog team. An elderly Native couple and their 12-year-old grandson were trapped by icing conditions on the Chandalar River late last fall in the foothills of the Brooks Range. They had started out from Venetie for their home at Gold Camp with some friends in a riverboat, but the trip was interrupted when the friends shot a moose and returned to Venetie with the meat. The couple, Mr. and Mrs. John Frank, who are both over 80 years old, and their grandson elected to remain on an island to await their friends' return, but in the interim ice began running in the river and the boat couldn't make it back.

The trio waited until the river froze, and then started to walk out. Although spotted from the air by helicopter, weather conditions prevented their rescue. Finally Allen Tritt of Venetie mushed his dog team through a heavy snowstorm and brought them safely to the village. Actually they'd done pretty well on their own. By the time of their rescue they had covered 60 rugged miles in a week. But, said the grandfather, "probably good thing dog sled come. No caribou. No meat. Mealtime come--three bites, that's all."

Big Expansion for Kodiak's Oldest Store
January 1966

Kodiak's oldest mercantile establishment, O. Kraft and Son, is opening a new enlarged dry goods, supermarket and men's store which covers a full acre. The firm was founded 63 years ago by Otto Kraft, who came to this country well before that. Otto arrived in Kodiak aboard a sailing schooner in 1885 when the Russian language was still spoken on the island and Russian money was in circulation. He managed the North American Commercial Company trading post at Woody Island before starting his own business in 1903. Today his grandson, Walter O. Kraft, is president of the firm.

R.R. Terminal Rebuilt
January 1966

The biggest reconstruction job following Alaska's disastrous 1964 earthquake, the rebuilding and relocation of the Alaska Railroad terminal at Seward, is all but completed. The $11 million project included dredging out channels for ocean going vessels at a site near the head of Resurrection Bay, some two miles from the old demolished docks, and using the gravel as fill for 55 acres of tidelands. The U. S. Army Corps of Engineers said that the dredging job alone provided enough fill to gravel a walk six inches wide to circle the equator. After that, a forest of steel piles were set, concrete slabs were placed atop, a spaghetti of tracks laid, and Seward was back in business.

60th Year as a Nun – A Special Event
February 1966

STUDENTS AND STAFF at little St. Mary's Mission School on the Lower Yukon held a special celebration October 5th in honor of Sister Thecia who marked her 60th year as an Ursuline nun. And although they couldn't be there for the occasion, hundreds of former students scattered throughout Western Alaska still remember the culinary skill which earned Sister Thecia the reputation as "the best baker on the Yukon."

Sister Thecia is 81 years old, and has served in Alaska for 46 of those years. She was born in the little Italian village of Azzano Dacimo and entered the Ursuline Order in Cividale, Italy. She served for a time in Rome and at Salvi, then in 1919 was sent to Pilgrim Springs on the Seward Peninsula in Western Alaska. Cooking and domestic work were pretty hard then with no electricity, oil or running water. In 1941 she was transferred to Akulurak, and in 1951 to St. Mary's Mission, where her bread continues to be the staff of life for some 200 students and staff of eight Ursulines, two Jesuit priests, two brothers and eleven men and women teachers.

Last moments of historic St. Michael's Greek-Russian Orthodox Cathedral as flames sweep upward towards its graceful dome and cross. A landmark since 1848, the church was built when Sitka was the capital of Russian America

Charred, ruined and sheathed with icicles in ten above zero weather, the Sitka Bazaar, a general merchandise and gift store, was one of more than 20 businesses destroyed in the fire. Damage was estimated at more than $3.5 million.

Silhouetted against the smoke and flames, volunteer firemen watch helplessly as the fire breaks through the roof of Sitka's Lutheran Church. They battled for more than four hours before containing the blaze.

The Historic Heart of Alaska: St. Michael's Cathedral and Much of Downtown Sitka Destroyed by Fire

All photos by Martin Strand

April 1966

THE HISTORIC HEART of Sitka and, indeed, of Alaska—St. Michael's Greek-Russian Orthodox Cathedral—was destroyed January 2 in a fire which wiped out much of Sitka's downtown business district. No lives were lost and no one was injured, but before the wind-whipped flames were brought under control the city had suffered a loss of more than $3.5 million.

The fire started shortly before seven o'clock in the morning somewhere around Porter's Clothing Store. It raced along the waterfront side of Lincoln Street, then jumped across and continued unchecked on the other side. The beautiful old cathedral, which stood alone like an island with the street branching around it, was doomed.

In all, 21 businesses were wiped out, including the Alaska Hotel, the Coliseum Theater, television station KSA-TV, the Sitka Printing Company, Sitka Bazaar, Russian Bell Gift Shop, Gracy's Beauty Shop, Franklin's Triune Service, Sitka Realty, Porter Spaulding Insurance, Elliott's Stationery Store, Etolin Paint and Ceramic Store, Bingham's Kleenette and a number of other offices. Also destroyed was the Lutheran Church and part of the Cathedral Arms Apartments.

While volunteer firemen frantically fought the flames in ten above zero weather, parishioners and priests groped through the smoke to save the cathedral's priceless gold icons and religious art treasures. As the fire neared the church they took down the heavy doors inlaid with gold and silver and hauled them away. But a painting which could not be removed from the wall in time and some irreplaceable records stored in the church tower were lost.

The graceful blue-gray cathedral, described as the finest example of Russian architecture in the United States, was completed in 1848. At that time Sitka as the capital of Russian America and one of the major seaports of the Pacific, prided itself as being the "Paris of the West." The cathedral's octagonal belfry and towering carrot-shaped spire formed a backdrop in 1867 for ceremonies marking the transfer of Alaska from Russia to the United States. Though the capital of the Territory of Alaska was moved from Sitka to Juneau in 1900, Sitka remained the spiritual seat of the Greek-Russian Orthodox Church in Alaska.

Even as the wreckage of the cathedral still smoked, plans were made to rebuild. Charred spikes ten to fourteen inches long, hand-wrought before 1848 in the old Sitka foundry and used to join the logs of the structure, were retrieved from the ashes to be presented to any person donating $100 or more for the reconstruction. Blueprints of the original church have been located in the Library of Congress, and it is hoped that the church can be rebuilt in time for Alaska's 1967 Centennial celebration.

Smoke billows over Sitka's waterfront from fire which raged unchecked through several blocks of the downtown business district early Sunday morning last January 2. The black round smudge in the center of the picture is the pyre of famed St. Michael's Cathedral. The arrow-shaped building at upper right is the Pioneers' Home for Alaska oldtimers which was not threatened.

No Winter Respite for Cook Inlet's Booming Oil Industry

March 1966

NORMALLY oil activity in Alaska cools off with the weather. Not so this season. Within one short week last November the following announcements came from various sectors of the booming Cook Inlet oil industry:

--Award by Union Marathon Oil Company of California of a construction contract for a unique one-legged "mushroom" drilling and production platform to be used in its Trading Bay well site area, with completion scheduled for this spring.

--Discovery by Union Marathon of another oil well four and a half miles south of its Trading Bay discovery, bringing the known oil fields in the Inlet up to six.

--Award by Pan American Petroleum Corporation of construction contracts for two new drilling and production platforms (these with four legs), their second and third in the Inlet.

--Completion by Shell Oil Company of the Inlet's first oil production pipeline, stretching from its Middle Ground Shoal platform to the Kenai Peninsula shore.

--Announcement by Pan American that its new Inlet gas well, located about 35 miles southwest of Anchorage, had tested at a rate of 19 million cubic feet a day.

The following week, as frosting on the cake so far as the State of Alaska was concerned, the U. S. Court of Appeals held that Alaska has sovereignty over inland waters where the headlands are not more than 24 miles apart. That meant that lands in Cook Inlet south of the Forelands adjoining rich state-owned oil fields also will come under state juris-

Mac's Foto Service
Off shore drilling in Cooks Inlet. The Chigmit Range appears in the background.

diction. The Appeals Court ruling reversed a decision which held that the lands were the property of the federal government.

The only sour note in the happy harmony came late in November when the third oil and gas lease lottery for federal lands on the North Slope of the Brooks Range fell flat. Only 148 of over 1,600 blocks of land available drew bids, and while some 10,000 offers had been expected only 1,954 were filed. Commented a Bureau of Land Management official: "There probably are several reasons why there wasn't more interest in this sale...No one knows as yet just what is going to happen on the North Slope. If there had been an oil well gushing in after one of the first two drawings, you'd have seen a lot of people at this one."

Nome's Name
August 1966

The Nome Nugget has dredged up an interesting story on how Nome got its name. Seems an early British map maker on British ships in the area during the period of 1845-51 put down (?Name) off what is now Cape Nome on the chart. A later map draftsman misread the note and "?Name" became "Nome."

Ship Aground... 'Breaking Up'... Crew Endangered
March 1966

"ODUNA advises aground.... Breaking up....Unable to get off." That was the terse message received at Adak late last November from Captain Otto Karbbe, skipper of the Alaska Steamship Company's freighter ODUNA. It touched off another massive rescue effort in the stormy North Pacific, which has seen many of them over the years.

The 10,000-ton vessel had been groping her way through a savage gale on her regular Aleutian run from Adak to Seattle, with stops scheduled at Sand Point and Kodiak. Her radar had not been operating properly, and shortly after daybreak on November 26 she ran hard aground between rocks and the high cliffs on Itakan Peninsula at the south end of Unimak Island. There she was wedged, breaking up under the pounding seas. So precarious was her position that she could not even once launch life boats for the 37 crewmen aboard.

Combined rescue efforts by the Air Force, Coast Guard, Army, Navy and civilians were launched at once. But it was an Air Force helicopter pilot and his crew, along with the Seattle tugboat, ADELINE FOSS, who really pulled it off. The tug, en route from Amchitka to Seward with a tow, was the first to arrive on the scene. She managed to pass a line to the stricken ship with a breeches buoy attached, whereby nine of the ODUNA'S crewmen made their escape. The other 28 crewmen were taken off by an Air Force helicopter, under the command of Captain Gerald Belanger, which battled winds of up to 50 miles an hour to lift the men from the rolling decks of the listing ship.

"I can't elaborate enough on the efforts of Captain Belanger and his crew," said Captain Karbbe, after all were safely ashore and the ODUNA was left to her fate. "What he did was beyond words...we owe a great deal to him."

Aleuts in Servitude?
January 1966

Charges that Aleut residents of the lonely Pribilof Islands were being held in servitude by the Bureau of Commercial Fisheries, which manages the islands and their fur seal resource, have been found to be untrue by a special investigative committee. In a report to Governor William A. Egan, the commission said that while there was room for improvement in employment and living conditions on the islands, most of the dissatisfaction stemmed from conditions which prevailed some years back and have now been corrected. However, legislation is being prepared which would permit the islanders to own their own homes and provide some measure of local autonomy. The servitude charges were leveled by the bi-weekly newspaper, TUNDRA TIMES.

Coal for the Eskimos
March 1966

NO MORE of those weak willow-wand fires for the Eskimo people of barren Anaktuvuk Pass. They've got a big TD-9 International tractor equipped with bulldozer blade now, and they plan to use it to dig coal out of the hillside.

For generations the people of the little village isolated deep in the Brooks Range have gathered willow branches for fuel, packing them five to six miles on their backs or by dog sled. And for generations they've known about the coal deposits some 30 miles from their village, but had no practical way to dig it or transport it back.

Then last spring Raymond Paneak made an appeal for a tractor at a meeting in Fairbanks which was attended by representatives of the Office of Economic Opportunity and a number of other federal agencies. Gerald Ousterhout of the Bureau of Indian Affairs took on the job of coordinating the effort.

Just the right tractor finally turned up as surplus property at the Clear Air Force Station. It was driven to the airfield, dismantled, and flown via Alaska National Guard plane to Anaktuvuk where there was no unloading problem because the whole village turned out to help. It will be on loan to the community indefinitely, as long as they maintain it and pay for operating expenses.

Quake Upsets Boundaries
September 1966

As an aftermath in Anchorage of the 1964 Good Friday earthquake, the largest civil case in the history of the state was filed in Anchorage July 1.

The Superior Court action seeks to readjust boundaries of over 200 pieces of Anchorage property. The quake had shifted land in the area from K Street to the Inlet and from Ninth Avenue north to the Inlet about nine feet west and four feet north — result, legal descriptions don't any longer fit the facts.

1966

PHOTO BY JOE RYCHETNIK

A Huge Plume of Ash from Mount Redoubt
May 1966

Mt. Redoubt, 10,197 feet, at the base of the Alaska Peninsula, across Cook Inlet from the Kenai Peninsula country, has been putting on an act again, throwing great clouds of volcanic smoke to 45,000 feet. This photo, taken in late January of this year, shows smoke billowing out of a new crater. Pilots on their way down the Peninsula and to Bristol Bay say the mountain has been much more active this winter than in many years past. At press time, still another "old actor" among the Aleutian Range volcanoes, Mt. Pavlof, 8,215 feet, far down near the very tip of the Alaska Peninsula, was reported belching.

Prehistory in Back Yard
March 1966

WHAT could be nicer for a professor of biology than to find a "prehistoric bog" right in his own back yard! Dr. Leonard R. Freeze has one, just a few hundred feet from the administration building at the Alaska Methodist University in Anchorage, and he thinks it is the only campus in the country with its own private bog. "It is invaluable to our classes," says Dr. Freeze. "All of us go down in waders and collect specimens." Treasures found there thus far include five kinds of little carnivorous plants and some tiny Alaska orchids.

Luxuries from Spuds
March 1966

NEARLY thirty years of potato farming in Alaska have paid off for Mr. and Mrs. Irvin Evenson of Sand Lake. He's one of the few full time farmers in the North who can make the grade without having to work "out" during the off season. Evenson came to the Matanuska Valley near Anchorage from Wisconsin in 1936 and made 60 cents an hour clearing land for the colonists. In 1943 he and his wife moved out to their own homestead and started small with an acre of potatoes. Now they have 30 to 35 acres in cultivation and grow about 500 tons of potatoes a year, most of which go under contract to the military. With the hardest years of land clearing and equipment buying behind them, Mr. and Mrs. Evenson can allow themselves a few luxuries. They have a pleasant home beside a little lake, their own light plane, and two years ago they went to Russia on a "People to People" agricultural tour with a group of 30 farmers.

Marauding Moose Gets Fiery Response from the Gentle Sisters
March 1966

THE GENTLE SISTERS at Providence Hospital had their hands full late last fall holding their own against a marauding moose mother and her calf. Not only did the moose chew up most of the garden, but they rattled the screens and smeared up the windows drooling over the house plants inside the convent.

"It's hard on the heart to hear a noise at three a. m., look out the window and see a moose staring right back at you," said Sister Barbara Ellen, hospital administrator. The sisters shouted, banged pans and finally rang the convent bell, but the moose were unmoved.

"They got right down on their knees to get at our border plants," she said. "Their pose was reverent, but not their manners."

The problem was reported to the city police, who were sympathetic, but no crime had been committed, except possibly trespass, and a convent isn't designed for a winter stakeout or armed guard. The Department of Fish and Game was notified and an agent inspected the depredation. He advised the nuns that they had a right to use rifles to protect their lives and property, but that was too much for the soft-hearted sisters. Finally he left a supply of Roman candles with Sister Barbara Ellen with instructions to shoot in the general direction of the munching monsters. So the New Year's fireworks display came a little early at Providence Hospital, but it did the trick.

Fears Unjustified... Little Damage in Big Blast
February 1966

WHEN LONELY Amchitka Island far out the Aleutian Chain was chosen as the site for an underground nuclear detonation, there was a lot of knuckle-gnawing by conservationists over what might happen to the thousands of sea otters in the area. But they weathered the blast just fine. So perfect was the shot, buried 2,300 feet in the volcanic rock of the island, that it caused only a lift of several feet at ground zero, and there was virtually no damage to wildlife in the area or anything else for that matter. A team of experts from the Fish and Wildlife Service and the University of Washington could find only a couple of dead ling cod and two or three birds. And they're not even sure that the blast was to blame for those.

The sea otters had been hazed away from the island with gunfire and fireworks shortly before the detonation last October 29. Afterward the experts checked for possible dead otters but found none. They did find quite a few live otters, however, in numbers comparable to those sighted before the blast. The automic device, with four times the power of the nuclear bombs that devastated Hiroshima and Nagasaki during World War II, was touched off to test the United States' ability to distinguish between earth waves caused by natural seismic disturbances and those generated by underground atomic blasts. For the record, its seismic magnitude registered at about 5.75 on the Richter scale.

Defector Defects Back to Siberia
March 1966

ONE OF THOSE two Russian defectors who came drifting over to Alaska in an open boat late last summer has decided to go home. After three months in the United States, 30-year-old Gregory Sarapushkin told the State Department he wanted to return to Siberia where he has a wife and son. He was turned over to the Soviet Embassy in Washington. His companion, Peter Kalentenko, 34, still is here and his request to stay is under consideration. The two caused quite a stir last August when they arrived at the village of Wales on the Arctic Coast, saying that they had become lost while on a hunting and fishing expedition off the Siberian Coast. They asked for asylum while aboard a U. S. Coast Guard vessel which was taking them back to their homeland.

Among Things to Come –
June 1966

INDICATION OF things to come in a looming industrial future for the Cook Inlet basin as a result of growing oil production is the recently announced news that a multi-million dollar ammonia plant is in the works.

Collier Carbon and Chemical, a subsidiary of Union Oil of California, will build the giant plant to use natural gas and produce 530,000 tons of ammonia and prilled urea. Tokyo Gas and Chemical Co. will be associated with Collier and completion of the plant is slated for 1968.

Buffalo Defense... Just Standing There When Struck in Rear by Auto
February 1966

LEAPING to the defense of Delta Junction's famed buffalo herd, Editor-Publisher W. Don Nilsson of The Delta Midnight Sun took off editorially recently when the old rumor cropped up that the shaggy beasts were charging automobiles on the Alaska Highway again. What touched it off was a car-buffalo collision, the first in quite a spell. "Shades of Old Black Joe!" somebody said.

Old Black Joe was reputedly a rogue buffalo who tangled with a dozen or so automobiles traveling the highway in the late 1950's. In the first place, Nilsson wrote, Old Black Joe didn't do all the charging he was charged with. There were a number of loners in the herd at that time, and it just made a better story (even to the police) to say that Old Joe had collected another victim. And in the second place, Nilsson contended, the recent charging charge obviously couldn't apply to the "new" Old Black Joe because he was hit in the rear.

1966

June 1966
Moose are common on the roads and byways of Fort Richardson, near Anchorage. Photographer James Peacock, took this shot of a mama moose and calf moose on the reservation.

Largest Timber Sale Ever... St. Regis Wins
April 1966

ST. REGIS Paper Company of New York was the successful bidder for 8.75 billion board feet of timber in North Tongass National Forest of Southeast Alaska, a sale described by the Forest Service as the largest in its history. The firm's final bid was 5.65 per thousand board feet for timber logged during the first five years on the basis of economic conditions. The figure was $2.35 above the Forest Service's advertised rate of $3.30.

The only other bidder at the sale, held in the Forest Service's regional office at Juneau, was Champion Papers Incorporated of Hamilton, Ohio. Both firms submitted sealed bids at the minimum level, and the bidding continued on an oral basis through 23 rounds until St. Regis hit the $5.65 mark and Champion dropped out.

The terms of the contract require St. Regis to establish a pulp mill in the area no later than July 1, 1971. The mill, together with any related facilities such as lumber and plywood plants, must be equipped to handle at least 175 million board feet of timber a year. The timber involved is predominantly Sitka spruce and western hemlock located on the mainland in the Taku Inlet area south of Juneau, on the west side of Admiralty Island, and in the Yakutat area.

Cutting operations will be planned by the Forest Service on a five-year basis with stringent multi-use concept requirements to protect wildlife, salmon streams, waterfowl nesting grounds and rcereational areas.

Close Call in Icy Waters of the Tagish
March 1966

BIG GAME GUIDE Doug Low of Whitehorse had as close a call as anyone would care to think about in the icy waters of the Tagish River just before freeze-up. He was crossing the river in an aluminum boat one morning to check on his pack horses in the area when the boat capsized and flipped him into the river. First he tried to swim, but soon realized he was becoming paralyzed with the cold. He managed to catch hold of the boat but was too weak and numb by that time to climb into it, so he just hung on and paddled over to the ice which had formed for a distance of about a hundred feet from the shoreline. There he clung and hollered for help.

About that time 17-year-old Robby Rose, who was taking a stroll on nearby Tagish Bridge, heard the sounds, but thought they were moose calls. His family was in the market for a moose, so he hurried to his home near the bridge, routed out his mother and stepfather, Mr. and Mrs. Archie Currie, and they all piled in the family car to go have a look. They had gone only a short distance when they realized the calls were those of a human being, and spotted Doug hanging onto the ice.

Robby and Archie rushed back for a boat, managed to get Doug into it, and took him across the open water to the far side of the river where they started a roaring fire. Meanwhile Mrs. Currie hurried to the trading post run by Harold White, who took off with his dog team to fetch the half-frozen man after phoning to Whitehorse for an ambulance. Doug was transferred from the dog sled to the Currie car and eventually to the ambulance which they met on the road. He landed in the Whitehorse hospital for a few days, but made a complete and speedy recovery.

Eskimo's Shot from Hip at Six Feet Kills Polar Bear
April 1966

POLAR BEAR HUNTERS, confronted with the need for tags, equipment, guides, planes, cover planes, etc., might be interested in this manner of going about it, as related by David C. Kagak, correspondent for the *Fairbanks Daily News-Miner* at the Eskimo village of Wainwright.

"First polar bear caught yesterday by Frederick Ahmaogak about 14 miles away from village on his way home from camping trip with his brother Ben. Both were traveling home in stormy windy weather. They sighted one bear which was eating from their seal meat which was stored away for winter use. Both shot at the bear but they wounded the bear, and one of their dogs loosed from their team went after the bear. The loose dog finally bit the bear on his throat and the bear clawed him away. But Frederick was close enough to shoot at the bear six feet away. He shot the bear, aiming his rifle from his hip. The size of the bear is about 6½ to 7 feet tall."

Sled Dogs Attack Tot
July 1966

A TWO YEAR OLD Kotzebue boy was bitten by sled dogs in April when he became entangled in the harness of a running team. He was saved from possible death by the quick action of a Alaska Department of Fish and Game protection officer.

Little Mike Gallahorn was dragged about 250 feet, face down on rough ice of a Kotzebue street in the accident. During the time he was being dragged, the dogs slashed at the boy and an eleven year old lad was trying desperately to stop the sled with little success.

Hearing the child's cries, Don Dexter, Alaska Department of Fish and Game employee, rushed into the middle of the dogs and laid about with his fists. He succeeded in beating the dogs off the child and threw the youngster clear, then fought his own way free and rushed the boy to the hospital.

Young Gallahorn suffered severe abrasions and deep puncture wounds, but after minor repairs was released from the hospital.

Enraged Bear Pursues an Unarmed Prospector
August 1966

A story out of Edmonton is a hair-raiser about a man, 60, who held off an enraged black bear for several miles until he could secure his rifle.

Fred Lypa of Edmonton, a prospector, was working several miles from his tent camp about 250 miles north of Yellowknife when he turned to find a bear with forepaw raised as if to strike. He yelled and the bear backed off.

Picking up his axe, his only weapon, Lypka shouted again, but the bear stood firm. Cautiously Lypka began moving backward, succeeding in staying a rush by the bear with repeated shoutings and dropping matches in the dry grass.

Once he turned to run, but the bear stayed with him and only frantic shouts held him off again. Seven hours later, the exhausted Lypka, his voice almost gone, reached his tent and his rifle. A shot from six feet broke the bear's back.

Canadian Press reports three men were severely injured last fall in western Alberta by grizzly bears.

June 1966
Sixteen year old Kathy Shapley of Craig was the winner in a design contest for creation of the Alaska State Medal for Heroism, authorized by the Alaska Legislature in 1965.

Miss Shapley's design, seen above, won over 428 other offerings.

Whaling Season
June 1966

FIVE WHALERS were to open the 1966 whaling season out of Coal Harbor on the west coast of Vancouver Island in Quatsino Sound April 1. The plant of Western Canada Whaling is jointly owned by British Columbia Packers and Taiyo Fishing Co. of Japan.

In 1965, the whale catch was 859 whales. In 1964 the fleet took 880 animals. Economists declare the industry is worth one and a half million dollars annually to British Columbia economy.

Record Elk Kill on Afognak Island
June 1966

HUNTERS BAGGED MORE ELK this past season on Afognak Island near Kodiak than in any season past—142 animals—but the kill is still less than 10 percent of the total herd. The season has been running from August 1 through December 31, but most animals have been taken from mid-October through mid-November, according to Alaska Department of Fish and Game biologist Sterling Eide of Kodiak.

The Forest Service has built shelter cabins and trails in the area and guides have been offering horseback hunts. These are two factors which have stepped up interest and success for Afognak area hunters.

69-Foot B.C. Log for Sitka's Indian Canoe
July 1966

HERM KITKA comes of a long line of dugout making Tlingits at Sitka. He was recently sent to Vancouver, B.C. to find a monster cedar log from which he will carve a great Indian canoe for Sitka's part in next year's Centennial.

Kitka made the trip with the purse seiner Martha K. and towed back a 69 foot log that measures seven feet at the butt and four feet in diameter at the small end.

The only difference from a hundred years ago, Kitka remarked wryly, is that in those earlier times he "would have sent slaves to do the job."

Jail 'System' Fails: No Free Trip
April 1966

THAT SLICK OLD SYSTEM of getting arrested in Barrow just to get a free ride to Fairbanks didn't work so well last winter. The Barrow jail, which serves as a temporary detaining point for prisoners awaiting the southbound flight to the state jail, was being remodeled and the erring ones were sent outside during the daytime to work in the ferocious Arctic weather. That meant they couldn't sit comfortably in nice warm quarters while contemplating life in the big city following their release from the Fairbanks jail. Cut the crime rate down considerably.

On the Road to Klutina Lake
* * * *
A Giant Spruce Burl

May 1966

This giant white spruce burl is 47.8 inches in diameter. Forester Duncan Gilchrist of the Bureau of Land Management took the photo with Fred Rungee of BLM's Glenallen Resource Area admiring the phenomenon. It's on the access road to Klutina Lake.

Polar Bear Trophies Removed from Competition... Decision Applauded
June 1966

SECRETARY OF THE INTERIOR Stewart L. Udall has commended the Boone and Crockett Club for its recent decision to eliminate polar bear from the list of animals eligible for big-game record competition.

The club is the official keeper of North American big-game records, the interior department said in disclosing that Udall wrote President Robert M. Ferguson at the Musem of Natural History in New New York:

"I wish to commend the Boone and Crockett Club for its forthright action in eliminating the polar bear from the list of wild animals acceptable in future big-game hunting competition...

"I agree with you that using aircraft and other motorized equipment largely removes the important sporting element of fair chase in the hunting of polar bears."

Alaska prohibits use of aircraft for hunting polar bears in the state's territorial waters, but aircraft hunting is carried on outside the three-mile limit.

The 1965 harvest of polar bears from Alaska contributed about $450,000 to the state's economy, the U.S. Fish and Wildlife Service said.

Season remains open for polar bear hunting in Alaska, however, with a permit now being required for next year's season opening January 1 and running to April 30. November 30 will be deadline for applications for 350 non-transferable permits, resident or non-resident, drawing to be held in December.

In addition, with limit set at one bear and no cub or bear with cubs to be taken, a hunter taking a bear will have to wait three more years before he can go out after a second bear. This latter rule will not apply to residents, many of whom use bear meat for food, but no airplane will be allowed in the chase.

On another regulatory front, trophy hunting of wolves in the Nelchina area (Unit 13), and in that portion of Unit 14 north of the Kashwitna River, will be permitted from October 1 through November 30 with the stipulation that no aircraft may be used. Bag limit is one wolf.

Running Water for the Homes of Unalakleet
April 1966

RUNNING WATER is just about on tap for the villagers of Unalakleet who up to now have been hauling it by the bucket in the summertime and in the form of ice by dog team in the winter. The new $300,000 sanitation system, first of its kind in Alaskan villages, was sponsored by the U. S. Public Health Service with residents supplying the labor.

It's a pretty complicated system. Water is pumped from a series of shallow wells a half mile from the village and stored in a 40,000-gallon elevated water tower. A portion of the water is then heated by oil-fire boilers and circulated through 9,000 feet of four-inch cement-lined cast iron pipe. Underground service connections contain thaw wires.

Each resident is supplied with a sink and seepage pit for waste disposal. Those who agree to provide a bathroom and keep the interior of their homes heated at all times also get flush toilets.

Under the old system residents paid about five cents a gallon to have their water hauled in. Estimated monthly cost for the new system is about $12.50 for a single fixture. If all goes well, similar systems will be installed in other villages, with Kotzebue next in line.

Farthest North Swimming Pool: Not for Bathing, But for Water Storage

December 1966

THIS MAY come as somewhat of a surprise but our country's farthest north swimming pool is located at Point Barrow. It is a beautiful blue-green plastic pool that fairly shimmers in the brilliant twenty-four hours of Arctic sunshine during the summer months. But don't expect to find it surrounded by bikini-clad bathing beauties. It's not that kind of pool.

John Nusinginya, a 38 year old Eskimo, born and reared in Point Barrow is the owner of this exceptional swimming pool. Nusinginya has already made Barrow proud of him with his fine record in the State Legislature at Juneau and his newest enterprise is again focusing attention on his home town.

Potable water has always been a problem in Point Barrow. In the winter, ice had to be cut from the lakes located out on the tundra or fresh water ice cut from the frozen ice pack in front of the village. Either way, it was hard work and meant a long haul by dog team. Most homes in the village had blocks of ice stacked beside them to be melted for water as needed. In the summer, water had to be dipped from the lakes and hauled to the village by the individual home owners. The tundra is muddy and springy in the summer months and the water haul was hazardous and at times, impossible. You often saw mothers and children out with cooking pots digging snow from unthawed spots to melt down for water. It was back-breaking work at best.

Then John Nusinginya came up with his unique method of providing water for the village. He had this beautiful plastic swimming pool shipped in and set it up on his property at the edge of town. He installed a four inch Wisconsin air-cooled pumping engine at a tundra lake approximately four miles from the village and is pumping water through a pipeline into his swimming pool which holds 21,000 gallons. From the swimming pool, he pumps water into small water tank vehicles for delivery to the homes.

That takes care of the water problem for Barrow during the summer. For the winter? Mr. Nusinginya has that one figured, too. He is filling one hundred pound size plastic bags with water from the swimming pool and freezing it. These are being stored until the winter freeze takes place and it will no longer be feasible to pump water in over the tundra. The hundred pound bags of ice will then be sold to the home owners for melting during the winter, until the pumping into the swimming pool can be resumed the following summer.

The portable swimming pool stores water at Barrow.

Ice blocks cut in winter keep for summer use in this sod house.

Blocks of ice stored outside of Barrow's soda fountain and pool hall will be melted for water.

'Dear Uncle Sam...'
June 1966

SOMETIMES the work of Selective Service isn't easy, even when everybody is cooperating to beat the band. Alaska's Selective Service director, Lt. Col. Dan Mahoney, tells of mailing an ex-Army man a questionnaire relative to his reserve status and receiving the following reply two months later:

"The reason for the delay in returning this questionnaire is that I receive mail only once a month. This fact can be confirmed by the postmaster at Port Williams.

"The above personally made two attempts to deliver your letter, but due to weather failed.

"My exact location on the island of Shuyak (north of Kodiak) is one-half mile west of the Geodetic Survey marker in Carry Inlet. It's the marker that's well in the inlet and not the one at the mouth.

"The cabin is about 25 yards from the beach and is visible from the beach.

"I am at the above location twice a week but if I am not at the cabin I will be on the (trap) line, which goes around the east side of Carry Inlet, down the west side of Western Inlet and around part of Big Bay.

"I hope the above information is of some help."

Top Pay in Alaska for Government Workers
August 1966

According to the Department of Commerce, as of October, 1965, Alaska had 14,200 federal civilian employees, slightly down from 1964; 6,700 State government employees, up 400 from the year previous, while local governments had 5,800 on the payroll, up 700. Total payrolls for these employees was $8,539,000 for October, 1965, a little over a million higher than a year ago.

Average monthly earnings for all government employees in Alaska last October was $742, the highest in the list of 50 states. California was second with a $651 average, New York third with $565 average.

Alaskan school payrolls averaged $717 per employee, highest for the U.S. with California again second at $698. Average Alaskan monthly pay for instructional personnel at the local school level was $772. California, in that category, scored a higher $784 average.

A Break in the Iron Curtain... Russ Hunters, Alaskan Eskimos Visit on Ice
September 1966

Russian hunters and Alaskan Eskimos visited on the ice some ten miles west of Gambell on St. Lawrence Island early in June. St. Lawrence Island Eskimos said the Russians were in a 20 foot boat, hunting oogruk and walrus and were only killing the mammals for the skins and blubber, leaving the meat.

Apparently the Russians were part of a fleet of eight boats and a mother ship.

Neither Russians nor Eskimos could speak the other's language and all conversation was by sign. They traded cigarettes, and St. Lawrence Island Eskimo Tim Gologergen, a National Guard captain, said the men were friendly, but he deplored the waste of a valuable resource.

The Alaskan Eskimos spotted the Russian hunters and their boat atop an ice pile looking for walrus. Contacting their other Alaskan Eskimo boats by walkie-talkie, they and the other three boatloads of hunters took out after the Russians. The Russian craft was slow, and the outboard motor powered Alaskan skin boats quickly caught up to the Russians, who apparently were afraid of the American craft and sent up flares, but handshakes and cigarette exchanges quickly followed.

Said one Alaskan Eskimo, "When I give him American cigarette, he throw away his own . . . lighted the American cigarette and started taking big smile."

Russians also apparently cast envious looks at the Alaskan outboard motors, the St. Lawrence Islanders reported.

The St. Lawrence Islanders also said the Russians "mustn't have washed up for days from the looks of them . . .," oil stain covering boat and men.

Judge Finally Loses Long Battle for Natives' Traditional Rights
August 1966

Back in Ottawa, Territorial Judge J. H. Sissons' long fight to preserve what he calls traditional hunting rights of Eskimos and Indians in the Northwest Territories ended in defeat recently in the Supreme Court of Canada.

Judge Sissons has been throwing out hunting charges brought against northern natives since 1959.

His rulings said that Eskimos and Indians enjoy traditional hunting rights under a 1763 royal proclamation and game ordinances of the territories could not apply to them.

The judgement upheld a charge of abandoning game against Sigeareak, a Whale Cove Eskimo. His lawyers admitted he killed five caribou and took only parts of them home, contrary to territorial law.

Judge Sissons, now 74, retires in July after 12 years as first justice of the territorial court. His decisions have been noted for their consideration of Eskimo and Indian cultures. His most recent case illustrates his attitude towards the Eskimo.

At Spence Bay he presided over a murder case in which two Eskimos were accused of killing a mentally-deranged woman. He told the six-man jury that the law flows from the people and that the Eskimo society must be judged on its own terms. Mercy killings are condoned by Eskimos.

One accused was convicted of shooting the woman and Judge Sissons gave him a two-year suspended sentence. The second was acquitted.

Too Many 'Friends' for Oil-rich Village
June 1966

THE VILLAGE OF TYONEK, across Cook Inlet from Anchorage, is oil rich from lease payments and the "forgotten" Indian tribe that makes up the population of Tyonek is suddenly finding itself a popular call for traveling salesmen with everything from television sets to stock plans for sale.

Chief of the Moquawkie Tribe, Albert S. Kaloa, Jr. has a sense of humor, but he felt the word should be passed that his people are getting a little tired of red hot deals and high pressure conversation. He ran the following ad in the Anchorage newspapers:

"We never had so many friends! And we like them all! However, please don't call on us till our village is complete, without prior permission from the Tribal Council. Contact us thru our attorney at 277-3132.

"Salesmen note the above. The scalp you save may be your own. Get the message?"

New Beginning for Stricken Seward
September 1966

They called it "another beginning" in Seward late in June when the city hosted dignitaries to a dedication of the Alaska Railroad's new $10 million complex of dock, yards and warehouses that once again makes Seward a major seaport for Interior Alaska.

The Alaska Steamship company renewed freight service into Seward with the motorship Tonsina.

The 1964 earthquake had put Seward out of business for railroad and steamship service and Department of Interior decision to rebuild piers at Seward despite developed facilities at Anchorage and Whittier was long a nip and tuck deal as to whether or not Seward would be put back into business as a major port or abandoned.

A new wharf built for Alaska Railroad is designed primarily for the handling of containerized cargo. It is 736 feet long, 200 feet wide, and has two 50 ton cranes.

In addition to rebuilding of Alaska Railroad steamship handling facilities at Seward, there is also talk of moving rail and barge services from Whittier to Seward, at the same time opening a tunnel road access to Whittier from Portage on the Anchorage side of the mountains.

August 1966
This giant halibut coming up from the hold of a fishing boat at Petersburg in May of this year, was delivered by Capt. Arel Mathiesen on his first trip of the 1966 season—weight 373 pounds. Biggest eastern Pacific halibut officially reported, according to the International Halibut Commission, weighed 495 pounds, and was taken many years ago, also in the Petersburg area. The western Atlantic reports a bigger specimen, also many years back, of 690 pounds. Sport fishermen in Alaska have been known to take halibut to 250 pounds.

Middleton Island Lures Oil Bidders
October 1966

Middleton Island is getting most of the attention these days as the Alaska oil picture constantly changes. Recently, State lands officers held the 16th competitive oil and gas lease sale and took on $7,034,760, of which about four and a half million was bid for rights to drill on Middleton Island, west of Cordova and Yakataga.

Oil has long been known on the main shore near Katalla and Yakataga, but badly fractured structures have led many geologists to surmise that better structures might exist on Middleton, farther from the mountain building effects along the main shore.

The Last Gazette
December 1966

Published for eleven years by the Business and Professional Women's Club of Seward as a public service, the Seward Petticoat Gazette entered Alaska's press history with its last edition on Sept. 29. Largely a volunteer production, the mimeographed Petticoat Gazette was the seaport city's major news media, contributing its profits to community projects. A commercial newspaper, the Seward Phoenix Log, began publishing in October.

Too Many Fish
December 1966

Running out of help before they ran out of fish, Southeast Alaska canneries have had their best season since 1951. Petersburg Fisheries, Inc., received 870,000 pounds of chum salmon in one day. The cannery's total chum poundage last year was 700,000. Cannery operators in both Wrangell and Petersburg reported pleading with housewives to help get the bonanza in cans. The weekly share of one seine boat crew member hit $2400.

Pilot Outwits Robbers Who 'Chartered' Plane
August 1966

Juneau pilot Ken Loken had an interesting charter early in June. Two men got him to fly to Sitka where they promptly revealed themselves as holdup artists, sticking up the Pioneer Saloon for $2,500 and then demanding at gunpoint that Loken fly them to Canada.

Loken stalled, maneuvered over populated places so his course could be noticed, then pretended to run out of gas near Ketchikan, landing at Lunch Creek, some fifteen miles north of the First City where his bandit passengers took off for the woods and were soon captured, a bloodhound named Annie leading State Trooper John McConnaughey and his M1 carbine to their hiding place.

The two men, Larry Crews, 26, and James Harkenson, 27, of Everett, Washington, were to be arraigned at Sitka. Kidnaping and airplane hijacking charges were pending.

While in the air, the duo admitted to Loken they were the persons who had a few days earlier stolen one of Loken's airplanes and abandoned it undamaged, but out of gas on a beach near Juneau.

House Moved by Sea to Make Room for Stores

July 1966

A Ketchikan home, constructed some years ago by Ketchikan contractor Carl Foss, was moved recently to help make way for a new shopping center. Paul Wingren, Wingren Food Stores, will build a big "Convenience Center" with 55,000 square feet of buildings, including a variety of stores at a cost of around $750,000. It is hoped the center will be open by late fall. The old Foss home was towed approximately fifteen miles down Tongass Narrows and around to Herring Cove on its big log raft to a new location. House movers like this kind of an operation—there are no city streets to block, no overhead wires to cut, and there is always a tide to help.

1966-67

New Life Ashore for Old Steamship
June 1966

THE WELL KNOWN old steamer Princess Louise of the Canadian Pacific will become a fancy restaurant near Los Angeles, according to reports of promoters.

The Princess Louise was built in Vancouver in 1921 for the Skagway run and ran that route and others until her retirement in 1962.

81 Below Zero!
December 1966

Memories of the bitter winter of 1947 were revived as the Canadian Department of Transport closed down its weather station at Snag in the Yukon. It was Feb. 3, 1947, that the Snag station recorded a temperature of 81.4 degrees below zero, coldest reading in North America's history. The cold was so intense that humans walking left vapor trails, and a patch of fog remained for several days above a tie-up area for dog teams.

Lesson for Eskimos: How to Can Walrus
October 1966

Eskimo women on St. Lawrence Island have been getting Government lessons in how to take care of their walrus. Eskimos used to eat some fresh, let some freeze or dry, and pickle quite a little in seal oil. If Gladys Musgrove, extension service home economist at Nome has her way, the St. Lawrence women will soon be adept at canning their walrus meat in pressure cookers.

On a recent trip to Savoonga, hunting had been good, but shipments of other pressure cookers had gone awry and Mrs. Musgrove felt for a time she was trying to cope with an impossible problem of "maybe 25,000 pounds of walrus and only one pressure cooker."

The women put up 240 one pound cans in the first three day cooking demonstration, borrowing extra canning equipment from the Lutheran ladies of Nome.

Holikachaget – Kaput!
July 1966

THE ONETIME VILLAGE of Holikachaget properly passed into the limbo April 3 when the folks of Grayling on the Yukon officially dedicated their new town built by Holikachaget (or "Holikachuk") people who had moved down off their low bank location on the twisting Innoko River to the mouth of Grayling Creek on the Yukon.

Seven new homes at the new townsite were erected in 1963. Federal and State funds helped the town grow. A school was built. A well was drilled and a new post office was established. Officials from many agencies helped the local folk cut cake and ribbons for the dedication.

The old Holikachaget location on a slough off the Innoko, was silting up, freight rates were high. Summer fish camps are nearer at the new site and Grayling is located closer to good wood and water supplies.

Unexpected Gift
September 1966

Al Kulan, Whitehorse, Yukon mining man whose original discoveries are credited with sparking the Ross River staking rush, has given the city of Whitehorse $25,000 to plant trees in the Yukon capital city as a centennial project.

Said Kulan, "The pleasure is all mine." Said Mayor Howard Firth, "I think this is the first time anyone has given Whitehorse money."

Indian Repays State for Old-age Assistance
December 1966

An interpreter explained to Gov. William A. Egan that Mrs. Jessie Kasko, 88-year-old resident of Douglas, was repaying $12,865.95 to the State of Alaska because it is part of her Tlingit Indian heritage to "demonstrate gratitude for favors received." Income from inherited timber lands near Haines made it possible for Mrs. Kasko to repay the state for past old age assistance payments.

September 1966

This is the last remaining covered bridge in Alaska. It is over Texas Creek, near Hyder, in a once booming mining district. Built in 1927, is is no longer used. Its purpose was to connect Hyder with the Chickamin mining district. The road to the bridge is impassable today, one of the main structural timbers needs repair and a portion of the shed was long ago destroyed by a snowslide.

KARL F. MIELKE

Alaska's Last Covered Bridge

1967

To Alaska in '40 with 37 Cents
* * *
Now he's Governor
January 1967

A young Kansan who landed in Anchorage in 1940 with 37 cents in his pocket, washed dishes on his first job and slept in an abandoned cabin, was to take office Dec. 5, as Alaska's first elected Republican governor.

Succeeding William A. Egan, governor since statehood, Walter J. Hickel, now a millionaire hotel owner and developer won the state's highest office in a cliff-hanging election that wasn't decided until a count of absentee ballots confirmed his slim plurality of 1,080 votes.

Second big Republican winner was Anchorage Attorney Howard Pollock, who unseated Representative Ralph Rivers for the state's lone Congressional seat.

Returned to the U.S. Senate with a 3 to 1 vote margin over his Republican rival, Dr. Lee McKinley, was Senator E. L. Bartlett.

Going to Juneau in January with Governor Hickel will be a Republican-dominated 20-member Senate and 40 Representatives, a complete reversal of the Democratic-controlled Fourth Legislature.

Also along will be Secretary of State-elect Keith Miller, relatively unknown Anchorageite who displaces veteran Hugh Wade as "assistant governor."

Seven proposals calling for issuance of $62.5 million in bonds for highway, airport, ferry, school and campground facilities were passed by wide margins.

ANCHORAGE TIMES PHOTO BY ALICE PUSTER

Governor and Mrs. Walter J. Hickel

Native Rights Asserted
January 1967

"**Treaties and laws** of the United States and Russia were passed to protect the rights of natives to our lands, but these measures have over the years been ineffectively enforced. It has now become necessary for the native people of Alaska to make a determined stand to protect what is rightfully ours."

Approved by 300 representatives of Alaska's 43,000 Indians, Eskimos and Aleuts, this declaration served notice that the state's first settlers want a final settlement on lingering land claims to more than 200,000 square miles. A 19-member committee named at the big October meeting in Anchorage will press to have the U.S. Court of Claims settle their case. Even as the Tyonek-sponsored native gathering was in session, 14,000 Eskimos in the Yukon-Kuskokwim delta filed claim to 12,000 square miles, and Kodiak Island natives filed claim to the entire Kodiak Island archipelago and surrounding continental shelf.

Historic Clerical Robes
January 1967

Dating back to the late 18th century, the clerical robes worn by Alaska's first Russian bishop, the Rev. John Veniaminov Innocentus, now hang in the University of Alaska Museum. Bishop Veniaminov reached Unalaska in July, 1828, and subsequently served at Kodiak and Sitka. The robes were presented by Dr. Harold McCracken, explorer, author and director of the Whitney Gallery of Western Art in Cody, Wyoming.

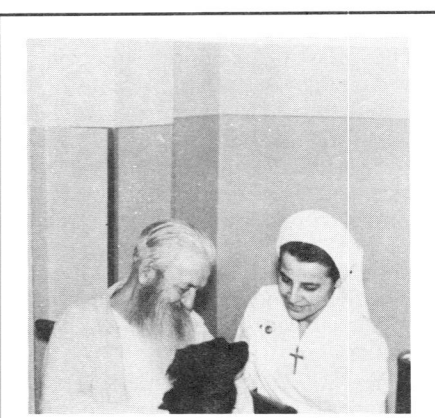

ALASKA SPORTSMAN PHOTO

February 1967

George Nelson, 75, trapper and a prospector at Cape Yakataga, spent nearly all of 1966 as a patient in Providence Hospital, Anchorage, recovering from injuries which cost him his left leg. Word reached the hospital that the sourdough's old dog had died, ending an 18-year-friendship. Determined that the cheerful trapper would not return alone to his cabin, Sister Philias, director of Providence nurses, rescued Peppy, a cocker spaniel from the Anchorage dog pound. Photo shows Sister Philias as she presented Peppy to Nelson just before Christmas. Equipped with a new artificial leg and a new dog, the sourdough trapper is happily back in his Cape Yakataga cabin.

Touchdown ★ ★ ★ President in Anchorage after Asian Tour

January 1967

The world's most powerful executive called Anchorage "home" for nine hours on November 1 and 2. The third president to visit Anchorage, President Lyndon B. Johnson and Mrs. Johnson landed at Elmendorf AFB at 11:37 p.m., November 1, and departed for Washington, D.C., on the last leg of a 17-day, 31,500-mile Asian tour at 8:36 a.m. on November 2.

Highlights of the interval between touchdown and takeoff included a greeting by more than 4,000 Alaskans, an unscheduled appearance at a bonfire, battling through friendly crowds as he entered and left the Anchorage-Westward Hotel, and a report to the nation on his trip.

Most significant event of the presidential visit was signing of two bills important to Alaska. President Johnson signed into law a bill sponsored by Sen. E. L. Bartlett which gives Pribilof Island residents more self-government and the right to gain title to land occupied by homes. Also earning the presidential signature was the fish protein concentrate act which calls for construction of one fish protein plant and lease of another. The fact that he selected Alaska for the signing has been interpreted by some officials as indicating one of the two plants will be located in the state.

President Lyndon B. Johnson is greeted by young Alaskans on arrival at Elmendorf AFB.

New U.S. Trawlers Bigger than Russia's
February 1967

Two new giant trawlers, larger than any Russian trawlers seen off the Pacific Coast, are being built at the Maryland Shipbuilding and Drydock Company in Baltimore for American Stern Trawlers Inc. of New York. One will go into service in the Atlantic and the other will fish for ocean perch, rockfish and other bottom fish in the North Pacific. These are species the Russians and Japanese now are taking without competition from American fishermen. The U.S. Bureau of Commercial Fisheries will pick up half the $10,458,000 tab for construction of the two 292-foot vessels under a new law which authorizes federal subsidies to make up the difference in building costs between U.S. and foreign yards.

Phone Man of Year
January 1967

Pioneer Sol Urie of Seward has Alaska's most unusual telephone—ivory figurines of animals and birds replace the usual dial numbers. The special phone was presented to Urie, whose communications service in Alaska dates back to 1922, as Alaska Telephone Man of the Year. A veteran of the WAMCATS, which preceded ACS, Urie still assists in providing Seward with telegraph and telephone service.

Galloping Glaciers
January 1967

Things on the move in Alaska include more than a dozen glaciers which are advancing at a gallop, according to experts of the U.S. Geological Survey. Among the ice fields which are running 10 to 100 times faster than normal—as much as two feet an hour—are Bering Glacier, largest in North America. The king of the continent's glaciers has moved about 4,000 feet in one area since 1963. None of the restless ice is near any Alaskan settlement.

Woman's Logic Conquers Post Office
February 1967

Mail from Alaska to South Viet Nam is going direct from Anchorage to Southeast Asia these days because an Anchorage woman revived the belief that a straight line is the shortest distance between two points. Mrs. Devon T. Quirk, whose husband is serving in South Viet Nam, could not understand the logic of trucking surface mail from Alaska to Seattle and then flying it to South Viet Nam, when Saigon-bound planes pass through Anchorage almost daily. Senator E. L. Bartlett saw the sense in Mrs. Quirk's views and so did the Post Office Department. Surface mail and parcels weighing less than five pounds now travel direct from Anchorage to the Southeast Asia war zone.

Chair from Sitka Castle for Governor Hickel
February 1967

In a new place of honor in Governor Walter J. Hickel's office is a heavy carved teak chair which once graced Lord Baranof's "castle" in Russian Sitka. The arms of the chair are formed by the carved heads of two elephants, and Hickel, Alaska's first elected Republican governor, calls it his "Mr. Republican chair." It is owned by Louis Jensen of Sitka Marine Service who told Hickel during a campaign swing-around that if he became governor he could use the chair as long as he was in office. The chair was flown to the Capital City the day before Hickel's inauguration and moved into his office just moments after he was sworn in. Although it will hold a permanent place there, the governor won't use it as his business chair. It doesn't swivel.

The Mosquito Totem
January 1967

Telling the tale of how the mosquito came into being, a 49-foot totem pole has been erected on the University of Alaska campus. Carved from yellow cedar by Amos Wallace, Tlingit Indian from Juneau, the eight-figure totem was commissioned by the University Alumni Association. The artist based his work on a 22-inch model carved between 1850 and 1900.

100th Anniversary
February 1967

An eight-cent airmail stamp, commemorating the 100th aniversary of Alaska's purchase from Russia, will be issued March 30 at Sitka. March 30 was chosen as the issue date because it is also "Seward Day" in Alaska, honoring William H. Seward, the U.S. Secretary of State who negotiated the purchase of Alaska for $7.2 million. Sitka was chosen as the issue site, because that's where the official transfer ceremonies were held. But it's hard to tell why an eight-cent airmail denomination was chosen because all first class five-cent mail goes by air in Alaska anyway.

Two Survive Crash
February 1967

A pair of Juneau prospectors spent four relatively sleepless nights while awaiting rescue last November after their helicopter crashed in the Chisana River area about 50 miles south of Northway. Walt Reams and Bud Lown had been scanning some cliffs at an altitude of about 150 feet looking for signs of copper deposits when a piston blew and down she went. They were much too low to make a soft landing. The helicopter turned on its side, and the rotors ground into the snow and rock and disintegrated.

Walt and Bud were okay, except for some bumps and bruises, and they had plenty of survival rations, along with guns, shells, an ax and a shovel. Everything, in fact, but the sleeping bags they'd overlooked in loading that morning at Scotty's Roadhouse. Well, they'd forgotten the sleeping bags, but they'd remembered to leave something else very important at Scotty's—instructions that if they weren't back by 5 p.m. to come looking.

With the temperature at 20 below zero, they built a big fire and hauled the seats out of the wrecked helicopter so they wouldn't have to sit in the snow. Then they took turns sleeping, each making sure the other woke up at regular intervals to move around and keep from freezing. Finally rescue came in the form of an Army helicopter from Ft. Greely.

"Ready to go?" asked the beaming pilot.

"Been ready for four days," said Walt.

Fur Processing Criticized by Senator
February 1967

U.S. Senator Ernest Gruening of Alaska says he doesn't think a firm experimenting with the processing of fur seal skins is doing such a hot job. And he's asked Secretary of the Interior Stewart L. Udall not to contract with Pierre Leclede Fur Company of St. Louis for any further processing of Alaska seal skins. Gruening says the sale of 3,500 Leclede-processed skins brought an average price of only $73.03 at auction last September, compared with $131.74 in April for skins processed by the old pros in the business, Fouke Fur Company. The State of Alaska gets 70 per cent of the profits from the government's management of the Pribilof Island fur seal herd.

1967

Bag Limits? Not in Those Days of Easy Hunting

January 1967

These two interesting hunting photos were typical of the early 1900's in America, when quantity seemed more the order of the day in declaring the success or failure of a hunt. Alaska and the Yukon were no exception. Mrs. George Slater, widow of a man who spent over twenty years in the North after he left his Connecticut home in 1898, sent us these shots from his effects.

The larger photo was of a "moose and sheep hunt" in 1912 and was taken in Fairbanks. Mastodon ivory and the prehistoric buffalo horns over the doorway were undoubtedly dug up in frozen muck of the Chatanika area placers.

The man with the axe is identified as "John Valentine"—the man at the stove George Slater, and the other man, James, or "Russ" Moore to whom the cabins belonged.

In the smaller photo, the caption refers only to a bag of "geese and swans" from a time when swans were legal birds and bag limits were unknown.

45,000 Reindeer
March 1967

There are now about 45,000 reindeer in Alaska in fourteen major herds, according to Dick Birchell, agriculture extension specialist for the Bureau of Indian Affairs. Reindeer, a semi-domesticated caribou, were introduced to Alaska at the turn of the century. Under present laws, only natives are allowed to own herds.

Chena River Landmark Destroyed by Fire
March 1967

The Fairview Hotel, an old Fairbanks landmark on the Chena river, built about 1910, was completely destroyed in a pre-Christmas fire. Sammy, the well known cat belonging to Mrs. Lee Steele, manager, was the only casualty. Occupants of the old frame building which had served as a men's rooming house since 1943, had just moved over to the nearby Steele Hotel following a furnace failure and frozen pipes which made living there too uncomfortable in the minus zero temperatures. Most of the roomers were old-timers in the Fairbanks area, and many lost all their possessions as they had intended to move back when heat was restored.

"Well, the place finally warmed up," was the comment of one of the former occupants, most of whom watched it burn from the lobby of the Steele Hotel. "After that furnace gave out, you had to go outside to get warm."

Cause of the fire is still unknown. Firemen were able to save the adjacent log cabin Chamber of Commerce and USO buildings from damage even though the sawdust insulation in the old hostelry made the fire difficult to extinguish. The building had recently been purchased by Don Pruhs and Wally Burnette.

Oldtimers recalled the days prior to the construction of a dike at Mile 18 on the Richardson Highway when the hotel stood on pilings in the Chena River. During break-up each spring, ice hitting against the piles would shake the building like an earthquake. Often flood waters would cover the lobby floor.

Fallout in Alaska... Nuclear Test Plans Stir Explosion of Protest
March 1967

An announcement by the U.S. Atomic Energy Commission of plans to set up an underground nuclear testing site at Amchitka Island in the Aleutians, with alternate sites in northern Alaska east of Point Lay in the Brooks Range, met with strong opposition from Alaskan native groups and from conservation organizations. Location of a test site for continuing experiments will depend upon geologic structure of the earth, according to a spokesman for the A.E.C.

The Arctic Slope Native Association and the newly-formed Alaska Federation of Native Associations have sent telegrams of protest to federal and state officials stating their opposition to the establishment of atomic test sites in Arctic Alaska. Earlier, the National Audubon Society said it would "vigorously oppose" using Amchitka Island for atomic blast tests.

Amchitka is located within the Aleutian Island National Wildlife Refuge, and is a major breeding ground for the once almost extinct sea otter. The Alaska Conservation Society is also concerned with the A.E.C. proposals, having been active in the opposition that cancelled Project Chariot, a proposed above ground atomic test at Cape Thompson near Point Hope several years ago.

When Operation Longshot, an 80 kiloton atomic underground blast, was completed off Amchitka in October, 1965, officials of the A.E.C. and the Defense Department assured conservationists that there would be only this one blast and that adequate measures to protect wildlife would be undertaken.

Investigations by biologists during the Project Chariot program revealed that people who regularly live on a caribou diet have a radiation body count far higher than the average American, even though fallout in the Arctic has been much less than in other parts of the United States. This is because of the unique relationship between caribou, the lichen they feed upon, and the large part that caribou play in the diet of those living in the far north. Lichens absorb nourishment directly from the atmosphere instead of through the ground.

Last October the Defense Department denied a report by Jessen's Weekly newspaper that the Atomic Energy Commission planned to renew tests in the Aleutians. Newly elected Governor Walter J. Hickel stated that he feels the state of Alaska should cooperate with the A.E.C. in this project in the interests of national defense.

Two Awards for Skagway's 'Cleaner' Image
May 1967

Shades of Soapy Smith in reverse! The town of Skagway, plagued in gold rush days by the reputation of the notorious badman, has come up with a far better connotation for the sudsy stuff. First it won top prize in the state's Clean-Sweep contest for cities of its size, and then went on to collect a certificate of honorable mention in the National Cleanest Town Achievement Award contest. Practically the whole town turned out in two general clean-ups of public and private property, including lots belonging to absentee owners. Paint was applied, and shrubs and flowers planted. The award was made on the basis of "before" and "after" pictures put together in a scrapbook and entered in the national contest.

Anchorage-Whittier Oil Pipeline

One of Alaska's biggest winter construction projects is laying an eight-inch petroleum pipeline which will link Anchorage with Whittier. Workmen of the Mullen and Dravo Co. are shown burying a section of the 60-mile line in Indian Pass, high in the Chugach Mountains south of Anchorage. A new 13,250-foot tunnel must be punched through the mountains ringing Whittier to bring the line to tidewater. With a capacity of 1,000 barrels of petroleum per hour, the new pipeline is sceduled for completion next September.

1967

B.C. Pulp Boom
March 1967

British Columbia's pulp industry, going at a pretty lively clip right now, is expected to almost double production within the next ten years. A special report by the B. C. Hydro and Power Authority says that three new pulp mills began operation last year, bringing the total in the province to 17. In addition, six other mills are in the active planning stage, and four other companies have extra timber reserves allocated for mills, necessitating expansion of existing facilities. All of the new mills are expected to have an initial capacity of from 250,000 to 350,000 tons annually and each will represent a capital investment of from $50 million to $100 million, the report says. That will add up to a total investment of about $1.5 billion and an estimated production by the mid-1970's of some six million tons of pulp a year.

Wrangell News: All Good
March 1967

Bordering on boomtown status in forestry production, Wrangell faced the new year with nothing but good news. Lumber export through the Wrangell Lumber Company's big "E" mill was up about 35 per cent over 1965, with every indication of further growth in the year ahead. The firm handled more than 148 million board feet of lumber, largely to the Japanese market, through the ports of Wrangell, Haines and Ketchikan. And the town's importance in the forest products field was hailed with the christening in Japan of a big new lumber and pulp carrier named the WRANGELL MARU.

In addition to all this glory, plans were announced at year's end for the construction of a $1.5 million veneer plant at Shoemaker Bay near Wrangell by the Puget Sound Plywood Company of Tacoma, Washington. The new plant will be operated in conjunction with the old Alaska Pacific Lumber Company sawmill there, which also has been purchased by the Puget Sound firm.

The Wrangell Lumber Company is building, too, with a $400,000 chip mill and a new $100,000 office building scheduled for completion this spring.

Minerals Sought Again Despite Earlier Duds
March 1967

Interest is perking up again over mineral deposits on McLean Arm at the southeast tip of Prince of Wales Island, site of a number of mining duds over the years. Dynasty Explorations, a Canadian firm, filed 300 mining claims there recently. McLean Arm has been tapped for gold and uranium in the past, but never very profitably. Gold mining was confined to the beach and yielded only a few thousand dollars. More recently a rather extensive uranium operation was undertaken, but profits never matched expectations and it was abandoned. Speculation in Ketchikan is that Dynasty may be looking for iron or copper.

Life of a Land Otter
* * * *
A Home in Kodiak, Vacation in Germany

February 1967

Katja, pet land otter of Mr. and Mrs. Rudi Reimnitz of Kodiak, plays in Anchorage's snow while waiting to board a plane for a vacation in Germany with his masters. Shown here with her pet, Mrs. Reimnitz reported Katja was found on a fishing expedition near Kodiak.

ANCHORAGE TIMES PHOTO BY ALICE PUSTER

Noted Russian Poet Warms to Alaskans... 'Simple and Direct'
February 1967

Flying into Fairbanks unheralded and un-announced, the well-known Russian poet, Yevgeny Yevtushenko, was able to accomplish his purpose — meet Alaskans and fellow writers on an informal, person-to-person basis without the fanfare of the press. As a result, several Alaskan poets may fly their own plane to Russia to visit him.

A phone call to a University of Alaska professor revealed the Russian's identity. He accepted an invitation to visit the University Writer's Workshop class on the condition there would be no reporters or persons not members of the class there. From here the thirty-three year old poet spent a night with students and professors of the creative arts in a round of dining, dancing, and general philosophical discussions at various Fairbanks night spots.

Out of this came an invitation from Yevtushenko for a group affiliated with the Writer's Workshop who call themselves the "Flying Poets" to visit him in Moscow next summer.

"Alaska is the best state I have been in," the poet announced. "The people are simple and direct. I am a Siberian, like you are Alaskans."

The Russian bard also visited the Indian village of Minto and Nome and Kotzebue on the Arctic coast. When interviewed at the airport in Fairbanks as to the purpose of his visit, he jokingly answered that he was "here to buy Alaska back for Russia."

He was accompanied on his trip by Albert Todd, professor of slavic languages at Queens College in New York.

Popular 'Dormitory' Closes Its Doors
April 1967

Anchorage's best known winter dormitory closed its all-night doors February 15. Postmaster George Byer announced that due to increased vandalism, the city's main Post Office lobby would be closed from midnight to 6 a.m., every day. The same policy will be extended to branch offices, warned Byer, unless the nighttime users display better manners.

Historic Drink
April 1967

Visitors to Kodiak will be able to drink as well as see the island city's production of "Cry of the Wild Ram," based on the life of Alexander Baranov. The Kodiak Mirror reports that three special drinks have been concocted to honor Alaska's first Russian governor. Named simply, "The Ram," the most potent includes one ounce Vodka, one ounce 151 proof rum, one ounce lime juice.

Thermometer Registers 72 Below Zero... 150-Mile Winds:

One Death and Incredible Hardships are Fate of First Climbers to Conquer Mount McKinley in Winter

May 1967

Dogged by bad luck ever since they started for the top of 20,320 Mt. McKinley in late January, three members of an eight-man climbing party clawed their way to the summit to make the first winter ascent of the highest peak in North America. Art Davidson, 22; Dave Johnston, 24; and Ray Genet, 35; all of Anchorage, Alaska, reached their goal on February 28, thirty days after they had been landed on the Kahiltna Glacier by bush pilot Don Sheldon at the 7,000 foot level.

A freak accident on comparatively gentle terrain resulted in the death of Jacques Batkin, 36, the second day of the climb. He fell through the snow crust into a hidden crevasse, usually thought to be snow-filled at this time of year. Sheldon, who kept tabs on the group throughout their assault, landed to take out the body and Genet, who made arrangements for Batkins remains to be returned to his native France.

It was nip and tuck if Genet would get back to rejoin the group which had gone on ahead with the climb, but Sheldon was able to set him down on the glacier again.

The climbing team, which consisted of leader Gregg Blomberg, 25; of Bremerton, Wash.; John Edwards, 35, of Cleveland, Ohio; Dr. George Wichman, 39, and Shiro Mishimae, 31, of Anchorage, in addition to the summit trio, kept in touch with Sheldon by short wave radio until the 14,000-foot level where radio batteries went dead and visual contact was obscured by storms.

Despite the fact they had food for forty days, concern began to grow for the fate of the expedition on the thirty-fourth day after a week of winds of over 100 miles per hour and temperatures estimated to be minus 50 degrees or colder.

When two climbers were finally spotted on March 6 by a distress signal stamped into the snow at 10,200 feet, a massive rescue operation was put into operation which saw members of the Mountain Rescue Unit of Seattle (which included McKinley and Everest conqueror, Jim Whittaker), Air Force planes and helicopters, veteran Alaskan mountaineers, and bush pilots converge on the small village of Talkeetna under the coordination of McKinley Park ranger Wayne Merry.

While attempting to buck extreme turbulence and land a rescue team on the mountain, fliers spotted three climbers at the 17,000 foot level, signalling that they were all right. By this time two other members seemed to be missing at a lower level.

The full story of the climb was not learned until Davidson, Johnston, and Genet were plucked from the mountain as they were making their way downward. Despite an ordeal that made their survival seem incredible, they were a bit incensed at having to be "rescued."

The seven men had all reached the 19,000-foot level ready for the summit push on Feb. 27, but were turned back to their 17,300-foot camp by high winds. Davidson, Johnston, and Genet made the successful ascent on February 28 at 7 p.m. with the temperature at 72 below.

After placing the deceased Batkins' hat there, they cramponed down to a bivouac at 19,000 feet in the dark. During the night, they awoke to find a wind "tearing us up," at an estimated 150 mph. Gusts tore their tents, packs, and scattered their cooking gear. They sought survival in the shelter of rocks.

With Davidson's and Genet's hands stiff with frostbite, Johnston dug a snow cave in which the trio spent six days in the raging storm. Although they had only two days' food supply with them, they found rations that had been cached in the rocks by a previous climbing party.

In the meantime, the four other members of the group had tried to reach them from the 17,200 foot camp, but were turned back by the storm. Finally they split up in parties of two, with Blomberg and Edwards starting down to a base camp at 8,200 feet where they had left another radio, so they could call for assistance from there. Wichman and Mishimae were to stand by at the 10,200 foot

Mt. McKinley climbing team: l. to r., rear: Art Davidson, Dave Johnson, Dr. John Edwards. Foreground, l. to r.; Gregg Blomberg, Dr. George Wichman, Jacques Batkin (kneeling) (and killed in fall), Shiro Nishimae. Not shown, Ray Genet, who reached top Feb. 28 with Davidson and Johnson.

camp where they had cached additional food, ready to try to reach the upper party, now feared dead, when the storm abated.

The successful climbers were painfully making their way between the 17,200 foot camp and the 10,200 foot level, when Army helicopters evacuated them. Later, the other two parties were located and also picked up. All were amazed and a little disturbed at the massive rescue operations at Talkeetna poised to come to their aid.

Sheldon flew all but Dr. Wichman directly to the University of Alaska campus where the climbers underwent extensive laboratory tests and "de-briefing" examinations under the auspices of the Institute of Arctic Biology and the Arctic Health Research Laboratory. Results were compared to those of a similar battery of tests given to them just before they left for the climb. This information, coupled with tests that the men gave themselves during the ascent will be used to detect the effect of cold, exposure and high altitude on the body.

"We have evidence that when a person is exposed a long time to the cold, there are some changes in his physiology that result in a net impairment of his over-all performance," said Dr. Jack H. Petajahn, Chief of the physiology section of the Research Center. "Although a person may adapt to the extremes of high altitude, he may do so at a cost to his over-all physical and mental well-being."

Davidson and Johnston sustained severe frostbite and were hospitalized at Bassett Army Hospital, Fort Wainwright. Their injuries are such that they may lose some toes, according to medical sources.

ANCHORAGE TIMES PHOTO BY ALICE PUSTER

New Sea Otter Herds
February 1967

Alaska Department of Fish & Game biologists have added ten more sea otters to the 23 animal transplant of a year ago to waters off Klag Harbor north of Sitka.

Signs are the transplant will be successful and new sea otter herds will take the place of those that swarmed the same area a hundred years ago.

Still unknown, however, is what sort of a market sea otters will create when actual quantity harvesting of growing Aleutian herds begins. Many years ago when sea otter were worth $500 to $1,500 a pelt, one of the prime factors in keeping prices up was the insatiable demand of wealthy Japanese for Prince Albert coats with sea otter collars, a style now long forgotten.

Gifts for Museum
May 1967

An intricately carved walrus tusk depicting an interlocking design of marine and land mammals . . . the old Yukon steamer RELIANCE'S pilot wheel, which once served as a hat rack in the Governor's Mansion. These are among the items that are now a part of the permanent collection in the Alaska State Museum, thanks to the generosity of former Governor George A. Parks.

Parks came north in 1907 to do mine inspection work in the Whitehorse area for the Venture Corporation of London. He served in the U.S. Army and then returned to Alaska in 1920 to take charge of the General Land Office. In 1925 he was appointed governor of the territory by President Coolidge, and held the post until 1933 when he returned to his position as cadastral engineer. When he left the governor's office he decided to loan his collection of artifacts and mementos to the territorial museum.

Parks retired from service with the federal government in 1948, and now makes his home in Juneau where he is associated with the R. J. Sommers Construction Company. And with a brand new state museum nearing completion as the Capital City's centennial project, he decided to make his collection a permanent gift to the state.

College Scholarship
May 1967

A four-year college scholarship for any university was awarded to Fairbanks High School student, Jerome Davis, as one of the 292 outstanding Negro students in the USA. He is a honor roll student, and vice-president of Lathrop High School's student body. He plans to major in pre-law at either Dartmouth or Princeton.

The scholarship is made available to outstanding Negro applicants by the National Merit Scholarship Corporation, contributed to by 55 different corporations, foundations, and individuals. Davis was selected from a list of over 3,000 candidates. Achievement scholars were selected for their outstanding ability and potential for future accomplishment.

Will this gold dredge near Fairbanks, and other prehistoric-looking dredges in the North eventually sink into the muck to lie among the other prehistoric remnants to be discovered and wondered about in another time when other men may choose to root again in the earth?

Silent Witnesses to the End of an Era... Mammoth Gold Dredges Abandoned
February 1967

Like the sternwheel steamers that now rest abandoned along the banks of the Yukon at Whitehorse and Dawson, the huge gold dredges of Alaska and the Klondike are one by one being laid up in the midst of their tailings to become silent witnesses to the end of an era and the glory that was gold mining in the Far North.

The last active dredge in the Dawson area, No. 8, was silenced on Sulphur Creek November 15. Shortly before, No. 6 at Granville sprang a leak and sank while digging its own grave where it was to be decommissioned. No. 11 on Hunker Creek and No. 9 on Upper Sulphur had already discontinued operation. Next season will be the first summer since they were put in operation in 1905 that dredges will not be working in the Klondike.

In Alaska the last Nome dredge closed down in 1962. All dredges are now silent on the creeks in the Fairbanks area. Only at Hogatza in the Koyokuk, and at Chicken in the Fortymile will the once numerous behemoths of the Fairbanks Exploration Company be scooping up pay dirt next year.

Lack of rich enough ground to work at the present price of gold and high operating costs are the reasons for the demise of the gold dredges which, like the Dinosaurs, may one day sink into the ooze to become an archaeological relic for some distant civilization to unearth.

Cross-country 'Ski-athon'... 140 Contestants Start, 88 Finish the Course
May 1967

In an event that bids to become as popular as the fall Equinox Marathon at Fairbanks, 140 cross country skiers swarmed across the starting line in a mass start in the first spring Equinox Ski-athon to be held there.

Eighty eight contestants finished the 20 kilometer (12 mile) course that looped around the Skarland Memorial Ski Trail in the hills north of the University of Alaska. Ages of competitors ranged from seven to forty-nine, and abilities from top high school and college racers to strictly "Sunday skiers."

Lance Parrish of the Lathrop high school ski team posted the fastest overall time of 1 hour 25 min. and also took first place in the men's division. Following him in second place was Chris Haines, Lathrop; Joe Stansk, U of A, third; and Tim Quintal, Lathrop, fourth. Fifty skiers in the men's division (high school or older) completed the course.

Rose Ernst, Lathrop ski team member, led a field of 23 women competitors to win first place with a time of one hour and 51 minutes. She was followed by her team mate, Diane O'Conner, then Ginny Wood, and Joan Foote, in that order.

Fifteen boys and girls of junior high school age or younger crossed the finish line led by Tony Knuutila with a time of two hours, 22 min. Tim Whipple was second; Doug Dean third; and Jeff Dean fourth.

The Thirsty Alaskans
May 1967

Alaskans have a mighty dry throat if recent figures presented to the State Legislature are accurate. Consumption of alcoholic beverages in the state in 1966 was 4,074,626 gallons, or an average of about 15 gallons for every man, woman and child in Alaska.

Kenai Gas for the Lights of Tokyo
May 1967

Liquefied natural gas from the Kenai Peninsula and North Cook Inlet will help light and heat the world's largest city by the spring of 1969.

Philips Petroleum Co., and Marathon Oil Co., have signed a 15-year contract with Tokyo Electric Power Co., and Tokyo Gas Co., Ltd., for delivery of 960,000 tons of liquefied natural gas a year starting March 1, 1969.

Staggering in size, the project will require construction of a liquefaction plant north of Kenai at an estimated cost of $30 million. Japan will pay about $30 million a year for the liquefied gas. Tokyo Electric will get about 75 percent of the gas, and plans to construct two generating plants of 350,000 KW each by 1969. Marathon Oil Co. will build two refrigerated tankers, each capable of carrying 450,000 barrels of the liquefied gas to the Tokyo market.

1967

International Curling Bonspiel: A Skip Urges Rink to Sweep a 42-pound Rock across the Sheet and into the House
May 1967

More than 200 curlers took part in the 32nd annual International Bonspiel sponsored by the Fairbanks Curling Club. Teams from Canada, and Alaska, including one from such off-the-beaten-track places as Inuvik in Northwest Territory and Bornite in Alaska (both above the Arctic Circle) competed around the clock for three days of round-robin play-offs. The men's championship was won by the Danny Norris rink from Inuvik, and top honors for the women went to the Dolores Jackovich rink from Fairbanks.

A curling Bonspiel is not a competition for hairdressers. It's a sport developed in Scotland in the 16th century that resembles a cross between bowling and spring housecleaning. It has more protocol and esoteric terms than tennis. Teams are known as "rinks," captains are called "skips," tournaments are "Bonspiels," one of which is called the "Beef and Greens." The game is played on ice (called the "sheet") with teams of four players, each endeavoring to slide 42-pound "rocks" into the "house," a series of circles painted on the ice at the opposite end of the lane.

As a curler releases his rock, he gives it a twist with the handle on top to guide it along the ice to the position indicated by his "skip" in the "house." The skip then judges the path and momentum of the rock and calls for his players to sweep in front of the stone to guide it to a winning position. The harder the ice is swept with special brooms the easier the rock glides as the heat from the sweeping melts the ice in front of the spinning "rock," reducing the friction.

Introduced to Canada by early Scot settlers at the end of the 18th century, curling has spread across the north, ranking next to ice hockey as a national sport. Once known as "an old man's game," it is now played enthusiastically both in Canada and the northern USA by all ages and both sexes. Most curling now takes place on indoor "sheets."

Steve Harris brushes the bottom of his stone before he sends it sliding.

Players sweep ahead of the stone to give it smooth run. Shown here are Fairbanks gals (l. to r.), Janet Dean, Barb Clarke, Dolores Jackovich, and Bev Birklid at the International Curling Bonspiel.

Reindeer Meat Surplus
June 1967

Northwest Alaska's supply of reindeer meat greatly exceeds the ability of the local market to absorb it, according to Mrs. Myrtle Johnson, partner in Northwest Reindeer Processing Co.

Mrs. Johnson reported that her firm slaughtered 1,058 deer in the Solomon area last fall to meet anticipated needs of Northwest towns and villages. The Nome market was flooded after 149 of the animals had been killed, Mrs. Johnston told the Northwestern Alaska Chamber of Commerce.

On another reindeer front, the Bureau of Indian Affairs is attempting to sell 10,000 pounds of reindeer meat for the Hooper Bay Native Store. Warmer weather is forcing the sale, with orders being filled at 56 cents a pound.

While reindeer meat is a slow seller, the BIA accepted bids until mid-May for reindeer antlers. In order to meet increasing demand, 100 sets of antlers with skull portions attached will be available after the round-up in August. Fifteen hundred pounds of non-velvet antlers suitable for cutting and drying will also be harvested.

'No' to Rampart Dam
June 1967

Hopes of promoters of a hydro-electric power project on the Yukon river at the Rampart canyon were dashed with the release of a negative report by the Department of Interior on its economic feasibility. The project has stirred up considerable controversy both within and without the state of Alaska. Those advocating the $1.3 billion dollar dam claimed that the resultant cheap power would bring industry to Alaska.

Those opposing challenged the concept that cheap power alone would make up for other drawbacks involved in setting up an industrial complex in Alaska. Conservationists objected to the loss of fish, waterfowl, and wildlife resources that would result with the flooding of an area larger than Lake Erie as a reservoir. Natives opposed the loss of their villages and hunting and trapping grounds.

The department of Interior report and the Bureau of the Budget recommend against Rampart dam on the basis that power produced by the project would cost more than the alleged three mill per kilowatt hour, and would not attract industry as claimed.

The transfer of power through Canada, even if permission could be obtained from that country, would not be competitive with power produced in the rest of the United States, according to the report. The cost of nuclear power is declining so rapidly that this also puts Rampart dam produced power out of the market.

The Bureau of the Budget analysis, according to Alaska Senator E. L. (Bob) Bartlett, arrived at a negative conclusion without reference to the half-billion dollar mitigation costs that the Fish and Wildlife Service had estimated it would take to try to restore wildlife resources lost if the dam were built. Proponents of Rampart dam had made the issue one of "ducks vs. people."

Pollution Control . . . This is the Time for Decision
June 1967

Spokesmen for big industry and bountiful nature met recently in Soldotna in an effort to work out a harmonious relationship. Arranged by the State Department of Health and Welfare, the meeting was called to consider issuance of a permit to Collier Carbon and Chemical Co., now in the process of building a $70 million dollar plant north of Kenai, to discharge industrial wastes into Cook Inlet.

The massive ammonia-urea plant will discharge 820,000 gallons of industrial wastes into Cook Inlet daily. Critical item in the process is the more than 7,000 pounds of ammonia gas which are included. Company officials reported that all the waste, except the ammonia, is drinkable. Led by Jim Rearden, Homer biologist, Department of Fish and Game officials advocated that the company act to prevent discharge of ammonia into Inlet waters. Collier Carbon and Chemical experts estimated that Anchorage is already dumping 4,000 pounds of ammonia into Cook Inlet each day in its sewage.

Putting the problem in perspective, Rearden stated: "Alaska at this time is not an industrial state, but we face a period of decision on pollution control which will set the pattern for the inevitable industrial development which will come to this land of immense and varied natural resource.

"For many areas in the rest of the nation, the unarguable fact is that water pollution in its varieties has been allowed to occur. The nation is now facing a tremendously difficult and expensive clean-up task. We in Alaska are in the fortunate position of being able to prevent pollution before it occurs."

A Reach Too Far
May 1967

The Alaska Division of Lands had to turn down thirteen filings for permits for offshore mineral prospecting recently. The applications were filed during the proper hours, all forms were filled out correctly, the required $20 filing fee accompanied each application, and there were no previous filings for the same area on record. However, the areas filed upon were not in the jurisdiction of the State of Alaska—they were in Siberian waters.

'Earthquake Park' for Slide Area of Turnagain Arm
March 1967

Known as Earthquake Park, this section of the Turnagain slide area will remain as it was after the great earthquake of March 27, 1964. A road was built into the area with Centennial funds last fall and a campsite and picnic area will be built this spring on level land overlooking the twisted earth.

Realistic War Games
May 1967

There is a trapper in Central Alaska who thinks the military makes their war games just a little too realistic. Reb Ferguson was mushing his dog team along his trapline near Shaw Creek when six men in white wearing strange patches stepped out of the spruce forest, ordering him to halt. Pointed rifles emphasized the command.

Disregarding his protests, he was searched, then ordered to accompany them to "headquarters." There his identity was established—and also that of his captors. Ferguson had been mistaken for an "enemy" by the "aggressor forces" in the recent Exercise Frontal Assault, winter war games in which more than 6,000 American and Canadian troops participated. The exercise took place in subzero temperatures near Big Delta.

At Last!
July 1967

One hundred years after becoming United States citizens, the 450 Aleuts on St. Paul Island in the Pribilofs are about to enjoy the full rights of their citizenship. Paving the way for implementation of the Fur Seal Act of 1966, signed into law in Anchorage by President Johnson last November, a task force of state and federal officials have been getting the St. Paul Islanders ready for self-government. The townsite is being surveyed and the people will soon gain patent to the land on which their homes will be built. Under a contract with the Department of Interior, the Aleut residents will take over all fur seal skins rejected as unsuitable by government inspectors. These will be used by island craftsmen and made available to Alaskan outlets. The government-owned grocery store will be taken over by the village on October 1.

Concern for Aesthetics
May 1967

At their annual Board of Director's meeting, the Alaska Conservation Society passed a resolution requesting the U.S. Forest Service to implement the sections of its Multiple-Use Management Plan which would preserve scenic and recreation values along the steamer and ferry routes of the Inside Passage.

Because of recent timber sales and increasing logging activity in the Tongass National Forest, the Society is concerned that commercial harvesting of timber shall not take priority over aesthetic and scenic values in certain areas which also have economic consequences to Alaska's growing tourist and outdoor recreational business.

A.C.S. officers were elected for the coming year. Bob Weeden, formerly editor of the Society's publication, the Alaska Conservation Society News Bulletin, was elected president; Dan Swift, a research scientist at the Geophysical Institute was named vice president; and Celia Hunter was re-elected executive secretary. Ginny Hill Wood will take over as editor of the Bulletin.

Sixty-seven dogs hitched to one sled and two trucks.

67-Dog Team Hauls Miss Alaska Sled – and Two Loaded Trucks
May 1967

The Twenty Mule Team of Death Valley had nothing on Fairbanks, Alaska where dog mushers under the supervision of veteran dog team driver, Jeff Studdert, hooked up 67 huskies that pulled a sled load of Miss Alaska and her court plus two heavily loaded trucks down Cushman street to commemorate the Alaska 67 Centennial.

Contrary to the myth of the vicious sled dogs of the north, the 67 straining malemutes were kept in line by one lead dog and photographers and onlookers roamed up and down the quarter mile line of dogs without incident. At times there was not a dog handler within 20 feet of the "team."

St. Regis Abandons Contract to Buy Timber... Pulp Mill Costs too High
June 1967

Giant St. Regis Paper Company of New York has pulled out of its contract with the U.S. Forest Service for purchase of 8.75 billion board feet of timber in the northern Alaska Panhandle. And all the firm left on the desk was its $100,000 deposit.

St. Regis had won the award in a tense oral auction in Juneau on December 17, 1965, for what was described as the largest single timber offering in U.S. Forest Service history. At that time the firm edged out the other lone bidder, Champion Paper, Incorporated, of Hamilton, Ohio, with a top bid of $5.65 per thousand board feet against Champion's $5.60. Both were well above the Forest Service's advertised rate of $3.30.

Before the sale could be finalized, however, the successful bidder was required to have completed surveys for a pulp plant within or adjacent to the area by August 1 of this year, and completed construction of the plant by July of 1971.

In a letter to Regional Forester W. Howard Johnson last April, St. Regis President William R. Adams said that anticipated high labor costs, both in constructing and operating a pulp plant, had prompted the decision not to go ahead with the purchase.

Since the auction, St. Regis engineers have inspected several mill sites in the Northern Panhandle, giving primary consideration to the Katlian Bay area northwest of Sitka and the Dupont area just south of Juneau.

The timber, all within the North Tongass National Forest, is located on the mainland south of Juneau, on the west side of Amirality Island, and in the Yakutat area.

Adams said that the quality and species of timber were substantial and economically workable, and that the cost of pulp wood delivered to a mill site was within reason.

However, he said, studies completed by St. Regis placed the estimated cost for a pulp mill far beyond a level which could produce a fair return on the investment.

Johnson said that the Forest Service would seek a legal determination as to whether the timber could be offered to Champion, the sole other bidder in the auction — but the question appeared to be academic. Since the 1965 conditional sale, Champion has merged with U.S. Plywood and has entered into long range plans in other areas, particularly with Southern pulp companies.

"We have every reason to believe that other pulp companies have indicated an interest in the Juneau unit timber sale," commented Governor Walter J. Hickel hopefully. "We are going to make every effort to interest these companies in coming to Alaska to utilize this vast resource."

In any event, it will probably take a number of months before a decision is reached as to whether the timber bloc will be put up for sale again, either in whole or in part. Meantime, only the brown bears and the conservationists are happy.

Alaska Marble for Memorial to William H. Seward
June 1967

Gerald Conaway, assistant professor of art at Alaska Methodist University, with seven ton marble slab from Tokeen on Prince of Wales Island, which he will transform into a memorial to Secretary of State William H. Seward. Conaway's design was selected as best submitted to Anchorage Centennial Commission for monument to be located on City Hall lawn. Conaway estimates 900 hours of carving away 1500 pounds of marble stand between him and finished memorial.

Younger Every Year
June 1967

Alaska is getting younger each year, according to the U.S. Department of Commerce. In 1960, a total of 39.3 percent of the state's population was under 18. As of July 1, 1966, the percent of residents under 18 was 43.8.

1967

Herring Roe
* * *
Less Than an Hour for $700,000 Yield

August 1967
Herring roe looks like seed pearls—and it's just about worth its weight in them. In two short, explosive harvests at Craig and Sitka this spring, 371,000 pounds of herring eggs on kelp were taken, valued at $700,000. In the Craig area, pictured here, over 1,200 pickers participated in the "season" which was limited to just twenty minutes by the State Department of Fish and Game. The Sitka harvest, which lasted forty-five minutes, drew a crowd of 800. The fishery, mostly for export to Japan where herring roe on kelp is considered a great delicacy, started to develop commercially in Southeast Alaska five years ago.

ALASKA DEPARTMENT OF FISH AND GAME

One Killed; Searcher Hurt
August 1967

A cliff in the rugged Lituya Bay area of Glacier Bay National Monument claimed the life of one man, and very nearly that of his would-be rescuer late last May. On a Saturday afternoon, 18-year-old Otis Bardwell of Anchorage left the oil exploration communications camp at which he was stationed to take some pictures. When he failed to return that night a helicopter search was begun on Sunday and a fellow worker, D. Scott Beugli of Portland, Oregon, started out to look for him on foot. Beugli picked up Bardwell's tracks leading to the edge of a cliff, then tumbled over it himself and landed near the body of his friend. Suffering from a broken leg and shock, Beugli was still able to radio a distress call with the portable transmitter he was carrying. The rescue operation involved hoisting the injured Beugli and Bardwell's body over 100 feet through overhanging trees to the helicopter.

Slow Whaling
August 1967

North Pacific whaling got off to a slow start this year, due to heavy fog, bad weather generally, and a catch which was running more to sperm whales, rather than the more profitable finback variety. The season lasts until October.

One of the major problems facing the industry is depleted stocks and the lack of a conservation agreement among nations whaling in the North Pacific. A proposal made at a conservation meeting in Washington, D.C. last spring called for a reduction in the harvest by ten per cent a year until the currently international catch of 3,000 annually is cut to 1,500. The proposal was acceptable in theory to all, but Soviet and Japanese operators balked when it came to signing a formal agreement.

Kenai Boom Continues... Liquefied Gas Plant, Chemical Complex – and More
July 1967

Alaska's copy of Pittsburgh and Houston compressed into one fast-growing town, the Kenai-North Kenai area is making favorable economic news at an accelerated rate in this Centennial summer.

Land transactions in the area are so active that both Anchorage newspapers recently started separate "Kenai" headings in want ad sections.

Phillips Petroleum Co., and Marathon Oil Co., are slated to start a twenty-eight-month project this summer which will result in a $50 million gas liquefaction plant in the East Foreland area. The initial labor force of 170 will expand to 355 as the project hits full stride.

Two 450,000 barrel tankers have been ordered by the two oil companies for transporting the plant's liquefied gas to Japan. The huge tankers are being constructed by a Swedish shipbuilder in Malmo, Sweden, for a price of $43 million.

A $70 million chemical complex being built by Collier Carbon and Chemical Corp., and Japan Gas Co., is under way with erection of clear span building 490 feet long and 179 feet wide. It will be used to store raw urea.

Further industrialization of the Kenai may come as a result of a recent inspection by representatives of Japanese industry and the Skelly Oil Co. The combine is considering construction of a $30 million methanol plant.

Construction of apartments, shopping centers and motels in the Kenai area is scheduled to start this summer, with costs of firm projects already topping $2 million.

And while the state is preparing plans for a Turnagain Arm causeway which will shorten the Anchorage-Kenai distance, the Alaska Railroad is eyeing 200 acres near Moose Pass as the possible site of a projected rail-oriented trucking center designed to speed freight to and from Kenai-Soldotna.

Opposite Kenai on the west side of Cook Inlet, the economic picture is no less bright. The Tyonek Indians rejected 1964 bids of $1.3 million for potential oil tracts, gambling that time was on their side. Their gamble paid off in early May when major oil companies bid slightly more than $2.6 million for the 13,000 acres.

The Tyoneks also broadened their economic base with recent purchase for $1.2 million of a 15,000 kilowatt gas turbine for generating electricity. The Indian village hopes the growing oil industry will be among its major power customers.

The oil richness of the west side of Cook Inlet was demonstrated in early May with Mobil Oil Co., announcing that its first development well on the Granite Creek platform near Tyonek was producing the black blood which is bringing new life to Alaska at a rate of 2400 barrels per day.

Parka Patent
June 1967

Parka designs can be protected by patent, as Alaska Airlines learned recently after having 160 parkas made which followed the design of Laura Wright, famed Fairbanks parka maker. A Superior Court judge in Anchorage awarded Mrs. Wright a judgment of $3,200 against Alaska Airlines or $20 for each parka made without her permission.

WALT PEIRCE

April 1967
There were 20 white foxes in this picture taken on the Dew Line in November of 1958 by Walt Peirce of College, Alaska. Walt said Canadian law did not permit any on-resident trapping and there perhaps had never been any local residents at "Cam D." The little white bundles, Walt writes, "were really in Utopia." Men of the station fed them table scraps. Walt said that while trying to photograph a white fox at close range, he dropped an outer mitt to work the shutter — the fox had the mitt the minute it hit the snow — Walt chased him — the fox tripped on the big mitt and Walt recovered his mitt, but in the three elapsed seconds, the mitt thumb of strong leather had been almost severed.

An Eye for Beauty
July 1967

A Fairbanks' woman's eye for beauty and appreciation of nature are being credited by conservationists as major factors in the establishment of the new 15,000-acre Chena River Recreational Area. Starting forty miles from Fairbanks on the Chena Hot Springs Road, and extending for fourteen miles, the area is ideal for hiking, boating, fishing, camping, photography and picnics. In achieving her two-year goal, Mrs. Magdalene Cassady had to overcome plans of the State Division of Lands to harvest the area's timber and chop it into five-acre river front tracts for sale. The U.S. Army Corps of Engineers once had plans for a dam on the Chena which would have partially drowned Mrs. Cassady's dream. Enlisting the support of the Fairbanks Garden Club and the Tanana Valley Sportsmen's Association, the determined woman got a bill introduced in the 1966 legislature, which failed to pass. Senator John Butrovich introduced a modified bill in the last legislature, and it was enacted. For the time being, Mrs. Cassady and her fellow Alaskans can continue to enjoy their undeveloped river valley.

Shrimp Capital, Too?
June 1967

Shrimp—little, medium and big—may trigger a new boom in already booming Kodiak, according to a survey by the Kodiak Mirror. Bulk of the 23 million pounds of shrimp harvested on the Pacific coast in 1966 came from Kodiak waters. Already the king crab capital of the state, which produced a record yield of 159 million pounds last year, Kodiak canneries are expanding to meet the nation's growing appetite for shrimp.

Evidence of the richness of the Kodiak area's shrimp beds, said the Mirror, is found in the 5,000 metric tons of shrimp caught by Russian trawlers in January and February. The entire Russian shrimp catch in Kodiak waters in 1966 was only 10,000 metric tons. Some fisheries experts predict Alaska can harvest 400 million pounds of shrimp annually.

One Kodiak processor admitted his firm is negotiating on an order for 60 million pounds of shrimp. Bix Bonney, who is constructing a new $1.4 million, automated processing plant commented, "The picture seems clear enough. Kodiak is going to boom with shrimp even bigger than it has with king crab."

More 'Marus' for Alaska
August 1967

Lumber carriers of the Japanese Kyowa Line are beginning to sound like a geographic roll call of Southeast Alaska Panhandle ports. With the *Sitka Maru* already in service, and the *Wrangell Maru* and the *Ketchikan Maru* due shortly, the *Haines Maru* made her maiden run to the Lynn Canal community recently. The vessel, capable of carrying about four million board feet of lumber, is under charter to Alaska Pulp Company, Ltd. and is expected to call at Haines about once a month.

JUNEAU EMPIRE PHOTO BY CHUCK HOYT

A New Look on the Stikine River... Wrangell to Telegraph Creek
August 1967

There's a new look on the Stikine River run between Wrangell and Telegraph Creek—and here she is. The new steel-hulled, 65-foot MARGARET ROSE, blue and white flagship of the Stikine Transportation Company, has replaced the old JUDITH ANN on the freight and passenger route, one of the most spectacular in the country. The new vessel will sleep 26 passengers, about double the capacity of the JUDITH ANN, and is topped by an observation deck. Cost of the three-and-a-half day trip (slow going upriver, down like a race horse) is $110, which includes meals. The MARGARET ROSE will depart Wrangell this summer every six days.

Caring for our Own
August 1967

Alaska reached a new level of maturity June 30, when the State Department of Health and Welfare terminated its contract for care of mentally ill, psychiatric and retarded patients at Morningside Hospital in Portland, Ore. Morningside had been a major care center for Alaskans since 1904. Patients returned from the Oregon facility are being cared for at the new Harborview Hospital in Valdez, Alaska Psychiatric Institute in Anchorage, and such other facilities as various nursing homes, the Sitka and Fairbanks Pioneer Homes and Jessie Lee Home at Anchorage.

'Grandfather' of the Chatham Area Tlingits
July 1967

Chief Billy Jones, who had walked the beaches of Admirality Island almost since Alaska's purchase from Russia, was laid to rest at Angoon last winter. He was about 98 years old (some said as old as 113). A humble man, he never referred to himself as chief, rather as "grandfather" of all the Tlingit Indian tribes in the Chatham Strait area.

Billy Jones led his people with dignity through the confusing transition into white man's ways. He served as early-day chief of police in his village, helped build the town hall in 1919, and packed timber for Angoon's three churches, the Greek Orthodox, Presbyterian and Salvation Army. After his death at Mt. Edgecumbe Hospital January 9, his body was returned to lie in state in Raven House, with a kerosene lantern flickering before the coffin, and a candle burning behind beside a Greek Orthodox cross.

Honor for Athabascan
February 1967

John Sackett of Huslia on the Koyukuk river is the first Athabascan Indian to win a seat in the Alaska state legislature. The 22-year-old youth was a full-time honor student at the University of Alaska and treasurer of the associated student organization before leaving for Juneau. He is also president of the Tanana Chiefs Conference. Sackett plans to make up the time he has missed from the University at a summer session so he can graduate next January. He intends to go on to law school after his legislative term.

Undersea Gold?
May 1967

Would you believe the Bureau of Mines has a Navy? Underseas explorations for gold deposits that can be economically worked under the present pegged gold price of $35 an ounce will be conducted this summer off the coast near Nome in the Bering Sea. The Bureau of Mine's ship, the RV VIRGINIA CITY will be used for the project in a cooperative effort with the geological Survey.

August 1967
Moose are as common as the name implies on Fort Richardson's "Moose Run Golf Course" and not infrequently a putter has to endeavor to concentrate while one of the critters watches.

MAC TAYLOR

Exploring an Old Mine
* * * *
Adventurous Boys Trapped 36 Hours on a Narrow Ledge

Octobe 1967

Teenaged boys and tight spots go together, but the three Juneau lads pictured here found one last summer that kept ground and air rescue units busy for two days. After being trapped for thirty-six hours on a narrow ledge overlooking the old Perserverence Mine's "glory hole" on the backside of Mt. Roberts, the boys were hauled to safety unharmed by a Coast Guard helicopter.

The trio, James Rosenberger, 17; his 16-year-old brother, Gary, and Peter Metcalfe, 15, had made a hobby for the past year of exploring the seventy-five-mile maze of shafts, tunnels and galleries in the old abandoned gold mine, armed with ropes and flashlights. On this particular occasion, however, they started a little late, tried a new tunnel, took a wrong turn, shopped for a shortcut back, and wound up out in the open again, half way up the 900-foot rock face of the glory hole just as darkness fell.

"We found a ledge where we could sit down," explained Peter, "and wait for someone to look for us."

The first to arrive on the scene were the boys' frantic fathers, Smokey Rosenberg and Vern Metcalfe, who showed up about two a.m. waving flashlights and shouting from the other side of the glory hole. Meanwhile, their equally upset mothers had notified the police.

The boys advised their fathers at the top of their lungs over the black expanse that they thought they could make their way back unassisted come dawn. But when the sun rose, the shale slide they'd scrambled down in the darkness looked like sheer suicide in the daylight. So it was time to sit back and wait again.

Mountain rescue units tried throughout the day and half the next night to reach the boys, but were stymied by ledges, overhangs and a touchy avalanche situation which sent rocks tumbling down over the cliff with every move. Finally the following morning a Coast Guard helicopter, its rotor blades whistling within ten feet of the face of the cliff, lowered a wire basket to the boys and cranked them up to safety.

Tired, hungry, but otherwise in good condition, the boys had this word of advice for their fellows: "Don't go climbing around the mine and the glory hole." Tom Sawyer could have told them that.

JUNEAU EMPIRE PHOTO BY DENNIS COWALS

Non-stop Jets for Sitka
July 1967

After years at the lonely end of a local airline loop, Sitka has been promised daily non-stop jetliner service to Seattle and Anchorage this summer. The service will be inaugurated by Alaska Airlines early in June, or just as soon as the gravel runways of Sitka's new airport have been paved. Alaska Airlines Vice President Robert Giersdorf says that while exact flight times have not yet been set up, daily flights will depart from Seattle fairly early in the morning non-stop for Sitka, continuing on to Anchorage, and then, after a short lay-over, to Fairbanks. Southbound flights will originate late in the afternoon. Immediate temporary authority for the Centennial Year service was granted by the Civil Aeronautics Board after Alaska Coastal Airlines, which recently merged with Alaska Airlines, withdrew its earlier objections to the Sitka service.

Mineral Wealth
August 1967

No less an expert than the director of the Interior Department's Bureau of Mines has reconfirmed the fact that Alaska is a mineral-rich state. Speaking to a Centennial minerals conference at Fairbanks, Dr. Walter R. Hibbard, Jr., said, "There is strong evidence that almost every mineral of commercial value can be found in Alaska and that discovery of new major high-value mineral deposits can be anticipated." He cited estimates that Alaska's mineral production could be increased 100 times to an annual value of $2.5 billion. A less optimistic view was presented by Dr. Raymond L. Smith, president of Michigan Technological University, who told conferees that Alaska's minerals research effort is too scattered. He advocated the establishment of an Alaskan science city to concentrate efforts at one point.

'Save the Whales'
July 1967

Citizens of Inuvuk, 165 miles north of the arctic circle in Northwest Territory, Canada, launched a "Save the Whales" campaign in an attempt to rescue a school of belugas trapped in a frozen inlet north of the community. Two hundred and forty pounds of chopped fish and lamb were airdropped to an estimated seventeen of the white aquatic mammals caught by freeze-up. Wood was dropped in an attempt to keep the two foot by ten foot breathing hole open until a compressor could be landed.

First Second Class City
October 1967

Nearly forty-five square miles in size, the city of St. Mary's was voted into existence recently by a vote of fifty for and eighteen against incorporation. Located on the Andreafsky river near its confluence with the Yukon, St. Mary's is the first second class city to be established in western Alaska.

Underwater Cables
August 1967

An underwater segment of Alaska's most ambitious electric transmission line has been completed with laying of four 22,000-foot cables from Point McKenzie to Point Woronzof. The underwater cable is part of a Chugach Electric Association project which will wheel thousands of kilowatts from a gas generating plant at Beluga River, forty-eight miles over a 138,000 volt transmission line along the west side of Cook Inlet, and under Knik Arm to Anchorage. Involving installation of two 15,000 KW gas turbines, the $10.5 million project is slated for completion late this year or early in 1968.

Two Youthful Hikers Injured by an Attacking Bear
October 1967

Another of the season's bear attacks was reported in Anchorage early in August when two youths were attacked by a bear, while hiking near Cooper's Landing in the Kenai.

Scott MacInnes, 14, and Michael Morelain, 15, both of Anchorage, got away with modest wounds, bites on the leg, back and shoulder for MacInnes and claw marks on the left hip and head for Morelain.

The boys said they were walking a trail, heard a grunt, and the bear, a brown or a grizzly, rushed out and first hit MacInnes who was in the lead, knocked him down and clawed him. Morelain had run behind a tree.

The bear left MacInnes, but returned, and young Morelain said he attacked the bear with a slingshot and a rock, the bear chased him and "ran right over him" when the lad tripped on a root, then Morelain managed to climb a tree.

Some time later Morelain helped MacInnes to a meadow and hiked fifteen miles out to the road and flagged a car. A military helicopter flew through bad weather to bring in the MacInnes boy, who spent the night in the hospital.

A New Foundation
September 1967

Literally as well as figuratively, that great burned-out hole in the heart of Sitka, where its beautiful Russian Orthodox Cathedral once stood, slowly is beginning to fill up. Work began last June on the first stage of reconstruction of historic St. Michael's Cathedral, which was built in 1844 and destroyed by a fire which swept Sitka's downtown business district on January 2, 1966.

With a little more than half of its $500,000 fund-raising goal in hand, the Sitka Historical Sites Restoration Committee has gone ahead with construction of a fireproof concrete basement which will serve as the foundation for the planned replica of St. Michael's. Meanwhile, the basement can be used as a meeting place for the congregation and housing for the famed icons and artifacts saved from the original church.

Before the rebuilding began, reconsecration and groundbreaking rites were celebrated by The Right Reverend Bishop Amvrossy at a small altar on the blackened, bulldozed site in front of a wooden cross which marked the location of the original main altar.

Change at Oldest School
August 1967

The oldest educational institution in Alaska, Sheldon Jackson at Sitka, closed its high school branch last June and henceforth will concentrate on its junior college program. Since its founding in 1878 by Presbyterian missionaries Sheldon Jackson and John C. Brady, the school has tried to meet needs not covered by public education. First it was a training institute for native boys, then a boarding grade school for boys and girls from Southeast Alaska. With the growth of the Bureau of Indian Affairs' primary education program, the grade school was closed in 1945. And now that the State of Alaska is working towards the establishment of its own regional high schools, Sheldon Jackson will shift its emphasis to its college program. At its 46th and last high school commencement, 17 graduating seniors received diplomas.

Whale Catch Declines
496 vs. 651
November 1967

North Pacific whaling just isn't what it used to be. The British Columbia whaling fleet called this year's season one of the worst on record. The five-vessel fleet owned by Western Canada Whaling Company, operating out of Quatsino Sound on the west coast of Vancouver Island, chalked up a total catch of only 496 whales, as compared with 651 last year. In addition to stiff competition from Russian and Japanese whaling operations, the market for whale oil and mink feed was depressed this year. Oddly enough, the only market to hold up at all was frozen whale meat for eating purposes. Under an international agreement, the big blue whales and humpbacks were protected during the season.

Fairbanks Flood
* * *
At Least Five Deaths, $200 Million Damage

October 1967

IN MID-AUGUST, President Johnson declared flood-stricken Fairbanks the second federal disaster area in Alaska in three years.

Governor Walter J. Hickel said he thought the flood would have a greater impact on the state than the Good Friday earthquake of March, 1964 because it affected more people.

At least five died in Interior floods and thousands fled homes at Nenana, Tok and Fairbanks. Damage was estimated at about $200 million. It was a raging, muddy mess.

Fairbanksans expect some rain in August. They also consider it routine for the Chena River, which normally flows peacefully through the center of the city to rise after breakup in the spring. Newsmen keep an eye on the "flood season" as mountain snowmelt causes the river to rise, but emphasis is usually on the bush villages.

Even where adverse weather is expected, few were prepared for the deluge which spilled muddy, oily water up to nine feet deep over America's farthest north metropolis. Almost six inches of rain fell in a six day period. Normal for the entire year is twelve inches. A heavy snow in the distant mountains silently added its burden to the Chena and on August 15 it rampaged through the city tossing and smashing everything in its powerful current.

Washouts cut highways and the Alaska Railroad, isolating Fairbanks except by air. Communications with the Outside faltered. The forty-two-acre Alaska-67 Centennial Exposition site, built at a cost of $7 million on a bend of the Chena, was reported virtually wiped out.

Bob Bondurant, who took these shots, is a private pilot, mechanic and young manager of Independent Rental Equipment Co. in Fairbanks. Bob went sleepless for three days straight, aiding in rescue efforts, operating a road grader and manipulating a camera when time allowed. There were some areas, with very deep water he was unable to reach.

He reported food lines took five hours to negotiate at the University of Alaska and three hours at Lathrop High School. Thanks to the fast cooperation of the military in the Fairbanks area, food was reported plentiful if not in great variety. Bob's summary of his part in the flood: "Finally, I was some place when something happened."

The brand new J. C. Penney store just opened its doors. The Anchorage store was destroyed in the 1964 earthquake.

Normally resounding to Malemute cheers, the Lathrop gym looks like a refugee camp. Many others stayed at the University of Alaska.

PHOTOS BY ROBERT E. BONDURANT
Water swirled around Municipal Utilities System headquarters and Public Safety Building. City crews did remarkably well under the circumstances.

Mama Grizzly Chastises a Photographer... Doctors Predict Full Recovery
October 1967

That cub bears sometimes have dangerous mothers was pointed out rather painfully when Jim McGowan, a seasonal ranger at McKinley Park, was clawed and bitten on the head and one arm when mama grizzly objected to his photographing her offspring. Although McGowan was what he thought to be a safe distance from the bears—far safer than many photographers have been observing this summer, the bear charged him after she had circled him and gotten his wind. Usually bears flee as soon as they get a human scent, but having poor eyesight, they often came closer to identify strange "animals" by smell. Then there is always the chance that a bear is a "Lee Oswald" type of the ursis world, with a grudge against human.

The mauling was witnessed by the ranger's wife from the road some distance away. McGowan was able to walk back to the road where he was driven to park headquarters for first aid and evacuated by air to the Fairbanks hospital. Although one eye was seriously injured, doctors expected he would make a complete recovery.

Despite their reputation, grizzlies have had an exemplary record for leaving people alone in McKinley Park. There have been only three other cases of maulings by bears in the park since its designation in 1917; in each instance, it was found that the bears had responded to reasonable provocation. There has never been a fatality caused by a bear. However, as park visitation increases and photographers become more bold, park officials fear more incidents.

Violence? Nothing New
November 1967

Evidence that violence is not a modern invention was unearthed recently by an archaeological expedition on St. Lawrence Island. Working near Gambell, a Swiss-American group headed by Dr. Hans-George Bardi of the University of Berne discovered a burial ground in which human remains were covered by whale and walrus bones. One well-preserved skeleton of a man contained sixteen ivory arrowpoints in his chest, skull and knees.

Viet Nam via Anchorage
July 1967

Eyes focused on the landing pattern for Elmendorf Air Force Base can testify to the vital role of this strategic complex in the Viet Nam war. An estimated 800 planes a month were passing through Anchorage in May, enroute to and from Southeast Asia. This activity will be doubled to 1600 flights a month in July, say Air Force spokesmen. About ninety percent of the Viet Nam flights stop at Elmendorf, the remainder at International Airport.

Test of Survival
September 1967

Keeping their cool, Juneau educator Robert L. Thomas and his nine-year-old daughter, Nancy, hiked to safety through incredibly rough country after their light plane crashed in the Yukon wilderness last June. The two were on the last leg of a flight home from Oregon when they were forced to turn back from Juneau because of bad weather. Although the gas gauge indicated fuel for a fifty-minute flight, the engine quit midway between Atlin and Teslin, Y. T.

Like survival experts, they patched up minor facial cuts suffered in the forced landing; fashioned packs out of their suitcases for supplies; got a fix on their location with an auxiliary radio receiver; left signals pointing in the direction they took, and struck out towards the road to Atlin about thirteen miles away. Four days later they made it.

"It was rough going," said Thomas, who is director of administrative services for the Alaska Department of Education. "Muskeg swamps, lakes, downed timber, beaver dams—you name it, we ran into it. There was plenty of food and water, but oh, those mosquitoes! They were nearly as big as birds, it seemed, and we ran out of repellent the first day."

Father and daughter were spotted from the air by search planes when they were only a short distance from the highway, and were picked up by car for the drive into Atlin. That was the only time the "cool" cracked. When Thomas was told that a Coast Guard plane participating in the search had crashed, killing three of the seven crewmen aboard, he sat down at the side of the road and wept.

Kick Fends off a Bear
September 1967

Three loggers working at False Island near Sitka knew just what to do when one of their number was attacked by a brown bear recently. The men were eating their lunch when the brownie charged over a hill and jumped 26-year-old Leo Beeks. Beeks wrapped his arms around his head, drew up his legs and kicked the bear in the face. Meanwhile, his companions raised a ruckus to turn the bear's attention, giving Beeks a chance to roll under a nearby log. The bear started towards the other two, then turned back to where Beeks had been, but wasn't any more, and finally retreated into the woods. Beeks got out of the ordeal with extensive bites on the arms and legs.

The Past Is Preserved
September 1967

Skagway residents are a forward-looking lot until it comes to their treasured vestiges of the past. At a recent bond election they okayed a new $150,000 Centennial Building, an $80,000 medical clinic and the purchase of a Back Hoe Loader to replace the old shovel and bulldozer. But they turned down, by a tight 73-72 margin, a proposal which would have replaced the good old wooden sidewalks on Broadway with cement.

Worst Salmon Fishing Season on Record... a Disaster in All Areas
November 1967

It was the worst salmon fishing season of the century. At Bristol Bay, where the poor red salmon run predicted turned out to be a disaster, one fisherman received a check for $1.53 which represented his entire season's earnings. In Prince William Sound, the first on-cycle year for earthquake-damaged spawning streams proved even worse than pessimistic forecasts. And in Southeast Alaska, where normal runs had been expected, canneries closed early when the fish just failed to show.

At mid-September, with the season all but over, the 1967 Alaska salmon case pack totaled only 1,443,448. That was more than two million cases under last year's pack of 3,860,832, and a good 100,000 cases below the lowest pack on record, 1,548,000 at the turn of the century in 1900. Only once since 1906 has the pack fallen below two million—in 1959 when the total pack for the year was 1,770,795 cases.

The pack was off this year in all areas of the state. In Southeast Alaska, it was down from 1,498,314 in 1966 to 401,966 cases; in Central Alaska, from 1,469,146 to 617,246 cases, and in Western Alaska from 893,372 to 424,488 cases.

By species, the 1967 pack consisted of 72,751 cases of kings, 666,385 cases of reds, 56,782 cases of cohos, 352,397 cases of pinks and 295,385 cases of chums.

As the season shaped up as the poorest on record, federal and state agencies moved to provide relief for now and help for the future. Surplus food was distributed in Northern and Southeast Alaska, and the Bureau of Indian Affairs set a $1.9 million relief program in motion for native fishermen and cannery workers, most of whom still owed money to local stores for credit extended through the previous winter.

Meanwhile, a $850,000 federal-state research program was launched under the State Department of Fish and Game to index and study salmon stocks, and to continue work in stream rehabilitation. And in Southeast Alaska, a three-way federal-state-private industry project on 108 Creek in Whale Pass may help determine the effects of logging on salmon streams.

PHOTO BY STEVE AND DOLORES MC CUTCHEON

This photo of idle seine vessels at Ketchikan underlines the sad story of the worst salmon pack year on record for the First City. Big New England Fisheries put up 2,000 cases this year. In a good year they'll do over 100,000.

Russian Refugees
September 1967

The vanguard of fifty families of Russian refugees who plan to settle in the Anchor River Valley on the Kenai Peninsula are already at work on building cabins. Fleeing originally to China, Hong Kong and Brazil before settling near Portland, the refugees from communism purchased a section of land at a recent sale for $14,100. They also purchased grazing leases on an additional 1500 acres adjoining the 640 purchased. Two of the group are now on the tract, and the families will move to Alaska as homes are constructed. All members in the colony have applied for U.S. citizenship, and children will attend public schools.

McKinley Climbers Die
October 1967

The names of six dead men have been added to the list of the more than 200 who have scaled Mount McKinley's 20,-320-foot South Peak. The six climbers paid for their successful ascent on July 18 with their lives. Joining them on the eternal snows of the great mountain was another climber who was ill and stayed behind at the 17,900-foot level, and whose body was later found by searchers. A rescue team later found two more bodies of the ill-fated expedition, but had to stop its search when a vicious storm struck the mountain. Further search and efforts to recover the bodies by helicopter were ruled out because of the altitude. In late August, a six-member team led by Vin Hoeman of Anchorage, who has climbed the highest points in all fifty states, was planning a new attempt to locate and bury all bodies and reconstruct events leading to the tragedy. The men who conquered the mountain and were conquered by it are: Jerry Clark, Mark McLaughlin and John Russell, all of Eugene, Oregon; Henry Janes and Walter Taylor of Lafayette, Ind., Dennis Luchterhand of Scarsdale, N.Y., and Stephen A. Taylor of Chicago.

State Trims Barbers
October 1967

The gold rush town of Skagway has been without the services of a professional barber for many years, but its menfolk have managed to stay reasonably trimmed on a "You cut my hair, I'll cut yours" arrangement. Some have developed quite a skill with the clippers and shears, and have been obliging enough to cut quite a few heads of hair. But no more.

One of the most accommodating of the amateurs recently received a letter from the licensing section of the State Department of Commerce which advised him politely that cutting hair in violation of the Barbering Act could bring about a fine of up to $500 and/or 90 days in jail. The printable portion of his comment was, "Sorry, boys. I've just given my last haircut." So if old-time Skagwayites start looking like modern-day hippies, it's not their fault.

September 1967 — DEDMAN'S PHOTO SHOP

Old Soapy Smith, gun in one hand and glass of suds in the other, has a new "bartender" at his original "Jeff's Parlor" saloon in Skagway, re-opened this summer as a museum. Soapy, in this case, is just a dapper, but not so dangerous dummy and the bartender is George Rapuzzi, lifelong Skagway resident and retired White Pass and Yukon Railway machinist, who has spent a lifetime collecting historical items of the gold rush era. Some of the items now on display were collected by Martin Itjen. Itjen first rescued the historic building during the 1930's and made it into a museum in connection with his Skagway "streetcar" sightseeing tours. The saloon, thrown up during the first months of Skagway's existence, has been closed for the past sixteen years. Rapuzzi has restored it and "stocked" it with a lifetime of treasures including two full mounted moose, their horns locked in a death grip, and Itjen's famous old streetcar still in running condition.

Oil May One Day Surpass the Fishing Industry
October 1967

The importance of oil and gas in Alaska's past, present and future was saluted with a round of Alaska Oil Progress Week activities in Anchorage in mid-July. Foreseeing the day when petroleum production may surpass commercial fishing as the state's main industry, Governor Hickel keynoted a banquet honoring the oil industry by predicting Alaska may advance from fifteenth position as an oil-producing state to the No. 5 spot by 1970. He estimated that by the end of 1968, Alaska will be producing 200,000 barrels of oil daily. Oil royalties and taxes paid to the state will exceed $30 million a year by 1970, according to the governor. In a thumbnail profile of the booming new industry the governor stated: "There are eight oil fields, four of which are rated as giants, having over 100 million barrels of recoverable reserves, and only one fully developed. We have sixteen gas fields, a compact but expandable refinery . . . a marine tanker terminal, over 200 miles of oil or gas pipelines, eleven permanent platforms in Cook Inlet; and when all are completed there will be a total of nineteen rigs on these platforms . . ."

As if to emphasize the governor's optimism, the state's twentieth competitive oil and gas lease sale brought bids of $19,369,805.07, a new record. One 2,560-acre off-shore tract in Cook Inlet brought a bid of $1,509.72 per acre for a total of $3,864,894.77.

The University of Alaska also felt the growing importance of the oil industry with receipt of a $25,000 unrestricted grant from the Pan American Petroleum Foundation, Inc.

'Centennial Jail'
August 1967

The little village of Kake on Kupreanof Island has come up with a good, practical project to mark this year's 100th anniversary of Alaska's purchase from Russia. It's a new community jail, named "Centennial Jail," to replace one that burned up last January.

Biggest, Fifth Fastest
November 1967

The nation's biggest state is also its fifth fastest-growing. The Census Bureau says Alaska's headcount rose 20.7 per cent between the 1960 census and last July 1, to a total of 273,000. Who's the fastest? Nevada, up a whopping 55.8 per cent since 1960 to 444,000.

First Sea Otter Sale
September 1967

One thousand sea otter from Alaskan waters will go on sale at the Seattle Fur Exchange January 30, 1968, the first such sale of pelts since 1911 when the animals were nearing extinction. With a population now approaching 30,000 animals stretching from the Aleutians to Prince William Sound, the otter harvest is biologically sound, according to Ed Shepherd, veteran Anchorage furrier who is co-ordinating the sale. The animals will be taken this fall and winter by Aleut hunters operating from Atka under supervision of State Fish and Game biologists. Shepherd predicts the auction may bring bids of $2,000 for individual pelts.

Oil Lures Eskimos
September 1967

The promise of fuel oil and improved housing has caused a majority of the 126 Eskimos living in remote Anaktuvuk Pass in Brooks Range to postpone plans for moving north to Umiat. A shortage of willows burned for fuel has been a prime reason for the earlier decision to move. The Bureau of Indian Affairs has promised to fly stove oil to the village.

Snettisham Project
September 1967

After five years of mostly talk, the proposed $40 million Snettisham hydroelectric project, twenty-eight air miles south of Juneau, finally is beginning to materialize. A $7,084,400 contract was signed recently by the Army Corps of Engineers with the Seattle construction firms of S. S. Mullen Inc. and Dravo Corporation. The work, which should be completed about this time next year, includes excavation for a road and airfield, construction of a permanent camp, boat and float plane landing facilities and a diversion tunnel to Lower Long Lake. The proposed dam, 800 feet across and 112 feet high with turbines generating 70,000 kilowatts from a power house at sea level, was first authorized by congress in 1962. If finished on schedule, it would put power on the line by 1972.

Elusive Boundaries
September 1967

The problem of Nome's confused property lines was spotlighted recently when Warner Gelzer asked Superior Court Judge William H. Sanders to grant his claim against the estate of the late Vallie Scott. Gelzer claimed that the Scott house protruded five feet over his property line. Judge Sanders denied the claim, but the matter inspired the Nome Nugget to speculate that seventy-five percent of Nome property owners don't know where their boundary lines are. A survey completed in 1957 was never accepted by the City Council. In pressing for a city survey, the Nugget editorialized: "It may be that civilization will catch up with Nome in this century."

1967

Cook Inlet Pollution: Difference of Opinion
December 1967

Pollution of Cook Inlet's waters has assumed major problem size, despite the finding of Thomas L. Kimball, executive director of the National Wildlife Federation, that he saw no sign of pollution on a September survey of Inlet waters.

A contradictory finding was posted a week later when Raymond W. Morris, aquatic biologist for the U.S. Water Pollution Control Administration, reported a flight over the Inlet showed him oil slicks originating from drilling rigs and docking facilities in the Trading Bay and Port Nikiski areas. "I have yet to fly down the Inlet without sighting some source of oil pollution emitting from the sunken vessels used for docks and breakwaters or from vessel or derrick barges moored at Nikiski," said Morris.

Seriousness of the problem was emphasized in mid-October, when the chief mate of the oil tanker, Atlantic Engineer, was arrested and charged with unlawful dumping of bilge oil in Cook Inlet in August. It was believed to be the first such arrest in Cook Inlet waters. A late October hearing was scheduled on the case. Said U.S. Attorney Richard McVeigh who ordered the arrest," I plan to vigorously enforce pollution laws in order to protect Alaska's fish and wildlife resources."

Highway Hazards
October 1967

You think you had trouble traveling the Alaska Highway this summer? Well, shed a tear for 17-year-old Verell Lanier who drove his 1930 Model A Ford Coupe home to Delta Junction, Alaska, from his granddad's farm in Alabama. The trip was not without incident, but he made it home safely despite a broken generator bracket, a broken fan belt, two flats, two blowouts, a leaking rear main seal, broken shocks, broken headlights, radiator cracked by rocks, and burned out wiring. He carried a water can (for the leaking radiator), extra oil (for the leaking seal), extra gas (for the five gallon tank), and a motorcycle strapped on the back (for just in case).

New Pioneers Home Opens in Fairbanks
September 1967

A source of pride for all Alaskans, the Fairbanks' Pioneers Home became a living reality as the first pioneers moved into it in early summer. Fully equipped and modern, the $2 million building can now care for sixty-three pioneers. It is divided into a thirty-seven-room guest wing and a twenty-six-unit nursing wing. First contingent to move in were eighteen pioneers transferred from the Sitka Pioneers Home. Processing of applicants from Interior Alaska is continuing and it is expected the new facility will soon be filled to capacity. Present law requires that residents be sixty-five years old with at least fifteen years residence in Alaska.

LAEL MORGAN

Centennial at Sitka – Where It All Began
September 1967

Opening of Sitka's attractive new Centennial auditorium above kicked off the historic celebration in the city where it all began 100 years ago. The new structure, used throughout the summer for exhibits and local theatre productions, is valued at $1,270,000. In photo on right, smiling Fred Baughn, Sitka postmaster, displays Alaska Purchase Centennial Stamp. It is the first commemorative stamp ever issued at Sitka and the third for Alaska. Photographer Lael Morgan, who offered these shots, has literally covered Alaska from Ketchikan to Barrow.

Collision in Fog ... Cruise Ship, Freighter
September 1967

The Alaska cruise ship Glacier Queen, southbound from Ketchikan, was feeling her way through a dense fog off Hamner Point in the late evening twilight on June 9 when she collided almost head-on with the Japanese freighter *Nickerei Maru,* outbound from Kitimat, B.C. A gaping gash seventy-five feet long was torn in the cruise ship's starboard bow above the waterline, while the freighter sustained a small hole in the bow and a snapped anchor. Both limped into the port of Prince Rupert, seven miles away.

Of the ninety passengers aboard the *Glacier Queen,* only four suffered minor injuries of cuts and bruises. But for all it was an unnerving experience. Many were in the lounge watching a movie when the collision occured. "Everyone went down like rows of dominoes," one of them said. "I was in the last row and hit my head on the projector—but wasn't hurt."

The passengers were flown the following day to Vancouver, B.C., where the cruise, operated by Westours, Incorporated, originates. After a temporary patch job, the *Glacier Queen* also went south for permanent repairs which were rushed to completion so that the vessel missed only two sailings and was back on her run by the first of July.

Longest Day, Sharpest Quake in Fairbanks
September 1967

June 21, 1967, will be remembered by Fairbanksans not as the longest day of the year but the date of the sharpest earthquake to jolt the city in thirty years. Rated as 6.8 on the Richter scale, the quake caused no deaths or injuries, but resulted in property damage to the State Court Building, FAA control tower and various stores. The U.S. Coast and Geodetic Survey station at College recorded 2,000 earthquakes in the first twenty-four hours after the initial big one.

Snowmobile Race
May 1967

Driving a Johnson Skee-Horse, Marv Dickerson of Anchorage, was named winner of the "world championship" 150-mile snowmobile race from Talkeetna to Anchorage. Dickerson was Class "C" as well as over-all champion. Richard McGahan in a Polaris and Lon Barner in a Ski Doo finished second and third in the race in which more than 200 machines started and less than half reached the finish line.

Fort Yukon Ceremony
October 1967

Using a Union Jack hand-crafted by Fort Yukon seamstresses, the residents of the former British trading post re-enacted on August 9, the ceremony by which Fort Yukon became part of the United States in 1869. The flag-raising ceremony took place at a replica of the old Hudson's Bay Company Fort which was rebuilt as a centennial project by the old town on the Arctic Circle.

Long-lost Luggage
October 1967

Lost luggage turns up in the strangest places. A visiting clergyman from New Jersey found his this summer on display in a Yukon museum. "Hey, that's mine!" shouted the Rev. Mr. R. C. W. Ward of the Trinity Episcopal Church in Keanrye, N.J. when he spotted a battered wooden trunk in the Old Log Church at Whitehorse. And sure enough, it was. Faded labels on the box still bore traces of his father's penciled handwriting, addressing the trunk to his son.

Mr. Ward said the trunk was brought around the Horn from England to Victoria by his grandmother, and followed him to the Yukon when, as a young student, he served in the Teslin, Carnacks and Selkirk parishes, but it went down with the *Casca* in Rink Rapids on the Yukon in 1936 while Mr. Ward was en route to a church meeting in Dawson. Delighted to find the family treasure, he was told that the trunk had turned up in the basement of the Bishop of the Yukon's house in Whitehorse, and was placed in the museum five years ago. After its long journeys, Mr. Ward decided to leave it there.

Do-It-Yourself Road
July 1967

Seward's do-it-yourself Resurrection River Road now extends nearly nine miles from the city, and is passable to the glacier. The Seward Chamber of Commerce is advocating borough, state and federal assistance in pushing the road through Resurrection Pass to a point on the Sterling Highway near Cooper Landing. The entire community of Seward pitched in with volunteer labor and equipment to complete the first nine miles of what residents hope will be a shortcut to the west side of the Kenai Peninsula.

1968

FROM KETCHIKAN TO BARROW

Flyers Survive Crash in Arctic
January 1968

The old adage that when you are down in the arctic, you are not necessarily out was proved again when three flyers attempting to establish a route for small aircraft between Alaska and Scandinavia were found after being missing nine days.

Thor Tjonveit, on leave from Wien Air Alaska, Rolf Storhavg, twenty-two year old co-pilot from Oslo; and Einar Pedersen, chief navigator for Scandinavian Airlines; crash-landed their twin engine Piper airplane on the tundra about sixty miles northeast of Old Crow. When one engine quit, pilot Tjonveit turned north from his course for Inuvik, his first intended refueling stop after leaving Fairbanks. The plane was losing altitude with one engine out, and the pilot hoped to reach an emergency landing field on the coast. When it became apparent that they could not clear the intervening mountains, he made a controlled crash landing. Despite cuts, bruises, and a broken arm for Pederson, the trio were able to walk away from the crash and set up an emergency camp near the wreckage. They had supplies for a month.

Bad weather and the fact that they were not on course hampered a search that involved both military and private planes from Canada and Alaska. Chance and a pilot's whim resulted in a Wien search plane crew extending their flight a little longer and farther than their assigned search area. Pilot Bob Shinn was just turning to avoid mountains when his co-pilot, Ron Wood, saw something bright out of the corner of his eye moving on the ground below. A low pass over the area revealed the lost fliers in bright coveralls waving vigorously.

Taken to the hospital in Inuvik by helicopter and a cargo plane, the men announced their intention to make another try in the spring in another plane over the same route.

"We are convinced that small planes can safely fly between Alaska and Norway," Pederson stated.

Disappears without a Trace... Another Old Timer Lost in Wilderness
February 1968

After having survived the Fairbanks flood in which he was reported drowned, old timer Glen Traxler, 65, has disappeared without a trace in the wilderness eighty miles east of Chitina. During the August flood, a body found in a cabin was identified as that of Traxler. Later, pilot Jack Wilson flew supplies into a camp where Traxler had been prospecting with his partner George Gilbertson in the McCarthy area, to discover Traxler there, alive and well.

However, a month later, Traxler appeared to be really dead although his body has not yet been found. In mid-September, guide Tom Truestead and a party shot a moose about half a mile from the headwaters of the Chitina River between Hawkins Glacier and Canyon Creek. Their plane's wing was damaged, so they got another pilot, Fred Potts, who homesteads at Spruce Point, to fly them out, telling him he could have the meat. He in turn flew to Traxler's and Gilbertson's camp and told them that if they would pack out the moose to an airstrip on a gravel bar on the Chitina River he would fly them out and they would split the meat.

Traxler took him up on the bargain and was dropped off at the strip with an axe, saw, rifle, pack-board, and sleeping bag. When Potts returned two days later, Traxler's camping gear was still on the bar, and the moose untouched. Traxler has never been seen since, nor has there been any sign of cloting such as would have been left had he been molested by a bear. The river is not considered swift or deep at this point. He had been in good health and spirits. He has a son, Eugene, of Juneau; and a daughter, Mrs. Lenaya Hill, of Fairbanks, who still hope he may prove to have been presumed dead twice.

PHOTO BY BARBARA KALEN

Skagway Landmark Bows to Bulldozer
February 1968

Another Skagway landmark, the old White Pass & Yukon Railroad hospital, bowed to the bulldozer recently to make way for construction of a new clinic. Built in 1899 to take care of railroad employees, the old structure gradually came to serve the whole community after the closure of the gold rush town's two other hospitals, the Bishop Rowe and the Red Cross. But with the development of air travel in Alaska, the old hospital was used less and less as townsfolk went elsewhere for modern medical treatment. Finally it was condemned for public use by the state fire marshal, and the WP&YR turned it over to the City of Skagway. The new clinic will be built on the same site with the use of Centennial funds, and will be known as the Skagway Centennial Health Center.

1968

A First in the Land of Wide Open Spaces
* * *
Parking Garages for Anchorage

HENRY S. KAISER, JR.

March 1968
Alaska's vast open spaces aren't found in cities. As a result, this new parking garage for Penney's Dept. Store is open and operating. The first such facility in the state, it has been followed by the second parking garage—that of the Anchorage-Westward Hotel.

Come and Get it!... Giant Water Tank for Kotzebue... Five Gallons, 15¢
March 1968

Drawing water from a forty by eighty foot storage tank at fifteen cents per five gallons may be a far cry from running water in the tap, but it is a big improvement, healthwise, for the residents of Kotzebue who have traditionally hauled drinking water in frozen or liquid state from polluted nearby ponds and streams.

The new one and one-half million gallon tank, installed by the U.S. Public Health Service, is the first step towards a community water supply system for this Arctic Eskimo village. The next phase will be to pipe it through heated ducts to central distributing points about town, and eventually, perhaps, into homes.

Water is obtained from Devil's Lake, three miles distant, and kept from freezing in the tank by a circulating pump that runs the water through an oil-fired boiler which keeps the temperature a little above forty degrees Fahrenheit. Operating somewhat like a giant Coke machine, water is obtained by dropping tokens in a meter. Commercial haulers can get water in 250 gallon quantities.

Both the Public Health Hospital and the school expect to switch over to tank water soon, from the desalinated well water they now use.

Long Live the Yukon, Long Live the Pioneer! ... And a Curse on Parking Meters
January 1968

There is one editor on the Whitehorse Star who doesn't think that progress is always the greatest. In a recent editorial in the paper, (whose motto, incidentally, is "Illegitimus Non Carborundum—loose translation: "don't let the _____ grind you down"), the editor comments on the changes made in Whitehorse since his arrival twenty years ago.

"There were no stores behind Third Avenue ... There was no plumbing in most houses and mostly wood furnaces constructed out of 100 gallon oil drums ... Beer parlors closed when the last customer left ... Water was 25c for a five gallon gas pail full and it was customary to give the driver a drink of OP rum. If you came after the third customer it was 25 cents a half pail.

"There have been many changes since then. Some good, some bad ... We like indoor plumbing and oil heat and are willing to give up a small part of freedom to enjoy it ... but ... parking meters are too damn much, and I say Down with them. Citizens arise, cast out these cast iron collectors. Viva la Yukon, Viva la pioneer, A curse on parking meters, may they rust in hell.

"Whitehorse is nowhere big enough to need parking meters. (Note: Whitehorse is the capital city of Yukon Territory). They will not pay for someone to check them, for two men to collect the money, for maintenance ... The city has been sold a bill of goods by a super salesman. If he sells refrigerators as well as parking meters, God help the Eskimos!"

'War' on the Trail... Dog Mushers vs. Motor Mushers
March 1968

Like the old range wars between the cattlemen and the sheepherders, a bitter feud is developing between dog mushers and snow machine operators over the use of traditional dog team trails in the Fairbanks area. After "iron dogs" interfered with the first two preliminary dog races which had several hundred dollars at stake for the winner, the battle was joined.

Cross country skiers in both Fairbanks and Anchorage also have come to look upon the sudden population explosion of snow machines as a scourge of the north. The mechanical sleds have played havoc with their ski trails and training areas. One pass over a cross country ski trail by a snow machine wipes out the two tracks and ruins the trail until another can be set after a fresh snow fall. Coaches of both high school and university ski teams in the Fairbanks area have had their racing program plagued by sno-gos carving up training tracks.

Snow machines have not only confused dog team racers by making false tracks and rutting up the racing trail, but on several occasions have actually been on the trail during a race, forcing a team off the trail. After one such heated encounter in which the dog musher minced no words in tongue-lashing the motor musher, a fence was put across a dog trail between the time the course setter had inspected the trail in the evening and the race was run the next day. This caused several teams to miss the trail altogether and others to lose valuable time breaking a new trail around it. Dog mushers suspect the fence was installed by some snow machine operators irate at being kicked off the dog musher's trails.

Organized motor mushers are as aroused as dog team drivers and cross country skiers about the problem and want to cooperate with other winter sport devotees. It is the "maverick" snowmobile operator, quite often youngsters, who cause most of the problems. The solution seems to be in enacting laws requiring the registration of snow machines so the few causing the trouble can be singled out, and developing separate trail systems for each sport. Dog mushers and skiers point out that they aren't opposed to motor mushing for those who want mechanized recreation, but they object to the "iron dogs" taking over and spoiling trails they have cut and maintained themselves by hard labor.

The Aleut League
February 1968

Aleut leaders from throughout the Alaska Peninsula, Aleutian and Pribilof Islands gathered in Anchorage in December to form the Aleut League, representing an estimated 7,500 Alaskans of Aleut descent. Flore Lekanof, first president of the new organization, described the purpose of the Aleut League as preservation of the Aleut cultural heritage, promotion of economic development, and fair treatment for Aleuts on land claims and aboriginal rights. Other officers are Tikhon Stepetin, St. Paul Island, first vice president; John Gunderson, Sand Point, second vice president; Carl E. Moses, Unalaska, secretary-treasurer.

Policeman Killed
March 1968

The first Anchorage police officer to be slain while on duty, Benjamin F. Strong, 29, died of a single bullet wound on January 5, while trying to stop the robbery of a Government Hill liquor store. Strong had volunteered for the off-duty stakeout watch. Two brothers, Willie and Dewey Gray, have been charged with first-degree murder. Both men were wounded by Officer Strong during the robbery attempt.

Caribou Shoot-out
January 1968

After waiting nine years, the Eskimos at Anaktuvuk Pass had a caribou shoot-out in mid-October, and when the 10,000 animals had moved south through the pass, the isolated village had its meat supply for the winter. Biologist Ken Neiland of the Department of Fish and Game was present for the three days of action, and described the harvest of 200 caribou. He reported that in 1948 an over-anxious hunter had turned the herd, but this year patient villagers allowed part of it to pass, some bands moving within 400 yards of the school, before firing. The last comparable migration passed south through Anaktuvuk in 1958.

Big Scallop Catch
March 1968

A thirty-hour fishing effort recently produced a 40,000-pound catch of scallops for the Virginia Santos to emphasize the apparent scallop riches of Kodiak waters. A New England scallop expert described the Alaskan scallops as "exceptional by East Coast standards." The first large scallop harvest was processed by King Crab, Inc.

Poor Prices for Pelts
February 1968

Poor prices on pelts plagued Panhandle trappers this year, due to a large carryover of furs from previous years and a shift by American furriers to buying on foreign markets. Wild Southeast Alaska mink is expected to bring a top of only $15 for extra large skins. Predicted highs for other species include $14 to $17 for marten, $25 to $32 for Alaska otter, $35 for beaver, and $55 to $60 for wolverine. The trapping season for most of the Panhandle ended January 22, although a spring season on land otter and beaver will open February 15 in some units.

The price decline appeared to be a continuation of a trend noted in the fall auction of fur seal skins from Alaska's Pribilof Islands. This year the State will receive only $332,256 from the sale of the skins. That figure represents receipts from the sale, less the cost of administration of the Pribilof Island operation.

Ores via White Pass
February 1968

Ores from Anvil Mining Corporation's big new operation at Ross River in the Yukon will be shipped over the historic White Pass & Yukon Railroad after all. The route was nailed down recently with the signing of an eight-year contract for hauling 30,000 tons of lead and zinc concentrates a month by rail from Whitehorse to the ice-free port of Skagway, Alaska. Earlier, the two communities got the scare of their lives when reports were circulated that Anvil would bypass the railroad and transport its concentrates all the way by truck to tidewater at Haines, Alaska.

With the deal set, White Pass also announced plans for a $10 million improvement program, including the construction of a $4 million bulk loading storage terminal at Skagway, and the addition of special railroad equipment. Work on the new facilities will begin immediately since the mine is expected to go into production in late 1969. Approximately 175 truck, rail and shop employees will be added to operate the new equipment.

Under the plan, the concentrates will be hauled 230 miles from the Ross River area to Whitehorse, and then be transported 110 miles by rail to Skagway for water shipment. Anvil spokesmen expressed the hope, however, that the railroad would eventually extend its line to a point near the mine to eliminate the shift from truck to train.

'Typewriters' Seized
January 1968

As if by magic, four boxes shipped from Sitka as typewriters had been transformed into slot machines when uncrated recently by State Troopers at Kodiak. Outlawed in Alaska several years ago, the rare typewriters were expected to end up being topped by sledge hammers before a final journey to the garbage dump.

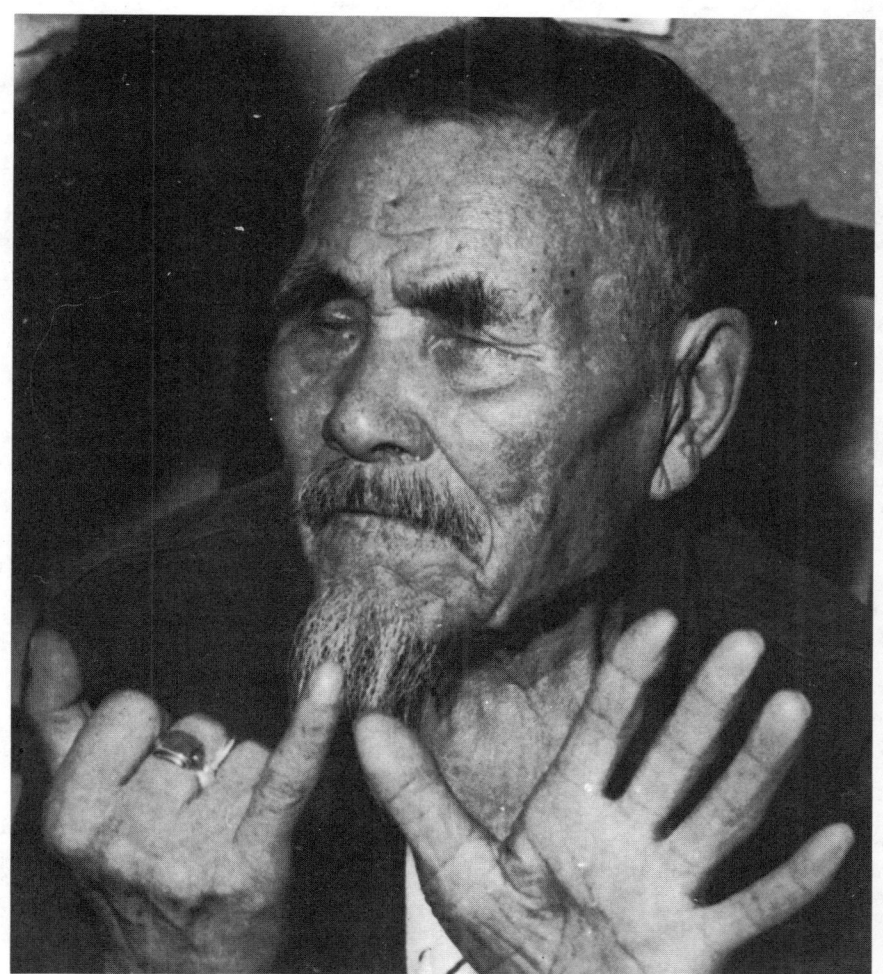
BETZI WOODMAN

Aged Aleut Has Lived All Alaska's 100 Years... Plus a Few More
February 1968

Evon Olympic wasn't greatly impressed by Alaska's 1967 Centennial celebration in terms of number of years. Small wonder, as he was reportedly born six years before Russia sold Alaska to the United States! The bearded Aleut, now believed to be 106, recently underwent cataract surgery at Alaska Native Medical Center in Anchorage. The former reindeer herder is called "grandpa" by nearly everyone in South Naknek where he now makes his home with daughter Eftikia Arsaknok. Evon has at least 17 grandchildren and several great-grandchildren. A scar on the old man's head shows where he was nearly scalped by a wounded brown bear years ago. He associates that encounter with witch doctor influence.

New Daily Paper Planned for Fairbanks
January 1968

Fairbanks will become the smallest city in the U.S. with two independent daily newspapers on Dec. 4, 1967, when Jessen's weekly moves into daily publication. Presses were scheduled to roll for the first time in three months on Friday, Nov. 17, and the paper would continue as a weekly for the next three weeks, as it has been since it was founded in 1942.

E. F. Jessen, long-time Alaskan and owner of the weekly, points out that his paper had never missed an issue until the disastrous flood hit on August 14 of this year. Even a serious pressroom fire in 1948 failed to halt publication, which continued on presses borrowed from the Fairbanks Daily News Miner.

Both the presses and the building structure were heavily damaged in the flood, with losses estimated at $400,000. Jessen praised the Small Business Administration for its role in both his and Fairbanks' recovery. "They're doing a wonderful job," he said.

Under the name "Jessen's Morning Daily," the new paper will be delivered to subscribers by 6 a.m. each day in the city and environs, according to present plans. Initial press run is estimated at 10,000 copies. The most modern offset printing equipment available has been installed, capable of turning out up to 20,000 papers per hour. Limited color reproduction facilities are also included in the revised set-up.

Assisting Jessen, who at 77 considers himself semi-retired, will be Al Phelps, formerly of the Nome Nugget, as business manager, and Tom Snapp, who will continue as editor. A staff of over 40 will be employed, 13 of them in the newsroom.

With its entry into the daily field, Jessen's will replace the Anchorage Daily News as the farthest north morning newspaper in the nation. Jessen's even covets the title of the farthest north daily newspaper, since its offices are a few hundred yards north of those of the Fairbanks Daily News Miner.

Jessens' will continue to emphasize local news, carrying on its traditional "old Alaska home flavor," the publisher noted.

To Avert Another Disastrous Season... A Moratorium on Fishery Licenses
March 1968

Faced with another possible disaster year on Bristol Bay and generally poor salmon runs in other areas of Alaska, the State Board of Fish and Game slapped a statewide moratorium on the number of salmon net gear licenses that may be issued this year. Long talked about, but never actually tackled, the board's gear limitation order is expected to face a court test.

The order came at the conclusion of a marathon eighteen-day meeting in which the board sought a solution to the knotty problems of assuring adequate escapement for off-year salmon runs and providing some sort of a break for Alaskans whose subsistence depends on the once-rich fishery.

With this in mind, the board also set up a sliding scale for the issuance of net gear licenses on Bristol Bay, based on credit points for those who held licenses in either 1966 or 1967, and for "hardship cases" which would be determined on an individual basis by the State Commissioner of Fish and Game.

Under the statewide moratorium order, net gear licenses in 1968 would be limited to the number issued in either 1966 or 1967. Trollers would not be affected. Licenses would be granted on a credit point system similar to that established for Bristol Bay.

In other major action, the board ordered the first saltwater bag limit for silver salmon in Southeast waters—a daily limit of six. It also reduced the silver salmon limit to three in Cook Inlet and waters of the Western Kenai Peninsula.

In connection with Southeast Alaska's herring spawn on kelp harvest, which has grown unwieldy to say the least over the past few years, the board ordered that all participants must be licensed commercially and must register in person one day prior to the opening of the fishery in each of the three major districts, Craig, Hydaburg and Sitka. Individual harvest quotas will then be set, based on the number of pre-registrants. Last year so many fishermen showed up that one "session" lasted only twenty minutes.

No Profit in Gold
June 1968

GOLD WOULD HAVE TO BRING IN $70-$75 PER OUNCE to put mining operations on a break-even basis, according to James A. Williams, director of the state Division of Mines. However, he added costs of operation vary with conditions. He stated that he thought copper had the brightest future of any ore in Alaska at present. Little uranium mining has materialized in the state, with the exception of one operation on Prince of Wales Island in the Panhandle. He also cited cinnabar from which mercury is extracted as a mineral that might become important in Alaska. Known deposits are centered in the Kuskokwim area between Sleetmute and Dillingham.

Williams said that the mineralized areas of the western United States have produced sixty times the per-square-mile output of Alaska which has just as favorable ground for mineral deposits.

Bridge to Japonski
February 1968

A bridge linking Sitka with nearby Japonski Island has been programmed, hopefully, for completion by 1971. And it won't be a toll bridge either. State Highways Commissioner Warren C. Gonnason says the bridge is one of the priority items in a five-year, $70 million special highway program which Congress has authorized for Alaska, but has yet to appropriate. If Congress comes through with the funds, construction of the $3.3 million span will begin in mid-1969.

For years, Sitkans have been trying to figure out the financing for a bridge to Japonski Island where Bureau of Indian Affairs and U.S. Public Health Service facilities are located. Last year new urgency for the structure was added with completion of a new state airport on Japonski, which provides direct jet air service to Anchorage and Seattle. The island is now served only by shuttle ferry.

First, Cordova's '63 Fire; then the Big Quake... Now, Another Fire
June 1968

THERE WAS a story to write, a fire to report, and one of the worst disasters in Cordova's history. It was all covered by the Cordova Weekly Times in a manner that would win praise from a big metropolitan daily.

Just as the paper was going to press on April 4, a fast-moving fire enveloped the Ocean Dock complex. It was press time, so Editor and Publisher Harold E. Bonser and Mrs. Alta Kowalke remade the paper, while Mrs. James H. Roberts covered the fire.

Although lacking the electronic gimmicks of big city journalism, Bonser and his crew were no strangers to disaster reporting. There was the 1963 fire which gutted the heart of Cordova, the 1964 earthquake, and now this.

Mrs. Roberts reported: "Fire hit the Ocean Dock this afternoon, and has virtually wiped out a major portion of the area. The Alaska Steamship Co. Dock, office and warehouse; the Standard Oil buildings and dock, and Parks Canning Co., have been hit badly..."

Complete with photos, the Times' story concluded: "From appearances, Standard Oil and Alaska Steam are wiped out, and Parks' main cannery building is about gone. It looked as though the fire hadn't hit their warehouse when I left to get this issue to bed."

Bonser reported that replacement of the lost facilities would cost between $4 and $5 million.

"Our pressing need is for a dock, and the cost of this is figured at $1.5 million," said Bonser.

The full effects of the fire were still being assessed on April 11, when Editor Bonser wrote: "Hope our town continues in the past tradition, and takes this blow to its economy more or less in stride, using the embers of this fire to rebuild bigger and better than ever before, as we have done thus far after each preceeding disaster."

The Royal Fur: First Sea Otter Sale in 58 Years
April 1968

CLEARING ITS RACKS and North America's legal supply of 826 sea otter pelts, the State of Alaska grossed $141,000 in the first sale of the once royal fur in fifty-eight years. When the shouting ended at the Seattle Fur Exchange on January 30, Governor Walter J. Hickel expressed pleasure at the average of $170 per skin, although it was far below the pre-sale prediction of $1,000 a skin. Best bid was $9,200 paid by Neiman-Marcus of Dallas for four prime skins. Low single pelt price was $40. Of the total skins, only 500 were harvested from the Aleutians in 1967, the remainder being the low grade residue from scientific harvests conducted in the last five years. In determining its profit margin, the state will have to deduct the $54.44 it spent in harvesting each of 500 animals in 1967, plus the costs of promotion and the sale. Biologist John Vania assured the buyers from leading European and American fashion houses that another sea otter sale will be conducted next year, predicting that the present herd of thirty to fifty thousand animals can be expected to provide a sustained yield of 500 skins a year. Among the buyers was a Finnish furrier whose exiled Russian customers wanted to recapture the feel of the royal fur. Now that sea otter is back on the market, its future is in the hands of designers who are now deciding if it is ready to return.

Alaska's Marine Highway Expands... Service Starts to Puget Sound
February 1968

In a major expansion of Alaska's growing transportation system, direct weekly passenger and ferry service between Panhandle ports and Puget Sound was inaugurated last December by vessels of the Southeast Alaska Marine Highway System. It marked the first scheduled service since 1954 over what was once one of the world's richest passenger routes.

The direct water link with the Lower 48 was established after the British Columbia government announced that its ferry *Queen of Prince Rupert* would not be returned until late spring to its run between Kelsey Bay on Vancouver Island and Prince Rupert, B.C., normal southern terminus of the Southeast Alaska ferry system. The Canadian ferry has been out of service for repairs since it ran aground last August.

That decision was termed "disastrous" for Alaska's transportation needs by Governor Walter J. Hickel, and at his request, the Coast Guard reclassified the waters of the Inside Passage along the British Columbia coast as "lakes, bays and sounds," clearing the way for use of Alaska ferries on the route.

The winter schedule calls for departures from Ketchikan at 10:15 a.m. each Thursday and arrivals at 8 a.m. each Saturday in Seattle at the Black Ball Ferry Line's Pier 30.

While the new link was set up initially as an emergency operation, the State is exploring the possibility of leasing another vessel so that the service can be continued year-round until a new fourth and larger vessel is added to the Southeast system, hopefully in 1970. Meanwhile, the Puget Sound ports of Bellingham and Anacortes are putting in strong pitches, along with Seattle, for permanent designation as the system's southern terminus.

Passenger fares range from $55.50 from Skagway, at the northernmost end of the system, to Seattle, to $36.50 for passengers from Ketchikan to Seattle. (Prince Rupert passengers to Seattle will be charged the same $36.50 fare as Ketchikan-Seattle travelers.) The price of berths run from $18.50 per person between Skagway and Seattle in a two-berth deluxe cabin to $6.50 per person in a four-berth cabin (sold only as a unit).

Vehicle fares range from $198 for a car 11 to 20 feet in length, including the driver, between Skagway and Seattle, to $131 between Prince Rupert or Ketchikan and Seattle. The rate is scaled all the way up to vehicles 56 to 60 feet long, which would be charged $755.75 between Seattle and the northern road link at Haines.

March 1968 Completed in August of 1967, this new highway bridge over the Tanana River at Nenana links Fairbanks with Healy, which makes the north end of the future Fairbanks-Anchorage Highway a reality except for paving.

HENRY S. KAISER, JR

Better Caribou Harvest
March 1968

Snowmobiles are improving the harvest of the Nelchina caribou herd, Biologist James Hemming told the annual weeklong meeting of State Division of Game personnel in Anchorage in January. Speaking of increased use of snow machines as a hunting vehicle, Hemming told fellow agents, "We are glad to see the increased access. We needed the harvest. People are getting off the road with them. In this respect we are doing a lot of good with these machines." Hemming also revealed that earlier estimates of 80,000 to 100,000 animals in the Nelchina caribou herd have been scaled down to 61,000. Loren Croxton, regional game division supervisor of Anchorage, told his fellow workers that the moose, caribou and brown bear harvests in 1967 were below those of 1966.

He Led His People up from the Stone Age
May 1968

Word has been received of the death of **HOMER MEKIANA**, well-known Eskimo leader of Anaktuvuk on Christmas Eve. Villagers spent five days digging a grave for him in the frozen tundra.

Living a stone-age existence until the early 1950s, the people of Anuktuvuk had little contact with the white man until then. In 1951, a U.S. post office was established, and soon after, a school, a trading post, and semi-regular bush plane service.

Mekiana served as the first postmaster, and still held that position when he died. He was also the weather observer, welfare agent, Wien Air Alaska agent, licensing agent for the Fish and Game Dept., elder of the Presbyterian Church, and correspondent for the Fairbanks Daily News Miner.

Formerly a nomadic inland Eskimo group that followed the caribou herds, the Anuktuvuk people began to settle permanently at the present location of their village with the coming of schools and a trading post. Lately there has been some talk of moving the village because it is running out of firewood within a day's dog team trip radius.

Plans for Dutch Harbor
June 1968

A TARGET for Japanese bombers just twenty-six years ago, Dutch Harbor is now being readied as a major refueling site for Japan's North Pacific fishing fleet. Southwestern Petroleum, Inc., of Newport Beach, Calif., paid $43,000 for a 14.9 acre piece of waterfront, once a part of the Dutch Harbor Navy base. The proposed refueling site was one of eight parcels sold by the General Services Administration in a bid sale which brought in $244,750. Disclosure of the California firm's plans to refuel the Japanese fishing fleet had resulted in opposition from Alaska's coastal towns and the state's fishermen.

Optimism at Prudhoe Bay: New Oil Field May Dwarf Cook Inlet ... Perhaps Rival the Fabulous Middle East
June 1968

WITH PRUDHOE BAY STATE NO. 1 WELL on the Arctic Slope flowing at 1,152 barrels of oil per day with 1.32 million cubic feet of gas, there is talk of this area surpassing Cook Inlet and perhaps even rivaling some of the large oil fields in the Middle East. Drilling is now almost at the 10,000 foot level and will proceed to 13,000 feet, according to officials of the Atlantic Richfield company.

Although this flow is about twice the average of the Swanson River field on the Kenai Peninsula, it is 390 miles north of Fairbanks and about 800 miles from year-around tidewater ports. Possibilities of pipelines from the Arctic well to the Midwest are being talked about, but it takes a lot of oil to fill a pipeline. However, a second well is being drilled at Prudhoe Bay State No. 2 in this area, and if it comes in as well as the first one more will follow. There are now over fifty producing wells in the Kenai area, and more than fifty in Cook Inlet.

Last of the Old Savoy
June 1968

THE OLD SAVOY BAR BUILDING on Second Avenue in Fairbanks will soon be no more. Built originally of logs in 1906, it has survived fires and earthquakes and the vicissitudes of remodeling, but last August's flood was too much. Its underpinnings are no longer sound, and the City Council has decreed it must come down. The structure was once on First Avenue where it was known as the Seattle Rooming House, then it was moved to its present location and another story added.

Pollution Law of '99
May 1968

REBECCA is the name of a 735-foot tanker that made maritime history on February 19, when she was seized by state troopers at Nikiski Dock north of Kenai and charged with pumping ballast that left an oil slick 200 to 300 yards wide and extending about twelve miles from Homer Spit to Seldovia Bay. Arrested under an 1899 law that prohibits dumping ballast in navigable state waters, Captain Elmer V. Johnson pleaded innocent. He was released after posting $1,000 bail, and will face trail later. The Rebecca was delayed thirty-six hours while the state filed a $200,000 damage suit against the owners. First by-product of the case was realization that Alaska's anti-pollution laws are toothless, a condition which the State Legislature is attempting to remedy. State District Attorney Douglas B. Baily reported that he had to rely on an 1899 law to prosecute the case.

Lucky Hunters
January 1968

All the meat doesn't come from those best-planned hunts. Norm Becker and George Truelson drove way to the end of the Dempster Highway north of Dawson without spotting a thing, and were on their way home to Whitehorse when their camper broke down. While waiting for a tow back to town, they took a look around and ran smack into a herd of thirty caribou. After downing one apiece they decided to whistle for a moose, and, sure enough one showed up right on cue. They had a fair tow bill to pay, but figured it was worth it.

Then consider the case of Yukon big game outfitter Danny Nolan. Investigating a crackling noise on a frozen pond at his ranch near Takhini Hot Springs, he spotted a grizzly bear dragging a calf moose off the ice. He shot the bear, and finding the moose done in, skinned it out for meat.

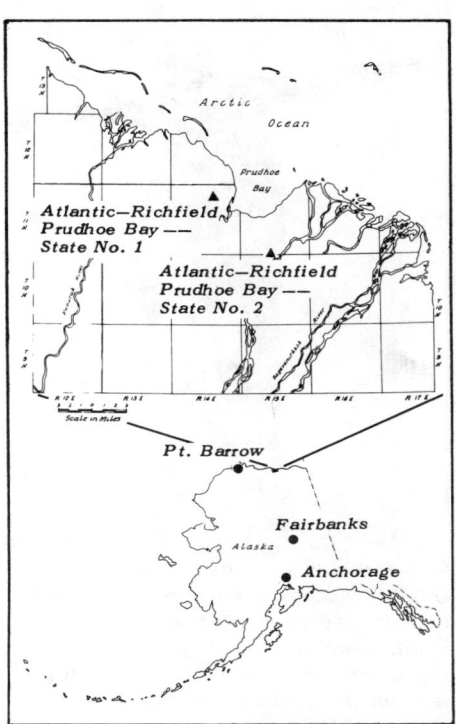

Map shows Atlantic Richfield—Humble's Prudhoe Bay State No. 1 well, where gas and oil have been discovered. The companies are planning to drill State No. 2, about seven miles southeast of No. 1.

Marine Highway Popular
May 1968

THE ALASKA MARINE HIGHWAY SYSTEM IS CARRYING MORE PASSENGERS AND VEHICLES than forecast by traffic projections several years ago, according to Robert Urquhart, traffic manager for the state-operated ferries. Urquhart told the Alaska Surveying and Mapping Convention in Anchorage that it was estimated the state vessels would carry 46,500 passengers and 13,250 vehicles in 1966. "Our records show that in 1966 we actually carried 134,500 passengers and 30,250 vehicles," said the traffic manager. The 140,800 passengers and 32,325 vehicles carried on the ferries in 1967 produced revenue of three and one-half million dollars. Acquisition of one or more foreign vessels is needed to continue meeting demands made on the ferry system, Urquhart told the state's surveyors and map-makers.

Against All Odds
* * *
Ice Pool Winner Two Years in a Row
July 1968

MATHEMATICALLY, THE ODDS WERE ALMOST IMPOSSIBLE, but Hugh Boyd of Ninilchik won the Nenana Ice Classic two years in a row. He held a ticket on Alaska's favorite guessing game which said the ice would go out on the Tanana River at Nenana this year at 9:26 a.m. on May 8. And it did. Boyd shared $112,000 with four other ticket holders including a pool from Dairy Queen of Fairbanks, another pool composed of Fort Yukon Northern Commercial Co. employees and families, and Mr. and Mrs. Robert C. Nelson of Petersburg. Each ticket was worth $28,000 before taxes. Last year, Boyd, 70, was one of fourteen lucky ticket holders. He's been in Alaska since 1943 and is retired. Boyd lives on Social Security and has never been to Nenana on the Alaska Railroad.

1968

Fred Richardson, a member of the U.S. Army Corps of Engineers, is 47, but he's an avid ski jumper and had been instrumental in promoting jumping in Anchorage. Here he is shown taking a leap off the 30-meter hill at Alaska Methodist University.

This is the 30-meter ski jump at Alaska Methodist University. The new facility was completed early in 1968 and already a sizeable ski jumping program has been developed in Anchorage. The first sanctioned jumping tournament was held Feb. 22.

Ski Jumps Mushroom in the Anchorage Area ... From None to Five in Only Six Months

June 1968

SIX MONTHS AGO Anchorage was without a ski jump. Today there are five of them in the area and nearly fifty skiers are participating in a jumping program which began in mid-January.

It all started with a man named Ralph Anderson, a Wisconsin-born ski jumper, who moved to Anchorage in 1965. Anderson, who started jumping at the age of seven, was coach of the Central Ski Association's Junior National Team in Wisconsin, and when he moved to Anchorage he had an urge to continue his coaching.

Not only did Anderson find no jumpers in Anchorage, there wasn't even a jump!

Anderson convinced Alaska Methodist University it should construct a jump near its ski area. The site was a natural and close enough to Anchorage for jumpers to come out in the afternoons and evenings to practice. The thirty-meter jump was completed early in 1968.

At the same time, Mt. Alyeska was putting up jumps of various sizes around the base lodge. Before it was over, there were three jumps at Alyeska — a fifteen-meter, a twenty-meter and a forty-meter.

By the end of February a fifth jump had been constructed in the area, this one at Russian Jack Springs, just inside the Anchorage city limits. This facility, of fifteen-meter calibre, was constructed by the Parks and Recreation Department.

The most eager to try jumping were youngsters. Many of those using the AMU hill are but ten years old, but they are among the best.

The jump also attracted a handful of girls and drew out some oldtimers as well, including forty-year-old Rolf Halle, a former member of Norway's national Noric ski team.

Next year Alaska hopes to field a jumping team for the Junior National Ski Championships which will be held at Mt. Alyeska. The first Alaska State Jumping Tournament was held February 22 at AMU and was sanctioned by the United States Ski Association.

—*By Bill Fox.*
Anchorage Daily News

Ten-year-old Bruce Fenn is one of Anchorage's youngest jumpers and also one of the best. Bruce usually gets at least 50 feet off the jump at AMU and also jumps off the bigger 40-meter hill at Mt. Alyeska.

Jet Runways for Barrow
April 1968

THE UPGRADING OF THE RUNWAYS AT BARROW, northernmost community under the American flag, to accommodate jet aircraft was closer to reality as the result of an agreement reached between the state and the Bureau of Land Management. Title to 660 acres of land that surround the Barrow airport was turned over to the State of Alaska, which can now proceed with the lengthening and widening of the present runway in cooperation with the Federal Aviation Administration.

The present field was the point of take off for Carl Ben Eielson's spectacular flight to Spitzbergen in 1928. Built on permafrost, it was designed to be paved, a necessity for jet aircraft. Wien Air Alaska hopes to be using a Boeing 737 on this run by late this year.

New Look in Aviation
April 1968

ALASKA'S AVIATION INDUSTRY has a new look this spring with two long familiar names disappearing as the result of mergers recently approved by President Lyndon Johnson.

Wien Alaska Airlines is the new name resulting from the merger of Northern Consolidated Airlines and Wien Air Alaska. The new firm will use the corporate structure of NCA. Anchorage-based NCA served sixty airports from King Salmon to Unalakleet to Fairbanks. Wien Air Alaska serves ninety-eight points in a 300,000 square mile area extending from Juneau to the Arctic Coast. New Boeing 737 jets have been ordered to serve larger communities on the Wien Alaska routes.

Cordova Airlines was officially absorbed into the Alaska Airlines system early in February, thus extending Alaska Airlines' intra-state service from Kotzebue in the Arctic to Juneau and Dawson City in the Yukon.

Fairbanks-based Interior Airways began three daily flights from Anchorage to Fairbanks in February, and followed this with purchase of Anchorage's Alaska Aeronautical Industries from Jack Peck. The new acquisition will extend Interior's service to Kenai, Swanson River, Soldotna and Beluga. Interior President James S. Magoffin points out that his firm, which now maintains a facility at Sagwon on the Arctic Slope now links the Cook Inlet oil fields with the Arctic exploration area.

A Dry Eagle
January 1968

Incorporated as Alaska's first "first class" incorporated city sixty-six years ago, Eagle voted itself a dry throat in October by a vote of nine to three. In voting to prohibit sale of intoxicating liquor within the city limits, Eagle residents also named Mrs. Esther Merley as Mayor of Alaska's newest dry village.

'Grandma' Doing Fine
March 1968

Mrs. Minnie Tucker, known to many Alaskans as Grandma Nataruck, is doing fine at the Alaska Native Medical Center in Anchorage despite her believed age of 103 and a fall at her Fairbanks home that fractured a hip. In fact, she had been doing her chores around her cabin where she lives alone after her fall, but decided to report to St. Joseph's Hospital because, "Her hip kept hurting." She was treated for arthritis until an x-ray showed a bone was cracked. She had been shoveling snow when she fell.

She can remember her early childhood at an Eskimo village at Golovin bay, and recalls talk of the purchase of Alaska from Russia.

Holdouts Finally Move to New Valdez
April 1968

STARTED WITH AN EARTHQUAKE AND TIDAL WAVE nearly four years ago, the process of making colorful, old Valdez a ghost town was finally completed in February, when the last residents moved to what residents call the "new town." Despite warnings that continued residence was precarious, a few diehard Valdezans held on for nearly four years. Started from scratch four years ago, the new Valdez is now home for about 1,000 Alaskans. If the Legislature provides funds, the spirit of the old Valdez will be retained in a park on the old townsite complete with historic buildings.

Flood's After-effect
January 1968

Despite early predictions that the Fairbanks flood would cut down the enrollment at the University of Alaska this fall because of financial set-backs in this area, the enrollment figures show a drop of only thirty-two students compared to last fall. The total enrollment at the College campus is now 1,847. Registration increased in almost every category except that of part-time students.

"This loss can easily be seen as an after-effect of the flood. People are simply too busy this semester working on homes and businesses to take courses at the University in their spare time," stated assistant registrar Ann Tremarello.

$2.10 Hourly Minimum Is Highest in Nation
March 1968

Alaskans began collecting the highest state minimum wage in the nation on February 1, when the new $2.10 per hour wage became effective. Reflecting the higher cost of living in Alaska, the state law is pegged at fifty cents an hour above the federal law, which now requires a minimum wage of $1.60 per hour.

Lost Mine Lures Trader
September 1968

JOE NETRO, well-known trading post operator at Old Crow, Yukon Territory, is ready to retire at 71, so he can have time to go looking for a lost gold mine. Except for three years he spent trapping in Alaska, Joe, who was born at Old Crow, has spent all his life in the tiny Indian community on the Porcupine River.

Getting in supplies for his isolated trading post has always posed problems. In the early days, Yukon River steamers out of Whitehorse dropped his supplies off at Fort Yukon, and Joe transported them 300 miles upstream along the Porcupine in his own boat, "The Otter." After World War II, there were no steamers, so Joe's freight went the long way round, from Vancouver, B.C. to Seattle, via steamship to Seward, rail to Nenana, and river barge to Fort Yukon, where Joe took it over. Lately a Dawson City riverboat team has been delivering his supplies each summer.

Joe and his wife Hannah live in Old Crow with five of their nine children, while four daughters work or go to school in Whitehorse.

Success at Prudhoe Bay... Second Well Strikes Oil
September 1968

THE PETROLEUM WORLD'S SPOTLIGHT shifted to Alaska's Arctic Slope in late June with Atlantic Richfield's announcement that its Sag River No. 1 had penetrated 200 feet of oil-bearing sand at the same level as Prudhoe Bay State No. 1, which has been tested at 2,415 barrels per day. Located on a 90,000-acre lease 390 miles north of Fairbanks and 150 miles southeast of Barrow, the two wells are seven miles apart. "A significant oil and gas discovery," was Atlantic Richfield's description of its second successful wildcat in the Arctic. Ripples of optimism rolled over the state as geologists speculated the Arctic Slope will rival the fabulous Middle East fields and dwarf the rich Kenai-Cook Inlet basin. By mid-summer there were predictions of pipelines linking the Arctic with Seward or Valdez, and some government officials indicated the Arctic strike would improve chances of a rail link from Fairbanks to the Gubik field. Even before the Sag River strike, Graden Laufbaum, Union Oil geologist, told the Kenai Chamber of Commerce that the Cook Inlet Basin will have 250 wells producing 300,000 barrels of oil a day by 1971. Such production will move Alaska from tenth-ranking oil and gas state to the number five spot.

Can You Hear the Northern Lights?
May 1968

OLDTIMERS IN ALASKA HAVE LONG VOWED THAT THEY COULD "HEAR" THE NORTHERN LIGHTS. This is disputed by scientists, but they concede that auroras do make low-tone sounds inaudible to the human ear. Dr. Charles R. "Buck" Wilson at the University of Alaska's Geophysical Institute is studying this phenomenon of infrasonic pressure waves created by the aurora borealis.

Auroral sounds were first detected after setting up the first infrasonic observatory in the northern aurora zone with four sensitive microphones capable of picking up the low sound waves. Units have been placed around the Fairbanks area at the corners of a five-mile square. Signals are transmitted to a recording device at the Institute on the University campus over local telephone lines. Scientists can then calculate the direction, elevation, and speed of the incoming waves from the relative arrival times of the sounds at each of the four microphones.

Another recording system has been set up at Palmer, so that the same signals can be recorded at both places and the location of the source computed by triangulation. Dr. Wilson hopes to determine the basic physical process in the aurora which generates the infrasound. This would help solve the question of just why the aurora moves as it does.

Costly Muktuk
September 1968

THERE IS A BOUNTIFUL SUPPLY OF MUKTUK in the villages of Alaska's northwest Arctic coast, but the Eskimos of Kotzebue have found that appeasing a hankering for the whale delicacy is costly. Caught in Point Hope up the coast, black muktuk is selling for $2.25 a pound in Kotzebue.

Fast-growing Kenai
January 1968

Proclaiming itself the "world's fastest growing city," Kenai observed two notable events this fall. The old Russian village got its first paved sidewalks, curbs and gutters. Natural gas was made available to residents at the same time. And on Oct. 4, City Manager William Harrison announced building permits were issued for one million dollars worth of single family dwelling units. Harrison reported that nearly 11 million dollars in improvements were added to the Kenai scene between January 1, 1967 and October 4.

Icefield Conquered
August 1968

THE FIRST DOCUMENTED CROSSING OF THE HARDING ICEFIELD, a 9-day trek that started at the head of Kachemak Bay and ended at Seward, was completed in late April by Vin Hoeman, Dave Johnston and Bill Babcock of Anchorage and Yule Kilcher of Homer. During their 90-mile journey, the hikers encountered a three-day snowstorm and 60mph squalls.

August 1968

At left, a polar bear on the Arctic ice pack north of Point Barrow is about to become a participant in a research program conducted by the Alaska Department of Fish and Game, with assistance from the U.S. Bureau of Sport Fisheries and Wildlife. After tranquilizing the bear by "shooting" him with an injection from a helicopter, a researcher (center) approaches the bear with caution. At right, a blood sample is drawn from the animal for comparison with bear in other areas of the world. When released the bear will wear a brightly colored neck belt, two ear tags and a large number painted on his fur. Purpose of this work is to determine if the same bears or groups of bear appear off Alaska's coast each year. This study is part of international studies being conducted by Alaska, Russia, Canada, Norway, Iceland and the United States. In another phase of Alaska's program, several polar bears have been "wiretapped."

1968

'Iron Dogs' Catch On
May 1968

ACCORDING TO A REPORT FROM THE ESKIMO VILLAGE OF WALES, westernmost community in the United States, the people there are hooked on snow machines, and they are fast replacing the dog team as a means of winter transportation in that area. The "iron dog" is faster, more practical, and more economical to operate—it doesn't eat when it's not working. However, as far as dependability goes, the villagers still concede that the sled dog has the edge. No one has yet to walk back because a dog team stopped operating.

Railroad to North Slope
November 1968

The oil-rich Arctic North Slope which has attracted world attention to Alaska will be tied to the state's established transportation system by a railroad, if the recommendations of Governor Walter J. Hickel's NORTH Commission are followed. An August meeting in Fairbanks resulted in a unanimous commission decision to press for a $210 million extension of the Alaska Railroad into the Arctic. Atlantic Richfield and Humble estimate that the Prudhoe Bay-Sag River field contains five to ten billion barrels of recoverable oil, but the North Commission heard Governor Hickel predict that the entire North Slope contains forty billion barrels. The Commission called for a crash construction program that would complete the Arctic link by 1971, the same year that major oil companies predict North Slope oil will be flowing through a pipeline to world markets. With pipeline route surveys being rushed there has been no announcement as to the pipeline terminus. Speculation ranges from a port on the northwest coast to "somewhere in southcentral Alaska."

Defensive Seamanship
August 1968

WHOEVER HEARD OF DEFENSIVE DRIVING AT SEA? There are so many Russian fishing vessels operating in the Kodiak area that the Kodiak Mirror recently devoted a half page to quoting Russia's maritime "Rules of the Road." The editors explained they printed the Soviet regulations as a service to Alaskan fishermen who may have to maneuver their way among the foreign ships.

Lake George – Landmark
October 1968

Lake George, largest of fifty-four self-dumping lakes in Alaska and Canada, was officially dedicated as a national landmark on July 26. The site is inaccessible except by plane or a long hike, but the landmark plaque is located just north of the old Knik River bridge. The fifteen-mile long lake is forty-four miles from Anchorage and twenty-seven miles from Palmer.

New Alaska Ferryliner
* * *
Grandest Ship in the North Pacific

September 1968

Newest, grandest ship in the North Pacific Ocean is the State of Alaska's elegant ferryliner **M/V Wickersham.** Built in Norway and sold to the state by Swedish interests for nearly $7 million, the vessel has been valued by U.S. shipbuilders at better than twice that figure. The vessel can hold more than 1,000 passengers, can accommodate 384 in berths, and can carry 140 vehicles on its car deck. Pictured above is: view of the ship underway; right, official christening of the **Wickersham** at Juneau, June 27, by Mrs. Walter J. Hickel, wife of the Governor.

ALASKA AIRLINES' PHOTOS BY BOB AND IRA SPRING

Waiver Sought to Expand Ferry Service
October 1968

Ketchikan editor Lew Williams has been tapped by Governor Hickel to head the governor's "JAR" (for Jones Act Relief) task force. Serving with Williams on a committee which is attempting to "JAR" an Alaska waiver from the national maritime regulations will be Anchorage Mayor George Sullivan; Anchorage attorney W. C. Arnold; Fairbanks businessman Red Porter; Don Dickey, manager of the Alaska State Chamber of Commerce; Wrangell businessman James Nolan; State Attorney General G. Kent Edwards; Alaska Public Works Commissioner Harold Strandberg; and Patrick Ryan, the Governor's Administrative Assistant.

Unless a waiver is obtained from the federal Jones Act (actually a series of federal acts and regulations), the state's newly acquired ferryliner *Wickersham* will continue to be limited to carrying passengers only between a foreign and an American port. Presently passengers may board the ship northbound only at Prince Rupert and may disembark at any of the Alaska ports of call. They cannot, however, reembark northbound. Southbound passengers may embark at any Alaskan city, but can disembark only at Prince Rupert.

Nuns Give up Hospitals
September 1968

A COMBINED TOTAL OF 140 YEARS OF SERVICE given Fairbanks and Juneau by two orders of Catholic nuns ended July 1. The Sisters of Charity of Providence, who had operated St. Joseph's Hospital in Fairbanks since 1908, leased the facility to the City of Fairbanks for three years of interim use while a new Community Hospital is built. Already renamed the Fairbanks Community Hospital, the pioneer facility will be operated by the Lutheran Home and Hospital Society. With roots in Alaska history dating back to 1886, St. Ann's Hospital in Juneau, operated by the Sisters of St. Ann, was turned over to the Greater Juneau Borough for operation on July 1. Unable to finance a new hospital, the Sisters leased the old hospital to the borough for use while it builds a new hospital near Salmon Creek. The Juneau nuns also closed St. Ann's Grade School.

Single Girls Fare Well
November 1968

"How does a single girl do up here?" asked a member of the Royal Commission on the Status of Women at an August hearing in Whitehorse. "She has a whale of a time," came the answer from a male in the audience. A territorial official offered this further explanation: "Because a great number of single, virile men come to the Yukon, therefore single, feminine women also come and we have no problem recruiting government office staff."

Wickersham's Home Is Historic Monument
July 1968

JUDGE JAMES A. WICKERSHAM, a man of many firsts in Alaska, scored again in mid-May, even after his death. Wickersham's former home in Fairbanks became the first historical monument to be so designated by the state. The Wickersham House, to be moved to the Alaskaland site and restored, dates back to 1905. It was the first Fairbanks home built of sawmill lumber, not logs. Judge Wickersham was Alaska's first delegate to Congress. He named the city of Fairbanks in 1903. He led the first expedition ever to attempt to climb Mt. McKinley and introduced the bill which created Mt. McKinley National Park. He introduced Alaska's first statehood bill in 1916. Standard Oil Company of California has purchased the land in downtown Fairbanks where the Wickersham home stands. The company donated the building to the Tanana-Yukon Historical Society. In recent years the home has fallen into disrepair. A furnishing and restoration fund for the building is being sought by Alaskaland from the federal government and private foundations. The state will provide 50 per cent of maintenance and operation costs. Pioneers of Alaska privately raised the money to move the building to Alaskaland.

'It Could Have Been One of My Little Boys'
* * * *
Eskimo Mother Saves Youngster's Life

September 1968

TIMOTHY EVON, five year old son of Mr. and Mrs. Joseph Evon of Bethel, owes his life to the courage of a petite little Eskimo mother, Mrs. John Kinegak, thirty-five, also of Bethel, Alaska.

Returning from a movie during a severe summer rain and lightning storm, Mrs. Kinegak heard someone yell, "There's somebody in the river."

The mighty Kuskokwim at this point in Bethel does not have a sloping bank. But Ella Kinegak did not hesitate for a moment. Fortunately she can swim (few Eskimo women in this area can swim), but even so, the icy waters are a challenge. With the aid of eleven-year-old Ricky Strauss, also of Bethel, Mrs. Kinegak got out to a boat and got to where just a tiny hand was showing above water. Mrs. Kinegak got the boy ashore, then applied artificial respiration until he revived sufficiently to be brought to the Bethel Hospital.

When asked how she mustered the courage to plunge into the icy, storm-tossed Kuskokwim River, Mrs. Kinegak said, "All I could think of was—it could have been one of my little boys."

Timothy Evon has been released from the hospital with no ill effects from his icy dip.

—N. E. HAMPTON

PHS ALASKA NATIVE HEALTH SERVICE

Ella Kinegak and five-year-old Timothy Evon.

Nonedible Swimmers
October 1968

The Eskimos on Little Diomede were looking for edible walrus in late July, and what did they find? Two nonedible swimmers garbed in hot water-heated rubber swimsuits who had just spent eighteen hours in swimming from Wales on the Alaska mainland to Little Diomede. Ben Schlossberg, Jr. and Steve Friedland, both twenty-seven, did the swimming accompanied by a trawler and a cameraman who recorded the adventure for posterity. The big adventure was climaxed with a side swim to the Russian side of the international dateline where three balloons were anchored with twenty-pound weights. Certain to confuse the Siberians were balloon messages which read: "Broderick Crawford for President," "Let it all Hang Out," and "Sock it to me."

Amchitka Defused
August 1968

DEFUSING THE NORTH END OF AMCHITKA ISLAND was completed this summer by eight Army ordnance experts from Fort Richardson. The touchy job was necessary to make the area safe for crews preparing the island for nuclear testing. In clearing the south end of the island last year, the demolitions specialists found more than two million blasting caps, 2,000 rounds of twenty millimeter ammunition, six 250-pound and one 500-pound bomb, all relics of World War II when Amchitka was an advance base.

Third Generation Flier
October 1968

Two generations of Wiens have made the name synonymous with Alaskan aviation, and now a third is on its way. Robert Wien, sixteen, son of Mr. and Mrs. Robert P. Wien of Fairbanks, soloed in a Cessna 150 on August 4. Young Robert's father is a Wien Consolidated Airlines captain and his grandfather was Ralph Wien, one of four brothers who blazed the state's air trails.

Scallop Capital?
September 1968

NORTH AMERICA'S NEW SCALLOP CAPITAL is the title being polished for Seward by New England scallopers who have found more bountiful beds in the Gulf of Alaska. Led by the *Viking Queen* which delivered a record catch of 50,000 pounds on its first trip, the *Ouringondy*, *Smaragd* and *Bountiful* had delivered more than 200,000 pounds of the delicacy to Seward's new scallop processing plant by mid-July. The movement of the scallopers from their former home port of New Bedford, Mass., to Alaska has added fifty-five families to Seward's population. With few regulations now applying to harvesting of scallops, the State Department of Fish and Game is expected to issue new rules in the near future to protect Alaska's newest seafood resource. Scallop meat delivered to Seward now brings a wholesale price of $1.40 a pound.

Oil Eclipses Gold
March 1968

The value of black gold produced in Alaska in 1967 was more than eighty-eight times greater than the value of the precious yellow metal that has contributed so much to the state's wealth and history. Year-end reports by the U.S. Bureau of Mines disclosed that last year's mineral production of $129.9 million, included crude oil and natural gas worth $88.2 million, while gold production dropped below the million mark for the first time in more than sixty years. Reflecting offshore drilling successes in Cook Inlet, the crude oil value jumped from $44 million in 1966 to $84.6 million last year. As the New Year started, daily production from the Cook Inlet and Swanson River fields was topping 140,000 barrels a day.

Honors for Eskimos
November 1968

New firsts have been achieved by two widely separated young Eskimos. Edmorris Milligrock, eighteen, a Nome Eskimo who can't speak his native tongue is the first Eskimo to enroll at Harvard University. A four-year scholarship took Edmorris on his first trip outside the state. Far to the east, Markoosie, twenty-seven-year-old Canadian Eskimo from Resolute Bay, N.W.T., became the first Eastern Arctic Eskimo to earn a commercial pilot's license. He is now flying for the Resolute Bay Charter Service owned by Weldy Phipps.

Why Not Moose Milk?
November 1968

Moose milk, muskrat stew, spruce needle soup. These tidbits may be among the Arctic and sub-Arctic's contributions to a hungry world, according to Dr. Ian M. Cowan, dean of graduate studies at the University of British Columbia. Speaking at the nineteenth Alaska Science Conference in Whitehorse, Dr. Cowan said, "We should be studying the moose in captivity, cultivating the moose for its milk, wool and meat. There are fascinating potentials here. Why aren't we trying aspen as fodder? Are spruce needles edible? Who knows? No one has tried to use them." He described muskrat as "far superior to rabbit, both in flavor and nutritive content." The conference, first held outside Alaska, attracted more than 300 who heard 150 papers on a variety of subjects. Chairman of the conference for 1969 is Victor Fisher, director of the Institute for Social, Economic and Government Research at the University of Alaska.

No Limit for Guides
November 1968

Although the Alaska Fish and Game Board had sought to limit the number of bears taken through guides to a total of three per year per guide, the regulation has been declared invalid and there will be no limit on the number of grizzlies or brown bears a guide can take. In a decision prepared by state Attorney General G. Kent Edwards for Fish and Game Commissioner Augie Reetz, Edwards concurred with protesting guides who said the regulation was more restrictive than the one published in the public notice of regulations under consideration. The published proposal would have limited the kill of bears to eight per year per guide.

Kodiak Ranks near Top
August 1968

TEN MILLION DOLLARS IN FISHERY LANDINGS during 1967 ranked Kodiak as the nation's third busiest fishing port for the second year in a row. As in 1966, Kodiak's fishery business was exceeded only by San Pedro, Calif., and New Bedford, Mass. Alaska's title as the nation's most productive fishing state in 1966 was lost last year to California and Texas. For the first time in nearly a century, salmon did not lead the state's seafoods in poundage in 1967. King crab led the pack with 135 million pounds, followed by salmon with 131 million.

Faro: Yukon's New Town
November 1968

Slated to come alive in September, 1969, Faro, the Yukon's newest town is fast taking shape. Clearing and grubbing of the townsite has been completed, and an access road is being built from Faro to the Anvil Mine near Ross River. A $662,572 contract was recently awarded for construction of streets and installation of water and sewer lines.

54 Walrus for Food
October 1968

Wainwright hunters assured the village of a good winter meat supply when they bagged fifty-four walrus in several days of midsummer harvesting of huge herds.

'Greenland Halibut' – Masquerade Is Over
November 1968

"Greenland Halibut," the lower-priced, lower-grade flounder which has been masquerading in recent years as a halibut—and creating havoc with the true halibut market in the process—will now have to be marketed under its true name, not "halibut." This good news for Alaska halibut fishermen and processors came from the U.S. Food and Drug Administration in the form of an order prohibiting the labeling of any fish as "halibut" other than *Hippoglossus hippoglossus* (the true Atlantic halibut) or *Hippoglossus stenolepsis* (the true Pacific halibut, harvested in Alaska waters)

Food and Drug Commissioner Herbert L. Ley Jr. specifically objected to the labeling of "flounder" or "Northern Flounder" as "Greenland Halibut." He commented: "The Name 'Greenland Halibut' has been accepted in the scientific community as the name for food fish of the species *Reinhardtiu hippoglassoides*, which is a variety of the fish commonly known as flounder. For this reason the Food and Drug Administration in the past has not objected to the use of the name 'Greenland Halibut' in the labeling of this species.

"There is now, however, sufficient information available to the administration to show that the ordinary individual who prefers the true and more expensive halibut may purchase fish labeled as 'Greenland Halibut' under the impression that it is a kind of halibut, which is not the case. The Food and Drug Administration therefore concludes that (such fish) is misbranded." In the future, said Ley, the fish shall bear the name "flounder" or "Northern Flounder."

October 1968

Subscription and Newsstand Prices Going Up

After January 1, 1969, a 12-month subscription to Alaska Sportsman will be $6 a year instead of $5. Newsstand per-copy price will go from 50c to 60c.

All subscriptions received prior to January 1, 1969, will be honored at the existing $5 rate.

November 1968
Biggest steelhead ever taken from Anchor River, and probably the largest ever taken by rod on the Kenai Peninsula, is this eighteen-pound beauty landed by D.E. "Pete" Lynds of Anchorage on September 5. Pete used a cluster of red eggs in a deep hole near the mouth of the river to land his prize after a twenty-five minute tussle. Thirty-six inches long, the fish had a girth of eighteen-and-a-half inches.

Home Building Boom
February 1968

Home building in Anchorage bounced back with a bang in 1967 with a total of 622 new homes constructed in the Greater Anchorage area. John Mercier, new president of the Home Builders Association of Alaska, reported 1967 construction was up sixty per cent from the previous twelve months. Average value of Anchorage homes built last year was $34,000, according to Mercier.

Cyanide for Coyotes
March 1968

A cyanide-shooting coyote-getter is being used by the Bureau of Indian Affairs to control predators near reindeer herds in Northwest Alaska, but no wolf poison is being distributed, according to Commissioner Urban Nelson of the State Department of Fish and Game. Nelson's finding followed an investigation of complaints the BIA was engaged in a wolf-poisoning program.

U. Graduates 300 Plus
July 1968

GRADUATES from America's farthest north university topped 300 for the first time this year. A record number of 114 master's degree candidates boosted the total to a new high at the University of Alaska on May 20. Total graduates from the university now number more than 2,510. The University of Alaska's first graduate, John J. Shanly, class of 1923, now lives in Buffalo, N.Y.

Boy's Dig: Clue to Past
December 1968

The first sourdough hunted moose and caribou in interior Alaska 11,000 years ago, and the key to this archaeological breakthrough was the artifact collection of a young Alaskan. The trail which led back to nine milleniums before Christ and added 5,000 years to the previous known presence of man in Alaska began in 1962.

Mrs. Paul Kirsteatter of Healy Lake showed a Darmouth College anthropologist the collection her ten-year-old son had dug from the family's garden plot. Dr. Robert A. McKennan studied Freddy Kirsteatter's arrows and spear points, and returned in 1966 for further digging. He was joined by John P. Cook, now a University of Alaska archaeologist. "We found a sequence of artifacts, animal bones and charcoal hearths extending from what we later learned was the 11,000-year level to recent times," said Cook. During the summer of 1967, Cook and his helpers dug more than fifty five-by-five-foot squares to depths of three to five feet.

Wilderness Hideaways Open to Entry... but It Isn't All That Simple
December 1968

Alaskans with visions of acquiring their own "wilderness hideaway" began making their dreams come true on October 15, as the State Division of Lands initiated its "Open to Entry" program on almost three million acres of choice fishing, hunting and scenic land.

Traveling by plane, boat, car, snowmobile, train and on foot, the land seekers are moving into designated areas ranging from the Gulf of Alaska to the area just north of Fairbanks. More than 400 application forms were issued by the Anchorage office on the first day.

The new program results from Chapter 157 enacted by the 1968 Legislature to speed "transfer of state land into private individual hands so that the land may be beneficially occupied and used."

Bulk of the land open to entry is located in the Susitna Valley, extends north along the route of the new Anchorage-Fairbanks Highway to Fairbanks, south along the Alaska Highway to Tok, and south along the Glenn Highway from Tok. There is sea frontage available near Seward and on Kachemak Bay.

Unless a land seeker has a clear idea of just where he wants to stake out his entry, the range and type of "open to entry" land is staggering. For the person who just wants land, an intelligent selection cannot be made without careful study of seventeen maps prepared by the Division of Lands which show forty separate areas ranging in size from a few acres to more than a million.

Names long familiar to Alaskan sportsmen are included in the "open to entry" areas. They include such adventure-related names as Thumbs Cove and Day Harbor near Seward, Tutka Bay and Sadie Cove near Seldovia, Caribou Lake near Homer, Alexander and Lake Creeks, and the Talchulitna, Skwentna and Yentna Rivers in the Susitna Valley, the Goodpaster and Clearwater Rivers near Big Delta, the Chatanika and Salcha Rivers near Fairbanks, Healy Lake and the Gerstle River east of Delta Junction.

The seeker of wilderness acres under the new Division of Lands program will soon find that it is no free and easy giveaway of choice tracts. None of the three million acres are directly accessible by main roads. And, although there are a half a million, five-acre tracts theoretically available within the "open to entry" areas, much of the acreage is swamp or mountainside.

Determined to prevent large speculators from tying up large blocks of the continent's best recreational lands, Division of Lands officials have certain protective devices built into the program.

Known in landsmen's language as an "entryman," each applicant must personally stake his entry, which cannot exceed five acres or include more than 400 feet of water frontage. The state is reserving the right to establish pedestrian access along streams, lake shore or other water frontage. Existing trails through an entry are presumed to have an easement. Each individual is limited to one tract.

Assuming the entryman has paid his $10 filing fee and $40 first year lease payment, he can use the land for a total of ten years by paying the annual $40 lease. Once his lease is approved, the entryman can apply to purchase his tract, providing he pays the cost of having it surveyed. He will be charged the fair market value of the land at the time of entry.

Land specialists point out that the cost of having a remote tract surveyed by qualified surveyors could add up to a sizeable investment.

Trapped between a Bear and a Forest Fire
November 1968

There's such a thing as too much excitement from hunting, and Doug Ballard of Eagle River had it on a recent sheep hunt. Left to guard sheep meat on the main fork of Eagle River while his partners packed out, Doug discovered a bear approaching down the canyon. A forest fire blocked his escape in the other direction. Caught between the bruin and the flames, he attracted a State Fish and Game plane by waving a yellow poncho. The plane notified Air Force Rescue at Elmendorf which dispatched a helicopter to rescue the trapped hunter.

Giant Timber Sale ... 1,000 New Jobs Predicted
November 1968

The Juneau Unit Timber Sale—biggest in the history of the U.S. Forest Service—a whopping 8.75 billion-board-feet over a fifty year period—was completed September 12 in the Regional Office of the U.S. Forest Service.

Somewhere in or near the sale area, U.S. Plywood-Champion Papers, Inc., will construct a forest products manufacturing facility (both pulp and sawmill) at a cost in excess of seventy-five million dollars.

More than 1,000 new jobs are forecast by the U.S. Forest Service at the plant and in the woods. In announcing U.S. Plywood-Champion's intention to purchase the timber, the firm did not disclose the probable location of the mill which will process 600 tons daily of unbleached pulp. The company is known to be considering Juneau, Sitka, and possibly other areas as well.

Construction is expected to begin about 1971 and will be completed by mid-1973. The company has until July 1, 1970 to submit to the Forest Service general plans showing the structures to be constructed and the machinery and equipment to be installed.

Said Regional Forester W. Howard Johnson, who signed the agreement for the U.S. government: "This is the largest sale of timber ever made by the U.S. Forest Service. It marks a milestone in the plans conceived many years ago to establish a pulp industry in southeastern Alaska. A major portion of the overmature hemlock and spruce timber in the area is primarily valuable for pulp. Therefore, processing of pulp is considered basic to the orderly development and full utilization of the forest resources of this region.

"Strict requirements are contained in the timber sale contract to prevent damage to salmon streams from logging and to modify logging practices for the protection of waterfowl resting, nesting, and feeding areas. Cutting area layout will consider the needs of recreational uses. Proper compliance will be required with all state and federal laws, including those for water pollution control," Johnson concluded.

Hazard for Fliers
October 1968

The Far North has found a new air traffic hazard—roving reindeer. Several hundred animals from the Bureau of Indian Affairs model herd swarmed over the Nome airport on August 1, stopping all plane traffic. Normalcy returned when herders and airport personnel drove the reindeer the full length of the runway and back into the tundra.

Caribou Comeback
October 1968

Missing from the Kenai Peninsula for more than half a century, caribou are making a comeback in the area dominated by moose. A herd of twenty of the animals was seen recently near the Kenai airport, and sightings are becoming more common each month. The new herd was started with eighteen transplanted animals in 1965.

50 Years a Guide
October 1968

Famed Yukon Territory big-game guide Johnnie John celebrated his seventieth birthday, and fifty years of outfitting, July 10. In Whitehorse to help him mark the occasion were daughters Mrs. Hazel Lovelace of Sacramento and Mrs. Ada Haskin of Skagway. John advises all concerned he's not retiring, but he has sold his business to Dennis Callison of Toad River Lodge. He'll be taking it easier as boss of the base camp for the hunting season in the Primrose Lake valley area.

Link to the World
November 1968

Biggest excitement at Point Hope these days is to make telephone contact with Anchorage, Seattle or any point in the world. One of the oldest and most remote settlements on the continent, the Arctic Eskimo village was recently provided with three telephones which tie into the Alaska Communications System and its links with the world.

September 1968
"Why, it looks just like a wedding cake, waiting for the candy bride and groom to be set on top!" This reaction by a recent Juneau visitor upon viewing the new Alaska State Museum building for the first time does not decrease Juneau's pride in the structure, which local residents helped to finance, through a special sales tax, as an Alaska centennial project.

Dangerous Mission
November 1968

Cordova fishermen are still singing the praises of a Coast Guard Albatross rescue plane which landed in seas ripped by seventy-five mile-an-hour winds on the Copper flats to rescue one boatman and recover the body of a second. Norman Campbell, skipper of the *MV Whistler*, and Norman Selanoff, crewman, took to the sea in life jackets when the *Whistler* sunk. Jim Foode and Bob Dettinger dropped a two-man raft from Foode's plane. Campbell reached the raft. Meanwhile, the Coast Guard plane arrived, landed and recovered Selanoff's body while Campbell paddled to the plane six hours after the sinking. High winds and seas prevented the rescue plane's takeoff and it was towed to sheltered waters by the Salmo Point, a tender skippered by Dave Kulper.

First Fisheries Course
May 1968

THIRTY YOUNG ALASKANS from southwest coastal villages are enrolled in the first fisheries course of its kind offered in the state. Conducted at the Kodiak Regional Vocational School, the first year course is designed to teach basic skills needed by an ordinary deckhand. Students learn net mending, hanging cork and lead lines, splicing, and are introduced to marine biology, conservation and fisheries regulations by Pete Resoff, teacher and commercial fisherman. The curriculum calls for field trips to vessels in Kodiak for firsthand lessons from the old pros. A more advanced and specialized course will be offered next year. "These courses are in the process of being developed." said Resoff," "and we hope to gear them to the definite needs of our own regional Alaskan students who are not academically inclined."

Surplus Musk Ox
June 1968

TRANSFER OF FIFTEEN YOUNG MUSK OX from the overcrowded range of Nunivak Island to nearby Nelson Island has given mild and temporary relief to the surplus musk ox problem. Conducted in March by state and federal biologists, the tricky transfer involved use of tranquilizers, a helicopter and small cargo plane. The new arrivals joined seven other musk ox moved to Nelson Island in an earlier transplant.

Indian Chiefs
July 1968

INDIAN CHIEFS AND VILLAGE COUNCIL PRESIDENTS from thirty-two interior Alaska villages gathered in Fairbanks May 15 and 16 for the annual spring Tanana Chief's Conference. Chief of the chiefs was young John Sackett, 23, of Huslia. Principal business under discussion was state and federal land claims legislation.

1969

Henry S. Kaiser

January 1969
Like your art traditional or modern? The Anchorage Museum of Fine Arts gives you your choice. Left, "Waiting for the Whale to Surface" by Fred Machetanz tells the same story as "The Hunters" by Dean Brennan. The styles are different as night and day.

'North Slope Oil' – The New Year's Magic Words
January 1969

Easiest 1969 forecast for Alaskans is that the words "North Slope Oil," will dominate state news in a wide range of fields. Raymond Peterson, chairman of the board for Wien Consolidated Airlines, put the barren Arctic in proper focus when he reported recently in Seattle: "The North Slope has been a catalyst, focusing in a dramatic way the interest of the oil and mineral exploration world on Alaska."

Already owning the land on which Atlantic Richfield-Humble made the Prudhoe Bay strike, the State of Alaska moved in late 1968 to sew up more potential oil land by making application for 1.8 million acres of federal land now under federal lease. The new move will add a belt twenty-four miles wide just south of the Prudhoe Bay acreage already under state control.

While teams of financiers visited Fairbanks and Anchorage, Commissioner of Public Works reported the state is studying the possibility of constructing a North Slope airstrip for the new jumbo jets. And the traffic problem in Fairbanks was so aggravated by Arctic-bound freight that Governor Hickel found funds and material needed to build a new Chena River Bridge which will shorten the route from the Alaska Railroad to Fairbanks International Airport by two miles. The Shipbuilders Council of America speculated that North Slope Oil may result in construction of as many as twenty five 50,000 ton tankers. As part of the North Slope's continuing spin-off, Atlantic Richfield recently announced plans to construct a $100 million refinery near Bellingham, as well as a topping plant on the North Slope for daily production of 42,000 gallons of diesel fuel.

Large enough to accommodate four-engine freight planes, a 4,500-foot runway is being carved out of the wild North Slope by Standard Oil Co. of California. Heavy equipment for the job was flown from Fairbanks to Sagwon, from where it was to travel down the Sag River to the construction site midway between the Arctic Ocean and Sagwon.

Million-pound Harvest
January 1969

Its potential still not defined, Alaska's new scallop industry produced one million pounds of scallop meat during the period from early summer until November, according to a report by the State Department of Fish and Game. Principal scallop beds located thus far are in the area between Cape St. Elias and Cape Fairweather, and near Kodiak Island.

End of an Aviation Era
January 1969

November, 1968, marked the end of another era in Alaska aviation. Western Airlines has replaced its Lockheed Constellations with turbo-prop Electras. The "Connies"–pride of the Pacific Northern Airlines fleet for a decade beginning in 1955—operated, before the advent of jets, from Seattle to Ketchikan, Juneau, Yakutat, Cordova, Anchorage, Kenai, Kodiak, and other points on the old PNA (now Western) route. While WAL schedules pure jet Boeing 720's on its primary routes to and within Alaska, the Electras (which carry approximately double the old Constellation load) will see service from Anchorage to Kenai, Anchorage-Kodiak, Kodiak-Seattle, and Anchorage-Juneau. The airline operates three types of Electras—an all-passenger model with room for ninety-four travelers, a passenger-airfreight combination aircraft, and an all-cargo version.

$4,300 an Hour
February 1969

All signals are "Go" for construction of an earth station on 250 acres of land five miles from Talkeetna, according to James McCormack, chairman of the Communications Satellite Corp., who was assured at a recent Anchorage meeting that the state supports the proposal to join the sophisticated space communications network. Bids were to be opened in mid-February for the project which will cost an estimated $7 million, and is slated for completion in 1970. Twenty-four to thirty persons will be employed at the Talkeetna station which will maintain contact with a satellite serving the Pacific area. The Alaska station will transmit telephone traffic, data and television to the western states, Canada, Japan, Australia, Philippines and Thailand. McCormack reported that the television rate of $4,300 per hour is likely to limit Alaska's use of the COMSAT system for live television shows.

Slaughterhouse
January 1969

Financed and operated by the state, a $60,000 reindeer slaughtering plant has been constructed at Nome. The first such facility built with state funds, the new plant was needed to meet new federal laws regulating slaughter and sale of meat. Until such time as a private operator takes over the plant, Dr. Fred Honsinger, state veterinarian, will manage it. Twelve of Alaska's seventeen reindeer herds numbering 30,000 animals are located on the Seward Peninsula.

Automated Lighthouses
January 1969

Long familiar beacons on Alaska's coastline are about to flicker out, and others will be tended by automated devices rather than lighthouse keepers. Destined to disappear, according to the 17th Coast Guard District, are light stations at Tree Point, Five Finger, Point Retreat and Eldred Rock. Manned stations which will be either automated or disestablished are those at Cape Decision, Cape Spencer, Cape St. Elias, Cape Hinchinbrook and Scotch Cap on Unimak Island. The Coast Guard reports savings of $15,000 each for stations which are automated, and annual savings up to $80,000 for stations closed down.

Thunder over Alaska
January 1969

Thousands of Alaskans seldom if ever hear thunder, but there is no shortage of sky noise in the Far North. A research study conducted last summer by the Weather Bureau to develop better methods of forecasting fire-producing thunderstorms disclosed that there was a minimum of 493 thunderstorms in the state from May 19 to August 28. Big boom day for the summer was June 17, with twenty-two storms reported across the Interior and Arctic. A number of federal and military agencies joined in the state's first thunderstorm count.

The Changing Scene
January 1969

More snowmobiles and more cash-paying jobs worked a major change in the fishing profile of the Arctic-Yukon-Kuskokwim area in 1968, according to the Department of Fish and Game. For the first time since records were kept in 1961, the 30,000 natives in the area sold more salmon than they used to feed themselves and their dog teams. Improved job opportunities and fewer dog teams are credited with the sale of 637,425 salmon last year and a subsistence catch of about 550,000 fish. With snowmobiles rapidly replacing dog teams in the villages, fisheries biologists expect the subsistence catch will continue to decline. In 1961, natives in the same area used 645,732 salmon for themselves and their dogs, selling 316,902.

Yukon vs. Outsiders: Put Up or Shut Up
February 1969

Said the headline in the Whitehorse, Yukon *Star*: "Asks Bennett to Put up or Shut up." The Bennett referred to was W.A.C. Bennett, Premier of British Columbia, who recently repeated a proposal he had expounded previously, namely that B.C.'s borders be extended north in order to include the Yukon Territory. Yukoners didn't seem to be any more enthusiastic about the proposal this time.

Said Territorial Councillor John Dumas, when he moved that the Council invite Bennett to Whitehorse to discuss the matter, "Bennett is a fine old gentleman who has served his country well but is now entering the twilight years... and sometimes wanders in his political thinking. He knows he may not survive the next election and something dynamic is needed, so he has reached into his old oaken bucket and brought up the same deal he offered back in 1947. Its just another case of someone wanting to ravish the north: He wants our land, Ottawa wants our resources, and Edmonton our history."

Baranof Mansion Is Historic Monument
January 1969

Lord Baranof's Mansion, oldest Russian structure remaining in Kodiak, will be designated a national historical monument, according to George Hall, Alaska's National Park Service coordinator. Hall told a meeting of Kodiakans that the National Park Service will request funds in the next budget for restoration of the mansion.

More Oil Refineries
February 1969

Alaska's single refinery in North Kenai will soon be one of three in the area. Joining the Standard Oil Co. plant will be the Western Frontier Oil and Refining Co., with a refining capacity of 5,000 barrels of gas a day, and the Alaska Oil and Refining Co., which will produce 20,000 barrels of jet fuel daily. Speculation as to where the independent refineries would obtain needed oil was ended with a recent announcement by Governor Walter J. Hickel that the State of Alaska will soon start accepting its twelve and one-half per cent royalty payment "in kind," meaning in oil. Present production in the Cook Inlet basin will entitle the state to about 20,000 barrels of oil a day. State officials have not confirmed that the state's oil will go to the independents, but informed observers are convinced that the two new refineries expect to buy their raw material from the state.

Telling It Like It Is
January 1969

Leave it to an Eskimo to tell it like it is. The Department of Fish and Game reported these answers from a Selawik Eskimo in reply to a questionnaire concerning sport fishing: "1. I did not sport fish. I fish for living. 2. Sport fishing is not known though you fish with tackle. 3. Eskimos do not let fish go because it was small. 4. If we do let fish go because it was small we will call it sport fishing."

(News-Miner photo by Paul J. Noden)

January 1969 — Top hunter in Fairbanks' Hunter School is seven-year-old Stanley Thomas shown here with 63-inch moose rack from a bull the second grader bagged in September.

More Protection for Alaska's Bald Eagles
February 1969

Bald eagles, national bird of the U.S.A., will gain additional protection in southeast Alaska under the terms of an agreement recently announced by the federal departments of Interior and Agriculture. The Bureau of Sport Fisheries and Wildlife (Department of the Interior) will locate and mark trees in which eagles nest. The U.S. Forest Service (Department of Agriculture) will revise logging contracts to insure protection of these trees.

Forest Products Dominate Alaska's Exports
January 1969

According to a United States Department of Commerce report, Alaskan exports during the first seven months of 1968 increased by nearly $7 million over the similar period in 1967. Total exports came to $37,305,991. Forest products continued to account for the bulk of Alaska's exports. Largest customer was Japan with Canada, Europe, Australia, Eastern Asia, India, Africa, and Central and South America also receiving shipments.

A Bump Test
January 1969

Highway engineers will know by spring if the jarring bumps produced by paving frost heaves can be eliminated by using heavy layers of insulation below the pavement. Test patches of both rigid and poured foam-type insulation have been located in a frost-heave area twelve miles south of Anchorage on the Seward Highway.

ACS up for Sale
January 1969

The nations's major telephone companies are now preparing bids for purchase of the far-flung Alaska Communications System. Purchase offers will be opened in March, and, if approved by the President and Department of Defense, the Air Force-operated system could be transferred to private ownership as early as July 1, 1970. In making bids for the Air Force-operated ACS, prospective purchasers must show a plan for lowering the present rate structure, expansion of facilities and improved public service. Included in the sale are toll centers in Anchorage, Fairbanks, Juneau and Ketchikan, twenty-two stations operated by ACS personnel, fifteen agent stations, thirteen marine radio and bush radio stations. The purchaser will acquire 740 miles of open wire lines and 368 miles of multichannel submarine cable. ACS employs 837 civilians and 139 military personnel.

Pioneer Pilots Honored
January 1969

Three pioneer Alaskan aviators were among fifty honored guests at a New York dinner in early December hosted by the Explorers Club in tribute to the aviation industry. Bob Reeve, president of Reeve Aleutian Airways; Ray Petersen, chairman of Wien Consolidated Airlines, and Noel Wien, president of Wien Consolidated were honored at the Waldorf-Astoria Hotel dinner attended by 1,000 persons.

Snowmobiles in the News: Lack of Gas Plagues Hunters, Trappers... Widespread Thefts... A Horse to the Rescue

February 1969

Snowmobiles don't need races to make news in Alaska where the ownership to population ratio is probably the highest in the nation. Police blotters reflect the popularity of the machines, with more than 100 stolen in a single week in Southcentral Alaska late in 1968. The lower Kuskokwim villages of Tununak, Toksook Bay, Newtok, Nightmute and Chefornak were virtually immobilized in November, when a supply of fuel for the gas-eating machines was lost in a barge mishap. And trapping and hunting at Anaktuvuk Pass also ground to a screeching halt in November when the local store ran out of gas. Shame came to a snowmobiler whose rig broke down on a hunt near Willow and he had to be towed home by a horse. But it was pride that showed in Kodiak when seven snowmobiles driven by members of Kodiak Motor Mushers' Association rescued seventeen Port Lions youngsters stranded at Anton Larsen Bay by an early December storm.

(USFS photo)

Winter picnics? Every Sunday when the weather cooperates, Southcentral Alaskan snowmobilers gather at Turnagain Pass on the Seward Highway for fun in the snow. Cross-country skiers frolic in an area set aside for their special use.

1969

Church Rededication
January 1969

Renovated and rededicated, the oldest Russian Orthodox church in Alaska, Church of the Holy Resurrection in Kodiak, was rededicated on September 22 by His Grace, Bishop Theodosius of Sitka. The recent ceremony was a prelude to the 175th anniversary of the founding of the Russian Orthodox faith in Alaska which will be observed at Kodiak in September, 1969. The first church was established at Three Saints Bay on September 24, 1794.

From Tent to House
February 1969

Among the first families to move into fourteen new homes completed in late 1968 under a special Alaska State Housing Authority project at Bethel were an Eskimo couple with nine children who had been living in a tent. Designed to alleviate substandard living conditions in the Bethel area, the project will provide up to 200 homes for needy residents. Supported by state and federal agencies, the Bethel home ownership program includes a housing factory which provides on-the-job training in plumbing, carpentry, electrical and painting trades. By mid-November the Bethel Housing Committee had received eighty applications for the homes. While Bethel's first new home dwellers were getting settled, the Alaska State Housing Authority was reviewing applications sent to 174 native villages eligible for participation in the $10 million housing program authorized by Senate Bill 1915. If fully funded by Congress, the special project could provide as many as 2,000 homes in remote communities by 1972.

$1 Million Stretch
January 1969

The *Tustumena*, state ferry on the western Alaska run, will be lengthened by fifty-five feet this winter, according to an announcement made in Kodiak by Governor Walter J. Hickel. Requiring eighty days, the stretching operation will cost more than $1 million.

The Good Old Days . . .
June 1969

Now I do not have any dog teams anymore. At present I only have one little pup. Maybe I should have stuck to good old dog teams still. And I wouldn't have gotten dirty all over when I am fixing Ski-Doo. When I had dog teams I only used to buy web and make harnesses and snaps and rings. And harnesses last you long time. Those were the good old days.

Joseph Lincoln
Toksook Bay correspondent
FAIRBANKS DAILY NEWS-MINER

February 1969

It wasn't official when this headline was written on November 19, but the Kodiak Mirror was so proud of its position as one of the top—if not the top—fishery ports in the nation, it broke out the big type to tell the world. In recent years, Kodiak has rated third behind New Bedford, Mass., and first place San Pedro, Calif., in value of fisheries landings. With a record seafood production total of $39,600,680 in primary wholesale value for 1968, Kodiak expects to be just what the headline says.

Grim Time for Aviation
February 1969

Fifty Alaskans died in three plane crashes that marked November and December as grim months for aviation. Worst of the accidents came on December 2, when a Wien Consolidated Airlines F-27 propjet plunged into Foxes Lake, twenty-three miles east of Iliamna, carrying a crew of three and thirty-six passengers to their deaths. So severe was the weather in the remote area 150 miles southwest of Anchorage that bodies could not be removed from the crash site until December 5.

On November 21, a twin-engine Aero-Commander piloted by famed Arctic pilot Bob Fischer crashed after takeoff at Barrow, killing the pilot and six members of the Governor's Employment Advisory Commission. Only survivor was Werner Bohrer, Nome businessman, and a member of the commission. The pilot and three passengers of a Sea Airmotive Cessna 180 failed to show up at Beluga in early November after takeoff from Anchorage. An extensive search failed to find any trace of the missing aircraft, and it is presumed to have crashed in Cook Inlet.

Bear Mauls Hunter
January 1969

A bear attacked and mauled Charles Merle Wells, 43, October 21 after Wells apparently killed a deer, left it along a roadway and headed for his automobile. Wells, who had been hunting at Fish Bay north of Sitka, died October 23. A party of six Fish and Game officials combed the area in an attempt to locate the bear after the attack but succeeded in finding neither the bear nor the deer.

Bounties Curtailed
February 1969

Bounties are no longer paid on coyote and wolverine as a result of action taken by the Alaska Board of Fish and Game at its December meeting in Anchorage. In addition to eliminating the $30 coyote and $15 wolverine bounties, the commissioners voted to stop paying bounties on wolves taken in a wide area of Southcentral Alaska and on Chichagof, Baranof and Admiralty Islands in Southeast Alaska. Fifty dollar wolf bounties will be continued in other areas of Southeast Alaska, western, interior and Arctic districts. Biologists argued before the appointive there is no biological justification for the bounty system.

Qiviut Knitting . . . There's a Faster Way
February 1969

Eighteen months is too long for knitting a sweater from musk ox qiviut, even if it does sell for $200. Mrs. Katie Tootkaylook of Mekoryuk on Nunivak Island should now be able to speed up her sweater-making after traveling to Fairbanks for special instruction in the art of carding and spinning the rare musk ox hair. On completion of her second sweater, Mrs. Tootkaylook planned to give spinning lessons to other Nunivak Island women now working with qiviut. Assurance that the craftsmanship of Eskimo skin sewers will be continued comes from Nome where the Rural Alaska Community Action Program is conducting a refresher course in making mukluks, after-ski boots, slippers, sealskin and fur hats, parkas and Eskimo fur dolls. With most of the students finding quick sales for their work, the course is self-sustaining.

Automation Protested
March 1969

Southeast Alaska sportsmen, businessmen, and aviators are protesting a decision by the U.S. Coast Guard to phase out manned light stations in the panhandle, and replace them with automatic unmanned equipment.

Plans, as announced by the USCG, call for the automation and demanning of the following light stations in 1973:

Cape Decision, Cape Spencer, Cape St. Elias, Cape Hinchinbrook and Scotch Cap Lights. Stations which would be phased out and replaced with a number of smaller automatic aids would be Tree Point, October, 1969; Mary Island, March 1969; Five Finger, May 1970; Eldred Rock, May, 1969; and Point Retreat, October, 1970.

In opposing closures, it was pointed out personnel manning the stations more than simply take care of the lights. They make weather reports, operate navigational beacons, relay messages by mariners and in addition to handling surface traffic, the stations also frequently aid small aircraft and some scheduled airline planes.

Kenai Sets the Pace
June 1969

Kenai is setting the pace for the state's economic growth, according to a recent report of the University of Alaska's Institute of Social, Economic and Government Research. Per capita income in the City of Kenai increased 263 percent from 1961 to 1967, jumping from $7,257,777 in 1961 to $36,839,576 in 1967. Total evaluation of real and personal property in the Kenai Peninsula Borough jumped from $180 million eighteen months ago to $245 million at present.

Weather Tantrums
March 1969

December displayed terrifying weather tantrums in two remote Alaskan sites, bringing death to three fishermen in one siege and threatening a military installation in another. Benjamin Golodoff, only survivor of four fishermen aboard the *North Sea*, 105-foot crabber, which was sunk near Cape Sarichef in heavy seas whipped by a gale topping eighty knots, said the ship received a warning before it went down that winds with triple the eighty-knot range could be expected. A veteran North Pacific fisherman, Golodoff said he had never before heard such a weather warning. Dying in the storm were Edwin T. Grabowski, Bellevue, Washington, and Elmer Olsen and Paul Hensen, both of Seattle.

Air Force men stationed at Sparrevohn are still talking about the 115 mph winds which assaulted their camp at the 3,300-foot level with the mercury showing forty below zero. Despite a chill factor of 175 degrees below zero, men and machines never stopped functioning. At the height of the storm, an airman was blown seventy-five yards in the air and 200 feet down the mountainside.

1969

Anchorage Times photo by Alice Puster

A workman at the Sag River well site demonstrates the type of cold weather outfit essential for men laboring to find black gold on the frigid North Slope.

Anchorage Times photo by Alice Puster

Close by the Arctic Ocean, Atlantic Richfield-Humble's new Delta drilling site is seen from the air in mid-day winter twilight. Officials have announced no drilling results will be released until after the state's next competitive bid sale of North Slope acreage next fall.

A Highway of Ice for the North Slope
* * *
Alaska's First Oil Millionaires

February 1969

A 420-mile road that didn't exist in November and will disappear in May is the most exciting thoroughfare on the continent this winter. Extending from Livengood to Stevens Village where it crosses the Yukon, north to Bettles and through Anaktuvuk Pass to Sagwon, the ice road got the go-ahead from Governor Walter J. Hickel in November as thousands of tons of freight for North Slope drilling operations piled up in Fairbanks. First segment from Livengood to the ice bridge over the Yukon was completed by State Department of Highways crews, followed by contractor completion of the remaining 360 miles in January. Alaska's trucking industry expects to move 50,000 tons of freight over the unique road before it is wiped out by spring thaws in April. And while bulldozers and trucks were making transportation history, the North Slope produced its first Alaskan millionaires. Thomas J. Miklautsch, Fairbanks pharmacist and city councilman, and Cliff Burglin, Alaska-born businessman, exchanged a half-interest in their 4800-acre Prudhoe Ibay oil lease for 36,364 shares of General American Oil Co. stock worth more than $2 million. The two Fairbanksans purchased their lease for one dollar an acre in January, 1967.

A Billion-dollar Pipeline May Carry Oil from Alaska's Arctic by 1972

April 1969

The biggest single construction project in Alaska's history—construction of an 800-mile pipeline from the North Slope to a deep water port in Southcentral Alaska at a cost of nearly a billion dollars—has given new dimension to the true size of Alaska's Arctic oil fields. Although most observers believe Valdez will be the southern terminus of the forty-eight-inch pipeline, the three oil companies who announced the overland link will be completed in 1972, indicated a final decision may not be made for six months. Capacity of the $900 million pipeline, one of the longest and most costly in the world, will be half a million barrels of oil daily—more than twice the present production of the Kenai-Cook Inlet field. Subsidiaries of Atlantic Richfield, British Petroleum and Humble Oil and Refining will construct the line which will require more than half a million tons of steel... Several weeks before the tri-company pipeline announcement, Marvin Andresen, a Fairbanks petroleum geologist, predicted the North Slope will be producing 2.5 million barrels of oil per day by 1980. At present tax and royalty rates, state income from such production would be about $1.2 million every twenty-four hours.

Test Drilling off Nome
April 1969

Nome's hopes for a rebirth of gold mining are riding on samples of sea bottom being taken from drill sites on the Bering Sea ice four miles west of Nome. A joint venture of Shell Oil Co., and American Smelting and Refining Co., the drilling is sampling what is believed to be a submerged ancient beachline. Bedrock is reached twenty to sixty feet below the sea bottom. No results have been announced, but panning of the sand and gravel brought up in core samples was continuing in a Nome laboratory in mid-February.

Thanksgiving Day Storm
February 1969

A great many Ketchikan residents didn't have time to give many thanks last Thanksgiving Day. Some found little to be thankful for, except for the fact that there were no fatalities or serious injuries when winds of more than 100 miles an hour roared through the city tearing roofs off homes, toppling three radio towers, and disrupting power. Also badly bruised by the devastating winds was the nearby Indian community of Metlakatla where two homes were blown off their foundations and the community dock was severely damaged.

First Foreign Consulate
April 1969

Ties between Alaska and Japan will be strengthened early in 1970, when Japan establishes a consulate in Anchorage. Approved by the Japanese government and funded early in February by Japan's Diet, the first foreign consulate in the state will be manned by at least two Japanese diplomats assisted by Alaskans. During the period from January 1, 1968, through last October, Alaska's exports to Japan totaled $40.9 million. Japan maintains consulates in Seattle and San Francisco.

Reindeer for Korea
April 1969

A herd of more than 200 Alaskan reindeer are sampling the feed near Cheju City, an island resort off the southern tip of Korea. Purchased from Golovin herders, the animals were airlifted to Anchorage, and then put aboard a chartered Northwest Airlines 707 jet in mid-January for the long ride to Korea. Korean businessmen who hope to import as many as 1,000 reindeer from Alaska, paid $20,000 for the charter flight to counteract reindeer horn tonic smuggling from North Korea. Principal ingredient in a combined general health-aphrodisiac brew prized by well-to-do Koreans, Alaskan reindeer horns have been imported by South Korea since 1962. Horns of the transplanted herd will be harvested in May when they are in the velvet. Established practice is to boil a thin slice of antler in water until it produces a gelatin-like substance to which herbs are added. Taken for fifteen days in spring and fall for maximum benefits, a two-week supply of the tonic costs about $150.

'Copter Tows a Ship
February 1969

Add a new trick to the bag carried by Coast Guard rescue helicopters—towing a ship in trouble. It happened recently in Kizuyak Strait near Kodiak when the *Fairmount,* skippered by Bill Berestoff, lost power and was drifting onto rocks. A Coast Guard helicopter answered the rescue call, dropped a line to the *Fairmont* and towed the vessel more than a mile to safety.

Self-help Welfare
April 1969

An entirely new concept of making welfare payments is being tested at the Indian communities of Tanacross and Dot Lake on the Alaska Highway. Under the self-help program the Bureau of Indian Affairs deposits a sum of money each month in a Tok bank. The village council surveys the community's needs, including older residents who need help or special care, and then assigns unemployed natives to do the required work. Length of work periods will depend on size of the recipient's family. No funds for wages or other expenses will be paid without approval of a board of three members, a secretary and treasurer. Money unused will stay in the bank until there is enough to buy material or equipment that will benefit the entire village. BIA officials hope the new approach will reduce the need for welfare agents, enabling needy natives to explain their needs to their own leaders.

Fires Sweep Timber Lands
March 1969

The worst fire season in eleven years burned 1,090,000 acres of Alaska timber in 1968, according to the Bureau of Land Management. A total of 446 fires did the damage which was second only to 1957 when more than five million acres were destroyed.

1969

Bad Luck for Japanese
May 1969

Registering two violations and one wreck, February wasn't a good month for Japanese vessels fishing Alaskan waters. It started on February 3, when the *Kukuyoski Maru* went aground 210 miles southwest of Adak, and each of twenty-four crewmen were airlifted to safety by an Adak-based Navy helicopter. Three days later, a Japanese fishing vessel sailed into Juneau for refueling, and was apprehended for having thirty-seven illegal halibut in its hold. Ten days later the *Fukuyoshy Maru* docked at Kodiak to get medical aid for two injured crewmen, and was seized by the U.S. Coast Guard for having 220 halibut in violation of the International Convention for High Seas Fisheries of the North Pacific. Both seized ships were released to Japanese authorities for prosecution.

Phone Link for Villages
May 1969

The communications gap between Alaskan villages will soon end, according to Representative John Sackett of Huslia. He reported to the *Tundra Times* that a system of radio-telephone links will tie in with the existing White Alice system. The new program will be activated in the Nome-Kotzebue section with sixteen villages tied into a common network.

First Eskimo Trooper
May 1969

The first Eskimo to serve as an Alaska State Trooper is now on duty in Fairbanks. He is Lorenz Schuerch, born in Nome and raised in Kiana. A graduate of the Troopers' Training Academy at Sitka, Schuerch hopes for a bush assignment after completing his year as a probational rookie.

Boom in Bootleg Booze
April 1969

Kotzebue's boom in bootleg booze was the target of irate citizens at the town's first council meeting of the year. Although they voted for a dry town and disbanded the former municipal liquor store, the citizens complained that liquor is easy to come by. One of the town's three known bootleggers imports six cases of whiskey a week from Nome, and makes a profit of $180 a case, according to one irate resident. State and local police said they needed formal complaints filed to take action.

The Snowmobile... Changing Way of Life in the Arctic
March 1969

N.E. Hampton

Bethel itself is a flat, treeless area in the Kuskokwim delta approximately 400 miles west of Anchorage and about eighty miles from the Bering Sea coast. The problem of trees for Christmas is handled by the Public Health Hospital folks in a modern manner. About twenty snowmobiles with sleds behind took off last year to cut trees several miles up river from the village. Doctors, dentists, nurses, microbiologists, technicians, cooks, maintenance workers and clerical personnel along with members of their families were piled on sleds and snowmobiles along with plenty of warm robes and thermos jugs of hot coffee. They came back with plenty of trees for everyone who wished one—not the large symmetrical trees that one might choose from a big city lot—but Christmas trees just the same.

Snowmobiles have changed the way of life in the Arctic. Many feel it is cheaper to trade in their snowmobiles on a new model each year than to maintain a team of huskies—though some of our Eskimo friends insist the snowmobile lacks the nose to find the way home in a storm.

Anchorage Times photo by Alice Puster

March 1969

Somewhere in this crowd of 309 snowmobile racers entered in the first running of the Midnight Sun 600 race from Anchorage to Fairbanks is Tony Burkel of Roseau, Minn., who finished first with an overall time of 17 hours, 46 minutes. Second was Jim Austin of Anchorage with a time of 17 hours, 52 minutes. Photo above shows mushers at Anchorage starting line for three-day, 600-mile race. Strangest anti-cold outfit (right) developed by motor mushers for the Midnight Sun 600 race was this brainchild of John Daley. He rigged up an auxiliary generator to run a hair dryer modified to serve as a heater and defroster.

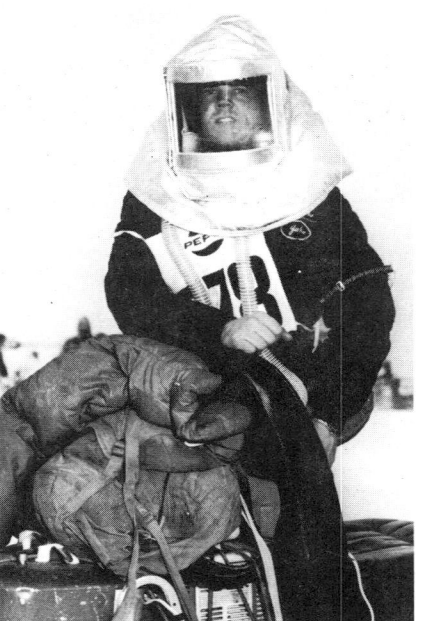

Anchorage Times Photo by Alice Puster

Record Cold Grips the North: Industries Forced to Shut Down; Water Supplies, Shipping Threatened
April 1969

Shove a stick into a can of kerosene, and if it leaves a hole in the congealed fluid you know it's about seventy degrees below zero. That's the test used by crews working on the ice road to the North Slope, and it symbolizes the cold that gave 1969 a frigid start from St. Lawrence Island to Petersburg and Wrangell.

Residents of southeast towns, their reservoirs depleted of fresh water, were taking delivery from city trucks. Skagway, Haines, Douglas and Ketchikan were among those hard hit by water shortage and frozen pipes. Schools were dismissed for varying periods and salt water was pumped into mains to guard against fire. Emergency sanitation kits were provided by the State Disaster Office. Blasted with sixty knot winds at ten below zero, a ship docking at Skagway was described as "looking more like an iceberg than a ship." Villagers at Gambell on St. Lawrence Island had to move out of their homes when high winds threatened to shove ice and water into the town site. Skilak Glacier acted up, sending a rare winter flood down the Kenai River and damaging more than twenty homes in the Soldotna area. The first half of January was the coldest ever recorded in Fairbanks with an average of forty-four below zero for the first fifteen days. Anchorage had the fifth coldest January in fifty-two years. It dropped to sixty-five below at Ross River in the Yukon and for two weeks Dawson City was numbed by a mercury that didn't climb above minus fifty-five degrees. Usually warm Kodiak was enjoying such unusual winter sports as ice-skating and snowmobiling, meanwhile worrying that its dwindling water supply might not survive the start of a frigid February. Kodiak stockmen have asked for emergency help to save cattle floundering in unusual four feet of snow. The intense cold and deep snow in Southcentral Alaska drove moose into populated areas where an average of one a day was killed by motorists. Paratroopers engaged in the military exercise, "Acid Test I" near Fairbanks early in February, braved chill factors of 150 below zero as they jumped into simulated combat. And the policy for school children at Dawson City was "no school when the temperature drops below sixty degrees in the classroom..." The cold siege, which developed into the coldest January in southeast Alaska in more than fifty years, had economic ramifications ranging from curtailed lumber and fishery operations in southeast Alaska to a three-week halt in work on the North Slope road. Ice fog put the brakes on air cargo flights to the North Slope. Cook Inlet's ice was so hard that eight ships, including four large tankers, were damaged in plying the Upper Inlet. One ship showed an ice-made gash twelve feet long and nine inches wide. The *Whitehorse Star* used this headline to speak for most Northerners about the winter of 1969: "We've Been Getting Rotten Cold Weather."

One of the heaviest ice fogs in recent years gave this street sign in Anchorage a brand new image.

Anchorage Times photo by Alice Puster

How Much Oil?
May 1969

How much? This question continues to dominate conversations throughout Alaska, and the various answers will set the pattern for the state's future. Oil executives ask it in pondering the true size of the Arctic Slope's oil reserves. Some geologists have expanded original estimates of five to ten billion barrels of recoverable oil to a high of fifty billion barrels. State legislators and administrators are asking how much they can expect from the sale of nearly three million acres of North Slope acreage next fall. A recent newsletter of the Alaska Education Association stated: "Oil men here in Juneau expect the state to realize about $150 million on this one land sale. Wow!!" The same newsletter speculated that state oil royalties from Prudhoe Bay "could approach $5 million a month" by 1972. Both legislators and oil executives were asking in March just how much, if any, the state's severance tax on oil production should be increased above the present four percent. Preliminary answers to how much oil will be flowing through the 800-mile Arctic Slope-North Pacific pipeline were given legislators by L. K. Chency, Atlantic Richfield executive. He estimated 300,000 barrels a day will be flowing through the line by 1972, increasing to as much as 600,000 barrels by 1975, and a maximum of 1,200,000 barrels by 1980.

Togiak's No-nos
June 1969

Live in the Eskimo village of Togiak on the Bering Sea and you'll have to abide by ten basic rules of conduct adopted by the village council, including these:

"School kids should be home by nine p.m., ages up to eighteen years. If the council catches a school kid after nine p.m., the kids will be required to work the following day. At nine p.m. the curfew bell will ring and the kids should be home by then."

"No movies after 9 p.m. When a council catches on third offense, the movie owner will have to work. No movies on Wednesday, Saturday and Sunday. (Church Service days.)

"There shall be no drinking alcoholic beverages in this village or making anything to make a person drunk.

"If an aircraft brings in a drunk person, the drunk person will be put in the village jail.

"There will be no stealing in the village. If you've borrowed something return it to the owner.

"Tie your dogs, whether they are good or bad. Loose dogs will be killed.

"There shall be no fighting in this village. Don't go into another person's house mad."

Longest Trapline?
June 1969

State game agents have a nomination for the world's longest trapline. They report it extended last winter from Big Delta to the Canadian boundary, a distance of 150 miles, and included 500 traps.

Hockey Fans, Players Shielded from Cold by Plastic Igloo
May 1969

The problem for most skating rinks is keeping the ice cold. In Fairbanks, it's a question of how to keep skaters and spectators warm enough to enjoy ice sports. A variation of the age-old Eskimo igloo has solved the problem for the University of Alaska hockey rink. The structure is a huge 280 by 124 foot vinyl-coated fabric bubble that keeps its shape by air blowers.

The structure, a product of Air-Tech of Clifton, New Jersey, took less than a day to inflate. It can be deflated in four to five hours and can be moved to another location.

In nearby Fairbanks, ice hockey for grade and high school students, figure skating classes, and ice skating for the public in general, is being enjoyed under cover this winter at the Big Dipper. This is the huge old Air Force hangar from Tanacross that was dismantled, transported 200 miles, and reassembled for a youth recreational center through volunteer labor donated by students and townspeople.

Ginny Wood

Keeping the spectators and players warm rather than the ice cold is the major problem in promoting ice hockey in Interior Alaska. The University of Alaska recently solved this problem by erecting a plastic bubble, held erect by air pressure, over its hocky rink.

Barrow to Fairbanks... A First by Snowmobile... Nearly 800 Miles in 18 Days
June 1969

Four men on four snow machines made the first overland snowmobile trip from Barrow to Fairbanks, covering nearly 800 miles in eighteen days. The four, Jack Frantz, Jim Peacock, Luther Leavitt and Bud Stevens are all from Barrow.

Leaving Barrow on March 14, the party headed south on the Ikpikpuk River to its headwaters, then overland to the Colville River, twenty miles west of Umiat. They headed down the Chandler River to its source, then over to Anaktuvuk Pass, where they hit the Winter Haul trail to the oil field, which they followed into Fairbanks.

Temperatures along the way ranged from fifty-five below to fifty above. The first day out they hit a blizzard with forty mile-an-hour winds. They slept out most of the way, hauling food, camping gear, spare parts, and four fifty-five-gallon drums of gas on four ahkio type toboggans. Although one machine broke through the ice on the Colville River and had to be pulled out by the other three, and two toboggans had to be abandoned when they were shattered on rough terrain, no serious difficulty was encountered, according to the men.

Another group of snowmobilers composed of three men and three machines who left the same day from Barrow for Fairbanks were the object of an intensive search when they were overdue for eighteen days. They had holed up in an Eskimo hunter's tent during the storm after they got off course. They returned to Barrow under their own power, having exhausted their supplies.

Ports Vie for Terminus of North Slope Oil Pipeline
May 1969

The prospect of greatly increased port activity as a result of North Slope oil operations has stimulated new rivalry among Southcentral Alaska communities. Valdez is considered by most observers as the most likely site for the still unannounced southern terminus of the 800-mile, $900 million pipeline from the Arctic. Beating the drum for Anchorage as the pipeline terminus is Robert Vroman, chairman of the Matanuska-Susitna Borough. Accessible electricity and railroad right-of-way were cited by Vroman as favorable factors. Valdez retaliated by emphasizing availability of land and its ice and silt-free harbor. The Kenai Peninsula Council of Chambers of Commerce got into the act by urging that the big pipeline terminate on the Kenai Peninsula. Meanwhile, Seward mounted a community-wide campaign aimed at investigating the Alaska Railroad's alleged preference of Whittier as a port.

Oil Spill on Ice-clogged Cook Inlet... Submerged Object Rips Tanker
May 1969

Pollution-endangered Cook Inlet lost a round in early March when the 28,000-ton, 628-foot tanker *Yukon*, carrying crude oil from Drift River terminal, hit a submerged object south of Kalgin Island, dumping thousands of gallons of oil into the ice-clogged waters. The four punctured tanks were cleared of oil at Port Nikiski, and original estimates that more than 200,000 gallons of crude were lost were revised downward. Officials of the Federal Water Pollution Control Administration rated the spill as "major," and causing them "serious concern." Although it had not reached shore, the spill was considered a potential threat to waterfowl, sea otter, clam and crab beds and salmon. Three weeks earlier the State of Alaska filed suits in Superior Court seeking $250,000 in damages for two oil pollution incidents which occurred last fall. A pipeline break which resulted in a 46,200 gallon spill brought a $200,000 action against Shell Oil Co. and Pan American Petroleum Corp., and a 100-barrel spill for which the City of Anchorage and Anchorage Plumbing and Heating Co. were blamed found both defendants in a $50,000 suit filed by Assistant Attorney General Robert L. Hartig.

Anchorage Times photo by Alice Puster

Oil tanker YUKON lies dead in water after hitting a submerged object in Cook Inlet which ripped four tanks and dumped thousands of gallons of crude oil into Cook Inlet.

In the Stone Age 20 Years Ago: Then Came Store, Mission, School, Bush Plane – and Now a Road (of Sorts!)

May 1969

Twenty years ago it was a settlement of Stone Age people living on a caribou-hunting, subsistence economy. There was little contact with the white man's culture. Then came a white trader to set up a store, then missionaries, scientists to "study" the inhabitants, and finally a school, an airstrip, and scheduled "bush" plane service. The village at Anaktuvuk Pass was on its way into the midtwentieth century.

Now, for better or for worse, it has made it all the way. One day in February the hundred-odd Eskimos that make this their permanent home watched the huge tractor of the Alaska Department of Highways clatter past the collection of sod and frame huts, dragging the mobile road camp behind it. Anaktuvuk Village is now connected to the rest of the world by a road.

Of course, it isn't exactly a super highway, this Winter Haul Trail. It has been pushed through in a few months from Livengood at one end of the Elliott Highway, 547 miles north across an ice bridge on the Yukon river, through Bettles, Anuktuvuk Pass and beyond to Sagwon and the new booming oil fields on the Arctic coast. It can only be used when the ground is frozen and the snow below melting temperatures. But thousands of tons of supplies will have been trucked over it before breakup, in the new "stampede" for black gold.

Located on the exact divide of the Brooks Range, Anuktuvuk Pass offers the only land route through the mountain barrier. "Cat trains" (tractors pulling sledges) have followed this route before, but never have trucks and cars been able to cross the Arctic circle from Fairbanks.

Construction crews blazing the Winter Haul Trail have been plagued with overflow ice on the John River north of Bettles, seventy below temperatures, drifting snow, and winds up to seventy miles per hour. Back in Juneau, legislators argue whether or not the Trail legally constitutes a "road" and what authority shall fund and maintain it. Already highway lobbyists urge that the Trail become a permanent all-year-round highway, and other winter trails-cum-highways be built to Kotzebue, Unalakleet, and elsewhere.

The cloverleaf turnoff to Anaktuvuk Village is still a long way off in the future, but the days of dog team transportation will soon be history.

Elaine Mitchell
Aerial view of Winter Haul Trail, taken some twenty-five miles north of Livengood.

Next Big Quake: When?
August 1969

Records indicate that Alaska has magnitude eight or greater earthquakes every ten years comparable in shock force to that of the San Francisco earthquake of 1906. Research which may result in accurate earthquake forecasting is under way at the University of Alaska's Geophysical Institute.

Seismologist Eduard Berg is in charge and he and his associates will implant borehole seismometers thirty feet into bedrock at widely separated locations. They will study the data given off by them and correlate it with other sources of information in an effort to establish a repetitive pattern of crustal deformation and failure, strain and resulting earthquake.

The project will keep the scientists deeply involved for the next several years, and the time may come when they will be able to alert Alaskans and others of earthquake dangers. As of now, however, the scientists decline to predict the day when they will be able to bring this about.

Conservationists Gather for Alaska's First Workshop of Wilderness Problems
May 1969

Some 70 representatives of conservation groups and government agencies gathered in Juneau in mid-February for Alaska's first workshop on wilderness problems.

Initiated by Robert B. Weeden, president of the Alaska Conservation Society, W. Howard Johnson, regional forester, and Bob Howe, superintendent of Glacier Bay National Monument, and arranged by Rich Gordon and other members of the Sierra Club group in Juneau, this historic workshop offered participants a rare opportunity to discuss in detail the provisions of the Wilderness Act of 1964.

The emphasis of the workshop was on the training and energizing of people who have a deep love for wildland values and who will become the leaders in future activities of the organizations of which they are members.

Brought together for these exchanges of facts and ideas were members of the Alaska Conservation Society, the Juneau and Anchorage groups of the Sierra Club, the National Wildlife Federation, the Southeastern Alaska Mountaineering Association, the Yukon Conservation Society, and key personnel from the Forest Service, National Park Service, the Bureau of Sport Fish and Wildlife, the Bureau of Land Management, the Department of Fish and Game and the Division of Lands.

Each of the government agencies presented its policies and practices with regard to the setting aside of wilderness areas for study and possible eventual inclusion in the National Wilderness Preservation System. The U.S. Forest Service unveiled its new publication *Alaska's Wilderness in Perspective*, its first official policy statement on the subject.

John Hall, Assistant executive director of the Wilderness Society, and Brock Evans, Pacific Northwest representative of the Sierra Club, discussed the practical and political aspects of preserving wilderness, citing the long-drawn-out struggle for the North Cascades National Park as an example of citizen initiative and persistence at work to achieve a desired goal.

An Alaskan Wilderness Council was created during the session devoted to specific Alaska wilderness proposals. Composed of representatives of all conservation groups, the council elected Celia Hunter, Alaska Conservation Executive Secretary, as chairman. Immediate goals of the council will be the study of all presently proposed wilderness areas and a statewide inventory of other outstanding sites.

The council will also spearhead action to support the wilderness area selection proposed for inclusion within the National Wilderness Preservation System.

Yukon Territory's First Albino Moose

June 1969

Yukon big game outfitter Alex Van Bibber of Champagne, Yukon, took the territory's first albino moose on October 3, 1968, in the Blanchard River area of southern Yukon, just north of the B.C. border and east of Mile 94 of the Haines Road.

Van Bibber first spotted the cow moose while on a hunt, guiding William Portman of Oklahoma City on September 30. Later he and a group of hunters from Whitehorse; John Gatey, Jr., Francis Chambers, Francis Fromme and Alex's wife, Sue Van Bibber, returned to the area and bagged the albino during the Yukon's open cow moose season, along with two other cows and a light colored bull with a horn spread of sixty-three inches.

The albino was palomino color, with pink eyes, lips and pink hoofs, was about three years old with bad teeth, warts on the neck and near the tail.

Courtesy of Whitehorse Star
Alex Van Bibber, Yukon big game outfitter, with territory's first albino moose.

First on Winter Road
June 1969

The first freight trucks to roll into Sagwon, on March 1, the terminus of the Winter Haul Road to the new oil fields on the North Slope near the Arctic Ocean, arrived twelve days after leaving Fairbanks. The drivers where Terry Zunker, Elwood Mintken, and Scotty Haskins, who logged 166 hours of actual driving time. The ice road to the oil fields had just been completed to Sagwon three days earlier.

Walrus Prefer Russia
August 1969

Bering Sea walrus are showing a clear preference for a certain rocky beach on Soviet-owned Big Diomede Island, according to a recent report of the Alaska Department of Fish and Game. Prepared by Biologist John J. Burns, the report disclosed that by mid-November, 1968, a herd of 2,000 to 3,000 walrus occupied most of the available beach on Big Diomede, where the animals are apparently not hunted by resident Russians. Concentration of walrus on the Soviet side of the international date line did not apparently harm the harvest by Eskimo hunters on Little Diomede. The Americans took 565 walrus in 1968, more than one-third of the total Alaskan kill.

Last Dog Team Patrol
July 1969

Another era of North Country history came to an end this spring when the Royal Canadian Mounted Police completed its last dog team patrol. In the future such patrols will be carried out by airplane or by motor toboggans. Constable Warren Townsend and Special Constable Peter Benjamin arrived back at their starting point, Old Crow, on April 5 after twenty days of rough going, covering 500 miles. The dogs suffered cut feet on the icy trail and one animal had to be destroyed. Temperatures dropped as low as forty-one degrees below zero and one morning the winds were so severe the travelers' tent was torn from its moorings. The patrol had been scheduled from Old Crow to Fort McPherson, then Arctic Red River, Inuvik, Aklavik, and back to Old Crow. Because of the condition of their animals, the constables canceled the Aklavik portion of the journey.

Indian Priorities
July 1969

How will Alaska's 53,000 natives spend the millions they are expected to receive from Congress in final settlement of land claims? If they follow the example of the Thlinget and Haida Indians, who were awarded $6.5 million by the U.S. Court of Claims, the state's Indians, Eskimos and Aleuts will allocate the money for scholarships and assistance for professional and vocational training, special services for the elderly, housing and loan funds, community development funds and either a revolving fund for loans or establishment of a Thlinget-Haida bank. The six-point money utilization program was recently adopted at the annual convention of the Central Council of Thlinget and Haida Indians of Alaska, and has been submitted to Congress for approval. Reelected president of the council was John Borbridge, Jr., of Anchorage. Other officers are Charles Nelson of Ketchikan, Roger Lang of Sitka, Kenneth Leask of Seattle and Richard Kito of Petersburg, all vice-presidents; James Thomas of Yakutat, secretary; and Harvey Marvin of Sitka, treasurer.

Oil Roundup: Big Sale Awaited; Valdez Gets the Nod; A Transport Squeeze
July 1969

Giants of the oil industry have now identified the North Slope acreage they want to bid on in the state's sale of leases for an estimated 700,000 acres in mid-September, and from now until the bids are opened Alaskans concerned with the state's economic future are holding their collective breaths. Confidential nominations for the presumed rich acreage were opened June 16 by officials of the State Division of Lands, and the tracts up for sale will be made known in July.

Estimates of sale income range from a state administration low of $11 million to Senator Vance Phillips' prediction the sale may add $500 million to state coffers, and a more recent forecast by the *Wall Street Journal* which quoted industry sources as predicting it might be history's first billion dollar lease sale . . . Covering operations in a cloak of supersecrecy, fourteen oil companies will have twenty-five drilling rigs working 'round the clock by midsummer to provide clues as to the value of the state-owned acreage which borders Prudhoe Bay on both the north and south . . . And while politicians started polishing schemes for spending the expected September windfall, booming Fairbanks got the word that Atlantic Richfield will construct a 5,000-barrel-a-day refinery near the interior city. Operation is slated for 1972 when the Trans-Alaska Pipeline from the North Slope to tidewater on the Gulf of Alaska is completed. The *Fairbanks News-Miner* claimed Valdez has already been designated as the southern terminus for the 800-mile pipeline, with about 200,000 tons of Japanese-made pipe to be delivered to Valdez, 250,000 tons to Fairbanks and 50,000 tons to Prudhoe Bay. First deliveries are expected in October, according to the *News-Miner* . . . Already responsible for a Far North transportation revolution, the North Slope oil rush is continuing with Fairbanks International Airport the focal point and Anchorage International and Whitehorse airports serving as satellites. Helicopter buffs were bug-eyed in May as Rowan Drilling Co. flew in two Sikorsky S-64E helicopters for North Slope work. Costing $2.2 million each, the air cranes can haul ten-ton loads. Governor Keith Miller indicated he will ask for an initial $6 million to establish a rail link into the Arctic. So much sea traffic is expected along the Arctic Coast that the Weather Bureau is speeding establishment of a special forecast service for the icy sea lanes. Even the Communications Satellite Corp. (COMSAT) was told its services may possibly be required in the communications-shy vastness of the busy Arctic . . . A new dimension was provided for measuring the massive $900 million pipeline when federal and state power experts reported it would require 620,000 kilowatts. The entire state's present capacity is 680,000 kw . . . The speculative dreams spawned by the North Slope were refueled in May as a California firm began an aeromagnetic survey of 300,000 square miles of the Bering Sea's continental shelf for fifteen major oil companies. Completing oil's encirclement of the state was drilling activity on the Alaska Peninsula and announcement by Tenneco Oil Co. that it will soon drill an offshore well three miles east of Middleton Island in the Gulf of Alaska . . . In proposing a task force to look after nature's interests on the North Slope, Interior Secretary Walter J. Hickel commented, "We often consider much of the north country a preserved wilderness, but in fact much of it is in jeopardy." The Alaska Oil and Gas Association promised it would cooperate with all agencies to protect the North Slope's environment, and various conservation groups are demanding more men and money to help the Arctic survive.

Alaska Sportsman

Biggest birds migrating north to Alaska in April were these giant flying cranes. Counterparts of similar helicopters used in Vietnam, the huge S-64E Sikorsky aircraft are the first in commercial use. Shown here at Anchorage's Merrill Field before moving to the North Slope oil fields and workhorse assignments, the two machines cost $2.2 million each and are owned by Rowan Air Cranes, a subsidiary of Rowan Drilling Co. Nearly 90 feet long, with a rotor diameter of 72 feet, the air cranes cruise at 130 miles an hour and can lift 20,000 pounds.

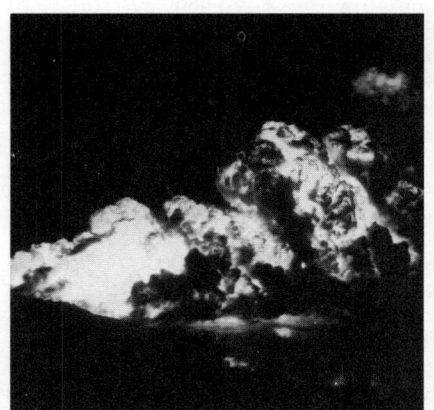

This conflagration was produced during testing of the Sag River No. 1 oil well on the North Slope late in 1968. Oilmen report some tests are mild and controlled affairs, but those involving gas often include such spectacular displays. Owned by Atlantic Richfield and Humble Oil, the Sag River No. 1 well was a key in defining the extent of the vast Prudhoe Bay oil field.

MacKenzie River Bush Flying Service Has Indian Owner, Eskimo Pilot
June 1969

Reindeer Air Service with headquarters in Inuvik, NWT, on the Mackenzie River fifty miles south of the Arctic Ocean, is not unique as far as northern bush flying operations go—except for one fact. Reindeer Air Service is owned and operated by Fred Carmicheal, an Indian; his chief pilot is Tommy Gordon, an Eskimo.

Inuvik, built from scratch by the Canadian government about twelve years ago to replace Aklavik, has become a center for government administration agencies, air and waterway transportation, and education for primary and secondary schooling of natives in the District of Mackenzie. Although two-thirds of the 3,000 inhabitants are Indian or Eskimo, most commercial enterprises are operated by white men. This makes Reindeer Air Service unique.

Carmicheal, who has fifteen years of flying experience behind him at the age of thirty-three, chose the name of his flying service because he started out as a reindeer herder in that region. His company owns two twin-engine Beechcrafts, a Cessna 185, and three Cessna 180's. Soon he will add an Otter for hauling freight.

Shrimp in Spotlight
June 1969

Shrimp have moved into the spotlight once held exclusively by king crab as Kodiak's glamour seafood. Figures released by the Bureau of Commercial Fisheries show 1968 landings of shrimp at Kodiak added up to 34,497,491 pounds compared to 21,050,009 pounds of king crab. Now the principal shrimp port on the Pacific Coast, Kodiak's 1968 shrimp production showed an increase of more than 130 percent over 1967. Latest BCF statistics indicate 115 millions pounds of fisheries products were landed at Kodiak in 1968, making it one of the nation's top fishing ports.

Who Filed First? Lie Detectors Needed
April 1969

Lie detectors may be needed to determine exactly who filed the first claims on potentially rich copper ground along the Alaska Highway south of Whitehorse. Close to the New Imperial Copper Mine property, the land was released by the Defense Department and opened for staking at midnight on January 1. Open acreage indicated space for sixty to seventy claims, but 146 have been filed in the Whitehorse office of Blake Baxter, mining recorder. One staking party of twenty-six men claim to have driven stakes at 12:001—one second after midnight on January 1. Other filings show stakes driven at one minute after midnight in thirty below zero weather. Baxter said it may take several months to decide conflicts. Some claim seekers have suggested that use of lie detectors might help solve the problem.

Musk Ox Back Home
July 1969

Forty-eight musk ox made the long voyage back to the homes of their ancestors in April when the shaggy animals were flown from overpopulated Nunivak Island to Barter Island. Musk ox disappeared from the area now included in the Arctic National Wildlife Range more than 100 years ago. Meanwhile, approval of a special fall hunt by the Department of Fish and Game Board to thin the 750 musk ox remaining on Nunivak must hurdle the opposition of Interior Secretary Walter J. Hickel before rifles can be readied.

August 1969
Wildlife artist Bill Berry shows his wife, Liz, and Celia Hunter, Executive Secretary of the Alaska Conservation Society one of the panels he and George West of the Institute of Arctic Biology painted as a start for a Nature Center planned for what was once Creamer's Dairy near Fairbanks. The Conservation Society sparked a campaign for donations to save the farm from subdivision when it went out of business two years ago.

Ginny Wood

'We're Thankful'... Seven Bowhead Whales for Barrow
August 1969

"Quweasukpuktugut," which means, "We are very thankful" in Eskimo was the headline used by the *Tundra Times* to report a harvest of seven bowhead whales by Barrow whalers. The joy of the whaling harvest was described by Mrs. Joe Slwooko of Gambell on St. Lawrence Island, correspondent for the *Nome Nugget*: "This time it is Stanley Oogevaseuk's boat, his son, Alex, is a striker. He did just the right way in handling the whaling. Oh, it was a great catch he did for the spring! Everyone was happy now. The people will be coming with their snow machines from Savoonga... Now we can have a chance to give them a gift, every one likes muktuk. But the men and boys are busy cutting up the whale. When it is all cut up in pieces and laid on the icy shore, the older men will give advices for dividing. It is divided among all the boats and so every one has a share. And there is to be sure a share for the women of the captain's tribe, called his 'sisters.' So it always is a great pride for a woman of the captain's tribe to receive a share of baleen and tail muktuk. It is another way of the tradition we still have right along with our modern ways."

Heroism Medals for Two in Angoon
August 1969

Department of Public Safety Commendations for Meritorious Service have been awarded to two residents of Angoon, a southeastern Alaska Indian village. State Fire Marshal Wallace Dawson made presentations honoring Joseph W. Johnson, Sr. and George B. Johnson, Sr.

The citation for Joseph Johnson reads, "At 5:30 a.m. of March 1st, 1969, the Harold Demmert residence was in flames and the Village of Angoon in danger of being completely destroyed by fire. Mr. Johnson, by his timely actions, alerted the village, a bucket brigade was formed, and the village of Angoon was saved."

George Johnson's citation states: "Mr. Johnson, without regard to his personal safety, saved the lives of the six members of the Harold Demmert family when their home was completely destroyed by fire..."

Alaska-sized Cabbage!... 72 Pounds
January 1969

Max Sherrod won $25 at the 1941 Matanuska Valley Fair for a record 36-pound cabbage. Proof that Valley vegetables are getting bigger and better came in September when Sherrod harvested the 72-pound giant shown here, a new world's record. His best previous head weighed 70 pounds. Palmer's vegetable king is shown holding a 53-pound turnip, also a new record. Sherrod's successful seed was O.S. Cross, a new hybrid developed by a Japanese plant breeder.

Frontiersman Photo

Flier at 76
June 1969

Still licensed to fly at seventy-six, Vern Bookwalter recently marked his fiftieth year as a pilot. He does more mining now than flying, but he took and passed his airman's physical examination just to keep his ticket current.

Bookwalter learned to fly World War I Jennies and flew the first air mail between Seattle and San Francisco in 1926. He is one of the few pilots still alive who belongs to the OX5 Club. Last winter he worked for Munz Northern Airlines in Nome, but this summer he is back on the creeks prospecting for gold.

Logs for Progress
August 1969

Logs are the key to building activities going on this summer in three Indian communities ranging from Klukwan north of Haines to Mentasta on the Glenn Highway and Minto on the Tanana River. Federal poverty program funds are being used to construct an authentic tribal house and community hall at Klukwan as a focal point for preserving Thlinget Indian culture.

When the Mentasta restoration project is completed, tourists traveling the Glenn Highway will see log housing typical of early Indian construction. A log store will display bark utensils, fish and meat drying racks and art and craft products.

Minto villagers, meanwhile, are clearing land and cutting logs for their new community which will be located high above the Tanana's waters which often flooded the old village. The Bureau of Indian Affairs and Alaska State Housing Authority are assisting in building the new Minto which will be ready for occupancy by the autumn of 1970.

Honor for Thlinget
July 1969

Rare recognition came to Alaska in April when Archie W. Demmert, sixth grade teacher at Sitka and a member of the Raven Clan of the Thlinget Indians, was named to the National Teacher of the Year Honor Roll. A grandfather and widower, Demmert was one of five finalists in the competition conducted by the Council of Chief State School Officers and *Look* Magazine. Demmert was the first Indian finalist in the seventeen-year-history of the national competition. "No Alaskan has added more to the quality and length of schooling among natives than this gentle, iron man," said the citation to Demmert.

Fisheries Outrank Oil
August 1969

Oil hogged the headlines, but it was Alaska's commercial fisheries that rated first among the state's industries in 1968. Total value of Alaska's commercial fishery products last year was a record $217.5 million, a cool $36.5 million above the value of oil production for the same period.

Flying on Thin Ice...

Anchorage Daily News photo by Vern Coryell

...Saved by a 'Copter

Alaska Sportsman Photo

July 1969

A good weather forecaster is not necessarily a good judge of ice strength, as Dave Evanson of the Anchorage weather forecast office proved in late April. Taking off from Campbell Lake on skis, Evanson decided to make a practice landing on Lake Spenard. As these photos show, the plane settled snugly into the ice until rescued by a friendly helicopter.

New Life for Plan to Move the Capital
September 1969

Twice buried by voters, the proposal to move Alaska's capital has been revived with appointment of a Capitol Site Review Committee by Governor Keith Miller. Claiming to see rumblings of a move to push the capital out of Juneau, Miller named a nine-man group, dominated by editors and publishers, to conduct hearings on the issue in Juneau, Anchorage, Fairbanks and Nome. The Kenai Chamber of Commerce fanned the embers by circulating an exploratory letter which stated, "It is essential that the capital be accessible by road and air and that it be closer to the people." By mid-July petitions for a new capital were being circulated which asked that it be located on a site accessible by road and rail but not in Anchorage or Fairbanks.

Last Holdout Loses to Parking Meters
August 1969

The last holdout against parking meters in the Far North has fallen to the coin-eating machines. Yellowknife, capital of the Northwest Territories, has purchased 125 meters. Whitehorse, capital of the Yukon, fought a losing battle against the meters in 1968. Alaska's capital city of Juneau, and Fairbanks, Ketchikan and Anchorage installed meters many years ago.

More Coal than Oil
July 1969

OIL is the magic word on the Arctic Slope these days, but long after the last drop of black gold has been extracted from north of the Brooks Range it will be coal that captures the world's attention. The May bulletin of the State Division of Mines and Geology reports that coal-bearing rocks cover 58,000 square miles north of the Brooks Range and west of the Itkillik River and contain an estimated 100 billion short tons of coal. On the basis of the consumption of coal in the U.S., the North Slope could meet the entire nation's coal needs for 100 years.

Dormitory Program for Native Students
July 1969

When new 200-bed dormitories for native students are constructed at Fairbanks, Sitka and Bethel under a new education concept of the Bureau of Indian Affairs, they can look to trailblazing Tok High School for guidance. Without fanfare, the state-operated school at Tok began Alaska's first dormitory program for outlying students last fall. Surplus ACS housing in the interior town was converted to dormitories, and the first such program ended in May with thirteen boys and nine girls completing a school year of dormitory living. Abandoning the idea of rebuilding Mt. Edgecumbe School, the BIA will now spend $9.6 million in constructing dormitories and expanding schools at Kotzebue and Barrow. Democratic Representative Julia Butler Hansen of Washington commented on the new approach to native education: "Children from remote areas will be able to live in dormitories near public schools but be close enough to their homes so they can be with their families on weekends."

Old Crow's New School
August 1969

Old Crow residents are busy hauling logs needed to rebuild the Yukon's farthest north school which was destroyed by fire in April. While work continues on the four-classroom structure slated for completion in November, Old Crow students are attending school in temporary classrooms. Because they join their parents in muskrat harvesting on Old Crow flats each spring, pupils have summer vacation from April 15 until July 2.

Now It's Official! Rebirth for Town Devastated by '64 Quake
August 1969

Certain to become a collector's item, this front page of the mimeographed *Valdez Breeze* shouted the announcement by Governor Keith H. Miller that means rebirth for the old Prince William Sound town virtually destroyed by the 1964 earthquake. First pipe for the 800-mile, forty-eight-inch pipe line which will pour North Slope oil across Alaska and into Valdez is expected this fall from Japan. Rated the largest single private construction project in the nation's history, the $900 million pipe line will run from Prudhoe Bay to Bettles, cross the Yukon River between Rampart and Stevens Village, pass within a few miles of

Girl Survives Crash
September 1969

Only survivor of a plane crash near Wrangell that presumably killed her parents is Lorna Lyman, eleven, Wrangell youngster who swam ashore near Ideal Cove and spent a night alone after the four-place plane piloted by her parents, Mr. and Mrs. Dean Lyman, crashed in thirty-five feet of water. "She was a real plucky little kid," said Stu Nielsen, crab fisherman who spotted Lorna on the beach the day after the accident. "The gnats, mosquitoes and white socks were awful. They'd almost eaten that little girl," Nielsen told the *Petersburg Press*.

Attacks by Eagle, Wolf
August 1969

Attacks by a golden eagle and a wolf inflicted injuries on young northerners in the Yukon in May. Patricia Ann Glowa, four, of Watson Lake, was treated in Whitehorse and Edmonton for severe bite wounds from a wolf kept at Watson Lake for breeding. A few weeks later ten-month-old Shawn Lewis of Anchorage was parked with his parents, Mr. and Mrs. Jerry Lewis of Anchorage, near Takhini Bridge north of Whitehorse, when a golden eagle swooped down and scratched his face. Young Shawn was released from Whitehorse General Hospital after being treated for superficial cuts. The eagle was killed by the boy's father and turned over to the RCMP.

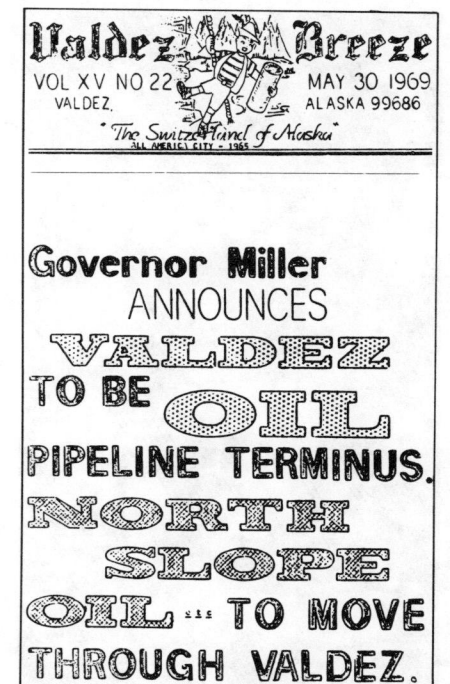

Fairbanks and Big Delta and border the Richardson Highway to Valdez. More than 1500 men will work to get the pipe line "on stream" by 1972, when it will move up to 500,000 barrels of oil a day into huge storage tanks near Valdez. Berths for three super tankers will be constructed adjacent to the storage terminal.

Unspoiled Talkeetna?
August 1969

"Unspoiled by tourist traffic," says the 1969 MILEPOST in describing the colorful and quaint village of Talkeetna, 118 miles north of Anchorage on the new Anchorage-Fairbanks Highway. But the old mining town will have to display rare skill to keep its special character. Work is now under way on a $3.6 million Communications Satellite (COMSAT) station two and one-half miles northeast of Talkeetna that will make it the nerve center of a sophisticated network extending from Canada and Alaska to Australia. Completion of the station which will employ up to thirty persons is scheduled for September 30, 1970. The 100-foot antenna to be erected in the once sleepy village of ninety persons will maintain contact with a satellite floating high over the Pacific Ocean. Traffic handled through Talkeetna will flow to Anchorage through a microwave link.

Meat from Outside
April 1969

Of the meat consumed in Alaska ninety-eight percent is shipped in from Outside, according to the Central Alaska Stockmen's Association. It is estimated between forty and fifty million pounds of meat valued at thirty to forty million dollars is imported annually. The stockmen are seeking legislative assistance to increase their share of Alaska's meat market.

'Alaska Will Never Be the Same Again'! International Oil Giants Pay $900 Million for Drilling Rights in Prudhoe Bay Area

November 1969

"Alaska will never be the same again," predicted Governor Keith H. Miller as he addressed a packed house in Anchorage's Sydney Laurence Auditorium on September 10, minutes before Alaska's twenty-third oil lease sale got underway. Seven hours later the world knew the governor was an accurate forecaster as international oil giants paid $900,220,590.21 in bonus money for the right to drill on 450,858 acres of tundra and sea bottom extending from the Colville Delta to the Canning River country. In the span of a single day, the state had increased its treasury balance more than 10 times. Figured on a per capita basis, the record-breaking sale netted each Alaskan $3,169. In addition to topping the previous record sale of offshore land near Santa Barbara by nearly $300 million, the Alaska sale saw a record bid of $72,113,000 by a combine of Amerada-Hess, Getty, Marathon, Placid and the H. L. Hunt interests for a 2,560 acre tract. The no-limit poker players paid an average of $28,233 per acre for the presumably oil rich tract. Following nearly a year of hectic and super-secret seismic work and exploratory drilling, the sale indicated major oil companies have either found new fields or the Prudhoe Bay discovery field extends more than 100 miles from east to west. While Bank of America officials were preparing to speed the state's oil checks to banks across the nation for cashing and later purchasing of federal securities, Governor Miller commented: "It's close enough to a billion dollars that we can all feel very happy." Commissioner of Natural Resources Tom Kelly accepted a total of 164 high bids for a total of $900,041,604.41. Fifteen bids were rejected.

ALASKA magazine photo by Dick Montague

Here's how it looked backstage at the Sydney Laurence Auditorium as State Division of Lands workers and Bank of America officials tallied lease bids and accompanying checks that brought more than 100 times the purchase price paid Russia in 1867.

ALASKA magazine photo by Dick Montague

As this sign shows, not every Alaskan was happy with the state's big oil lease sale. This man was among several who protested with signs near sale site.

Chances Are Increasing for Survival of Alaska's Valued Wilderness Areas
November 1969

Bits and pieces of wilderness throughout Alaska are winning both recognition and a chance at survival. Hearings will be held in Anchorage on November 13 concerning designation of two small islands in Kotzebue Sound and a larger island in the Aleutians as national wilderness areas. Puffin and Chamisso Islands in Kotzebue Sound support extensive colonies of horned and tufted puffins, Pacific kittiwakes and murres. Total size of the proposed Simeonof wilderness refuge is 25,270 acres, which includes more than 14,000 acres of submerged tidal land. It is home for sea otter, hair seal and 55 species of birds... Named as head of a Bureau of Outdoor Recreation group to survey the potential of establishing a parkway in now inaccessible Chitina Valley located 50 miles northeast of Palmer, former Senator Ernest Gruening expects to present recommendations to Secretary of Interior Walter J. Hickel by mid-November. Gruening describes the valley as "the most magnificent under the American flag."... Officials of the National Parks Service of Canada and the U.S. National Park Service joined in a three-day hike over the Chilkoot Trail from Skagway to Bennett. Purpose of the late summer trip was to plan for joint development of the famed route to the Klondike... Forest Service plans for a 15-mile road up Petersburg Creek were discussed at a recent hearing in Petersburg. Said the *Petersburg Press* of the project, "The road has drawn almost as much fire as Custer did from Sitting Bull."

First Woman Trooper
November 1969

Frances Jean Howard, 25, a tall and attractive brunette, has been named Alaska's first woman state trooper. A native of Grants Pass, Oregon, Miss Howard began working for the Department of Public Safety in February, 1968, in Juneau as a clerk typist. She was promoted to radio dispatcher last July and has been administering driver's tests and serving court papers. After attending the Alaska State Trooper Academy at Sitka, her duties are expected to include special work with juveniles and women prisoners.

Communications Revolution in Alaska
September 1969

A communications revolution is underway in Alaska with RCA Global Communications, Inc., in the process of taking over the Alaska Communications System on a bid of $28.4 million. RCA backed up its bid with a promise to spend $27,683,000 on upgrading the statewide system in three years after the transfer is completed in 1970. Establishment of the new system will cut a three-minute day call from Anchorage to New York from the present $7 to $4.75. A similar call from Juneau to Seattle will drop from $3.50 to $2.70 under the RCA toll table. The successful purchaser of the historic ACS hopes to extend phone service to 124 Alaska communities which now have poor or no communications. Statewide direct dialing is expected by 1971. While RCA won the right to run the state's civilian phone network, it lost its present contract to operate the White Alice and BMEWS systems for the Department of Defense. New operator will be Federal Electric Corp., Paramus, New Jersey, with total bids of $86,172,000 for the three year contracts. Topping off the communications revolution, about half of Alaska saw the moon landing of Apollo 11 astronauts through an elaborate Department of Defense-sponsored live telecast on three Anchorage television stations.

Ready for the Big Blast on Amchitka Island
September 1969

Despite opposition of some Alaskans, including former Governor William Egan, the Atomic Energy Commission is ready to detonate a one and two-tenths megaton nuclear device on Amchitka Island in the Aleutians in late September or October. Appearing in appeasing sessions at Juneau, Anchorage, Fairbanks and Kodiak, a team of top AEC officials headed by Commissioner Frank Castigliola explained the fall test is a calibration shot to determine whether the Amchitka site is ready for bigger blasts in the future. The explosion will be triggered at a depth of 4,000 feet in Amchitka's rock. Dismissing fears that the test might produce an earthquake or tidal wave, Commissioner Castigliola told Alaskans he'll be on the island when the test is fired. The AEC team reported that prior to the autumn explosion an additional 250 to 300 sea otter will be moved from Amchitka waters. Meanwhile, Senator Ted Stevens has suggested atomic power might be used to blast a new harbor on Alaska's Arctic coast.

'Fore!'... New Nine-Hole Golf Course for Anchorage
September 1969

The unfamiliar shout of, "Fore!" began ringing across the slopes of Russian Jack Springs in Anchorage in August, as the city's new nine-hole golf course came alive. Synthetic greens and tees made of Astro-Turf are the key to the new course. Laid down like a carpet, the covering known as "Astro-Turf" cost $116,000. Without a municipal golf course since 1966, Anchorage duffers pay $3 a round, $1.50 after 6 p.m. Single season tickets are $150, with family tickets $200.

Boat Hits Iceberg; Three Die
November 1969

Three persons died when the fishing boat *Monroe* from Petersburg struck an iceberg and sank August 29 near Sumdum Glacier, 40 miles south of Juneau and about 67 miles north of Petersburg. The skipper of the boat, Tom Stewart, and one passenger, Mrs. Kelly Hofstad, were rescued by the Coast Guard after spending four hours on a makeshift raft in the 47-degree water. With them was the body of Andrew Edward Hofstad, 21, husband of Kelly. Hofstad was a fishing boat captain and a member of a long-time Petersburg family. The Coast Guard also found the bodies of Kathleen Ann Hogan, 22, of Pleasant Hills, California, who was employed as a waitress at a Petersburg restaurant, and Joseph Peter Baines, 30, a crewman on the *Monroe*.

A Parched Alaska
September 1969

Ice lenses melted in the permafrost beneath the Elliott Highway leaving depressions in the road. Water was so low in Interior Alaska rivers that river boats had difficulty delivering freight. Hundreds of wells went dry in Southcentral Alaska and the town of Palmer was without water for thirteen hours in late June. Small creeks dried up in the Cook Inlet area. The Department of Agriculture reported crops were showing "stress and damage." It was all part of the parched picture of Alaska in midsummer of 1969. Even Petersburg and Wrangell, in the heart of Southeastern Alaska's rain forest, were so rain-shy in late June that restrictions were placed on water until early July showers came to the rescue. Record June temperatures were registered throughout Alaska and the Yukon and the precipitation record for Anchorage from July 1, 1968, to June 30, 1969, was a scant 8.38 inches, lowest in fifty-three years of record-keeping.

Weather Vagaries in the Largest State
October 1969

Headlines in widely separated Alaska newspapers on August 5 magnified the vagaries of the largest state's paradoxical weather. While forest fires were burning above the Arctic Circle, "FAIRBANKS GIRDS ITSELF FOR POSSIBLE NEW FLOOD," was the headline used by *Jessen's Daily* to report an early August surge of the same Chena River which nearly drowned the city in 1967. Although the river stopped rising just below flood stage, the threat caused some stores to build sandbag dikes and a few low-lying homes were evacuated. "FOREST FIRE HITS KENAI," was the headline of the *Cheechako News* on August 5 as flames from one fire were stopped in the city limits and more than 4,000 acres were burned in a second fire in the Swanson River area. "RECORD RAINFALL IN JUNEAU," told *Ketchikan Daily News* readers their sister city to the north had been washed with 13.43 inches of rain in July, wettest July on record in the capital city.

World's Tallest Authentic Totem Pole
November 1969

Department of Economic Development photo by Fred Belcher

Thlinget Indians from Kake (left of totem) and Chilkat Dancers from Port Chilkoot pose with world's tallest totem pole at its dedication August 22 in Port Chilkoot. The 132½-foot long, red cedar totem was commissioned by the town of Kake and will be exhibited at Expo 70 in Japan before permanent erection in the Southeastern Alaska town.

The world's tallest authentic totem pole, a 132½-foot shaft of Alaskan red cedar, was dedicated August 22 at Port Chilkoot to all Indians of Southeastern Alaska. The totem will be exhibited at Expo 70 in Osaka, Japan, and will be erected on a bluff at a tourist park in Kake, a town of 550 persons on Kupreanof Island. It will be the first totem in Kake since 1926 when missionaries made the natives burn theirs because of the totems' supposedly pagan symbolism.

Kake contracted with Alaskan Indian Arts Inc. in Port Chilkoot to carve the giant totem for $10,000. Carl Heinmiller, director of the non-profit corporation, and four other carvers designed 14 major crests and figures, representing the various Indian clans. The totem is topped by a giant eagle and includes legendary carvings of a half man, half sockeye salmon figure and the figure of an Indian ripping a sea lion in half.

The Kake totem is more than 10 feet taller than the former record holder in Victoria, B.C. It will be taken to Japan on a lumber ship.

Pulp, Lumber Will Be Sold to Japan... Big U.S. Firm Still Hasn't Selected Mill Site
September 1969

U.S. Plywood-Champion Papers, Inc., in announcing recently a $600 million contract for the sale of Alaska pulp and lumber to Japanese interests, pledged that specific measures would be taken to insure forest and wildlife conservation and environmental control over manufacturing operations. The contract was announced by Gerald A. Jackson, president-Alaska Division. He said the agreement calls for sale to Tokyo-based Kanzaki Paper Manufacturing Company, Ltd., of approximately $40 million worth of unbleached pulp and lumber annually for a period of fifteen years.

Site for U.S. Plywood-Champion's $75 million Alaska mill complex has yet to be announced. Said Jackson, "We are forming an advisory committee of conservation experts to assist us in every phase of our planning for mill design and operation as well as for our forest operations and timber harvesting. The team will be composed of well-known scientists and leaders in the fields of fish and wildlife, oceanography, multiple use, and reforestation."

Alaska Ranks Third
September 1969

Alaska trails Connecticut and New York in per capita income, but is next in the procession, according to Frank Murkowski, commissioner of economic development. He reported the state's per capita income totaled $4,124 in 1968, with a growth rate of nine and three-tenths percent.

Eva McGown: 'Alaska's Only Living Leprechaun'
September 1969

On the evening of June 24 a birthday party was held on the Steamer *Nenana* at Alaskaland for "Alaska's only living leprechaun," better known as Eva McGown... and to hundreds of visitors and Fairbanksans merely as "Eva." Mrs. McGown reached Fairbanks via stagecoach from Chitina in February of 1914, only a few weeks removed from the "auld sod."... On the day of her arrival she was married to Arthur McGown, then a partner in the Model Cafe. Although a widow for many years she has continued to make the All-America City her home and since early in the war years has been its official greeter and hostess. The city fathers, in a singular gesture of appreciation, set aside the entire week as Eva McGown Week. At the party Mrs. McGown admitted to being a youthful eighty-six.

Windblown Trees
September 1969

The staggering damage that can be done to forests by a windstorm was pinpointed recently by the U.S. Forest Service. It reported that in the Wrangell Ranger District alone twenty-five million board feet of timber were blown down by a storm last Thanksgiving Day. Greatest damage was recorded on Zarembo, Etolin and Shrubby Islands.

1969

Youngsters Strike Gold
September 1969

Eldorado! Bonanza! These old gold words echoed along Nome's historic waterfront in June and July as the city's youngsters followed in the wake of crews removing ancient boardwalks to mine for lost coins. And the enterprising stampeders dug hundreds of dollars in silver coins and gold pieces from the rich ground exposed by the dismantling crews. A diamond ring worth $200, a $20 gold piece, dollars, half dollars and other assorted coins were uncovered by the pint-size miners. "There hasn't been so much excitement since 1898," said the *Nome Nugget* in reporting on the gold rush that will end as concrete sidewalks replace Front Street's wooden walkways.

December 1969

The state is about to move in on us and surface some of our streets and put down concrete sidewalks, curbs and gutters. They call this progress... It seems to me that if we here in Nome want to wade through mud sometimes and get dust blown in our eyes at other times, it should be our own damned business...

—Albro Gregory, Editor
NOME NUGGET

Anchorage Growth
November 1969

The 1989 population of Greater Anchorage will be 258,000, according to a recent prediction by the trends and projection committee of Operation Breakthrough. The most recent census gives Greater Anchorage a population of 113,000. Operation Breakthrough officials described the forecast as "quite conservative."

Yukon's Klondike
December 1969

Canadians other than Yukoners who use the term "Klondike" in advertising or promotion are liable for prosecution. The Registrar of Trade Marks has been given notice that anyone using the term "Klondike" must get permission of the territorial government. Because it is not retroactive, the new move will not stop Edmonton from continuing use of its "Klondike Days" celebration.

Lighthouse 'Demanned'
July 1969

Mary Island Light Station, some twenty miles south of Ketchikan, has been decommissioned by the U.S. Coast Guard as a manned facility. Automated lighthouse and foghorn equipment, however, has been installed at the station as a continuing service to mariners. Decommissioning ceremonies took place at the historic facility (created in 1902 by the now defunct Lighthouse Service), on April 15. The USCG is automating a number of Alaska stations for economy reasons. Next to be demanned in the Ketchikan area will be Guard Island.

Unified Government
December 1969

Voters in the City of Anchorage and Greater Anchorage Area Borough used ballots in October to start the process of unifying the two local governments now concerned with 40 percent of Alaska's population into a single governing body. With both city and borough residents approving the concept of unification, the voters also elected an 11-member charter commission which has the mission of producing a charter document acceptable to 120,000 residents of Greater Anchorage. If all goes well, the state's largest metropolitan area could have a single government by 1972.

Summer on the Icefield... 17 Feet of Snow
December 1969

Despite severe weather conditions, the Juneau Icefield Research Program completed another season in the icefields between Juneau and Atlin, B.C., last September. "It has been the most unusual summer in my 25 to 30 years experience up here," said Dr. Maynard Miller, director of the program. "From mid-June to September 10 we had 17 feet of snow above the 5,000-foot level."

The Summer Institute of Glaciological and Arctic Sciences of Michigan State University was organized in 1960, and since then has been held each summer to provide academic and field training for potential polar and mountain scientists.

This year 40 men from all parts of Canada, the United States, Japan, Czechoslovakia and Sweden studied the movement of glaciers straddling the Alaska-Canada border, and the effects of glaciers in the Atlin area.

A group of 16 walked across the icecap last summer, making a complete traverse of about 100 miles. They went from sea level to 7,200 feet, visiting 12 of the institute's camps in their eight-week trip. It was the third time Miller had crossed the icefield. Last year he made the trip with a group of 12, and in 1952 he and two others crossed the cap.

Old Days, Old Ways
November 1969

The old days and the old ways were relived recently in the Northwest Territories when 70 residents of Rae began a long trek by canoe into the edge of the Barren Lands in search of caribou. The hunt was financed by the Canadian Department of Welfare to assist Rae residents in getting a winter meat supply. The animals were boned and the meat dried before the return home via 79 portages.

Women at Work
December 1969

Forty percent of Alaska's salaried workers are women, according to the U.S. Department of Labor. And of the working women, forty percent are wives and mothers, compared to a national average of thirty-three percent. Greater Anchorage's work force of 32,935 in 1968 included 12,500 women. Juneau's labor force of 5,600 included 920 working mothers.

Alaska Sportsman
September 1969
Shown here as she competed in the U.S. Junior National Ski Championships at Mt. Alyeska last March, Barbara Britch, seventeen, of Anchorage, is the first girl to win the United States Ski Association's Finlandia Trophy. A June graduate of Anchorage's West High School, Barbara is a former U.S. Junior National Cross Country Champion.

Spearfishing – It's Legal
December 1969

A straight-shooting spear arm is a new requirement for winter anglers in Tanana River drainage. The first season for legal spearing of whitefish on all tributaries of the Tanana River above the Kantishna confluence began October 1 and continues through March 31. Holders of a current sport fishing license can spear all species of whitefish except sheefish, according to George Van Wyhe of the Department of Fish and Game. There are no size or bag limits nor spear size limitations for the new way of fishing.

Delay for Snettisham
December 1969

The $50 million Snettisham hydroelectric project near Juneau was temporarily shut down late in September. Work stopped on the project after the U.S. Army Corps of Engineers ran out of funds to let bids for additional contracts. Some $7 million has already been spent.

Plans originally called for Snettisham to begin providing power to the Juneau area by December of 1972. However, Army Corps officials have expressed concern that it may be mid-1973 before power is on the line due to the lack of funds. The Johnson administration originally budgeted $8.6 million for the project this fiscal year. The Nixon administration budget slashed the allotment to $2 million and it was further cut to $1.2 million. Then on October 2 the House Public Works Subcommittee approved an appropriation for Snettisham of $5,350,000, which awaits congressional approval.

Food for Ducks
August 1969

Ducks stopping at the Copper River flats this fall will find a special nine-acre table of good food waiting for them, thanks to efforts of Cordova sportsmen, the U.S. Forest Service and the Alaska Department of Fish and Game. Through a combined effort more than $900 was raised for purchase of seed which has been planted in ponds covering nine acres. The new duck plants were needed to replace those lost during the 1964 earthquake upheaval of the Copper River delta.

Fizzling Spectacle
September 1969

Once rated a midsummer spectacle, Lake George's breakout has fizzled for the third successive year, and scientists are predicting that nature may have canceled one of its most exciting shows. With Knik Glacier again failing to butt up against Mt. Palmer forty-five miles northeast of Anchorage, the sealing process needed to dam up Lake George didn't take place. For nearly fifty years prior to 1963, the Lake George dumping act was an annual event. It missed in 1963, but the show was staged annually for the next three years. There has been no sudden outpouring of Lake George waters since 1966.

Fire on Platform A
45 Men Evacuated
July 1969

Forty-five workmen were evacuated from Shell Platform A in Cook Inlet near Kenai in late April when fire threatened the $5.5 million structure. Firefighters brought the upper level blaze under control after six hours. Main valves to producing wells controlled from the platform were shut off and there was no pollution from the fire. The platform was back in full operation several days after this photo was taken.

Anchorage Times photo by Alice Puster

1969

Big Boom, No Waves
December 1969

"BOOMSDAY!" shouted the headline in the *Kodiak Mirror* which announced the test of a 1.2 megaton device on Amchitka Island would be conducted on October 2. With Alaskans and others around the Pacific rim keyed up for predicted earthquakes, tidal waves and radiation exposure, the blast at the bottom of a 4,000-foot hole went off as scheduled, but without dire consequences. Tom Brown of the *Anchorage Daily News* described it as a "seismic whimper." Rapped by Governor Keith H. Miller and Representative Chet Holifield of California, chairman of the House atomic energy committee, for needlessly scaring thousands of persons, opponents of the nuclear test promised they would continue working to stop further explosions on Amchitka. Although it has several unused shot holes on Amchitka, the Atomic Energy Commission was quiet concerning future testing on Amchitka.

Trophy Meat to Charity
December 1969

Men who are hungry and down on their luck will be served steaks and roasts from trophy moose and caribou in Anchorage this winter if a meat salvage plan endorsed by big game guides, the Department of Fish and Game and the Salvation Army succeeds. Triggering the idea of utilizing wild game which is often wasted, especially on the Alaska Peninsula, was Ottokar Skal of Moose Pass, who arranges hunts for European sportsmen. Under the plan the state and guides will cooperate in getting the meat to peninsula airports where the Salvation Army will pay for its transportation to Anchorage. Freight rates on the meat will range from seven to 15 cents a pound.

'Fat Little Sister'
September 1969

Best known woman on Amchitka Island answers to the improbable name of "KL7—Fat Little Sister" (KL7FLS). Bearing the strange moniker is Mrs. Paul Filmore of Eagle River who stretched an earthquake-born interest in amateur short wave radio to serving as the communications link between 600 Atomic Energy Commission employees on Amchitka and the outside world. Honoring her two years of providing Sunday afternoon phone-patch service for the Amchitkans and their families throughout the nation, the contracting firm on the island recently presented Mrs. Filmore with a silver tray with an inscription describing her as "amateur ham radio operator of the year."

Elbow Room in Alaska
October 1969

Alaskans suffering from that hemmed-in feeling can find relative relief from the most recent census figures. Average population density for the nation as a whole is 60 persons per square mile. Alaska's density is four-tenths of one person per square mile.

175th Anniversary of Church in Alaska
December 1969

Members of the Russian Orthodox Church in Alaska began a year of celebration on September 24, the anniversary of the founding of their faith in North America. It was on September 24, 1794, that eight monks reached Kodiak Island after traveling more than eight months. The 175th anniversary observance began with special services at St. Michael's Orthodox Cathedral in Sitka conducted by His Grace, Bishop Theodosius. It continued at the Church of the Holy Resurrection in Kodiak with a diocesan assembly from September 24 to 28. Climax of the celebration will come on August 9, 1970, when Blessed Father Herman of Spruce Island is officially listed among the saints of the Russian Orthodox Church.

Oil Riches Pour In . . . Pipeline Approval Nears
December 1969

The most palatable figure in the smorgasbord of numbers emerging from Alaska's ballooning oil outlook is word from Governor Keith H. Miller's office that the more than $900 million in oil bonus money from the September sale of North Slope leases is earning the state about $7,800 each hour, or $187,500 a day. To assist in wise utilization of the windfall, the governor will propose establishment of a new Department of Treasury to the next Legislature . . . With major North Slope operators revealing estimated sizes of their recoverable reserves by bits and pieces, most experts now expect 15 to 20 billion barrels of oil will be recovered from the Prudhoe Bay and adjacent fields . . . More specific details on the North Slope potential were due at the November 13 meeting of the Alaska Oil and Gas Committee in Anchorage when operating rules are considered, including a proposal to allow one well for every 640 acres as contrasted to the present single well for each 160 acres. Such a revision would save the oil companies money and please conservationists by reducing damage to the tundra.

Less pleasing to conservation groups throughout the nation were growing signs that approval of the 800-mile Prudhoe Bay to Valdez pipeline is rapidly approaching. In mid-October only approval of the Senate and House Interior committees for lifting the native land freeze along the pipeline route was needed for construction to start. With shiploads of pipe reaching Valdez from Japan simultaneously with job-seekers and new workers, city officials appealed to Governor Miller for assistance in meeting a housing crisis. Officials of Trans Alaska Pipeline System now expect actual construction on the $900 million project, largest in the nation's history, to start early next spring. First phase work will include laying four 100-mile sections of pipe between Valdez and the Yukon River and dock and terminal construction at Valdez . . . Biggest blemish on September North Slope operations was the rupture of a rubberized, pillow storage tank owned by British Petroleum. Fifteen thousand gallons of fuel were spilled into the tundra and ocean. State officials who inspected the area reported little if any damage was done to fish and wildlife.

Family Gold Mine
* * *
Nugget Tops a Pound
November 1969

A pound of gold! Judy and Candy Tillotson found this sixteen and one-half ounce gold nugget recently in their father's sluice box on Spruce Creek near Atlin, B.C., 120 miles south of Whitehorse. From Minneapolis, Minnesota, the family comes to the Atlin Creeks to work during the summer and this year did well. The nugget is worth anywhere from $1,100 to $1,500. In the cleanup they also found two four-ounce nuggets.

Whitehorse Star photo

Ice Road in Trouble
December 1969

Better known as the ice road to the North Slope, the Walter J. Hickel Highway won't be the scene of much trucking activity during the winter of 1969-70. Governor Keith H. Miller has decided that the $433,000 appropriated by the last Legislature for reconstruction and maintenance of the highway is only about one-third of the amount needed. The governor's decision against reopening the road was based on a ruling by the attorney general that the $600,000 anticipated in trucker tolls could not be used for general roadwork. Pushed through at a cost of about $766,000, the road project activated by former Governor Walter J. Hickel was used by truckers for only about a month and carried 7,464 tons of freight to the North Slope from Fairbanks.

Cook Inlet Courier

September 1969

While Secretary of Interior Walter J. Hickel and captains of industry dedicated the maze of tanks and tubes that comprise the $50 million Collier Carbon and Chemical Corp. plant in North Kenai, it was an array of five aquarium tanks on the company dock that attracted the attention of Cook Inlet fishermen. Each aquarium contains 100 red salmon smolt from the Kenai River. The two-month test involved exposing some of the smolt to water that is part of the Collier plant's discharge and includes ammonia, and the remainder to fresh Cook Inlet water. Collier biologists are convinced the tests will prove the plant's waste discharged into the Inlet at high tide is not harmful to fish.

Record Prices for Halibut: Nearly 40¢ a Pound
December 1969

Halibut is a flat fish that produced some fat paychecks for Alaska's fishermen during the last season. Leading the pack in port landings was Kodiak with more than 6.5 million pounds, followed by Petersburg with nearly 5 million pounds and Ketchikan in third place with 3.1 million. Prices during the season approached a record 40 cents per pound.

Eskimo Tongue-twisters
November 1969

Try Point Hope's new street names if you are good at tongue twisters. Mayor Henry Attungana and the village council recently authorized using authentic Eskimo names to identify their streets. Included are "Oungasiksikaaq," "Qaqmaqtuuq," "Piskitaagvik" and "Tulunkgigruk." "We wanted to always remember the good things we had long ago and not so long ago," explained Mayor Attungana.

Rail Yard for Valdez?
December 1969

Railroad buffs will be surprised to know that while the Alaska Railroad is removing rails from its unused spur line between Palmer and Jonesville, it has moved to acquire 50 acres of land near Valdez for a terminal yard. Although Valdez is several hundred miles from the railroad's main line, the ARR needs the new terminal yard for storage of rail cars now reaching Valdez by freight barge.

1970

Coming Soon: Big Oil Producers on the North Slope

January 1970

The Prudhoe Bay field on Alaska's North Slope will soon be home for oil wells, each capable of producing 10,000 barrels of black gold daily. The field, which is roughly defined as about 40 miles long and 22 miles deep, includes three oil-producing zones. These new and vital statistics were revealed at a hearing conducted in Anchorage by the Oil and Gas Conservation Committee in mid-November for the purpose of establishing rules for development of the Prudhoe field. Atlantic Richfield and British Petroleum, which hold some of the richest ground in the field, advocated a change in present State rules, recommending only one well for every 640 acres in contrast to the present allowance of one well for every 160 acres. Standard Oil of California argued for retention of the 160-acre-per-well rule.

The hearing, conducted by Homer Burrell, director of the State Division of Oil and Gas, and attended by 450 oilmen, failed to reveal the detailed picture of the Prudhoe Bay richness that was expected.

Staff photo by Richard W. Montague

A view of the wellhead of Put River No. 1, British Petroleum's discovery well on the North Slope near Prudhoe Bay. The well is currently capped, but can be put into production once arrangements have been completed to bring the crude oil to world markets, either through the projected Trans-Alaska Pipeline or by sea-going tanker through the Northwest Passage.

Atlantic Richfield attorneys claimed that complete disclosure of all field information would bring frowns from the Securities and Exchange Commission. It was explained that unitization of the field is likely, with one major operator representing a number of companies. British Petroleum, Mobil, Humble, Phillips and Standard of California are probable field partners if unitization is approved.

The three oil pools in the Prudhoe field were given names at the hearing. The Prudhoe Bay Sand pool, richest of the three, ranges between 8,110 and 8,680 feet; the Prudhoe Bay Lisburne pool is located between 8,785 and 10,450 feet, and the Prudhoe Bay Kuparuk River pool encountered oil between 7,070 and 7,765 feet. As the two-day hearing started, British Petroleum revealed that it encountered oil in seven of nine wells drilled within 10 miles of its discovery well. "It looks better all the time," said Burrell, in promising that his committee would formulate a preliminary set of ground rules for the Prudhoe Bay action early in 1970.

Trainloads of Pipe for Oil Line to Valdez
February 1970

From Valdez and Seward to Anchorage and Fairbanks and points in between, Alaskans are watching huge lengths of pipe move into position for ultimate welding into a single strand that will extend 800 miles from Prudhoe Bay to Valdez. Even before Congressional committees approved modification of the native land freeze to grant a right of way for the $900 million project, Japanese freighters had delivered nearly 80 miles of pipe to Valdez. Trainloads of 40-foot lengths of the 48-inch pipe began rolling last December from Seward through Anchorage to Fairbanks, where 35 miles had been stored by early January. Actual construction on the Trans-Alaska Pipeline System, largest private construction job in history, will not start until an exact route is approved and engineers are convinced that certain permafrost problems can be solved. An important segment of the route was completed in December when a new highway from Livengood reached the Yukon River. In aiming for a 1972 completion date, TAPS will have to comply with a 34-page booklet of construction rules developed by the Department of Interior. Among beneficial spin-offs from the big project will be hiring of 300 Alaskans to be trained this year at Mt. Edgecumbe School in Sitka and Beltz School in Nome. First target of the industry-supported program will be the training of machinists, welders' helpers and other semi-skilled workers... While the North Slope grabbed headlines, the Swanson River oil field quietly produced its 100 millionth barrel of crude oil on November 14, a little more than 12 years after Richfield Oil Company started the new oil era with its discovery well... And a new phase in refining started January 1, when Tesoro-Alaskan Petroleum Corporation began buying state royalty oil for refining at its new $18 million plant. The North Kenai refinery will produce jet fuel for the U.S. Air Force and diesel fuel for the Alaska market.

Dawson Restoration
February 1970

"Few have not heard of the fabled Klondike, the site of the greatest gold rush in history," said Canada's Minister of Indian Affairs and Northern Development in announcing a $1.7 million program for renovating four historic sites in the Yukon. Extending over eight years, the program will include acquisition, preservation and restoration of old Dawson City buildings, establishment of a gold room at Bonanza Creek, rejuvenation of the *SS Klondike* at Whitehorse and preservation of the Presbyterian Church at Bennett. Dawson City structures assured of continued existence as a result of Minister Chretien's announcement are the old Post Office, Robert Service's cabin, original Commissioner's office and Royal Canadian Mounted Police quarters, a small hotel, general store and blacksmith shop.

Wrangell Storm Downs Power Lines... Candles Fight the Darkness
January 1970

Residents of Wrangell resorted to candles for light during a city-wide brown-out that lasted for several days in early November. The brown-out resulted from a storm that blew trees across power lines and from a combination of mechanical problems that crippled the city's power plant. The Alaska Wood Products mill, about six miles south of town, put its power plant to work for the city, but the auxiliary power was delayed when an underground cable overheated and burned. New cable had to be strung to connect AWP with the city. Then a 300 KW diesel plant cracked a cylinder and dropped off the line, leaving Wrangell with about half of the power generation capacity it requires. Two other generating plants had been out for some time due to mechanical problems.

Residents were asked to turn out all unnecessary lights and to use power only for their refrigerators and furnaces. The Wrangell Elementary School was closed for a day because there was not enough power to heat the building, and many street lights were turned off.

A spare cylinder for the diesel generator arrived in Wrangell and was to be installed by November 6, ending the brown-out. However, the city light plant reported that power output would be dangerously low until two new Ingersoll-Rand generators could be put on the line in late November.

New Life for Juneau Hydro Project... More Power for Anchorage Area
February 1970

Bids on construction of the main dam at Snettisham hydroelectric project near Juneau have been solicited by the Alaska District of the U.S. Army Corps of Engineers, and are scheduled to be opened February 13. The contract is expected to exceed $10 million and extend over three and one-half years. Work on the $50 million project was halted last September when the Army Engineers ran out of funds for additional contracts. The Nixon Administration requested only $2.2 million for the project, but early in December, Congress approved $5,350,000 for it. In addition to the main concrete dam, which will be 800 feet high and 115 feet long, the contract includes related facilities. About $13 million has already been spent on the project for a diversion tunnel, docks, airport and access road... The growing electricity appetite of Greater Anchorage and the Kenai Peninsula will be appeased by recently granted REA loans of $9,010,000 to the Chugach Electric Association and $3,817,000 to the Homer Electric Association. The CEA loan will provide for the addition of transmission lines from the Beluga River generating station to Anchorage. The HEA loan will finance 255 miles of distribution lines to serve 1,132 new customers.

Alaska Deposits Grow
February 1970

One-fifth of total deposits in six of Alaska's larger banks belong to the State of Alaska, according to Commissioner of Revenue George Morrison. In distributing $19,590,000 of the September oil lease bonanza to the six banks in late November, Morrison reported the six had a total of $34,525,000 on deposit from the North Slope sale. The second round of deposits was made following assurance that the money would be used to increase the banks' lending capacity. The seven banks not getting a second helping of state deposits will be eligible for another serving when they show a need for additional loan funds to the State Investment Committee. Banks receiving the last round of state deposits were National Bank of Alaska, First National Bank of Anchorage, Alaska National Bank of Fairbanks, First National Bank of Ketchikan, B. M. Behrends Bank of Juneau and Bank of Petersburg. The new year started with Commissioner Morrison holding to his prediction that the state's $900 million earned from the North Slope lease sale will earn $67.6 million in interest by next September.

Boom vs. Pop
February 1970

The nuclear test blast which jarred Amchitka Island in the Aleutians last October 2 was a small pop compared to the big boom being planned for the island in late 1971. Top officials of the Atomic Energy Commission reported on past operations and future plans to a six-member panel appointed by Governor Keith H. Miller to evaluate the official report. Dr. Charles Williams, deputy director of the AEC Nevada test site, reported that work will start this winter on drilling a 5,875-foot hole for the next test, which will be several times larger than the one megaton Milrow blast which was widely opposed. Major General Ed Giller, AEC military applications officer, said the next tests code named "Cannikin" will not be ten times larger than the Milrow test. He emphasized that the test shot will not be fired without President Nixon's approval. The Alaskan panel was told that the last test triggered no tidal waves or earthquakes, and did no damage to Amchitka's sea otters, eagles and fish.

Asbestos via Alaska
February 1970

Asbestos mined at Clinton Creek in the Yukon is being shipped to market via the Taylor Highway and Alaska Railroad. The new routing resulted from a prolonged Canadian shipping strike last fall. It led to winter maintenance of the Taylor Highway by state crews for the second time since it was constructed. Hauled from Clinton to the Alaska Railroad at Fairbanks, the Yukon asbestos is mined from what is believed to be an extension of a large deposit discovered on the Alaskan side of the border near Eagle. By mid-December, Sourdough Freight Lines of Fairbanks was trucking 250 tons a day from Clinton Creek to Fairbanks.

Heavyweight Battle: The Cabbage Kings of Matanuska
January 1970

Ray Rebarchek and Max Sherrod of Palmer are determined to prove that there is apparently no limit to how big an Alaskan cabbage can grow. The lively competition started last fall when Rebarchek claimed the cabbage crown with a pair of 70-pounders. Sherrod showed up two weeks later with a 72-pounder. This fall Rebarchek regained the title with a heavyweight that weighed in at 73 pounds, an all-time record for the state. Both pioneer farmers are now gearing up for 1970 and the next round in the battle of the big cabbages.

Kodiak Fights to Save Historic Baranof Mansion
February 1970

Determined that Kodiak's oldest building and one of the oldest on the west coast must stay alive for future generations, Kodiak residents have pooled talents, time and money to halt deterioration of the Baranof mansion. With the venerable structure disintegrating while awaiting action to make it a national monument, the Kodiakans pitched in to patch the building from foundation to roof. Joining to give the early headquarters of the Russian American Fur Company a reprieve were the Kodiak Rotary Club, Kodiak and Aleutian Islands Historical Society, Mrs. Kodiak Tour Guides, Girl Scouts, Rural Alaska Community Action Program and various individuals and businesses.

Haines Says Yes to Merger with Port Chilkoot
January 1970

Haines voters approved overwhelmingly a merger of the cities of Haines and Port Chilkoot at an election in early October. The cities plan to take into one government entity the borough area between the two communities and some of the residential area south of Port Chilkoot. After the merger annexation will be considered to extend the city limits to the crossroads north of Haines on the Haines Highway. The borough in the Haines area is of the third class. Port Chilkoot is a city of the second class and Haines is a city of the first class.

Dedman's Photo Shop

Aerial view of WP&YR shops at Skagway. A fire October 15 leveled the roundhouse at left center, plus five more buildings immediately surrounding it. Although the major portion of rolling stock was unharmed, and the railroad will maintain uninterrupted service, two of the new heavy-duty diesel locomotives just received this summer were lost, plus a small switch engine, an old steam locomotive, a caboose, one parlor car, and a flat car. The major portion of the loss, estimated to be in the millions of dollars, is in equipment, tools and spare parts used and stored in these repair facilities.

Dedman's Photo Shop

Shown here is one of the WP&YR's new locomotives, lost in the disastrous fire. The men tried valiantly to haul this engine out through the wall after the turntable area was too hot to work, but the cable attached to a bulldozer snapped, and the engine was lost. Most of the rolling stock was saved, due in large part to the efforts of the firemen, who included just about every able-bodied man and teen-age boy in Skagway. Buildings at left in this picture caught fire minutes after this photo was taken.

White Pass Rail Shops Leveled by Fire
January 1970

A fire of undetermined origin leveled the major portion of the White Pass and Yukon Route railroad repair facilities October 15 in Skagway. Damage was estimated at several million dollars. Six major buildings and two new locomotives were destroyed by the raging fire fed by gasoline, kerosene and oil. Fuel drums exploded as the fire grew. Burned to the ground within 90 minutes after the first alarm were the roundhouse, blacksmith shop, machine shop, boiler room, wash-and-lunch room and oil room. Also destroyed by the blaze were a small switch engine, a steam engine used as an auxiliary boiler, a parlor car, one caboose and a flatcar.

Firefighters, including all able-bodied men and most teen-age boys in the town of 800, were hampered by insufficient water pressure. Some hoses carried water from town hydrants four blocks away. Water was also pumped from the river.

Following the fire, WP&YR crews cleared away debris and filled in the turntable pit. Switches and "Y's" will replace the turntable. Temporary wooden structures were to be erected over pits which are essential for repair work and maintenance on diesel engines.

A new permanent facility with steel buildings is scheduled for construction in the spring.

13-Inch Rain, Massive Slide
* * *
Power Plant Destroyed

February 1970

A massive rock slide buried Ketchikan's new Lake Silvis hydroelectric power plant at 2 a.m. November 28, wiping out 40 percent of the Ketchikan Public Utilities' generating capacity. No one was at the plant at the time. Pieces of plywood, insulation and roofing tile from the 30-foot building that housed the plant were found floating in the lake.

Governor Keith Miller asked President Nixon to declare Ketchikan a disaster area, explaining the Ketchikan area's dependence on electricity, and the fact that no replacement equipment of adequate size is available in Alaska. The Governor requested assistance in providing 2,000 kilowatts of power. An application for disaster status has been sent to the regional Office of Emergency Preparedness in Everett, Washington, to obtain funds for a power source to replace the buried plant.

The slide, which covered the building with mud and rocks, came after heavy rains in November had soaked the Lake Silvis area with approximately 42 inches of water. A total of 12.99 inches of rain fell at Lake Silvis between 4 p.m. November 27 and 3 p.m. November 28. The slide also took out about 400 feet of a rock and gravel road to upper Lake Silvis.

The plant was built as part of a $2 million expansion program and went on the line in September, 1968. The loss has been estimated at not less than $1.5 million.

Power was still on in all areas of Ketchikan in early December, but orders had gone out to conserve it. There was no threat of power brown-out as long as the rains continued, according to Elmer Titus, KPU manager. He said the volume of water coming off the hills was sufficient to keep the company's two other plants generating at capacity.

The U.S. Army Corps of Engineers has been searching the state for emergency generation plants, and OEP was investigating the possibility of moving a ship into Ketchikan to provide backup power.

Ketchikan Public Utilities
Left, Ketchikan's Lake Silvis hydroelectric power plant before the slide; right, the building is buried under rocks and mud.

Ever-changing Skyline... Oil Boom Spurs a Building Boom in Anchorage... Hospital, Hotel, Stores – and More
February 1970

A photo taken of Anchorage's skyline in the morning is obsolete by evening, just one of many indicators of the phenomenal growth surging through Alaska's largest city as it enters a new decade. Spurred by the oil boom, new arrivals have reversed the old trend which saw an exodus of seasonal workers to the south as winter approached. Major credit for the unprecedented reversal of old patterns is the $900 million oil lease sale on September 10.

School enrollment in the Greater Anchorage Borough has jumped more than 3,000 since last June, and with several hundred new pupils being added each month double-shifting in as many as a dozen elementary schools may be required when classes start in September, 1970. The borough school roster showed 19,297 students in June, 1965, compared to nearly 31,000 at the end of October.

The city's Joint Housing Referral office reported 78 units vacant in October, 1968, and only 18 in October, 1969... With Elmer Gagnon, director of the Federal Housing Authority for Alaska, reporting a 96 percent housing occupancy in late 1969, FHA officials report at least 3,000 living units will be needed in 1970 to just stay even with the population boom. One of the spin-offs of the housing crush is acceleration of the trend toward mobile home living. By November there were 3,671 spaces in 116 mobile home parks in the Greater Anchorage Borough and many more in the planning stage...

...Building permits issued by the City of Anchorage totaled $13.9 million in 1968, and building supervisor James Hall expected a slight increase for 1969. Then came the record oil lease sale, and now he expects this year's total will approach $26 million, the figure he had earlier predicted for 1970. His current guess is that 1970 may see $50 million in permits issued. Outside the city, borough officials report a 70 to 80 percent construction increase over 1968...

...Among the major projects under way or scheduled to start in 1970 are a $13 million expansion of Providence Hospital, a $6 million addition to the Anchorage-Westward Hotel which will give it more than 600 rooms, a new office building for Union Oil, an expansion of the Atlantic-Richfield building, new Northern Commercial Co. complex, expansion of Penney's, the largest Valu-Mart center in the Northwest, a 14-story Royal Inn, a 250-room Holiday Inn and $26 million expansion at Anchorage International Airport... The state is offering land near the airport for a new hotel, the Anchorage Municipal Port is preparing for a $2 million addition, a multi-story hotel is being built in Spenard, the Cherrier Brothers are completing a spacious apartment house in the downtown buttress area, and the Alaska State Housing Authority has approved an $8 million program for construction of shops and offices on the land reclaimed following the earthquake...

...Taking the bloom from the boom for new arrivals is the harsh fact that new jobs aren't being generated as fast as new job-seekers are arriving. The State Manpower Center in Anchorage reported in November that the city had 1,000 more jobless—most of them unskilled—than at the same time in 1968. "Don't come to Alaska without a definite job offer," is the warning being given by the State Department of Labor, union officials and Chamber of Commerce offices in reply to a record number of inquiries concerning job prospects.

Educational TV for Alaska's Youngsters... A Demonstration Project
April 1970

Most exciting educational news in Alaska this spring is keyed to a satellite in the Far North sky. Governor Keith Miller has gained approval from the National Aeronautics and Space Administration for a television demonstration project that is expected to bring educational TV programs directly to Fairbanks, Nome, Kodiak and Fort Yukon, and indirectly to pupils in Barrow, Bethel, Cordova, Wrangell, Petersburg, Haines, Skagway, Hooper Bay, Little Diomede, Juneau, Sitka and Ketchikan. Never before attempted in the United States, the test program will determine whether children in small towns and villages can advance faster through use of educational television than through regular teaching alone. COMSAT already has ground stations earmarked for Fairbanks and Kodiak, and when additional units are located in Nome and Fort Yukon programs will be received through NASA's ATS-1 satellite now aloft. Video tapes of the programs will be provided the 12 other towns included in the state test program. Proponents hope the network will be established in time to give Alaskans a view of the next moon shot... Senator Mike Gravel has asked for $45,000 from the State Legislature, which he says will extend Armed Forces television programs to residents in a 31,000 square mile section of Bristol Bay. Installation of TV towers and translator stations at Naknek and Dillingham, according to Senator Gravel, would permit broadcasting of programs from the Air Force TV station at King Salmon.

Alaska Escalates War on Pollution
February 1970

A tool needed to combat pollution was fashioned by Governor Keith H. Miller in December with activation of the Alaska Air Pollution Control Commission. The Governor told a Remote Sensing Symposium in Anchorage that Alaska has a "unique opportunity to avoid the destructive mistakes that have been made in other states." In addition to state commissioners of Health and Welfare, Economic Development, Natural Resources and Fish and Game, new members of the Commission are Dr. Charles Ribar and Charles Sargent of Fairbanks, Clifford Judkins and Mrs. Elmer Rasmuson of Anchorage, and Dean Morgan of Ketchikan. The commission will set air quality standards and establish rules and regulations for enforcing its orders. Boroughs and cities have five years to meet state standards... The Greater Anchorage Borough moved into the forefront of the anti-pollution scene with a law so stringent that it could prevent fireplace blazes and cigarette smoking if rigidly interpreted... The state's major cities entered the 1970's with water pollution high on the list of pressing problems. Ketchikan has been warned by the U.S. Public Health Service that its water supply failed in late 1969 tests to meet minimum standards for drinking water. Sewage disposal problems loom large for Ketchikan, Anchorage and Fairbanks. Greater Anchorage is now dumping 12 million gallons of raw sewage into Knik Arm each day. Included in a $39 million master sewerage program now under way is a sewage treatment plant at Point Woronzof which will dilute the waste to one part of sewage to 2.5 million parts of water. Completion is slated for mid-summer in 1972... Fast-growing Fairbanks is seeking solutions to worsening pollution of the Chena River. An injunction was sought late in 1968 to prevent dumping sewage in Noyes Slough... A state sanitarian recently told Ketchikan borough officials, "The sewage disposal practices at Ketchikan result in serious bacterial contamination of the adjacent waters of Tongass Narrows."

For Sale: A $128 Million Railroad
April 1970

Carrying a price tag of $128 million, the Alaska Railroad is listed "for sale" in President Nixon's new budget. Among prospective buyers—the only one of record—is the State of Alaska. Governor Keith H. Miller recently told the NORTH Commission: "It is possible the federal government will ask the state to assume ownership of the line. I want the state to be properly prepared to consider such a request when it comes. I want you to thoroughly evaluate the question of state ownership of the Alaska Railroad and make recommendations to me as soon as possible." ARR officials in Anchorage report they've heard sales talk in the past, but no buyers have bid for the colorful, 470-mile railroad that showed a profit of $418,000 last year.

No More Smoke: Mill-waste Burner Finally Closed — In Use Since '03
January 1970

A thing of the past that won't be missed in downtown Ketchikan is the mill burner smoke that until recently was a familiar nuisance to residents of the city. Unchippable waste at Ketchikan Spruce Mills sawmill formerly went into a wigwam burner by way of a high conveyor. The waste is now transported to the Ketchikan Pulp Company's boilers at Ward Cove, six miles north of town, to assist with the generation of steam and electrical power there.

Ketchikan residents have lived with the wigwam burner and its output since 1903, when the first sawmill began operations at the downtown site. In the past 66 years it is estimated that more than three-quarters of a billion board feet of logs have been processed, with residues being fed into the burners. The wigwam burner will remain in place, but will not be rekindled except for emergency service, according to Dave Murdey, timber and lumber manager for Ketchikan Spruce Mills.

Staff photo by Laurie McNicholas

Ketchikan Spruce Mills has cooled its wigwam burner, ending a smoke nuisance in downtown Ketchikan.

Juneau Rejoices... U.S. Plywood Selects Berner's Bay for Huge Mill Complex
February 1970

"WE'VE GOT THE MILL!"

That banner line across the front page of Juneau's *Southeast Alaska Empire* reflected the town's gleeful reaction to the announcement that U.S. Plywood-Champion Papers, Inc., had selected Echo Cove in Berner's Bay, about 40 miles from Juneau, as the site of its $100 million wood products complex.

The announcement, which came December 15 in Juneau from Gerald A. Jackson, president of the company's Alaska Division, ended more than a year of speculation about whether the company would locate its sawmill-pulp mill at Berner's Bay or at Katlian Bay near Sitka. Jackson stressed that the site selection had been based on scientific findings. Engineers, economists and ecologists were unanimous in the selection of the Echo Cove site at Berner's Bay. Ecologists reported that Berner's Bay is much less productive than Katlian Bay in all aspects of marine and surface riches and does not have the considerable commercial and sport fishing potential of Katlian Bay from the standpoint of salmon, herring, halibut, shrimp and trout fisheries. Katlian Bay also surpasses Berner's Bay in valuable marine mammal and bird populations dependent upon these species, the ecologists said. They pointed out that the Berner's Bay site is superior to Katlian Bay for effluent disposal operations. Katlian Bay has a shoal or sill across its western end which presents a barrier to free circulation of water in and out of the bay below a depth of about 50 meters.

Jackson said some preliminary work will be done in 1970, but actual construction of the mill would not begin until 1971. The pulp and sawmill "will probably go on the line simultaneously," he said.

The Forest Service now is extending the Glacier Highway three miles to Yankee Cove under a $3 million contract. About 7.4 miles remain to be built to carry the road to Echo Cove. W. Howard Johnson, U.S. forester for Alaska, said he would "like to see the entire construction completed by mid-1971."

State Commissioner of Economic Development Frank Murkowski said the mill "should result in some spectacular changes" in the Juneau community, including 600 to 800 jobs, a broader tax base, a "very significant" expansion of facilities, and "perhaps additional air transportation."

Craig-Klawock Road
January 1970

A ten-mile highway that links Craig and Klawock on the west side of Prince of Wales Island with Hollis on the east coast was opened in October by Governor Keith H. Miller. Future plans call for ferry service between Ketchikan and the landing at Hollis.

Alaska Native Brotherhood Meets in Kake
February 1970

Richard Stitt of Juneau was elected grand president of the Alaska Native Brotherhood at its 57th annual convention, held in mid-November at Kake. The 110 delegates who came from all over the state endorsed the land claims bill prepared by the AFN, and voted to oppose continued commercial sale of herring eggs. Stitt said that opposition was based on three factors: Roe has been a source of food for larger fish such as the king salmon; last year's herring spawn was not encouraging and the drop has been attributed to the loss of roe and roe has been a traditional source of food for native people.

Among speakers at the convention was Walter Noerenberg, acting commissioner of Fish and Game, who told delegates that Southeast Alaska can expect a run of 28 million salmon in 1970. The fish run he referred to would be about the same size as experienced in the big fishing year of 1968.

Thlinget Culture
January 1970

An educational project is under way in Klawock which aims to revive interest of native youngsters in school work by including special courses on the language, culture and history of their Thlinget ancestors. Extending from the third through eighth grades, the special project is financed by a $2,655 grant from the U.S. Office of Education.

1970

Forced Landings
* * *
Fliers Defy Arctic Rule... and Live to Tell It

March 1970

Three hardy and lucky airmen have proven in two separate accidents in the Alaskan and Canadian arctic that you can walk away from a downed plane and survive in midwinter. First to defy the old rule that survivors should stay with their aircraft was Bev Woslyng of Inuvik, N.W.T. Crashing his plane in the mountains northeast of Inuvik early in November, Woslyng stayed only one day at the plane, which had been far off course, before deciding to seek survival by walking. Eighteen days later he met an Eskimo who took him to an oil camp. Asked to describe his reaction to the 30 below zero cold which he endured without shelter for more than two weeks, Woslyng told an Inuvik radio reporter: "You can't get rid of it, so the only thing you can do is try and get away from it. It's up to you. There's nobody to help you. You build a fire. You do anything you can, that's all. And just remember that every step is one less....."

Anchorage Times photo by Robin Smith

Practically new when he started his 50-mile walk to Umiat in 40-below-zero weather, Brendan Kilmurray's boots were much the worse for wear when he reached safety.

Anchorage Times photo by Robin Smith

The toe of Brendan Kilmurray's battered left boot looked like this at the end of his 50-mile hike to Umiat following a helicopter failure on the North Slope in late December.

Ron McNeil, 34, and Brendan Kilmurray, 29, were heading south from Umiat with a Bell helicopter when the electrical system began failing. They landed on the Chandler River on December 23, and stayed with the machine until New Year's Day. Search planes passed over their emergency camp several times without sighting the men or their fire. They began 1970 by starting to walk to Umiat. A storm with minus 40 temperature forced them to seek shelter for two days in a snow cave. Their 12-day ordeal ended January 3, when they walked to a Wien Consolidated Airlines radio shack after walking an estimated 50 miles from the downed helicopter. Said Kilmurray of their chilling experience, "It got so cold we reached a sort of plateau where we didn't get any colder. We just stayed cold."

Klukwan Potlatch
January 1970

A potlatch to celebrate completion of a new tribal house was hosted last October by the entire community of Klukwan, located 22 miles north of Haines on the Haines Highway. The old Thlingit Indian custom of potlatch was revived by residents of Klukwan—population 95—as a means of saying "thank you" for the assistance given by federal and state agencies in financing their new building. The tribal house will serve as a tourist attraction, a showroom for native artisans' works and a community center. Nathan Jackson, a renowned Thlingit artist, created the exterior design on the gable of the new structure. The building has heating and fluorescent lighting.

Anchorage Praised for 'Terrific' Response
March 1970

Hanoi and Moscow didn't look good, but Anchorage emerged from H. Ross Perot's late December effort to fly relief packages to an estimated 1,400 American prisoners in North Vietnam as "the city that cares." Rebuffed in Laos, Perot made a last ditch effort to deliver the 25 tons of mercy packages via Moscow. On reaching Anchorage, he faced the problem of repackaging the medical supplies and food into small packages weighing not more than six and one-half pounds in order to meet Hanoi's specifications. The call went out that Perot and his small staff needed help in completing the big repackaging job. Nearly 1,000 Alaskans of all ages responded and completed the giant task in Western Airlines' hangar in six hours on December 29. The humanitarian gesture was stalled the next day at Copenhagen when Perot's chartered Boeing 707C was denied permission to proceed to Moscow. Billionaire Perot purchased a full page ad in the *Anchorage Daily Times* on January 12 to thank Anchorage for its "terrific" response, describing the city's humanitarian reaction as the highlight of his world-girdling odyssey.

Live Network TV for Southeast Soon... But Not for Other Parts of State
May 1970

Television fans throughout Southeastern Alaska may be able to receive live commercial programs on their home sets in the not-too-distant future, but for the rest of the state such entertainment is a long way off, according to R. D. (Chuck) Jensen, vice-president of Midnight Sun Broadcasters, which owns stations in Ketchikan, Juneau, Sitka and Anchorage. Ketchikan is the only city in the state now receiving live television broadcasts from the Lower 49. The city receives its live programming from the Canadian Broadcasting system, which runs many United States network programs, including all major sports events.

The Canadian television signal at Prince Rupert, B. C., 90 miles south of Ketchikan, is picked up by a mountaintop translator near Ketchikan and then distributed by cable throughout the city. Jensen says his firm is studying the feasibility of placing translators throughout Southeastern Alaska to carry the Canadian signal to the rest of the region. But, he added, extending live television to the rest of the state is a greater problem.

Noting proposals by Federal and state lawmakers throughout the state as part of an educational television program, Jensen said he believes the satellite program will be too expensive. He also pointed out that educational television by satellite will not spread popular entertainment shows such as "Bonanza" and top athletic events.

Jensen suggested that a video tape recording center be established to make tapes for distribution to communities in the north equipped for television.

Bethel Regional High School to Open in '71
May 1970

Two hundred students from a 100,000 square mile area of western Alaska will be attending Bethel Regional High School in the fall of 1971, according to James Harper, state director of regional schools. Work on the Bethel school, which will join existing regional state high schools in Nome and Kodiak, is scheduled to start this summer. Constructed by the Bureau of Indian Affairs, a dormitory for 100 boys and 100 girls will be included in the high school complex.

February 1970

H & M Photos Services

Two men who have given their names to Fairbanks' schools renewed an old friendship at the recent dedication of James C. Ryan Junior High School in the interior city. At left is Dr. James C. Ryan, pioneer Alaskan educator, with Mr. and Mrs. Dave Adler. Adler Elementary School was named in honor of the pioneer Fairbanks businessman and friend of education.

Non-Alaskan Urges – Keep the Mafia Out!
May 1970

"Even we non-Alaskans want no Mafia influence and corruption in our Last Frontier," was the message received by ALASKA magazine from Dr. H. J. DiMeola, a physician in Hartford, Connecticutt. His concern resulted from an article by Charles Grutzner in the latest issue of Harvard Business Review. Grutzner reported airlines, shipping firms and the state's oil fields are high on the list of "growth industry" targets for organized crime. The $900 million North Slope lease sale last September triggered the Mafia's interest, according to Grutzner. "The bosses of organized crime apparently feel that if they are going to extend their operations as far as Alaska, it will be for more substantial gains than those of gambling or loan sharking," wrote Grutzner in the article, "How to Lock out the Mafia." The underworld is interested in Alaska-serving shipping and airlines because of "the possibility of using the ships, especially those under foreign registery, as conduits for the international movement of 'hot' cash and goods, including narcotics." Best anti-Mafia medicine wrote Grutzner is an aroused business community which cooperates with law enforcement agencies.

Historic Sternwheeler
January 1970

Work on restoring the *S.S. Klondike*, retired Yukon River sternwheeler, to its former glory is under way at Whitehorse. Typical of the sternwheelers that plied the Yukon for half a century, the Klondike was constructed in the 1930's. The project is being financed by Canada's National Historic Sites Service.

New Kasaan Totem Park
February 1970

A request for withdrawal of a 14-acre tract of land in the South Tongass National Forest from operation of mining laws has been submitted to the Bureau of Land Management by the U.S. Forest Service. The tract, known as the New Kasaan Totem Park, is located on the east side of Prince of Wales Island on the north shore of Kasaan Bay, approximately one-half mile west of New Kasaan.

Situated on the land are trails, totem poles, a community house of the Haida Indian tribe and a native cemetery containing the grave of Chief Son-I-Hat of the Haidas. The Forest Service said mining activity would not be compatible with public use.

50,000th Phone
June 1970

Boasting more telephones than in all the rest of the state combined, the City of Anchorage Telephone Utility installed its 50,000th phone in late March. Twenty years ago Anchorage led the state with 4,200 telephones in its system.

One of the World's Richest Oil Wells... Put River No. 1 on Alaska's Prudhoe Bay
April 1970

Unknown to ALASKA magazine's editors at the time of its appearance, that photo of Put River No. 1 oil well on page 37 of the January, 1970 issue was a historic picture. Standard Oil of Ohio, which shares an interest in British Petroleum's discovery well, revealed recently that Put River No. 1 flowed at a rate of 21,500 barrels of oil per day during a test. Such a staggering production figure makes it the richest well in Alaska and North America and one of the world's biggest. Industry experts speculate that when the well is put into production it will be controlled at 10,000 to 12,000 barrels per day. ... The question of when the giant well and others will start pouring North Slope oil into the Trans Alaska Pipeline System remained very indefinite in mid-February. Secretary of Interior Walter J. Hickel assured TAPS officials the 800-mile pipe line "will indeed be built," and Richard Dulaney, a top TAPS executive gave State Senate President Brad Phillips "absolute assurance" that the pipe line will be built to Valdez and not through Canada. Senator Ted Stevens said, "They will be laying pipe up there this year," but Dr. William Pecora, chief of the U.S. Geological Survey, told the State Senate permafrost problems could delay the pipe line "a year or more." ... Meanwhile, contractors were busy moving equipment into position north of the Yukon River for construction of a 375-mile pipe line work road. In support of the project, the State Department of Highways asked for $250,000 from the Legislature for maintenance work on that stretch of the Hickel Highway between Bettles and Sagwon. In planning for the pipe line, TAPS has requested permits for three airfields, three communications sites, 10 campsites and 100 potential gravel pits. ... The first shipment of state royalty oil from Tesoro-Alaskan Petroleum Corp. was loaded aboard a Japanese tanker in late January. The 250,000-barrel shipment was destined for Tokyo, which will receive regular shipments from Tesoro-Alaskan's new North Kenai refinery. ... Prospects that Alaska's oil patch will grow in size came with the announcement by the Department of Natural Resources that it plans to offer 75,000 acres in Cook Inlet and 100,000 acres in Bristol Bay for lease in July. Later in the fall 150,000 acres of North Slope land will be put up for sale. The state expects the 1970 sales will bring in $40.5 million.

(See page 112 of this anthology for the oil well picture referred to above. –The Editors)

'Heritage in Peril'... Totem Pole Preservation
May 1970

"Alaska Totems—A Heritage in Peril" is the new and official name of the state's totem pole preservation campaign, and Dennis Demmert of Ketchikan is the new paid, full-time coordinator of the project. The project received a big boost early this year when a bill appropriating $50,000 to assist in totem pole preservation efforts sailed serenely through the State Legislature.

Purpose of the project, which was initiated last summer, is to rescue 44 poles located in abandoned Thlinget and Haida Indian villages near the southern tip of the Southeastern Alaska panhandle. The poles will be stored until they have lost the dampness which causes their deterioration, and will be treated with preservative. When the project is complete, Ketchikan will be home of one of the largest collections of authentic poles in the United States. The collection will be housed on property donated by the City of Ketchikan near its tiny city park.

Cost of the project, including retrieval of the poles, a storage-laboratory facility, preservation work on the poles and a facility for housing, interpreting and exhibiting them will total approximately $215,000, according to Jane Wallen, director of Alaska State Museum. In addition to the $50,000 state grant, the Smithsonian Institute in Washington, D.C., has agreed to provide the balance of the funds needed from various souces.

The totems to be housed at Ketchikan will be collected early this summer from unoccupied Indian villages under Mrs. Wallen's direction, according to current plans.

The removal early this year of two of only five traditional poles of the 1880's remaining in permanent preservation in Alaska from their long-time location—poles popularly known as the Old Witch totem in Juneau and the Wayward Husband totem in Ketchikan—enabled Mrs. Wallen and Demmert to learn handling techniques that they will put to good use when work starts at village sites this summer.

Alaska State Museum photos by Jane Wallen

The weathered Old Witch totem, left, ended a 16-year vigil near Juneau Memorial Library and another traditional pole popularly known as the Wayward Husband, right, was removed from its Ketchikan location just last February as part of the State of Alaska's totem pole preservation project.

Oil Spills Continue in Kodiak Island Area
June 1970

Oil spills continued to plague the Kodiak Island area in April. A faulty valve in a Navy storage tank released 90,000 gallons of fuel oil into Woman's Bay. Early hopes that rapid evaporation and quick use of absorbent straw would reduce damage were wiped out when biologists found thousands of marine animals, ranging from clams to starfish, had been killed by the spill. ...First clear-cut pollution violation by a foreign ship came in early April when the Soviet refueling ship *Mozyr* dumped oil in servicing Russian shrimp boats inside the three-mile limit near Marmot Island. The Coast Guard arrested Captain V. C. Sherstovitof, who paid a $1,500 fine in U.S. District Court in Anchorage. ...And the American owners of the *Eagle Leader* paid a $900 fine in the same court in Anchorage for failing to keep a ballast dumping log book aboard the vessel. The ship was boarded on February 5 by inspectors investigating a Kachemak Bay oil slick.

Native Council to Move
April 1970

Plans to transfer Thlinget and Haida Central Council headquarters from Anchorage to Juneau were announced early in February by John Borbridge, Jr., president and general manager of the council. The move will place the headquarters nearer most of the 14,000 Indians in the group. Borbridge, who is also first vice-president of Alaska Federation of Natives, said the Central Council will continue close relations with the statewide group. He said the move to Juneau is scheduled to take place shortly after the Thlinget and Haida annual convention April 16-18 in Anchorage.

ACS Sale to RCA Awaits Alaska Okay
June 1970

Sale of the Defense Department's Alaska Communication System (ACS) to a subsidiary of RCA Corporation was approved in principle late in March by the Federal Communications Commission. President Nixon approved sale of ACS on June 25, 1969, under a federal law providing for disposal of the Alaska system, subject to authorization by the FCC and Alaska Public Service Commission. The FCC said it would withhold final action until PSC approves the transaction.

The FCC said RCA Alaska Communications, Inc., would purchase the ACS facilities for $28.5 million and has agreed to invest another $27.5 million in improvements over a three-year period. It will also make immediate rate reductions averaging some 29 percent on interstate service and 40 percent intrastate.

The agency said RCA would purchase some 90,000 circuit miles and would lease another 480,000 circuit miles from the Defense Department, the Alaska Railroad, Canadian National Telegraph, AT&T and General Telephone and Electronics Co. In addition to covering Alaska, the circuits will extend into Canada and the "lower 48."

1970

A Milestone in Yukon's History

Anvil Mining Corp.

April 1970

Completion of this processing plant 135 miles northeast of Whitehorse was the third most important event in the Yukon's history, Commissioner James Smith told top Canadian government officials and industrialists gathered for dedication of the Anvil Mining Corporation's $65 million complex. Employing 300 in the production of lead and zinc concentrates, the new industry will soon make Faro, the project town located 12 miles from the plant, second largest city in the Yukon. A thousand tons of concentrate are being trucked daily to Whitehorse for rail shipment to Skagway and loading aboard ships for Japanese and German smelters.

Clouded Future for $100 Million Project Near Juneau... Conservationists Sue to Block Timber Sale
May 1970

An injunction to prevent construction of the proposed $100 million pulp mill-sawmill complex at Berners Bay near Juneau by U. S. Plywood-Champion Papers, Inc., and to nullify sale of timber to the company was filed February 11 by the Sierra Club, acting jointly with the Sitka Conservation Society, in U. S. District Court in Anchorage.

In September, 1968, the U. S. Forest Service and the company signed a 50-year contract calling for the sale of 8.75 billion board feet of timber in the North Tongass National Forest on the mainland south of Juneau, on the west side of Admiralty Island and in two areas near Yakutat on the Gulf of Alaska.

The complaint specifies a number of alleged irregularities in the timber transaction between the Forest Service and the company, and contends that construction of the mill would violate the multiple use and sustained yield act, which requires that uses other than logging, such as recreation, watershed and wildlife development be given consideration in the balanced planning of national forests.

Defendants in the suit are Clifford Hardin, U.S. Secretary of Agriculture; Edward Cliff, Chief of the U. S. Forest Service, and Howard Johnson, regional U.S. Forester for Alaska.

Robert Weeden, Alaska conservation representative for both the Sierra Club and the Alaska Conservation Society, said: "If the suit is successful, I think we would see a concerted and comprehensive examination of all Forest Service management policies in Southeast Alaska in an attempt to find out whether there are better ways of achieving a balance in their management program between the timber industry and the recreation-wildlife habitat protection-wilderness aspects."

Weeden, who noted that the court action was not against USPCP, said he had been encouraged by the fact that the company's advisory board of ecologists had been established for a five-year period. "As far as I know, this step by USPCP is the first time a pulp company that big has shown this much interest in environmental problems." Weeden was a research biologist with the Department of Fish and Game for ten years before assuming his present post.

Jack Calvin, a member of the board of directors of the Sitka Conservation Society, said the court action "isn't something sudden. It has been worked out very carefully over a period of time."

W. Howard Johnson said in Juneau that the Forest Service plans to go ahead with its contract with USPCP despite the suit. "No delays are foreseen which might alter the early development plans," he said. He stated that the sale offering "was made fully in accord with laws and regulations long used in selling national forest timber," and that the contract contains requirements for protection of forest resources including fish and wildlife.

Sitka and Juneau, both of which were in the running as locations for the mill, had waited more than a year for the site selection decision. USPCP announced last December that the mill would be located at Echo Cove in Berners Bay, about 40 miles north of Juneau.

State Budget's Whopping Increase... from $149 Million to $242 Million
March 1970

"Most historic legislative session in Alaska's history" was the description given the Sixth Alaska legislature by Governor Keith H. Miller on January 14, when he charted a course into the future in his state of the state address. The next day he submitted a general budget proposal of $242,229,000 for the fiscal year starting July 1, a whopping increase over the current general fund appropriation of $149,100,600 for the fiscal year ending June 30. Key to Governor Miller's program which calls for reducing or eliminating several taxes while expanding operations for nearly every department of state government is the $900 million paid for North Slope oil leases last September. Massive expansion can be carried out in the fields of education, transportation, law enforcement, health and welfare, fish and game, natural resources and capital improvements without depleting the windfall of nearly a billion dollars, the Governor told Alaska's 60 legislators. He proposed a constitutional amendment which would permit establishment of a $500 million permanent investment fund for the benefit of future generations, investing $300 million in high yield securities and depositing $100 million for the state's banks to assist in home and business loans. . . . "I pledge total effort on the part of this administration to ensure a proper balance between development and our unspoiled natural environment," said the Governor in his opening address. He called for an "environmental coordinator" in his office to join efforts of the newly established Division of Environmental Health with other departments. Other environmental improvement moves proposed include assisting cities with water and sewage facilities, tax incentives for industries installing anti-pollution equipment, greater authority for the Division of Oil and Gas in dealing with industry conservation problems. A 300,000-acre Denali State Park was proposed to compliment Mt. McKinley National Park on the south. The governor called for stepped-up planning for multiple use development of the Wood River-Tikchik Lakes area in the Nushagak drainage. Accepting the challenge of President Nixon to stop degradation of environment, Governor Miller called on the Legislature to support his recommendation that the nation establish a national institute of environmental sciences in Alaska.

Anchorage Times photo by Alice Puster

April 1970

Protected from sub-zero cold, snow and wind by a coat of heavy plastic, workmen are busy this winter in putting the finishing touches on the Union Oil Company's six-story headquarters in Anchorage. The protective covering is being used on a number of Alaskan projects to permit construction throughout the winter.

Wolf Bounty in Doubt
April 1970

While some legislators are working to eliminate the $50 bounty on wolves, the newly formed Alaska Sports and Wildlife Club of Kodiak has requested that the wolf bounty be increased to $100.

'A Threat of Economic Disaster': Oil Pipeline Project Bogs Down in a Maze of Suits and Regulatory Hurdles

Trans Alaska Pipeline System pipe trucked in from Valdez and stockpiled in Fairbanks is inspected by TAPS personnel. Each pipe is 40 feet long, 48 inches in diameter and averages 10,000 pounds.

June 1970

Distress signals were flying throughout Alaska in mid-April as plans for construction of the Trans Alaska Pipeline System from Prudhoe Bay to Valdez bogged down in a maze of court actions and objections by U.S. Geological Survey experts who must give approval before the 48-inch line for moving hot oil 800 miles from the Arctic to tidewater can be built. All seven members of a House conservation subcommittee signed a letter to Interior Secretary Walter J. Hickel requesting he delay issuing the TAPS permit pending further investigation on effect of the pipe line on environment.

Rated the largest single construction project by private firms in the nation's history, the estimated cost has now topped $1 billion. An emergency meeting of Fairbanks contractors, businessmen and labor officials in early April resulted in estimates that stoppage of all work on the project would result in sudden unemployment of several thousand men in the Interior. The *Fairbanks Daily News-Miner* reported delay in the big project "could be close to an economic disaster to all of Alaska, since we are depending so heavily upon income from the huge Prudhoe Bay oil fields to finance many social, educational and welfare projects for the betterment of our people." The feeling of many Alaskans was reflected by Rep. Tom Fink of Anchorage, who told fellow legislators, "Day by day the picture seems to get darker." The *Anchorage Daily Times* asked: "Is it time for Alaskans to consider the possibility the proposed Prudhoe Bay-to-Valdez pipe line may never be built?"

Governor Keith H. Miller moved to salvage the northern segment of the project by requesting a road right of way from the Department of Interior for the 350-mile pipe haul road which will extend from the Yukon River to Wiseman, cross the Brooks Range through Dietrich Pass and proceed to Prudhoe Bay. Speeding the Governor's action and offer to have the state build the road, was the fact that millions of dollars worth of construction equipment is in staging areas north of the Yukon River and will be idled for a full year if the project is halted. Not until the Yukon freezes next winter can most of the heavy equipment be moved out if the project is killed or delayed. TAPS, however, indicated it would not go ahead on the $120 million pipe haul road which will parallel the pipe line without solid assurance that it will receive the pipe line permit from the Department of Interior. . . .Original hopes that the pipe line would be completed and royalty money would start pouring into state coffers by 1972 have been abandoned. State financial leaders now face the probability that royalty revenue from the North Slope may not show up until 1973, 1974 or later.

While problems involved in moving North Slope oil to market mounted, so did estimates on the size of the black gold pool in Alaska's arctic. R. A. Brown, Jr., president of Canada's Home Oil Co., one of eight firms in the TAPS consortium, said new drilling results indicate North Slope oil reserves range from 50 to 100 billion barrels of oil. He said such reserves could produce three million barrels daily by 1980, adding that cost of the TAPS project has now risen from $900 million to $1.3 billion. . . .Even as the pipe line project was stymied, Secretary of Transportation John Volpe announced the green light has been given to a $3 million engineering feasibility study of a transportation corridor to northern and northwestern Alaska. The San Francisco firms of Tudor, Kelly and Shannon will do the study. In reporting the go-ahead to Senator Stevens, Secretary Volpe said, "I know you share my beliefs that the result of this study of proposed new transportation routes will be invaluable to Alaska's development and the growth of the economy."

March 1970

The 800-mile Trans Alaska Pipeline System from Prudhoe Bay to Valdez won't come within 150 miles of Anchorage, but Alaska's largest city recognized the importance of the giant artery by displaying this 27-foot length of 48-inch pipe on the City Hall lawn during the Christmas season.

May 1970

Spanning the Yukon River between Stevens Village and Rampart, this 2,250-foot ice bridge has been the key link in moving thousands of tons of equipment across the big river in preparation for building roads and camps needed for construction of the 800-mile Trans Alaska Pipeline System. The movement schedule called for nearly 10,000 tons of material to move over the seven-foot thick ice bridge before breakup in May.

1970

Woman Attacked by a Bear, Faints; 'Grizzly Bear' Comes to the Rescue

June 1970

Anchorage Daily Times photo by Alice Puster

Theresa Gratias, two and one-half, traces the scratches left on the face of her mother, Mrs. Dave Gratias, in a strange April encounter with a grizzly bear at Mile 82 on the Denali Highway. Growling of her chow brought Mrs. Gratias out of the cabin where she and her husband had spent the winter. The dog broke its chain, and in following it around the cabin Mrs. Gratias stumbled over a grizzly bear cub. Sensing the mother was near, she raced for the front door behind which Theresa was sleeping. Barring the door was the mother grizzly. Mrs. Gratias slipped in trying to escape and the bear grabbed her arm. The family's 175-pound St. Bernard got into the act by nipping the bear's hindquarters and sending it to the woods. Mrs. Gratias fainted on the cabin porch, regained consciousness to find her rescuer licking her face. Name of the heroic St. Bernard, shown below, who is credited with saving his mistress from a severe mauling: Grizzly Bear. Mrs. Gratias' scratches didn't require hospital care.

Anchorage Daily Times photo by Alice Puster

When Mrs. Dave Gratias left her Denali Highway cabin in early April, following the encounter with a grizzly bear, she had to leave her 175-pound St. Bernard named "Grizzly Bear." The dog, who drove the attacking grizzly away from his mistress, caught a later train at Cantwell and is shown here greeting Mrs. Gratias on his arrival in Anchorage.

11 Men and 65 Dogs... Fort McPherson's Reenactment of the Famed Dawson Patrol
June 1970

Eleven men and 65 sled dogs entered Dawson City in the Yukon on Friday, March 13 to end a 415-mile dog team trek from Fort McPherson, N.W.T.

The historic reenactment of the famed Dawson Patrol, which was started in 1899 and continued until World War II, was the main feature of Fort McPherson's contribution to the Northwest Territories Centennial celebration.

Departing Fort McPherson on February 16, the nine Indians and two white men in the patrol, made the trip in 20 camps, although they could have completed it in 15. Four of the Indian mushers were over 60.

Roster of the patrol that drove into Canada's history books and the hearts of Dawson's welcoming crowd included: Andrew Kannizi, 78, chief guide and a member of the Dawson Patrol in 1914; Keith Billington, patrol leader; Bill Antaya, area administrator for Fort McPherson and Arctic Red River; William Vittrekwa, 76, second guide and hunter; George Robert, 60, trail breaker William Teya, trail breaker; Jim Vittrekwa, cook; Fred Vittrekwa; Abe Koe, trail breaker; Peter Nerysoo, woodcutter, and Abe Vaneltsi, youngest of the mushers who celebrated his twenty-fourth birthday on the trail.

When Keith Billington, a public health nurse, conceived the idea for reviving the Dawson Patrol, he put a notice on the community billboard calling for 11 drivers. He got 50.

Women of Fort McPherson caught the Centennial project spirit and spent hundreds of hours making parkas and moccasins from caribou hide, adding pompons and beaded emblems with the words "NWT Centennial Project—Dawson Patrol." Each of the 65 dogs sported a colorful jacket, shoes—when needed—and pompons.

"A good trip," said old Andrew Kannizi, 78, who first made it more than 50 years ago.

Jim Stirling

George Robert, 60, poses with his lead dog after winning Dawson City's Moosehide Race on the Klondike. A member of the Dawson Patrol, both George and his dog are wearing special outfits made for the occasion by Fort McPherson women.

Each man carried 500 pounds of food and supplies, including tents and axes. The patrol followed the old route from Fort McPherson south to the Peel and Trail Rivers, then over the Caribou Mountains and down to Mountain Creek and Wind River. Turning up the Little Wind River to Little Wind Pass they passed the spot where Inspector Fitzgerald's patrol met death early in the century. They moved up Waugh and Michelle Creeks to the Blackstone River near Chapman Lake about 74 miles up the Dempster Highway from Dawson.

"It was 59 below when we left Fort McPherson," said George Robert," but the snow was not deep and we made good time."

Days on the trail started about 8 a.m. Following breakfast, the dogs were fed harnessed and the patrol moved until noon when there was a brief lunch stop. The dogs were rested in midafternoon and camp was made each night about 6 p.m.

William Teya shot a caribou and George Robert bagged a moose.

"We go real good after eating the moose," said Robert.

Billington, a public health nurse, took the pulse of the Indian mushers at intervals during the trip.

"My pulse rate was around 60 after we'd been on the trail for a time," said Billington. "These men were only registering around 40 beats a minute."

Friday's entry into Dawson City was restaged on Saturday for the benefit of late arriving guests, including a plane load of celebrants from Inuvik and Fort McPherson.

Seven of the patrol members participated in Dawson City's dog team races extending three miles down the Klondike River and return. Winner of the race was George Robert, 60, and the oldest musher competing.

The rousing Dawson City reception ended, the patrol members and their dogs boarded a plane and were flown back to Fort McPherson. Their return trip was made in three hours.

Jim Stirling
Whitehorse, Y.T.

$1 Billion Formula
June 1970

A billion dollar formula for settling the land claims of an estimated 60,000 Alaskan Indians, Eskimos and Aleuts was approved by the Senate Interior Committee in mid-April. The proposed bill, which must now win Congressional approval, includes these provisions: Payment of $500 million by the federal government over 12 years, two percent of all oil revenues from public lands and lands not patented to the state until $500 million has been paid, grants of four and one-half million acres of land with full title and mineral rights. An additional three million acres would provide only surface rights, and could not be claimed in parks or national forests. The bill calls for phasing out all operations of the Bureau of Indian Affairs in Alaska.

August 1970

The native culture class is doing a wonderful job of sewing Indian dance blankets. Only three boys are making their own blankets. The rest are all girls. This is something to see—eagles, raven, sockeye, dog salmon, whale killer designs. They learned close to 10 Indians songs, and Tlingit language is going good, also. This is the best thing that ever happened in Klawock.

—Fannie Brown,
Klawock correspondent
KETCHIKAN DAILY NEWS

Strongest Man, Strongest Dog in the Yukon
May 1970

Strongest man and dog in the Yukon were determined at the recent Sourdough Rendezvous in Whitehorse. Uwe Meyer, a photographic salesman at Hougen's, took a lunch break to pack a 750-pound load of flour 50 yards and win the strong back title.... In the animal world, it was Blackie, owned by Edwin Hager of Mayo, who won the single dog pull contest by hauling 1,050 pounds.

Louisiana vs. Alaska
August 1970

Louisiana caught more than a billion pounds of fish and shellfish in 1960—nearly three times as much as Alaska—but Alaska's catch lead all states in dollar value, according to the Fish and Wildlife Service. Alaska's 1969 harvest of 346.8 million pounds was valued at $71.1 million. California was second in dollar value with $62.1 million and Louisiana ranked third with $56.7 million.

Alaska Grows
August 1970

Preliminary census figures show Alaska with a 1970 population of 294,417, an increase of 68,250 persons over the official 1960 census. Greatest growth has been recorded in the Greater Anchorage Area Borough, which extends from Chugiak to Girdwood and includes the City of Anchorage, with a 1970 total of 123,631—41 percent of the state's population. Anchorage continues to dominate the state's cities with a preliminary 1970 census of 46,137, an increase of 1,900 over 1960. The Fairbanks North Star Borough total was about 44,000, but the City of Fairbanks initial count of 14,000 was expected to climb to 18,000 as a result of recent annexations. Other Alaskan cities showed these totals, with the 1960 census given first followed by the preliminary 1970 total: Ketchikan, 6,483 and 6,703; Juneau, 6,797 and 6,002; Kodiak, 2,628 and 3,660; Sitka, 3,237 and 3,327. Most recent population count for Nome was 2,375 and for Kotzebue 3,934.

Alaska Boating Deaths Exceed National Average
August 1970

The number of deaths caused by boating accidents in Alaska is 48 times above the national average, although the state has relatively few recreational boats—less than 15,000 registered—according to Rear Admiral Robert E. Hammond, commander of the 17th Coast Guard District in Alaska. Hammond told a mid-May meeting of Juneau Chamber of Commerce members that there were 96 known boating deaths in the state in 1969. Among natives, the death rate from boating accidents is higher than from any other single cause, he added. He urged boat owners to have their boats inspected by the Coast Guard Auxiliary, and urged that children particularly wear life jackets when boating.

Hammond is slated to leave his Juneau post in mid-June to become Chief, Office of Operations, at Coast Guard Headquarters in Washington, D.C. His successor is Capt. James A. Palmer, who will be promoted to Rear Admiral. Palmer has been serving as assistant superintendent, U.S. Coast Guard Academy in New London, Connecticut.

The Coast Guard has 16 cutters, five helicopters and five multi-engine aircraft stationed in Alaska. The aircraft operate out of air stations at Kodiak and Annette. The Coast Guard estimates that it contributes $10 million annually to the Alaska economy in military and civilian payrolls plus commercial contracts.

Anchorage Daily Times photo by Alice Puster

All this talk about oil on Alaska's North Slope hasn't made much of an impression on the caribou shown in this photo as they file past a British Petroleum drill site near Prudhoe Bay. By looking close you can find five caribou in the photo, two of which are within the third circle.

Eyes of the World Turn Toward Alaska's North Slope
August 1970

The international importance of Alaska's North Slope oil was evident in early summer as news concerning the state's petroleum resources was made in Tokyo and Paris. Japanese steel firms announced in Toyko that despite a setback in the Trans Alaska Pipeline System construction schedule they will continue to ship 48-inch pipe to Alaska until delivery of the full order of 800 miles of pipe is completed in February, 1971. Meanwhile, Japanese ships continue to deliver pipe to Valdez, and four barges will travel from Japan to Prudhoe Bay this summer with 30,000 tons of pipe. A flotilla of 33 tugs and 55 barges was scheduled to leave Seattle in July for a giant haul of about 150,000 tons of freight to Prudhoe Bay. . . .Speaking at a meeting of international economic officials in Paris, two top officials of Atlantic Richfield Company recently described the importance of North Slope oil. Robert F. Cox, manager of corporate planning for Atlantic Richfield and secretary of its executive committee, said, "By 1974 total production in the United States will start to decline unless oil begins to be produced from the new reserves in the North Slope." He added that current evidence indicates 12 to 15 billion barrels of oil reserves have been discovered on the North Slope. "Compared with other suggested means of transportation," said Cox, "the Trans Alaska Pipeline (from Valdez to Prudhoe Bay) offers the most direct and lowest cost route that can be completed at the earliest date for bringing oil from the North Slope to those areas in the United States which have the greatest need for major additional supplies of domestic crude oil." He predicted that by 1980, two million barrels of oil a day would be flowing through Valdez, much of which would be diverted by pipe line to the Midwest and East Coast. Rollin Eckis, vice chairman of the Board of Directors of Atlantic Richfield, told the Paris meeting, "We are fully convinced that our operations can and are being carried out in a manner that is completely compatible with preservation of the delicate environment and without material hazards to the ecology. This statement applies particularly to the proposed Trans Alaska Pipeline about which there has been so much concern. We believe that the problems will be resolved and construction of the Trans Alaska Pipeline will proceed so that North Slope crude oil will move into Pacific Coast markets to fill the supply gap there. Subsequently we expect North Slope oil to move into the Midwest and perhaps the East Coast of the United States as well."

Methods of Killing Fur Seals to be Studied Again
August 1970

The system of killing fur seals on Alaska's Pribilof Islands with a single blow to the head is being studied again this summer by representatives of the Humane Society of the United States and the International Society of the Protection of Animals. Representatives of the two agencies observed the Pribilof harvest in 1968 and 1969, according to Dr. Leslie L. Glasgow, assistant Secretary of Interior. Restoration of the herd from a low of 200,000 animals in 1911 to a current population of 1.5 million animals is regarded as a conservation milestone. The Humane Society of the United States is opposed to the Pribilof seal harvest largely because the major product is a luxury fur. Alternate methods being considered for killing the three and four-year-old males surplus to the herd include shooting, gas, drugs and electricity.

March 1970

I was well over 50 years before I even saw the North. This is a very good place to grow old in because there is so much to do, and age is no barrier. For instance, when my sister came to visit me, she was over seventy and was immediately offered two jobs.

—Deaconess Hilda A. Hellaby,
Anglican leader in the Yukon in
WHITEHORSE STAR interview

Lore of the Bush Pilot . . . Lands on Road to Refuel at a Filling Station
July 1970

Warren Enzler of Kenai added an anecdote to the lore of bush pilots of the north April 18, when he landed his out-of-fuel plane at a filling station along the Hart Highway in central British Columbia. Enzler was flying with two passengers from Fort Nelson to Prince George when he tried unsuccessfully to make radio contact with an airport. Believing that he was off course, he began flying around to get his bearings, and his fuel ran out. Enzler brought his plane down on the highway, taxied to the pump and gassed up, then took off again. Shortly afterward the pilot landed safely at Prince George. Enzler later learned he had been on course all along. His radio was on the wrong frequency.

1970

The Highest Pay...
September 1970

If Alaska now has the highest paid state legislators in the nation at $16,150 a year, Anchorage is on the trail to supporting some of the more highly paid local officials. The *Anchorage Daily Times* reported that an Anchorage City councilman who also serves as a member of the Greater Anchorage Area Borough Assembly now receives "something like $11,000 or $12,000 a year."

Musk Ox Hunt? Forget it
August 1970

Put your rifle away if you planned to participate in the musk ox hunt scheduled by the Department of Fish and Game on Nunivak Island for September and October and next February and March. The permit hunts were designed to cull 100 old bulls from the Nunivak herd. Secretary of Interior Walter J. Hickel passed the word to the state in mid-June that he would not permit the hunt on Nunivak, which is controlled by the Department of Interior. In his third such rebuff of hunt plans, Secretary Hickel said herd reduction could be accomplished by additional transplants. ...If you want to substitute a buffalo for a musk ox, the Northwest Territories can accommodate you. For the first time since 1961, the NWT Game Department will allow hunting of 2,500 buffalo which roam 2,000 square miles. The season runs from September 15 through December 31. License fees are $75 for nonresident Canadians and $150 for other nonresidents. Hunting headquarters will be at Hook Lake, 60 air miles northwest of Fort Smith, N.W.T.

Fairbanks Daily News-Miner photo by Charles Darby

September 1970

Not Lake Bennett at the height of the Klondike Gold Rush, but the Tanana River near Fairbanks on May 23, 1970—the day of the Tanana River Raft Classic. Sensation of Alaska's recreation world, the 1970 raft attracted 395 entries for the 60-mile drift to Nenana. Winner was "Worm Germ" which was driven by leg-powered paddle wheels. "Admiral" Merritt Helfferich, originator of the race in 1968, estimated nearly 2,000 persons rode the river road to Nenana. Almost as many visitors descended on the town of 500 to welcome the rafters at the finish line.

The Last Payment
August 1970

Just 35 years after he moved to the Matanuska Valley as a colonist, A. R. Carson made his last payment of $212.73 to the Alaskan Rural Rehabilitation Corporation. As part of the program of Palmer's annual Colony Days celebration, Carson's final payment was returned to him. Some of the original colonists paid off loans earlier than required, others needed refinancing. Carson was honored as the colonist who stuck to the original schedule, never missing a payment in 35 years.

High Bids for Land
August 1970

Desire for land ownership was demonstrated in May when Alaskans paid $50,000 more than the appraised value of 14 tracts near Delta Junction. The state valued the agricultural tracts at $145,000 and auctioned them off for $196,000.

Alaska's Longest Legislative Session... Funds for a North Slope Road
August 1970

The Sixth Alaska State Legislature adjourned at 3:55 a.m. Sunday, June 7, after a 147-day session, longest in the state's history. In the closing hours, the legislature approved a $314 million general fund budget, a $120 million appropriation to build a road to the North Slope, and increased the state's gas and oil severance tax. The North Slope road is to be constructed along the route of the proposed Trans Alaska Pipeline System (TAPS) pipe line. The bill authorizing and funding the road requires that the state contract for guaranteed repayment of the cost of the road, plus 7.5 percent interest. The severance tax has been increased from a flat rate of four percent to a graduated rate ranging from three percent to eight percent, based on the average daily production of a well.

The $314 million budget is more than double the current fiscal year's operating budget of $154 million, and exceeds by $72 million the budget proposed by Governor Keith H. Miller. A free conference committee on the budget composed of members of both legislative houses agreed on the $314 million total, well above the $264 million voted by the Senate or the $308 million presented by the House.

The budget includes $33 million for capital improvements previously authorized for construction through the sale of Alaska State Housing Authority (ASHA) revenue bonds. Some $13 million of the capital improvement funds are earmarked for construction of the state office building in Juneau. However, the legislature passed a resolution instructing the administration to attempt to sell ASHA bonds until October of this year on the projects that have been authorized.

The legislature set aside $100 million in a fund to provide a monthly income of $100 to Alaskans who are at least 65 and who have lived in the state 25 years.

Municipal support programs approved by the legislature included a $68 million school foundation program. The amount to be returned to local schools by the state is nearly double that of last year, when the program was first enacted. Also approved is a $6.2 million program of municipal revenue sharing which provides state contributions for police and fire protection, air or water pollution control, certain kinds of land use planning, road maintenance and health facilities, including hospitals.

Pay raises were voted for state employees, judges, legislators and teachers in state-operated schools. State employees will receive raises of approximately six percent in most grades, diminishing to nearly three percent at upper levels. Legislators upped their salaries from $6,000 to $9,000, and added another $4,000 a year for travel, secretarial expenses and sundry items. They also gave themselves a retirement program which does not require individual contributions.

The legislature passed a measure that will, in effect, give National Guardsmen the educational benefits of the G.I. Bill of Rights after they have completed a voluntary enlistment period.

Other major legislation enacted by the Sixth Legislature includes:

—A liberalized new abortion law which makes abortion a matter to be decided by a woman and her physician. Vetoed by Governor Miller on April 17, the bill later became law when the legislature overrode the veto by a 41 to 17 vote.

—A measure significantly strengthening the Public Service Commission won passage after a ten-year battle. The bill gives PSC jurisdiction in service area disputes and rates. It was opposed by several municipalities which operate power companies.

—A bill lowering the drinking age to 19 and dropping several other legal age limitations to 19.

—Laws creating Chugach State Park, covering some 512,000 acres in the Chugach Range—Kachemak State Park near Homer, which includes approximately 300,000 acres—and, at "zero" hour, Denali State Park, which abuts the south side of Mount McKinley National Park.

Orphaned Bear Cub in a New Home Near Juneau

July 1970

A tiny, orphaned black bear cub has found a new home with the Howard Lockwood family in Juneau's rural Riverside Park area. Lockwood found the six-to-eight-week-old, male cub crying and starving near the body of its mother April 17 in the Lemon Creek area, approximately five miles northwest of Juneau. The cub's mother had died three or four days earlier of an undetermined cause. With the enthusiastic help of his wife, Willette, and four children, Lockwood fed the cub milk and pablum from a baby bottle until the infant was able to eat from a bowl. They named the cub Apollo, because it was found on the same day that the Apollo 13 crew returned safely to earth. After three weeks, the cub was romping with the family dog in fields near the Lockwood home. Lockwood has obtained a permit from the Alaska Department of Fish and Game to care for the bear until it becomes necessary for Apollo to move on to other quarters, such as a zoo.

Rick Simpson

Mrs. Howard Lockwood feeds Apollo, an orphaned baby black bear cub, at her home in Juneau.

1970

Chief Shakes the Ninth: A Totem-raising Potlatch in Ketchikan ... and a New Leader in an Old Stikine Tribe

September 1970

Jonathon DeWitt, a 31-year-old Thlinget Indian in Ketchikan, was designated "Chief Shakes the Ninth," at a totem-raising potlatch held in front of his home June 27.

The 45-foot totem, first authentic house totem to be erected in this southern Panhandle community in seven decades (and the first to be raised by Chief Shakes' people in nearly 85 years), was carved and created in honor of young DeWitt by his father, Forrest DeWitt, Sr., also of Ketchikan.

Although both DeWitts now live in Ketchikan, the family hails originally from Wrangell, and are members of the Stikine tribe of Indians, over which Chief Shakes the First ruled, in the 1700's. The last Chief Shakes (the eighth), James Bradly, died in the 1940's. Until DeWitt succeeded to the title, the Stikines had been without an official chief.

Conferring the designation on DeWitt was Kelly James, a Stikine elder and himself the nephew of Chief Shakes the Eighth. Kelly led a delegation of Stikine people to Ketchikan for the occasion.

The pole, which Forrest DeWitt had been carving since November, 1969, is topped by an Eagle since Chief Shakes the Ninth is of the Eagle clan. (Thlinget Indians divide themselves into two clans, Eagles and Ravens. Eagles cannot intermarry with Eagles nor can Ravens marry Ravens. A person inherits his clan designation from his mother's side of the family.) The pole contains, as well, a killer whale, a legendary Indian hero named Nuts-te-keen-na, a brown bear, and additional figures out of Thlinget totemic lore.

The totem was raised into position in the old-fashioned manner, by rope and manpower. No less than 50 members of the Raven clan pulled and hoisted the cedar monument into its erect position. No vehicles or power machinery were utilized.

Throughout the afternoon, in celebration of the pole raising and the designation of the new chief, the Stikines performed Indian dances for an assembled crowd of spectators which at times numbered in the hundreds.

At the conclusion of the potlatch, as is customary, the new chief presented blankets to the Raven people in payment and in appreciation for their work in raising the pole.

In the evening, Ketchikan Jaycees sponsored a special dance at the Elks Club, in honor of the occasion. Again the Stikines performed traditional Indian dances, in full ceremonial regalia. Later, to the sound of a 20th century "rock" ensemble, townspeople and Indian visitors alike danced to music with a modern beat.

Mike Miller

The pole, topped by an Eagle, stands at the Ketchikan home of the new Chief Shakes. Carved from red cedar, the pole is painted with special Canadian paint containing crushed salmon eggs for the oil base, ground baked clam shells for white, crushed ochre for red, hemlock bark for red and brown tones, and pitch from spruce for binding properties.

Mike Miller

New Chief Shakes (the ninth) is Jonathon DeWitt, right. At left is his father, Forrest DeWitt, who carved a 45-foot totem pole honoring the new chief of the Stikine people.

Mike Miller

Hand adzes and old-time tools—no power machinery—were utilized by the senior DeWitt in carving Ketchikan's new totem pole. Here, during the carving process, DeWitt discusses progress of the monument with his daughter-in-law, Nancy, wife of the chief.

Now Kodiak Boasts: 'We're Number 2'
July 1970

"WE'RE NUMBER 2" shouted the bannerline in the *Kodiak Mirror* on April 22 to tell its readers that Kodiak has moved into second place among the nation's ports in the dollar value of fish landed in 1969. Preliminary statistics released by the U.S. Bureau of Commercial Fisheries put San Pedro, California, in first place with $40.5 million in value of fish landings. Kodiak's total was $18 million, followed by Brownsville, Texas, with $17.7 million and New Bedford, Massachusetts, with $17.4 million.

First Port Heiden High School Graduate
August 1970

First person in the history of Port Heiden to graduate from high school is Miss Laura Mattson, daughter of Mr. and Mrs. Andrew G. Mattson. Completing the eighth grade in Port Heiden, Laura transferred to the Bristol Bay High School in Naknek where she was graduated in May. She was one of 670 students enrolled in the state's boarding home program during 1969-70. The program started in 1966 with 160 students.

Anchorage Daily Times photos by Alice Puster

September 1970

Too many "zs" and not enough "rs" make these Anchorage street signs attractive for blooper-seekers. It should be "Breezewood Drive" and "Strawberry Road."

The First Plane – A Strange Thing
March 1970

When the first plane arrived in Aklavik, it was a strange thing, as people never saw one before. I was walking home when the plane came in very low. I ran behind the house where I will be safe, and people were running all over the settlement, with children crying with fright. One of my little girls asked me if those men were good. I said yes even though I was not sure myself.

—Mrs. Sarah Simon,
Ft. McPherson correspondent
THE DRUM, Inuvik, N.W.T.

1970

Belt-tightening Ahead
September 1970

Announcing that the state and the eight oil companies comprising Trans Alaska Pipeline System had been unable to devise an acceptable plan for North Slope road construction this year, Governor Keith H. Miller canceled his call for a special session of the state legislature scheduled for July 6. Miller had called for the session after TAPS officials announced June 12 they would not accept a legislature-approved plan for the state to build the $120 million road, which required that TAPS repay the cost of the project within five years at 7.5 percent interest.

Miller said he issued the call for the special session June 18 after he had "received reasonable assurances from TAPS a plan for construction of the highway could be worked out."

Admitting he was bitterly disappointed at the failure to get the pipe line road under construction this year, the governor warned in a statewide TV and radio address that Alaskans will have to "tighten our belts." He promised to work hard at cutting down on record $314 million expenditures authorized by the last Legislature.

"There must be a pipe line in Alaska's future if Alaskans are to receive the benefits from the oil on the North Slope," said Governor Miller as he announced formation of a 15-member pipe line commission in mid-July to study the possibility of state construction and ownership of a Valdez-Prudhoe Bay pipe line. He told the non-partisan panel headed by Dr. Robert Horchover of Juneau: "Future state revenues are largely dependent upon the commencement of oil production from the North Slope, and it has been delayed too long. We cannot continue to wait; we must have action now."

Construction of the 800-mile pipe line can't begin until an access road is built across tundra on federal land between the Yukon River and the North Slope. And the state can't collect royalties or severance taxes from its oil reserves until the proposed $900 million pipe line is carrying oil to the ice-free port of Valdez.

Staff photo
October 1970

Far from fancy, but plenty practical, homemade snowshoes such as these were used by Alaska's early trailblazers. This pair was made of birch and moosehide more than 40 years ago by the late William Besser, who trapped and fished near Moose Point on the Kenai Peninsula.

August 1970 — Staff photo

Visited by thousands of Centennial visitors to Anchorage, the Igloo Puk at International Airport "melted" during an attempted move to a new site. The giant plywood model of an Eskimo igloo was jacked up and loaded aboard trailers. It disintegrated after traveling about 200 yards.

Cities Unhappy with First Census Figures
September 1970

"Preliminary census figures are causing sobs all over the state," wrote *Ketchikan Daily News* Editor Lew M. Williams, Jr., in commenting on ramifications of first totals of Alaska's 1970 census. For one thing, the preliminary totals are expected to be very near the official figures to be released later this year, and Alaska isn't growing as fast as some had assumed. The State Department of Labor estimated in June that Alaska's population was 313,200, nearly 20,000 more than the actual preliminary total of 294,417.

Each person counted in a city is worth about $25 in shared state revenue, and every person in the state figures in allocation of some federal funds. The 1970 census will determine the geographic makeup of the state legislature for the next decade, and political power shifts are in the wind. Commented Editor Williams: "Anchorage with 14 of the 40 representatives in the legislature now has almost one-half of the state's population. Preliminary figures give the Anchorage borough in district eight 123,631 people. The City of Anchorage is credited with 46,137 of these—more than the Fairbanks borough or entire Southeastern area. . . .What it probably means in Southeastern Alaska is that the Wrangell-Petersburg district will be combined with the Sitka district and Haines-Skagway will be thrown in with Juneau. Cordova will disappear as a district."

Although they set the growth pace, neither Anchorage nor Fairbanks were happy with the 1970 preliminary totals. "Fairbanks' city pride took a rude jolt last week when preliminary figures issued by the Bureau of the Census fixed its population at only 14,336. The truth is, we're larger than that," said an editorial in the *Daily News-Miner*. "Last year Fairbanks shared revenues based on a city population of 20,000. A drop to 14,000 would be extremely costly." Fairbanks claims it should receive credit for nearly 4,000 persons annexed to the city this year. The Bureau of Census bases its count on a city's population as of January 1, 1970. Now that more residents apparently reside outside the City of Fairbanks, the weighted vote enjoyed by city councilmen who also serve on the Fairbanks North Star Borough assembly will be lost. Anchorage city officials are unhappy with a total that shows only 1,900 more city residents than in 1960. "We find 1,900 absolutely unacceptable," said a disgruntled councilman. The Greater Anchorage Area Borough added about 9,000 in the last 10 years to far outdistance the city in both total and growth rate. The Greater Sitka Borough slumped from 6,313 in 1960 to 5,965 in 1970. The Juneau-Douglas Borough showed a total of 13,338, but the City of Juneau dropped from 6,797 in 1960 to a total of 6,002. The new figures put Kotzebue and Bethel above Wrangell and Petersburg in state ranking.

'Historic Day'... Senate Okays Land Claims Bill
September 1970

"The most historic day for Alaskans since statehood," was the way Senator Mike Gravel described passage by the U.S. Senate on July 15 of a native land claims bill which appropriates $500 million in cash payments over a period of 10 years to the state's estimated 55,000 Indians, Eskimos and Aleuts. With a further provision granting the state's natives a two percent overriding royalty on oil and other mineral production from federal and state land until $500 million is reached, the settlement package totalled a billion dollars. Land provisions of the bill, passed by a vote of 76 to 8, call for a grant of 7.5 million acres in fee simple, plus 2.5 million acres on which only surface rights would be held. Pressed by the Alaska Federation of Natives, an amendment calling for land grants of 40 million acres was defeated. Congressman Howard Pollock, who must lead the bill through the House of Representatives, expressed confidence that it would pass, but probably with some changes.

A Forest Service Ally in Sierra Club Suit
September 1970

The Sierra Club lawsuit against the U.S. Forest Service, which seeks nullification of the federal agency's sale of 8.75 billion board feet of timber to U.S. Plywood-Champion Papers, Inc., is scheduled for trial August 17. USPCP has joined the Forest Service as co-defendant. L. Clair Nelson, vice president of legal affairs for the company, said that his firm had intervened because "we wanted to be side by side with the Forest Service in the defense of the suit." In addition to requesting that the timber contract be declared null and void, the Sierra Club is asking an injunction prohibiting the Forest Service from granting any permits, leases or title to land at Berners Bay to USPCP for a pulp mill.

The company conducted a town hall-type meeting June 18 in Juneau to give local citizens an opportunity to discuss possible impacts on the environment of the proposed $100 million pulp mill-sawmill complex. The meeting was packed, and members of the panel of ecologists retained by USPCP answered questions from the press, the audience and over the telephone for two hours.

Early in July the company signed a contract with a Tacoma, Washington, firm for a $400,000 well exploration project at the mill site to determine whether well water is available in sufficient quantity to supply the proposed mill.

Theft of a Log Cabin
August 1970

Thieves demonstrated a new high in bold determination when they zeroed in on the 20 by 24-foot log cabin of W. H. Swift of Fairbanks. The unbelieving owner reported the log-loving larcenists dismantled the cabin log by log and loaded the loot on his trailer to carry it away.

Yuk Dialect in Schools for the First Time
October 1970

Much of the strangeness of school was gone when school began in September for Eskimo first graders in schools at Bethel, Akiachak, Nunapitchuk and Napakiak. The youngsters, for the first time, were speaking their own Yuk dialect. The pilot program aimed at teaching the first graders in their native tongue was developed as part of the Alaska Rural Schools Project. English is being treated as a second language, with conversational instruction starting in the first grade. Project leaders expect the children will be able to read English by the third or fourth grade. The Yuk dialect will be used through the fifth grade. In developing a written language for Yuk, linguists used "a lengthened square" in Yuk to explain the English word "rectangle." "Washing machine" has become "an instrument for the removal of grime" in the Yuk dialect. Present plans call for expansion of the program as more teaching aides are trained in use of Yuk.

No Pipeline Permit Yet
October 1970

"Future" was the word stamped on all plans to move Alaska's North Slope oil to market as the 1970 construction season drew to a close without a permit being issued for construction of a 48-inch pipeline from Prudhoe Bay 710 miles to Valdez....On the first anniversary of the record $900 million sale of North Slope leases in September, 1969, the best hope that royalty-producing, job-making oil would start flowing came from Secretary of Interior Walter J. Hickel's Seattle announcement that he expected a permit for the pipeline would be issued by next spring....It appeared that TAPS, Alaska's best known acronym, translated into Trans Alaska Pipeline System, would hear "taps" as the eight-company TAPS consortium decided to reorganize under the name of Aleyska Oil Pipeline Service Co....Record shipments of pipe and oilfield supplies were delivered to Prudhoe Bay in August and more than 200 miles of Japanese-made lengths of the huge pipe was stored in Valdez by early September....Oil company executives said they were "very pleased" with results obtained thus far from hot oil pipeline tests being conducted near the University of Alaska....Canada's Minister of Public Works, Arthur Laing, said that oil pipeline tests being conducted near Inuvik, N.W.T. are showing no damage to permafrost and no disruption to wildlife....Commissioner James Smith of the Yukon made an inspection trip of Herschel Island, reported to be the best port nearest Prudhoe Bay, and said, "We're going to see some exciting developments up there." Canada is investing $500,000 in studies of Herschel Island and its potential as a tanker port....The Coast Guard cutter *Staten Island* conducted summer oil spill tests in the Arctic Ocean on both water and ice to gain knowledge for future emergency action....British Petroleum made a grant of $25,000 to assist in a study of the tundra biome ecosystem in the Arctic.

A New Klondike Strike ...$1,000 in Four Days
September 1970

Eldorado Creek in the Klondike blazed with new excitement this summer, 74 years after George Carmack made his historic strike. It all started when Albert Bolduc, 42, and his son, Ron, 23, both of Kelowna, British Columbia, arrived in Dawson City, bent on seeing the Gaslight Follies. They were four days early, so the elder Bolduc decided to try and find four gold nuggets for a ring. The Dawson City mining recorder reported there was a mining claim open on Eldorado Creek that could be worked by paying a $10 registration fee. In four days of panning, the Bolducs panned an estimated $1,000 in gold. Holders of adjoining claims rushed to the creek, hoping to duplicate the Bolduc's luck in finding nuggets where placer gold is common. The instant miners declined an offer of $5,000 for their claim, deciding to ponder the possibilities involved in their rediscovery of the Klondike's yellow metal.

A Plan for Cheaper Roads
September 1970

Synthetic foam is being eyed as the key to building cheaper and better roads in Alaska's arctic. Extensive tests conducted by ARCO Chemical Co., a subsidiary of Atlantic Richfield, and the University of Alaska have indicated that 20 inches of gravel laid over a layer of polyurethene foam is less disturbing to permafrost than 60 inches of gravel. The tests were conducted on a 1,000-foot road at Prudhoe Bay, and best results were obtained when gravel was laid over foam protected with a moisture-resisting sealant. Professor G. R. Knight of the University of Alaska estimated that foam-based roads would have a trouble-free life of 15 years. Use of the foam, say test engineers, could result in arctic road-building savings of $150,000 per mile.

Land of the Young? It's a Myth!
November 1970

Three men with a combined age of nearly 250 years used late summer visits to shatter the myth that Alaska is reserved for the young. Glen Wooldridge, 74, of Grants Pass, Oregon, led a six-boat expedition in a 650-mile safari on the Yukon, Porcupine and Tanana Rivers. Ralph Davies, 78, bagged a bull moose in the Alaska Range in late August that scored a near-record 251 7/8 Boone and Crockett points. Less lucky but more amazing was Gordon Jacobs, 93, of Hornbrook, California. He put 8,875 miles on his speedometer in his third solo drive to Alaska. During his travels around the state, Jacobs also did a bit of moose hunting. He plans to return next summer, hopefully with someone who will help him drive on his fourth trip over the Alaska Highway.

Wrangell's Floatplanes Must Yield to Boats
October 1970

Boats hold priority over floatplanes for use of the water in Wrangell's harbor. Because of several near misses of boats by planes taking off and landing, the City Council banned floatplane landings in the city's harbor except when weather makes them necessary.

Voting Age Drops to 18
November 1970

Thousands of Alaskan youths literally came of age this fall as new laws went into effect. Approval of a constitutional amendment in the state's August primary election by a vote of 36,590 for and 31,216 against, gives 18-year-olds the right to vote in the November 3 general election, provided they registered before October 20. Previously denied Alaskans under 21, recently-enacted laws that went into effect on September 25 give those 19 and over the right to purchase intoxicating liquor and work in places selling alcoholic beverages. The new law also makes them responsible for jury duty and authorizes them to act as incorporators of corporations and serve as special law enforcement officers.

Whitehorse to Share a World Premiere... Film Version of a Yukon Classic by Jack London

Co-starring in Jack London's "To Build A Fire," are Ian Hogg and Pepper, the dog. The two got to be such good friends on location in the Yukon that Pepper thought the actor was playing when he followed the script and prepared to attack the dog.

July 1970

The world premiere movie of Jack London's classic story "To Build a Fire" is slated jointly in Whitehorse and London sometime in July.

The British film crew who made the film, David Cobham Productions Ltd., left the Yukon for England April 9 to start working on the 14,000 feet of movie film shot on location in the Yukon.

Commissioned by the BBC in England, "To Build a Fire" will be shown in color as a 50 minute film. The film has also been sold to German television and to Westinghouse in America which plans distribution throughout the nation. Canadian, Australian and Japanese TV companies are also reported interested.

"To Build a Fire" tells of the cheechako who ventured out along with a dog at 70 degrees below zero in the Yukon bush. Despite his precautions, the extreme cold soon starts to numb his limbs and dull his senses. Soon it becomes apparent that to live he must build a fire and thaw his frozen limbs. His initial success and subsequent failure is the dramatic highlight of the story and the film which faithfully follows London's script—a classic man versus nature contest.

The cheechako is played by Scottish actor Ian Hogg and the dog, Pepper, a Yukoner through and through, was supplied by Fred Stretch, Whitehorse dog musher.

Much of the action was filmed at Old Crow, 600 air miles north of Whitehorse and north of the Arctic Circle. It was an average 20 below zero for the ten days the film crew was there. Jack London would have been pleased.

Anticipating problems with the co-star, Hogg and Pepper lived together for the entire location period in a shack, and not in a warm motel with the rest of the crew. But they got on so well that Pepper just thought Hogg was playing when the script called for the actor to attack the dog so he could use Pepper's coat to keep warm!

British Actor Ian Hogg applies "frost" to his beard with a mixture of icing sugar and greasepaint. His skin was treated to give it a blue-black pallor. At the time of the March-April filming of Jack London's short story "To Build A Fire," it was just too warm in the Yukon for natural frost to form on Hogg's beard.

The final product will be an ambition fulfilled for producer-director Cobham. "The story has always appealed and here was the place it had to be done. No place that was just cold in the winter and snow would do," he said in justifying the 14,000 mile round trip.

Jim Stirling

Diplomas for the Isolated
September 1970

Isolation is being eliminated as a barrier for Alaskans who want to receive high school diplomas. Commissioner of Education Cliff Hartman has announced that persons without access to community college programs can now obtain a high school equivalency degree through correspondence study. On completion of the study program, the applicant is given a series of two-hour tests on basic subjects in the state's high school curriculum. If he passes the exams, a high school diploma is awarded.

Season's First Whale
August 1970

The first whale kill of the season at Barrow in early May sent a steady stream of men, women and children by dog team and snowmobile out on the arctic ice to join in the sharing of a 55-foot bowhead whale. A 25-knot wind and temperature of 15 degrees above zero didn't dampen the enthusiasm of the Eskimos on the 12-mile, midnight trek over the ice pack to the whaling camp. By early May, Point Hope whalers were reported to have taken four of the huge mammals.

1970

Some Bounties End
August 1970

Payment of $50 wolf bounties ended July 1 in all of Alaska except in the southeast where wolves are a threat to deer. The action to end the bounty system on wolves was taken at a recent meeting of the State Fish and Game Board.

From ACS to RCA
November 1970

ACS, three letters long synonymous with communications in Alaska, is fading from the scene. Recent approval by the Alaska Public Utilities Commission of the offer of RCA Alaska Communications, Inc., a subsidiary of Radio Corporation of Alaska, to purchase the Air Force-operated Alaska Communications System, paved the way for an end to military operation of the state's long distance communications network. Approved earlier by Congress, the RCA Alascom purchase involves payment of $28,431,132 for the far-flung system, spending of an additional $27,683,000 on improvements within three years and rate reductions amounting to $40 million Purchase of an interest in the Bartlett earth station at Talkeetna and extending and upgrading service to 142 bush communities are involved in the improvement package. With a history dating back to 1900, ACS will turn over to RCA Alascom 48 communications stations and 714.8 miles of long distance telephone lines. Also involved are microwave and submarine facilities extending from Ketchikan to the Aleutians, and from the Canadian border to Nome.

Fire in Ketchikan
November 1970

A fire on Ketchikan's downtown waterfront August 24 caused an estimated $150,000 to $200,000 in damage. A Ketchikan Cold Storage building, a warehouse serving Tongass Trading Company, and the Tongass Marine Store were damaged by the fire, with the warehouse suffering the worst damage. Firemen suspect boys playing with fire may have started the blaze.

Ketchikan Chamber of Commerce

Juneau Challenges Ketchikan's Claim as Third Largest City

November 1970

The new sign pictured above was attached to Ketchikan's Welcome Arch on Mission Street in mid-August, after the KETCHIKAN DAILY NEWS proclaimed the city as third largest in the state. The newspaper based its claim on preliminary U.S. Bureau of Census figures for 1970, which showed Ketchikan with a population of 6,703 and Juneau with 6,002. The 1960 census counted 6,797 persons in Juneau, making it the state's third largest city, followed by Ketchikan with 6,483 residents. The DAILY NEWS' proclamation drew a retort from Juneau's newspaper, the SOUTHEAST ALASKA EMPIRE. The EMPIRE pointed out that on July 1, (three months after the 1970 census count), the area unified to become the new City and Borough of Juneau, with expanded corporate limits encompassing a population of 13,338. The EMPIRE also suggested Ketchikan ship its new sign to Juneau.

University – A Magnet
September 1970

Rising national concern for the environment is believed partly responsible for an increase of nearly 20 percent in applications for admission to the University of Alaska. By mid-June the university had received 1,408 applications compared to 1,206 by the same period in 1969. Wildlife Management and Interim Studies programs have attracted the most applications. "The Wildlife Management program is unique," said Ann Tremarello, assistant director of admissions. "Nothing quite like it is available elsewhere." Reversing the 1969 pattern, when Alaskans filed a majority of applications, the 1970 count showed 717 requests from nonresidents compared to 570 in 1969.

No Rush for Land
October 1970

Fewer than 4,000 acres of land have been filed on under the state's open-to-entry program which started on October 15, 1968, according to the State Division of Lands. The law allows staking of up to five acres of land, including not more than 400 feet of water frontage, in an area ranging from Fairbanks to Homer and Seward, and including about 2.5 million acres. As of early July, 760 persons had filed for land under the program, but none had yet requested purchase under provisions of the law. Land-seekers from as far distant as Florida, Massachusetts and Hawaii have come to Alaska in search of land under the new law. Practically all of the areas open to entry are inaccessible by car.

The Independent Voter
October 1970

Asserting their independence of either major political party, 46,614 Alaskan voters have registered "no party." As of July 28, the "no party" voters outnumbered the combined total of those registered Democrat (26,951) or Republican (16,516), according to Mrs. Thelma Cutler, state director of elections. Mrs. Cutler told a luncheon meeting of the Greater Juneau Chamber of Commerce that she expected 100,000 to 105,000 persons to be registered in time to vote in the August 25 primary election. She said that of the 294,000 population, possibly 110,000 to 120,000 might be eligible to vote.

North Slope Cleanup
November 1970

Alaska's North Slope—that section of it controlled by Standard Oil of Ohio and BP Alaska, Inc.,—will soon be clear of thousands of steel oil barrels that now mar its stark landscape. BP Alaska has used Hercules Airfreighters to move more than 4,000 oil drums from its lease acreage and the backhaul to Fairbanks is expected to end late this year. The barrels are worth $10 each in Fairbanks. The oil company is also flying non-burnable scrap metal to Fairbanks although much of it and many of the oil barrels were not left on the Slope by BP Alaska. ...In another phase of the Arctic cleanup, the Bureau of Sport Fisheries and Wildlife and U.S. Geological Survey made progress in scouring debris from the Arctic National Wildlife Range. Eight hundred five-gallon gas tins, more than 100 55-gallon oil drums and miscellaneous loads of abandoned camp equipment were cleared from the 8.9 million-acre range last summer. Much remains to be done, however, as Secretary of Interior Walter J. Hickel noted on an August visit to the Arctic. "There are over 100,000 drums still on the coast, and I am going to push to see that the Federal government does something about them," said Hickel. He reported that most of the oil barrels were abandoned by military and civilian users during construction and operation of the DEW Line.

Whales, Sharks Enliven Fishing in Alaska Waters

November 1970

Silver salmon brought cash prizes, but it was sharks and whales that produced special thrills for Alaskan fishermen in late summer. Darrel Allen of Wrangell hitched a brief ride aboard a huge humpback whale. When the whale's flipper got tangled in Allen's gear, it surfaced and the small troller's bow was riding high on the whale's back, its stern nearly flooded. "Each time he flipped that big old fin it sent cascades of water over the deck and darned near drowned me," Allen told the Wrangell Sentinel. "He had a very bad case of halitosis." Finally, the whale swam away, taking one of Allen's bow poles and lines as a souvenir. ..."The *Seven Hi* went up one side of that whale and slid back into the water," said Ted Telgenhoff of his collision with a whale in Frederick Sound. "She (*Seven Hi*) was clear out of the water for a time. It was so close I could see the barnacles," said the surprised skipper. ...A.G. Bunch and Dale Murphy were fishing in Seward's Resurrection Bay with 20-pound test line in mid-August, when they started losing halibut. Finally turning to nylon braided ski rope, they caught two sharks that weighed in at 450 and 300 pounds. Laid nose to nose, the sharks were as long as the 14-foot boat used by the anglers. Bunch and Murphy estimate there were 25 to 30 sharks in the school they encountered. ...Largest of more than 4,500 silver salmon caught in Seward's Silver Salmon Derby was a 16-pound, 15¼-ounce fish caught by Mrs. Miriam Thom of Elmendorf Air Force Base. It was worth $3,000 to the lucky lady. Donald Sherwood of Fort Richardson won $1,500 with a silver one ounce lighter than the winner. ...Fred Searle of Valdez won $1,000 for the biggest silver caught in the Valdez Silver Salmon Derby, a fish weighing 17 pounds, 10 ounces. ...Veteran Kodiak fishermen were bug-eyed when the *Alrita*, skippered by Otto Jangaard, delivered a 420-pound halibut to B & B Fisheries. Caught in Kodiak waters and worth $125, the giant was eight and one-half feet long.

1970

End of an Era
* * *
Street Paving Buries a Link with Nome's Past

Wilma Knox

November 1970

Start of work on paving Nome's famed Front Street, first in the city to be hard-surfaced, was a traumatic experience for Albro Gregory, anti-paving editor of the Nome Nugget. "Nome's glorious frontier past will be sliced off tomorrow when blacktopping crews place an ebony-colored band of mourning on our town's fabled Front Street," wrote Gregory in a black-bordered editorial on the eve of the paving project shown here. "It is an end of an era in Nome, and that is for sure. Something is gone that can never be restored; something good and close and saddening, like having to throw away a pair of treasured bedroom slippers."

Bow-and-Arrow Hunter
November 1970

Stalking within 18 yards of his quarry, Bob Hansen of Anchorage bagged a Dall ram in the Chugach Range with a bow and arrow. The sheep had a one and one-eighth curl and measured 39 inches. Hansen had previously shot bear, caribou, goat and deer with his 50-pound bow.

The Primary Election ... Governor Miller Wins
November 1970

Incumbent Republican Governor Keith Miller edged out his challenger, Representative Howard Pollock, in the state's gubernatorial primary race August 25, while on the Democratic side, former Governor William Egan outran Anchorage grocer Larry Carr by a better than 2-1 margin. Egan lost the governor's chair in 1966 to Walter J. Hickel, whose subsequent appointment as Interior Secretary elevated Miller to the post of governor from that of secretary of state.

Official returns from statewide races in the primary election, with absentee and questioned ballots counted, are as follows:

Governor: Republican—Keith Miller, 19,019, Howard Pollock, 16,602; Democrat—Larry Carr, 11,280; William Egan, 23,883; James Russell, 213. *Secretary of State*: Republican—Brad Phillips, 11,884; Robert Ward, 20,121; Democrat—Red Boucher, 14,703; Emil Notti, 12,759; Charles Sassara, 10,748. *U.S. Senate*: Republican—Fritz Singer, 1,335; Ted Stevens, 39,718. Democrat—Joe Josephson, 12,669; Wendell Kay, 16,627. *U.S. House*: Republican—C.R. Lewis, 17,345; Frank Murkowski, 22,034; B. Dickerson Stevens, 2,283. Democrat—Nick Begich, 28,785.

All five of the constitutional amendments on the primary ballot won voter approval. The tally: Amendments lowering the voting age from 19 to 18, for 36,590, against 31,216; eliminating a knowledge of English as a prerequisite for voting, for 34,079, against 32,578; changing the title of secretary of state to lieutenant governor, for 46,102, against 18,781; providing for election of the state supreme court chief justice by all the court's justices, for 44,055, against 19,583; providing that the court system administrator serve at the pleasure of all the justices, for 43,462, against 18,651.

Oil Pipeline from North Slope ... 'Monstrous Tube'? ... or Economic Necessity?
December 1970

The unbuilt Prudhoe Bay-Valdez oil pipe line dominates Alaska's political and economic scene as 1970 draws to a close even as it did at the year's start. Secretary of Interior Walter J. Hickel continued repeating his earlier prediction that he expects construction on the pipe line to begin "late this winter or early next spring." Speaking to the State Chamber of Commerce in Anchorage early in October, E. L. Patton, president of the Alyeska Pipeline Service Company, described the need for North Slope oil as "becoming more critical by the day." Calling for removal of all "artificial obstacles to the pipeline," Patton said, "This is a time when the desires of special interest groups must not take precedence over the demonstrated needs of our citizenry as a whole." Despite the Sierra Club's description of the proposed pipe line as a "Monstrous tube," Patton reported, "At this time we know of no technical or environmental problems which cannot be licked...We will of necessity disturb the environment. Our challenge is to assure that this disturbance will not result in anything beyond temporary scarring...We are proud of the performance of the oil industry in protecting the environment on the North Slope...We fully expect to be even more proud of our environmental accomplishments with this pipe line project. But we are not going to have anything to be proud of if we don't build the system."

...Governor Keith H. Miller told the State Chamber of Commerce, "For us to properly protect our environment we must have the financial means to budget for the necessary programs... Further delay of the pipeline project jeopardizes future state revenue and puts off the day when Alaskan crude oil can go to market and be utilized to help meet the power needs of our nation."

...Senator Ted Stevens told the Fairbanks Chamber of Commerce he believes ALPS will construct the line in 100-mile segments, starting on those which are free of major permafrost problems... A consultant for the W. J. Levy Corporation, adviser to the Legislative Council, said in Anchorage that 1974 seemed a "reasonable target" for completion of the pipe line... The Department of Interior expected ALPS would file a new application for a pipe line construction permit late this year... More than 500 miles of the 48-inch pipe needed for the world's largest non-government construction project is now stored in Alaska, 287 miles of it moving over the Valdez docks.

... "The litter situation is a lot better than it was," said a Bureau of Land Management spokesman recently in commenting on oil industry efforts to demonstrate concern for the environment. The BLM is assisting the big clean-up by designating half a dozen dumps for deposit of non-burnable material. Gulf Oil hired Eskimos to clear more than 33,000 acres on the Colville Delta of everything from oil drums, boxes and paper to old clothes. The Eskimos will use snowmobiles in November and December to remove the trash to pick-up points for transportation out of the Arctic... Out-of-bounds to visitors only a short time ago, the North Slope oil operations are now so relatively neat and clean that regular tours of the area are conducted for VIP's.

...And while Canadian government and industry leaders continue their push for a gas pipe line from Prudhoe Bay through Canada, their enthusiasm is not shared by the Indians at Old Crow, farthest north settlement in the Yukon. Chief Alfred Charlie recently advised the Minister of Indian Affairs and Northern Development that "oil exploration in Old Crow Flats should cease." He said it was the objective of the Old Crow people "to preserve to ourselves and our children the possibility of continuing our traditional practices so far as we desire, to preserve for the benefit of the whole Canadian nation an area of wilderness still untampered with."

Theft of Aged Eskimo's Winter Wood
November 1970

Mrs. Minnie Tucker, whose age is reckoned at somewhere between 109 and 111, will be warm this winter despite the thief who stole all the wood from the shed near the small cabin of Fairbanks' oldest resident. When the community learned of the theft, it rallied to the aid of the Eskimo woman who lives alone, cooks for herself and chops her own wood. Mrs. Tucker has now been "adopted" by troops from Fort Wainwright and Eielson Air Force Base as well as many Fairbanksans and a fuel supply is assured.

A Walrus Meat Freezer
August 1970

A huge freezer for storing up to 200,000 pounds of walrus meat is being constructed at Savoonga on St. Lawrence Island and will be ready for use by November. Designed by the Institute of Arctic Environmental Engineering at the University of Alaska, the electricity free unit will be maintained at between 0 and 20 degrees F. by thermal convection loops. Its principal use will be storage of walrus meat, a staple in the diet of Savoonga Eskimos. If the $93,000 pilot plant is successful, similar freezers may be developed for other coastal villages where food preservation is a problem.

Down Through the Permafrost

Anchorage Daily Times photo by Gladys Reckley

November 1970

Getting a close-up look at the problem-making permafrost in the Copper River Basin is Secretary of Interior Walter J. Hickel. He is shown conferring with Dr. William Pecora, chief of the U.S. Geological Survey, before descending 50 feet into an entry hole which penetrates permafrost near Glennallen. The Geological Survey constructed a number of such holes in the area last summer in an effort to find a safe method of constructing the Prudhoe Bay-Valdez oil pipe line.

Klukwan Mine Lease
September 1970

Iron rich lands near the Chilkat Indian village of Klukwan, 22 miles north of Haines, have been leased to the U.S. Steel Corporation of Pittsburgh. Members of the village council voted early in June to accept the company's bid of $55,000 for mineral rights to 589.29 acres of the Klukwan Reservation. The lease will run for ten years or as long thereafter as minerals are produced in paying quantities. The area has an estimated 500 million tons of material averaging about 13 percent iron and two percent titanium oxide, and is adjacent to a deposit containing about 1,500 million tons of similar mineralized rock on non-Indian land. New refining procedures have made the ore with titanium usable. The Bureau of Indian Affairs reports the steel company will study plans for developing the huge iron deposits on the reservation and other adjacent properties also under lease to the corporation.

Record Enrollment for University
December 1970

The University of Alaska's record-breaking 1970-71 enrollment of 2,693, includes students from 125 Alaskan towns, every state except North Carolina and 21 foreign nations. Neighboring Fairbanks leads as a student contributor with 852, followed by Anchorage, 208, and College with 207. Juneau contributed 85 and Nome and Kodiak each sent 30. California is home for 149 students, followed by Washington with 52 and New York with 49.

Strenuous Eskimo Games
November 1970

The first Northern Games staged at Inuvik, Northwest Territories, in mid-July was so successful that plans are already advancing for the 1971 event. Attracting contestants from Alaska, the Yukon and Northwest Territories, the games were so strenuous that winners of the blanket toss and high kick competition wore crutches when awards were presented. New to the Alaskan competitors were such contests as those for "Good Woman," boiling fish, dry fish making, roasting fish, tea boiling and bannock making. Events imported from Alaska and strange to Inuvik residents were the blanket toss and kayak races.

October 1970

Last time we were out hunting couple female walrus went after and man! We were scared almost to death and lucky we can see them in the water when they attacked our boat and Danny Oxereok who was running the outboard motor turned the throttle at full speed. The animal that attacked us swam inside the water and she was swimming very fast and good thing the old days are past, otherwise if we didn't have this good little engine a outboard Evinrude 18 hp this walrus would gave us a big hole and maybe put our boat upside down and we would be swimming this ice cold Bering Strait Sea.

—Clarence Ongtowasruk
Wales Correspondent
NOME NUGGET

No Handicap for this Fisherman

Alaska Department of Health and Welfare

November 1970

Robert L. Sidney, 22, of Juneau, center, caught both the 34-pound king salmon he is holding and the 32-pounder displayed by Russell Bartoo, right, during a day of fishing last summer at Berners Bay, approximately 34 miles northwest of Juneau. Looking on is Mrs. Margaret Bartoo, Sidney's mother. Sidney was permanently paralyzed from the chest down three years ago in a gymnastics accident.

Tracing the Mighty King Salmon... 2,000 Miles up the Yukon to Spawn
November 1970

For the king salmon driven by the urge to spawn 2,000 miles up the Yukon River in the creek of their birth, Wayne Wilson was the last hazard in 1970.

It was his task, as a worker for Alaska's Department of Fish and Game, to enumerate the salmon as they by-passed the Whitehorse dam through the fish ladder. He also netted a 20 percent sample of fish using the ladder, determining their sex and age and taking scale samples before returning them to the river.

The information was passed on to fisheries biologists in Anchorage, where it aided in estimating future runs and regulating commercial seasons on the lower Yukon.

The story of the long-swimming kings started several months before when they sought out the mouth of the Yukon River. Traveling about 40 miles a day, the fish swim upstream, stopping and feeding only rarely. It is estimated the salmon lose at least 25 percent of their body weight during their journey.

They fight their way through rapids, falls and past fishermen until they reach Whitehorse in the Yukon early in August.

When they reach the territorial capital, the fish are about 60 miles from the shallow creeks where they were hatched four, five, six, seven or more years earlier.

On reaching the dam and feeling the force of water coming over it, they seek the path of easiest resistance and find it in the fish ladder.

The ladder is 1,200 feet long and rises about 22 vertical feet in graded steps. When they arrived at the top of the

Jim Stirling

Biologist Wayne Wilson of the Alaska Department of Fish and Game holds a 42-inch king salmon he studied at Whitehorse, a few short miles from the end of its 2,000-mile journey up the Yukon River.

ladder, the kings found themselves prisoners of Wilson.

Making as many as six trips a day during the peak of the run, the biologist counted the fish in the pool, took his samples and released the salmon to continue their journey.

"There's still a lot we don't know about salmon, and this is a real good place to start trying to learn more," said Wilson.

The fish he studied this year varied considerably in size. Five and six-year olds usually scale from 10 to 18 pounds, while seven and eight-year olds can weigh just about anything. The 42-inch specimen netted and pictured here would run close to 50 pounds. Wilson estimated it weighed probably 70 pounds when it left the Bering Sea.

The 1970 total of 334 kings is comparable to 1969, although this year there were significantly more females than males.

The pioneering effort marked the first time the Alaska Department of Fish and Game had assigned a man to Whitehorse for the full duration of the run. Wilson is working toward a master's degree in biology at Central Michigan University.

—Jim Stirling

1971
FROM KETCHIKAN TO BARROW

Former Governor Egan's Comeback... Senator Stevens Is Top Vote Getter... Democrats Gain in House
January 1971

A former two-term governor of Alaska, Democrat William A. Egan, defeated incumbent Republican Governor Keith H. Miller by a 5,069-vote margin in the state's November 3 general election. Egan, 56, lost the governorship in 1966 to former Governor Walter J. Hickel in a close, bitterly-contested race. Miller, 45, moved up from the position of secretary of state to that of governor two years later when Hickel became Secretary of the Interior. Egan takes with him into office as lieutenant governor former Fairbanks mayor H. A. (Red) Boucher. Miller shared his slate with incumbent Lieutenant Governor Bob Ward. Unofficial returns in the statewide election, with absentee and questioned ballots counted and all but about six precincts reporting, gave Egan 42,212 votes to 37,143 for Miller.

Senator Ted Stevens (R-Alaska), was the state's top vote-getter with 47,478 votes to 32,367 for his Democratic challenger, State Representative Wendell P. Kay. In the race for Alaska's only U.S. House seat, Democratic State Senator Nick Begich defeated former Commissioner of Economic Development Frank Murkowski by a vote of 43,816 to 35,850.

The Democratic tide ran strongly in state House races with the Democrats increasing their plurality from 22-18 to 31-9. Democrats elected from the Anchorage area included two Negroes, the first of their race ever to win election to the state House. The Republicans lost their 11-9 edge in the state Senate, which is now even at 10-10.

A major suprise in the election was passage of a proposal for a state constitutional convention. The tally was 33,997 votes for, 33,678 against calling a constitutional convention. Prior to the election, administration spokesmen, various candidates and business and professional groups around the state had urged the defeat of the proposal on grounds that a convention is not needed at this time. The proposal appeared on the ballot only because the Constitution requires that the question must be placed before the voters once every ten years if a constitutional convention has not been held in that time. Delegates to the convention will be chosen at the next general election, unless the state legislature calls a special election for that purpose.

Voters approved by large margins all 11 general obligation construction bond propositions on the ballot, totaling a record $146.2 million. Approved were bonds for $10 million for airports; $2.3 million for park and recreation facilities; $5.5 million for highway maintenance shops and facilities; $29.7 million for the University of Alaska; $3 million for the Alaska remote housing program; $5.6 million for hospitals, medical facilities and mental health centers; $11 million for community water and sewer systems; $20.3 million for state-operated regional and district schools; $29.2 million for highway construction; $21 million for improvement and expansion of the Alaska ferry system and $8.6 million for construction of correctional facilities.

During the campaign, Miller and Egan locked horns on such major issues as native land claims and how to spend the state's $900 million of oil lease bonus money, with Miller taking the position that payment of the claims was the responsibility of the federal government, and that the state should not have to pay $500 million in royalties on the sale of state land and oil and gas leases. Miller also was on record as favoring establishment of a revenue-producing permanent fund with approximately $500 million of the oil lease money. In an interview following the election, Egan said establishment of a large permanent investment fund is "premature." Alaska first needs to handle the many problems it faces in improving life for its people, he said. He added that settlement of the native land claims remains his top priority.

A 'Moving' Session for Ketchikan C. of C.
January 1971

The late November planning session of the Greater Ketchikan Chamber of Commerce was certain to be "moving." It was held on the state ferry *Matanuska*. Members of the Petersburg Chamber of Commerce were invited to participate in the sessions providing they could be at the dock when the northbound ferry stopped at 1:30 a.m. on November 20, or at 1:15 a.m. on November 22 when it stopped on the return run to Ketchikan.

Bows ands Arrows Guard Big Planes from Big Moose
January 1971

Bows and arrows have been called upon again to prevent a confrontation between the big jet airplanes, including Boeing 747's, which use Anchorage International Airport and moose which also make claim to the busy runways. A special bow and arrow season conducted last year to reduce the danger of a moose-plane collision harvested more than 20 of the animals. The current season opened on November 1 and continues through March 31. Four moose were shot on airport grounds on the opening day, including a cow clipped at 45 yards by Bill Ryan, president of the Alaska State Archers Association. Hunt rules are specific on the size of bows and arrows allowed, and forbid more than 25 archers being in the field at one time. Bow and arrow hunters can't use snowmobiles in pursuit of their quarry, and a hunter can't stalk a moose on an airport runway unless accompanied by an airport security officer.

Is This the World's Largest Moose Rack?
January 1971

Perhaps the world's largest moose rack, this heap of horn was bagged last fall on the lower Matanuska River by Bruce Hodson, second from right. With a preliminary score of 264 Boone and Crockett points, 13 more than the current champion, Hodson's horns measured 79 1/8 inches. Guides Denny Thompson, left, and Bill Sims, right, look on as Fred Mueller shows the coin that cost him a chance at the record. Mueller and Hodson flipped a coin to decide who would shoot the 2,000-pound bull. Hodson won.

Anchorage Daily Times photo by Alice Puster

A Warm Christmas Thanks to RCAF
February 1971

Anaktuvuk Pass Eskimos are thanking the Royal Canadian Air Force for a warm Christmas and winter. When the Eskimo settlement deep in the Brooks Range ran low on fuel oil in early December, it was an RCAF twin-engine DeHaviland Beaver that came to the rescue. On assignment to Eielson Air Force Base for winter maneuvers, the RCAF Beaver made five trips to Anaktuvuk, for the Bureau of Indian Affairs, carrying 17 55-gallon drums of oil on each trip. The plane was able to land and take off in little more than 500 feet of the airstrip which was not cleared of snow because the village tractor was disabled.

Metlakatla's First Bank
January 1971

Metlakatla received its first banking office October 15 with opening of the Metlakatla branch of National Bank of Alaska. The community is located 15 miles south of Ketchikan, and has a population of 1,011.

Bog Saved for A.M. University
January 1971

The only nature-made bog laboratory on a university campus will be around for a long time, according to officials of Alaska Methodist University. Heeding a plea by AMU's "Save The Bog Committee" headed by Dr. Leonard Freese, professor of biology, the board of trustees recently voted to retain 40 to 60 acres of campus land in its original state. Despite the fact the bog could easily be filled to accommodate the busy and growing campus, the bog-boosters convinced university officials that it is a unique piece of real estate and should be unmolested by man. Complete with spongy vegetation surrounding a pond, the bog was described by Dr. Freese as "giving us a look back through the years almost to the ice age."

'Are You Listening, Ma?'

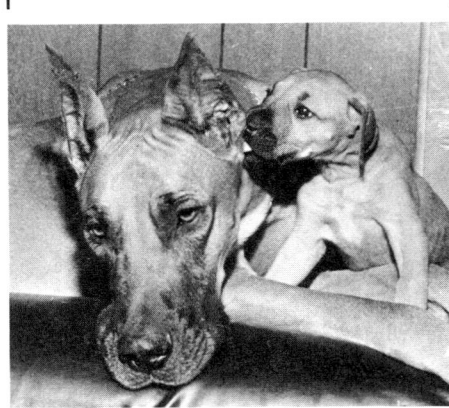

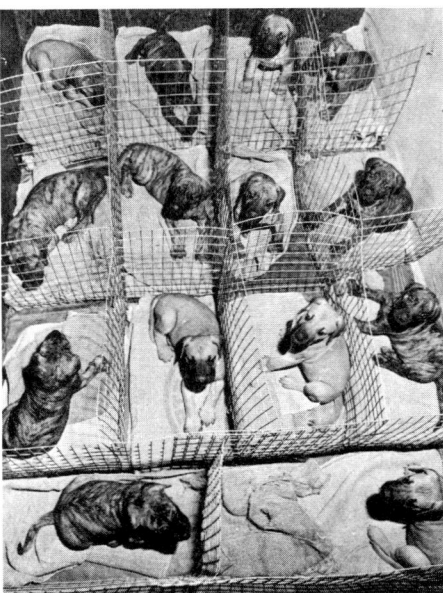

Anchorage Daily Times photo by Alice Puster

February 1971

"Are you listening, Ma?" might be what this puppy is asking Bella, Great Dane owned by Mr. and Mrs. Harvey Longenecker of Anchorage. Bella recently gave birth to the near-record litter of 14 pups shown here.

Hotel-Motel Boom in Anchorage
February 1971

Despite the addition of about 900 hotel and motel rooms in Greater Anchorage in 1969 and 1970, more are being planned by major builders if the economic indicators are favorable. Firms owned by H.L. Hunt, Texas oil millionaire, and his sons have indicated an interest in building a giant downtown complex of 20-story office buildings, hotel and retail stores. A Hunt subsidiary has purchased 66 lots in the Anchorage loop in recent years. Officials emphasize that their ambitious plans are keyed to completion of the Trans-Alaska pipe line. ...A need for more hotels throughout the state was a common theme at the recent meeting of the Alaska State Hotel-Motel Association in Anchorage. "The new hotels now being built in the Anchorage area are needed," said John Stevens of the Anchorage-Westward, outgoing association president. "This summer we won't have the problems that we've had in the past of accommodating the tourists and the business trade."

New Copper Mine? Hope Revived
February 1971

It may be that Alaska will again have a major copper mining operation, first in the state since the demise of the Kennecott mine northeast of Cordova in the 1930's. A consortium of three French mining companies has formed an Alaska corporation and plans to develop a copper-molybdenum property on the Alaska Peninsula in the Chignik area. The new company, SEREM of Alaska, Inc., expects to begin operations next spring on the property of Anchorage businessman Ward Gay. ...An attempt by Kennecott Copper Company to develop a mine on Ruby Creek in northwest Alaska stalled five years ago when a deep shaft was flooded. That property was turned back to an exploration subsidiary for further definition of the ore body.

Big Hunts Succeed
January 1971

Nutritious caribou meat has been provided hundreds of Indian families in the Northwest Territories as the result of successful hunts staged jointly by native hunters and the territorial government. Government planes made rendezvous in the remote Barrens with successful hunters and flew the meat back to settlements. More than 500 caribou were taken by 53 hunters from Fort Rae, who used canoes to reach their food supply. The government flew one plane load of caribou back to Fort Rae for the hunters in exchange for two more plane loads of meat for needy residents unable to hunt. Hides surplus to Indian needs were purchased by the government for distribution to Eskimos in caribou-shy areas. Northwest Territories officials estimate it cost about $4,185 to harvest 70,000 pounds of edible caribou meat—an average cost of slightly more than 13 cents a pound ... Alaska's government didn't sponsor any hunts in the fall of 1970, but those wanting a taste of reindeer—close cousin of the caribou—could buy fresh frozen reindeer roasts and steaks from Bering Sea Reindeer Products at Mekoryuk on Nunivak Island. Cheapest meat was reindeer chuck at 45 cents a pound. Boned loin was $1.25 a pound and tongue moved into the gourmet class at $2 a pound.

One-Horse Town?
January 1971

In the past we sat idly by while the occasionally discourteous visitor from the south has irreverently spoken of ours as being a "one-horse" town. We will no longer tolerate such degrading exaggerations, for we, in fact, have three horses which can be seen on any given day on our main drag. To locate the horses, one simply looks for a crowd of kids.

—George Smith
Fort Simpson correspondent,
NEWS OF THE NORTH,
Yellowknife, N.W.T.

A New Tactic to Save the Polar Bear
February 1971

A new tactic devised by Alaskans opposed to polar bear hunting is expected to give a one-year reprieve to a minimum of 50 bears from the harvest quota of 300 authorized by the Alaska Department of Fish and Game for 1971.

The new technique was used in the September drawing of 300 non-transferable permits from 492 applications received for the 1971 polar bear season, which opens February 1 and ends April 30.

A leader in the save-the-bear movement told ALASKA magazine non-hunting permit winners have paid the $7 big game license fee required for resident polar bear hunters and simply will not use the permit. The no-hunting proponents claim to have won permits for both the western area near Kotzebue and the northern area which includes Barrow. Ninety of the permits are for the northern area and 210 for the western area.

"Most polar bear are taken by airplanes and we consider this unsporting, as does the Boone and Crockett Club which no longer lists polar bear in its big game record book," said a spokesman for the non-hunters. "Some of us are simply opposed to taking polar bear by any means, and we think spending $7 to buy an extra year of life for one of these majestic animals is a good investment."

A Fairbanks resident who drew a permit he won't use commented: "We want to draw public attention to the nonsensical slaughter of polar bear. If the people of Alaska can't save the polar bear, then perhaps the U.S. Congress will step in and restrict polar bear hunting beyond the territorial jurisdiction of the State of Alaska."

Save-the-polar-bear advocates claim that Norway, Denmark and Russia prohibit killing polar bear, and Canada limits hunting to Eskimos who are given quotas.

"Some of us investigated the income realized by Eskimos in Barrow, Kotzebue, Point Hope and other villages from polar bear killing, and we have found it is virtually nil," said a no-hunting proponent. "It is only the white guide, usually only a spring resident, who really benefits."

Biologists claim that the bear population on arctic areas adjacent to Alaska can sustain a harvest of 300 animals in 1971. Department of Fish and Game officials admit they won't know how many bears will be spared by non-hunting permit holders until the season ends.

The Case of the Hijacked Musk Ox Wool: Now It Can Be Told... How Costly Qiviut Sold at Bargain Prices

March 1971

The case of the hijacked musk ox wool can be told now that two enterprising Fairbanks youngsters have retired from the business of selling bootleg qiviut—one of the rarest commodities on the market.

The animals at the University of Alaska Musk Ox Farm had been imported from the wild Nunivak herd and domesticated for a long-range project. They were government property; all the signs on the fence said so.

But did that include the wool stuck to the chain link fence?

Not to youngsters six and eight years old. The qiviut was off the animals and therefore free. Visitors collected it; why shouldn't they?

The dense, wooly undercoat is the finest animal fleece in existence, and garments made from it are warm and non-allergenic. It is removed by hand each spring and shipped East for spinning. Women in the Eskimo villages are taught to knit one by four-foot scarves that weigh less than an ounce, and the finished products are handled through a controlled market.

The two children, having heard opportunity knock, picked the wool from the fence, tied it in neat bundles of two sizes, 25 cents and 50 cents, and sold them in plastic bags to tourists. Business boomed...until the fence was bare of wool.

After consultation, the partners devised a desperate strategy. A few trips to the family garden soon established which vegetables would bring the animals to the fence. Brother fed the front end of the beast while sister, with her small hands, reached through the fence and plucked the back end. Shrubs helped to hide their picking operation from the herders and tourists.

This unique business continued for two summers. Then the children—astride new bicycles—found other interests.

The entire neighborhood, meanwhile, had been chuckling, including the parents of the children and the caretakers of the farm. All had been aware of what was going on but no one had the heart to curb such industrious enterprise. The tourists were charmed by the well-mannered, junior-sized businessman and woman. Who can resist red hair, freckles and dimples with a 25-cent bargain?

—Esther De Witt

Gown of ivory-colored qiviut over gold satin, modeled by Mrs. Laura Bergt, was included in a showing of qiviut fashions in Fairbanks in 1969. Eskimo women of Mekoryuk hand knitted the qiviut fabric for the gown, which is valued at $1,000. Mrs. Bergt, a former Eskimo Olympics chairman, is a community leader in Fairbanks.

Here's how the University of Alaska musk ox looked to the young qiviut hijackers who devised a system for relieving the shaggy animals of their high-priced wool.

Fired from Cabinet Job... Alaska Editors Praise Hickel's Performance
February 1971

Firing of Walter J. Hickel as Secretary of Interior on November 25 was noted by Alaskan editors with praise for the performance of the first Alaskan to be named to the U.S. Cabinet and speculation concerning the views of his successor, Rogers Morton of Maryland, toward the state which is most closely involved with the Department of Interior. Said the *Anchorage Daily Times*: "There is a great wave of national feeling that Mr. Hickel—under such heavy fire at the time of his nomination and during the first weeks of his administration—may well rank with the great secretaries....Instead of being the exploiter and developer he was alleged to be, he became the great protector of the environment....When it comes to dealing with Alaskan issues, Mr. Morton will be able to act much more freely and easily—with his own high regard for Walter Hickel certainly to be a contributing factor in decisions he may make..."

Commented the *Fairbanks Daily News-Miner*: "The growth in stature of Mr. Hickel as Secretary of the Interior has been noted and recognized throughout the country....If anything, one reason undoubtedly influencing Secretary Hickel's abrupt dismissal was that he has been doing 'too good a job!' In protecting our country's environment he has trod, not gently, upon some of the largest corporate toes in the United States....We share the apprehension of many Alaskans now as we view the future with a new Secretary of the Interior entering the picture shortly. Capable though he may be, it is highly unlikely that he will have any great knowledge of Alaska's problems, the very substantial value to the United States of Alaska's tremendous resources, or perhaps even does not realize that the Secretary of the Interior has far more influence in controlling Alaska's destiny than all Alaskans combined—including our governor....We reiterate our opinion that Alaskan Walter J. Hickel has done an outstanding job for all of the United States as Secretary of the Interior during the past two years...."

An editorial in the *Anchorage Daily News* included this assessment: "The former Alaska governor brought a vigor and alertness to the cabinet that has been unmatched in this administration....The loss of Wally Hickel from the Nixon Cabinet, indeed, is a loss for Alaska. But it is a loss for the nation, too."....Said the *Tundra Times*: "Walter J. Hickel may not have the finesse some people might like to see in a public figure, but he does have the stuff that makes men tick. If he has a somewhat rough exterior, we have also noted a generous streak of humanity in the man."

Governor Urges an Alaska Environmental Agency
April 1971

A state Department of Environmental Affairs is "urgently needed to meet the demands of the times for adequate recognition and protection of the Alaskan environment," Governor William Egan told the Alaska legislature January 14 in his State of the State address. The governor said he would propose legislation to establish a cabinet-level department "with responsibility for maintaining clean air and pure water throughout the state and establishing adequate environmental surveillance of the design and construction of major public and private works in the state, including pipelines." Egan also asked the lawmakers to begin planning for at least two other new departments—one for community affairs and the other for transportation.

Egan also presented to the legislature a proposed budget totaling $318,079,000 for fiscal 1972. Included was a request for $3,363,500 for creation of the Department of Environmental Affairs. The proposed budget is 1.2 percent higher than the $314,230,100 approved by the legislature for the fiscal year ending June 30.

Egan urged the lawmakers to "hold the line within reasonable limits" during the year until North Slope oil production reaches its full volume. He reported that the state's $900 million in oil lease revenue from the North Slope will shrink to $85 million by July, 1976, according to current estimates. But he said the bonus monies "have bought us time to plan for other ways of increasing state revenues. Anticipated revenues show a good increase in fiscal 1974-75," he said, "based on the informed estimate that 1974 is the earliest optimistic time during which oil can begin flowing to market" from the North Slope.

Historic Landing
April 1971

History was made on one of the Pribilof Islands last January when an HU-16 aircraft from Kodiak Naval Station touched down on a dirt airstrip, and became the first aircraft ever to land on St. George Island. Most of the island's approximately 150 native residents, who had spent three years constructing the 3,000-foot airstrip, excitedly met the aircraft. It was carrying State Senator Ted Stevens and his party, 1,200 pounds of Christmas mail, a Public Health Service doctor and a native of St. George who had been stranded on St. Paul Island for over a month by high seas. The pilot, Commander J.R. Lewis, ensured that the airstrip was safe by first circling the field and making one touch-and-go landing. The plane's successful arrival ended the island's virtual isolation and established a possibility of medical aid, emergency evacuation and mail delivery by other aircraft.

A Better Way?
March 1971

Alaskan natives, who have tanned animal skins for centuries, are now being taught a better method. In home tanning workshops, sponsored by the Cooperative Extension Service at the University of Alaska, natives learn to use a solution of salt and sulphuric acid to produce skins that are better tanned, less susceptible to odor, and better able to stand up to warm weather. The workshop was the idea of Gladys Musgrove, retired Extension Service home economist, who felt that sending skins out for commercial tanning was a dollar drain on the Seward Peninsula economy.

Apollo the Bear Pays a Visit to High School

Apollo's antics during his day at school kept Ginny Lockwood (shown with Apollo) on the run.

February 1971

Remember Apollo, the orphaned baby black bear adopted last April by the Howard Lockwood family of Juneau?

...... The Lockwoods cared for "Polly" throughout the spring and summer until he became a healthy, happy, 160-pounder, then reluctantly arranged for larger quarters for the bear on the grounds of Cortino Lodge at Mile 134.5, Haines Highway. Just before he left for his new home, "Polly" was treated to a day at Juneau-Douglas High School by Ginny Lockwood, 17, a member of the J-D High senior class.

Governor's Goals: Native Land Settlement ... Oil Pipeline ... Economic Growth
March 1971

"Three landmark objectives" to be achieved in Alaska in the next four years were outlined by Governor William A. Egan in his January 9 inaugural address: A just settlement of the Native land claims; construction of an oil pipe line from the North Slope to Valdez, in conjunction with planned environmental protection, and development of an Alaskan economic policy for growth without inflation.

More than 1,200 out-of-town visitors and Juneau residents participated in a gala weekend of formal inaugural ceremonies for Egan and Lieutenant Governor H.A. (Red) Boucher, despite icy winds which gusted as high as 100 miles per hour and plunged the chill factor to 35 degrees below zero in the capital city's worst weather of the season. An inaugural parade was cancelled, and the state ferry *Wickersham*, tied up at the city dock to provide urgently needed housing for inaugural visitors, was moved 14 miles north to the more sheltered Auke Bay ferry dock after wind and waves caused its mooring lines to snap and pushed the big vessel against the downtown dock. Another state ferry, the *M/V Taku*, which also housed out-of-town guests, was able to remain at city dock.

The inauguration, which represented a tremendous political comeback for Egan, marked the official beginning of his third term as governor of Alaska. He actually had assumed the office on December 7, as prescribed by the state constitution. Egan has lost only one election in a career that began in 1941. He was Alaska's first chief executive and served for two terms. Egan was defeated by Walter J. Hickel in a bid for a third term in 1966. Keith H. Miller succeeded to the governorship upon Hickel's appointment as Interior Secretary in January, 1969. Egan defeated Miller by more than 5,000 votes in the November, 1970, gubernatorial election.

At the time of his inauguration, Egan had named 10 persons to his 14-member cabinet, including Mrs. Irene Ryan as commissioner of the department of economic development. Mrs. Ryan becomes the first woman to fill a commissioner's post in Alaska government. Other new commissioners are George W. Easley, public works; Joseph R. Henri, administration; Charles Herbert, natural resources; Eric Wohlforth, revenue; Emery Chapple, Jr., public safety; Henry Benson, labor, and Kenneth Kadow, commerce. Other new cabinet members are John Havelock, attorney general, and Lt. Col. William S. Elmore, adjutant general of the Alaska National Guard.

The first session of the Seventh State Legislature convened January 11 in Juneau. Representative Gene Guess, D-Anchorage, was elected speaker of the House by a party line vote of 30-9. The Senate, with a membership evenly divided between Republicans and Democrats, was deadlocked in electing a president.

Oldest Pilot at 79
February 1971

The oldest active pilot in Alaska celebrated his 79th birthday at Nome on November 19. Vern Bookwalter has been flying for 51 years and holds pilot license No. 2530. His mail pilot license is No. 82. Using its front page to wish the pioneer flyer a happy birthday, the *Nome Nugget* said, "Oh, to be so young at such an age."

Boat Vanishes ... Two Adults, Six Children Missing
March 1971

A 30-foot gillnetter, the *Andrea*, with two adults and six children aboard, vanished December 2 in icy waters near Juneau. Extensive searches conducted by the Coast Guard failed to turn up a trace of the fishing vessel or its passengers. Missing are Mr. and Mrs. Warren Beardon and their five children, ranging in age from six and a half months to 17 years, and a family friend, Paul D. Kaiser, eight, all of Juneau.

The boat left Juneau November 25 on a hunting trip to Tracy Arm, 42 miles southeast of the capital city. In the following days, Southeastern Alaska was hit by high winds, rough seas and a chill factor constantly below minus 50 degrees. The operator of the *Andrea* radioed distress signals to the Coast Guard light station at Five Finger Island for several hours December 2, before saying the boat was going to be beached, apparently to keep it from sinking. Icing was heavy, he said, and the boat was listing. He reported that the *Andrea's* compass was inoperative and that the vessel was going in circles. The *Andrea* estimated her position to be probably north of Grand Island, 18 miles southeast of Juneau, before communications with the vessel were lost.

A week-long search of shorelines and all bays and inlets of Stephens Passage was conducted by two Coast Guard cutters—the *Sweetbriar* from Juneau and the *Cape Henlopen* from Petersburg—and two Coast Guard helicopters. Joining in the search were the Alaska State Troopers, the Civil Air Patrol and various volunteer vessels and aircraft, both commercial and private. Search efforts were hampered by winds gusting up to 70 knots and by sub-zero weather. The Coast Guard discontinued the search on December 10, but resumed efforts to find the *Andrea* on December 17, after an orange life jacket was found near Point Bishop, 12 miles southeast of Juneau.

Boy's Steelhead Apparently a World Record

March 1971

Apparently a world's record steelhead fell to David White, 8, last year while fishing for king salmon in the salt chuck out of Bell Island, near Ketchikan—42 pounds of fish that everybody thought was a king salmon until a taxidermist began to wonder when mounting it. He called University of Washington professors who checked the big fish out as no king but a monster steelhead. David's parents, Dr. and Mrs. Robert White, live in Seattle. His fish was 43 inches in length but few other details were recorded except that it took David quite awhile to catch the big brute out of a rubber boat in Bailey Bay not far from Bell Island.

No Little Shrimp Here!
March 1971

Large numbers of shrimp up to 10 inches long have been observed at depths to 500 feet in the Gulf of Alaska, according to petroleum geologists who have been scouting the sea bottom in a two-man submarine. The report of the giant shrimp was made by oil company personnel who recently reported on their findings to state and federal fish and game biologists. During one dive the mini-sub was embraced by an eight-foot octopus but managed to escape.

Walrus for Gambell: Unexpected Harvest
March 1971

Hundreds of bull walrus, driven by a strong west wind, piled up on beaches several miles from Gambell on St. Lawrence Island late in November. Led by a hunter who bagged four bulls on the rocks, Gambell's Eskimo hunters enjoyed an unusual winter harvest. One hunter reported that hundreds of walrus had climbed up on rocks on the island, while even more clogged offshore waters during the storm. The November migration of southbound walrus usually passes 30 miles from the St. Lawrence coastline.

Annexation Battle in Anchorage
January 1971

On the eve of its fiftieth birthday as an incorporated city, Anchorage lit a fuse that promised fireworks more spectacular than the display planned for the anniversary celebration. More than 300 persons crowded into Sydney Laurence Auditorium on November 10 to shout opposition to a city plan to increase its size from 16½ square miles to nearly 600. The City Council approved resolutions asking for annexation of the Muldoon area and watersheds east of the city, including Fort Richardson and Elmendorf Air Force Base, the Point McKenzie area across Knik Arm from Anchorage and Fire Island at the entrance to Turnagain Arm. A city administration recommendation that Spenard be included in the annexation move was voted down by the council. Justifying the annexation move on grounds it will increase the city's population and result in more than half a million dollars a year more in state funds for the city, city administrators have asked the Local Affairs Agency to submit the proposal to the Local Boundary Commission. If the latter approves following a public hearing, the Legislature has 45 days to reject the proposal. The Greater Anchorage Area Borough and Charter Commission oppose the idea of annexation without a vote by residents, and the Matanuska-Susitna Borough is fighting the city's move because the Point McKenzie Area, site of the proposed new city, Seward's Success, is now within the Mat-Su Borough. Anchorage's bid to broaden its land and tax base followed defeat of a unified charter proposal in early October. City residents approved the charter, but it was rejected nearly two to one by borough voters outside the city.

Fairbanks Daily News-Miner

Where the Tall Corn Grows...
January 1971

The sight of these palate-tickling ears of ripe sweet corn at the University of Alaska's Experimental Station near College can be credited to polyethylene. Dr. Don Dinkel, shown here with corn brought to maturity in less than three months, covered the rows of planted corn seed with polyethylene in conducting experiments to increase Alaska's crop potential. When seedlings appeared, the plant physiologist cut a hole through the plastic so they could continue growing. Use of the plastic increased soil temperature under the plastic up to 40 degrees above uncovered soil. Dr. Dinkel sees use of plastic covers as a tool that can greatly increase production of corn, squash, peas and other vegetables.

Back to Nature... Environmental Education
January 1971

School kids are going back to nature and the wilderness on the Kenai Peninsula. It's all part of the Kenai Peninsula School District's Environmental Education Program, a pacesetter for the nation. Initiated in 1969, the program involves selection of outdoor laboratory areas near each school on the peninsula. Special projects last fall included a week of camping at Kenai Lake during the last week in September for 60 sixth graders from Seward. During the last week in October, three seventh graders from Kenai Junior High School spent several days studying with game biologist Robert E. LeResche at the Kenai Moose Research Center in the Kenai National Moose Range. With environmental awareness being integrated into the total curriculum of peninsula schools, students at all levels are studying soils, wild plants, stream and water surveys and wildlife art. Eighty teachers are being given special training in the program. Indoctrination in the environmental education approach is planned for 1,200 persons from the South 49 in the next year, providing housing can be found.

Anchorage Profile
January 1971

The average Anchorage adult has a higher educational level than his national counterpart—and he is more likely to change homes. Dr. James Matthew, associate professor at the University of Alaska, turned up these facts in a recent survey. The median educational level of Anchorage adults, he found, is 12.4 years of education, compared to a national level of slightly above 10 years, but 26 percent of the Anchorage respondents "definitely planned to move within a year." Fifty-seven percent said they planned to remain in the community permanently. According to Dr. Matthews, the study also suggested that "a substantial number of new residents leave a community during the first year, but once they get beyond that point they tend to remain in increasing numbers in successive years."

Parking Meters – Again
January 1971

Now that the City of Whitehorse has legal title to its streets, parking meters have been restored to the Yukon's capital. Shortly after being installed in March, 1968, the meters were ruled illegal because the city did not have title to its streets. That oversight was recently remedied and 300 meters are now collecting coins.

For Ladies Only
March 1971

Ladies in Kodiak will be learning about fishing and seamanship this spring in a course designed especially for them. The importance of Kodiak as a fisheries port has led many of its female citizens to ask questions and their questions have led the local college to provide some answers. Among topics to be covered in the course are "Dungeness and tanner crab," "Safety at sea," and "Basic navigation."

Live TV – Super Bowl and Apollo Moon Flight
March 1971

Live television bounced into Alaska with a bang in January as the state's populous Southcentral audience saw the first live network sports broadcast from Anchorage's KTVA on January 3. Following the viewing of the Colts–49'er football clash, the Super Bowl game was broadcast live by KENI in Anchorage on January 17. Next came the Apollo moon flight in early February, with the show being picked up by the COMSAT Station at Talkeetna from the Intelsat satellite over the Pacific. Other signs that television will be playing a larger role in the lives of Alaskans include plans by RCA to construct a ground station at Lena Point near Juneau which would make possible live TV broadcasts between the Juneau-Sitka area and the rest of the state. And investigation is continuing on use of television to expedite exchange of medical information between South 48 medical centers, Alaskan cities and bush communities.

Impact Report: Nation's Need Outweighs 'Some' Environmental Damage

March 1971

The nation's compelling need for North Slope oil outweighs "some" damage that will be done to Alaska's environment in moving the oil to market. That was the gist of a 257-page Department of Interior report on the environmental impact of construction of a 48-inch pipe line from Prudhoe Bay to Valdez. Released in mid-January, the report called for mid-February public hearings in Anchorage and Washington D.C. on the $1.5 billion project. The document includes a route map designating 405 miles of the pipe line that can be buried, and showing 376 miles as "questionable," indicating nearly half of the line may have to be elevated in passing over permafrost areas. No phase of construction could be started without government approval.

Submitted to the Council on Environmental Quality and other federal agencies, the long-awaited report stated: "The government has developed the most stringent environmental and technical stipulations ever proposed upon industry for a project of this nature." Admitting that the pipe line would intrude on the Arctic, the Department of Interior commented:

"While the stipulations mitigate the environmental impact upon other resources, such as fish and wildlife and water quality, it is clearly recognized that no stipulation can alter the fundamental change that development would bring to this area. Whether this transition is adverse or advantageous is a matter of value judgment. For those to whom unbroken wilderness is most important, the entire project is adverse because the original character of this corridor area in Northern Alaska would be lost forever. To others, the opening of this remote country is a proper development which can be defended on both economical and recreational grounds, with the additional argument that this development would affect only a small proportion of Northern Alaska, an area nearly twice the size of California without one mile of state or federally controlled highways."

Governor William A. Egan described the report as a "sound move toward construction of the pipe line." He has made completion of the line a major goal of his administration, and asked the Legislature to appropriate $500,000 for state monitoring of the project. Commissioner of Natural Resources Charles Herbert, whose department will be closely involved with the pipe line, said he was pleased with the report. Former Secretary of Interior Walter J. Hickel repeated his conviction that the pipe line can be built with minimum danger to the environment. Although he claimed some conservation leaders joined in developing the report, initial reaction from the Sierra Club, Friends of the Earth and Wilderness Society was adverse.

Alyeska Pipeline Service Company

Nearly 400 miles of 48-inch pipe are shown in this aerial photo of Alyeska Pipeline Service Company's storage yards at Valdez. The new town of Valdez is located at the top left of the picture.

Alaska Oil and Gas Association

Eskimo snowmobilers finish the task of cleaning 33,000 acres on the Colville River Delta on Alaska's North Slope of abandoned oil barrels. The barrels and other debris were collected in piles last year, awaiting winter movement to a collection point on Neukshat Island.

Fairbanks Daily News-Miner photo by Sue Lewis

Waiting for word that work can start on the trans-Alaska pipe line, this snow-shrouded camp of Alyeska Pipeline Service Company is located on the Dietrich River northeast of Bettles on the south slope of the Brooks Range. The camp is maintained by a skeleton crew.

Moose, Caribou Thrive on Each Other's Range
April 1971

Moose are thriving in the caribou country of the North Slope, and caribou are booming on the moose range of the Kenai Peninsula, Alaska Department of Fish and Game biologists report. "There is a surprising abundance of the animals (moose), particularly in the Sag and Colville River areas," reported Dr. Robert Rausch, ADFG research coordinator, following an aerial survey of the North Slope from the Canadian border to Point Lay, 175 miles southwest of Barrow. He reported observers saw between 1,500 and 2,000 of the animals which have been on the increase above the Arctic Circle. . . .No less surprising is an estimate by Paul A. LeRoux, ADFG biologist on the Kenai Peninsula, that caribou transplants have increased 500 percent in the last four years. Figuring that 25 to 30 caribou survived transplants in 1965 and 1966, LeRoux calculates there are now about 200 animals on the Kenai Peninsula. More than 100 caribou have been sighted between Resurrection Creek and the Chickaloon River. Smaller herds are located north of the Kenai airport and east of Swan Lake. "If growth continues at the present rate, hunting on a limited basis could be initiated in the next few years," said LeRoux.

Skiing Draws Japanese
March 1971

Alyeska's ski slopes had a distinct oriental flavor on a recent weekend when 85 ski buffs traveled from Japan to the resort south of Anchorage for five days of skiing. Excursion fares for groups of more than 40 Japanese skiers are $250 per person. One of the Tokyo skiers reported that it takes as long to reach Japan's best ski areas by bus and train as it does to fly to Alaska.

The Talented Eskimos
March 1971

Eskimos often show extraordinary talent as map-makers, mechanics and artists. A University of Alaska assistant professor of educational psychology suggests in a recently-published paper that these well-known talents may reflect the same sort of intellectual abilities that serve engineers, pilots and research scientists.

In one study, Dr. Judith Kleinfeld reports, "Village Eskimo students surpassed urban Caucasian students in their ability to recall complexly structured images." Unusual skills of Eskimos in perceptual analysis and image memory are illustrated by many examples such as an Eskimo's amazing ability to find his way through monotonous tundra or jumbled piles of sea ice; his resourcefulness in repairing complicated machinery, and the precise detail of his drawings.

Possible reasons for these exceptional abilities and their educational implications are discussed in her paper, "Cognitive Strengths of Eskimos and Implication of Education," which was published by the University's Institute of Social, Economic and Government Research.

A Bear Hibernates Beneath a Mobile Home
April 1971

"Shh! Don't wake up the bear!" Thus have many mothers scolded children, and usually "the bear" referred to is a tired daddy. But in the case of a family near Clear, the warning could be quite literal. The *Fairbanks Daily News-Miner* reports that during the winter, a black bear stirred from his den, wandered around, and ended up beneath a mobile home. The man of the house, father of small children, quickly boarded up the bear's entry hole so that he could ponder the situation and decide what to do. The bear, unconcerned, fell asleep. The homeowner called the Fish and Game Department. At last report, the men involved were trying to figure out a way to remove the animal without harming it or endangering the family, the bear was still snoozing, and the mother, no doubt, was still tiptoeing. And spring is slowly coming . . .

Moose at the Bus Stops
March 1971

So many bold moose have been driven onto Fairbanks area roads by unusually deep snow that parents have been warned to watch their children until the school bus arrives. Kim Domke, 10, of Chena Hot Springs Road was knocked down and mauled by a moose while waiting for a school bus. A neighbor saw the attack and used his car to drive the animal away from the girl who escaped with a few cuts and bruises.

1971

The Mischievous Stork
April 1971

The mischievous stork braved January temperatures in the Far North and made two surprise visits within a week, bringing babies to the bewildered occupants of a helicopter and a ferry! Curtis Louie, seventh child of Mrs. Regina Louie, made his dramatic entrance 8,000 feet above the wintry Canadian wilderness, as Trans North Turbo Air pilot Cliff Armstrong and Dr. T. Albertini, Whitehorse, Yukon, were rushing Mrs. Louie, 26, from her home at Iskut Lake, in northern British Columbia, to the Whitehorse hospital. The premature boy arrived just before the helicopter reached Atlin, British Columbia, where it touched down in 44 below zero weather before continuing to the hospital. According to Mrs. Louie, history was in a sense repeating itself, for she, too, was born somewhere along the trail between Telegraph Creek and Atlin—but on the ground.

Six days after Curtis Louie was born, the passenger list on the *M/V Malaspina*, an Alaskan state ferry, made an unexpected jump from 99 to 100, when Mrs. David Rowland, en route with her grandmother and two-year-old son to join her husband in Ketchikan, gave birth to a girl. The *Malaspina* was in the Inside Passage near Fraser Reach, British Columbia, when Miss Carla Malena Rowland made her appearance. A nurse who happened to be on board, Mrs. Laure Heidelberger, Skagway, assisted in the delivery, and afterward received a hearty ovation from fellow passengers in the ship's cocktail lounge. Mrs. Rowland and her new baby were hospitalized at Prince Rupert, British Columbia, where they were reportedly doing well.

Totems on Garbage Cans ...Tlingits Protest
April 1971

Use of totem designs to decorate City of Ketchikan trash cans has been protested by the Alaska Native brotherhood and Sisterhood camps in Ketchikan and Saxman. Tlingit Indian leaders claim use of the totems on the cans is desecration of emblems of tribal significance to the Raven and Eagle clans.

Boating Fatalities Climb
April 1971

Alaska may set a new national record for boating fatalities in 1970, according to the Coast Guard. The state's 1969 toll was 110 boating deaths, second only to California, which had 117. Incomplete figures show that Alaska surpassed its 1969 total in October, 1970, but a Coast Guard spokesman said in January that final figures would not be available for some time. "When you consider there are in excess of 250,000 boats in California and only 17,000 in Alaska, there is something radically wrong," said Lieutenant Commander Richard N. Westcott, chief of the boating safety branch of the 17th Coast Guard District. Carelessness, poor maintenance and lack of safety equipment are major causes of the high death rate, Westcott said.

Heavy Ice Blocks Tankers in Cook Inlet

Last January and in early February, unusual cold produced heavy ice in Cook Inlet which prevented ocean-going tankers from reaching crude oil terminals in the upper Inlet. At times seven and eight tankers were anchored in Kachemak Bay off the lower Inlet, awaiting improvement of ice conditions. This is a view of two waiting tankers across the ice piled up on the inside of the Homer Spit, in Kachemak Bay.

Staff photo

Chill Factor to 100 Below... Records Shattered in Alaska's Bitter Winter
April 1971

Brutal, mean and bitter were some of the milder adjectives used to describe the record-shattering cold endured by Alaskans in January. From Ketchikan to Kotzebue, from Kodiak to Kaktovik the verdict was the same: January made 1971 a tough winter. The peak (or pit) was reached on January 23 when the thermometer at Prospect Creek, a site on the proposed Prudhoe Bay-Valdez pipeline, recorded 79 degrees below zero, toppling the previous minus 76 reading at Tanana in January, 1886, and establishing a new Alaskan and U.S. record. "Now that it is all over, the cold wave of January is something to remember—because some day we will want to tell cheechakos about it when they ask, 'Does it ever get very cold here?'" commented the *Anchorage Times*. The state's largest city had set a new record of 21 straight days during which the temperature dropped below zero, and more than a week when the high for the day was below zero. Adding to the chill factor were hurricane winds which raked the state during mid-January... Fairbanks schools closed four days—a rare happening—as the temperatures dipped to 60 below zero. Moose-human and moose-dog encounters were frequent, and game biologists predicted a heavy loss to starvation. The exasperation of Interior Alaska was expressed by the *News-Miner* in these words in late January:

"Fairbanks is slowly but surely suffocating in its ice fog; is being strangled by its traffic, and faces the prospect of high if not flood waters from a record fall of snow... The thick, choking fog—a serious form of pollution—has become a way of life when the mercury drops to 30 below zero or lower."...Cook Inlet was so choked with ice that tankers had difficulty reaching the Drift River Terminal and production of offshore wells was cut back to stay within the terminal's storage capacity... "Key-Key-Key-Riminey, But It's Cold, Cries Ancient Key-Bird," said a headline in the *Kodiak Mirror* on January 25. The ice was so thick in Women's Bay, usual mooring site for Coast Guard vessels, that the Coast Guard cutter *Confidence* had to be moved to the city dock to avoid being imprisoned by rare sea ice. Residents were warned against walking on the ice on seldom-frozen Women's Bay....A new January low was recorded at Dawson City in the Yukon when the mercury plunged to 69 below on January 18....The new sport of snowmobiling was introduced at Wrangell, where boats moved the machines to the frozen Stikine River for jaunts on the ice....The Scow Bay correspondent for the *Petersburg Press* reported, "The snows came and they came and came....No one is suggesting that it isn't winter."..."It seems nothing works," commented the *Valdez-Copper Basin News* in reporting on struggles to keep cars moving and homes warm....Mabel Johnson of Kotzebue told the *Nome Nugget*, "This has been the winter of many storms....When the chill factor hovers around minus 100 degrees, one wonders whether it is worth battling all these elements."...State Senator Chancy Croft, his wife and three children had a frightening encounter with the cold when their car stalled near Tok at 78 degrees below zero, and they waited 13 hours for rescue....Problems born in January were hatching in February as frost penetrated below 10 feet in Anchorage to freeze water mains and warmer weather sent water over solidly-frozen creeks.

Three New Ferries Planned... 'Wickersham' to Be Sold
April 1971

Governor William A. Egan unfolded plans January 14 for construction of three new state ferries, including one ocean-going vessel, and eventual sale of the foreign-built ferry *M/V Wickersham*. In doing so, he substantially revised plans for ferry system expansion outlined in a $21 million bond issue approved by the last legislature and passed by the voters in the November general election. Previous plans called for lengthening of each of the three *Malaspina*-class ferries by 56 feet, and acquisition of two small ferries for use in Southeastern Alaska.

The proposed new program would cost $36 million. "This revised program should satisfy the predicted needs for capital improvements for the system in Southeastern Alaska for at least the next eight years without further general fund financing except on a short-term loan basis," Egan said. Breakdown on the financing would be $21 million from bond funds; $8 million from federal funds available under terms of the Federal Highway Act of 1971, which for the first time provides ferry construction money, and an estimated $7 million to come from the sale of the *Wickersham*.

The $36 million would be spent this way: $17.5 million for a new 407-foot, ocean-going vessel to replace the *Wickersham*; $8 million total for two new 235-foot vessels; up to $9 million for lengthening *Malaspina*-class ferries, and $1.5 million for new port facilities at outlying communities in Southeastern Alaska.

The Swedish-built *Wickersham* was purchased by the administration of former Governor Walter J. Hickel. It is the largest ship in the Alaska state ferry fleet, with a capacity for up to 1,300 passengers and more than 100 vehicles, and can berth 384 persons. Under restrictions of the Jones Act, the *Wickersham* cannot carry passengers or freight between U.S. ports and must use a Canadian city at the southern end of its Southeastern Alaska Panhandle runs. Because of this situation, Egan said, "more than $500,000 of likely revenue escapes us each year."

"It is my hope that when the Congress... is convinced of our intent to build a new vessel in America, Alaska will be granted a temporary certificate of exemption from the Jones Act for the foreign-built *Wickersham* until the new vessel is completed," Egan said.

Public Access Okayed
March 1971

The railbed from Palmer to the former coal mining community at Jonesville has been made available for use by snowmobilers, horsemen and hikers as the result of an agreement between the Matanuska-Susitna Borough and Alaska Railroad.

Rough Ride for Lady Snowmobiler in Championship Race

April 1971

Lady snowmobilers in Alaska face rough rides as Mrs. Betty Hight of Anchorage proves in this sequence shot by Alice Puster of the ANCHORAGE DAILY TIMES during the January women's championship race from Anchorage to Big Lake and return. Mrs. Hight's machine balks as she heads up a hill at Peters Creek at left. Her snowmobile got away from her in center photo, and the action ended with both the machine and driver upended.

Record Cold Lingers
June 1971

The winter of 1971 continued its assault on Alaska right through March and into April. All-time lows of 41 below zero at Kenai and 24 below in Anchorage were set just two weeks before the calendar said spring had arrived. And as a proper postscript for the record winter, the National Weather Service reported in April that the new U.S. record of 79.2 degrees below zero recorded at Prospect Creek on January 23, was in error. Due to a slight defect in the thermometer used by Weather Service Observer Wilbert Weisz, the true temperature was minus 79.8 degrees. In line with Weather Service policy, the reading is now entered in the records at 80 degrees below zero. Forty feet below the sea's surface near Kodiak a state fisheries biologist found the water temperature was below freezing in March. At least 200 sea otters died on the north side of the Alaska Peninsula in March

ALPS photo
Wilbert Weisz holds record-breaking thermometer at Prospect Creek.

when unusual cold sealed bays and lagoons with ice, thus keeping the otter from their sea bottom food supply. Several dead walrus washed up on Bristol Bay beaches, a sign of severe ice conditions. The Coast Guard icebreaker, *Glacier,* made a cruise far north into the Bering Sea in March and reported ice seven to 10 inches thicker than normal . . . As late as April, moose were still floundering in snow that blanketed an area from Fairbanks to Homer. A 70-car Alaska Railroad freight train was stalled by snow near Summit for two days in early March, the first such holdup in more than a decade. Nearly 500 Fairbanks area property owners had signed up for flood insurance by early April. The weight of nearly four feet of snow was bending roof trusses in Interior Alaska. The University of Alaska's Cooperative Extension Service reported the February snow load was five times heavier than in 1970, with 46.8 pounds per square foot in Fairbanks on March 1 and 63.4 psf at Cleary Summit. While nature was deciding whether Fairbanks would face a late spring flood, local, state and federal officials continued planning for the worst. Symbolic of the severity of the past winter was a resolution passed by the Northwest Territories Council asking that Canada's Department of National Health and Welfare conduct a research project into the causes and cures of "Arctic Hysteria," known to most northerners as cabin fever.

Effort to Block Timber Sale Fails . . . Sierra Club Suit Dismissed in District Court
June 1971

The Sierra Club's suit seeking to halt a Forest Service contract for the sale of 8.75 billion board feet of timber to U.S. Plywood-Champion Papers, Inc., was dismissed March 25 by Judge Raymond E. Plummer in U.S. District Court in Anchorage.

The 64-page decision said the manufacturing and mill construction requirements contained in a contract between the Forest Service and USPCP "are lawful and their imposition does not violate the requirement of sale for fair market value."

The judge also ruled that the Secretary of Agriculture, in approving the sale, "gave due consideration to all the use values enumerated in the multiple-use sustained-yield act . . . "

The court found that the Sierra Club filed its action "unreasonably" late, that the club had not exhausted administrative appeals through the Interior Department and the delay had "exacerbated" the lumber company's investment of more than $3 million in planning funds to implement the "good faith" agreement with the Forest Service.

The company's expenditures included $100,000 for a panel of environmental experts which selected Echo Cove in Berners Bay, 34 miles northwest of Juneau, as the site of a proposed $100 million pulp mill. On February 10, 1969, Plywood-Champion signed a contract to sell all of the mill's output for 15 years to the Kanzaki Paper Manufacturing Company of Tokyo.

Selection of the Echo Cove mill site was announced by Plywood-Champion in December, 1969. On February 10, 1970, the Sierra Club, together with the Sitka Conservation Society and guide Carl Lane, filed suit to stop the sale.

The plaintiffs charged that the 1968 timber sale "together with previous timber sales, had irrevocably and for the first time in any national forest committed the Forest Service to an inflexible schedule of harvesting all of the virgin-growth forests in Southeastern Alaska to the exclusion of all other legitimate uses." However, the federal court's decision held that the "contract requirements for designation and marketing of timber satisfies the requirements of applicable law."

The plaintiffs have 60 days in which to appeal the ruling to the Ninth Circuit Court of Appeals in San Francisco, and Sierra Club spokesmen said that a decision would be made before the appeal period ended.

'Waqaa' – Will It Sell?
June 1971

"WAQAA," pronounced "Quah-caw" will be Alaska's new greeting for visitors if the University of Alaska's Division of Statewide Services has its way. As part of a tourist-related education program conducted by Dr. Mildred Matthews, the new approach hopes to make the Eskimo greeting as symbolic of Alaska as "Aloha" is for Hawaii.

Billion-dollar Question:

The Oil Pipeline Still Tangled in a Web of Red Tape

May 1971

While Department of Interior specialists sifted through hundred of pages of testimony given by 205 witnesses who appeared during five days of hearings on the trans-Alaska pipeline at Anchorage in late February, it became apparent to Alaskans that the proposed 800-mile Prudhoe Bay to Valdez line has moved to the center of the national and international stage. Following Secretary of Interior Rogers C.B. Morton's early March appearance before the House Interior Committee, Representative Nick Begich of Alaska said it might be seven years before work is started on the pipeline. Senator Mike Gravel told the State Legislature in Juneau that only President Richard Nixon could get the pipeline started this year. "If we don't get a pipeline permit in the next 45 days, we won't get one for two years," said Senator Gravel in Anchorage on March 10. "The pipeline issue has caught the public fancy... Congressmen are getting tons of mail and not very much of it favors the pipeline," said the senator. Throwing more cold water on the hopes of pipeline advocates was an early March statement by Interior Secretary Morton that it would be a "matter of months" before the environmental impact statement required by the Environmental Quality Act of 1969 is completed. Countering suggestions from both Canadian and U.S. leaders that the pipeline should be re-routed through Canada to the Midwest, Governor William A. Egan commented on March 8:

"Should, in fact, North Slope oil be left in limbo, and if a miracle occurred and our Canadian friends permitted pipeline construction through Canada, thence through other American states to Chicago, it is my estimate that it could not be earlier than 1985 before Alaskan oil would be on stream... In the meantime, long before 1985, Alaska's fish and game programs, environmental health and parks and recreation programs, educational and capital improvement programs would of necessity have been reduced to relative insignificance... It must be kept in mind that the State of Alaska would have to make the decision as to whether we permit a pipeline to cross state lands on a route entering Canada... The state cannot permit a reckless change in routing which would create serious damage to the ecology of the Arctic"... In his appearance before the three-man Department of Interior committee conducting the hearing on Interior's draft environmental impact statement, Governor Egan said, "Alaska cannot be a viable state and a total natural preserve at the same time."... Commissioner of Revenue Eric Wohlforth testified that even if North

ALPS photo

Construction camps located along the proposed right-of-way will house workers when construction on the trans-Alaska pipeline begins. The camps include mobile modular housing units, modern utilities (including sewage treatment plants) and microwave communications. Heavy equipment can be seen stored at the camp awaiting commencement of road construction.

> 'Alaska cannot be a viable state and a total natural preserve at the same time.'
> –Gov. William A. Egan

Slope oil starts flowing in in 1975-76, Alaska will not be able to meet its operating expenses by 1980... The most pessimistic state testimony was given by Commissioner of Labor Henry Benson who said Alaska's unemployment rate of about 25 percent is the nation's highest. "Without pipeline activity, we may anticipate one out of three unemployed in 1972, and without the pipeline activity by 1973 we must anticipate a migration from the state and a diminishing population"... Commissioner of Natural Resources Charles Herbert reported that the pipeline would have to stand as high as a three-story house if it were to carry as much oil as described in an anti-pipeline ad. "Gross exaggeration, misstatements of facts and hectic appeals for money are weapons used by charlatans for private gain—they cannot serve conservation," said Herbert... A parade of state legislators, mayors, councilmen and Chamber of Commerce members asked for early issuance of a construction permit to Alyeska Pipeline Service Company which was formed by seven major oil companies to transport North Slope oil. "We have submitted more than 2,000 pages of detailed exhibits and material dealing with every significant issue raised in connection with our application for project approval," said ALPS President E.L. Patton. Claiming that his company was ready to start work on the billion-dollar project, Patton testified, "It should be obvious to anyone who thinks about it that the project cannot maintain in Alaska a capability adequate to go forward if the decision to go forward is delayed indefinitely. Moreover, the cost to the entire country in loss of resource potential far outweighs any speculative benefits to be derived from further delay."

Few witnesses asked that the pipeline be halted or the project abandoned. There were, however, a number of statements questioning the routing through Valdez. The Alaska Conservation Society opposed use of Valdez as a terminal, as did witnesses for other conservation groups. The majority asked

ALPS photo

The University of Alaska at College, near Fairbanks, has been one of the prime sites for research carried out for the proposed crude oil pipeline to be built across Alaska. Six hundred feet of warm pipe were buried in the permafrost, as shown here, to verify Alyeska's mathematical models describing heat flow and permafrost melting and to test the pipeline's effect on vegetation.

> 'There are real live people in this equation, with children, futures and hopes. Do not forget them.'–Vide Bartlett

for further investigation of proposals for rerouting the line through Canada. The Cordova District Fisheries Union, representing 500 Prince William Sound fishermen, voted prior to the Anchorage hearing to oppose use of Valdez as a terminal. "We are not opposed to the pipeline per se, but we are trying to stop the terminus being located on Prince William Sound," said Knute A. Johnson, chairman of the CDFU. Following the hearings, the CDFU voted a fund of $10,000 for court action needed to block an oil terminal at Valdez.... Pro-pipeline testimony most quoted by Alaskan editors was delivered by Vide Bartlett, widow of Alaska's late senator. A resident of Fairbanks, Mrs. Bartlett said, in part: "The worry about environmental damage that could possibly occur in Alaska is not as great a worry for us as it is for those who do not live in Alaska. We understand our environment. We have seen the development of our natural resources and the changes in our environment resulted in betterment for our people... I, who grew up in Cleary Creek, 30-odd miles from Fairbanks, cannot now find the city of Cleary which had a population of 20,000 in 1905 nor can I find the claim where we lived that my father mined. Our faith in nature reclaiming her own is well-founded... My knowledge of Alaskans—natives and old-timers and newcomers—has convinced me they will not allow this line to be built to destroy what they value above all—wildlife and the beauty of the great land. Life in Alaska is not easy. It demands a fierce respect in exchange for a harsh grace. This is not oil versus wilderness. There are real live people in this equation, with children, futures and hopes. Do not forget them. Let's get on with the job."... Diametrically opposed to Mrs. Bartlett's views was David Brower, president of the Friends of the Earth, who said in an Anchorage address on March 10:

"There should be a plan to keep Alaska's oil in the ground... Alaska has

> 'Keep Alaska's oil in the ground.... The pipeline is totally bad news for Alaska.'–David Brower, president, Friends of the Earth

more valuable things than the oil industry. The most valuable thing here is the extraordinary stand of the last great wilderness... The pipeline is totally bad news for Alaska."... Despite creeping pessimism, the Alyeska Pipeline Service Company was continuing plans for construction of the controversial pipeline. Plants for coating more than 650 miles of pipe now in Alaska are expected to be operating at Valdez, Fairbanks and Prudhoe Bay by early summer...

1971

Vacant: One Eagle Nest
July 1971

If a pair of bald eagles decides to set up housekeeping in an abandoned, old nest on Montague Island, they'll find it ready for use. It wasn't until after the Kenai Lumber Company of Seward was awarded a timber cutting permit on Montague by the U.S. Forest Service that the old eagle's nest was discovered in the sales tract. Forest Service officials met with Kenai Lumber executives and it was agreed that 7.5 acres surrounding the nest tree would not be logged. Bird experts report that bald eagles have been known to return to once-abandoned nests.

Some Win, Some Lose
April 1971

Alaskans spent more than $2 million in spelling B-I-N-G-O, guessing on ice breakups, trying to catch prize fish and other contests in 1970, according to the Department of Revenue. In a report to the Legislature, Commissioner Eric Wohlforth said 211 non-profit bingo permits issued by his department brought in $1.2 million, followed by lotteries and raffles which accounted for $391,155. Ice guessing contest and fish derby winners pocketed more than $100,000 in each category. State income from issuing the $10 permits was $3,940. . . . Establishment of a territory-wide sweepstakes in the Yukon is up in the air, with both a Whitehorse group known as the Yukon Betterment Society and the territorial government wanting to operate the lottery. Whitehorse Mayor Bert Wybrew, a member of the YBS, told the city council that the territorial administration has refused to approve the YBS idea of a Yukon-wide lottery, indicating that such a venture should be government-administered.

An Anchorage Pet for 11 Years

Anchorage Daily Times photo by Alice Puster

April 1971

Oley, a hair seal who defied biologists' predictions he couldn't live in captivity to become, perhaps, Anchorage's best known pet, died in January at the age of 11. A star resident at the Anchorage Children's Zoo, Oley was raised by Mrs. Sammye Taplin and was known to thousands of Anchorage school children. He was featured performer in a Japanese film on Alaska. With hundreds of Alaskans helping to keep Oley in food, Mrs. Taplin estimates she cut up about 12 tons of fish for him.

A Farrier in Alaska:
Traveling Blacksmith Makes House Calls to Shoe the State's Growing Horse Population

May 1971

A growing number of Alaskan horses are wearing studded horseshoes, thanks to Henry R. Ferguson, until recently the state's only farrier.

Proof that the art of blacksmithing is far from dead, Ferguson was on the scene

Farrier Henry Ferguson heats a horseshoe in the forge of his mobile shop. A farrier is a blacksmith who shoes horses, as distinguished from a blacksmith who does not shoe horses or a horseshoer who is not a blacksmith.

and ready to go to work when horses started making a sensational comeback in Alaska. Greater Anchorage alone is home for more than 2,000 horses.

Many Alaskans think the horse is the best all-weather, off-highway transport, and such innovations as rubber snow pads and studded horseshoes make Alaskan horses more sure-footed on snow and ice.

The dean of Alaskan farriers, Ferguson even makes house calls. His half-ton pickup with a smokestack poking through the roof is a familiar sight from Palmer to Soldotna.

For the 10 years or so that Ferguson was the only farrier in the state, he and his truck ranged busily from Fairbanks to Homer. Now life is less hectic for him, and he welcomes the addition of a new farrier to the Alaskan scene. "We need the help," he says. "We need more farriers and good horseshoers."

—Ruth Edmonson

Ferguson burns an imprint of the shoe into the hoof of a tranquil customer, Sid. The horse, owned by Donna Crites of Anchorage, is a mixture of quarter horse and thoroughbred.

A Brave Mountaineer
June 1971

Ray Genet has looked down from the top of Mount McKinley's 20,320-foot peak more times—seven—than any other man but the Anchorage-based mountain expert completed one of his toughest assignments on another peak on March 27. On that date, after failing in two previous tries, the Swiss-born mountaineer reached the wreck of a twin-engine National Guard Beechcraft at the 14,800-foot level of Mount Sanford in Alaska's Wrangell Range. Genet confirmed the deaths in the February 19 crash of U.S. Army Major Steven Henault of Fort Richardson and Lt. Col. William Caldwell and Sgt. Herbert Alex, both of Anchorage and Air National Guard members. Genet and Dave Johnston were moved to Mount Sanford by Army helicopter in late February, but vicious winds and cold confined them to an ice cave for days. They were evacuated without reaching their objective. Accompanied by Rex Post, a Pan American Airways pilot who had climbed with him on Mount McKinley, Genet made his second try to reach the wreck in mid-March. Post suffered mountain sickness and in descending with Genet to relieve his condition, the Seattle climber died in his sleeping bag. Determined to finish his grisly task, Genet was flown to the 13,000-foot level on March 27, and by mid-afternoon had reached the wreckage and confirmed the deaths. Storms struck again and he had to remain on Mount Sanford until March 29, when he was airlifted from the peak. Genet has been awarded the Outstanding Civilian Service Medal by the U.S. Army for his work. A certificate of Appreciation for Patriotic Civilian Service was issued to Dave Johnson.

Acts of Heroism... Many Saved from Drowning
June 1971

Acts of heroism saved two youngsters and a man from drowning in Gastineau Channel at Juneau last March. Denise Dunker, 6, was fishing from a downtown dock with her brother Michael, 16, and two sisters, when she fell into the water. Michael immediately jumped in after her, unmindful of the fact that he could not swim. Attracted by the screams of the other Dunker children, Charles Elrod, a National Guard sergeant, ran under the dock, dived into the water fully clothed and pulled out Michael, who was floundering 10 to 15 yards from the dock. Meanwhile, Bill Bernhardt and Mike Sturrock, two charter aircraft pilots who were loading their floatplane at a nearby dock, jumped into a skiff and rowed toward the Dunker children. Bernhardt spotted the top of Denise's head beneath the water and swam to her. He clung to a dock piling, holding the unconscious and seemingly lifeless girl above water until Sturrock picked them up. Bernhardt, Sturrock and others applied mouth to mouth resuscitation and heart massage to Denise for 20 minutes before they finally felt a pulse in her throat. She was taken to a local hospital and is recovering.

In a separate incident, taxi driver Frank See, Jr., and his passenger, Warren Price, rescued Joseph Paul Gregory, 24, from his automobile March 28 after it left the Glacier Highway and landed upside down in Gastineau Channel at high tide. See and Price entered the icy water, kicked in a car window, forced open a door and pulled Gregory to safety.

Two Ketchikan men received certificates of appreciation from the Coast Guard March 1 for rescuing three persons fron Tongass Narrows last year. Cited for their courage and prompt action in pulling three men from waters near Ketchikan and Pennock Island in separate incidents were Ted Grant, 22, a welder for Ketchikan Welding Company, and Robert T. Baade, sport fisheries biologist for the Alaska Department of Fish and Game.

A Rugged Eskimo:
Removes Steel Splinter from His Own Eye
July 1971

The Naval Research Laboratory at Point Barrow cites Charlie Hopson as the type of man it is seeking for duty in the Arctic. Station manager for Ice Island T-3, a floating laboratory, Hopson was cutting a steel cable in mid-January with the temperature at 47 degrees below zero. A three-quarter inch splinter of steel imbedded itself one-quarter inch into the Eskimo's right eye. It missed the pupil but there was heavy bleeding. Holding his eye lid open, he walked back to camp and used a pair of needle-nose pliers to remove the steel. He was later flown to Barrow where a surgeon approved the Alaskan's surgical technique. With no permanent damage to his eye, Hopson was soon back at work on his ice island.

No Canning in Ketchikan; First Time in 70 Years
June 1971

Once known as the "Canned Salmon Capital of the World," Ketchikan will be without an operating salmon cannery this summer for the first time in 70 years. The *Ketchikan Daily News* reported that neither the Ward Cove Packing Company plant nor those of the New England Fidalgo Company will operate. As many as one million cases of salmon were packed in a single season in the 11 canneries that once operated in the Ketchikan area. More than 400 fishermen and cannery workers would have been employed by the two canneries. Win Brindle, president of Ward Cove Packing Company, blamed the decline of Ketchikan's salmon industry on the State Department of Fish and Game and logging near salmon streams.

Spare That Moose!
April 1971

Canada's Director of Civil Aviation has issued a circular advising pilots to avoid flights below 1,000 feet over moose. The circular was issued following a finding that an increase in oil and mineral exploration in Canada's Far North by planes and helicopters was having a detrimental effect on wildlife, especially moose. "Studies on moose have shown that a hard three and a half mile chase in winter is usually sufficient to kill the animal," said the circular.

The Popular New Archangel Dancers: A Cultural Revival of Sitka's Russian Heritage
July 1971

It was early in 1969 that Stella Conway, housewife, mother and 12-year resident of Sitka decided to revive and interpret Sitka's cultural past and at the same time entertain the ever-increasing number of tourists visiting the picturesque city known in the Russian era as New Archangel.

In less than three years, the New Archangel Dancers have established themselves as one of Alaska's most exciting performing troupes. They have appeared more than 200 times in the "other 49," Canada, and throughout Alaska.

British-born Mrs. Conway enlisted the aid of Mrs. Karen Grussendorf, a teacher and director of the Sitka High School Girls Drill Team. Mrs. Grussendorf, an experienced dancer, became choreographer for the New Archangel Dancers.

Steeped in a rich Russian heritage which includes Castle Hill, site of the castle where Russian managers ruled until 1867, the old Russian orphanage, blockhouse, cemetery, art treasures of the Russian Orthodox Church and Sitka National Monument, the city's Russian community came to Mrs. Conway's aid with ideas for costuming and developing authentic Russian dances. The dancers cut out and sewed the first set of costumes, except for hats and boots, which were purchased.

After only a month's practice, the group gave its first performance early in 1969, and before that year ended had given 25 performances, including three aboard Matson Line cruise ships.

It was late in January, 1970, that the New Archangel Dancers faced what was probably their most critical and one of their most appreciative audiences. In Sitka as guests of Alaska Airlines were Vladimir Orlov, vice-president of Russia's Intourist Board, and Alex Savin, economic adviser to the Ministry of Foreign Trade.

The Soviet officials were so moved by the Sitka dancers that they rushed to the stage to join in the dancing and singing!

On the practical side, Orlov and Savin suggested the Alaskan women not hold rigidly to basic steps but be creative in order to fit the music and mood.

Firm evidence of their popularity came early in 1970 when one troupe of eight dancers performed at the Governor's Ball in Juneau on the same day that a second group of equal size was appearing at a travel agents' meeting in Portland, Oregon.

Largest audience to applaud the New Archangel Dancers was at the Alaska Travel and Trade Show at Costa Mesa, California, in March, 1970. Performing twice daily, the dancers were seen by thousands who visited the show.

More than 80 performances were given for tour ships stopping at Sitka last summer. The 1971 repertoire includes such dances as the Korobushka, Karapiet (a Russian two-step), and the Kohanashka, Troika, Hopak and Koketa which are built around a basic polka step. New dances being perfected for the coming season include the Horse Head dance and the Ribbon dance, the latter originating near the Chinese border.

The colorful city that was the cultural capital of the Pacific Rim more than a century ago is in the process of recovering some of its past glory through the talented feet of the New Archangel Dancers.

—Pat Smith

R. V. Smith

New Archangel Dancers strut their stuff in Sitka's Centennial Building.

Whitehorse Star

June 1971

Martha Benjamin of Old Crow, Canadian cross-country ski champion in 1962, now mushes her own dog team in the races at the Sourdough Rendezvous. She finished seventh this year, but won the "most colorful musher and team" award, a new trophy put up by Murdoch's Gem Shop of Whitehorse. Her team is the beautifully-matched Siberian husky team formerly owned and raced by the RCMP at Old Crow.

Six Dozen Hot Cakes Every Day... for Starving Moose

Fairbanks Daily News-Miner photo by C.H. Darby

May 1971

Doing her bit to feed starving moose that have invaded the Fairbanks area is Mrs. Tilly Brockman of 6 Mile, Chena Hot Springs Road. A 35-year Alaskan, Mrs. Brockman cooks six dozen hot cakes each morning, and demonstrates here her technique for dispensing them to hungry visitors.

1971

A Friend in Need...

University of Alaska News Service

August 1971

Only three weeks old and rejected by her mother after a difficult birth, this 40-pound musk ox will weigh nearly 500 pounds by the time she is two years old. But meanwhile, she needs a friend...

University of Alaska News Service

...and a friend is found! Dee McConnell, wife of chief herdsman at the University of Alaska's Musk Ox Project farm near Fairbanks, provides "58-Girl" with a snack of formula milk. Named by her number and sex, "58-Girl" is the first farm-born musk ox to be reared this way. She is one of 20 calves (11 females, nine males) born this spring, bringing the total stock to 90. The herd began with 33 musk oxen captured six years ago on Nunivak Island.

Inoffensive Rainbird
June 1971

Complaints by the Alaska Native Brotherhood and Alaska Native Sisterhood camps in Ketchikan have resulted in removal of totem emblems from City of Ketchikan trash cans. The City Council solved the problem by ordering the totems painted over with an inoffensive rainbird design.

New Alaska Record: A 90-pound King Salmon for My Birthday!

Story and photo from Rev. Orville E. Carter

September 1971

We had been fishing for about two hours and I had caught one cod. "This just isn't our day," said my host and guide, Charlie Jim Jr., a lifetime resident of Angoon on Admiralty Island in Southeastern Alaska.

We were trolling in about 20 feet of water in Favorite Bay when we decided to return home. There were large clumps of kelp in the water, and when I felt my hook grab as I started to reel in, I assumed I had snagged.

Charlie stopped the motor so I could take the line in and free my single herring on a bare hook. I took in about 10 feet of line, when the sluggish weight that was to become the largest king salmon caught on sports tackle in Alaska came alive.

A retired Assembly of God minister from Rochester, Minnesota, I was in Alaska on my sixth trip since 1964. My wife De Ette and I were visiting Reverend and Mrs. Gordon Olson, Angoon's missionary pastor, and I was assisting him in conducting revival services.

I had fished for 50 years, but never for Alaska salmon. It seemed appropriate that I should observe my 67th birthday on May 22 by accepting Charlie Jim's invitation to try for salmon. I bought my license in the morning at Carl Jacobson's store in Angoon and we shoved off in Charlie's 16-foot open boat at 1 p.m. Young Frank Tom, 11, had joined us.

Largest sport-caught king salmon recorded in Alaska, my record fish filled this cart which was used by myself, left, and Charlie Jim Jr. to haul trophy to Angoon village.

We jigged for and caught herring needed for bait, and Charlie trolled slowly toward Favorite Bay. I was equipped with an old rod borrowed from Charlie, a Model 49 Penn Reel, 30-pound test line and a single hook on which Charlie had threaded a herring.

When the big strike came, I told Charlie to start the motor and head for open water. The fish made a run and I let the line out. We didn't see him for 30 minutes, and then he surfaced.

"It's a record! It's a record!" shouted Charlie as we saw the size of the giant king. It completely dwarfed the largest fish I had caught previously, a 14-pound great northern pike landed in Minnesota.

I brought him within 15 feet of the boat, when he made a fast run across the bow, catching the line on an anchor ring. I told Charlie I figured the fish was lost.

Charlie quickly scrambled over the forward decking, and hung headfirst over the bow in a precarious position to free the line.

I then knew the fish was still on as he took off down channel, taking nearly all of the line. As I brought him back in, I sensed he was tiring. It was about 45 minutes after he struck that we brought the huge fish to the side of the boat. Efforts to bring him in with a landing net were futile. As the fish came alongside the boat, Charlie used a club to end the struggle. It took both of us to haul my first salmon into the boat.

When we reached the Angoon dock, the whole village soon gathered around, and everybody was taking pictures. A scale was produced and the big red king's weight was recorded at 90 pounds. Its length was 49 7/8 inches and girth was 37 3/4 inches.

After about an hour, we used a cart to move the fish to the home where we were staying. I had laid out plywood, and was preparing to butcher the fish when Carl Jacobson said it shouldn't be butchered because he was sure it was a record. He ran to his store, checked State Fish and Game statistics, and returned with the news that my birthday king was a new record for the state.

We needed an official weight, so the fish was loaded into a jeep and hauled to the boat dock, where it was loaded aboard a boat for a ride across the bay to a licensed fish buyer who certified the weight at 87 pounds. I am told, considering the time the fish was out of the water, it would be reasonable to assume it had lost three pounds in weight.

The record king was flown to Juneau for mounting by Chandler's Taxidermy Studio and was to go on permanent display in Carl Jacobson's store in Angoon. I consider it just fisherman's luck that my name appears on the plaque, but I won't soon forget my 67th birthday and the unexpected present I caught in Favorite Bay near Angoon.

Navy Sails Away
August 1971

The Navy's Alaskan Sea Frontier and 17th Naval District sailed away from Kodiak and into extinction in early summer, ending an important chapter in Alaska's military history. Inspired by an estimated annual savings of $569,000, the Navy disbanded its Kodiak base, assigning Alaskan responsibilities to the Western Sea Frontier in San Francisco and the Hawaiian Sea Frontier in Honolulu. The Navy's Fleet Air Alaska has been transferred from Kodiak to the Adak Naval Air Station. About 2,200 Navy personnel and their dependents at Kodiak were transferred to new stations. The now disbanded Alaskan Sea Frontier was responsible for 4.8 million square miles in the North Pacific. Kodiak leaders hope that an expanded Coast Guard role in Alaska will lead to that service filling the gap left by the Navy's departure.

Alaska Baby Boom in the Decade of the '60s
July 1971

Most of the population increase in Alaska during the '60's resulted not from newcomers entering the state but from Alaskans having babies. Census figures show an increase of more than 74,000 people from 1960 to 1970, with immigrants accounting for only 14,000. Births far outweighed deaths, reflecting the fact that more than half of Alaska's residents are under 24 years of age. The state's 1970 population officially numbered 300,382.

Also shown in the Bureau of Census' final report is a trend toward more modern and expensive housing in Alaska. The number of homes without indoor plumbing declined by more than 4,000, although 23,536 new housing units have been built since 1960. The number of one- and two-room cabins declined, too, from a high of 21,422 in 1960 to 18,519 in 1970. Slightly more than half of all Alaskan residents own their own homes, but 18,000 pay more than $200 rent per month.

Native and non-white residents represented 23 percent of the state's total population.

Water by Truck
August 1971

Bulk deliveries of water are now being provided for its residents by the City of Bethel. Charges for the truck-delivered water range from four cents a gallon for small amounts to two cents a gallon for users of 5,000 gallons a month. An extra charge of $20 is made for persons whose tanks need filling on Sunday.

Optimism for Oil Pipeline... 'All Bases Covered'
September 1971

"All bases have been covered and we're ready to proceed." Secretary of Interior Rogers C. B. Morton told Alaskans in late June that is the trans-Alaska pipeline message he hopes to give President Richard Nixon and his Council on Environmental Quality in September.

Reflecting the optimism that Secretary Morton spread on his first official visit to Alaska was a headline in the *Anchorage Daily Times* on June 23, which read, "MORTON PREDICTING SEPTEMBER PERMIT." Even pessimists detected a pro-pipeline attitude in comments such as these made by the Interior Secretary on his Alaska visit: "This pipeline, if it is built—and I think it will be—will be a monument and a turning point in our civilization that will mark a new relationship between man and the rest of nature." . . . "We're going to have such a good case that we're going to win it and that's the whole ball game." . . . "It seems perfectly compatible to me that here in this great land, known for its beauty, vastness and tenderness, should be the place where man decides to put the biggest proposition that he's ever put at one time on the crust of the earth—namely a 48-inch pipeline across this state."

In announcing that he had extended the land freeze until Congress adjourns or enacts legislation settling native land claims, Morton made it clear that he would not necessarily wait for a claims settlement to issue a construction permit to Alyeska Pipeline Service Company which has now supplied him with all information needed to make a final decision. He advised Cordova fisheries leaders that they would be wiser to work with the state and oil industry to seek ways to protect Prince William Sound from pollution than to fight the project in court.

Last of the Nevada Bar
September 1971

Soaked in more than 60 years of history as a thirst-quencher for dry Alaskans, Fairbanks' Nevada Bar is no more. The structure built in 1909 was first known as the Magnet Hotel and then the Nevada. It was condemned by the Fairbanks City Council because it failed to meet city building standards. A last wake for the old bar included a reading of sad regrets from the governors of Nevada and Alaska. Commented the *Fairbanks Daily News-Miner* on the Nevada's special charm: "Steeped in history nearly as old as the city, the Nevada has been a home to some, retreat for others and a madhouse on Friday evenings."

Midsummer Tales... Some Whopping Fish Stories
September 1971

A midsummer harvest of just a few of the fishing tales that intrigue Alaskans included these piscatorial whoppers: While trolling in Chichagof Pass near Wrangell for king salmon, Mrs. Herman Johnson accidentally hooked a 40-foot whale that surfaced 20 feet from her husband's small boat. Johnson grabbed the rod, cinched down on the drag. "We were lucky to save the rod and reel," Mrs. Herman told the *Wrangell Sentinel*. "Would you believe we only lost 40 feet of line, a sinker, a leader and one choked herring?" . . . Dr. Dennis Smedley of Ketchikan disqualified himself and his 50-pound, eight-ounce king salmon from winning the top prize of an $8,500 boat in Ketchikan's King Salmon Derby. The doctor's action followed his learning that one occupant of his boat did not have a derby ticket as required by contest rules. The boat was won by Eldred Tisserand with a 44-pound, eight-ounce fish . . . The largest fish caught in the big $52,272.57 Ketchikan contest was also flipped out of the running. Mrs. Walt Northrup hooked onto a lost line and pole, on the end of which was a 54-pound king . . . Winner of Sitka's derby was Joyce Pearson's 59-pounder . . . For sheer financial suspense, nothing could beat the prize in the Golden North Salmon Derby staged at Juneau from July 16-18. A specially-marked king was released as the derby started, and it was worth $10,000 to the catcher. And Al Zuvor, Petersburg commercial fisherman, had more than his share of big fish luck in one day. A shark made a clean hole in his net, followed by a whale which made a mess of the webbing . . . The previous 249-pound record for a halibut caught on sports gear was displaced by a 258-pound halibut caught near Homer on June 11 by Dorothy Miller, Palmer school teacher. She needed 70 minutes to land the seven-foot fish . . . James Odeman of Anchorage won the Ninilchik King Salmon Derby with a 37.3-pound fish . . . A 30-pound, seven-ounce lake trout won the Tagish Lake Derby for Cal Scouten of Whitehorse . . . Making ripples as a junior angler was David Bruce, 10, of Mount Edgecumbe, who caught a 64-pound king near Olga Strait . . . Anchorage area kids got a finny break when the Department of Fish and Game released 500 half-pound rainbow trout in Chester Creek.

$27 a Barrel for Oil
August 1971

With fuel oil costing $27 a barrel, and some homes requiring five barrels a month, the Gambell village council has asked the state to assist in providing better housing for 400 residents. Reporting that the present homes "are inadequate and poorly built from scrap lumber," and "in danger of high seas and shore waves," the council requested that new homes be built at a less dangerous site. The eight council members claim their village has been excluded from previous government housing programs.

The Snow Machine—Here, There, and Everywhere!
May 1971

With junked snow machines now becoming common sights in Alaska's outpost villages, the University of Alaska began a program of repair and maintenance in March that may lead to a reduced rate of abandoning the machines that are replacing dog teams. Carl Bowie, a former Kotzebue resident, visited major Eskimo villages for more than a month, conducting both day and evening classes on snow machine repair and maintenance. "Many snow machines are abandoned each year. They wouldn't have to be if their owners could easily and quickly repair them," said Bowie, who is teaching the classes for the University's Division of Statewide Services.

Anchorage Daily Times photo by Alice Puster

Snowmobiles are so popular in Anchorage that a course was recently conducted for 58 Central Junior High students. Shown here explaining the insides of a motor is Bill Byers of Craig Taylor Enterprises.

September 1971

It seems that machine-automation is taking over this village because during the Christmas Races there was actually one dogteam that took part in the dogteam races. Rest of the races were all sno-machine races. I hope that somebody will raise dogs this year so that, God willing, we will have complete dogteam race in Christmas this year.

—Ray H. Ningeulook
Shishmaref correspondent
FAIRBANKS DAILY NEWS-MINER

May 1971

Now making tracks as far south as Ketchikan, snow machines are even traveling by water as the vehicles' popularity mounts in the state's coastal towns. Six Wrangell snowmobilers used boats to move their machines to the frozen Stikine River for 15 days of riding in the back country. Another Wrangell group of four machines was moved by boat to Mill Creek for an overnight drive to Virginia Lake. Fifteen members of Kodiak's Sno-Bruins snowmobile club loaded their machines aboard the M/V *Alma B* in mid-February for a trip to Port Lions and winter trips to Terror Bay Flats, Viekoda Bay and Barbara Lake.

A Whale of a Ride!
September 1971

Two young Kodiak fishermen survived a whale of a ride in late June, living to tell a story that could only be topped by Jonah. Bob Williams, 16, and his brother, Dave, 14, were using a 25-foot skiff to check halibut gear in Chiniak Bay. A 50- to 60-foot whale surfaced directly beneath their boat, lifting the skiff and its 50-hp engine completely out of the water. Clinging to the boat which was tilted at a 45-degree angle, the brothers rode an unknown distance before the whale submerged. After ending their free ride, the youths found themselves in a pod of whales, one of which bumped the boat so hard it knocked Dave to his knees. They expressed the belief that if their boat had been smaller and less sturdy it would have been overturned or crushed.

Rampart Dam: New 'No'
September 1971

Rampart Dam, a $1.3 billion project proposed for the Yukon River, was virtually written off as an impossible dream late in June by the U. S. Army Corps of Engineers. Brigadier General Roy S. Kelley, division engineer from Portland, Oregon, reported that a 12-year study of the giant project by district and division engineers had produced a recommendation that "a project for hydroelectric power generation at the Rampart Canyon site, Yukon River, Alaska, not be undertaken at this time." General Kelley reported the Corps of Engineers found the Rampart Dam project would have "a benefit-to-cost ratio of 0.96 to 1." The most ambitious plan for Rampart would have created a dam 530 feet high and resulted in a mid-Alaska lake larger than Lake Erie. At the time of conception it was boosted as the world's largest hydroelectric project. Former Secretary of Interior Stewart Udall had earlier indicated the Bureau of Reclamation's rejection of the project. Even die-hard Rampart boosters admit that the Corps of Engineers verdict has drowned all dreams of a dam at Rampart.

WAMCATS Pioneers
September 1971

The pioneers—old and new—who kept Alaska's communications lines up and operating for 70 years are hoping to strengthen bonds developed while serving in the WAMCATS and ACS. Tracing their history back to May, 1900, when the Washington-Alaska Military Cable and Telegraph System was established, the WAMCATS Pioneers held their 14th reunion in Seattle, Washington, on May 21. Three of the members are in their 90's and few are younger than 60. Arthur Fernandes of 320 NW 51st Street in Seattle was the moving force in organizing the pioneer radio operators, telegraphers and linemen. Thirty-two of an estimated 150 WAMCATS still living attended the Seattle meeting. The WAMCATS became the Alaska Communications System (ACS) on July 1, 1936, and ACS, in turn, was replaced by privately-owned RCA last January.

1971

An SOS in the Sand
October 1971

An SOS stamped in sand on a bank of the Alsek River in the Yukon's Saint Elias Mountains resulted in the August 1 rescue of a young man from Washington state who had spent 38 days in the wilderness. Gary Anderson, 23, and his father, Kenneth Wayne Anderson, 55, were en route from Anchorage to Juneau on June 24, when their floatplane was forced to land on the river. It capsized and the elder Anderson was swept downriver. Gary reached shore and walked downriver for three days searching in vain for his father. He spent the next 35 days at an empty hunter's camp, at the junction of the Alsek and Tatshenshini Rivers, where he lost more than 50 pounds but survived on roots, potato peelings and discarded scrambled eggs from an old campfire. The formal search for the missing plane had been suspended June 30, a month before Anderson was found by a family group on a Sunday flight.

Loser: City of Douglas
April 1971

A decision by the Alaska State Supreme Court apparently has brought to an end the efforts of the City of Douglas to remain an independent municipal entity. In a ruling announced in mid-January, the state's highest court reaffirmed a Superior Court decision dismissing the suit which challenged the right of the City and Borough of Juneau to include Douglas in the new unified municipality.

In 1970, Douglas residents voted 71 percent in opposition to unification but the measure was passed on the strength of "yes" votes in Juneau and outlying service areas. Douglas went to the courts in June to challenge the constitutionality of the state's unification law, but Superior Court Judge Edward V. Davis ruled that the law is constitutional. An appeal to the Supreme Court followed.

July 1971
Tradition to the contrary, a one-legged cache is better and lasts longer than the standard four-leg model, according to Sonny Holmberg. William Woolard of Medfra provided this photo of Holmberg's one-poler on the Nixon River near McGrath.

© Nancy Simmerman

November 1971
Left high and dry and pointed the wrong way by an ebbing morning tide on upper Turnagain Arm, this unlucky Little Piked whale (also known as a Pike or Lease Rorqual) was kept alive by compassionate passers-by. Bob Bella of Girdwood was one of those friendly humans who used a hubcab to pour water on the approximately 16-foot-long whale until the incoming tide that evening allowed a group of men to launch him back into the briny deep. The little drama took place between Girdwood and Portage in May. Note the distinctive white band on the fore flipper. This species of baleen whale rarely exceeds 33 feet and is generally found in waters close to shores. (But seldom ON shores!)

International Incident... Where's the Boundary?
September 1971

A fishing incident in the waters of Dixon Entrance nearly flared into an international boundary dispute May 16, when a Canadian fishing vessel, the *Anthony J.*, ignored orders from a U.S. Coast Guard cutter to be escorted into custody. The boundary between U.S. and Canadian waters in Dixon Entrance has been disputed for some time.

The Coast Guard said in its report of the incident that the cutter *Cape Romain* observed the *Anthony J.* in a position within 2.5 miles of U.S. territory near Cape Chacon on Prince of Wales Island, and informed the *Anthony J.'s* master, Jack Secord, that he was being taken into government custody and would be escorted to Ketchikan. He was told he could pull in his halibut gear.

Secord signified he understood and admitted he was within the three-mile limit, but said he questioned the U.S.-Canadian border line. According to his charts the border is one-half mile offshore. Several hours later the *Anthony J.* cut its gear and made for Prince Rupert, B.C. Secord ignored orders from the *Cape Romain* to stop, saying that he was doing so under orders from the Canadian Department of Fisheries. A Canadian spokesman confirmed the orders.

The *Cape Romain* chased the *Anthony J.* into international waters off Cape Chacon, where the Canadian fishing vessel *Masset Maid* appeared and began to harrass the *Cape Romain* by making repeated passes within 100 feet of the cutter. After about 45 minutes the Coast Guard, in consultation with the Department of State, decided to avoid overt action and broke off pursuit of the *Anthony J.* three miles off Rose Point Overfalls Shoal Lighted Buoy, where Canadian territorial waters start in that area. The *Anthony J.* proceeded into Prince Rupert.

Canadian Fisheries Minister Jack Davis announced on May 18 that Canada had made a formal protest to Washington over the incident. He said the U.S. government had been advised that the *Anthony J.* was in Canadian waters when it was "accosted" by the U.S. Coast Guard cutter. He added that Canadian vessels will continue to fish in the area where the *Anthony J.* was approached. Davis ordered a Canadian Fisheries patrol boat into the disputed waters to pick up $2,000 worth of halibut gear left behind by the *Anthony J.* The recovery mission met no opposition.

Secord said the *Cape Romain* uncovered its guns at one point during the chase. A spokesman for the 17th Coast Guard District in Juneau said the uncovering of the cutter's machine gun was normal procedure, but that there never had been any intention to fire.

Award for Skipper
September 1971

Credited with saving the lives of 70 people from seven nations, Captain Harold Payne of the Alaska Ferry *Malaspina* has received an Award of Commendation from Governor William A. Egan. When the burning Norwegian motor vessel *Meteor* issued a Mayday call on May 21, 1971, the *Malaspina* heard it and sped to the stricken ship. All 66 *Meteor* passengers and four crew members were rescued and taken to Vancouver.

Strange Discoveries
November 1971

When it comes to finding strange objects, Ray Henricks of Lutak Inlet near Haines has an entry hard to beat. The *Chilkat Valley News* reports that when he went to tend his salmon net in early August, Henricks picked a dozen salmon plus three salmon steaks packaged in a plastic bag. "I've never before caught salmon already prepared," commented Henricks.

A Knik Arm homesteader found a rain jacket attached to an empty can. It contained a note from a hunter near Lake George on upper Knik River which reported that he had suffered a heart attack and needed help. The homesteader notified rescue officials who dispatched an Air Force helicopter to the designated emergency site. Searchers found an old SOS on a sandbar, and recalled that they had rescued a stricken hunter from the area in August, 1970. A check with the Palmer hunter rescued a year previous revealed that he did send the note attached to the can down the Knik River. It was found a year later.

Slightly faster service was recorded for the bottle which was tossed into the Pacific near Osaka, Japan, on November 22, 1970. It was found on Blashke Island near Wrangell early in July by Oscar Oglend of Wrangell.

She Lives Alone, Cares for Herself ...at Age 111

Fairbanks Daily News-Miner photo by Sue Anderson

November 1971
Living alone and caring for herself, Mrs. Minnie Tucker celebrated her 111th birthday at Fairbanks on Friday, August 13. The centenarian-plus Eskimo elder was born at Rocky Point on the Bering Sea just before the Civil War started. She received gifts and cards from throughout the nation as the result of a wire service story last year which reported theft of wood she needed for her wood stove.

1971

Dr. Jake Jacobson, Kotzebue, loads his Cessna with portable dental equipment as he prepares to make "village calls."

Ken Cash

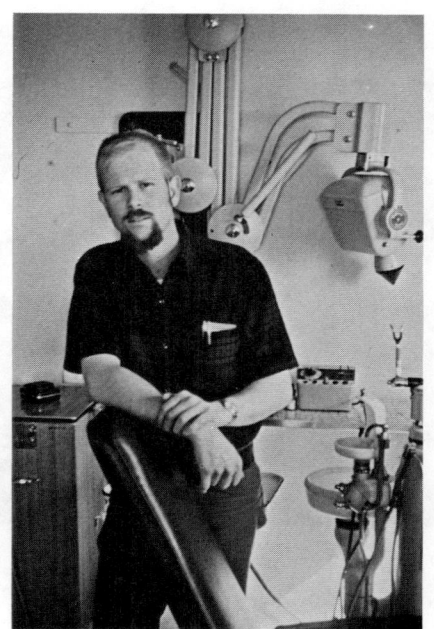

Ken Cash

Dr. Jacobson was one of the youngest men to graduate from his college of dentistry. He didn't want "to waste time."

Flying Dentist in Alaska's Bush Country:
He Makes 'Village Calls' in a Cessna 180 ... Logs 20,000 Miles a Year

November 1971

Dr. Jake Jacobson, a tall, wiry man topped by a volcano of red hair, is a qualified assistant guide and a licensed commercial pilot.

He is also a practicing dentist with an unusual office.

Much as a general practitioner used to make house calls, Dr. Jacobson makes "village calls." From his home base in Kotzebue, he travels to the bush with his office on his back: completely portable equipment that fits into his Cessna 180 with room for 400 pounds to spare.

With the help of Dick Olsen, Anchorage dental equipment repairman, he reduced the usual dental machinery to traveling size. The dental suction is provided by parts of an old vacuum cleaner, the catch-all is a Kodak developing tank, and the sprayer's water source is a modified windshield squirter from a Volkswagen.

The total unit, as complete as some dental offices in Alaska, includes a laboratory and a portable x-ray. Dr. Jacobson has assistants in each village, so all he needs is a place to land, a power supply, and a few patients.

Although relatively new to the state, Dr. Jacobson has been headed here since the age of five, when he spoke to some Alaskan trappers. Raised in Arizona, he also lived in New Mexico and Montana, and received his training at the University of Oregon. One of the youngest to graduate from that dental college, he says, "I never liked school, so I saw no reason to waste time."

In 1967 he began a two-year job with the U.S. Public Health Service, and learned to fly in order to reach the villages. In January, 1971, he completed his 103rd trip.

He has visited 56 villages. While he is not the only traveling dentist he is probably the farthest ranging, logging 20,000 miles a year.

Most of his trips were made for the Public Health Service. Some were under federal or state contracts, and the rest were private. He feels that the contract business should be expanded, so that more dentists might become involved with bush work.

He is happy in his work. "The bush is where it's at," he says. "Beyond the need for dental care that exists, the people are a type I can identify with. They are there because they choose to be. Independent. Conservative. Appreciating the needs, opportunities, supplies. And they have the ability to improvise."

In other words, Alaskans like himself.

By Ken and Sandi Cash

New Bartlett Hospital
November 1971

Juneau's new, 67-bed Bartlett Memorial Hospital officially was opened July 17. Mrs. Vide Bartlett unveiled a portrait of her late husband, Senator E. L. (Bob) Bartlett, during dedication ceremonies. The two-story structure, located just off the Glacier Highway three miles north of the downtown area, replaces the hospital built by the Sisters of Saint Anne, who came to Juneau in 1886. The sisters left the capital city in 1968, transferring operation of the hospital to the Greater Juneau Borough. Future plans call for construction of a medical arts building on a site adjacent to the new hospital.

Sitka's O'Connell Bridge
July 1971

John O'Connell Memorial Bridge is the name selected for the 1,225-foot span that will connect Sitka with Japonski Island, Governor William A. Egan has informed the Sitka Borough assembly. The bridge is under construction, and scheduled for completion in 1972. The governor's action came in response to resolutions from the assembly and various civic organizations in Sitka urging that the bridge be named in honor of O'Connell, a former Sitka mayor and state legislator who died February 14.

The End of an Era
September 1971

The Kasaan post office on Prince of Wales Island, established in 1900, was closed May 31. Only eight people still live in the once-thriving community.

Guns, Snowmobiles ... Native Way of Life
November 1971

Largely dependent on seals and walrus for their basic meat supply, the average hunter at Savoonga on Saint Lawrence Island owns 3.4 guns, and his counterpart at Gambell on the same island uses 2.7 firearms to harvest food. These statistics were reported to the recent twenty-second Alaska Science Conference by S. Burgess of the Institute of Arctic Biology at the University of Alaska. Land vehicles, predominantly snowmobiles, are more than twice as common at Savoonga as dog sleds. Gambell residents spend an average of $560 a year per person at the village store and $800 each for mail orders.

Herder Clubs a Wolf
June 1971

A Golovin reindeer herder proved recently that a four-foot club is almost as good as a rifle when it comes to protecting your animals from a hungry wolf. Spotting a black wolf chewing on a reindeer it had just downed, Martin Aukonuk, 35, grabbed a club, jumped on his snow machine and gave chase. He caught up with the wolf and clubbed it to death.

Sierra Club to Appeal Loss of Its Timber Suit
October 1971

The Sierra Club has renewed its efforts to block the sale by the U. S. Forest Service of 8.75 billion board feet of timber in Southeast Alaska's Tongass National Forest to U. S. Plywood Champion Papers, Inc., by filing a notice of appeal with the U. S. Ninth Circuit Court of Appeals. The club will ask the appellate court to reverse the decision of U. S. District Court Judge Raymond Plummer, who dismissed the club's suit against the Forest Service last March. Sierra Club attorney Warren Matthews said on July 19 that it would be premature to say when the actual appeal would be written. At stake in the outcome of the court battle is a proposed $100 million pulp mill which Plywood-Champion plans to build at Berners Bay, 34 miles northwest of Juneau.

Buddhist Marker for 235 Japanese Who Died on Attu

August 1971

A sacred Buddhist marker in the Army cemetery at Fort Richardson, near Anchorage, marks the mass grave of 235 Japanese soldiers who died on Attu Island during the Aleutian campaign of World War II. They were part of a 3,000-man Japanese force, of which only 29 survived Attu's recapture by American troops. In the Allied plot of the cemetery lie the bodies of Canadian and Russian airmen. American soldiers who fell in wars from World War II to the present conflict are buried in the main cemetery.

The Northern Lights... ...The Southern Lights

University of Alaska

A World Apart ...and Yet so close

November 1971

Like mirror images, the northern and southern lights flicker over the earth's poles in almost identical patterns, as shown in photos taken simultaneously at conjugate points in the north and south. Such photographs, taken by the University of Alaska's Geophysical Institute during airborne experiments, have established the occurrence of conjugate aurora, and now researchers are puzzling over why the auroras are not always identical and simultaneous in both

Taken a world apart at the same instant on March 26, 1968, these almost identical photos show the aurora borealis of the northern hemisphere, at left, and the aurora australis of the southern hemisphere.

hemispheres. Auroras over Alaska are generally brighter than the auroras observed south of New Zealand, and higher-latitude auroras are slightly displaced from their expected position.

Storm Erupts over New Alaska Charts
November 1971

State Department cartographers caused bigger fall storms in Alaskan waters than the usual autumn winds as they unveiled new charts which have greatly reduced the amount of water the state believes it should control. Governor William A. Egan was so provoked by the new charts, which limit Alaska's territorial waters to three miles seaward from island shores, that he asked President Richard Nixon to investigate and correct what he described as the surrender of "thousands of square miles of precious sovereignty."

Alaska has long considered waters inside lines projected between outer islands as being under state jurisdiction. The new charts, which now guide U.S. Coast Guard operations, result in some traditional inland waters being designated as "high seas." The Governor told President Nixon, "The cartographers have allowed the high seas, including the contiguous zone, to invade every historic bay and channel of the Alexander Archipelago more than six miles wide, as well as the Bristol Bay fisheries and other waters on the periphery of the Alaskan land mass and related islands. I cannot stand by and let this happen."

Confusion over the boundary line between Alaskan and Canadian waters off Prince of Wales Island led in late August to the arrest of a Canadian halibut vessel near Nunez Rocks and a subsequent flight by the *Masset Maid* to Prince Rupert, British Columbia, with the arresting officer aboard. Frank Sharp, 40, Department of Fish and Game protection officer from Ketchikan, was the principal in the case in which ADFG agents confiscated Canadian halibut gear within the three-mile limit claimed by Alaska south of Prince of Wales Island, and the Canadians "confiscated" Officer Sharp. The *Masset Maid's* skipper contended that although he was within three miles of Alaskan land, he was inside the Canadian boundary established in 1903 which extends from Cape Muzon eastward to the mouth of Portland Canal. Puzzled fishermen agreed that harmony was unlikely to return to the troubled waters until the United States and Canada redefine fishing boundaries.

Anchorage Daily Times photo by Alice Puster

Trucks Marooned...

Ten huge trucks were marooned on August 10, when Granite Creek roared over its banks and chewed away both approaches to the Glenn Highway bridge. An Air Force helicopter plucked 19 people from the isolated area, including two families whose homes were washed away by the flood.

Heavy Flood Damage
* * *
Road, Rail Links Are Severed by Rampaging Rivers

October 1971

Southcentral Alaska became an island the second week in August as sudden floods cut road and rail links to the rest of the state. Hundreds of southbound and northbound motorists were temporarily stranded as the rampaging Matanuska and Susitna Rivers and their swollen tributaries cut the Glenn Highway and washed out the Alaska Railroad's main line near Houston. Governor William A. Egan asked that the Matanuska Valley be declared a federal disaster area to assist scores of families who suffered home, property and crop losses. First estimates indicated damage would exceed $4 million, with the worst residential flooding in the Bodenburg Butte area. No deaths were reported, but several hundred persons were left homeless and given temporary shelter in a Palmer school. Second only to the Fairbanks flood of August, 1967, the Matanuska Valley disaster was triggered by a record rainfall

Anchorage Daily Times photo by Alice Puster

Train Derailed...

Southcentral Alaska's rail link with Fairbanks was cut near Houston on August 9, when the flooding Little Susitna River weakened the roadbed and caused this derailment of 11 northbound cars and five engine units.

of nearly three inches on the first weekend in August. On August 10, the Matanuska River reached a level of 13.3 feet, highest ever recorded since measuring began in 1949.

Pipeline – Clean, Empty As the Army Gives It Up
October 1971

If anyone has a use for it, the Army's 432-mile, eight-inch pipeline from Haines to Tok is clean and empty. Following a Department of Defense decision to close down the 432-mile segment between Haines and Tok, Army petroleum crews completed the task of flushing the line in mid-August. The line was filled with 145,000 barrels of fresh water which was found to be free of contamination and was drained at 12 stations along the route. Finally, scrapers and "sypho pigs" were sent through the line with compressed air to remove all remaining fluids. Military petroleum needs for bases north of the Alaska Range are now being filled by Alaska Railroad tank cars from Whittier and Anchorage.

111 Passengers Die in Worst Plane Crash
November 1971

Grief swept over Alaska in September as virtually every corner of the state was closely identified with some of the 111 passengers killed in the September 4 crash of an Alaska Airlines 727 jet on a mountain 21 miles west of Juneau. Site of the worst single plane accident in the history of American aviation was the 2,500-foot level on a steep 3,500-foot mountain. Recovery of victims was a nightmarish task requiring more than a week. Even as the National Transportation Safety Board was probing the cause of the accident, the Federal Aviation Administration announced additional electronic equipment will be installed in Juneau to assist pilots in determining distance from the airport. Starting in Anchorage, the fatal flight had made stops in Cordova and Yakutat and was descending for a last stop in Juneau enroute to Seattle when it smashed into the mountain. The crash ended the lives of 15 state employees and 13 students enroute to Sheldon Jackson Junior College and Mount Edgecumbe School, both in Sitka. Five Kake school teachers died in the accident as did five soldiers from Fort Greeley. The seven-member Alaska Airlines crew was known throughout the state.

Sign of Progress?
August 1971

Another sure sign of civilization will be added to Yukon living on August 23, when letter carriers start delivering mail to Whitehorse residents. Four mailmen will drive mailmobiles and three will travel on foot in initiating the Yukon's first home delivery of mail.

Fence Divides Busy Street

Staff photo

September 1971

Lois Drive, one of Spenard's busiest streets, was narrowed a bit in June when James Wanamaker claimed the 23-year-old road encroached on his property at the corner of Northern Lights and Lois. Wanamaker moved to reclaim his property by constructing this wooden fence down the roadway, taking a maximum of about 15 feet from the former thoroughfare. The State Department of Highways has indicated it must ask the Superior Court to decide who owns the contested road.

Northern Champions: Tea Boiling, High Kicking, Logging, Fishing...

November 1971

Each summer produces a list of winners of various and assorted contests that give the North a special flavor. Here's a sampling of 1971 champions: New queen of the Eskimo Olympics staged at Fairbanks is Mary Keller of Nome...King and Queen regent of Fairbanks' Golden Days were William Shaeffer and Mrs. Grace Harkness....Winners of the Good Woman contest at Inuvik's (Northwest Territories) Northern Games in late July were Jane Charlie of Fort McPherson and Naomi Atatahak of Coppermine.

Tea-boiling champion at the Inuvik meet was Mrs. A. N. Blake of Fort McPherson, and the bannock-baking winner was Annie Elvioyak of Cambridge Bay...Joe Kasak of Barrow won several events at Inuvik, then retained his title as two-foot high kick champion at the Eskimo Olympics with a jump of six feet, six inches. Fred Titus amazed several thousand visitors at the Fairbanks event by walking 860 feet with a 17-pound weight attached to one ear to set a record. Jenny Felder won the blanket toss contest for the third time. Morgan Sageak of Barrow won the body weight contest by hauling four men a distance of 38 feet, five inches.

Don Barton of Boise Cascade won the All-Around Logger trophy in a meet at Sitka...Al Kuchta of Juneau won the State Goldpanning Championship at Fairbanks, facing tough competition from Cathy Searfus, 10, of Fairbanks, junior title winner...Jim Wilke and three crew members won the Great Nome Raft Race by traveling five miles in 96 minutes.

Named to the U. S. National Nordic Ski Team were Barbara Britch, Margie Mahoney and Chris Haines of Anchorage and Marianne Van Enkevort of Fairbanks.

Worth nearly $200 a pound, a 16-pound, ¼ ounce silver brought first prize of $3,000 in the Seward Silver Salmon Derby to Terry Weber of Anchorage. More than 3,000 anglers entered the derby, competing for $18,000 in prizes, not including a marked fish insured for $10,000 which went uncaught....Jimmy Burzinskie, 14, of Valdez, won $1,000 and his town's 19th Silver Salmon Derby with a 15 pound, 11½ ounce fish....The biggest silver salmon taken on sports tackle in the Homer area was landed by Mark Walatka, nine, who brought home an 18-pounder. And the same area provided a new contender for largest halibut landed by a sports fisherman, a 267-pound giant caught near Land's End by Frank E. Browder of Englewood, Florida....Betty Jean Banta was judged new queen of the Ninlichik Fair.

Fairbanks Daily News-Miner photo by Karen Perdue

No game for weak-eared men, this Eskimo Olympics contest shows Jimmy Kilbear of Point Barrow, at right, taking on his sixth challenger in the ear pull contest at the Fairbanks event. His left ear swollen from victories in earlier contests, Kilbear was later defeated by Joe Kaliak.

Fairbanks Daily News-Miner photo by Karen Perdue

New Miss Eskimo Olympics is Mary Keller of Nome, shown here with her court, left to right, Katherine Itta, Miss Mt. Edgecumbe; Lillian Venes, Miss Bethel, and Johanna Harper, Miss Fairbanks Native Association. Miss Keller's coronation took place July 31 at Fairbanks.

New Women's Record
December 1971

Mrs. Atlas Bailey of Fairbanks caught a 62½-pound king salmon in Cook Inlet near Ninilchik last July, believed a new state record for women, but it is the king that got away she won't soon forget. Fishing with her husband and a friend in a 17-foot canoe, Mrs. Bailey told the *Fairbanks Daily News-Miner's* Ed Martley that she got a strike at high tide. The fish fought for 77 minutes before it escaped, moving the canoe seven and one-half miles from where it was first hooked. At one point the great king was brought alongside the canoe and spanned the distance between two thwarts. Bailey estimated its length at seven feet. (The record king caught last May 22 at Angoon by Rev. Orville E. Carter was 49 7/8 inches long.) Two days later Mrs. Bailey hooked and, after a 65 minute fight, landed her 62½-pound king.

AMU Survives a Crisis
December 1971

New president of Alaska Methodist University in Anchorage is Dr. John O. Picton, 48, formerly an executive in the Northwest Regional Education Library in Portland. The state's only degree-granting, four-year private college, AMU survived a financial crisis that threatened to close the university. Governor William A. Egan's office, AMU trustees and regents of the University of Alaska developed a formula in late July that insured operation of the school which was then about $1.2 million in debt. Cooperation of Anchorage banks which are owed more than $600,000 by AMU has enabled incoming cash, including a $100,000 grant from Atlantic Richfield Company, to be applied to operating expenses rather than debt retirement. Other elements of the life-saving program include purchase of AMU's library by the University of Alaska for $350,000. The state has also asked that a special $400,000 fund set aside for construction of a joint University of Alaska-AMU library on the AMU campus be released for operating expenses. Governor Egan also requested that AMU follow through on fund-raising goals which call for raising $1,250,000, of which $400,000 is to be raised within Alaska. The governor indicated he would not consider the idea of a state loan to AMU unless the present program fails to solve the problem.

Alaska Adds Its Losses from the Longest West Coast Dock Strike
December 1971

Losses in time, money and higher shipping costs were being calculated by Alaskans in October as a Taft-Hartley Act injunction gave an 80-day respite from a 99-day strike of West Coast docks, the longest in history. The first post-strike Sea-Land container ship reached Anchorage on October 15, more than three months after the ILWU strike was called. Although stores in major Alaskan cities offered essential consumer goods throughout the strike, some stores in smaller towns were showing bare shelf space when the strike ended. Both private and government construction projects were delayed by the strike. Some Anchorage schools scheduled to open in August have been delayed until January. Automobile dealers reported 1971 models were still coming in when showrooms should have been displaying 1972 models. Playing key roles in reducing strike hardships in populous Southcentral and Interior Alaska were Alaska Trainship, Alaska Hydro Train and Canadian National, all of which increased railcar-barge service to Alaska during the strike. Also coming to the rescue were airlines and Alaska Highway truckers. Lynden Freight increased its over-the-highway tonnage four to five times during the strike, moving as much as a million pounds in some weeks.

Roadhouse Lost in Fire
December 1971

A major repository of Interior Alaska history was lost in late September when fire destroyed Miller House 114.5 on the Steese Highway. Established in 1896, the state's oldest roadhouse in continuous existence was built by Fritz Miller, later operated for nearly 40 years by the late Frank and Graziella Miller, no relation to the founder. Some antiques were saved before the rambling structure was destroyed.

Women Win
March 1971

The Northwest Territories has followed the lead of Alaska and the Yukon in electing women to decision-making positions in government. Mrs. Lena Pederson of Coppermine became the first woman to serve on the Northwest Territories Council when she was elected as councillor from the Central Arctic. Three natives were elected to the council in the December elections in which the number of elective seats was increased from seven to ten. Four more council members were appointed by the Canadian government.

'Environmental Blight'...

December 1971

Competition between the Chugach Electric Association and City of Anchorage Municipal Light and Power Utility produced this jungle of power poles at 13th Avenue and Cordova Street. The Alaska Public Utilities Commission described the scene as "environmental blight" and ordered the city to remove its poles.

A Dog-killing Wolf
December 1971

Invasion of Wrangell's outskirts by a dog-killing wolf is believed to have ended with the trapping and killing of a 105-pound male wolf by Jim Keline of Juneau, a Department of Fish and Game trapper. The wolf protection move was taken following an attack on a Samoyed dog which was partially eaten, chasing of another dog and numerous sightings near Wrangell's airport.

Fish Hatchery Staffed by Students
December 1971

Junior and senior students in Ketchikan High School are assisting in the operation of Deer Mountain Hatchery, which was vacated by the state Department of Fish and Game. One hundred thousand fertilized pink salmon eggs donated by the state are the first concern of the fisheries-minded students. Under an agreement with the Ketchikan King Salmon Derby committee, which owns the hatchery building, king salmon will be raised in the hatchery which is supervised by Carroll Fader, vocational education director for borough schools, and Jim Jenkins, a marine biologist.

Historic Landmark

November 1971

Kenai's Russian Orthodox Church of the Assumption of the Virgin Mary was dedicated on August 28 as a National Historic Landmark. Constructed in 1894 on the site of an earlier Russian church constructed in 1849, the Kenai Church shown here is considered one of the finest examples of a 19th century Russian Orthodox Church constructed on the vessel or quadrilateral ground plan. The designation plaque at the ceremony was presented to the Rt. Rev. Theodosium, Bishop of Sitka and Alaska, by Ernest J. Borgman, Alaska chief of the National Park Service.

Conflicting Signals... When Will $2 Billion Trans-Alaska Oil Pipeline Get the Nod?
December 1971

Flecks of green were added on September 26 to the amber caution light that has been flashing for months as to whether the 789-mile trans-Alaska oil pipeline from Prudhoe Bay to Valdez will be granted an essential construction permit from the Department of Interior. Optimism that the $2 billion project will get the full green light came during an Anchorage visit by President Richard Nixon and Secretary of Interior Rogers C. B. Morton.

President Nixon all but endorsed the massive project when he said, "Based on the information now at hand, I do not believe that the apparent conflict between oil and the environment represents a permanent impasse. Instead it presents a challenge—a challenge to our engineering skills and a challenge to our environmental conscience. I believe we can meet that challenge, proving that natural resources—in the Arctic and elsewhere—can be developed and transported in a responsible manner which respects environmental values."

On his second trip to Alaska in two months, Interior Secretary Morton said in Anchorage that he now expects the final impact statement for the Prudhoe Bay-Valdez line will be completed in December. Considering court actions expected to follow granting of the permit, Morton indicated the pipeline construction might start by next spring. "This work of man (the pipeline) can be put on the ground," said Morton. "It will be a great new step in developing a new sense of orderly development on the crust of the planet."

Pipeline prospects were not brightened in October, however, as the conservation and native claims issues converged to produce storm clouds. The Arctic Slope Native Association filed a suit in Washington, D. C., which asks the U. S. District Court to invalidate the sale of North Slope leases by the state in 1969 for $912 million. The ASNA charges that the North Slope land selected by the State in 1964 violated the Alaska Statehood Act.

With the Native Land Claims settlement advancing through Congress, a new barrier to the issue involving 55,000 native Alaskans came when 12 national conservation groups asked President Nixon to oppose a proposed land settlement of as much as 40 million acres until a statewide land use plan has been developed. Qualified Alaskan observers see the latest conservation move as a tactic which would delay both the pipeline and a native land claims settlement for a year or more. In asking for a concerted offensive against both the pipeline and native land claims, the Sierra Club advised members: "Conservationists... feel the national interest should be put first, and that these lands should be reserved by the federal government before the natives, the state and private interests select what they want."

One phase of the pipeline picture was completed in late October when the last load of 48-inch pipe was delivered to Valdez, bringing a grand total of 822 miles of the Japanese-made pipe now stored in Valdez, Fairbanks and Prudhoe Bay. First load of the pipe under the $100 million contract was delivered to Valdez on September 1, 1969.

No mad rush for promising Alaska oil land was apparent in a Tyonek Indian offer to sell leases on 7,978 acres near Cook Inlet's rich offshore wells. Not a single bid was entered.

Answering claims that much of the North Slope oil is destined for the Japanese market, Governor Egan replied, "I have been assured there are no plans to sell North Slope crude to Japan."

A prediction that oil will be an important element in Alaska's economic bloodstream for decades to come was made recently by Thomas Marshall, chief geologist for the Division of Oil and Gas. He listed untested areas of the North Slope, the Norton Sound-Point Hope, Cook Inlet Basin and Gulf of Alaska as probable sites of giant oil reserves known as "elephants."

Barrow and Welfare
April 1971

"It's almost a welfare economy," said three members of the University of Alaska's Department of Business Administration, following a recent visit to Barrow. Noting an unemployment rate of 30 percent, Dale Swanson observed, "There's Naval Arctic Research Laboratory money, some tourist money and welfare." Despite Barrow's economic problems, the University visitors noted many Barrow businesses in the town of nearly 2,200 "are run as efficiently as any in Alaska."

History in the Making...

December 1971

History was made at Elmendorf Air Force Base on September 26 when President Richard M. Nixon welcomed Japan's Emperor Hirohito to the United States. The Alaskan meeting of the two heads of state marked the first time a reigning Japanese Emperor had set foot on foreign soil and the first such meeting with a President of the United States. Returning from his European tour, Emperor Hirohito stopped briefly at Anchorage International Airport on October 13, where he was greeted by Governor William A. Egan. Flight time, via regular commercial airline, from Anchorage to Tokyo is approximately seven and one-half hours; from Washington, D. C., to Anchorage flight time is about six hours.

A Mountaineer's Death
July 1971

Dr. Grace Hoeman, Anchorage anesthesiologist and one of Alaska's foremost mountain climbers, was killed in an avalanche which swept down Eklutna Glacier on April 12. Also killed in the slide was Hans Van Der Laan, who had joined Dr. Hoeman and John Samuelson on a trek into the Chugach Range. Samuelson escaped the slide and reported the burial of his companions. Despite an intensive search, the bodies had not been found by mid-May. Dr. Hoeman had edited the article "Crossing the Harding Icefield," which appeared in the May issue of ALASKA magazine under the name of her late husband, J. Vin Hoeman, who was killed in an avalanche on Mount Dhaulagiri in the Himalayas early in 1969. Dr. Hoeman led the first successful ascent of Mount McKinley's South Peak by an all-woman team in the summer of 1970.

Sitka Votes Unification
December 1971

By a vote of two to one, Sitka voters in late September approved unification of the borough and city governments to follow Juneau's lead in forming a unified local government. Six assemblymen and a new mayor were to be elected November 2.

Failure of Anchorage's attempt at unification in an election last August has triggered a move by the city to establish its own borough government, thus eliminating the powers of the existing Greater Anchorage Area Borough to administer certain programs within the city. Watching the success of Anchorage's exploratory move are Kenai and North Kenai, both of which are unhappy in the Kenai Peninsula Borough and are toying with the idea of establishing their own borough.

The idea of requiring a five cent deposit on metal and glass beverage containers didn't appeal to Juneau voters who rejected the proposition by a vote of 1,799 to 861... A move to establish fourth class cities in the Glennallen and Copper Center areas was turned down by voters in September... And Nome suffered shrinking pains from a vote of the State Supreme Court which ruled that land belonging to the U.S. Smelting, Mining and Refining Company, which was annexed three years ago, must be taken out of the city limits. The court also ruled that the City of Nome must return $30,000 in property taxes paid by the mining firm.

How Not to Get Lost
December 1971

Students in seven schools throughout the Yukon Territory are learning to travel in the wilderness without getting lost. Known as orienteering, the new course teaches young Yukoners how to use a map and compass. Orienteering has certain elements of an outdoor sport, and teachers were instructed on its use as such. As part of the physical education curriculum, students are timed around a course on which they must find designated checkpoints on a map.

1972

Preserving the Totems in Sitka Monument
January 1972

Each year 60,000 visitors walk the shady paths of Sitka National Monument, site of a Tlingit fort in 1804, and learn about the Indians' last major stand against the Russian settlement. And they admire one of the finest collections of totem poles in existence today.

Last May four houseposts and 13 totem poles were gently lowered from their various stations for their first major preservation treatment since 1939. Only "Fog Woman," the tallest totem in the collection, remained in place.

The 13 totems were part of a group of 20 poles brought to Sitka in 1903, after Territorial Governor John Brady visited the villages on Prince of Wales Island to obtain the poles from their tribal owners.

After being displayed at the 1904 Louisiana Purchase Exposition in St. Louis, some of the poles were in such poor condition that they were sold. Others were shown at the Lewis and Clark Expedition in Portland, and at the

Visitors to Sitka National Monument in the summer of 1971 found the south end looking like some weird cemetery. The site is where most of the 18 Haida and Tlingit poles throughout Totem Park were taken for preservation treatment. The original $20,000 fund request is now estimated to cost an additional $15,000. The "Raven" pole (foreground) is Haida; the frog is on the "Crane People" pole and thought to be Tlingit.

> **Governor Brady obtained the valued totems from their tribal owners and brought them to Sitka in 1903.**

close of 1905 returned to Sitka, where they were placed in Sitka's public park. In 1910 the park became Sitka National Monument.

Chief Son-I-Haat of Kasaan had personally given the "Fog Woman" and four accompanying houseposts to Governor Brady in 1901. Brady donated them to Sitka National Monument, completing the total of 18 poles that are there today.

Two totems, the "Crane People" and "Wedding" poles, are Tlingit in origin; the other 16 are Haida.

In 1939 four of the cedar totems were completely recarved, and five were repaired. Thirty years later an inventory of the poles revealed that they urgently needed restoration and preservation. Officals decided upon an intricate and lasting "double diffusion" treatment.

In the past the totems have been painted many times without removing the old paint, as it was thought that paint was the best preservative. In the more recent process, however, totems first receive three applications of a paste-like commercial paint remover. Before each application the surfaces of the poles are steam-heated to a minimum of 70 degrees.

Then a large pit is dug and made leakproof. Two poles at a time are submerged in a solution of sodium fluoride for eight days, then the solution is pumped to a holding tank and the poles soak for 12 days in a copper sulfate solution. The two chemicals react to inhibit growth of fungus causing the rot.

After the totems are dry, they are sprayed with a solution of pentachlorophenol, wax and resins in mineral spirits. Time is then allowed for the mineral spirits to evaporate. The penta preserves the wood, resins stabilize rotten wood fibers and wax inhibits further moisture penetration.

Officials hoped for a return to authenticity when the totems were repainted. The original carvers had only highlighted the main features of the totems, leaving much of the natural wood exposed. This technique allows more moisture to escape and thus helps to preserve the totems.

"Crane People" pole, original location.

—Pat Smith

Dr. Joe Clark, a Wisconsin U.S. Forest Service wood pathologist, has recommended treatment and methods for Sitka Monument totems, which he considers the finest in Alaska. This "Cormorant" Haida pole shows how cracks appear. The rounded depression in the back wing near the body is rot. It will be carefully removed and replaced by today's Native descendants in preserving their cultural history.

1972

Snowmobile Classic: 70-Mile Race ... 18 Below Zero

Anchorage Daily News photo by Henry Peck

February 1972

Masks were in vogue for the Wasilla Grand Prix snowmobile race on December 11 and 12 as drivers roared over the 70-mile course in temperatures that hit 18 below zero. Three Anchorage youths paced the field in the $20,000 race. Jack Cox, 16, won first prize money of $6,000, largest single prize in Alaska snowmobile history, with a two-day time of 3:38:08. Taking second prize of $4,000 was Guy Rearick, also of Anchorage, who finished just ahead of Wes Hamrick who won $2,000 for third.

Anchorage Daily News photo by Henry Peck

Traveling at a high speed in 18-below-zero weather added this icing to the mask of Harry Johnson, who was among 70 snowmobilers from a starting field of 198 who finished the Wasilla Grand Prix in December.

Closing of a Landmark
January 1972

Anchorage lost a landmark in October when the 55-year-old Parsons Hotel at Third Avenue and H Street closed its doors. Known for friendly simplicity, moderate rates, and informality, the hotel was built by miner Fred Parsons before Anchorage was incorporated as a city and changed ownership several times. Decision to close the hotel was made by the present owners because the expense of renovating the old structure was not deemed practical.

A Cover Story
January 1972

The old adage, "You can't tell a book by its cover," was verified in Kodiak last fall when a bookstore there discovered that two copies, ostensibly of Walter Hickel's book, "Who Owns America?" had nothing to do with politics. Due to a mixup at the bindery, the text inside the Hickel-autographed cover was that of another book, "Sex and Sanity," by Melvin Anchell, M.D. Ermalee Hickel, wife of Alaska's former governor and the nation's former Secretary of the Interior, requested one of the mis-bound books to present to her author husband.

The Ring of Progress
April 1972

Anxious to try the new-fangled system known as direct distance dialing, Alaskans in 37 Southcentral Alaska communities were so active in telephoning their way into the modern communications era they nearly swamped the system on February 6. RCA Alaska Communications, Inc., which plays the key role in linking Alaska with the rest of the world, said the number of long distance calls on cut-over day was about 200 percent above average.

Despite an intensive education campaign, phone officials report that many subscribers don't understand how to use the new system. The initial result was an overload on calls for operator assistance.

Only in Anchorage could users dial the area code and number of party to be called. In all other communities, callers had to dial a prefix number, then the area code and Outside number. Direct distance dialing will be extended to the rest of Alaska later this year.

Expensive Fishing
January 1972

The most expensive foreign fishing venture in Alaska's and the nation's history took place near Baranof Island in Southeastern Alaska in late October, and the intrusion in U.S. waters cost the Japan Whaling Company a total of $115,710 in fines and court costs. Contrite culprit in the case which resulted from Coast Guard apprehension of the *Ryushu Maru No. 5*, a 190-foot vessel, inside the 12-mile limit was Captain Masazo Kitada. U.S. District Judge Raymond Plummer of Anchorage imposed a fine of $30,000 against Kitada, and the Japan Whaling Company paid an additional $85,000 to settle civil claims against the seized vessel. U.S. Marshal's costs added $710. In asking and getting the heaviest fine ever levied against a foreign fishing vessel, U.S. Attorney Kent Edwards said, "We do not intend to tolerate continuing violations of this type." The Japanese crew was returned to the vessel in early November and sailed for Japan, ending a five months cruise. Alaskan officials indicated that the arrest of Captain Kitada was made before a single fish was caught in prohibited waters. The Japanese captain told the court, "My whole life is not long enough for me to pay all these debts."

The Native Land Claims Settlement: 962 Million Dollars and 40 Million Acres
February 1972

"NATIVE LAND CLAIMS SETTLEMENT SAILS THROUGH CONGRESS" shouted the double-banner headline on the *Anchorage Daily Times* on December 14, 1971. Two days later, hundreds of native leaders from throughout Alaska gathered at Alaska Methodist University to formulate plans for managing the $962.5 million and 40 million acres of land authorized by Congress to extinguish claims unsettled since the U.S. purchase of Alaska in 1867.

The new law provides for selection of up to 22 million acres by 220 villages. The land will be selected from up to 25 townships (900 square miles or 576,000 acres) surrounding each village. Such lands are reserved from other use until the village selections have been made in the allotted four years. Villages will gain subsurface rights and village size will be a factor in determining the amount of land to be selected.

An additional 16 million acres will be selected by 12 regional corporations which will administer the settlement. This land will be selected on an equal rights basis with the state. A final two million acres will be designated by the Secretary of Interior for use by native groups too small to qualify as a village, for urban native land grants and for cemetery and historical sites.

The state will be granted full title to about 26 million acres now classed as tentatively approved, and including the Prudhoe Bay oil fields. Native selections will not be made within two miles of any home rule or first class city or within six miles of Ketchikan, and no land may be claimed within an existing wildlife refuge.

The money provision calls for Congressional appropriations of $462.5 million over an 11-year period. The remaining $500 million will be paid from a two percent mineral royalty on state land. The funds will be administered by 12 regional corporations and will be allocated to regions on a population basis. The law provides for a thirteenth regional corporation to administer funds for natives not permanent residents of Alaska.

The statewide land freeze which has been in effect since January, 1969, will end 90 days after the bill is signed into law by President Richard Nixon. During this period, the Secretary of Interior is authorized to withdraw up to 80 million acres for inclusion in national park, forest, wildlife refuge and scenic river systems. Authority is granted the Secretary of Interior to withdraw land he deems necessary for a corridor for the Prudhoe Bay-Valdez oil pipeline.

"It is not a perfect bill by any means. It is not as generous as the natives had hoped it would be. The land settlement is larger than many non-natives had wished," said the *Anchorage Daily News*.

'A tremendous Christmas package for Alaska's Natives.'

"Various other groups will be offended by provisions which affect their special interests. And conservationists will not be satisfied with many of the bill's provisions. Yet despite these parochial complaints, we believe the bill is one Alaska can live comfortably with and that this will be recognized in the future."

Said the *Anchorage Daily Times*: "... Alaska's natives—who have long sought recognition of aboriginal claims—have been handed a tremendous Christmas package. The hope is that it turns out to be all good things to Alaska's native citizens. And also a fine, progressive thing for all the people of Alaska and for the future of the 49th State."

Fairbanks Daily News-Miner.

An Unexpected Visitor

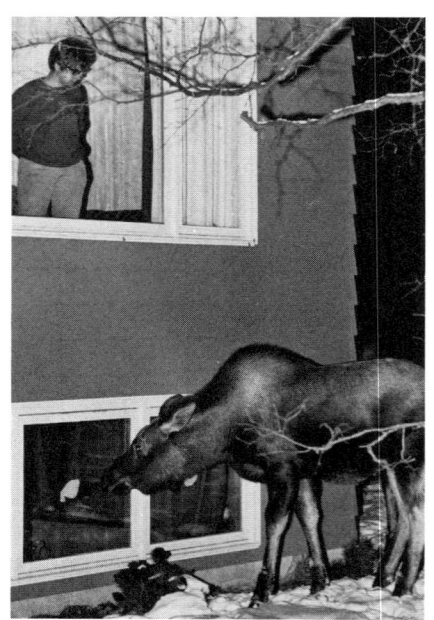

February 1972

While Mrs. Robin Smith watches from inside her Anchorage home, a visiting moose peeks through a basement window.

Anchorage Daily Times photo by Robin Smith

Comeback for Beaver
February 1972

Beaver have made such a comeback in the Yukon, through natural re-population, that they are now being under-harvested by trappers. So says Yukon Game Branch director J. B. Fitzgerald, who added that their increased numbers are occasionally posing problems for highway crews.

Beaver at times build dams on a creek on the downstream side of a road, causing water to back up and flood the road. Fitzgerald's department has issued special permits to the road crews to destroy such beaver dams but workmen find, after dismantling a dam, that the animals build another one overnight.

There are three methods of handling the problem: beaver are either trapped and moved away, explosives blow up the dam or trappers in the area are allowed to trap out of season. There is very little damage to a colony when a dam is blown up as the main beaver house is usually some distance from the dam, Fitzgerald said.

The Game Branch uses a clamshell trap to capture the beaver for relocation. The traps do not injure the animals but someone has to be stationed nearby to rescue the animals from drowning. Beaver have been known to trip the trap by pushing pieces of material ahead of them.

There was a time when beaver could not be trapped south of the Yukon River, when their numbers had dwindled, and the 1958 forest fires near Whitehorse killed a large number. But now they have re-populated and there are fewer trappers to harvest them.

More Power – Soon
March 1972

Juneau's Snettisham power project, largest hydroelectric complex in Alaska, may be providing the capital city area with electricity by next December, according to a major contractor on the $50 million job. Kirk Fox, project manager for Taku Contractors, reported recently that major portions of the work are completed but "it's going to be a rough job next summer to get power on time." Fox's firm built the outflow tunnel, gate system and underground powerhouse and plugged the diversion tunnel. Installation of powerhouse equipment and generators and construction of the power line to Juneau remain to be done. When completed, Snettisham will provide Juneau with 70,000 kilowatts, five times the present peak load

How to Walk on Ice
March 1972

Ice-walking is the name of a new mini-course taught this winter to students at Nome High School who want to learn the secrets of moving safely over the Bering Sea's ice. Designed for young fishermen and seal hunters who venture onto the frozen sea, the course was taught by local ice-walking experts. Students in the special course, one of many offered high school students, learned how to determine ice-thickness and other safety tips.

Ordeal on the Mountain: Freezing Winds at 100 Miles an Hour... A 1,000-foot Fall... A Timely Rescue

March 1972

Bruce Tornberg of Seward was accustomed to all the hazards involved in bringing television service to small towns in Alaska. He had packed heavy equipment up and down mountains with high winds, snow, and even an occasional bear to complicate his work. But when he and his son, Kurt, 13, tried to bring television to the people of Whittier last October, they ran into more trouble than even they could anticipate.

After several attempts to airlift their gear had been delayed, a helicopter finally dropped off power cable at various points on the mountain, where Bruce and Kurt would connect and string the cable down the mountain into Whittier. The chopper's final trip was to the top of the mountain to deliver the Tornbergs, their camp gear and equipment for the television translator.

As the pilot prepared to leave, he mentioned that tailwinds were beginning to pick up. It was 10 to 15 degrees above zero.

Wind was nothing new to Bruce and Kurt. They set up the tent, buttoned down everything tightly, and climbed into their down sleeping bags.

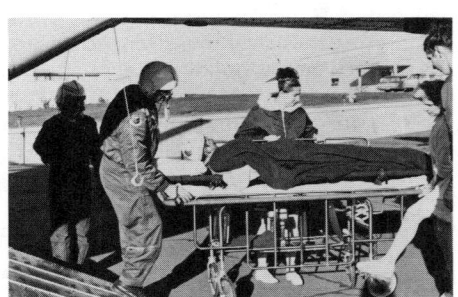
USAF photo

Now recovered from injuries sustained in a 1,000-foot fall down a mountain near Whittier last October, Kurt Tornberg is shown as he arrived at Anchorage's Providence Hospital aboard an Air Force helicopter.

At daybreak the tent began to pull at its moorings. Then it ripped apart. When Bruce's snugly-fitting stocking cap was torn from his head and disappeared, he knew that they were in trouble.

With winds over 100 miles an hour and whirling snow stinging their faces, the two were already cold, and it was impossible to reestablish their camp and wait out the storm. It was time to cache what was left of the tent and the television equipment and leave. They wrapped their gun and a few personal belongings in the sleeping bags and started down. Bruce hoped there would be less wind farther down the mountain. There never was.

Kurt was extremely cold, and the wind made breathing almost impossible. They had descended several hundred feet before they realized that they had missed the only access down, the place where they had planned to run the power cable.

Bruce tried to coax Kurt into retracing their steps, but Kurt was too cold, and the wind was impossible to walk against. Bruce wondered if he could even make it back himself. He dug out a small snow drift behind a rock and leaving Kurt there, went in search of another way down.

The numbing cold distorted Bruce's sense of steepness. Finding what appeared to be a possible route down, he dropped his sleeping bags first, intending to follow them. When they disappeared into oblivion, he changed his mind.

After scouting the area further, he returned to Kurt and encouraged him to get back on his feet by telling the boy that he had found a way down. They trudged on. At each impasse Bruce would again encourage Kurt and be rewarded with renewed effort.

Finally they came to such a precipitous wall that they could only inch their way down, scooting on their bottoms with Kurt's legs hooked around Bruce.

Suddenly Kurt slid around in front of Bruce and the two of them began to tumble down a crevasse.

Bruce managed to maintain a sort of controlled fall, missing outcrops of rock along the way, until his fall abruptly ended with his face crashing through the crusty snow. After a moment he realized that the snow had prevented any bones from being broken by the crunching impact.

But Kurt was still tumbling, helter-skelter, faster and faster. Bruce saw him bounce into the air several times and finally stop at a spot about 1,000 feet below where their fall had begun. He could see his son's still figure, his torn rain gear flapping in the wind.

He made his way to Kurt and examined him, horrified by the amount of blood that one three-and-a-half-inch gash in the head could produce. As he tried to revive the boy, Kurt kept shaking his head, flinging off blood like a wet dog shaking off water. Bruce yelled at Kurt above the howling wind, and the semi-conscious boy responded by moving each of his arms obediently.

Bruce dragged Kurt down to a more sheltered spot by two boulders which would also identify the location, removed his outer clothing and covered Kurt with them. He then continued the descent alone to find help.

By sheer grit Bruce managed to make it to the road. He saw a truck, but he was

Jo Ann Tornberg

Kurt Tornberg as he looks today, fully recovered from his injuries.

He could see his son's still figure, his torn rain gear flapping in the wind

---

so cold in the driving wind that he couldn't speak. He collapsed on the road.

Afer the truck driver got him into the truck, Bruce revived enough to say that his son was still on the mountain. A search team was quickly formed, and Bruce pointed to the place where he had left Kurt.

When the rescue team arrived with a stretcher at the two boulders, they found only some blood and Kurt's hat.

Kurt had revived, and bewildered, followed Bruce's footsteps through the snow to emerge at the foot of the mountain. He saw a truck turn around and tried to signal by throwing his coat into the air. He was in a gully, but the truck driver did see something in the air. Thinking that the wind was blowing things off the truck, he looked carefully and saw Kurt trying desperately to climb the steep embankment.

An Air Force helicopter flew the Tornbergs to an Anchorage hospital, where Kurt was sutured, x-rayed, and treated for concussion and frostbite, and Bruce thawed out on his own.

A re-examination of the mountain convinced Bruce that once they had missed the cable route, the course they took—fall and all—was the only way they could have gotten off the mountain alive.

A second attempt to install Whittier's television translator was postponed until late spring.

—*DOT BARDARSON*

1972

March 1972

Surviving 90-knot winds and a 50-foot Bering Sea wave that sheared away her flying bridge, the crabber LYNDA is shown on her side at Cape Labin on Unimak Island. Captain Knute Johnson and his crew of three were removed from the beach in a daring Coast Guard rescue. Whitney-Fidalgo Seafoods, owner of the vessel, expects to recover the stout ship. The same early November storm hit Dutch Harbor on Unalaska Island with gusts measured at 142 miles per hour. Governor William A. Egan authorized $20,000 in emergency state funds to assist villagers in repairing damage.

Teller's Public Bath
March 1972

Anyone in the Teller area who feels the need for a bath has only to supply his own towels and soap, according to Council President James Isabell. Built with a grant from the State Rural Development Office, Teller's new public bathhouse and laundry includes coin-operated washers and dryers. There are separate tubs and showers for men and women. Baths and showers are free in the first such facility on the Seward Peninsula.

An Infusion for AMU
March 1972

An agreement that will provide expansion space for the University of Alaska's Anchorage campus and funds for Alaska Methodist University was signed early in January. It provides that the University of Alaska will be given a 99-year lease on 142.5 acres of AMU land, and for which AMU will receive full payment during the first 10 years of the lease. Amount to be paid will be determined following an appraisal of the acreage. AMU had proposed a price of $7.5 million, advising state officials that it could not continue operations beyond March without an infusion of funds. The memorandum of understanding signed by the two universities calls for elimination of duplicate college efforts in Anchorage, provides for University of Alaska use of unused AMU facilities and a common calendar for 1972-73 to avoid course duplication.

'Copter Saves 'Beluga'
February 1972

Biggest "beluga" in the north is being kept afloat and snow-free by a Fairbanks helicopter. Given its name because of its size and resemblance to a stranded whale, the inflated fabric building, which is used at the University of Alaska to protect hockey rinks in winter and tennis courts in summer, has a snow problem. The first time a heavy snow threatened to sink the "beluga," workmen climbed atop its frail body. The structure collapsed before they could start shoveling. It was finally determined that the best way to clear snow from the flimsy covering was with low-flying helicopters. Merric Inc., a Fairbanks helicopter firm, was awarded a contract to keep the snow from "beluga's" back.

January 1972

Amchitka Island earth cracks near the site where a five megaton nuclear device was detonated on November 6 are inspected by James Schlesinger, chairman of the Atomic Energy Commission, right, and an Army adviser. Although it induced protests, petitions, pickets and fear throughout the world, the AEC test blast performed almost exactly as the AEC predicted. No radiation was leaked and no earthquakes or tsunamis were triggered by the largest such U.S. blast.

Signing up to Share in the Native Land Settlement
May 1972

Extending to the far corners of the earth, the task of enrolling as many as 100,000 Alaska Natives of one-quarter or more Eskimo, Indian or Aleut descent is now under way.

Required for all persons hoping to share in benefits of the Alaska Native Claims Settlement Act, enrollment must be completed by March 30, 1973, under terms of the recently-enacted law. All qualifying Natives who were born on or before December 18, 1971, are eligible.

Key man in the process is Gary T. Longley, 39, a Nome-born Eskimo and veteran Civil Service employee, who was named enrollment coordinator by the Bureau of Indian Affairs in early March. Starting in late March, enrollment enumerators began traveling to villages by plane, snowmobile, boat and dog team in making the crucial count.

Longley estimated 60 percent of the enrollment would be completed by the end of April. Headquarters for the far-flung project is the Kaloa Building in Anchorage.

Actual number of Natives eligible for enrollment is estimated by Longley at 80,000 to 100,000. He expects as many as 150,000 persons may apply for enrollment. Information on the enrollment process may be obtained by writing: Enrollment, Pouch 7-1971, Anchorage, Alaska 99501.

Two major problems facing Longley and his staff are enrolling eligible Alaska Natives who now live throughout the world, and establishing eligibility for older Natives whose birth has not been recorded in government or church records.

A media campaign is being developed to advise out-of-state Natives on the enrollment process. Information requested on the enrollment form includes name, Social Security number, last known address, sex, date of birth, degree of Native blood, residence as of April 1, 1970, and the village and/or region in which the applicant is enrolled.

With Native villages and regional corporations deep in the process of becoming incorporated, a badly needed $560,000 was appropriated by the Legislature in early March as first payment by the state on the $500 million it must pay from mineral royalties under provisions of the Settlement Act.

A Sled Dog's New Life
March 1972

The last RCMP sled dog will live forever in the hearts of many Canadians enthralled by the North—and in full view as well. The remains of Rex, one of the dogs in the last two teams retired in 1970 in favor of snowmobiles, will be mounted with care by taxidermist Terence Morgan for the RCMP Museum at Regina, Saskatchewan.

No Heat ... 45 Below Zero
May 1972

It's not just the Mayo Clinic in Rochester, Minnesota, which makes medical history. Some kind of record was chalked up at Mayo in the Yukon this winter when an 80-year-old woman survived after being found unconscious in her unheated cabin when the temperature was 45 degrees below zero.

When brought to Mayo Hospital, Mrs. Susan Blanchard had a body temperature of 77 degrees, no pulse and no heart beat, but she was moaning slightly. Normal body temperature is 98.6 degrees and Dr. James D. Clark and his staff of nurses worked six hours to raise the woman's body temperature slowly, one or two degrees each hour. "Ma Blanchard," as she is known to many Yukoners, survived the experience, and says she isn't going to let the fire go out next winter.

Fur Prices Soar
March 1972

Prices for furs almost doubled since 1970 at the first winter auction in Regina, Saskatchewan. More than 50,000 pelts were sold for $172,000, almost double the 1970 total. A string of 52 wild mink pelts brought $41 per skin, compared with $25 the previous year. Adam Cooke, manager of the Saskatchewan fur marketing service, said the furs were first class and fetched more than expected. He said the reason for the higher-than-usual prices might be an economic recession in Europe. "Three-quarters of our skins go to Germany, Italy, Switzerland and Britain, and I reckon that people are buying as an investment," he said. "A lot of trappers all over Saskatchewan who supplied these skins had a very happy Christmas."

Sign of Life for an Old Ghost Town ...
January 1972

In 1900 a wave of gold stampeders got part way up the Middle Fork of the Koyukuk River, got cold feet, and turned around and departed. The point where they turned was named "Coldfoot." In 1902 Coldfoot boasted one gambling hole, two roadhouses, two stores, seven saloons, and ten prostitutes. By the 1920's it was a ghost town. Recently the Alyeska Pipeline Service Company established a construction camp at Coldfoot, hauling in modular housing, as well as construction machinery for building the proposed trans-Alaska pipeline. A skeleton crew is kept at the Coldfoot Camp. From the above recently constructed sign it appears that the skeleton crew was down to two when the sign was erected. The shoe is painted blue—about the same blue as a half-frozen foot.

State Ponders Using Schools Year-round
April 1972

The need to provide classroom space for Alaska's booming school population led the State Board of Education recently to endorse the concept of the rescheduled school year. Although not yet adopted, the idea of utilizing schools 12 months of the year is being studied by the state's more populous school districts. Slated for consideration during the current Legislature is House Bill No. 467 which would allow school districts to adopt a rescheduled school year on a voluntary basis, and provide up to $25,000 for each district planning year-round use of schools.

Dean, Department of Education Alaska Newsletter, commented on the proposal destined to change the state's education pattern: "The most obvious advantage of the rescheduled school year is the release of classroom space. Many school districts are facing a crisis due to the shortage of facilities. Under a continuous learning year, a substantial portion of the student body is always on vacation; this accounts for an effective capacity increase of 20 to 33 percent...

"Shorter vacations scattered throughout the year would permit students, parents and teachers to participate in a wider variety of activities—winter sports, fall hunting and spring fishing."

Old Eskimo Custom Upheld by Court
May 1972

Custom adoption of children, as practiced by Canada's Eskimos, is legal and binding, the Northwest Territories Court has ruled.

In a milestone decision concerning Native rights, Justice William Morrow ruled at Yellowknife that the traditional verbal agreements to give or accept children for adoption are legally binding within the social and moral code of the Eskimo community, though no court procedure is involved. The ruling, the first on the legal status of such adoptions, was handed down in a case where the mother of a child given to friends in 1959, sought to have the child returned to her.

Judge Morrow appointed lawyers to argue both sides of the case and held a hearing to determine the legal status of the child and the custom adoption. In a judgment which filled 19 pages, the territorial court stated, "This custom of handling surplus children was obviously born of necessity, the need of the primitive community to survive. The coming of the white man with police and court discouraged the custom of killing the unwanted or surplus baby, so the custom of giving them out in adoption has probably increased and become more important than ever before."

The Dwindling Herd
May 1972

Fanciers of reindeer meat were recently notified that a slump in the size of the Nunivak Island herd may eliminate butchering of the animals next fall for commercial sale. Daniel T. Olrun, Sr., general manager of Bering Sea Reindeer Products, reported, "Our deer population has dwindled to 4,188 animals from an estimated 16,000 in 1959." Olrun said that 300 Nunivak reindeer were butchered during the winter, but this quantity fell far short of filling orders. He attributed decline of the herd to "unsatisfactory management by the federal government."

Big Game for Archers
January 1972

Four caribou, three moose, two Dall sheep and a black bear were taken by Alaskan archers in recent hunts, according to the Alaska State Archery Association. Bob Berry took a moose and two caribou and Bob Hansen got a sheep and caribou. Longest shots were from 45 yards, and the farthest any animal traveled after being hit was 150 yards. Bow weights ranged from 55 to 73 pounds.

Waiver for Alaska Ship
May 1972

The M/V *Wickersham*, pride of Alaska's fleet of state ferries, became a full-fledged Alaskan ship early in March when Congress approved a waiver of the Jones Act, which will allow the 1300-passenger ferry to carry travelers between U.S. ports. Under provisions of the Jones Act, the foreign-built ferry could sail only between one U.S. port and a foreign port.

Engineering the first such waiver of the Jones Act was Congressman Nick Begich who won support for his bill by noting that the state has already signed a $19.5 million contract for a vessel which will replace the *Wickersham*. The waiver granted by Congress extends for a maximum of 36 months and excludes freight shipments. The new replacement ferry is expected to be completed in 27 months.

With the *Wickersham* now allowed to sail directly from Seattle to Alaskan ports, and between Alaskan ports, Congressman Begich predicted "vastly improved service on the Alaska Marine Highway." He added that the ferry purchased by former Governor Walter Hickel "will cease to be a financial liability for the state."

Cabin Fever...
January 1972

Women and newcomers are more subject to cabin fever than long-time northerners, according to Dr. A. Patrick Abbott of Whitehorse, a psychiatrist with Canada's Northern Health Services. In a report to the Northwest Territories Council, Dr. Abbott reported:

"The syndrome is much more common in women. A danger is that this change in mood will cause deterioration in the marriage, sometimes to the point of a marriage breakdown." Observing that employers carefully check the adjustment capability of potential male employees to northern living, the Yukon psychiatrist recommended assessments also be made of wives. Characteristics of the malady also known as "arctic hysteria" are depression, irritability, easily-provoked anger and a breakdown of relationships with whom the sufferer is living. Advocating use of radio and television in planning new Far North communities, Dr. Abbott reported that until recently a new community in the Yukon could receive regular radio broadcasts only from Radio Moscow. "Surely such a situation must lead to a feeling of being utterly isolated from the rest of Canada," he commented.

Kodiak, Naval Base Cut off by Slide

Island Times photo

March 1972

Kodiak's Pillar Mountain started sliding early in December, blocking the only road link between the city on one side and the Naval Base and new state airport on the other from December 6 to 24. Black mass in center of photo marks the slide which sent huge boulders over the roadway. The city approach is shown at bottom of photo and the new city dock now under construction is just beyond the slide. By early January controlled traffic was allowed on the vital link, but State Highway Department engineers emphasized that more problems lie ahead. The new lower road was constructed after the 1964 earthquake to replace the higher road now buried by the slide.

Island Times photo

Pressed into service to provide a water link between Kodiak and the Navy Base after the Pillar Mountain slide blocked the only road, the fishing vessel ENDEAVOR departs Gibson Cove for Kodiak's city dock. The slide blocked 250 children from reaching school in December, and resulted in planes and other ships working to link the rock-divided island community.

Shortest Day, Longest Shadow...

March 1972

Shadows are shorter now, but they made Anchorage Daily Times photographer Alice Puster a giant at high noon on December 21, when she took this photo to depict Anchorage's shortest day and longest shadows.

1972

Widespread Hardship from Winter Storms

April 1972

Winter mauled the North Pacific rim in January and February, inflicting hardship on an arc extending from Prince Rupert, B.C., to Kodiak. Suffering most were Prince Rupert, Juneau and Kodiak.

Snow and mud slides on the Yellowhead Highway east of Prince Rupert blocked both rail lines and the road which links the city with the rest of Canada. An air controllers strike complicated the problem, leaving Prince Rupert isolated and dependent on the British Columbia and Alaska Marine Highway ferries for contact with the outside world.

An avalanche in Juneau's Last Chance Basin on January 19 knocked out the city's water supply for five days. Some areas of the city were without water entirely while other areas had sporadic supply until complete service was restored the following Monday.

The record snowfall which may have triggered the avalanche provided ample water for those who took to the Alaskan way . . . one gallon of snow equals five cups of water; and it takes five **gallons** of water to flush a toilet.

The airborne avalanche tossed a tree across power lines which put the main water pumps out of action. As work progressed to clear a trail to the pumps, a check valve in the one-million-gallon reservoir malfunctioned and the entire water supply drained back into Gold Creek.

City repair crews worked 'round the clock to restore the water system only to find that the line itself had been damaged by the snowslide. A temporary "patch" was installed, and later a more permenant repair was accomplished.

High winds topped 80 miles an hour and blew down Juneau's KINY radio tower in late January.

Hardest hit was Kodiak, where a prolonged cold spell extended into February and idled seafood processing plants. An estimated 2,000 cannery workers, fishermen and supporting workers were left jobless by the depletion of Kodiak's 210 million gallon reservoir to less than 24 million. Rationing was being considered in mid-February, as prospects for warm weather needed to restore the reservoir appeared dim.

A cold spell in 1971 idled the processing plants for a month in March and April, and there were fears that the 1972 siege might be longer and much more costly. Meanwhile, Kodiak Island ranchers reported some of their cattle were starving because access roads were blocked by 10-foot drifts and the animals could not be reached with feed.

Elaine Mitchell
Photo taken from Basin Road, Juneau, clearly shows the path of the avalanche, January 19, which damaged the city's water line. The cloud of snow apparently bounced off the barren spot in the center of the photo, becoming airborne and came to rest across Gold Creek on the Basin Road—and up the hillside.

Southeast Alaska Empire photo by Mike Todd
January winds gusting to 80 knots toppled this 500-foot tower of radio station KINY in Juneau.

Jim Moltion
Winds that hit a peak of 125 miles per hour sheared away the roof from the Composite Building on Shemya Island on January 5 and deposited the section in foreground 1,000 feet distant. Stripping the section of roof at right, the Aleutian storm blew for 12 hours and sailed some roof sections 1,500 feet from the building.

Anchorage Daily Times photo by Alice Puster
Heavy snow whipped by stiff winds created problems for small plane owners near Anchorage in mid-winter. Leif Lie is shown working to free his "snowbird" at Lake Hood.

A New Mining Town?
July 1972

A new town on the Bering Sea coast 80 miles north of Nome is being planned by the Lost River Mining Corporation. Created to serve the mineral fields of fluorite, tin and tungsten several miles inland, Lost River City is expected to have a population of several thousand, a year-round dock facility and a modern airport. The 356-square-mile townsite is on well-drained gravel free from permafrost and located six miles from the mine complex. Its port would permit drastic reductions of freight costs to such towns as Nome and Teller.

Lost River Mining Corporation, a subsidiary of Pan Central Exploration Ltd. of Toronto, has been working toward development of a large mine on the Seward Peninsula since 1970. A final feasibility study is due in a year, data is being gathered for a possible environmental impact statement, and the company has opened a full-time office in Anchorage. Murray Watts, president of the corporation, estimates that the mineral reserves at Lost River will support "a 4,000 ton per day operation for 20 years," and said that most of the more than 200 employees of the operation will be Alaskans. No underground mining is expected until the seventeenth year.

To date the firm has spent more than $1.6 million in capital outlays on the project and expects to spend $2 million this year. Production could begin within two years after a decision is made to go to development. Fluorite has a number of industrial uses, but the bulk of it is used in the production of aluminum.

Teaching on the Tundra
February 1972

If the Northwest Territories Department of Education approves their plan, teachers and pupils at the arctic coast community of Igloolik will move out of their classrooms to the tundra during the last two weeks of June. At the Eskimo hunting camps, they would learn the traditional ways of the older people who have lived on their own resources for much of their lives.

"That's what the people really want," Igloolik council chairman Josiah Kadlutsiak told NWT Commissioner Stuart Hodgson when he met with the settlement council recently. When the Commissioner found it was also what the teachers wanted he too waxed enthusiastic and promised to submit the proposal to school authorities. So, this spring, the white teachers of Igloolik may find themselves taking a few lessons from their Eskimo students.

Nuclear Plant Success
April 1972

Mission accomplished: After nearly 10 years of operation, the SM-1A nuclear power plant at Fort Greely will be decommissioned. It has successfully proven the feasibility of building and operating a nuclear power plant in the remote Arctic; and it is no longer needed as a research and development facility.

Sharon Clegg
May 1972
This strange-to-an-Outsider sign on a Nome store window was considered worth photographing by Dr. Sharon Clegg, D.V.M., during a recent visit to the Norton Sound city. The Eskimo name for a large bearded seal, oogruk meat is a staple food on Alaska's northwest coast.

A Gain for Women
June 1972

Alaska's population during the sixties apparently became younger, whiter, more female, and increased more than that of the nation as a whole. Statistics included in a recent publication issued by the state Department of Labor indicate that Alaska's population grew by 34 percent during the decade of the sixties, while the population of the nation as a whole grew by 14 percent.

Although each racial group increased in numbers, only white percentages rose, from 77 to 79 percent. The black percentage of the population remained at three percent, and the Chinese, Japanese and Filipino percentage remained at one percent, while Eskimo, Aleut and Indian percentages dropped slightly. The percentage of all Alaskans 24 or younger jumped from 53 percent in 1960 to 55 percent in 1970. But the most noticeable trend of the decade was a nearly 41 percent increase in the number of females, although the male population grew by 27 percent, and men still comprise 57 percent of the population.

Anchorage Daily Times photo by Alice Puster
June 1972
Cook Inlet was still packing a heavy load of ice on April 11, when the second barge of the season headed for Anchorage. Shown as it bucked ice pans near Kenai is a Pacific Western Lines barge with mobile homes and general cargo enroute from Seattle to Anchorage.

Biggest Borough
May 1972

Larger than 40 states and dwarfing any local government in the nation, the petition for a North Slope Borough has been approved by the State Local Boundary Commission. Last step in the process leading to establishment of the first class borough, which will include virtually all of Alaska north of 68 degrees, will be an election in the next few months at which an estimated 3,500 residents of the area will approve or reject the proposal. Strongly supported by Eskimo leaders, the new borough is expected to win easy endorsement. The oil industry, whose Prudhoe Bay field and several hundred miles of the proposed trans-Alaska oil pipeline are within the North Slope Borough, opposed creation of the new borough. Some sources indicated establishment of the local government entity might be challenged in the courts. Eskimo-dominated population centers in the proposed borough are Point Hope, Wainwright, Barrow, Kaktovik (Barter Island) and Anaktuvuk Pass. The borough's boundaries are similar to those of the Arctic Slope Native Association, one of 12 regional corporations being established under the Alaska Native Claims Settlement Act.

Top Shrimp Port
January 1972

Kodiak's claim as the world's top shrimp port appeared cinched by mid-October as landings at the island city totaled 64,493,600 pounds for the first nine and one-half months of 1971. Some fisheries observers predicted that Kodiak's 1971 shrimp poundage would reach a record 75 million pounds. Kodiak shrimp landings have soared from slightly over 32 million pounds in 1969 to more than 49 million in 1970. Meanwhile, the state's seafood capital expected to tally nearly 10 million pounds of halibut during 1971, making it top U.S. port in halibut landings.

Fairbanks Landmark: Fire Destroys Nordale Hotel . . . . Four Die
May 1972

The Nordale Hotel, a Fairbanks landmark since 1906, was destroyed by fire February 22, bringing death to at least four Alaskans. By early March those identified as perishing in the blaze in which 11 persons were injured were Eva McGown, Earl Simpson, Sven "Whitey" Thorpe and Helen Langton. Forty-four persons were registered at the time of the fire which moved so swiftly through the sawdust-insulated structure that some occupants had to jump from windows. Five Fairbanks area fire departments fought the flames with more than one million gallons of water. Also destroyed were Martin Victor Furs, the Alaska Insurance Agency and Nordale Barber Shop. The original Nordale Hotel, which Tony Nordale built beside the Chena River in 1906, was destroyed by fire in 1923. Nordale then purchased the building which bore his name for nearly 50 years.

—*Steve Preston*

Steve Preston

Only a shell of Fairbanks's Nordale Hotel remained the day after the historic structure was struck by fire.

'No Way to Start' Oil Pipeline Work Before Another Year . . . Cost Estimates Climb from $900 Million to $3 Billion
June 1972

"We see no way of starting construction before about a year from now," said Edward L. Patton, president of Alyeska Pipeline Service Company, in a talk to the Fairbanks Petroleum Club on April 11, thus giving a new time frame for the proposed 789-mile trans-Alaska pipeline from Prudhoe Bay to Valdez.

The ALPS president made it clear that the new timetable for the long-delayed project was contingent on Secretary of Interior Rogers C. B. Morton granting ALPS a right-of-way permit this spring. And Morton's decision was to be based on information contained in thousands of pages in the six volumes titled "Final Environmental Impact Statement—Proposed Trans-Alaska Pipeline," which was released on March 20. No less important in the decision-making process were three volumes released at the same time which relate to the economic and security aspects of the pipeline project.

"We fervently hope the Secretary of Interior will decide to issue the right-of-way permit," said Patton. "Such an announcement will put us into court against the Wilderness Society and Cordova fishermen, and we would expect the court hearings and appeals procedures to take at least the remainder of this year, so we see no way of starting construction before about a year from now."

If the permit is issued, and assuming court tests will extend through this year, the ALPS president said his company will concentrate on detailed construction and engineering plans. "We think this kind of detailed effort would enable us to complete the 600,000 barrels-per-day base case in late 1975, if we start no later than next spring," said Patton.

The original cost estimate for the 48-inch pipeline, largest private construction project in history, has soared from $900 million in 1969 to $3 billion. With cost of the line having a direct bearing on state income from royalty and severance taxes, some Alaskan leaders are pushing for barrel tax on Prudhoe Bay oil to insure income. Advocated by Governor William A. Egan, a proposal for state ownership of the pipeline was sidetracked in late March by a negative Senate vote.

Undersecretary of the Interior William T. Pecora put the trans-Alaska pipeline into focus when he described it on March 20 as the "most complex, most costly, most ecologically sensitive, most criticized, most carefully scrutinized, most long-awaited" project.

While Alaskans and other Americans took sides for and against the $12.7 million Department of Interior Environmental Impact Statement, ALPS president Patton and his staff kept their "cool," maintaining that, "Our extensive research has shown that the trans-Alaska pipeline can be safely built with minimum disturbance to the Alaskan environment. Just as we have taken no shortcuts in conducting our research, we will take no shortcuts in the construction of the pipeline system. We respect and appreciate Alaska's environment, and we will protect it."

Natural gas made news when the Northwest Project Study Group, a consortium of oil and gas giants that hope to pipe North Slope gas to the U. S. Midwest, reported that cost of the proposed 2,500-mile line had escalated from an estimated $2.7 billion to about $5 billion.

Already providing power and light for Tokyo, natural gas from Kenai-Cook Inlet fields may assist Los Angeles and other Southern California cities in meeting a developing energy crisis. Pacific Lighting Service Company reported in Anchorage that it hopes to develop a liquefaction plant on the North Kenai that will tap Alaska's gas for benefit of Californians. Cost of the plant would be about $130 million and target date for completion is 1976.

1972

May 1972
When the spring sun climbs higher and there is smoke in the chimney there are icicles on the eaves of Alaskan cabins. The March icicle screen on this cabin north of Kasilof on the Sterling Highway all but obscures the windows.

Beware...
Year of the Big Snow Is Yet to Come!
August 1972

Buy high boots and a big shovel for 15-foot drifts if you plan to live in Southcentral Alaska in the year 2000 and if the long-range weather forecast of Bernt Balchen, arctic expert, is correct. During a recent visit in Anchorage, the man who explored the South Pole with Admiral Byrd, pioneered transpolar aviation routes and once commanded Alaska's Tenth Rescue Squadron, predicted that the Arctic Ocean will be open if present warming trends continue.

Noting that explorer Fridtjof Nansen recorded more than 40 feet of ice under his ship *Fram* during the 1893 expedition, Balchen claimed that winter ice on the Arctic Ocean is now only eight feet thick in winter and four to five feet in summer.

Opening of the Arctic Ocean, according to Balchen, will shift the track of North Pacific storms and dump up to 15 feet of snow on Anchorage during a "normal" winter in the next century. Balchen sees dry winters for the central United States and a winter temperature dip of 10 degrees in southern states. Balchen said five scientific reports published since 1953 support his contention that the Arctic Ocean will be an open sea by the year 2000. An increase in carbon dioxide in the atmosphere is the major cause of the climatic change now in progress, according to Balchen.

March 1972
Thousands of spectators now line Anchorage's Fourth Avenue to watch hundreds of sled dogs compete in the Fur Rendezvous World Championship Races—but it wasn't always so. This 1939 photo shows three young Anchorage mushers ready to start a one-dog Fur Rendezvous race that has grown into a national sporting event. No local Rendezvous fan could identify these pioneering young mushers.

The Big Payoffs
July 1972

Fifteen tickets with 11:56 a.m. written on them were worth about $7,000 each on May 10, when the Tanana River ice moved at Nenana and put the winning time into the payoff records of the 56-year-old Nenana Ice Classic. With more than 220,000 tickets sold this year, Nenana contest officials estimated prize money would total $108,000.

Individual and pool winners included: Frank Depner, Soldotna; NBA Soldotna Club; Ed Kjera, Fairbanks; William Halleran, Anchorage; Michael Dimentieff, Kenai; Virginia Tessier, Anchorage; ECB Employees Club, Anchorage; Milton and Ora Dickerson, Valdez;

Also holding winning tickets were the Seven Club, Anchorage; Sea-Land Pool, Fairbanks; Gary McNeil, Anchorage; Fred Bailey, Wasilla; Anatoly Lekanof, Anchorage; Hadfield Bar Pool, Naknek; and King Ko Inn, King Salmon.

In other contests, winner of the Chena Ice Classic was William E. Bunch of North Pole who won between $2,800 and $3,000 when he guessed the Chena River ice would go out at 5:08 p.m. on April 23; the clock stopped at 5:18 p.m.

Biggest single sled dog racing winner of the past season was Peter Sangris, 35, of Detah, NWT, who won $7,500 for finishing first in the Caribou Carnival Race at Yellowknife in March with a time of 16:40:31 for the three-day, 150-mile marathon.

Alaska Spelling Bee champion for 1972 is Joe Vissers, 13, of Orion Junior High School on Elmendorf Air Force Base. He won the title by outspelling 102 other competitors.

'Deadly Shooting!'... Eskimo Hunters Show Oil Rig Crews a Thing or Two
July 1972

Eskimo workers on oil rig crews in Canada's High Arctic are showing the white men a thing or two about hunting. Steve Hume, on the northern beat for *The Edmonton Journal*, reported from Kristoffer Bay, one of the arctic drill sites, that hiring Eskimo workers can have substantial side benefits for southern-based oil companies.

According to drilling supervisor Wally Kuysters, a polar bear began creating havoc at the Ellef Ringnes Island site, and efforts to drive it away were useless. Workers worried about their skins every time they stepped out of their quarters, and the bear was disrupting camp activity.

"We didn't know what to do because the bears are protected, so we called Rea Point for advice," said Kuysters. "They told us to hang tough and they'd think of something. On the next plane was an Eskimo with his hunting license, a rifle and two shells. He was one of the new workers at Rea Point and he said he'd been sent up to solve our bear problem.

"Two shells, mind you. I couldn't believe it. I tried to get him to take a box of ammunition from our stores but he just laughed and said he had one too many shells already. He went out and shot that bear, then brought back the extra shell as a present. I've never seen shooting that deadly before!"

Another Eskimo point of view has been provided for some of the animal-loving workers from Edmonton and Calgary. At Kristoffer Bay the drill site was frequented by arctic foxes—until the first native crew arrived from Pond Inlet, a trapping community on Eclipse Sound, 500 miles north of the Arctic Circle. Firearms are prohibited on Panarctic drill sites by company regulation, but the Eskimos were happy to make-do with odds and ends of wire, which they used to make snares.

One Pond Inlet employee went home with his pockets full of wages and his arms full of a spare-time bonus of 38 prime arctic fox pelts. Some of the southerners were incensed that the cute, fluffy white animals had been trapped, until a visiting member of the RCMP bluntly told them that the Eskimos had done the camp a favor.

"Foxes are very susceptible to rabies," he said. "They look nice running around your camp until they get rabid and go mad—then they are a real pain in the rear."

Boat Crippled in Rough Seas... Plane to the Rescue
May 1972

Following the tradition of Alaskan pilots, who often land their planes in unusual places under unusual circumstances, Chuck Traylor of Wrangell rescued a 21-foot cruiser and its three occupants from rough water and rocks near Station Island in January by using his float plane as a tow boat. The cruiser was without power and drifting toward danger when Traylor intercepted the distress call, landed, fastened a tow line to a float strut, and maneuvered the boat to smooth water. He called the two-hour operation "scary."

Gastineau Revival
August 1972

The now-vacant Gastineau Hotel in Juneau is expected to provide 41 new apartments for the city's elderly, handicapped and displaced residents. In the first such project in Alaska, the old hotel is being rehabilitated under the National Housing Act of 1968 to provide 26 one-bedroom and 15 efficiency apartments. Completion of the project is expected in December.

May 1972
While winter means funtime, it also means chores. Our water has to be hauled on a sled pulled by a snow machine from a creek. The men and boys all get on that job, and it is quite a task to keep eight families in water. At night it is like the olden days—heat the water, pour it into the tub and line up. We mothers usually are last in, and as one mother described it, "It's like taking a bath in a warm pond with moss, needles and silt." If a neighbor kid happens to be over for the night, they think nothing of following the rest of the crowd. Only in Alaska do you find such happenings.
—Donna Galla
Logging camp correspondent
WRANGELL SENTINEL

Aleut Basketry: Preserving an Ancient Art

June 1972

The ancient art of Aleut basketry is being kept alive largely through the efforts of Mrs. Anfesia Shapsnikoff of Unalaska. Shown here during a demonstration at the University of Alaska, Mrs. Shapsnikoff has traveled to several Aleut villages, Kodiak and Anchorage as well as the University in an effort to save the basketry tradition from extinction. Her instruction in Aleut communities includes finding reeds from which the baskets are made, and proper care of the fragile grasses. Photos shown here were taken by Barry McWayne, staff photographer for the University of Alaska Museum.

Photos from the UNIVERSITY OF ALASKA MUSEUM

The blade of grass . . .
Main hope for continuing the ancient art of weaving Attu baskets lies in the skilled fingers of Mrs. Anfesia Shapsnikoff of Unalaska. She is shown selecting a blade of grass to be used in a demonstration.

. . . it must be moistened
The grass must be moistened to make it flexible.

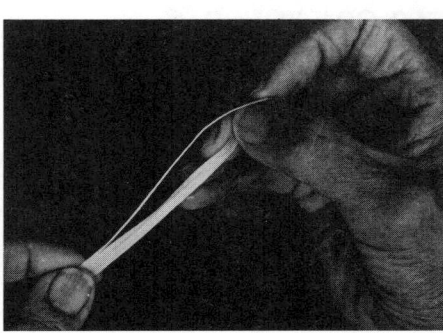

. . . and split.
The moistened grass is split into the proper thickness with the thumb nail.

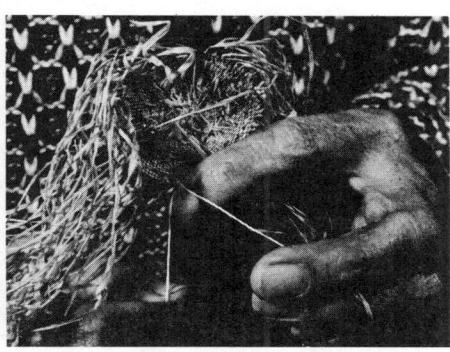

Weaving by touch.
When a woman is weaving the bottom of a basket, it is between her and her hands so that weaving is done almost entirely by touch at this stage in the growth of the basket.

Creating the design.
Mrs. Shapsnikoff demonstrates with a rubber band how the embroidery thread is twisted over the grass strands to create a design on the outside of a basket.

Retaining the shape.
When a basket is not being worked on, a wooden mold is placed in it to retain the proper shape.

Some superb examples.
These baskets, all done over glass bottles, are from the collection of superb Aleut basketry donated to the University Museum by Mr. William Brown of Seattle.

1972

One Step Closer... But Alaska's Future Still Rests with the Courts

July 1972

Alaska's major newspapers used red, yellow and blue bannerlines and maps to announce on May 11 that Secretary of Interior Rogers C. B. Morton had decided to grant a right-of-way permit for construction of the 789-mile trans-Alaska oil pipeline from Prudhoe Bay to Valdez.

"Momentous and tremendous news for Alaska," said Governor William A. Egan. "It is a great day for the nation as well." Senator Ted Stevens called Secretary Morton's decision, "The most significant day since the passage of the Alaska Statehood Act. . . . this means we're over the top."

Oil industry officials joined Egan, Stevens and other leaders in agreeing that a major battle had been won in the effort to move ahead on the world's largest private construction project, now estimated to cost more than $3 billion, but the war was not decided.

The fate of the project closely entwined with Alaska's economic future now rests with the courts. Alyeska Pipeline Service Company, which will build the line for seven major oil firms with North Slope wells, said it was "extremely gratified" with Morton's decision.

"Alyeska Pipeline Service Company is deeply committed to constructing and operating the safest and most secure oil transportation system in the world, and every precaution will be taken to safeguard against environmental risks," said the ALPS announcement. Its plans frustrated since 1970, when conservation groups won an injunction halting work on the line, ALPS made it clear in May that it plans no work on the giant project until the courts have made a final decision, and this may not come until late this year.

Unhappy with Morton's decision, the Wilderness Society, Friends of the Earth and other environmental organizations announced they will continue to fight the line of 48-inch pipe which will bisect Alaska.

"We will continue to oppose a trans-Alaska pipeline," said Dr. Edgar Wayburn, past president of the Sierra Club.

George Alderson, legislative director for Friends of the Earth, commented, "We will do our best to keep the thing tied up until details of studies of alternatives can be done."

Congressman Les Aspin of Wisconsin, a leading advocate of building the line through Canada, described Morton's decision as a "blatant example of the interests of the oil industry superseding the public interest." He predicted the project would be stopped in the federal courts.

Governor Egan, however, said, "I am confident that the injunction and lawsuits will be resolved at an early time so that construction can begin on this largest project of all times."

"Completion of the trans-Alaska line would require at least three years from date of approval, thereby permitting the delivery of oil by about 1976," said Morton in announcing his decision. "According to best estimates, the trans-Canada line would involve at least three to five years additional time for completion. . . . It is in the interest of national security, balance of payments, and reliability of energy supply to achieve early delivery of North Slope oil to reduce our dependence on imports. . . .I am confident that my decision now in favor of a trans-Alaska pipeline is in the best interests of the nation and the American people."

Only three days before Morton's decision, ALPS had reported that construction of an oil line through Canada would delay by at least five years delivery of badly needed North Slope natural gas to the Midwest. ALPS reasoned that oil must be flowing before natural gas is produced, and use of the Canadian route would greatly delay production of North Slope oil.

Standard Oil of Ohio emphasized the richness of the Prudhoe Bay field in April when it announced that a new well completed northwest of Sohio's discovery well was tested at 27,000 barrels of oil per day, a new record for Prudhoe Bay. . . .Charles E. Spahr, Sohio board chairman, told a recent stockholders meeting that by the time the trans-Alaska pipeline is completed it will be able to move 800,000 barrels a day rather than the 600,000 previously planned.

SS Arco Sag River, second of five new tankers being constructed for Atlantic Richfield Company to move North Slope oil from Valdez, was christened at Sparrows Point shipyard in late April. The 70,000-deadweight-ton tanker is 810 feet long.

Gulf Oil Corporation was planning an early summer start on drilling a wildcat well near Port Heiden on the Alaska Peninsula. And the state moved ahead with plans for a competitive oil and gas lease sale of tracts on the north end of the Kenai Peninsula

Staff photo

February 1972

Anchorage, Kenai, Fairbanks and Valdez are now vying for the title of "Oil Capital of Alaska." It was a different story 60 years ago, when Katalla, east of Cordova on the Gulf of Alaska, was the unchallenged "Oil and Coal Center of Alaska," as this bar coin proclaims. Walter M. Stephen, pioneer Alaskan surveyor, picked this coin up at the Northern Hotel when he was in then bustling Katalla in 1911.

Wanted: Rural Free Delivery

Staff photo

May 1972

The sign on this mailbox, along the Nabesna Road, which runs into the Wrangell Mountains from the Tok Cutoff, suggests that Alaskans are trusting and neighborly. The state kept the 43-mile road open last winter for the second consecutive year, and about 10 families wintered there. Photo was taken in early March.

High Prices for Land
August 1972

State land sold at auction in Petersburg in late April went for 246 percent of the appraised value, despite an attempt by the State Division of Lands to drive down area property prices by dropping the assessed value. The first such sale in the community since 1964 attracted more than 200 people, and most successful bidders were local residents. All 20 residential lots were sold in the first round, under veterans' preference bidding, and together with two commercial and 13 private recreation units brought in a total of $171,285. Located north and south of the town, with a few across Wrangell Narrows, the lots ranged in size from one-half acre to seven acres and were sold for prices between $1,800 and $9,800.

A Rising Tide of Job-seekers... Pipeline News Sparks an Invasion
August 1972

Warnings of government, union and industry leaders have apparently failed to stem a tide of presumed job-seekers pouring over the Alaska Highway in hope of finding work on the still moth-balled trans-Alaska pipeline.

The U. S. Immigration and Naturalization Service reported that 6,551 passengers in 2,697 vehicles entered Alaska via highway in May, 1972, compared to 5,313 passengers in 2,323 vehicles in May, 1971. In noting a 38 percent traffic increase over the April, 1972, total of 4,738 entries, District Immigration and Naturalization Service director Jack L. Jobe commented, "The generally optimistic outlook for the beginning of construction of the oil pipeline from the Arctic Coast to Valdez is apparently bringing in an ever-increasing number of citizens interested in employment . . . in this undertaking."

Secretary of Interior Rogers C. B. Morton's May 11 announcement that he would issue a permit for the giant project is believed to have started the invasion of work-seekers. In mounting a campaign to halt or slow the influx of job-seekers, government, union and business leaders emphasize that Alaska has the highest unemployment rate in the nation and there is little hope that work on the 789-mile pipeline will start before 1973 at the earliest. Now the subject of litigation expected to reach the Supreme Court, the pipeline could be postponed beyond 1973, according to some oil industry sources.

'The Sea Is Our Farm – It Feeds us, Clothes us...'
Congress Gets an Education in the Eskimo Way of Life...
An Eloquent Plea for a Harsh but Valued Heritage
August 1972

Their entire way of life threatened by proposed legislation which would eliminate or greatly curtail their use of sea mammals, Alaska's coastal and island Eskimos gave eloquent testimony in Washington, D. C., Bethel and Nome in recent hearings on bills now being considered by Congress to protect sea mammals.

Testimony of Allen D. Alowa of Savoonga before a Senate subcommittee in Washington included these statements: "It is not my wish that I am here. I should be at home making preparations to insure that my children will be fed and warm the next winter. . . . Life is constant activity, for one day of relaxation could mean starvation for a family. . . . All meat-bearing foods which Americans place on their tables every day come from animals killed one way or another. We too kill animals and sea mammals because somehow that's how it was meant to be. We do not waste at all. Our men die yearly trying to bring every bit of the sea mammal home to be used. To waste is to die.

"If the ivory and hide are not made into beautiful objects that people on the mainland will buy, there will be no money to buy gas and ammunition for the next hunt. If there is not another hunt there is no food. . . . We are not in Alaska for America to gawk at or play with, nor to be a ploy of conservationists. We know better than any proclaimed conservationist what it means to conserve that which you depend upon. We're not a documentary to be talked about, we're for real. We live this life I have described. We love our Alaska. We live there, and often we die very young there. But it is home. It feeds us. . . . What shall you send us in replacement of a life we have known for hundreds of years—social workers and drugs to dull our days?. . . Lets us who live so near to nature and its temper determine how we will live in balance. How much more evidence do you need than the hundreds of years we've made it work?"

More than 100 witnesses testified at hearings conducted in May at Nome and Bethel by Senators Ted Stevens and Mike Gravel. The majority appeared in support of S. 3161, introduced by Senator Stevens and which would allow Alaska Natives to take sea mammals for both subsistence and for sale of craft work derived from sea mammals. Excerpts from testimony at the Alaskan hearings follow:

> 'What shall you send us in replacement of a life we have known for hundreds of years – social workers and drugs to dull our days?'

"Learning to hunt and carve are equivalent to a masters in college," said Paul Tiulana. "Now this bill has taken away my diploma."

Testified Edwin Tunguk, 80, of Golovin: "Someone outside in the United States want to cut this seal hunting off. They must have seen something I haven't."

"For generations, we have been taught to conserve because we live off the environment," stated Sharon Orr of St. Lawrence Island. "If this bill passes we will have to be solely dependent on welfare. The people do not want to live on welfare. It kills their pride in themselves."

Dave Stone, a Point Hope whale hunter, testified: "In Point Hope our very lives revolve around the migratory cycle of the oceanic mammals. There are virtually no jobs available in Point Hope. The 1970 state manpower survey showed 64 percent of the population had an average income under $3,000 and the cost of living is double that of Seattle. Obviously, it is virtually impossible to meet the cost of oil, rent, lights and food without any monetary supplies. Any money that we can gain from our limited use of the sea mammal products is sorely needed."

John Apangalook of Gambell commented: "I would say the one who introduced this bill (HR 10420) needs an education in the Eskimo way of living."

"The Bering Sea Eskimos cannot grow food like the farmer does," said Simon Pushruk of Anchorage. "The sea is our farm, and we get our food from the sea. We live on seal, walrus meat, crabs, fish, sea birds and their eggs and, when luck comes our way, polar bear meat. We carve ivory, sew seal hides and other furs for money to buy coffee, milk and flour. We wear clothes we make using furs we get for ourselves."

Velma Koontz of Savoonga wrote: "We receive more benefit from killing one walrus than those people (Outside) receive from killing one cow, both in pounds of meat, dollars per animal profit or any way you want to figure it."

Commented the *Anchorage Daily News:* "We would like to see some of the bill's sponsors try to explain to a septuagenarian walrus hunter from St. Lawrence Island why he must throw away the walrus tusks after he has made his kill. This is America's highly-touted efficiency?"

Commented the *Tundra Times,* Alaska's Native weekly newspaper: "Whaling is a way of life among the Arctic Eskimos. It is a tradition as sacred as beef. Take beef away from the world and there would be calamity. Take the bowhead whale away from Alaska Natives, and there would be more than calamity. It would be genocide. It would be the end of the rich cultures. It would end the spirit and drive of those people."

It was reported at the Alaska hearings that sole income for 10,000 Natives comes from arts and crafts products, most of them made from sea mammals. Walrus, seal and whale meat make up 90 percent of the diet in some coastal villages.

Admitting that his amended and liberalized bill faces a tough fight, Senator Stevens predicted in early summer that the sea mammal protective legislation which is finally passed will provide for Native use of the mammals for food and arts and crafts.

Anchorage Daily Times photo by Robert Koweluk

August 1972
The worst flooding in years threatened villages on the lower Yukon and Kuskokwim Rivers in late May and early June. Located downriver from Bethel, Napaiskak is shown here under siege by river ice on one side and swirling floodwaters on the other. Several hundred villagers were given temporary shelter at Bethel and St. Marys during peak flooding.

The Restoration of House and Totems on Shakes Island

Ketchikan Daily News

August 1972
Shakes Island community house and its 10 attending totems have been restored and are again attracting visitors to the Wrangell Island site which was occupied by seven Chief Shakes dating back more than a century. Lew Williams, editor of the Ketchikan Daily News, *strikes a typical tourist pose beside the Eagle Totem.*

Ketchikan Daily News

Dick Stokes, president of the Wrangell camp of the Alaska Native Brotherhood, examines one of four corner posts from the original community house which have been incorporated in the structure rebuilt with a $31,000 state grant.

Ketchikan Daily News

New to the rebuilt Shakes Island community house is this decorative screen which serves as a backdrop for a small stage on which Indian dancers perform. Although it is open for visitors, the restored island center will not be dedicated until next autumn.

1972

Point Hope Loses...
August 1972

Point Hope, a settlement with roots going back to prehistoric times, is losing its ancient battle with the sea and the town council is making plans to move to a new site about four miles east. Known also as Tigara, Point Hope's north beach is being eroded at a rate of nearly nine feet per year. The new site, which is to be surveyed this summer by the Bureau of Land Management, was known in whaling days as Jabbertown.

...and Point Hope Gains
August 1972

One of the most successful whaling seasons in more than a decade was observed at Point Hope from June 8 to 10 with a whaling festival. Muktuk, blubber and doughnuts made in seal oil were featured at the feast, which marked the close of a season in which 12 Point Hope crews took 14 whales. Point Barrow whalers had nearly equal luck, and whales were also taken by Eskimo crews at Kivalina and on St. Lawrence Island.

50 Moose Killed in a Special Hunt
March 1972

Fifty antlerless moose were harvested from Fort Richardson in a special permit hunt December 20-22. Open only to hunters who had failed to take a moose in regular seasons, the hunt attracted 2,860 applicants. Each of the 50 hunters—including three women—whose name was drawn was accompanied by a state or military game agent. The hunt was ordered to trim the Fort Richardson herd to manageable size and reduce danger to motorists.

Even Eskimos Seldom See This...

June 1972

Even in northern Alaska, a snow house is a rare sight today, and surely countless visitors are disappointed not to see one. To the delight of everyone on campus at the University of Alaska at Fairbanks this spring, a 10-foot diameter snow igloo was erected by engineering student Bill Kneeland as part of a civil engineering project. After completing construction, Kneeland spent the night in his snow-block house. The word "igloo" actually means "home" and Alaskan Eskimos seldom use snow houses except as temporary shelters during trips.

A Police Snowmobile
January 1972

Something new has been added to Bethel's snowmachine scene: a police snowmobile equipped with a red, police-car type blinking light and a loud siren.

Governor Pares Budget
September 1972

Line-item veto action by Governor William A. Egan in early July reduced by $11.3 million the $341.7 million general fund budget voted by the Alaska State Legislature in early June for the 1972-73 fiscal year. In explaining his budget-cutting action, Governor Egan said, "Regrettably, we cannot do everything we would like to do all at once."

Affected most by the governor's cuts was the University of Alaska, which had its legislature-approved funding pared by about $8 million. Despite the line-item veto action, first taken by an Alaskan governor, the total state budget for 1972-73, including federal grants and receipts, comes to a record $528.6 million.

Governor Egan said his action will enable the state's general fund to remain in the black until about mid-1978. He predicted that without his veto action, the general fund would go into deficit status about March, 1977.

Now It's a Guard Town
September 1972

A Navy town for more than three decades, Kodiak became a Coast Guard town on July 1, when the U. S. Naval Station and U. S. Naval Communications Station near the island city were turned over to the Department of Transportation for operation by the Coast Guard. Not to be utilized is the Marine barracks, the third Naval facility at the base started before World War II. Nearly 400 Navy personnel have been reassigned to other stations. Ninety-two civilian employees of the Navy have joined 333 Coast Guard personnel in operating the new Coast Guard base.

High and Dry... Till Tide Comes In

October 1972 — Bob McDannold

The seiner VELVET of Petersburg had a precarious start when the fishing season opened in Southeastern Alaska. Engine trouble resulted in the VELVET drifting toward shore. The tide went out and the vessel was high and dry on a rock in Bradfield Canal. The next tide lifted the VELVET from its awkward perch without a scratch.

Visitors Flood Park
October 1972

Predictions that a dramatic rise in numbers of visitors to Mount McKinley National Park would follow completion of Alaska Route Three from Anchorage to Fairbanks were quickly proven true this summer. Through June 30 of the 1971 season, 12,300 persons visited the Park. By the same date in 1972, the estimated figure had jumped to 80,700!

'A Great Day for Alaska'... Judge Refuses to Stop the Oil Pipeline... But Appeals Spell Still More Delay
October 1972

Cautious optimism surged through Alaska on August 15 as U. S. District Judge George L. Hart, Jr. of Washington, D. C., dissolved an injunction prohibiting work on the trans-Alaska pipeline which he issued in April, 1970.

Acting earlier than expected, Judge Hart's ruling against the Friends of the Earth, Wilderness Society, Environmental Defense Fund and Cordova District Fisheries Union served to revise the pipeline construction timetable, providing Judge Hart's lifting of his 28-month old injunction is upheld by two higher courts.

It was only a few weeks before Judge Hart's decision that Secretary of Interior Rogers C. B. Morton said on an Alaska visit that "litigation could go for as long as a year or 18 months." Pipeline proponents now foresee the possibility of a decision by the U. S. Court of Appeals by mid-October, after which the case is expected to go to the U. S. Supreme Court. There was some conjecture that if the Appeals Court and all parties to the action agree, the case may go directly to the Supreme Court.

Describing the case involving the 789-mile pipeline as "the most important environmental case now before the courts," Judge Hart concluded in dismissing the complaints:

"The Environmental Impact Statement (of the Department of Interior) reasonably meets all requirements of the National Environmental Policy Act which became effective January 1, 1970.

"The various right-of-way and permits necessary for the building, maintenance and operation of the pipeline are authorized by law."

Governor William A. Egan, who has declared completion of the pipeline from Prudhoe Bay to Valdez is vital to Alaska's future, said Judge Hart's decision was "a great day for Alaska."

While Department of Interior attorneys began work on a construction permit required for building the $3 billion pipeline, Alyeska Pipeline Service Company assured conservation groups that it will give at least 30 days notice before any construction starts. Although pleased with the lower court ruling, ALPS officials reiterated their intention to wait until court action is completed before starting the project.

During a mid-summer visit to Alaska, Secretary of Interior Morton commented, "The trans-Alaska pipeline is one of the most environmentally safe undertakings in American history."

He was preceded to the state by Vice President Spiro Agnew who blasted what he described as an "anti-progress campaign," and added, "Alaska oil is vital to our national economy and will, by 1980, avoid a further balance of payments deficit of about $2 billion per year. And, of course, oil is vital to the economic development of Alaska."

While top administration officials were supporting the pipeline concept, a $3 million engineering study financed by the State of Alaska and U. S. Department of Transportation proposed extension of the Alaska Railroad to the North Slope at an estimated cost of $2.38 billion. Such a railroad, said the consultants, could haul 1.25 million barrels of oil a day from Prudhoe Bay to Whittier. It would involve operating 18 oil trains a day, each with 111 tank cars.

Another plan for railroading North Slope oil to market came from the Canadian Institute of Guided Ground Transport. Released by Don Jamieson, Canada's minister of transport, the report said two million barrels of North Slope oil could be moved each day by using 20 trains a day, each with 168 cars.

With Alaska's pipeline project stalled in the courts, the state's newspapers gave front page space to the news that Occidental Petroleum has signed a nearly $3 billion contract with the Soviet Union for exploration of Russian oil.

Alaska's oil industry doldrums were confirmed by the Alaska Oil and Gas Association which reported that industry employment slumped from 3,385 in 1971 to 2,707 last year and the downward trend is continuing.

Dairyman of the Year
September 1972

The son of Matanuska Valley colonists, Bob Havemeister has been named Alaska Dairyman of the Year by the American Dairy Association. The honored farmer took over operation of his parents' 160-acre farm on Bogard Road between Wasilla and Palmer 11 years ago. With the help of his wife and two young sons, Havemeister milks 24 cows in a 60-animal herd of Holsteins. In observing dairy month in June, the ADA noted Alaska's 1,700 head of dairy cows produce 17.1 million pounds of milk each year, accounting for 35 percent of the value of the state's farm production. Ninety percent of Alaska's dairy industry is located in the Matanuska Valley.

Battle of the Charts
September 1972

Fireworks were promised by Governor William A. Egan if new State Department charts which redefine the state's territorial waters are used by foreign fishermen to invade areas long reserved for U. S. fishermen. Appearing before a Senate subcommittee at a May hearing in Juneau, the governor said the new charts "gave up thousands of square miles of previous Alaskan territory at the stroke of a draftsman's pen."

Warning that he would order the arrest of foreign vessels which use the charts, Egan said there is a danger that they may invite alien fishermen "to invade areas which but a short time ago would have been denied them by history as well as logic."

The conflict over the charts developed when the State Department followed the contour of Alaska's coastline in determining territorial waters, abandoning the long-used, point-to-point method of determining boundaries.

"The charts," said the governor, "not only fail to use the straight base-line concept in measuring Alaska coastlines, they also disregard over 90 years of U. S. jurisdiction and 10 years of state jurisdiction."

Most irritating to Alaskans is designation of areas in Chatham Straits, Frederick Sound, Icy Straits, Lynn Canal, Cook Inlet, Shumagin Islands and Shelikof Straits as international waters.

Plane vs. Canoe
August 1972

"It's not too much fun to be canoeing and have some plane come along and land and let a whole bunch of people out," said Bob Seemel, acting refuge manager of the Kenai National Moose Range, in response to complaints from float-plane pilots and fly-in fishermen over the closure to aircraft of some 65 lakes on the Kenai Peninsula. Estimating that some 5,000 canoeists use the lakes annually, Seemel said that airplane operators can travel farther than canoeists and should not want to deprive the canoeists of their recreation. "Many more lakes are open to aircraft than are closed," he pointed out, and said that these include good fishing areas.

SKAGWAY: 1920
Martin Itjen's Famous 'Streetcar'

Photos from DEDMAN'S PHOTO SHOP

October 1972

George Rapuzzi created quite a stir in Skagway recently when he drove the oldest sightseeing bus in Alaska from a warehouse to his Soapy Smith Museum. Martin Itjen built the vehicle in the early 1920's by attaching the body of the 5th Avenue Hotel horse stage which dated from around 1900, to a four-cylinder Packard. That model was built from 1904 to 1915 and features an aluminum engine and handmade fenders. Although the "Skagway Streetcar" carries a 1932 license tag—and that was about when it was retired in favor of a larger bus—it was operated during a Fourth of July parade in 1942. Rapuzzi reconditioned the engine so that the old relic could travel once again under its own power.

Builder of the old bus, Martin Itjen, came to Skagway in 1898, worked on the White Pass & Yukon construction crew, mined, and later diversified his interests, as Skagway's economy declined. He became a property owner and landlord, ran a taxi and transfer business, sold wood and coal, cleaned cesspools and served as the town undertaker. He had one of the first cars in town and ran a Ford dealership for many years. In the 1920's and 30's, his streetcar tours of Skagway were a smash hit, and so was Martin, with his handlebar moustache, German accent and fund of amusing anecdotes. This photo of him was taken in the 20's; the tractor was used for odd jobs and the roller for road building. Itjen furnished equipment and worked on the first section of an eight-mile road from Skagway to Dyea, completed in 1947.

—Barbara Kalen
Skagway, Alaska

1972

Last Hours of McKinley Hotel

Photos by Russ Wagner

November 1972

Known to visitors throughout the world, the 84-room old section of the McKinley Park Hotel was reduced to ruins by fire which struck the famed hostelry on the evening of September 3. Although heavily damaged by smoke and water, the new 50-room section of the hotel was saved from destruction. None of the 300 visitors and employees at the hotel were injured in the blaze. George Fleharty, president of Outdoor World Ltd., which held the concession for the hotel, estimated it would require about $1.5 million to replace the structure. Federal and state officials are urging that in planning for a new hotel the National Park Service consider a site from which Mount McKinley can be viewed. Russ Wagner of Anchorage recorded the rapid destruction of the McKinley Park Hotel on the evening of September 3 in this sequence of photos: 1. Smoke billows out of the front entrance of the structure built in 1938. 2. First flames appear above the building. 3. Almost totally enveloped in flames, the hotel is doomed and firefighters concentrate on saving nearby buildings. 4. By the morning of September 4 only smouldering ruins remain.

Surprises from the Sea
October 1972

Surprises from the sea were recorded in Alaskan waters last summer. Skipper Roger Howson of the *Lucinda J* knows the feeling of losing 33 fathoms of seine web to a 30-foot whale. Unable to cut the whale from the seine net, the *Lucinda's* crew spent four hours trying to drown it in Chatham Strait. Not drownable, the mammal broke free.

One benefit from Soviet and Japanese crab fishing in the eastern Bering Sea is the knowledge that king crab live longer than once believed. The National Marine Service Fisheries Service reports that 13 years was considered ancient for king crab. Then the return of 23 crab tags by the foreign fishing fleets showed all but one 13-year-old were older than the presumed maximum age. The NMFS had tagged 32,000 king crab in the Bering Sea in 1957 and 1959. One of the crabs was believed to have reached 18 years.

And a 10-inch cutthroat trout tagged at Petersburg Creek on June 15 was caught July 9 at Duncan Salt Chuck. It surprised biologists by traveling 40 miles in 24 days.

Strange catches for the summer included a 60-pound, 4-ounce king salmon caught in Saginaw Bay near Petersburg on a one-fourth inch herring jig. Andy Mathiesen of Petersburg and Ron Schmitt of Eberbach, West Germany, caught the king on the tiny hook after a 40-minute fight. It took five shots from a .357 magnum pistol for Jack Dauchy of Eagle River to kill a 256-pound halibut he caught in Sadie Cove near Homer. Dauchy said the seven-foot fish made a full load for his 14-foot skiff.

David Kutz

September 1972

Missing from Cordova is the Windsor Hotel, a landmark since 1911. Shown in the process of being demolished last spring, the old hotel will not be rebuilt.

Comeback for Gold if Price Tops $75 an Ounce
October 1972

The yellow metal that sailed into Seattle 75 years ago and set the stage for this year's first annual Klondike Festival may once again be synonymous with Alaska and the Far North.

Gold could make a comeback in Alaska if the price goes to $75 an ounce, according to Charles Herbert, Alaska's commissioner of natural resources. "There's gold all over the country," said Herbert in predicting that a $10 boost over the present price of about $65 an ounce would stimulate exploration.

Foreseeing environmental restrictions as putting brakes on some gold operations, Commissioner Herbert estimated that Alaska gold production, which now ranks far below gravel in value, would not rise rapidly until the 1980's.

He noted that prospectors invested nearly $7 million in gold exploration in 1969-70, recovering only 60,000 ounces worth about $2 million. He predicted the Nome area would become a hot gold spot if the price goes to $75 an ounce.

Canada's Discovery Mines reported recently that if the price of gold goes to $80 an ounce, it would be profitable to work claims at Indian Lake in the Northwest Territories which hold 13 million tons of gold-bearing ground that average $3 per ton at the $35-an-ounce rate.

Anchorage Values Soar
July 1972

Carry a fat checkbook if you want to buy property in downtown Anchorage. Following the first reassessment of the city's downtown core area since 1966, Greater Anchorage Area Borough assessor Pat McKee reported some choice property is selling at $25,000 per front foot. Evidence of the mounting value of downtown property was disclosed in the assessment of the J. C. Penney Company at Fifth and D Street, which rose from $3,814,128 in 1966 to $5,247,300 this year. The Captain Cook Hotel on Fourth Avenue between I and K Streets had an assessment jump from $2,659,104 in 1971 to $3,399,300 in 1972.

Down Payment... $500,000 Each for Alaska's Native Corporations
September 1972

Uncle Sam made payments of $500,000 each to 12 Alaska Native regional corporations on July 1, first step toward ultimate payment of $462.5 million authorized by the Alaska Native Claims Settlement Act. Selection of 40 million acres of land and payment of $500 million from state mineral royalties will complete the settlement. The way was paved for the initial payments when Secretary of Interior Rogers C. B. Morton approved incorporation plans for the 12 regional corporations. The U. S. Treasury payment schedule calls for $50 million to be paid to the Native corporations this fiscal year, $70 million during each of the next three years, $40 million during the sixth fiscal year and $30 million in each of the next five fiscal years.

While the search for out-of-state beneficiaries of the Settlement Act was intensified, enrollment officials in Anchorage reported that more than 61,000 Alaska Natives had filed for benefits due by mid-June. Final number of applicants is expected to reach 75,000 to 80,000 by the deadline on March 30, 1973.

Among the first major land acquisitions under terms of the Settlement Act was the July transfer of Wildwood Air Force Station near Kenai to the Kenai Native Association. The almost completely self-contained facility vacated by the Air Force will be used as an educational and training center. A first phase of the program involves using Wildwood to assist in educating 200 ninth-grade Native students who had been originally scheduled for education outside Alaska.

In a second land-acquisition move, the Cook Inlet Native Corporation asked Secretary of Interior Rogers C. B. Morton to grant it a 5,080-acre tract on the eastern outskirts of Anchorage known as Campbell Airstrip. The Native request adds a complicating factor in the competition for the strategic tract which is wanted by both the City of Anchorage and the Greater Anchorage Area Borough.

Before Disaster Struck...
October 1972

There was no hint of disaster to come when Miss Nobue Yakima, 31, left, and Mrs. Sachiko Watanabe, 24, prepared their equipment in Anchorage in early June for an attempted ascent of Mount McKinley as members of a five-woman Japanese climbing team. The two women shown above and Miss Mitsuko Toyama, 30, were last seen alive at the

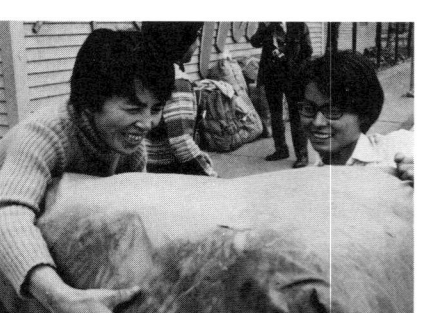

Anchorage Times photo by Dennis Cowals

19,000-foot level on June 29. Their bodies were found at the 15,000-foot level in July. It is believed they reached the summit and perished in a storm on the descent.

Widespread Troubles with Angry Bears
* * *
One Person Dead, Four Hurt

The damage done by a bear to Ken Shewchuk's plane near Beaver Creek on the Alaska Highway was nearly unbearable. Shewchuk damaged a wheel in a landing last spring, and before he could return for repairs a hungry and curious bear crashed through the cabin roof and exited through the fuselage. Shown after receiving first aid, Shewchuk's plane sustained $700 damage.

November 1972

Black and brown bears invaded man's domain in Alaska and the Yukon last summer and fall, leaving one Anchorage man dead and injuring at least four others in confrontations ranging from Ketchikan to King Salmon and Kotzebue Sound.

Killed by a 600- to 700-pound grizzly near Tazlina Lake on September 5 was Raymond J. Capossela, 35, an Anchorage guide. Witnessing the attack was Nelson Stimaker of Buffalo, New York, who was being guided by Capossela. Stimaker said the two men were trailing the bear, apparently got too close and it charged. The victim got one shot into the bear before it reached him. Stimaker managed to kill the grizzly with four shots, but not before it had inflicted mortal wounds.

An employee in Mount McKinley National Park was injured by a grizzly in mid-summer, two Michigan youths were mauled by a black bear that invaded the Dry Creek Campground near Glennallen on August 17, and John D. Minifie of Salem, Oregon, suffered badly clawed legs when a black bear chased him up a tree near Glennallen on September 6.

Hunger and overcrowding appeared to be major causes of the bears' war on humans. Juneau authorities received 50 bear complaints in a two-week period last summer. Garbage cans and open dumps were prime targets for the invaders. A black bear was shot in Ketchikan after it had killed a pig on the outskirts of the city, and a reindeer herder near Buckland shot a grizzly that was after his herd.

"There seem to be more black bears in the area this season than in any recent year," said Don Strode of Juneau, Southeastern Alaska supervisor for the Department of Fish and Game. In urging residents to keep garbage out the bears' reach, Strode also warned against intentional feeding of the animals.

Black bear are so numerous in Southeastern Alaska, according to Strode, that they have filled the available habitat. "This means that there is no space available for additional bears, but more are being born every year. These bears without established territories are now moving into populated areas and are becoming a nuisance."

A determined brown bear made two attacks on an army camp during an exercise near King Salmon, once shredding a mess tent and then driving two sergeants from their sleeping tent. The intruder was tranquilized and flown 30 miles away. Less fortunate was a black bear that was killed following a food foray into a construction camp at Blair Lakes Bombing Range near Fairbanks.

A woman at Mile 49 on the Richardson Highway shot a bear as it was invading her yard. Several bear were shot last summer as they threatened Harding Lake residents; another was killed as it attacked a fisherman near Clear Creek in the Tanana Flats.

A Juneau resident told a game protection officer in Juneau, "I am a believer in wildlife conservation, but the next time I find a bear under my kitchen sink, I'm going to shoot it."

J. B. Fitzgerald, director of the Yukon Game Branch, reported considerable bear activity in the Yukon last summer. The animals were live-captured at Canadian Customs on Six-Mile Road, Clinton Creek, Wellgreen Mine, Beaver Creek, Pine Lake, Kathleen Lake, Iron Creek and Whitehorse and moved to remote areas, according to Fitzgerald.

"We've spent a lot of man hours at this task, but we don't like to see these bears shot," explained Fitzgerald. "They are moved quite a way away and we hope it will be sufficiently far so that we don't have the same problem with them."

One of the few bears that entered Anchorage as a visitor last summer rather than an invader was this brown bear cub. The forlorn six-month-old cub weighed 35 pounds when he was brought to the Anchorage Children's Zoo after his mother was killed near King Cove. Sharon Dixon is introducing herself to the zoo's newest bear.

A Court-ordered Tie-up
December 1972

Claiming a Sierra Club injunction which virtually prohibits logging in the Tongass and Chugach National Forests threatens the state with economic hardship of "overwhelming magnitude," Alaska has joined the Department of Agriculture and U. S. Forest Service in fighting the court order.

Issued by District Judge Samuel Conti of San Francisco, the Sierra Club injunction restricts any cutting of timber or new road-building in national forests "which will change the wilderness character of any roadless or undeveloped areas." A trial on the issue was scheduled for November 6.

If not amended to exclude Alaska, which is the state hit hardest by the injunction, the order will eliminate 1,400 jobs and adversely affect 20 percent of the state's total payroll, according to Governor William A. Egan.

An estimated 90 percent of land in Alaska's two national forests is affected by the injunction which could stymie the planned sale of 187.2 million board feet of Alaska timber in 1973 and 1974. The Alaska Loggers' Association estimates that continuance of the injunction would adversely affect nearly 3,000 loggers and mill workers.

Polar Bear Rug Thefts
December 1972

The black market in polar bear rugs reached a new high in Anchorage in late September when a bearskin rug, claimed by its owner to be the largest in the world, was stolen from a chalet south of the city. State police report seven polar bear rugs were stolen in Anchorage in August and September. Largest of the "hot hides" was shot near Little Diomede Island in 1964 by Les Miller, Anchorage attorney. The owner estimates the 10½- by 10-foot bearskin rug has a black-market value of $10,000. Taxidermists throughout the nation have been alerted to watch for the stolen polar bear rugs.

N-Blast and Quakes
December 1972

Amchitka Island's five-megaton nuclear bomb blast in November, 1971, did not tie in with nature's earthquake-making apparatus, according to Dr. E. R. Engdahl, a geophysicist with the National Oceanic and Atmospheric Administration. Although the explosion nearly a mile beneath Amchitka's surface did produce 22 local quakes, Dr. Engdahl reported it "did not interact with natural earthquake-causing processes in that area." The post-blast quakes, said the scientist, resulted from collapse of the underground cavity caused by the blast. The largest such quake registered 3.5 on the Richter scale. All but one of the blast-related quakes occurred within 23 days of the test, and the scientist concluded that they "represent such a localized and short-term phenomenon that they cannot be considered a serious hazard of nuclear testing."

New Champions Reign: Whale Hunting... Duck Plucking... Logging... Bicycling...

October 1972

From Kotzebue to Ketchikan, summer produced new champions in an assortment of activities. Among them were Dan Snyder who won all three prizes in Kotzebue's Fourth of July Beluga Whale Derby. Juneau's Golden North Salmon Derby was won by Frank Williams with a 48-pound, 4-ounce king caught at Auke Bay. More than $30,000 in prizes was shared by the top 100 fishermen. A 62-pound, 4-ounce king won the Ketchikan King Salmon Derby for Shirley White. A king salmon that had more pounds than its catcher had years won the Soldotna Chamber of Commerce salmon derby for Fred May, 70, of Millheim, Pennsylvania. May's big fish weighed 72 pounds.

George Wigg of Wrangell is getting in the habit of catching gilt-edged salmon. Wigg won Wrangell's 1972 king salmon derby with a 55-pound, 5-ounce fish; he won the 1971 contest with a 54-pound king. Each fish was worth $1,000.

For the second consecutive year, Don Barton won the All-Alaska Logging Championship in competition at Sitka.

Captained by Del Hayward of Fairbanks, the *Scotty H* won the Yukon 800 riverboat marathon for the second straight year, making the run from Fairbanks to Galena and return in 19:05:14. The race was marred by the drowning of Roland Lord, a member of the *Miss Alaska Too* crew. First running of the Fairbanks-Nenana Bike Race was won by Vern Korslien who pedaled the 56 miles in 3:30:42 to beat 163 entrants.

Mickey Gordon of Inuvik, NWT, set a new record at the World Eskimo Olympics in Fairbanks by reaching a height of seven feet, one-half inch in the two-foot high kick. Joe Kaleak of Barrow retained his title in the ear-pulling contest by besting Gordon in a contest that required first aid for the Inuvik man's cut ear. Meanwhile, the Barrow Eskimo dancers won the drum dancing event at the Northern Games in Inuvik, an event which attracted competitors from 27 settlements. The duck plucking contest at Inuvik was won by Edith Josie, popular correspondent from Old Crow in the Yukon.

Maureen Brena, 12, won the Skagway Gold Panning championship for the fourth consecutive year.

Anchorage Daily Times photo by Alice Puster

November 1972
Caught less than 24 hours before the final gun of the 17th Seward Silver Salmon Derby, this 17-pound silver salmon won first prize and $3,000 for George Knapp of Anchorage, shown with his valuable fish. Second place and $2,000 was won by Dean Simons of St. Anthony, Idaho, with a 15-pound, 12¼ ounce silver. Caught by Betty Seaman of Anchorage, the third place fish was worth $1,500.

Sustained by Seaweed, Celery and Prayer...
December 1972

Stranded for a month on the west side of Lynn Canal, 50 miles from Juneau, a young Seattle man ate seaweed and wild celery, read Emerson and prayed. George Hardin, 22, was flown to the area near William Henry Bay on August 20 to prospect. He expected to be picked up either by boat on September 10 or by plane by September 15, but for reasons that remain unclear, no one realized that he was waiting. His food supply ran out by September 9 and he lost 40 pounds during the next two weeks. Although he spotted boats and planes in the vicinity, he was unable to attract their attention. Finally a crew of RCA employees in a helicopter found the distress note he had pinned to the door of a nearby repeater station and located his camp, where he lay in his tent, too weak to greet them.

Native Fire Fighters
October 1972

Fire-fighting history was made in July when the first all-Native crew hired by the Bureau of Land Management successfully controlled a large fire at Roundabout Mountain near Huslia. Fire boss for the project involving 120 Native men and women was Jim Commack. Jim Huntington was line boss, and Barney Attla and Roger Huntington served as division bosses.

Only support for the Native crew was provided by one helicopter and a B-25 water bomber. Past practice by the BLM has been to use Outside-trained experts to supervise fire-fighting teams. A few women were hired in Anchorage and Fairbanks to fight forest fires last summer, but the biggest concentration was in mop-up of a fire near Kiana, the job being handled by 31 women from Kiana and Selawik.

Gas for California?
December 1972

Liquefied natural gas from Cook Inlet plays a major role in providing Tokyo, the world's largest city, with fuel for power and heat, and the nation's largest state and city are hopeful of following in Japan's footsteps in easing a fast-approaching energy crisis. Evidence of the interest of California in acquiring a major share of Alaska's natural gas came in August when 40 California business leaders and editors toured arctic Alaska and Canada, seeing potential natural gas fields and emphasizing their need for fuel from the Far North.

"California has more gas users than any other place in the country—one out of every seven gas meters in the United States is in California," explained Joe Rensch, president of Pacific Lighting Corporation, whose subsidiary has 3.2 million natural gas customers.

Rensch predicted curtailment of service by the late 1970's unless new supplies of natural gas are found. He estimated that there are 26 trillion feet of natural gas at Prudhoe Bay alone, and that the total throughout Alaska and northern Canada approaches 1,000 trillion cubic feet.

"The Arctic's fuel field represents a responsibility to the industry for processing and bringing the fuel supplies to the citizens of Los Angeles," said Kenneth Hah, a Los Angeles County supervisor. "Now is the time, in 1972, to plan for 1976 when the energy crisis will be really felt."

Keith McKenney, vice-president and general manager of Southern California Gas Company's liquefied natural gas project, said in Anchorage, "It is in Alaska that we hope to bring our natural gas hopes to fruition." He reported that Cook Inlet gas is California's main target.

"Even if gas producers in this area do not wish to sell us the amount of gas we need, we plan to start the LNG (ship delivery) project serving Southern California anyway. If we move fast, we can have it by 1976," declared McKenney. California gas industry officials indicated that if necessary they would drill their own gas wells.

The Chief's Daughter
December 1972

The daughter of a Yakutat Tlingit chief has been named vice-president of Sheldon Jackson College. Mrs. Elaine Ramos, former director of special services at the two-year college in Sitka, is a graduate of Sheldon Jackson. The first Tlingit to become a registered nurse, Mrs. Ramos was instrumental in organizing the Southeastern Alaska Health Aid Program which has become a model for the state. The new vice-president has been a leader in the movement to revive the Tlingit culture and language.

Far-northern Tuna
November 1972

Seldom seen in Alaskan fish plants, 6,000 pounds of tuna caught off St. James Cape, midway between Ketchikan and Seattle, were delivered to E. C. Phillips and Son of Ketchikan in early August. A warm current in the North Pacific is credited with bringing the tuna north to the point where they were caught by the troller *Spring*, owned by Fred Olsen. The last big run of tuna was recorded in 1948, when 300,000 pounds were delivered to Ketchikan buyers. Biologist John Valentine of the Department of Fish and Game reported that tuna travel in water ranging from 58 to 70 degrees, and such warm currents are relatively rare off Alaska's coast.

Gain for Minorities
September 1972

The number of state jobs held by minority group Alaskans was nearly three times larger in March, 1972, than in 1971, according to the Alaska Human Rights Commission. Native employment rose from 442 in 1971 to 1,049 this year, and the number of black employees increased from 56 to 238. Pleased with the upward trend in adding minority group workers to the state's 9,305 employees, Governor Egan commented, "Increasing the employment of minority group members has been and continues to be a top priority of my administration."

Their First TV
December 1972

Many Yupik Eskimos in Bethel saw their first television broadcast in September, when KYUK-TV came on the air and area inhabitants clustered around the 50 or so television sets in the town of 2,500. Taped educational films supplemented with live local and statewide news were featured in the inaugural broadcast of the state-sponsored educational radio and television complex. Radio didn't reach the 20,000 residents of Alaska's western bush region until almost two years ago, now television will probe the wilderness as the station increases its radius to include most Kuskokwim and lower Yukon River villages. "The coming of television in Bethel marks the beginning of a new era for us," said Mayor John Guinn.

700 Compete in Alaska Marathon
December 1972

A big bloc of the more than 700 runners and hikers who competed in the Tenth Annual Equinox Marathon leave the starting line at the University of Alaska on September 23. Winner was Michael Fairchild of Putney, Vermont, who finished in 3:05:15. Mrs. Marcie Trent of Anchorage set a new senior women's record of 4:21:14, and Carole Hogins of Juneau did the same in the younger women's division with a time of 4:32:54.

Anchorage Daily Times photo by Jim Warfield

Alaska Maps Pipeline Plans in Hope of Early and Favorable Ruling on Appeal
December 1972

Despite the fact the fate of the trans-Alaska pipeline rests with eight members of the U. S. Court of Appeals in Washington, D. C., the $3 billion project is so important in Alaska's scheme of things that state officals have started to plan in anticipation of construction starting next year.

Emerging from oral arguments presented the Appeals Court on October 6, Attorney General John Havelock said he was "reasonably confident" the eight judges who will rule on the case will uphold an earlier decision by District Judge George Hart to allow the project to proceed. Havelock predicted, however, that the next court decision will be very close. The attorney general, Senator Ted Stevens and other lawyers believe there is a possibility that if the Appeals Court upholds Judge Hart the case may not go to the U. S. Supreme Court, especially if a majority of the court finds that the environmental impact statement prepared by the Department of Interior is adequate and the right-of-way width requested is legal.

Senator Stevens told the State Federation of Labor Convention in Fairbanks that final court approval for construction of the 789-mile line could conceivably come this year.

In an effort to stay abreast of the growth and problems that will come if the pipeline gets a green light, state agencies working on budgets for fiscal 1974 have been advised to assume construction will start next spring. The Alaska Division of Budget and Management has advised plans should be based on a state population of 355,000 by June 30, 1974, an increase of nearly 50,000 over the present total.

The State Department of Labor is developing regulations, also in anticipation of an early pipeline start, which will be needed to engineer compliance with new local hire laws passed by the last Legislature. Preferential hiring for a wide range of pipeline-related jobs will be given Alaska residents—those who have lived in the state for a year, maintain a home in Alaska and do not claim residency elsewhere.

The attraction of the pipeline project for the criminal element was the subject of discussion at the recent Alaska Criminal Justice conference in Anchorage. With as many as 18,000 expected new jobs attributable to the pipeline and support industries, the Alaska State Troopers and police departments in larger cities are mapping strategy to combat an expected upsurge in crime.

Racketeering was reported even before there was assurance the pipeline would be built. Alyeska Pipeline Service Company, which will handle the big job, has notified all state and federal employment agencies that fraudulent employment agents are extracting placement fees for attempting to place out-of-state workers in non-existent jobs. ALPS officials have notified employment services that they have no employment agents and have no jobs open. The fraudulent recruiters are reported to be concentrating on truck drivers, heavy equipment operators and engineers in Oregon, Texas, Montana and Wyoming.

"What we're trying to do," said an ALPS spokesman, "is to head this problem off before it reaches major proportions."

Meanwhile, the state conducted its twenty-fifth oil and gas lease sale in late September on lands bordering Upper Cook Inlet. The unofficial bid total for 155 tracts was $1,327,434.40. Highest bid of $260.40 an acre was made by Atlantic Richfield, Shell and Standard Oil Company of California for a tract adjacent to the Beluga River gas field. The joint bid totaled $330,337.

A Kayak for the University

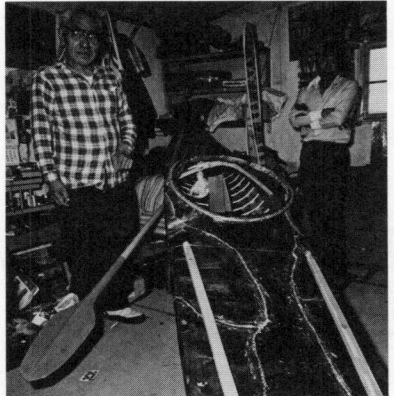

Staff photo

December 1972

Simon Paneak (left), Eskimo hunter of Anaktuvuk Pass, in his home with a 19-foot, 6-inch kayak he has constructed for the University of Alaska museum. Covered with four or five de-haired caribou skins sewn together with waterproof seams, the kayak's 138-piece frame was made of willow ribs with spruce longitudinals. Fastenings are rawhide, and no metal was used. The poles on deck are for propelling the boat in shallow water. The kayak is of the design used by Alaskan inland Eskimos for hunting caribou in lakes, and it is similar to those used by Paneak and other Eskimos on Chandler Lake in the Brooks Range, west of Anaktuvuk Pass, two decades and more ago. At right is Simon's son, Roosevelt Paneak.

A Tlingit Reader . . . Prayers, Potlatch Speeches
August 1972

First reader ever edited by a native speaker of the language is a Tlingit book produced through Sheldon Jackson College and Alaska Methodist University. Purpose of the limited edition reader is to help teach Tlingit speakers to write their language and to enable them to teach both writing and speech. Edited by Mrs. Nora Marks Florendo, Juneau, it includes keys to pronunciation, texts of potlatch speeches and various prayers and poetry.

1972

Road to High Adventure... Stewart-Watson Lake Highway
December 1972

Completion of the 400-mile Stewart-Watson Lake Highway through the rocky spine of British Columbia makes it possible—not easy, but possible—to travel from Anchorage to the South 48 with only 24 miles on the Alaska Highway.

Completed in October and still considered a pioneer road, recommended only for four-wheel drive vehicles, the new road to high adventure begins 12 miles west of Watson Lake on the Alaska Highway. It extends south 399.8 miles to Stewart, British Columbia, at the head of Portland Canal. The Stewart-Watson Lake Highway links with the Terrace-New Hazelton turnoff 39 miles east of Stewart. The latter extends 122 miles south to Hazelton, British Columbia, where it joins Yellowhead Highway 16.

Claiming to be first to travel the full length of the new route are five bicyclists who left Anchorage on June 15, and reached Missoula, Montana, on September 7. The only mileage they recorded on the Alaska Highway was 12 miles from Tok to Tetlin and 12 from Watson Lake to the Stewart-Watson Lake Highway junction.

Made up of Mr. and Mrs. Dan Burden, Mr. and Mrs. Greg Siple and John Lifkins, the Hemistour cyclists reached Stewart on July 29, seven days after leaving Watson Lake. They claim to be the first nontracked vehicles to travel the full length of the new highway which Burden described as a "beautiful route." The five cyclists reached Missoula, 3,103 miles from Anchorage, 84 days after their start.

Among the first motorists to ride the new highway was Stan Jones, of Seattle, former ALASKA magazine staffer, who logged the distance at 399.8 miles. He noted on his September trip that there was extensive construction along the previously built section from the Alaska Highway to Cassiar, British Columbia.

Major rivers crossed by the new highway, according to Jones, are the Burrage, Iskut and Bell Irving. He said the route abounds in magnificent mountain, glacier, river and lake vistas.

Testifying to the rigors of riding the new road are Mr. and Mrs. Don R. Anderson of Richland, Washington. The couple drove a four-wheel drive truck, pulling a 20-foot camper trailer in mid-September. The trip from Stewart to the Alaska Highway required 16 days, according to Anderson.

"It took six days to travel eight miles in one stretch," Anderson told the *Fairbanks Daily News-Miner*. "The mud was 24 inches deep."

The Andersons used an 8,000-pound winch to pull themselves from rough spots and move boulders. Their truck survived a bent flywheel, broken axle, smashed wheel and six flat tires.

A retired insurance agent, Anderson reported no gas stations in long sections along the new highway.

Permafrost Comes to the Aid of a Crusading Editor
December 1972

An old Alaskan enemy is coming to the aid of Albro Gregory, editor of the *Nome Nugget*, in his battle against Nome's new-fangled black-topped streets and concrete sidewalks. When the state moved in 1969 to install paving on Nome's Front Street and replaced wooden boardwalks with concrete, Gregory fought a losing battle to stop progress. Now, he is convinced that permafrost is his ally in the campaign against concrete.

In an early August editorial, Gregory reported: "Back in the spring of 1969 when workmen wantonly were tearing asunder one of Nome's most pleasing landmarks we cautioned the state that the 'replacements' could not last. And they are not. Hopefully, when all the concrete and asphalt has returned to the permafrost we will again turn to good old board sidewalks."

Claiming that the machines did not dig deep enough into the permafrost before back-filling, Gregory reported, "In some places where the blacktop and concrete have started to buckle it's like riding a roller coaster.... But it's just as well. In another two or three years the concrete and asphalt will have disappeared. All we'll have to do then is replace a board once in awhile."

Tourism vs. Industry
August 1972

One of Canada's best-known writers, Pierre Berton, has called for a two-year freeze of all industrial activity in the North. Speaking to 500 members of the Petroleum Society at Calgary, Alberta, the Klondike-born author and radio and television personality, said the North's greatest assets are wildlife, Native people, history and tourist potential.

"In my opinion, tourist trade will produce more dollars than minerals in 10 to 15 years," Berton said.

Citing construction of highways as one of the destroyers of the Arctic environment, he criticized Prime Minister Trudeau for his plan to build a highway from Alberta to the Arctic "with a wave of his hand."

Matanuska Luncheon
October 1972

Lunch at a Matanuska Valley farmhouse has proven such a popular feature of a Kneisel Travel Inc. tour that locals are joining tourists on the jaunt. For $13 the visitors get a $10 scenic spin around Palmer and a $3 lunch that includes fresh halibut, salad from the summer garden, homemade cinnamon rolls and rhubarb pie with ice cream. Hosting as many as 40 people at once, the Clyde Oberg family, long-time dairy farmers, serve their guests in the living room with its view of Pioneer Peak on one side and a colorful red barn on the other. "We've got it down to pretty fine science now," says Mrs. Oberg, and adds that the extra cooking has made their summer different from previous ones, but has not interfered with the farm work.

Photo by Department of Public Safety

Colorful uniform—winter gear of the State Troopers at Barrow is in evidence as they prepare to climb aboard their all-purpose truck for a local patrol.

Life of a Lawman in Barrow
December 1972

What is it like to be a lawman at the Far North post of Barrow?

It means that your post has a huge area of responsibility, the largest of any in the state: roughly, from Icy Cape southeast to the Brooks Range, and along the range eastward to the Canadian border, approximately 86,000 square miles.

The 4,000 permanent residents of the area live at Barrow, Wainwright, Kaktovik, Sagwon, Umiat, Anaktuvak Pass, at transient fishing and hunting campsites and at six DEW line sites. The population fluctuates considerably with the arrival and departure of oil industry workers.

You travel by snow machine and by small plane, usually a Cessna 180 but sometimes a Navy DC-3 operated by the Arctic Research Lab.

On a typical trip, you load your snow machine onto the DC-3 and fly to the DEW line site at the mouth of the Coleville River, then drive the machine upriver to Bud Helmricks' camp to investigate reported larcenies in the area. The temperature this day is 26 degrees below zero and there is a 20 knot wind. On an earlier trip, you flew into a fish camp on the delta to find and arrest a man accused of threatening one of the DEW line personnel with a knife.

Most of your time is spent in the village of Barrow. Your workday never ends. You consider yourself on duty and available for call at any time. An attempt is made to divide the day into 12-hour shifts so that either you or the other trooper at Barrow can be out in the field most of the time.

Almost all of your "business" relates to alcohol. Most disturbances run their course and are settled when the participants sober up. In some cases the intoxicated persons are taken to the community alcohol center for counseling. Concerned citizens work with the Alaska State Troopers, the city council, and Magistrate Sadie Neakok to operate this center for problem drinkers as an alternative to the courts.

As a trooper in Barrow, your uniform is different from those worn in the cities. Your wear fatigues, mukluks, insulated coveralls, parkas, and whatever else is necessary for warmth.

And instead of a patrol car, you have a snowmobile.

—*Morris T. Rogers and Lorenz O. Schuerch, Alaska State Troopers, Barrow*

Coast Guard Shepherds a Sloop's Hazardous Trip
December 1972

A 26-foot sailboat owned and operated by Craig Watson of Juneau can testify to the service offered Alaskan mariners by the U. S. Coast Guard. During a five-day trip from Wrangell to Juneau, the sloop was involved with three Coast Guard cutters and a helicopter. First, the cutter *Cape Coral* located the slow-moving boat in Stephens Passage and determined it was in no trouble. The next day a Coast Guard helicopter found the overdue boat. Then, the cutter *Sweetbrier* found the ship hard aground in Stephens Passage and towed it free. A day later the cutter *Cape Henlopen* found the boat with an inoperative outboard and broken tiller, which was repaired. The sloop arrived in Juneau without further assistance.

1973
FROM KETCHIKAN TO BARROW®

Sitka Park Expansion Strengthens Link with Russian Alaska

January 1973

A change in the designation of the Sitka National Monument to the Sitka National Historical Park has expanded boundaries, permits greater scope of historical interpretation and provides for the restoration of buildings and other historic sites. Signed into law by President Nixon on Alaska Day, the bill to expand and redesignate the historic area as a National Historic Park assures preservation of the remains of Russian Alaska in Sitka.

The Sitka National Monument was established to preserve the site of the 1804 Battle of Alaska, a last effort by the Tlingit Indians to rid themselves of foreign domination. One of the first acquisitions of the new National Park will be the old Russian Mission, which served as a school and orphanage as well as a mission and residence for the Russian Bishop of Alaska. Built in 1842, this building, which has three-foot thick timbers and a small private chapel, has deteriorated but will be completely restored.

During Alaska Day celebration of the new designation, Park Superintendent Dan Kuehn arranged for the firing of the old double-eagle Russian cannon for the first time in more than 100 years.

Until now, protection of Sitka historical buildings and sites was undertaken by the city, the state and private individuals, along with the Russian Orthodox Church. The National Park Service will continue to cooperate with these groups in preserving and interpreting Alaskan history. Focus of park development will be on three historical elements: Indians, Russian occupation and settlement and United States occupation. Cost of property acquisition is estimated at $140,000 and development and improvement costs at $691,000. Annual operating expenses are expected to be about $70,000.

Daily Sitka Sentinel photo by Thad Poulsen

Division Of Tourism

The Sitka Mission House, built in 1842, was a school for children of workers of the Russian-American Company and in 1849 became a seminary. Even after Alaska was purchased by the United States, the Russian Church financed teachers in the school, until 1917 when the church cut ties with Russia. The church continued to occupy the building until 1969; the bill giving national park status to the Sitka Monument authorizes purchase of the property from the Russian Orthodox Greek Catholic Church and restoration of the Mission and associated structures.

A major step in the restoration of Saint Michael's Cathedral in Sitka was accomplished in mid-October when the new cupola and cross were installed atop the structure. Before being raised, the cupola and cross were blessed in a ceremony conducted by the Rt. Rev. Joseph Kreta, administrator of the Russian Orthodox Church in Alaska, and the Rev. Cyril Bulashevich, both shown at left in lower photo. Completion of the cathedral's exterior—to be identical with the original built in 1848—is scheduled for next summer. Final phase will be completion of the interior.

Daily Sitka Sentinel photo by Thad Poulsen

Old Russian Cannon Booms Again...

Daily Sitka Sentinel photo by Thad Poulsen

January 1973

A highlight of the Alaska Day celebration at Sitka on October 18 was firing of this old Russian cannon from atop Castle Hill. Marking the first time the old cannon was fired in the annual observance, the authentic salute was arranged by Dan Kuehn, Sitka historian.

Division Of Tourism

Many of the Russian Church's historical objects housed in the small chapel of the Sitka Mission House were moved from the old Russian settlement at Fort Ross, California, when the Russians abandoned their southward expansion.

Most Intensive Search Ever... No Trace of Congressmen, Others Missing on Anchorage-Juneau Flight

January 1973

The longest, most intensive and sophisticated search ever conducted by the Air Force Rescue Coordination Center at Elmendorf Air Force Base had uncovered no clue by mid-November as to the fate of Representative Nick Begich, 40, House Majority Leader Hale Boggs, 58, of Louisiana, Don Jonz, 38, Fairbanks pilot, and Russ Brown, 37, an aide to Begich.

The chartered Cessna 310 carrying the party from Anchorage to Juneau was last heard from on October 16, just before entering Portage Pass. During the first 30 days of the search, Air Force, Coast Guard, Air National Guard and private planes had flown more than 1,000 sorties and logged more than 3,500 hours in the fruitless hunt for the missing men. Nearly 100 leads had been investigated by November 15, all proving to be negative as the search area exceeded 300,000 square miles.

High altitude photo reconnaisance planes never before used on a civilian search mission were ordered to cover the 560-mile flight route from Anchorage to Juneau. Detailed photos resulting from the classified camera equipment aboard the Air Force "spy" planes revealed no clues.

Despite the widely assumed presumption that he is dead, Congressman Begich's name appeared on the general election ballot, and Alaskans gave him 55 percent of their vote in the November 7 election. The Republican challenger, State Senator Don Young of Fort Yukon, received about 45 percent of the vote.

With state officials and leaders of both parties agreeing that chances of Begich's survival are very small, steps were being taken to fill Begich's seat. No timetable had been developed by mid-November, but it appeared likely that Alaskans will choose a new Congressman in a special election, possibly in February.

165

Republican Resurgence... Big Win for Stevens
January 1973

Alaskans followed the national trend on November 7 by giving the Nixon-Agnew ticket 58 percent of their votes in the general election thus maintaining the record of having favored President Nixon in each of his three presidential bids.

Statewide balloting was marked by a resurgence for Republicans, led by Senator Ted Stevens who overwhelmed his Democratic challenger, Gene Guess of Anchorage, with 77 percent of the vote. Missing Democratic Representative Nick Begich was re-elected with 55 percent of the vote.

With 10 Senate seats up for election, the Republicans changed a 10 to 10 balance in the last Legislature to 11 Republicans and 9 Democrats in the next session. Last year's lop-sided 31 to 9 Democratic control of House seats was altered by voters to read 20 Democrats, 19 Republicans and 1 Independent for the next Legislature. Defeated in the primary by Brenda Itta of Barrow, Democratic incumbent Frank Ferguson of Kotzebue ran as an independent write-in candidate in the general election, narrowly defeating Miss Itta.

Alaskans saw no need for a new constitutional convention, voting 68.3 percent against a referendum on the subject. Of eight bonding propositions, all were approved except No. 3, which called for $11.5 million for civic, convention and community recreation centers.

Winning voter approval were bond propositions involving $124.5 million, including $3.5 for health facilities, $10 million for highways, $18 million for University of Alaska projects, $24 million for airport construction, $16 million for state-operated schools, $20 million for flood control and small boat harbors and $33 million for water supply and sewer system projects. All Supreme Court, Superior Court and District Court judges on the ballot won retention of their seats.

Dancing Bears...

University of Alaska Museum photo by Barry McWayne
February 1973

Producing smiles for sick children in Fairbanks are these dancing bears which were brought to life on the walls of the pediatric waiting room in Fairbanks Memorial hospital by artist Bill Berry.

University of Alaska Museum photo by Barry McWayne

Widely known for his wildlife paintings, Fairbanks artist Bill Berry works on a gleeful mural in the pediatric section of Fairbanks Memorial Hospital.

Snowmobile Stakeout
February 1973

Stakes—hundreds of them—reveal the mounting influence of snowmobiles in Alaska's bush settlements. Governor William A. Egan recently reported that about 900 miles of snowmobile trails have been staked in the Nome-Kotzebue area and another 350 miles of winter trails have been marked in the Bristol Bay district.

$3 Billion Gas Line Planned for Alaska
February 1973

The role of Alaska as the site of the largest single private construction project ever planned may be doubled if El Paso Natural Gas Company achieves its goal of constructing a natural gas pipeline from the North Slope to a Southcentral Alaska port.

In announcing the $3 billion project in Anchorage on December 4, Howard Boyd, board chairman of El Paso Natural Gas, said his firm will spend $11 million on engineering and environmental studies relating to the proposed 790-mile, 42-inch buried pipeline capable of delivering 1.6 billion cubic feet of gas daily. In addition to the pipeline proper, the huge project would involve construction of a liquefaction plant and refrigerated tankers to carry liquefied natural gas to West Coast markets.

Cost of the natural gas project will about equal the $3 billion cost of the 789-mile trans-Alaska oil pipeline from Prudhoe Bay to Valdez, the fate of which is being decided by the federal courts.

Boyd said he is convinced that upcoming studies will confirm "that it is equally as cheap or cheaper to come down with an all-Alaskan line as to go through Canada." The chief executive of the largest United States natural gas company said it will cost $5 billion to build a 2,507-mile pipeline from Alaska to the U.S. Midwest. The proposed trans-Canada line is being advocated by a group of major United States and Canadian oil, gas and pipeline companies anxious to tap the 26 trillion cubic feet of gas estimated in the Prudhoe Bay field. Recent estimates indicate that if all goes well, mid-1977 would be the earliest date the trans-Canada line could deliver four billion cubic feet of gas per day through a 42-inch line.

Merrill Field Controllers... Best in the Nation
January 1973

Top air control tower in the nation in 1972 was at Merrill Field in Anchorage. Accepting the coveted "Earl F. Ward Memorial Award" on behalf of the 16 members of the tower team, at the Air Traffic Control Association's annual banquet in Chicago, was Fayette Harder, tower chief. The "Facility for the Year" was cited by the professional organization for its handling of an increased workload without experiencing any operations or systems errors, and for providing service to the 25 flight services and flying schools based at the field. The controllers also coordinate airspace use with adjacent military and civilian airports.

Return of Sanity – A Reversal of the 1971 Image of Caribou 'Slaughter'
January 1973

Sanity and sportsmanship returned to caribou hunting on the Taylor Highway last fall, and credit for correcting the "slaughter" image resulting from the 1971 season is going to the state departments of Fish and Game and Public Safety and the Bureau of Land Management as well as to hunters.

Determined not to tolerate a repeat of the 1971 action in which hunters harvested more than 2,300 animals from the 15,000-animal Fortymile herd, the government agencies prepared "Operation Caribou" pamphlets which outlined rules of the 1972 hunt, conduct that was expected and a basic primer on sportsmanship and conservation.

"Among the more obnoxious offenses reported last year were herd shooting, leaving gut piles on or near the road, harassing wild animals with snow machines, wasting meat and shooting from on or across the highway," said one of the pamphlets. The Department of Fish and Game warned hunters: "Remember, abusive, discourteous or unsportsmanlike conduct is just more fuel for the anti-hunting and anti-firearms groups."

More rigid policing by biologists and public safety officers resulted in a much cleaner, more satisfying hunt last fall, according to observers. To assist in solving the litter problem, the Bureau of Land Management assigned trucks in which hunters could dump camp and kill waste.

The 1972 harvest quota for the Taylor Highway hunt was 1,500 animals and by late October, the kill had reached slightly more than 1,100.

Larry Jennings, Department of Fish and Game biologist at Tok, and a prime mover behind the new hunting formula, said after the main hunting effort ended, "All hunters need is some good advice, some education on what is expected of them, and they do just fine."

ADF&G photo by John Trent

Hunter-originated garbage was loaded aboard pre-positioned Bureau of Land Management trucks on the Taylor Highway during the 1972 season.

$4,500 for Bearskin
January 1973

Bringing top bid at a mid-October church-sponsored auction in Fairbanks was a polar bear skin that produced $4,500. Conducted by Roman Catholics to raise funds for operation of Immaculate Conception Elementary School and Monroe High School, the HIPOW (Happiness is Paying Our Way) auction raised about $70,000. Among more than 500 items donated for the two-day affair were nearly two acres of land, 25 bales of hay, two gold-dredge buckets, three ounces of raw gold, five slaughtered hogs and a 50-foot well complete with six-inch casing.

An Aging Lead Dog's Bag of Tricks: He'd Feign a Limp, Upset a Load, Start Down a Wrong Trail – Just for Fun!

January 1973

Spook was given to our family nine years ago by a trapper who knew I wanted to have a dog team at our Alaska homestead. We needed one.

The trapper told my parents this lead dog was too old to keep up with the younger ones on the trail. He was pushing nine years, but still had enough spunk to pull a sled and would make a perfect "kid's dog."

I was 12 at the time, and Spook sounded like a good start for my first dog team.

Evidently the dog was never told he was past his prime, for when he arrived at Gold Creek, some 200 miles north of Anchorage along the Alaska Railroad, he got off the train with the dignity of a king.

A harness hung like the tool of his trade from his large 90-pound frame. Bold letters across the chest strap proclaimed, "Spook." His pale blue eyes, typical of Siberian huskies, made an eerie contrast against the thick black coat and testified to how he got his name.

After our introduction to his theatrics while pulling a sled, we were certain that somewhere in his mixed heritage was a touch of the devil.

Spook, we soon discovered, was a bottomless bag of tricks. Whether he was used alone or as leader of a team, he was never at a loss for some new antic to pull. On each sled trip, he had another lesson to teach me.

The dogs always pulled a flat-bottomed sled, because more could be placed in it, a fact that Spook failed to appreciate. He didn't hesitate to dump the sled when he felt the load was too big.

To accomplish this maneuver, he would get the sled traveling fast down a hill, then nonchalantly step off the trail. The sled would whip past him and stop with a sudden jerk, throwing items in all directions. Job accomplished, he would lie down and nibble at the snow, calmly ignoring my threats and grumblings.

After the sled was reloaded, he would once again start down the trail. If I hadn't bothered to lighten the load, however, his performance would be repeated as soon as the terrain provided an opportunity. This would continue until I carried some of the contents of the sled. Then, as if satisfied that I was doing my share of the work, he would trot down the trail without an encore.

Spook was both patient and determined. He spent years teaching me what was and was not allowed when I drove the sled. I learned, through quite a humiliating experience, that one taboo was threatening him with a whip.

He was leading four other dogs on a trapline check, when his continuous playful misbehavior sent me into a rage. My threatening display of power was met with a cool stare, and we traveled on to the next stop without event. But when I stepped out of the sled to check a nearby mink set, he led the team about 100 feet down the trail.

Noticing that he had stopped and lain down, I finished checking the set before following the dogs. Then, as I approached the sled, Spook casually got up, stretched, yawned and started the team moving again. He kept the sled just out of reach, and no amount of threatening or cajoling could get him to stop the nonsense. I could tell by the look in those devilish eyes that he was thoroughly enjoying the farce. This went on for about 100 yards, until he tired of the sport and allowed me to crawl wearily into the sled.

Spook was not a mean dog. He never growled or bit me. To him life was a big game, and irritating me must have supplied him with the ultimate pleasure, since he did it so often.

But he was a professional in his field, and in his more serious moments, his ability as a lead dog was obvious. He knew direction commands like a trooper. He could artfully back up in his tracks, and could, upon command, turn the entire team and sled around on a narrow snowshoe trail without tangling up one dog in the traces.

He never ran away with a sled, chewed a harness, or stole anything from the load, no matter how long he was left hitched up. What's more, he made sure none of the other dogs did, either. If a fight broke out while the dogs were in harness, Spook ended it with one deep-throated growl.

"Spook"
Melody A. Zager

Spook condescended to pose with me for this picture. I was 12 when we met, and he was already an experienced lead dog.
John Erickson

Although he could take his responsibilities seriously, he did like to dabble into the lighter side of life. He wasn't above feigning a limp, "innocently" starting down the wrong trail, or dumping a load, in order to add some levity to a day's work. But, as the years wore on, I resigned myself to the fact that it was better to have a clown for a lead dog than to have no lead dog at all.

> He worked nine years for the homestead. He never ran away with a sled, or chewed a harness, or stole. He was a teacher – and a clown.

This earned him nine years of full-time employment at the homestead.

Hauling wood for the furnace in the winter was one of the hardest jobs for the dogs. The loads were heavy and the freshly packed trails, which usually couldn't support their weight, caused them to sink considerably. It was necessary for every dog to pull his fair share. Spook, of course, saw no reason why the younger, more energetic dogs shouldn't bear this burden, while he just led.

One time, after a brief reprimand for shirking his duty, Spook succumbed to my wishes. For the next few weeks, from my vantage point behind the sled, I noticed with satisfaction that Spook was right in there, pulling with his every ounce of strength. Well! I thought smugly, maybe my opinions carry some weight, after all!

A few days later, however, as I stood somewhat to the side of the team, watching them maneuver an enormous load down the trail, I noticed that something just didn't look right.

Spook was apparently as industrious as ever. His ears were flat, tail and head down, body in a pulling configuration like the rest of the team.

Then I saw the tell-tale slack in the tow-line hooked to his harness. He wasn't pulling; he was faking it! I couldn't help but smile at the cleverness of the old warrior.

He continued the pantomime until he heard the tone of my voice, telling him the game was over. With a small wag of the tail, he gave me a sheepish grin, reminiscent of a little boy caught with a hand in the cookie jar. Then, displaying all the finesse of a good loser, he tightened up the tow-line and began to pull.

Now, after 18 years at lead, Spook enjoys the leisurely life of a house dog. He doesn't look as fearsome as the day we met. Maybe it's because I have learned from him, or maybe it's those white whiskers that have been collecting around his snout.

Still, every time I dig his old harness out of storage and slip it over his ancient frame, the mischievous glimmer in those ice-blues tells me that even "Old Scratch" is going to have his hands full, when Spook takes him for a ride down that last, long trail.

—Melody A. Zager

1973

A First for Women
March 1973

For the first time in its history, Unalakleet elected a woman as president of the village council early in January. She is Mrs. Agnes Ivanoof Baptiste, a graduate of the University of Alaska and an adult education teacher for the Bureau of Indian Affairs. Two other Unalakleet women serving on the five-member council are Betsy Pleasant, secretary, and Isabelle Millett, treasurer.

Joan of Whitehorse
January 1973

Armed with a pocketful of nickels, the newest heroine in Whitehorse is Joan Schrioch, 20, who serves as the Yukon's first anti-meter maid. Twelve applicants showed up for the unique job advertised by Bob Erlam, publisher of the *Whitehorse Star*, who is sparking the campaign and guaranteeing Miss Schrioch's wages.

Erlam spelled out his objective as being "to stop the over-zealous meter maids in the City of Whitehorse from issuing parking tickets—and therefore putting an end to the fantastic amount of fine money flowing into the city coffers."

In one two-hour period in early November, Miss Shrioch fed the nearly expired meters for 22 cars, saving the owners a possible $44 in fines. In doing her good deed, the anti-meter maid leaves an envelope under the windshield wiper which reads: "Help stamp out the too aggressive meter maids. I have just saved you a $2 fine by placing 5 cents in the meter. If you care to make a donation place it in this envelope and mail it." All income above that needed to pay Miss Shrioch's salary is given Mary House, a Whitehorse charitable facility.

Erlam claims that the meters drive business from downtown Whitehorse. Already paid for, the meters are no longer needed to assist in solving overparking and traffic problems, according to the publisher. City income from the meters during the first nine months of 1972 was more than $40,000.

January 1973
DRUM photo by R. Gauthier

Among the greenest thumbs in Canada's High Arctic is that of Father Joseph Adam, pioneer Oblate missionary, shown here with tomatoes in his greenhouse in Inuvik, NWT. Serving in the Northwest Territories for 36 years, Father Adam's gardens have been tourist attractions at Bathurst Inlet, Aklavik and Inuvik. Production in his new plexiglass greenhouse quadrupled that in cold frames. He raised three plantings of lettuce and radishes last summer in his 60- by 100-foot plot, located farther north than Kotzebue. His produce included cabbages, cauliflower, carrots, rhubarb, parsley, potatoes, beets and a wide array of flowers.

First Native Elector
March 1973

Harold Bell of Nome, first Alaskan Native to vote in electoral college balloting, was among the electors who cast Alaska's three votes for President Richard Nixon at Juneau in mid-December. Bell was joined by Waino Hendrickson of Anchorage, a former acting governor, and Clara Rust, pioneer Fairbanksan.

Santa's Busy Helpers
March 1973

A record-shattering million pieces of mail were handled in a single day just before Christmas by 130 workers in the Anchorage International Airport post office. Anchorage mail carriers delivered 890,000 parcels during the 1972 Christmas season compared to 664,000 in 1971.

Special Train Rushes Skagway Boy to Hospital
April 1973

It isn't everywhere in the world that residents of a small town can expect a railroad to lay on a special train to take a sick boy to the hospital, but it happens several times a year at Skagway, Alaska.

Most recent demonstration that White Pass & Yukon Route has a heart came in January, when weather conditions are at their foulest for the 110-mile narrow gauge railway between Skagway and Whitehorse, Yukon.

Fifteen-year-old George Stewart was in trouble with abdominal pain; the Skagway doctor decided it was appendicitis and called White Pass assistant superintendent Bob Bissell at 8:55 p.m. Bissell called up a five-man crew and had a train under way by 10:15 p.m.

The special unit ran to Carcross, Yukon, where a territorial government ambulance was waiting to transport the boy and his mother another 50 miles by road to Whitehorse General Hospital. He was operated on early Wednesday and well on his way to recovery hours later.

White Pass general manager Marvin Taylor estimates such an outing costs the company between $600 and $700, but no bill will be submitted.

Mean Old Grizzly Wrecks 27 Cabins
January 1973

A Salcha River grizzly bear known as "Old Raider" may be on the way to setting a new record as a cabin wrecker. From mid-September to mid-October, according to the *Fairbanks Daily News-Miner*, the mean grizzly had wrecked at least 27 cabins along the Salcha, ranging from within a mile of the Richardson Highway to 50 miles up the river. Reported to leave a 12-inch-wide track, Old Raider is suspected of being the same bear that wrecked nearly 50 cabins along the Salcha during the winter of 1969-70.

15 Below in Old Crow; New Freezers Arrive
February 1973

Welcome but unseasonal were the 20 freezers and refrigerators delivered to Old Crow families high above the Arctic Circle in the Yukon. Eighteen 22-cubic-foot freezers and two refrigerators were flown to the Indian village by the Department of Indian Affairs and Northern Development. They replaced a community freezer which did an unreliable job of storing caribou meat, a staple in Old Crow's diet. Months will pass, however, before the new freezers are needed. It was 15 degrees below zero when the freezer-loaded plane landed at Old Crow.

Court Rules for Alaska ... Lower Cook Inlet's $2 Billion Oil and Gas Reserves at Stake
March 1973

Offshore lands believed to contain $2 billion in oil and gas reserves are the property of the State of Alaska and not the federal government, said U. S. District Court Judge James A. von der Heydt of Anchorage in a mid-December decision which declared the waters of Lower Cook Inlet are owned by the State of Alaska.

Expected to be decided eventually by the U. S. Supreme Court, the five-year-old case was initiated in 1967 when the federal government halted a state proposal to sell oil leases in Lower Cook Inlet.

Major credit for the state's victory was given Robert De Armond, editor of **THE ALASKA JOURNAL**, and former executive editor of **ALASKA SPORTSMAN**, who was recently named to the Alaska Historical Commission by Governor William A. Egan. Robert Hartig, former assistant state attorney general who did much of the state's pre-trial work on the case, told the *Anchorage Daily Times*:

"Without Bob's work, if we didn't have it, it would have been impossible to prove that Cook Inlet was an historic bay.

"The judge found the facts overwhelming," said Hartig of a 250-page history of Lower Cook Inlet prepared by De Armond, who began research on the case in late 1967. "It was this document that the State of Alaska relied on in the case," said Hartig, now serving in the Legislature as a Republican representative from Anchorage.

The state estimates income from leases and royalties in the 4,000 square miles involved in the case could reach $263 million. "It is the first time in the history of the country that a state has won such a contest," said Attorney General John Havelock.

"Indications are that this will be some of the most valuable oil land anywhere in Alaska," said Governor William A. Egan.

Judge von der Heydt's decision brightened state hopes of eventually obtaining ownership of other historic bays and straits over which the federal government now claims ownership.

Pipeline Hopes Dashed Again:
Appeals Court Raises a New Barrier; Alaska Fears Another Two-year Delay

April 1973

A 53-year-old mining law has stalled plans for construction of the proposed 789-mile trans-Alaska pipeline and clouded the state's economic outlook.

Hopes that the 48-inch oil line from Prudhoe Bay to Valdez might possibly see a construction start in 1973 were dashed on February 9, when the U. S. Circuit Court of Appeals ruled that the nearly 150-foot right-of-way approved for the line by Secretary of Interior Rogers C. B. Morton is illegal. Unless Congress acts to change the Mineral Leasing Act of 1920, the pipeline right-of-way cannot exceed 50 feet, said seven Appeals Court judges in a 137-page decision.

> The country will have to make up its mind whether it wants to keep running or not.–Edward L. Patton, Alyeska Pipeline Service Co

Still being studied by attorneys in mid-February, the complex Appeals Court decision had the effect of continuing the injunction against the pipeline which was lifted last fall by U. S. District Court Judge George Hart. He had issued the original injunction in 1970.

Although it referred the right-of-way problem to Congress for solution, the Appeals Court in a 4 to 3 split, made no clear cut ruling on the National Environmental Protection Act as it relates to the $3 billion pipeline project.

With the energy crisis making the pipeline a national issue, it was Alaska that faced the most grim aspects of the court decision. While Governor William A. Egan expressed hope that Congress or President Nixon would act to get the pipeline moving, some legal experts predicted that the Appeals Court action meant a minimum delay of two years for the project expected to start in 1973. The Governor indicated the state would seek to get the case appealed to the U.S. Supreme Court.

Legislative leaders said the negative court action indicated extensive pruning would have to be done on Governor Egan's record $357.3 million budget for fiscal 1974. That budget required $129 million from the dwindling North Slope lease sale fund, and was based on an assumption that North Slope oil would be paying royalties to the state in 1976.

More than a week before the new court ruling dashed hopes of a 1973 start on the pipeline, E. W. Wellbaum, a vice president of Alyeska Pipeline Service Company, told a state legislative committee it was unlikely pipeline work would start in 1973 or that oil would be flowing to Valdez by 1976.

The Legislature was told by Governor Egan in January that at the present rate of spending, the nearly billion dollars banked from the 1969 North Slope lease sale would be exhausted by late 1977.

Shortly after the Appeals Court dimmed hopes of an early start on the pipeline, Edward L. Patton, president of Alyeska Pipeline Service Company, representing oil firms with major North Slope holdings, said:

"We are still confident that, in time, we will be allowed to construct the crude oil line. . . .The country will have to make up its mind whether it wants to keep running or not. It is particularly unfortunate for the nation that in this period of energy crisis, the people are unable to use the vast reserves of oil and gas on Alaska's North Slope."

Patton said the oil firms which make up ALPS had spent about $400 million on the pipeline project thus far. Not included is the industry investment of about $2 billion on the North Slope.

Other oil industry court involvement that has a bearing on the pipeline includes a January decision by Superior Court Judge Eben H. Lewis which affirms the legality of the North Slope Borough. Opposed by the oil

> Now Alaska will have to rethink its spending plans, which counted heavily on dwindling funds from the North Slope oil-lease sales.

industry because it includes Prudhoe Bay, which will provide most of the taxes for the new borough, the North Slope Borough case may be appealed to the State Supreme Court.

And attorneys for both the state and industry were preparing to start trial on an industry suit which seeks to abolish the right-of-way leasing law enacted by the last Legislature. Claiming the new law is unconstitutional, the plaintiff oil firms charge that the law could add $150 million a year to operating costs.

With North Slope oil locked up in legal snarls, the state has indicated it is interested in leasing promising offshore oil lands in Lower Cook Inlet, an area which an Anchorage U.S. District Court ruled late last year was owned by the State.

In reporting plans for an early leasing schedule, Governor Egan said, "Because of the national energy considerations and the solid legal grounds upon which the district court ruled, I would expect the federal government to abide by the ruling."

Natural gas from Prudhoe Bay won't be piped anywhere until an oil pipeline is constructed, but when it is finally available for piping, the natural gas won't damage the permafrost. That is the verdict of Canadian Arctic Gas Study Limited, which has closed down a test facility at Prudhoe Bay and two in the Northwest Territories. The Canadian company said its tests proved "that a natural gas pipeline can be operated in the Arctic without thawing northern permafrost."

Prudhoe Bay Job Gets off the Ground... in Model Form!
Palmer Sixth Graders Tackle a Big Construction Job

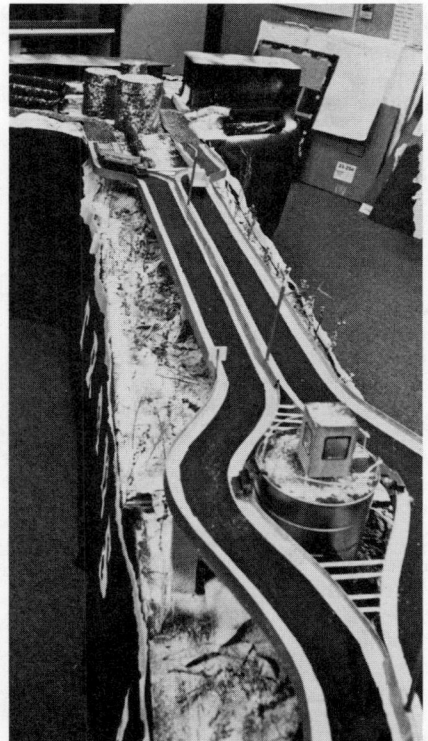

Anchorage Daily Times photos by Bill Kelder

April 1973

Above—The way to construct a trans-Alaska pipeline is simply to build it. And that's just what the sixth grade class at Sherrod Elementary School in Palmer has done. Unconcerned with court decisions, the students of Robert Siems and Charlotte Allen built two different scale models of a trans-Alaska pipeline, each involving different concepts. Shown here is a view of the Prudhoe Bay end of the pipeline built by Siems' class on a scale of 1-to-32. An elevated road extends over the pipeline. Left—Three members of a sixth grade class at Sherrod Elementary School in Palmer who built their own trans-Alaska pipeline as a class project put finishing touches on the Prudhoe Bay end of the facility. From left are Clyde Fischer, Dale Roland and Clinton Huling.

1973

A Terrifying Choice: Cut off His Own Hand, Or Die by Freezing
May 1973

His left hand self-amputated, Morris Hofseth, 53, of Napamute, sat up in his bed at Bethel's Public Health Hospital in early February and told how he had to use a hatchet to cut off his left hand on January 30 in a fight to escape freezing to death in a snowmobile accident.

Born in Napamute on the Kuskokwim River above Aniak, Hofseth is a father and grandfather. A retired Bureau of Indian Affairs employee, he and his family are among the last remaining inhabitants of Napamute.

The day of his terrifying ordeal began when he hitched a sled behind his snowmobile and started on a mail run for Aniak, 28 miles distant.

He said his rifle was riding next to him on the snowmobile. About 14 miles from Napamute, the rifle fell and Hofseth reached to retrieve it with his left hand. His left hand and coat were yanked into the vehicle's track, and he was thrown to the ground at the rear of the machine. The temperature was 30 degrees below zero.

Stunned, Hofseth lay entangled in the track for some time before realizing his desperate situation. He could not reach any of the tools in the front of the machine, but he noted a small hatchet was within reach.

He was successful in his struggle to disengage the sled and turn the snowmobile on its side. For five hours he worked to free his hand and forearm from the unyielding track.

"It was frustrating to have the tools so close and yet so far," he said.

Kuskokwim Kronicle photo by Larry Fulton

Minus the left hand he had to amputate to escape freezing to death on the ice of the Kuskokwim River following a snowmobile accident, Morris Hofseth of Napamute recovers in the Public Health Service Hospital at Bethel. The plucky Alaskan performed the crude surgery with a hatchet when he realized he would freeze to death if he didn't free himself from his snowmobile's track.

It was 30 below zero. His hand was caught in the snowmobile track. He was miles from help. Only a small hatchet was within reach....

He knew his feet and right hand were beginning to freeze and realized he had to amputate his hand or freeze to death.

Hofseth estimates he required at least an hour of work with the hatchet to sever his hand four inches above the wrist. He applied a tourniquet and walked three miles to the R and H Mining Company headquarters on the Rolmokofsky River. Dorr Holloway had difficulty in getting an emergency message out on the company's two-way radio. Reverting to a citizen's band radio, Holloway made contact and a bush plane from Aniak soon flew Hofseth to the Public Health Service Hospital at Bethel.

"Without that hatchet I would have been a goner," said Hofseth as he recovered from his ordeal and prepared to return home.

Nurses at the Bethel PHS Hospital described Hofseth as "the bravest man we have ever met," and Alaskans along the Kuskokwim rate his fight for survival as among the most harrowing in memory.

—Larry L. Fulton, Editor
KUSKOKWIM KRONICLE

January's Gift
April 1973

Talk about Alaska's warm winter wasn't heard in January as the entire state was walloped with bitter cold. Anchorage reported the fourth coldest January on record. Fairbanks had 14 days in late January during which the mercury never climbed above 30 degrees below zero—a new record for the Interior city. Nome went two weeks in January without a single above-zero reading and endured a cold week of nearly 40-below-zero weather.

Wind storms did damage from Palmer to Prince Rupert. Ketchikan closed its schools during a blizzard that knocked out power lines in late January. Kitimat, British Columbia was buried under 51 inches of snow that fell in three days. The Matanuska Electric Association handled 530 calls reporting power problems following a windstorm. Heavy damage was reported in Kodiak from a storm that hit the island city with gusts nearing 100 miles per hour on January 29. Frozen water and sewer lines kept the Bethel Regional High School closed for more than a week after the Christmas holiday.

95,000 Sign Up for Native Benefits
June 1973

A big surge of applications for enrollment under the Alaska Native Claims Settlement Act before the March 30 deadline sent to about 95,000 the number of applications received for benefits under the 1971 law, according to John Hope, coordinator for the Bureau of Indian Affairs enrollment center in Anchorage.

The total number of applications soared from 74,000 on March 22 to 95,000 at the deadline. The incentive was a share in 40 million acres of land and nearly one billion dollars in payments which are provided by the Claims Act.

Hope reported that about 15,000 applications came from Natives of one-quarter or more of Eskimo, Indian or Aleut ancestry who lived in the other 49 states and 19 foreign countries. As computers began the claims processing, Hope said he expects the total number found eligible for enrollment will be considerably less than 95,000. He estimated there are several thousand duplicate applications, and others will be found ineligible.

"I'm satisfied that we did everything in our power to get the word out," said Hope of the enrollment campaign. "On the basis of results, I'm completely satisfied with the enrollment effort."

Why Neglect Alaska?... $100 Billion in Metals, Staggering Oil Riches
March 1973

"It is folly to neglect the huge State of Alaska which, according to estimates prepared by the U. S. Geological Survey, may contain $100 billion in metals and 600 billion barrels of oil," said Alaska Commissioner of Natural Resources Charles Herbert in a mid-January address to the Alaska Press Club.

Noting that the United States is growing ever more dependent on mineral imports, Herbert expressed concern that mineral resources in vast areas of Alaska may be locked up in national parks, wildlife refuges, forests or wild and scenic river systems. He reported that Secretary of Interior Rogers C. B. Morton has only a year to withdraw 80 million acres for various federal uses as provided by the Alaska Native Claims Settlement Act.

"We must urge the Secretary (of Interior) and the Congress to provide in their decisions regarding the 80 million acres sufficient flexibility to permit the search for and recovery of mineral wealth from the tiny fraction of 80 million acres that might contain recoverable resources," Commissioner Herbert told his Anchorage audience.

Sharing Herbert's apprehension on Alaska resource development is the National Petroleum Council which recently reported to the federal government that "a rational balance must be achieved between environmental goals and energy requirements."

Requested by the Department of Interior, the NPC study titled "U. S. Energy Outlook" recommended "leasing policies and programs that open the public domain to mineral exploration and development in an orderly and timely fashion." The report noted, "Access to such areas is being seriously delayed or completely denied at the present time."

The NPC study stated: "About one-half of the remaining discoverable (domestic) oil and gas reserves are in the public domain, in Alaska and offshore areas.... Therefore, the importance of making leases available in these most prospective areas becomes apparent."

Doubt that construction will start on the $3 billion trans-Alaska pipeline in 1973 was expressed recently by Attorney General John Havelock. He speculated recently that a Supreme Court decision on the pipeline case may not come before next autumn.

Admitting disappointment that the U. S. Circuit Court of Appeals had not returned a decision before Christmas, Havelock said it is now possible that full-scale construction on the giant project may not start until 1974.

Elmer Rasmuson of Anchorage, chairman of the board of the statewide National Bank of Alaska, recently commented, "It looks as if the resolution of the pipeline matter will be delayed further. We are making our estimates in the event that the pipeline will not be commenced in 1973, but I hope we are wrong."

Cupid's Helper... Cold Bay Magistrate Flies 600 Miles to Officiate at a Wedding
June 1973

No Alaskan magistrate has a better claim to the title of Cupid's helper than Karl Heiker of Cold Bay. When Magistrate Heiker learned that Fred Landt and his fiancee wanted to be married in Nikolski on Valentine's Day, he boarded a Reeve Aleutian Airways plane for the 300-mile trip. While the plane was on the ground for 27 minutes at its regular Nikolski stop, Judge Heiker drove to town, united Mr. and Mrs. Fred Landt in marriage and was back in time for the return flight to Cold Bay. He had logged 600 miles on behalf of Cupid.

11 Polar Bears
March 1973

The quota of 11 polar bears for Native hunters at Sachs Harbor on Banks Island was taken late in 1972. All the bear were taken at Kellet Point west of Sachs Harbor.

Hamburger School
April 1973

Serving hamburgers to paying customers is routine school work for a group of ninth and tenth graders in Selawik. After school hours, four days a week, the hard-working youngsters operate the Northern Lights Restaurant, a business they opened in November with the help and supervision of teacher Kirk Meade and other adult volunteers.

The educational project began last summer, when a loan from the school board enabled the students to rent, remodel and furnish an old building. A sophomore does the bookkeeping, and other students gain classroom credits, not only for preparing and serving food, but for ordering supplies, pricing, advertising, assuming responsibility and learning about "profit and loss" and "depreciation."

Apparently they're learning their lessons well. The loan is being repaid with interest, expenses are being met and improvements, such as the recent addition of a jukebox, are being made. A future budget may even include wages!

Selawik is an Arctic Circle community with a population of about 500.

Ketchikan's New Airport... Dedication Soon

Ketchikan Daily News photo by Normand Dupre

June 1973

Slated for opening in late June and costing more than $12 million, the new Ketchikan International Airport on Gravina Island won't be officially dedicated until August 4. The terminal building for the airport is shown here with the main 7,500-foot runway just above the parking apron in mid-photo.

'Romantic' Hootch
March 1973

"This romantic name was founded in an Indian village 'Hootznahoo' wherein the brew originated during the rough and ready days of the Klondike Gold Rush of '98," says the label on bottles of "Yukon Hootch," now available in the Yukon.

Produced and bottled in Canada exclusively for the Yukon territorial government, Yukon Hootch is the territory's alcoholic salute to "Klondike '73," the territory's year-long celebration of the seventy-fifth anniversary of the Klondike Gold Rush.

Sales of the first 100 cases were described by Department of Liquor Control director Rollie Thibault as "absolutely phenomenal." A blend of Canadian and imported rums with a 40 percent alcohol content by volume, Yukon Hootch is available in 12- and 25-ounce bottles.

Thibault said the name "hootch" came from a Tlingit Indian settlement on Admiralty Island in Southeastern Alaska known as Hootznahoo and Hootchinoo, where the original drink was introduced to cheechakos heading for the Klondike.

Costly Wool
January 1973

It cost $1,300 a pound for the government of Northwest Territories to acquire three pounds of musk ox wool known as qiviut, according to *The Drum* of Inuvik, NWT. The expensive harvest had its beginning when the NWT Council accepted an offer of a Yellowknife minister to gather the wool in an area west of the Aberdeen Lakes. *The Drum* described the qiviut as "weather-beaten wool, tickey-tackeyed up with all manner of foreign bodies such as 'mud, twigs, dung and other things.'"

'Too Cheap Too Long'... Fur Prices Soar
June 1973

Soaring fur prices have pulled trapping from the doldrums throughout the Far North, and prospects for the future indicate the best and most experienced trappers may make up to $12,000 for a year's work.

"Fur has been too cheap too long," said Perry Green of Anchorage, one of the state's largest resident fur manufacturers and buyers. "There is more interest in real fur than ever and the law of supply and demand is finally working."

The demand, according to Green and other Alaskan fur buyers, is coming largely from Europe. One buyer estimated that 70 percent of Alaskan-trapped fur is going to Germany and Italy.

Green reported that he paid a top price of $55 for lynx last year. Top-grade lynx have brought up to $160 this spring. One of Green's buyers paid an average of $110 each for 62 lynx skins.

Among factors credited by the fur industry for the comeback of fur are desires of Europeans to convert devalued U.S. dollars into tangible furs and fears that proposed anti-trapping legislation may curtail the supply.

Twice as many beaver pelts were brought to Dillingham's annual Beaver Round-Up celebration this year as in 1972, and all were sold for higher prices—top skins bringing $55.

Worth $35 five years ago, premium wolverine are now bringing $130. Green reported that he bought first-quality arctic timber wolf skins for $80 in 1971, $110 in 1972 and recently paid $170 each for five wolf pelts from Canada's Arctic.

Muskrat prices were expected to reach $2 or more in late spring auctions, more than double last year's price. Alaskan buyers have been paying $65 for cross fox and $55 for red fox.

Although prices of some long-hair pelts are the highest in 40 years, one Anchorage fur buyer is predicting they will go higher. Several years ago he predicted arctic timber wolf would reach a price of $500 for a premium hide. With $285 paid for a Canadian wolf at a recent Canadian auction, his prediction seems within the realm of possibility.

Good news for trappers can be translated into a strain on the wallets of fur garment buyers. Green estimates the cost of parkas, especially those using seal, will be up 30 to 50 percent. He expects his cost of making parkas this year will equal the 1972 retail price.

Rabbit Jumps at the Chance...

Kenneth Roberson

March 1973

Fattest rabbit in Glennallen is the flying snowshoe hare shown here who has mastered the trick of jumping into Ken Roberson's bird feeder for daily snacks of bird seed, salad and bread scraps.

John Trent

Smiles on the faces of Lige and Susie Charlie of Minto as they watch state biologist Mel Buchholtz of Fairbanks measure their beaver skins reflect zooming prices being paid for Alaskan furs. Top-quality beaver pelts are now bringing $55 according to fur buyers.

Hmmm... Mosquitoes!
June 1973

Most unpopular species of Alaskan wildlife, the mosquito, was the object of a recent study by the Arctic Health Research Center in Fairbanks. If you want to impress your fellow fishermen, campers or hikers this summer, drop these fascinating facts about the outdoorsman's number one enemy: Only female mosquitoes bite, because they need more protein to mature their eggs. Their hum is lower than the male's mating buzz, and their antennae are not as bushy... Alaska has about a million more mosquitoes than people... At least 435 mosquitoes can bite one forearm in five minutes... If you wander nude around the tundra without repellent, you can feed 172,260 mosquitoes per hour, and each of the healthy pests can carry away about 2.57 cubic millimeters of blood. At that rate, a man could lose 25 percent of his blood within three hours, and die... Male mosquitoes (and the females, when they aren't bugging people or animals) feed on plant juices and nectars... A mosquito's life span can range from one or two days to about a week.

Failure of 'Success'
March 1973

Dreams of an $800 million project involving construction of an enclosed, self-contained city known as Seward's Success on Point McKenzie across Knik Arm from Anchorage folded in late December. The Great Northern Corporation, which planned to build an aerial tramway linking Anchorage with the site, failed to make an annual $41,255 lease payment for 3,209 acres of land owned by the Matanuska-Susitna Borough and the State Division of Lands.

Proposed as a car-free city, Seward's Success progress stalled, said its backers, when construction on the proposed $3 billion trans-Alaska pipeline was stalemated by court suits in 1970.

Costly Water Shortage
February 1973

A water shortage in Kodiak early in 1972 cost $7 million in 90 days, according to Gary Stevens, manager of Northern Processors, Inc. In a speech delivered to the Kodiak Lions and Rotary Clubs in November, Stevens emphasized the importance of fishing to the city's economy. Kodiak is the second largest fishing port in terms of dollar volume in the United States.

"It cost the city of Kodiak over $200,000 in lost revenue," he said. "It cost the state of Alaska over $1.4 million in lost taxes. It cost the people of Kodiak over $5.4 million in lost payroll."

Although the 90-day closure was not a total one, some 1,562 cannery workers, fishermen and other marine-related personnel were unemployed during the period. The local government's loss was in sales taxes, water revenue and wharfage and dock fees.

Man vs. Moose
* * *
Who'll Be the Goalie Here?

June 1973

"I'll be the goalie," was the way George Molnar, custodian for the Eagle River-Homestead Schools, interpreted the grunts of this moose when it invaded the schools' hockey rink in March. Molnar kept the goalie net between himself and the intruder before abandoning the rink to the moose, who had the ice to himself for several hours.

Dennis B. Johnson

Supreme Court Bows Out... Now the Pipeline's Fate Rests with Congress
June 1973

With the U.S. Supreme Court bowing out of the trans-Alaska pipeline case, hopes of Alaskans for construction of the controversial $3 billion project have shifted to the U.S. Congress. In refusing to hear an appeal of a February decision by the U.S. Court of Appeals which effectively blocked any chance of pipeline construction in 1973, the U.S. Supreme Court made Congress the battlefield on which the pros and cons of the issue will be fought.

Proponents are banking on a

Kite Flight on Mount Alyeska

Anchorage Daily Times photo by Dennis Cowals

May 1973

Strangest bird in the skies at Mount Alyeska this spring is this delta-winged kite shown carrying Ray Morris, 42, on a flight from the top of the main chairlift to the main lodge two miles below. An experienced pilot, Morris has a total airborne time of more than 40 minutes in his 16-foot kite. The flight from the starting point, 1,800 vertical feet above the main lodge, requires about four minutes, according to Morris.

worsening energy crisis and the spectre of oil and gas rationing as well as deflation and balance of trade deficits to win Congressional approval. Counteracting the initial gloom that hit Alaska with Supreme Court refusal to hear the case was an early April announcement by Secretary of Interior Rogers C. B. Morton that President Nixon wants him "to go all out—in pursuing the construction of the pipeline, which he feels is vital to the national interest."

Focal point of Congressional action in late spring was Senator Henry Jackson's Interior Committee which was considering bills to amend the Mineral Leasing Act of 1920, authorizing the wider right-of-way needed for pipeline construction. Other moves were being made to move the issue of compliance with the National Environmental Protection Act from the courts to Congress. Fireworks are expected in a clash between those wanting the pipeline to extend from Prudhoe Bay to Valdez and then move North Slope oil to the West Coast by tankers and members of Congress from the Midwest and East who want the line to cross Canada.

Senator Jackson made clear his pipeline preference when he told the National Press Club he hopes construction will start next year on the trans-Alaska pipeline. "It makes no sense to be importing oil from all around the world when we have one-fourth of the (nation's) reserves in Alaska," said the Washington Democrat.

In a letter to every member of Congress, Secretary Morton made it clear that he and the President favor the all-Alaska route. He noted that the trans-Canada line would be four times longer than the proposed trans-Alaska pipeline, and environmental damage to the land would be much greater.

"I am fully convinced that it is in our national interest to get as much Alaska oil as possible delivered to the U.S. market as soon as possible," wrote Secretary Morton. "I am equally convinced that prompt construction of a trans-Alaskan pipeline is the best available way to accomplish both of these objectives."

Formed to assist Alaska's Congressional delegation in pitching for the Prudhoe Bay-Valdez route, the Alaska Pipeline Education Committee established a headquarters in Anchorage. An appropriation of $100,000 was authorized by the last Legislature for use by the attorney general's office in advancing the cause of the pipeline. Attorney General John Havelock said in early April he hoped for action within "three or four months" which would open the way for a U.S. District court test on the pipeline impact statement's compliance with the National Environmental Protection Act. Havelock described Congressional action on the right-of-way issue as "somewhere between a lopsided probability and a virtual certainty."

Meanwhile, a new transportation proposal entered the picture when Premier Dave Barrett of British Columbia advocated moving North Slope oil by a railroad extension through the Yukon to link up with the existing British Columbia Railway. State and federal officials showed little initial enthusiasm for the trans-Yukon project.

Natural gas-shy Southern California will have its dwindling supplies replenished from the Kenai Peninsula and Cook Inlet fields without using a pipeline if plans of Pacific Lighting Corporation are achieved. In mid-April, the California-based firm was pushing ahead with plans for a $130 million natural gas liquefaction plant that would process 200 million cubic feet of natural gas per day. If the proposed schedule is met, California will be using liquefied gas from Alaska sometime in 1977.

1,063 Miles in 33 Days: The First Annual Sled Dog Race on the Iditarod Trail

June 1973

Spanning 1,063 miles and 33 days, the first annual Iditarod Trail Sled Dog Race became an exciting chapter in Alaska's sports history on April 3, when the last of 22 mushers completed the grueling run from Anchorage to Nome.

Winner of $12,000 first prize was Dick Willmarth, 29, of Red Devil, who was cheered by more than 2,000 Nome residents and several hundred visitors as he reached the finish line on March 23, just 20 hours, 49 minutes and 41 seconds after he started from Anchorage in thirty-third position.

Arriving with 8 of his 12 starting dogs and beating his nearest rival by more than 12 hours, Willmarth took a victory bath 13 days before the last musher, John Schultz, of Delta Junction, reached the finish line.

Second and third largest shares of the $50,000 prize money for Alaska's longest sled dog race went to Bobby Vent, 59, of Huslia, who won $8,000 for second, and Dan Seavey, of Seward, who pocketed $6,000 for third. Setting the pace early in the race, then slowed with sick dogs, George Attla staged a blazing finish to place fourth and pick up $4,000.

Cash prizes were awarded the first 20 mushers to reach the finish line, ranging from $3,000 for fifth to $500 for twentieth. Nome boosters took up a collection for the last two teams to reach Nome, thus giving every musher some prize money.

Willmarth gave major credit for his big win to Hotfoot, his five-year-old leader. "If it hadn't been for him I'd still be out there," said the new champion. "I got kind of scared between White Mountain and Solomon. You couldn't see a thing. My leader brought me in; I just had to stay on the sled and let him pick the way."

Looking to his sixtieth birthday in October, Vent was considered out of the money midway in the race when an ailing leg hampered him and his team dropped to six dogs. Refusing to quit, the pioneer musher running a team for the first time in more than 15 years—had only the minimum five dogs allowed when he reached Nome.

A Seward school teacher, Seavey finished with 11 of his 12 starting dogs still in the harness. Attla started with 16 dogs and finished with six, sickness taking a heavy toll.

Other leading finishers in order were Herbert Nayukpuk, Isaac Okleasik, Dick Mackey, John Komok and John Coffin.

Anchorage Daily News photo by Ralph Lee
Man with the biggest smile in the sea of faces is Dick Willmarth, shown taking off his jacket after crossing the finish line to win the Iditarod Trail Sled Dog Race from Anchorage to Nome. Practically everybody in Nome turned out to welcome the musher who paced a starting field of 34 teams to win $12,000 for his 1,063-mile run.

Henry Peck
With one dog in the basket and one trailing, the struggle on the long Iditarod Trail is reflected in the face of John Komok, who placed eighth. This photo was taken early in the race.

The long-cherished dream of Joe Redington of Knik, the Iditarod race followed the old dog-team mail route from Knik to Nome, unused for 50 years.

Pre-race pessimism turned to optimism as the battle of men and teams against the elements gained media coverage and public attention as the teams crossed mountains, were stormbound, sped down the Yukon River ice and skirted the Bering Sea on the long run to Nome.

Despite a $30,000 debt to raise prize money, the Iditarod Trail committee is convinced that the future of the race is assured.

The mushers were cheered at every village along the route, but it was in Nome that the men who completed the race were made to feel they were champions. Fire sirens were sounded every time a team approached the finish line, and a welcoming crowd was on hand for every team's arrival. Nome staged three banquets for teams in the 33 days between the first and last finish.

"No single event has generated as much excitement here since the days of the Gold Rush," said Nome's mayor Robert Renshaw, who declared, "Anyone finishing the race is a champion."

Linda Billington
Pace-setter early in the long race was George Attla, shown here just a few miles after the race start in Anchorage. Despite losing most of his team to sickness, Attla finished fourth.

Permits for Fishermen
June 1973

Seventy days shorter than its 1972 predecessor, the first session of the Eighth Alaska Legislature ended April 7 after 90 days of deliberations that resulted in a 1974 fiscal budget of $352.9 million, about $4 million less than requested by Governor William A. Egan.

The majority of legislators agreed that the most far-reaching action of the session was passage of a bill to limit the number of commercial fishermen who can compete in the state's fisheries. Asked for by Governor Egan in an effort to protect both fishermen and dwindling stocks, the bill calls for a three-member commission which will draft regulations for the new system.

Having no effect on 1973 fishing operations, and providing for issuance of interim-use permits in 1974, the new system will be applied in full force in 1975. Senator Bob Palmer of Ninilchik, who was involved in drafting the legislation, said, "The basis of the program is to let in all those who would be significantly harmed if they were kept out and then buy them out on a voluntary basis.... I think it's going to take at least five years before we see anything significant at all happen here."

A Costly Hoax
May 1973

It cost $9,000 to $10,000 for Ketchikan police and school officials to determine that a telephoned bomb threat was a hoax. The February incident resulted in evacuating Ketchikan High School at 10:30 a.m., and eventually dismissing classes for the day.

Furs Fit for a Queen

Margie Bauman
June 1973
Wrapped in furs fit for a queen, Nita Sheldon, 21, of Noorvik, was crowned Miss Fairbanks Native Association at the annual FNA potlatch in Fairbanks in mid-March. A junior at the University of Alaska, Miss Sheldon is researching the lost culture of the Kobuk area.

Dr. J. K. Hilliard
June 1973
David J. Williams Sr., one of Alaska's most renowned Tlingit carvers, is shown in his Hoonah workshop with his last work of art, a cedar bowl. Dr. J. K. Hilliard of Sitka took the photo on March 5. The artist, who had taught carving in London, lectured on Tlingit culture at Washington State University and whose work is represented in the Smithsonian Institution, died at Mount Edgecumbe on March 12 following a stroke. He was 68.

Pipeline Ban a 'Crime'... An Independent Alaska?
June 1973

When Joe Vogler, Fairbanks miner and real-estate developer, decided to circulate petitions asking for establishment of the sovereign nation of Alaska, he had no idea that his bold solution for solving the state's problems would make him a celebrity.

A few weeks after Vogler circulated 500 petitions, each with 30 spaces for signatures, all were signed by Alaskans who endorse his idea that Alaska would be better off controlling its own destiny and going it alone.

"The response has been beyond my wildest expectations," Vogler told the *Pioneer All-Alaska Weekly* early in March. "I never dreamed the people would respond like this."

The petition that is bringing a positive reaction from Alaskans reads simply:

"We, the undersigned residents of Alaska, do hereby respectfully and without malice or rancor, petition the President and the Congress of the United States of America to grant us and our land free and independent sovereignty, under the auspices of the United Nations, from this day forth."

A 30-year Alaskan and graduate of the University of Kansas Law School, Vogler admits it was the latest anti-pipeline ruling of the U.S. Court of Appeals that triggered his move for independence.

He described the court's pipeline ruling as "a crime in the annals of American jurisprudence." Unhappy with the invasion of foreign fishing fleets, new restrictions on logging Alaska's forests and the Jones Act, Vogler said, "We're totally controlled by groups outside Alaska. We should control our destiny and not be a colony. Compared to the things we're subjected to, King George (III) was a gentleman."

Now being sought for television, radio and newspaper interviews as well as speaking engagements, Vogler commented, "I never realized there was such a deep undercurrent of dissatisfaction."

He noted that as a sovereign nation, Alaska could set the price of gold at $150 an ounce and make it possible for gold mining to flourish in the new nation. "We could back up our currency with gold. Our income taxes would be paid to Alaska.... We could establish our own fishing limits and make our own laws regarding the development of our resources without interference from Outside."

"We're out to get 150,000 signers," said the independence-minded Fairbanksan. "We have no cutoff time, no deadline."

A Diluted Ice Pool... 58 Winning Tickets
July 1973

The Nenana Ice Classic, an Alaskan harbinger of spring for nearly half a century, set a new record when the Tanana River ice tripped the timing wire at Nenana at 11:59 a.m. on May 4.

A new high of 58 tickets from throughout the state were marked with the winning time, and the number of persons claiming a share in the estimated $110,000 prize was believed to top 500. The share of some of those in the larger pools was less than $100.

Less competitive, the Chena Ice Classic in Fairbanks, produced only one winner, Pacita Helms of Fairbanks, who won more than $1,700 by guessing the Chena tripod would start moving at 1:13 p.m. on April 12.

A No-growth Mood?
August 1973

Unlimited growth of Alaska's largest city doesn't appeal to a large segment of Anchorage's population, according to a recent survey conducted by the Rowan Group, Inc., a political consulting firm with contracts throughout the nation.

In conducting a study related to location of the $71 million federal complex planned for Anchorage, Rowan personnel interviewed 573 Anchorage residents over 19. Forty percent felt there was already more than enough development in Anchorage, 44 percent regarded it as about right and 13 percent indicated there was too little development. "This is a very substantial anti-development mood," said the Rowan report, "and it is especially apparent to long-term Anchorage residents."

Thirty-seven percent of those surveyed agreed that "a maximum population for the Anchorage area should be established, and that steps should be taken to discourage growth when the population reaches this level." The Rowan Group noted that in 24 states where it has conducted surveys since 1971, only in Colorado and Oregon has the concern about growth been greater than it is in Anchorage.

$100 a Month Bonus to Pioneers over 65 – Needy or Not
February 1973

About 3,800 pioneer Alaskans were mailed $100 checks in February, as the State of Alaska made first payments under its unique longevity bonus program. Enacted by the last Legislature, the program provides that any Alaskan who reaches 65 and can show 25 continuous years of Alaskan residence is entitled to the bonus, regardless of need.

For those pioneers who need the bonus most, however, the program may be less a blessing than the Legislature intended. Some state officials fear that for some recipients of the monthly bonus there may be a cut in federal old age assistance benefits. Present law requires that persons eligible for old age assistance grants must have less than $250 a month income from all sources.

"The federal government says that you have to take money from whatever source is available," explained Commissioner of Administration Joe Henri. "Under that requirement, the $100 bonus would be supplanting federal money with state money. In some cases, our recipients will not qualify for old-age assistance."

Commissioner Henri expects there may soon be about 4,000 applicants, of whom an estimated 1,700 are receiving old-age assistance grants. The last Legislature appropriated $2.2 million to pay for the program from the state's general fund, but Commissioner Henri expects the annual cost will reach $5 million.

Dream House: A Non-Melting Igloo
July 1973

It had to happen! Canadian Eskimos at Baker Lake, NWT, have ordered an igloo from a Toronto firm. Shelter Limited, architect Jeremy Jenkin's firm, built a children's camp using seven imitation igloos of wood, coated with polyurethane foam. The Eskimos at Baker Lake decided that a Toronto-built igloo was just what they needed for meetings of the Arctic Christian Fellowship. It would be bigger than anything they could build of snow, and it wouldn't melt in the summer. They ordered a custom-made dome 40 feet in diameter and 20 feet high with 10 triangular windows.

Property-tax Relief for Senior Alaskans
May 1973

A statewide program of relief from property tax burdens is now in effect for senior Alaskans whose incomes are less than $10,000 a year. Deadline for eligibility applications for the state's senior citizens (65 or over) property tax exemption law was January 15. The forms are available at city and borough tax assessors' offices.

Real property covered by the exemption includes dwellings, a dwelling within a multiple dwelling and mobile homes. "The State of Alaska will reimburse municipalities in full for all tax revenues lost due to operation of this statutory exemption," said Governor William A. Egan.

Halibut Quota Reduced — Is Japan to Blame?
April 1973

The International Pacific Halibut Commission has reduced by two million pounds the catch Canadian and United States fishermen will be allowed this year, and it also wants Japanese catches curbed.

The six-member commission, three each from Canada and the United States, released its recommendations after its annual meeting in Petersburg last January.

Commission Director Bernard Scud of Seattle said examination of halibut fillets from Japan, marketed in North America, showed some "were definitely from fish less than the minimum size agreed to by the North Pacific Fisheries Convention."

"The commission is extremely concerned about continuing low stocks and believes this condition is due in a large part to intensive foreign fishing," the commission reported.

It said the commission would make "strong representations" to both the Canadian and U. S. governments about Japanese violations "and will urge appropriate measures to prevent further violations."

Last year's halibut catch in Canadian- and U. S.-controlled waters was 41.5 million pounds, a 30-year low, Scud said.

The Iron Bars on Saint Herman's Alaska Cabin... Why?
July 1973

The iron bars which I recovered from the remains of the cabin once occupied by Saint Herman of Alaska, first North American saint of the Russian Orthodox Faith, now resemble a cross.

But there is no doubt that these bars I first saw 50 years ago in the windows of Father Herman's old cabin on Spruce Island near Kodiak were installed for protection. And I have often wondered why there were bars on the cabin of this beloved monk.

Canonized in Kodiak's Church of the Resurrection on August 9, 1970, Father Herman had served in North America from 1794 to 1837. Most of those years he spent in Alaska at Monk's Lagoon on Spruce Island.

A small cabin was standing in a clearing a few hundred feet down the trail from Father Herman's chapel, known as Elovai Mission, when I first visited the site in 1923. This was known as Father Herman's cabin.

A barred window with four panes of glass was set in the south wall and another the same size in the west wall. The cabin was habitable in 1923, although it appeared no one had lived in it for many years. The ceiling was barely six feet high.

I recall wondering at the time why there were iron bars in a monk's house. There are no wild animals on this four-by-seven-mile island, and I had always understood the relationship between Father Herman and the Native people was harmonious.

My theory about the bars is that relations were not always the best between the Russian and Aleut people during that era 150 years ago. I am of Russian and Aleut descent on my mother's side, and I will admit that renegades crop up now and then in Native settlements.

Assuming there were such characters during the Russian era, it is likely that when Father Herman's cabin was built other Russian priests and workmen demanded that iron bars be installed.

As I recall Father Herman's cabin, the log walls were hewed with dove-tailed corners—a sure sign of Russian craftsmanship. The casings and floor were made of whipsawed and hand-planed lumber. The roof was gabled and covered with crude shingles. I doubt there is a builder's plan for these early cabins in either Alaska or Russia, and so it is unlikely an explanation for the iron bars will be found in historical records.

The elevation of Father Herman to sainthood revived my interest in the iron bars several years ago, and I made a trip from my home at Pleasant Harbor to now-deserted Monk's Lagoon. The wood had rotted away and the iron bars lay there like two crosses.

Except for my two sets of bars, all that remains of Father Herman's log cabin are traces of rotted log walls and a depression which marks the location of a shallow cellar under the cabin.

Will the reason for the installation of the iron bars that now resemble a cross remain a mystery?

—Edward Nikolia Opheim Sr.

Edward Nikolia Opheim Sr.

Father Herman's original cabin was located in this clearing at Monk's Lagoon on Spruce Island near Kodiak. The photo was taken when prelates of the Russian Orthodox Church visited the site. At right is the grave of Archimandrite Gerasim, 20th century disciple of Father Herman, who lived here from 1937 until his death in 1969, and who was responsible for recovering many of the Saint's relics.

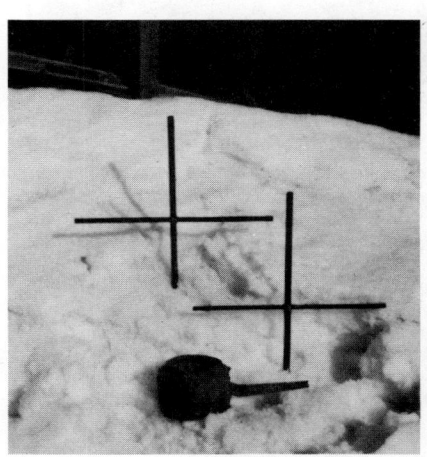
Edward Nikolia Opheim Sr.

The iron bars which I found in the remains of Father Herman's cabin now resemble crosses. The handmade copper kettle in the foreground was found near Monk's Lagoon and dates back to the Russian era.

A Gold Room for the University of Alaska... Thanks to One Who Struck It Rich
April 1973

"The Gold Room," established by heirs of Clarence J. Berry, is nearing completion at the University of Alaska's museum at Fairbanks. A vault-type display case will house gold in all its forms; ore, nuggets, dust and likely some worked gold. Also on exhibit will be artifacts from the gold rush period, including some of Berry's steam points—considered a pioneering development in mining frozen ground.

Berry, originally a fruit farmer in California, was one of the first to strike it rich in the Klondike at the end of the last century, and one of the few prospectors who held on to his fortune and enlarged it through investment. The Berry Holding Company, created by family members after his death in 1930, has pledged $25,000 to build the Gold Room, will also offer three $1,000 scholarships and this year donated $3,000 to the college as an unrestricted gift.

Berry himself was known for his generosity. In front of his Klondike cabin stood a can full of gold, a bottle of whiskey and a sign reading "Help Yourself." Pierre Berton, who wrote of Berry in his book, *The Klondike Fever*, also described him as "sober, honest, hard-working, ambitious and home-loving, and he stayed that way. Of all the original locaters on Bonanza and Eldorado, there is scarcely one other to whom these statements apply."

Logging by Balloon

Alaska Loggers Assn. photo by James Ouellette

August 1973

Soaring over the tall timber near Kake on Kupreanof Island in Southeastern Alaska is this huge logging balloon known as "Soderberg's Air Force." Pat Soderberg is using the 113-foot high, 105-foot diameter balloon in his Clear Creek Logging Company's operations. Containing 530,000 cubic feet of helium when filled, and with a lift capacity of 25,000 pounds, the balloon weighs 6,200 pounds. Capable of logging a perimeter of 3,000 feet, the high-sky operation, first of its kind in Alaska, results in less environmental damage than traditional methods.

Aid for Native Artists
August 1973

The Canadian government has taken steps to protect original Eskimo carvings and to prevent the making and sale of copies without the carver's permission. The Hon. Jean Chretien, Minister of Indian Affairs and Northern Development, recently reminded the conference on the Fine Arts of the Arctic in Ottawa that many years ago, Munamee of Cape Dorset made a carving which the government presented to Her Majesty, Queen Elizabeth. Not long ago, a manufacturer in the south made copies of this carving for sale, without Munamee's permission. The federal department took action on Munamee's behalf and no more copies will be made. The man who made them has apologized and will pay damages to Munamee.

"This is the kind of action I am prepared to take, to help you protect your art," Chretien told the delegates at the conference, who included artists from Alaska and Greenland, as well as Yukon, Northwest Territories and northern Quebec. "If you think we need new laws to help you, then I would like to hear your suggestions."

Milk Wine
September 1973

A patent for making nonintoxicating wine from milk has been granted to a Palmer priest and his brother who claim to be the world's only producers of milk wine. The patent was issued to Father Emmet R. Engel and his brother, George, who make the wine in fifth and gallon containers in a small plant between Palmer and Wasilla.

Father Engel reports his now-patented recipe is adapted from a formula developed centuries ago in Bohemia and handed down to him by his grandmother. He claims to have spent 44 years in perfecting his unique product, which is transformed from powdered milk into wine in 111 days.

Record Brown Bear Kill
August 1973

The highest spring kill of brown bears in the Kodiak National Wildlife Refuge since the permit system was established in 1968 was recorded last spring, according to Gerry Atwell, refuge manager. The harvest of 70 or more bears in the season which ended May 15 came from an estimated population of 2,000 brown bears on the refuge.

Atwell told the *Kodiak Mirror* he attributes the increased bear take to a shortened bear season on the Alaska Peninsula, elimination of polar bear hunting and rumors that brown and grizzly bear may be protected as endangered species. Among those issued permits for hunting on Kodiak were residents from 14 states, Holland, Canada and West Germany.

Noting that the bear harvest is being closely watched by federal and state biologists, Atwell said, "If the pressure is going to be steady—and maybe increase—a shortening of the spring season may be necessary." He said that division of the refuge into 75 hunting units aids in providing quality hunts by dispersing hunters. Largest bear of the recent season was a male with a skull size of 29 and 7/16 inches, taken by Henry Buxman of Wiggins, Colorado, in a hunt guided by Eldon Reese.

Grizzlies See Red!
September 1973

You can't make friends with a grizzly bear by dousing her with fire retardant containing red dye and fertilizer. This lesson was learned in early summer by the Bureau of Land Management, according to the *Fairbanks Daily News-Miner*. Called to the scene of a small fire, the first plane dropped the retardant. Smoke jumpers in a second plane looked down to see a mother grizzly and two cubs—all wearing red coats—racing through the timber in search of the source of their misery. Finding no way to convince the three mad bears that the retardant, dye and fertilizer were harmless, the smoke jumpers decided not to jump.

The Fine Points of Haida Basketry

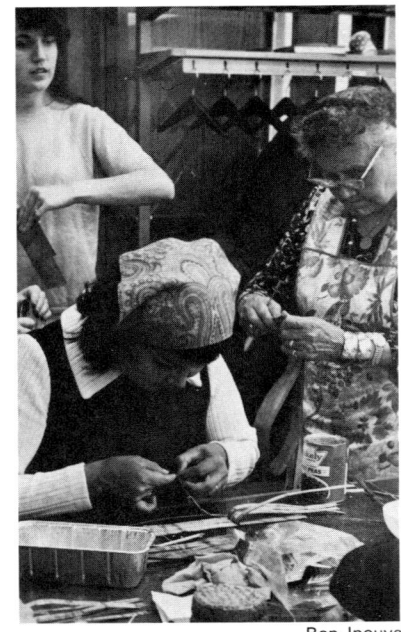

Ron Inouye

August 1973

Winner of a first prize award in basketry at the recent Alaska Festival of Native Arts in Anchorage, Mrs. Selina Peratrovich of Ketchikan, at right, demonstrates the art of splitting cedar bark for Ketchikan students. The Ketchikan artist uses traditional Haida Indian techniques for her cedar bark and spruce root works, which are highly prized by museums. Sponsored by the State Museum and Alaska State Council of the Arts, Mrs. Peratrovich's recent Ketchikan course covered basketry techniques from gathering and processing to the finished product.

$200,000 Reward!
August 1973

Dramatic rescues are almost routine for bush pilots in the Far North, so when young Randy D'Aoust of Yellowknife spotted an overturned canoe on the Talston River last July, found the four Americans who had lost the canoe and flew them to safety, he thought that was the end of the matter. Then, about Christmas-time, the 18-year-old received word that money was being invested for him by the grateful survivors and he would receive at least $200,000 on his twenty-fifth birthday.

Suddenly the North's most eligible young bachelor, Randy declared that "happiness is a lot more important," and that the money won't change him. "I quit school in grade eight," he said. "All I ever wanted to do was be around airplanes, and that's what I'm doing."

Randy was flying supplies into a fish camp on the south shore of Great Slave Lake when he spotted what he thought was a canoe. After making his delivery, he flew back over the area for a closer look and confirmed his suspicions. Searching the river, he located the four tourists who were, he recalls, "in pretty bad shape. They'd been chewed up by flies and they'd been without food for about 10 days."

Moose – Double Hazard
June 1973

Don't tell Debbie Wentland, 20, of Birchwood that moose aren't a hazard on Alaska's highways. In the span of just a few minutes on a March evening, Miss Wentland was involved in two moose-vehicle collisions.

Her car collided with a moose at Mile 11 on the Glenn Highway north of Anchorage. The Eagle River ambulance was called to carry the injured girl to a hospital.

The ambulance struck a moose at Mile 3, enroute to Providence Hospital. Miss Wentland escaped with lacerations, as did the ambulance, which completed its trip to the hospital, and the moose which it hit. The moose struck by Miss Wentland's car had to be killed and her vehicle sustained $400 in damages.

Alaskans Find Limits in Ducks Unlimited
August 1973

Ducks Unlimited has hatched a nestful of problems with refusal of the national headquarters to use funds to develop, restore and maintain waterfowl breeding grounds in Alaska. Shortly after the annual meeting of the Alaska chapter of DU in Anchorage in April, at which it was announced that Alaska was setting a membership pace for the nation, John W. Hendrickson, chapter chairman, resigned. He was joined by Alvin Krevie, the chapter secretary and Mike Hershberger, treasurer.

Claiming that DU's national officers refuse to divert funds for Alaska waterfowl projects, Hendrickson said, "The president and trustees state that their purpose is only to raise money for developing, preserving, restoring and maintaining waterfowl breeding grounds in Canada."

Alaska's fledgling DU chapter had more than 300 members at the time of the officers' walkout. Hendrickson said he will continue to work for conserving and increasing Alaska's ducks and geese through the Alaska Waterfowl Association.

Russia Flights Canceled
September 1973

The only flights which carried passengers west from the United States into the Soviet Union were stopped early this summer when international negotiations met a snag. Attempts between the two countries to work out a reciprocal agreement allowing Soviet carriers to fly vacation packages to Anchorage failed and the Russians denied landing rights to Alaska Airlines' scheduled flights over Siberia, forcing the cancellation of five special package tours. The 500 or so vacationers, including about 50 Alaskans, who held tickets for the jaunts had to forego their visits to Russia or else fly over Europe like everyone else. This would have been the fourth year of the tours.

Boats in Sad Shape
August 1973

The sad shape of many Alaskan boats was confirmed recently at Ketchikan when a three-man Coast Guard boat safety inspection team inspected 42 boats and found 80 percent were in violation of Coast Guard regulations. Most common offenses were inadequate fire extinguishers and lack of flotation devices.

Victory over TB
August 1973

Twenty years after it opened its doors as Alaska's major health facility for the care of tuberculosis patients, the Alaskan Native Medical Center closed its tuberculosis ward.

Commenting on the victory over the disease which has decimated many Native families, Lillie McGarvey, chairman of the Anchorage Service Unit Native Health Board, said, "Alaska Native Medical Center was designed and built as a tuberculosis hospital, and when it was opened in 1953, it was soon filled to capacity. There was a long waiting list."

Although the disease is still a threat, Mrs. McGarvey said it has been reduced to the point where tuberculosis patients are treated in regular medical wards at ANMC.

"We would like to thank the federal, state and private medical people who helped in the almost total eradication of tuberculosis in Alaska," said Mrs. McGarvey.

Halibut Fishing: The Lady Skipper and her All-daughter Crew

September 1973

Halibut fishing is no longer reserved for sturdy Alaskan males. Captain Joyce Jones of Valdez, skipper of the halibuter VI, and her all-daughter crew sailed out of Valdez in mid-June to join the halibut fleet. The lady skipper is shown topside. Her crew members are, left to right, Tammy, Jamie and Lore Jones. Jarvis Jones, husband and father of the all-female crew, works with the State Department of Highways.
(Valdez-Copper Basin News photo by Wanda Day Boelts)

Senate's Approval of the Oil Pipeline Cheers Alaskans... But Fearful Observers See More Obstacles Ahead
September 1973

A one-vote margin in the U.S. Senate on July 17 advanced the trans-Alaska pipeline project from "proposed" and "pending" to "probable" in the eyes of Alaskan boosters of the $3.5 billion project to construct a 48-inch crude oil pipeline 789 miles from Prudhoe Bay to Valdez.

"Trans-Alaskan Pipeline Authorization Act" is the simple title of the precedent-shattering bill which won passage on a 49-48 vote.

Reflecting growing concern of Congress in easing the energy crisis, the amendment sponsored by Alaska's Senators Mike Gravel and Ted Stevens prohibits further judicial review and calls for immediate issuance of a pipeline construction permit by the Secretary of the Interior. A subsequent move for reconsideration by Senator Allan Cranston of California was defeated when Vice President Spiro Agnew broke a 49-49 tie by supporting the Alaskan position.

Even as the Senate was voting for the Alaskan-sponsored amendment to Senator Henry M. Jackson's bill, which authorizes increasing the right-of-way for pipelines from 50 to 150 feet, the House Public Lands Subcommittee voted 13 to 3 in favor of its own right-of-way bill. The House legislation, which also waives further judicial review, was approved July 24 by the House Interior Committee and headed for the floor of the House for consideration.

"This kind of action in the Senate will be followed through in the House," said an optimistic Governor William A. Egan. Some observers predict both Senate and House will vote by October on a trans-Alaska pipeline bill expected to emerge from a joint conference committee.

The Senate's interest in getting action on the long-stalled project was most evident in the decisive 77-21 vote for Senator Jackson's right-of-way bill. Impatience with continuing delay was demonstrated a week earlier when Minnesota Senator Walter Mondale's motion to delay any pipeline action until the merits of the trans-Alaskan vs. trans-Canadian lines could be studied was defeated 61-29.

Learning the hard way that predicting a start on the massive project that will involve 8,000 to 10,000 workers on the pipeline proper and create another 10,000 supporting jobs is a risky game, Alaskan leaders were nevertheless optimistic that the Senate vote cleared a major hurdle.

Most rosy prediction on a possible work start came from Department of Interior Undersecretary John Whittaker who told a Canadian audience that the project could be under way in six months. Some oil industry officials in Anchorage were optimistic that actual pipeline work would be started by mid-1974, while others suggested early 1975 is a more logical date.

Despite the Senate-passed amendment which declares the Alaska pipeline impact statement meets all requirements of the National Environmental Policy Act, and is not subject to judicial review, conservationists and others, including Senator Jackson, believe the matter must be decided by the courts.

In passing the Gravel-Stevens amendment, Senator Gravel said the Senate ruled that "the impact statement demanded by NEPA is sufficient under the terms of that Act."

Prior to the voting, Senator Gravel stated, "In reality, the question can be decided either by the Congress or the courts. If we make the decision, the courts will be relieved of the responsibility. If we defer, then the courts will be compelled to make the decision. Both of us have the authority to make the decision. Our decision will have the same validity as the court's decision... The Alaska pipeline will be built some two years sooner with my amendment than without it."

Welded to Alaska's economic future, the pipeline was scheduled for completion in 1973 by industry planners back in 1969. It was assumed oil royalties would be fattening the state's treasury this year. With delays piled on setbacks, the earliest Prudhoe Bay royalty money can be banked is now 1977. And Governor Egan told the last Legislature that at the present spending rate the nearly billion dollars gained from the 1969 North Slope lease sale, which has dropped below $700 million, will be exhausted by late 1977. On the positive side, once Prudhoe Bay is producing 1.5 million barrels of oil daily, Alaska's income from North Slope oil is projected at about $377 million a year.

The Unblinking Frog of the Cohoe Clan...
September 1973

An unblinking wooden frog from Southeastern Alaska engages in a stare-down contest with four young Alaskans from Southwestern Alaska at the Anchorage Historical and Fine Arts Museum. Part of the international exhibit "The Far North: 2,000 Years of American Eskimo and Indian Art," the huge frog was carved in Sitka in 1902 as an emblem for the Cohoe Salmon Clan of the Tlingit Indians. Intrigued by the frog are, left to right, Charlie Peterson of Mountain Village, Frankie Pete of Bethel, Chris George of Nightmute and Mark Leary, Bethel. The exhibit of more than 350 pieces of art will remain in the museum until September 9. (Anchorage Daily Times photo by Alice Puster)

Best Use of the D-2 National Interest Lands... Is the Tendency to Think Too Big?
September 1973

Preliminary recommendations on best use of much of Alaska's 80 million acres of D-2 "national interest" lands have been made to Secretary of the Interior Rogers C.B. Morton by the Federal-State Land Use Planning Commission.

Culminating intensive summer work sessions and an earlier round of public hearings at which nearly 1,000 persons testified, the commission's recommendations will be considered by Secretary Morton in making his final recommendations to Congress no later than December 18, 1973. The 80 million acres of "national interest" lands will be designated by Congress as national forests, national parks, national wildlife refuges or wild and scenic rivers no later than December, 1978.

The package being passed to the Department of the Interior by the 10-member Alaskan commission includes some major problems. Larry Lynn, assistant secretary of Interior, warned that Native corporations may have to encroach on the D-2 lands in order to acquire the 40 million acres authorized by the Alaska Native Claims Settlement Act.

Dr. Max Brewer, commissioner of the State Department of Environmental Conservation and a member of the FSLUPC, noted that the federal government has designated use of 421 million acres of Alaska's land, when there are only 365 million acres in the state.

"The cart is before the horse when lands are committed to a management agency or a form of management before their potential uses can be known or management plans evolved," Brewer told his fellow commissioners. "Alaska is big, and thus the tendency to think big in committing huge blocks of land — 10 million acres or more at a crack. However, proper designations can be made only when there is some freedom of action in designating both natural boundaries and proper size of lands, after thorough study."

Warning against creation of "paper parks," Attorney General John Havelock told a Fairbanks audience that the bids by federal agencies for control of the D-2 lands is "senseless." He said, "The key to good land planning is not who is the landlord but what happens to the land... So little is known about most of Alaska's public domain as to make permanent specific use commitments unwise."

Joe Josephson, Anchorage attorney and co-chairman of the FSLUPC, told a Ketchikan audience that extended delays in designating uses for the D-2 lands could lead to another federal freeze.

Taking his place on the FSLUPC in midsummer was co-chairman Burton W. Silcock, who was named to the post by President Nixon. Silcock was Bureau of Land Management supervisor for Alaska for seven years before being appointed national BLM director in 1971.

Anxious Whale... Her 40-foot Baby in a Gill Net
September 1973

What do you say to a 70-foot long mama whale when you've accidentally trapped her 40-foot baby in your gill net? Cordova fisherman Glen Carlson must have said the right thing, because mama kept her cool and refrained from wreaking havoc on Glen's boat, the *Viking*, or on any of the other boats standing by to help.

Reported Lone E. Janson in the *Cordova Times:* "She would come up and take a good look at the situation, then submerge and raise herself up under the net, trying to lift it off the little whale. When several tries at that did no good, she came up and took another good look, then, with a huge commotion, Whap! — she cut the net with one swipe of her tail... the net drifted free and apparently she got her baby loose, because Glen recovered his gear about a mile away... lines, corks and leads intact."

The mammals were believed to be rare blue whales, which are among the largest in the world.

Homestead Land for a Nature Park
September 1973

"People have to have room, too; but they have to give a little space to other living things." Acting on this philosophy, Mr. and Mrs. Robert Johns recently sold 58.75 acres of their homestead property near Turnagain Arm to the Anchorage borough to be maintained in its wild state as a park. Worth $110,000 if it were developed and subdivided, the property brought the Johns only $60,000 and the guarantee that wildlife will continue to have Furrow Creek as a natural corridor from the Chugach Mountains to Cook Inlet.

Hiking, cross-country skiing, picnicking and other recreational activities which do not require facilities will be allowed in the park, but no natural vegetation will be cut for trails and parking will be restricted to the periphery. A sewer interceptor will be constructed through the park, but the borough has agreed to restore the area completely afterward.

"I've lived with the birds and animals all these years, and I've seen how one by one all the creeks that flow to the Inlet have been developed and closed off, so that the living things can't get down any more," said Mrs. Johns, who with her husband homesteaded the area in 1947. "Furrow Creek is just about the only access they have."

A quarter of the parkland is tidal flats and bluff which are part of the Potter Marsh bird sanctuary.

Iceberg Sinks a Barge
July 1973

The barge crew at Icy Bay on May 1 had reason to believe they were in the North Atlantic's iceberg alley. Propelled by gale winds, a huge iceberg calved from Malaspina Glacier crashed into and sank a 150-foot barge owned by Sandstrom-Anderson Construction Company. The iceberg also knocked out 80 pilings which the company had installed for a log pond. Valued at $150,000, the sunken barge was refloated and put back in operation within a week.

Modular Jails for Eskimo Villages
August 1973

The need to confine prisoners in cells or lock them in schoolrooms is about to end in at least three remote Eskimo villages. New modular units which include detention cells, a small courtroom and offices for magistrates and constables are scheduled for placement this summer at St. Marys, Emmonak and Kiana. Costing about $33,000 each, the 14- by 60-foot facilities were built at Bellingham, Washington, and barged north. The purchase was made possible through a $100,000 grant from the federal Law Enforcement Assistance Program.

Expected to serve the needs of 10 to 15 neighboring villages, the new jail-courtroom buildings are equipped with chemical toilets, heating and fire-sprinkler systems. The structures are mounted on skids, and if danger of flood or fire threatens, they can be hauled to safety.

A New Flagship
September 1973

A new flagship was added to Alaska's fleet of ferries in early May with the launching of the $19.5 million *Columbia* at Lockheed Shipbuilding and Construction Company in Seattle. The 418-foot vessel will enter service early next year on the Southeastern segment mainline run of the Alaska Marine Highway. It can carry 1,000 passengers, 184 automobiles and a crew of 80, and has 324 berthing spaces. Entering service at about the same time will be a 235-foot feeder-line vessel now being built in Wisconsin.

The 2,200-mile Alaska Marine Highway, connecting Alaska to Seattle and to British Columbia and linking some 17 communities within the state, now has five vessels operating throughout Southeastern Alaska and one each on routes connecting Whittier-Cordova-Valdez and Anchorage-Seward-Kodiak. The first ferry, the *Malaspina*, went into service 10 years ago.

The *Columbia* is the fourth Alaska ferry built by Lockheed, which also built the *Malaspina*, *Matanuska* and *Taku*. The new vessel will replace the *Wickersham*, a foreign-built ferry which is operating under a temporary waiver on the Jones Act.

Blinded by a Bear at Age 17... a Ph.D. at 31
September 1973

Blind since he was mauled by a bear north of Juneau at 17, Lee D. Hagmeier, 31, was awarded his Ph.D. in educational philosophy at the University of Washington commencement exercises in early June. Barely surviving the savage attack, the plucky Alaskan completed high school, graduated summa cum laude from Chico State College in 1967 and received his master's degree from the University of Washington in 1969. The full story of Dr. Hagmeier's youthful ordeal and subsequent victory was told in "The Bear All Juneau Remembers" by John Jensen in the January, 1970, issue of ALASKA® magazine.

(See also page 28 of this volume for an additional report on Lee Hagmeier's ordeal.
– The Editors)

EPA's Plan to Limit Fairbanks Autos: 'Senseless'!
September 1973

Fairbanks will be warmer next winter if anger at the Environmental Protection Agency can be converted into heat. The city-federal agency feud approached the boiling point this summer when the EPA announced its plan for solving the carbon monoxide problem in Alaska's second largest city might include banning use of private autos in downtown Fairbanks during the coldest winter months.

Described by Mayor Harold Gillam as "senseless," the EPA plan which was to take effect August 15 included such other elements as improved traffic flow, development of a mass transit system, vehicle inspection and maintenance program, requiring catalytic-converter exhaust control devices on vehicles and allowing cars to idle for no more than five minutes.

The State Department of Environmental Conservation has said it will not develop an arbitrary plan to make Fairbanks conform to federal standards by 1975 as required by the Clean Air Act of 1970. EPA officials have declared that Fairbanks must limit its carbon monoxide level to 15 parts per million in any eight-hour period.

The EPA claims that carbon monoxide standards established by the Clean Air Act were exceeded in downtown Fairbanks on at least 112 days between October 1, 1972 and March 31, 1973.

As one of 28 cities in the nation with severe clean air problems, Fairbanks was described by the EPA as "geographically and meteorologically closed... the encircling hills and frequent inversions hold in pollutants, and the rigorous winter climate complicates the use of ordinary modes of transportation, of which the automobile is far the most commonly employed."

Said an EPA summary: "The proposed regulatory mechanisms to accomplish the reduction in vehicle miles traveled are the complete exclusion from the downtown area of Fairbanks of all private automobiles, coupled with the development of an efficient, convenient, reliable and safe system of public transportation."

Anger was the common reaction of Fairbanks' leaders to the EPA plan. "The economic impact may see us asking for federal aid for businesses much like as in floods," said Borough Mayor John Carlson.

Soaring Gold Prices Revive Nome's Dream of Riches
September 1973

Soaring prices of gold on the world market are reviving dreams of past riches in the Nome area, according to Albro Gregory, editor of the *Nome Nugget*. Gregory reported that U-V Industries is using a new drill for exploratory work near a now idle dredge site, and there is speculation that the company may activate two dredges in 1974. "It is highly possible that within our own confines we are going to see a brisk resumption of gold mining," wrote Gregory, "especially if a new less-expensive method of thawing permafrost proves itself in the coming months."

A Colorful Offense
August 1973

Budding artists had best resist the temptation to "pretty up" the miner whose countenance appears on Yukon vehicle license plates. For painting the miner "various colors," John Russell of Whitehorse was fined 50 cents by Justice Harr Maddison. Territorial law prohibits making the miner more colorful than he already is.

Suddenly It Was an Airport
September 1973

"All of a sudden it was an airport," reported the *Ketchikan Daily News* in describing the first landing of an Alaska Airlines jet at the new $14 million Ketchikan International Airport on June 30.

Despite problems with the ferry *Abnaki* which transports passengers between Ketchikan and the airport on Gravina Island, borough airport manager Fred Baxter said in early July, "Things have gone as well as can be expected under the conditions, with an incomplete airport and all."

When the regular ferry slip for the borough-owned *Abnaki* is complete, the airport ferry will be able to make two trips an hour across Tongass Narrows. About 1,500 passengers moved through the airport in its first three days of operations.

Activation of the new airport marked the end of an unusual passenger transfer operation which involved flying passengers from the landing strip on Annette Island to Ketchikan in an amphibian Grumman Goose. Alaska Airlines celebrated the end of the Goose flights with a full-page ad in the *Ketchikan Daily News* which said simply, "Goodbye Goose." The new airport was scheduled to be officially dedicated on August 4 and 5.

A Ghost Ship on a Clear Sunday
May 1973

A ghost ship closely resembling the legendary *Flying Dutchman* was sighted in the waters of Southeastern Alaska in February by three crewmen of the State ferry *Malaspina*. The chief mate and two sailors, one at the helm and one at lookout, were standing watch on the bridge early on a clear Sunday morning, as the big ferry moved north toward Ketchikan. When the ship was abeam of Twin Island, Revillagigedo Channel, a huge gray vessel suddenly loomed about eight miles dead ahead broadside and dead in the water. For ten minutes the seamen watched it and reported that it looked "exact, natural and real," with their binoculars even revealing sailors moving on board. Then the mysterious ship vanished.

None of the three men had made such a sighting before, but the *Flying Dutchman* is familiar to mariners the world over. The famed ship is often associated with the Cape of Good Hope, South Africa.

Optimism Flows... Construction Could Start by the Turn of the New Year

October 1973

Open optimism is flowing from Alaska this fall in the wake of a 356-60 vote by the U.S. House of Representatives on August 2, calling for immediate construction of the 789-mile trans-Alaska pipeline from Prudhoe Bay to Valdez.

The House action ran parallel to that of the Senate which approved its version of the bill on July 17 with a 77-20 vote. Key vote in the House came on an amendment offered by Rep. John Dellenback of Oregon which would have retained judicial review provisions for environmental aspects of the bill. The amendment was rejected by a 221-198 vote, paving the way for the six-to-one approval of the bill waiving further court action.

With a Joint Conference Committee slated to coalesce the House and Senate versions into a single bill in September, there seemed little doubt that the legislation would be signed into law by President Nixon, probably in October. In a pipeline conference with Alaskan leaders before the House vote, the President was quoted as saying, "Let's get on with the job."

Despite the fact that construction of the then $900 million pipeline was considered "imminent" in September, 1969, after oil companies paid more than $900 million for North Slope leases, Alaskan leaders were growing bullish in predictions that four years later work was really "imminent" on the project that now has a price tag of $3.6 billion.

While court tests on the constitutionality of the pipeline bills still are possible, proponents feel that the massive pro-votes in both the House and Senate have provided momentum that may be slowed but cannot be stopped.

Governor William A. Egan stated in early August that he doesn't believe an oil industry court suit against pipeline legislation enacted by the 1972 Legislature will delay the project. He indicated that conciliatory discussions are under way with the oil industry, and an out-of-court settlement is considered a possibility. Some Republican legislators have suggested that a special session of the Legislature may be required this year to enact remedial legislation.

Pipeline price tag – once $900 million – has grown to $3.6 billion.

Alaska's Congressional delegation has speculated that Secretary of the Interior Rogers C. B. Morton will issue the necessary construction and right-of-way permits as soon as the pipeline bill is signed into law, and construction could start this year.

"It is entirely possible we could have the actual construction activities begin around the turn of the year," said Governor Egan.

E. L. Patton, president of Alyeska Pipeline Service Company, which will build the pipeline, said after the favorable House vote that he hopes "full scale" construction of the pipeline could begin in 1974, with oil flowing through Valdez by 1977.

Secretary Morton was expected to consider details of the pipeline project during a late August visit to Alaska, and Secretary of Labor Peter Brennan inspected Prudhoe Bay and toured the pipeline route in early August.

The importance of Alaska's oil to the nation and world became more apparent with recent disclosure that the government estimates Naval Petroleum Reserve No. 4 west of Prudhoe Bay contains reserves of 15 billion barrels of oil. The current estimate for Prudhoe Bay is 9.6 billion barrels of recoverable oil.

Commenting on the impact of the pipeline on Alaska, Senator Mike Gravel said, "The quality of life for every Alaskan will be changed by the action of the Congress approving the pipeline. The benefit to each of us will be somewhat unbelievable. We will have a remarkable legacy to pass on to our children."

Meanwhile, two giants of the natural gas industry are seeking the most-favored position in getting natural gas from Prudhoe Bay to market. In direct competition for the estimated 30 trillion cubic feet of natural gas in the Prudhoe Bay field are Arctic Gas, which is backed by major developers of Prudhoe Bay, and El Paso Natural Gas Company, one of the nation's largest gas suppliers.

The former hopes to construct a natural gas pipeline from Prudhoe Bay through Canada to the U.S. Midwest. El Paso is planning a pipeline from Prudhoe Bay to a Southcentral Alaska port, liquefying the gas and shipping it to the South 48 in LNG tankers.

Red Smoke?
November 1973

Smoke presumed to have come from forest fires in Siberia posed problems for Interior Alaska flyers during a brief period in midsummer. A helicopter pilot got lost in the imported haze and had to get radio assistance to find his way back to McGrath. Prior to the arrival of the wind-carried smoke cover, none of which could be traced to Alaskan fires, Siberian weather reports obtained by the National Weather Service had mentioned smoke. The smoke was reported down to 6,500 feet at Kotzebue and up to 14,000 feet north of Fairbanks.

Canada Bans Fuel, Hyder Doesn't Care
October 1973

Alaskans hardest hit by the Canadian government's decision to stop exporting petroleum products to the U.S. are the fewer than 100 people living in Hyder, Alaska, at the head of the Portland Canal, according to the *Ketchikan Daily News*.

Lacking an oil dock or gas station, Hyder residents have driven six miles across the border to Stewart, British Columbia, and filled their tanks in the Canadian town, which also provides them with telephone and electricity service.

"The Canadians now are refusing to sell fuel to Hyder residents," reported the Ketchikan newspaper. "But we have it on good authority that the State of Alaska isn't worried about this little threat to the Hyder economy. Stewart, B.C., exists only because of the Granduc Mine and 10 miles of road between Stewart and the mine run through Alaska. When the state highway department runs out of fuel, it is going to close the road."

Strange Encounters... Wildlife in the News
October 1973

Strange encounters between northern birds, animals and man made unusual wildlife news last summer:

□ A Canadian helicopter crew came to the rescue of two eaglets near Yellowknife last July. Unable to fly and their 30-foot-high nest in the path of a fast-moving forest fire, the 18-inch eagle chicks were rescued by Bob McKillop, Canadian forestry officer, despite attacks by the enraged parents. The lucky birds were flown to Yellowknife where they celebrated their escape by eating a six-pound lake trout.

□ Attacks on Fairbanks joggers by goshawks protecting a nest ended in July when the chicks learned to fly. Joggers had earlier complained to the Department of Fish and Game that they were subject to dive-bombing attacks as they passed the nest 25 yards from the trail.

□ Two campers in Mount McKinley National Park were cuffed and slapped by a grizzly sow and two cubs who caught them in their sleeping bags about 11:45 p.m. at the headwaters of Big Creek. The New Jersey residents were not seriously injured. And golfers at Kemano near Kitimat, British Columbia, faced a new hazard last summer — seven grizzly bears took up residence near the golf course.

□ Wolf lovers won a victory of sorts when Magistrate Carl Heinmiller of Haines dismissed a state charge brought against Eunice Benson, who imported a pair of wolves from Oregon. Heinmiller suggested that the state issue a permit for the wolves which were raised in captivity and are held in a pen.

Buildings, Tanks Barged 3,500 Miles to Prudhoe Bay

October 1973

Shown (top photo) as it was ready to depart Seattle in July, this structure is one of five now being assembled at Prudhoe Bay to provide a 95,000-square foot operations center and living quarters for up to 150 workers. Each section is 50 feet wide, 45 feet high and 125 feet long. Organized by BP Alaska Inc., Prudhoe Bay operator for Standard Oil Company of Ohio, last summer's 3,500-mile sea haul to Alaska's arctic coast involved eight barges carrying 20,000 tons worth $30 million. The operations camp will cost $18 million when it is completed. Fresh water (bottom photo) is a critical factor in Prudhoe Bay operations, and these water tanks, each with a million-gallon capacity, were barged north to help meet the demand when the BP Alaska section of the oilfield is in full operation. (BP Alaska Inc.)

The Six-Week Cruise of a Ghost Ship
December 1973

No one in Kodiak doubts the seaworthiness of the *M/V Patriot*, a 36-foot fishing vessel that cruised the stormy Gulf of Alaska for nearly six weeks last summer without a man aboard.

The vessel was being towed by the *M/V Chief* to Kodiak from Seattle on June 11, when the tow line broke. The powerless craft seemed in such trouble that two crewmen were taken aboard the *Chief*. It was presumed the *Patriot* had sunk in the heavy seas.

The U.S. Coast Guard cutter *Winona* found the plucky *Patriot* about 60 miles off Yakutat in late July. The vessel had little water in her hold and was in good shape.

Donation for AMU: 780-Acre Farm
August 1973

Alaska Methodist University nearly tripled its 400 acres of campus in late May when Miss V. Louise Kellogg, a member of AMU's board of trustees, announced she has donated her 780-acre Spring Creek Farm to the university.

To be known as the Kellogg Campus of AMU, the gift from the Matanuska Valley civic leader is the largest in the history of the university. "I don't know what it is worth because I've never tried to sell it," said the woman who began her farming operations in 1948.

"In deciding the best future for the farm, I wanted to insure that it would remain intact and useful," said Miss Kellogg, who stipulated in the gift that the 780-acre tract can never be sold and must remain intact and undivided. Another provision allows her to continue residing at Spring Creek Farm as long as she lives.

In requiring that never more than half of the land will be cleared, Miss Kellogg said, "I feel it is convenient for men and moose and ducks and geese to get along together."

AMU officials indicated Spring Creek Farm will serve as a center for studies in liberal arts, health sciences, the environment and intercultural relations.

Fisherman, Halibut Die in Struggle
September 1973

A battle between a lone fisherman and a big halibut ended in death for both, according to Alaska State Troopers who recently recovered the body of Joseph T. Cash of Petersburg from his troller *Flicka* at Eagle Point on Kupreanof Island. As reconstructed by the troopers, Cash is presumed to have landed a 150-pound halibut. In thrashing around the deck, the fish is believed to have broken Cash's leg and severed an artery. The fisherman then apparently tied himself to the troller's winch, dying before he could reach help.

75-Minute Battle for 70-Pound King... A Derby Winner

September 1973

Winning Ketchikan's King Salmon Derby, this 70-pound, 4-ounce fish has done much to finance a college education for Milton George, 19, who caught it near Blank Point, south of Ketchikan. Nearly 20 pounds heavier than its nearest rival, the winning king won a cabin cruiser worth $7,700 for the young Alaskan. He sold the boat to acquire funds for college. Norman Jackson, left, was with George when he landed the big king after a 75-minute fight. (Bill Weiss)

Record Attendance at State Fair
December 1973

Topping the 100,000 mark for the first time, attendance totals for the Alaska State Fair at Palmer this year reached 104,457, about 6,000 more visitors than last year. Two weekends of good weather were credited with the increase.

As always, big vegetables attracted the interest of many of the visitors, who saw a 20-pound turnip, a four-pound radish, a 1.5-pound tomato, a 3.25-pound celery, a 2.25-pound cucumber, a 2.25-pound beet, a 1.5-pound carrot, a 5.25-pound head of lettuce and a 47-pound head of cabbage.

A One-Auto Village
August 1973

New addition to the scene at Fort Good Hope, in Canada's Northwest Territories, is a car — the only one of its kind in the settlement. It's a taxi, operated by Mary Al Wilson which explains the name MAW Taxi. Residents of the Mackenzie River village find it pretty exciting to phone for a cab.

Wolf Bounties Revived
December 1973

Dead elsewhere in Alaska, the wolf bounty system was revived for game districts one, two and three in Southeastern Alaska on November 1. Appropriated by the last legislature, $10,000 is available for the program which allows $50 for each wolf. The bounty will be paid only for wolves taken in the three game districts near Ketchikan, where wolf predation is worst.

Safe Passage for Swans
December 1973

Whistling swans had safe passage through Alaska during their migration this fall, although it was proposed by the Alaska Department of Fish and Game that 1,000 permits be issued for taking of the huge white birds.

Dan Timm, ADF&G waterfowl biologist, recently disclosed that the federal bureau of Sport Fisheries and Wildlife had rejected the state's request for a special swan season due to pressure from anti-hunting groups who want no liberalization of hunting laws. Timm stated the proposed permit hunt for swans was justified biologically.

The state's wild duck population was estimated at 4.5 million last spring, a 12 percent increase from 1972, and representing more than 10 percent of all North American ducks. Last year's waterfowl harvest by Alaskans was about 85,000 ducks and 10,000 geese.

North Slope Train Studied
December 1973

Will future travelers to the North be able to take a train from the "lower 48" through Canada into Alaska and up to North Slope? Railroad officials in British Columbia and in Alaska are enthusiastic about the idea, while admitting that it might be difficult to gain support for the project from pipeline-harassed politicians or private citizens. Walker Johnston, general manager of the Alaska Railroad, met with British Columbia railroad leaders recently at Governor William A. Egan's request to discuss the project and review the Canadians' optimistic four-part study of an Alcan Railroad which would transport passengers, minerals and cargo between Dawson Creek and Prudhoe Bay.

Created by Congress in 1923, the federally owned Alaska Railroad was authorized to build 1,000 miles of track but now extends just under 580 miles.

75,000 in Anchorage
December 1973

Anchorage now boasts a population of 75,000, according to City Manager Robert Sharp. The big jump came through annexation to the city of Elmendorf Air Force Base and Fort Richardson, adding 18,000 residents and more than 30 square miles of area.

ALASKA® staff

December 1973

For the fourth time in 55 years, a burial house was erected in late September over the grave of a famed Tlingit Indian chief in the Russian Orthodox cemetery in Juneau. Jack Yackwan (note the different spelling on the gravestone, reproduced above from a charcoal-on-rice-paper rubbing) died December 29, 1918, and was buried near Glacier Avenue, where his gravesite was vandalized several times and restored in 1939 and 1958. Highly regarded as a diplomat and peacemaker, Chief Yackwan was the son of Chief Yees-Gaa-Nalth of the Auke tribe. In rededicating the grave the Kag-wan-ton tribe of Juneau (another altered spelling) was host to Kag-wan-ton tribal members from Sitka, Hoonah, Klukwan, Haines and Anchorage, as well as the Yakutat Coho tribe. And, in honor of the rededication, Juneau's mayor proclaimed "Kag-wan-ton Day."

McKinley Tourists Approve the Rail-car Housing
December 1973

Use of 12 Alaska Railroad cars for housing and serving guests at Mount McKinley National Park was so successful that plans for replacing the cars with more permanent facilities are being sidetracked by George Fleharty, who operates the hotel concession.

Fleharty's train-hotel idea was inspired as an emergency plan to replace the main section of the old park hotel which was destroyed by fire on Labor Day last year. With profits for July and August up 25 percent over 1972, Fleharty is reconsidering earlier plans to establish a conventional hotel facility.

"We have had so many good reports concerning the place that we have decided to see if it will work out permanently," said Fleharty. The new complex can handle twice the number of visitors as the old hotel.

Park Superintendent Daniel Kuehn reported in early September that recreational use of the park in July was up 52 percent over the same month in 1972. During the three peak summer months this year, a total of 35,844 visitors used the shuttle buses compared to 23,591 in the same period in 1972.

Street of Ill Fame Becomes Historic Zone
December 1973

KETCHIKAN—Once the center of Ketchikan's night life and the heart of its red light district, Creek Street is assured a place in the city's history. The Ketchikan Gateway Borough Assembly has approved an ordinance establishing the Creek Street Historic Zone, first step in a detailed plan to preserve the street's colorful past while adding a cloak of respectability.

Phone Network Grows
December 1973

From Akiachak to Wales, from Moses Point to Sheldon Point, from Hooper Bay to Scammon Bay and in 37 other outlying Alaskan communities, the 1973 holiday season will mean a chance to talk to and hear from the rest of the world.

Part of RCA Alaska Communications program to improve and expand Alaska's communications network, the bush phone system now includes 43 villages. More will be added starting next April, and the program will be completed in mid-1975, when about 142 villages will have bush phones.

Powered by batteries, the remote phones have the same capability as any telephones. Bush numbers are dialed in the same way an Anchorage resident dials a Fairbanks number.

With few exceptions, most of the bush phones are the responsibility of the village president or village council. Most remote of Alaska's communities now reachable by telephone is Little Diomede Island in the Bering Strait, almost astride the line dividing the Soviet Union and United States. The number for Little Diomede is 443-2945.

Moose Range Too Big?
December 1973

A 22 percent reduction in the size of the 1.75 million-acre Kenai National Moose Range is being advocated by the Kenai Peninsula Borough Assembly. Borough Mayor Stanley F. Thompson noted that the Moose Range now makes up 17 percent of the borough. The resolution passed by the assembly stated that "man, not moose, is an endangered, unique species when too confined to limited areas of suitable land."

Claiming that the present refuge is larger than needed to protect the moose herds, Thompson said, "We find the moose live quite well out of the moose range around here." The 449,228 acres which the assembly wants removed from the range includes land near Tustumena Lake, Point Possession and most of the existing Swanson River oil field. The assembly proposed adding about 51,848 acres near Bradley Lake at the head of Kachemak Bay to the range.

Honor for Women Who Haul Firewood 100 Miles
December 1973

Two Alaskan women who haul firewood 100 miles rather than deplete the meager supply of trees near their camp have been named joint winners of a "Connie" award by the Society of American Travel Writers. Honored for "outstanding contributions to a quality travel environment through conservation and preservation" were Celia Hunter and Ginny Wood, operators of Camp Denali just outside Mount McKinley National Park.

Of the six 1973 "Connie" awards made at the annual SATW meeting in Rapid City, South Dakota, the Alaskans were among four individuals selected. The official citation stated: "Celia Hunter and Ginny Wood are outstanding examples of concerned citizens who would preserve the natural beauty of America's last frontier while providing a quality travel experience for those who would appreciate the natural and scenic environment of this rugged country."

383-Pound Halibut Is Worth $200
August 1973

Worth more than $200 at current prices, this 383-pound halibut was biggest of a boatload caught off the Aleutians and delivered to Sitka aboard the WESTWARD, out of Seattle. Skipper Marvin Olsen is shown with the fish which weighed 112 pounds less than the largest Pacific halibut ever recorded.

Sitka Daily Sentinel photo by Thad Poulson

$10 Million Offer for the Ferry 'Wickersham'
October 1973

Ten million dollars put an end to the hopes of some Alaskans that the M/V Wickersham might be retained in the state's ferry fleet. Describing the price offer of $10 million from an unidentified foreign buyer as "highly satisfactory," Governor William A. Egan announced the sale will be consummated on October 31, following a drydock inspection of the 363-foot vessel. The buyer has the option of cancelling the offer until October 31.

Following appeals from various Alaskan city councils and chambers of commerce that the Swedish-built vessel be retained in Alaska service, Commissioner of Public Works revealed that the ferry purchased in 1968 for $6.9 million was the most costly in the state's fleet, losing more than $1 million a year. He said keeping the Wickersham would place a needless burden on Alaskan taxpayers and break faith with Congress which had granted a temporary waiver of the Jones Act. Governor Egan said money from the sale arranged by a London shipping firm would help pay for the M/V Columbia now being readied in Seattle to start serving Alaskans early next year.

Desperate for Housing in Ketchikan
December 1973

The severity of Ketchikan's housing shortage was dramatized in late July by a new arrival who ran an ad in the Ketchikan Daily News offering a $100 reward to the first person "providing a successful lead to a nice three-bedroom apartment or house." Dave Comklin told the newspaper he placed the ad because "I heard housing is hard to find here."

Real Estate Deal in Whittier
August 1973

The biggest Alaskan real estate transaction in months was culminated in early May, when residents of Whittier voted by a five-to-one margin to issue $250,000 in general obligation bonds for the purchase of 97 acres of federally owned land in the town of Prince William Sound. Included in the purchase are the fourteen-story Hodge Building and five-story Buckner Building, two of the state's largest structures with a combined total of more than 500,000 square feet of space. A former military shop, post headquarters and communications building and the central heating and power plant are included in the sale. Voters also approved (66-13) a proposition which allows the city to lease a portion of the first three floors of the Hodge Building to the U.S. Army for five years at annual rental of $126,000.

Five-Acre Wilderness Tracts Suspended from Entry ... Many Abuses Cited
November 1973

Abuses and exploitation have forced suspension of Alaska's unique open-to-entry land program for at least a year. F. J. Keenan, director of the Division of Lands, announced that applications for five-acre wilderness tracts available under the program enacted by the 1968 Legislature would not be accepted after August 15, 1973.

Cessation of the program virtually eliminates chances of acquiring wilderness tracts without purchasing them directly from the state or private owners. More than 3,000 persons had applied for the five-acre tracts which could be selected from more than two million acres of state-owned land ranging from Seward to Fairbanks. The law required that the person applying for a tract must have personally staked it. Once approved, a five-year lease was issued for an annual fee of $40. The tract-holder had the option of gaining ownership by having the tract surveyed and paying fair market value at the time of staking.

Abuses that led to de-classification of open-to-entry lands and suspension of the program were mainly in three categories: speculators who were paid to locate and stake land for applicants in violation of the law; applicants who claimed to have staked land which it is believed they never saw; nonresident applicants claiming to be residents, thus skirting a new provision which limited open-to-entry land to Alaska residents.

The growing demand for wilderness tracts showed clearly just before June 12, 1973, when the open-to-entry program was closed to nonresidents. One young Californian flew to Anchorage on June 11, chartered a plane, flew to an open-to-entry area, staked his five acres and was back to file his application in the Anchorage Division of Lands office before 4:30 p.m.

During the period from May 1 to June 11, 1972, a total of 94 applications was filed for the five-acre tracts. The total zoomed to 232 during the same period this year.

In its bulletin for July, 1973, the Division of Lands reported: "It was thought that when the program was restricted to residents only, the activity would slow to a walking pace. However, that did not prove true. The resident activity is still very strong and the filing pace is slowing only a little."

During the suspension of the program, Division of Lands personnel will make on-the-ground inspections of questionable filings, and the attorney general's office will prosecute violators of the law.

In ordering a study of the now-closed open-to-entry lands as they relate to an overall state land use plan now being developed, Keenan said the Division of Lands will use the suspension period to evaluate what lands should be added or deleted when, and if, the program is reactivated.

Caribou Hazard
December 1973

Telephone lines strung along the Canol Road in the Yukon 30 years ago have brought death to at least 20 caribou in 1973, according to Mike Brine, coordinator of the Yukon Resources Council. Telephone poles along the little-used road have decayed and fallen, dropping the wire to a deadly level for passing caribou, which become entangled and starve.

Amchitka Island is Returned to the Sea Otters ... No More Nuclear Tests Planned
October 1973

Amchitka Island in the Aleutians has been returned to the sea otters by the Atomic Energy Commission. Headed by Dr. Dixy Lee Ray, AEC chairman, a group of officials gave the island a last inspection in mid-July and found that demobilization and restoration of the nuclear test site was 92 percent complete. All work was expected to be completed by the end of August.

"If we had any intention of using the area in the future, we wouldn't be pulling out now," said Dr. Ray, allaying fears of those opposed to further nuclear testing. The big cleanup of the island cost about $1 million, with $9 million worth of equipment transferred to other agencies.

Although the Cannikin test of a 5-megaton thermonuclear device, biggest and last conducted on Amchitka, is estimated to have brought death to about 700 sea otter, the AEC's final report placed the island's present sea otter population at more than 6,000 animals.

1974
From Ketchikan to Barrow®

Law Okays the Pipeline; Likely Cost Spirals to $4.5 Billion
January 1974

Construction of the long-delayed 789-mile trans-Alaska pipeline became the law of the land on November 16, when President Nixon signed into law the authorization bill for the $4.5 billion project, largest such undertaking in history.

Indicative of the urgency to find solutions to the worsening energy crisis, the way was paved for the president's law-making signature by a 361-14 vote for the bill in the House of Representatives on November 12, followed by an 80-5 favorable Senate vote on November 13.

A possible pipeline roadblock was believed removed on November 12, when the special 27-day session of the Alaska State Legislature adjourned after enacting eight pieces of remedial legislation offered by Governor William A. Egan. The legislation was required, according to the governor, to remove the threat of prolonged court battles against 1972 laws opposed by the industry.

Despite some predictions that Secretary of the Interior Rogers C.B. Morton would issue a construction permit for the giant project before January 1, and actual construction might start by April or May, there remained three possible barriers.

Environmental opponents of the pipeline may still force a court test of the constitutionality of the new Alaska pipeline law. Senator Henry Jackson of Washington warned that if the project is delayed further in the courts, he will move to have the federal government build the line.

Initial reaction of the oil industry to the compromise legislative package enacted by the special legislative session indicated it might be acceptable. Individual companies must act, however, to determine if changes in the 1972 laws are sufficient to drop pending court actions.

Finally, even if all other signals are "go," the seven oil companies which own Alyeska Pipeline Service Company expect to have problems in financing the project which has soared from an estimated $900 million cost in 1969 to the present $4.5 billion.

Wanda Day Boelts, Valdez-Copper Basin

January 1974
Going into State Department of Fish and Game record books as the largest chum salmon ever taken on sports tackle in Alaska is this 15-pound, 8-ounce beauty caught July 27 by Barbara Ross of Palmer at Jacks Bay near Valdez. The previous record chum was a 15-pounder taken in 1972 from the Naha River.

D-2 Land Proposals... Fireworks Promised in Congress
February 1974

The often-changed map of Alaska is due for its greatest change if Congress approves plans for 83.47 million acres submitted on December 18 by Secretary of the Interior Rogers C.B. Morton.

Acting under provisions of the Alaska Native Claims Settlement Act, Secretary Morton recommended about 32.26 million acres for national parks, 31.4 million acres for addition to the national wildlife refuge system, 18.8 million acres for national forests and about 820,000 acres for wild and scenic rivers. Congress has five years in which to act on the Department of the Interior recommendations.

First reactions to the Morton plan for Alaska's D-2 "national interest" lands promise that fireworks and feuds will figure in Congress' deliberations on the proposals.

If the proposals for adding 31.59 million acres to the National Wildlife Refuge System are accepted by Congress, Alaska will have nearly five times more wildlife refuge acreage than all other states combined.

Nearly Suffocated in Heavy Snow
February 1974

Nearly suffocated by drifting snow, dehydrated, his feet frozen, Tom Reeves went from "despair to a determination not to give up" during the five days he spent in late November near Drift River, 100 miles southwest of Anchorage.

Reeve's bout with the wilderness began when he and Don Beasley, both of Anchorage, discovered after a successful hunting trip that their small aircraft would not take off with a full load of moose meat. Taking part of the load to a nearby airstrip they hoped would be free from snow, Beasley was to return for Reeves and the rest of the load. Beasley never came back.

Reeves estimates that he walked 40 miles through waist-deep snow attempting to reach the airstrip, but finally decided he had a better chance for survival and rescue on the beach of the river. He returned to the beach, just in time to signal a small plane overhead. The plane, piloted by George Ioanin of Anchorage, landed and flew Reeves back to Anchorage. Reported in good condition after his rescue, Reeves thanks his father for "teaching me how to be a woodsman." Beasley was still missing in mid-December.

First Mini-TVs in U.S.
January 1974

Television sets were high on the Christmas lists of residents of remote Unalaska and Saint Paul as the two island communities prepared for January operation of the first mini-TV stations in the nation.

Sponsored by the Alaska Educational Broadcast Commission, the new television concept was approved by the Federal Communications Commission which waived certain technical regulations to get the program started.

Costing only about $7,000 per station, the new system involves a 10-watt television translator which serves as a mini-TV transmitter. It is modified to accept a signal from a video cassette player, and has an effective transmitting radius of five miles.

Initial programming will rely heavily on videotape cassettes of such programs as "Sesame Street" and "The Advocates" made by the Public Broadcast System.

Bursting Dam Unleashes a Flood in Ketchikan

January 1974

Rupturing of Carlanna Lake Dam on October 26 caused an estimated $2.2 million damage in Ketchikan. Millions of gallons of water cascaded through the break in the 20-foot high, 100-foot long dam, sending a flood-riding battering ram of logs and stumps into a major Tongass Highway bridge. Flood waters surged through a mobile home court near the creek, damaging vehicles and homes.

Although there were no deaths or serious injuries in the disaster, its aftermath was widely felt in the Ketchikan Gateway Borough. For a time after the flood, 2,000 residents of the North Tongass Highway section and Ketchikan Pulp Company workers were cut off from the city. Both water and electrical utilities were damaged in the sudden flood. Carlanna Lake was the source for 20 percent of Ketchikan's water.

City officials estimate loss of the dam and damage to other utilities will approach $1.2 million, and private property losses were figured at more than $300,000. Declaration of the damaged section as a major disaster area led to establishment of a state-federal assistance center to aid victims.

While work crews completed a temporary log and earth bridge on the busy Tongass Highway in early November, state and borough officials were rushing plans for construction of a permanent bridge.

Jane Hanchett, Ketchikan Daily News

Pushing a log battering ram, the flood triggered by a break in Carlanna Lake Dam on October 26 nearly severed the Carlanna Creek Bridge on Ketchikan's busy Tongass Highway. This aerial photo shows pedestrians crossing the battered bridge the day after the disaster.

More Food for Moose
January 1974

More food for moose is a current concern of the Alaska Department of Fish and Game. In exploring ways of creating or maintaining better moose habitat, the department is considering an experimental range rehabilitation program which would involve mechanically knocking down and crushing mature timber to permit development of good browse such as second-growth willow, birch and aspen.

During the 1940's and 1950's fires and land clearing by homesteaders resulted in more browse for moose; in more recent years, improved fire prevention and decreased homesteading has allowed the land to revert to a climatic stage. "If the needs of moose are not considered along with those of humans, moose and moose hunting are certain to become things of the past," said Ron Somerville, regional game supervisor in Anchorage.

Dempster Highway Progress
February 1974

Construction of the Dempster Highway in northern Yukon progressed another 17 miles last summer, but the road is still open to the public only as far as Milepost 178 from its junction near Dawson City.

Wiley Oilfield Hauling of Red Deer, Alberta, had been given a contract to construct 58.5 miles of the gravel road to Milepost 236.8, near Eagle River, just south of the Arctic Circle. Winter conditions stalled the project, which is expected to start up again in March, for completion by late summer of 1974.

When completed, the Dempster will meet with the Mackenzie Highway at Arctic Red River, NWT; last summer, part of the road common to the Mackenzie and the Dempster between Arctic Red River and Inuvik, NWT, was constructed. Arctic Red River will be Milepost 379 of the Dempster and Milepost 892 of the Mackenzie Highway, on the Great Circle Route.

91 Years Late... Reparation for U.S. Navy's Shelling a Tlingit Village... $90,000 for Angoon

January 1974

Ninety-one years after the U.S. Navy's vessel *USS Favorite* shelled the Tlingit Indian village of Angoon on Admiralty Island, the federal government's reparation offer of $90,000 for the ill-advised bombardment was accepted by descendants of Angoon residents who saw their village destroyed.

Every Angoon child knows the story of the attack that continues to rankle residents. As reconstructed by lawyers who worked on the case brought before the Indian Claims Commission four years ago by the Tlingit-Haida Central Council, the trouble started in October, 1882 when a Tlingit shaman who was fishing with two white men was killed in a premature harpoon explosion. Following accepted tradition, the Angoon Indians asked the trading company for whom the dead man worked to pay 200 blankets for his loss. Instead of making the blanket payment, the manager sailed to Sitka and reported to U.S. officials that the surviving white men were being held hostage, a charge that was not substantiated.

The Navy sent two ships to Angoon, landing about 100 sailors and marines, and asking payment of 400 blankets from the Indians. The Navy warned that if the blankets were not paid, the canoes would be burned and the village shelled. The Tlingits evacuated the village and four days after the shaman's death, the Navy commenced firing. There is no record of Indians being killed in the attack, although local legend claims six members of the tribe died in the shelling.

Nine days before the case was to go trial last fall, federal attorneys offered payment of $90,000 for property destroyed in the 1882 mistake. Villagers met on October 21 and approved acceptance of the $90,000 in reparations. According to Clarence Jackson, president of the Tlingit-Haida Central Council, the payment was less important to the people of Angoon than the admission that the U.S. had been wrong 91 years ago.

John Lyman

Angoon from the beach. The large building is the Alaska Native Brotherhood hall (reprinted from ALASKA GEOGRAPHIC, Vol. 1, No. 3).

Survival in the Wilderness: A Yukon Stove, Big Supply of Wood... But No Lounging about in Pajamas!

February 1974

Wood stoves are making a comeback in the North, and those who dread the possible emergency-induced switch from oil to wood as a home-heating fuel should have no fears, according to one of Alaska's best known woodsmen.

A noted guide and trapper, Oscar Vogel with his family survived many cold winters at Stephan Lake near the Talkeetna Mountains, relying on a wood stove for heating their two-room cabin and cooking.

"We had a Yukon stove with a cast-iron top and a drum in the stovepipe for baking," Vogel recalled for ALASKA® magazine. "We were never uncomfortable and never more healthy," said the Anchorage pioneer. He emphasized that any wood stove should have a metal protector under it and on the wall nearest the stovepipe.

Mrs. Vogel brought her daughter to the cabin when she was a month old in December, 1949. "It reached 40 below zero that winter," she remembers. "Our daughter's first bed was a wicker laundry basket. At night before retiring we'd put a big log, preferably birch, on the fire and close all the dampers. There were still coals for starting a new fire the next morning."

The Vogels' cabin measured 14 by 32 feet. "A well-built, well-chinked cabin holds heat for a long time," said Vogel. After our daughter, Mary, was a year old, we didn't keep a fire through the night. During the coldest spells, we'd wake up to find ice in the water pail, but I'd have kindling ready and 10 minutes after starting the fire the cabin was warm."

Those who switch to wood heat will learn not to lounge about in pajamas or robes, according to Mrs. Vogel. "When our daughter got up, she got dressed," she explained. "She never caught a cold because she was properly dressed. During my winters in the cabin, I always wore house dresses, cotton stockings and slippers."

Oscar found it required 90 trees, most of them spruce averaging six to eight inches in diameter and about 45 feet long, to heat the cabin for a winter. Lacking a chain saw, the Vogels generated additional heat by sawing their fuel supply by hand.

More than 40 years ago, Oscar spent a winter beyond the treeline on the tip of the Alaska Peninsula. "My only fuel was small alders and they were usually green," he said. "I'd get a fire going and load the oven with green alders. While the next load was drying out, the green wood was giving off a pleasant aroma. When the 'baked' alders were ready to burn, I'd fill the oven with a new load. Stayed plenty warm all winter."

Birch was in short supply and often green at Stephan Lake, but to improve its burning quality, Mrs. Vogel often preheated it in her drum oven.

"We worked hard during our years of using wood to stay warm in the wilderness, but we certainly didn't suffer," reported Vogel.

Those who have a good cabin, good stove and access to firewood need have no fears on the coldest days, according to the Vogels.

"In many ways those winters in our wood-heated cabin were the best of our lives," said Mrs. Vogel.

Oscar Vogel
The Vogels' cabin at Stephan Lake where a wood stove kept the family warm for many winters.

Oscar Vogel
Vogel cut his firewood on the shore of Stephan Lake and rafted it to the cabin site. Ninety trees were needed to feed the stove through a winter. Shown here is part of a winter's supply.

> 'We worked hard during our years of using wood to stay warm in the wilderness, but we certainly didn't suffer.'

D-2 – a New Version
March 1974

First to modify the controversial recommendations made to Congress by Secretary of the Interior Rogers C.B. Morton on future use of 83.47 million acres of Alaska's public interest land apparently was Secretary Morton himself.

The official recommendation submitted to Congress on December 18, in accordance with provisions of the Alaska Native Claims Settlement Act, called for including 83.47 million acres of federal land in either national parks, wildlife refuges, national forests or wild and scenic rivers.

Largely ignoring the recommendations of the 10-member Federal-State Land Use Planning Commission, the Morton proposals were attacked by Alaskans because they apparently would put vast areas in 10-year deep-freeze for further study, prohibit multiple use on all but national forest lands and make no provision for transportation corridors.

The new version of the plan recommends a three-year study of the 63.85 million acres proposed for national parks and wildlife refuges, a cutback from the 10-year freeze originally recommended for study purposes. Another modification would allow mining and oil development on 24 million of the 31.6 million acres designated for national wildlife refuges. It was also revealed that sport and subsistence hunting would be permitted in areas proposed for national parks. The Interior Secretary's cover letter also recognized the need for transportation corridors through areas to be withdrawn.

Bush Village Barter
May 1974

Four skin masks equal one month's mortgage payment for a family in Anaktuvuk, and in 13 bush villages from Kaktovik on Barter Island to Ouzinkie on Kodiak Island, other Native families are finding unique ways to pay 25 percent of the cost they are charged for their new houses.

By midsummer, 101 Alaska Native families will have moved into modern new homes being built by the Alaska State Housing Authority with a $3 million state bond issue.

Average cost is $28,181 for each new two-bedroom, 870-square-foot house. Many are equipped with running water and indoor toilets.

Ferry 'Wickersham' Is Still Making Waves... High Bidder's $10 Million Offer Soars
February 1974

Sitting quietly in a berth at Seattle's Pier 48, Alaska's MV Wickersham was making waves in mid-December that spanned the Atlantic and splashed along the North Pacific coast.

High bidder for the retired pride of the state's ferry fleet when it was offered for sale last September was Sol Lines Limited of Holland with an offer of $10 million. But Sol Lines was unable to come up with the money, so the state has told its brokers to find a new buyer.

The Wickersham's stormy career embroiled a 27-member Dutch-Portuguese crew that was to have sailed the 363-foot ferry to Holland. When the plight of the seamen marooned in Seattle became known, the Dutch government promised to assist in paying back salaries and $20,000 in food and hotel bills. Meanwhile, the state had to pay $50,000 to renew the Wickersham's Pan American certificate, a document that must be current before it can be sold.

Evidence that the Wickersham is still cherished by some Alaskans came in mid-November when the Alaska Municipal League, representing 50 local governments, passed a unanimous resolution asking that the vessel not be sold. The Ketchikan Daily News suggested in early December that the controversial ferry be used for a bridge between Ketchikan and the new international airport on Gravina Island. And the Anchorage Daily Times recommended that the "Wicky" be used as a hotel ship at Valdez to ease an anticipated housing crunch when pipeline construction starts.

Japanese Crab Pots... Confiscated Gear Is Sold to Alaska Fishermen
March 1974

Some of the 4,100 Japanese crab pots which were seized by the U.S. Coast Guard last July near the Pribilof Islands are back fishing again—only this time they are being used by Alaskan fishermen.

Confiscated when they were found within the 12-mile U.S. contiguous fishery zone, the pots and 15 miles of heavy nylon line were returned to Kodiak. About 100 Kodiak fishermen bid nearly $30,000 for about 4,000 pots which were auctioned at the National Marine Fisheries Service facility at Gibson Cove in late November.

The pots were sold in lots of 100, and bids ranged from $5 to $10 per pot. The NMFS retained about 150 pots for lending to fisheries programs of the state's colleges.

The Green Light
* * *
A Flurry of Activity with Pipeline Permit

March 1974

Streams of heavily loaded trucks began moving across a Yukon River ice bridge in late January, carrying supplies for construction camps needed to build the 789-mile trans-Alaska pipeline.

The winter movement of freight was just one sign of an upbeat tempo surging through Alaska following the issuance of a permit for the massive project on January 23 by Secretary of the Interior Rogers C.B. Morton.

A portent of the importance of the $4.5 billion project to Alaska came in December when the state's Associated Press, broadcasters and publishers named passage of the Alaska pipeline bill as the state's top news story of 1973.

Anticipating issuance of the key permit by Secretary Morton for the job that will employ a peak of about 13,000 workers, a record 348 job-seekers were waiting in line at Fairbanks' Laborer's Local 942 when the doors opened on January 2, 1974. Their objective was to get high on the list of workers who will be dispatched to pipeline and related jobs. The total number on the Fairbanks' union's rolls on January 2 was equal to the total for all of 1973.

The pipeline was certain to play a major role in deliberations of the State Legislature which met in Juneau on January 21. Departments of state government and individual cities were pressing for increased funds to meet problems resulting from an influx of pipeline workers.

Modular units manufactured in Calgary, Alberta, for housing pipeline workers north of the Yukon River began moving north over the Alaska Highway to Fairbanks, with delivery promised by March 1. The $5.9 million contract awarded by Alyeska Pipeline Service Company calls for 26 units, each with a 52-man capacity, a 390-man kitchen and dining hall and four larger kitchens and dining units.

Susan Andrews, Anchorage Daily Times
Work was proceeding in January on construction of a 75-foot wide, five-foot thick ice bridge across the Yukon River. This aerial photo shows outline of the bridge which is being used by heavy trucks hauling material needed to resupply camps established north of the Yukon for construction of the northern segment of the trans-Alaska pipeline.

ALPS, the company formed by seven major oil companies with North Slope holdings to build the largest single privately financed project in history, started meshing gears after a four-year wait for the green light. Peter DeMay, ALPS vice-president for construction, moved to Anchorage, in preparation for initial work in completing a pipe-haul road north of the Yukon River, construction of camps, preparing the difficult Keystone Canyon for pipe laying and site work at the Valdez terminal.

A decision was expected by mid-February on naming the firm selected to monitor construction of the 48-inch pipeline from Prudhoe Bay to Valdez, and the state and federal governments signed an agreement providing equal surveillance authority. Retired General Andrew P. Rollins Jr. will head the federal team of pipeline overseers, working with a staff of 40 based in Anchorage.

The tightening bond between Alaska and Southwest oil centers was emphasized by the application of Alaska and Braniff Airlines for direct service from Anchorage and Fairbanks to Dallas-Fort Worth and Houston, and a similar bid by Western and Continental Airlines for an Anchorage link to Denver, Oklahoma City, Dallas-Fort Worth and Houston.

Hoping to ease traffic pressure on metropolitan Fairbanks, the Department of Highways announced it plans to start work this spring on a by-pass road from Badger Road south of the city to Chena Hot Springs Road north of Fairbanks. It would send North Slope traffic around the city proper.

Meanwhile, interest in Cook Inlet's oil and gas was revived with a December sale of Lower Cook Inlet leases near Homer that was second only to the historic 1969 North Slope sale in profit for the state. Lead by major oil companies, bidders paid $24,824,927.50 for 64 tracts. Standard Oil of California bid $7.6 million for a single 2,477-acre tract in Kachemak Bay. It hopes to start drilling on the tract this year.

With the decision as to ownership of much of Lower Cook Inlet's potential offshore oil land still in litigation, Governor William A. Egan is pressing for a state-federal understanding that will allow leasing in the disputed area, pending a final court decision.

The importance of Cook Inlet to Alaska and the nation was underlined with the announcement that the McArthur Field 65 miles southwest of Anchorage has produced more than 200 million barrels of oil since 1967.

Cash for Natives
April 1974

First major cash benefits of the Alaska Native Claims Settlement Act were being received in February by members of some of the 12 Native regional corporations in Alaska. Initial payment to approximately 70,000 Natives approved for enrollment ranged from about $171 to nearly $1,000.

Troubles with names and addresses on enrollment lists delayed payments to 9,000 members of Fairbanks-based Doyon Limited until mid-February, and similar problems were expected to delay issuance of checks to 6,000 members of the Cook Inlet Region until mid-March.

First checks were received in early February by most members of NANA regional corporation with headquarters in Kotzebue, Bering Straits corporation in Nome and Sealaska corporation based in Juneau.

John Borbridge, president of Sealaska, estimated that individual cash benefits from the Settlement Act would range from $6,000 to $10,000 when the final federal and state payments to the $962.5 million settlement have been made.

Concerned that hustlers and confidence men may try to get their hands in the Natives' pockets, the office of the state attorney general for consumer affairs is going to conduct consumer protection seminars in Fairbanks, Bethel, Kotzebue, Anchorage, Kodiak, Juneau, Sitka, Petersburg, Wrangell and Ketchikan. It will use newsletters printed in English and Native dialects to expose money extraction schemes as they arise.

Meat, Fish Aplenty; No Need for Money

February 1974

When we live in the bush we don't have to worry about spending money. There is lots of things to eat. Meat and fish and some duck and any birds. If we stay in town all the time then we spend money every day. Everything costs too much so we spend a lot of money.

—Dora Gully,
Fort Franklin correspondent
NEWS OF THE NORTH,
Yellowknife, NWT

Miracle of Survival . . . Abandoned Infant Girl Survives Two Hours in Anchorage's Biting Zero Temperature

February 1974

Tiny but tough, a blue-eyed baby girl only four days old amazed hospital workers in Anchorage in early November by recovering from the lowest body temperature they had ever seen in a newborn infant. Wrapped in a towel and lying in a cardboard box, the abandoned infant lay in zero temperatures in the vestibule of a church for an estimated two hours before being discovered by a clergyman and rushed to Alaska's largest private hospital.

She was stiff, her skin was hard and waxy-blue and her temperature, at 75.5 degrees, was more than 23 degrees below normal—an extreme condition that even adults seldom survive. The barely breathing child was first wrapped in warm, wet towels and rushed to a radiant-heat bed in the special care nursery, then transferred to a 106-degree whirlpool bath for rapid rewarming. This decision was a calculated risk, for no one is certain whether extremely frozen persons should be thawed quickly or slowly.

Immersing the baby until only her lips and nostrils were above water, doctor and nurses knelt around the bath and tensely waited. After 10 minutes her temperature was up to 85 degrees and her skin was pinker; after another 10 minutes her respiration and heartbeat had improved enough for them to take her out of the hot bath. Nine days later little "Jane Doe," described by physiotherapist and mother of five, Mrs. Eloise Payne, as "a beautiful baby" was turned over to foster parents, leaving behind a fan club of adoring nurses in a hospital aptly named Providence.

1974

Woman Musher Drives Toward Second Win

Alice Puster, Anchorage Daily Times

April 1974

Roxy Brooks of Fairbanks drives toward the finish line and her second successive victory in the 1974 Anchorage Fur Rendezvous' Women's Sled Dog Race. Mrs. Brooks finished the three-lap race in 118 minutes, six seconds, only 40 seconds ahead of Donna Bruce of Anchorage. Third among the 10-team field was Shirley Gavin of Chugiak with a time of 121:44.

Eielson's Mail Flight Was Historic First
May 1974

On February 21, 1924, Ben Eielson donned three layers of clothes, loaded his Liberty DeHavilland biplane with survival gear, spare parts and 164 pounds of mail and took off on Alaska's first scheduled air-mail flight.

Fifty years later, the Cook Inlet Historical Society recalled that inaugural air-mail flight with a program and display of Eielson memorabilia at the Anchorage Historical and Fine Arts Museum.

For $2 a mile, Eielson flew between Fairbanks and McGrath, with erratic instruments and no radio. Taking off from McGrath, he started the biplane unassisted, because no one there had ever seen a plane before.

The pioneer aviator was killed in a 1929 crash, while on a rescue flight to an American vessel icebound near eastern Siberia.

New Use for Old Cans
January 1974

Old beer cans aren't just fading away in Alaska. They are being wrapped in reflective tape to brighten boundaries of the state airport at Dillingham.

The State Division of Aviation recently shipped 126 wooden stakes, reflective tapes and instructions for converting beer cans into runway markers to the manager of Dillingham's airport. The beer cans have been wrapped with red and white reflective tape, nailed to the stakes and spaced every 200 feet along the runway boundaries.

5,103 Homesteads since '08 ... But No More
June 1974

Homesteading in Alaska ended on March 29 with publication in the Federal Register of Public Order 5418, the document, signed by the Secretary of the Interior, which withdrew about 15 million acres of unreserved federal land from the public domain. Now reclassified as federal public interest land, the acreage, which was still technically open to homesteading, was located mainly in interior and western Alaska.

The Department of the Interior action, which ended an adventure-some, soul-testing era that began with the first Alaskan homestead in 1908, was taken under authority of the Alaska Native Claims Settlement Act. A major reason for the withdrawal, according to BLM officials, was to prevent would-be homesteaders from cutting off access to adjacent public lands.

The desire of Americans to acquire a maximum of 160 acres by homesteading resulted in several hundred letters each month to BLM headquarters in Anchorage, plus continuing personal calls at the office.

The 15 million acres now withdrawn were not good for homesteading, according to the BLM. The law requires that at least 20 of the 160 acres be cleared for farming, and the remote and inaccessible tracts, stretching from the Kuskokwim Valley to north of Kotzebue, were rated as poor farming land.

Federal land records indicate about 5,103 homesteads involving 593,217 acres have been patented in Alaska since 1908, most of them in the Fairbanks, Delta Junction, Glennallen, Palmer, Talkeetna, Anchorage, Kenai and Homer areas. The latest withdrawal does not affect mining exploration and operation in the 15 million acres.

Following last year's cessation of the state's open-to-entry program for wilderness tracts, the Department of the Interior reclassification now makes it impossible to acquire Alaskan land through other than purchase or lease from the State Division of Lands or private owners.

Alice Puster, Anchorage Daily Times

March 1974

Susan Fleischer, a one-dog musher sends her "team" over the pedestrian crossing recently completed over Anchorage's busy C Street. The overpass is heavily used by skiers, bikers and little girl mushers.

Endangered Wolf? Controversy Rages over Wildlife Poster
June 1974

A photo of a wolf on a National Wildlife Week poster has fanned new flames in the controversy over whether the wolf is an endangered species. Prepared by the National Wildlife Federation, the poster showed a wolf, with the overline "We Care About Endangered Wildlife."

Replying to the poster and its implications, Joe Nava, executive officer of the Institute of Arctic Biology at the University of Alaska, wrote Tom Kimball, president of the Native Wildlife Federation:

"Your poster will clearly give the broad impression that wolves are endangered. This is the impression that other organizations would like to give for the eventual purpose of eliminating the harvest of wolves.

"While some wolves may be endangered in some states, this is not the case in Alaska. We have healthy populations of wolves and the Alaska Department of Fish and Game is now considering more adequate wolf control in some areas so that the large game herbivore populations can be more equitably distributed between man and wolf for food.

"Alaska desires to retain management control over its wildlife resources, but pressure which is built up by such things as your wildlife week poster is forcing federal control of the resources on us."

Skookum Jim's Legacy
January 1974

Skookum Jim's gold nugget watch chain has found a final resting place in the MacBride Museum at Whitehorse. The famous gold nugget and diamond chain was seen by thousands of Yukon visitors, after it was purchased from Skookum Jim's estate in 1915 and displayed in the window of the former KeeBird Store on Main Street in Whitehorse. Since the store was sold three years ago, the valuable artifact had been stored by the Royal Canadian Mounted Police.

New Senior Tax Break
March 1974

Whatever your income, if you're an Alaskan 65 or over, the state will foot your property tax bill this year. Expanding the 1973 law, which allowed property tax exemptions for those over 65 but with an income less than $10,000 per year, the state retained only the age stipulation.

Robert Dozier, state assessor with Community and Regional Affairs in Juneau, estimates the program will cost Alaska $550,000 this year, but he adds, "It's all so up in the air we can't make any predictions." Under last year's property tax program, the state paid slightly more than $220,000.

1974

It Could Happen Only in Alaska...
January 1974

- Cade and Wade Goodridge are twin brothers who were born 165 air miles and four hours apart. Cade was born in Cordova on the morning of October 14 to Mrs. John Goodridge. Meanwhile, a medical evacuation plane arrived and flew Mrs. Goodridge to Anchorage's Providence Hospital, where Wade was born at noon. Both mother and sons were "doing fine" in Cordova in early November.

- There's no doubt that Ross "Tiger" Hodges of Soldotna met the solo requirements for his private pilot's license. On his sixteenth birthday in early October, young Hodges flew nine different airplanes ranging from a Cherokee 140 to a twin-engine Piper Aztec. His parents own Soldotna Flying Service.

- Most high school students wash cars to raise funds for school activities. The senior class at Delta High School has varied the technique—they are washing airplanes to raise money needed for a trip to Hawaii.

- While Boeing 747's roar overhead, bow and arrow hunters are again stalking moose in a controlled, either-sex moose hunt within the boundaries of Anchorage International Airport. Aimed at reducing the danger of moose-aircraft confrontations, the season opened November 1 and ends March 31, 1974.

Charles D. Evans

January 1974
Blazing down the ice at the Anchorage Sports Arena, these 10-year-olds prove the popularity of hockey in Alaska. Their tryouts started at 5:30 a.m. as volunteer coaches began selecting teams from more than 800 future hockey stars.

A Bridge to Town? No! 'We Love Old-style Life'
June 1974

Residents of Pennock Island, in Tongass Narrows at Ketchikan, want to keep it an island, inaccessible except by water. In response to a proposal that a bridge be built to connect Pennock to Revillagigedo Island and Ketchikan, 73 residents of the island signed a petition which states, "The undersigned residents and property owners of Pennock Island wish to voice our disapproval of the proposed bridge connecting Ketchikan with Pennock."

"We love the old-style life on Pennock and our boats and don't want to give them up for a bridge," said Mrs. Cindy Lorentz, an island resident. She also said, in a letter to *The Ketchikan Daily News,* "The plans for this bridge will not only ruin Pennock Islanders, cost a great deal of money, be highly impractical, but also of extreme importance, the only feasible route is on the south end of the island, and the entire south end is an Indian burial ground with many graves that should not be violated and should be protected and preserved."

One proposal would result in two bridges: one from Revillagigedo to Pennock Island, the other to connect Pennock to Gravina Island upon which Ketchikan's municipal airport is located. The airport is now reached from town by ferry.

Pennock Island is just over three miles long and a little less than a mile wide at its widest.

$5.7 Billion Proposed for a Gas Line from Alaska
June 1974

Before construction of the trans-Alaska oil pipeline was officially under way, its claim as the largest privately financed construction project in history was overshadowed by a proposed $5.7 billion, 2,600-mile gas pipeline from Prudhoe Bay through Canada to the U.S. Midwest.

Already causing political sparks in Alaska, Canada and Washington, D.C., the long gas line took on flesh and bones on March 21, 1974, when Alaskan Arctic Gas Pipeline Company filed applications with the Department of the Interior and Federal Power Commission for authority to build the line. At the same time Canada Arctic Gas Pipeline Limited filed similar applications with Canada's National Energy Board and the Department of Indian Affairs and Northern Development.

Formed by a consortium of 27 companies which claim to have spent $70 million in seven years of research and engineering, the joint application calls for moving four billion cubic feet of gas per day—about six percent of the present North American demand for gas. The proposed construction schedule calls for start of construction in 1976 and delivery of the first gas by 1979.

As proposed by Alaskan Arctic Gas, the 195 miles of pipeline in Alaska—from Prudhoe Bay to the Canadian border—would cost about $600 million and would require a peak work force of 2,500 men in the third winter of construction. In addition to tapping Prudhoe Bay's 26 trillion cubic feet of natural gas and that from the Mackenzie Delta fields, Alaska Arctic Gas has its eye on the estimated 300 trillion cubic feet of gas in Alaska's Arctic.

Opposition to the Alaskan Arctic Gas proposal is expected later this year from Alaska El Paso Natural Gas, which is planning to apply to the Federal Power Commission for authority to construct an 803-mile gas pipeline from Prudhoe Bay to a terminal near Cordova. The El Paso plan calls for liquefying the gas and moving it to the West Coast in LNG tankers.

Although major owners of the Prudhoe Bay gas fields are allied with Alaskan Arctic Gas, the El Paso strategy is to get a commitment from the State of Alaska for the state's 12 percent royalty share of Prudhoe Bay gas. There was early evidence that routing of the Prudhoe Bay natural gas would be a hot topic for politicians in the 1974 elections.

Free Fuel for Village... Environment Is Saved
January 1974

The village of Anaktuvuk Pass received free fuel, and a possible environmental threat to the Toolik River was removed this fall due to prompt action and cooperation between an oil company and state and federal agencies. During the summer, a weathered pillow tank at Home Oil's inactive drill site about 50 miles southwest of Prudhoe Bay developed a small leak, and state environmental officials (alerted by BLM) feared that two tanks containing 80,000 gallons of diesel fuel could rupture, spilling oil into the nearby Toolik River.

Home Oil offered to give away the fuel, and repaired the airstrip at the site so that a Hercules aircraft could land safely. The Bureau of Indian Affairs transported the fuel to the Brooks Range village, which has been plagued in recent years by chronic heating fuel shortages.

The High Cost of Illegal Fishing
June 1974

The cost of illegal fishing in Alaska's waters reached a new high on March 29, when the Japanese owners of the *Ebisu Maru* paid $300,000 for release of the vessel. The payment involved a $290,000 out-of-court settlement and a $10,000 fine imposed on Shoji Murosawa, 22, skipper of the vessel.

The Coast Guard Cutter *Midgett* seized the vessel on March 19 about five miles from Cape Tanak on the north coast of Umnak Island. Although the *Ebisu Maru* was outside the territorial three-mile limit, one of its long lines was within 2.2 miles of shore.

Appearing before U.S. District Judge James A. von der Hedyt in Anchorage, the young captain pleaded "no contest." The $10,000 fine was recommended by U.S. Attorney G. Kent Edwards. The owners paid $290,000 to settle a civil suit brought by the U.S. against the vessel, its equipment and catch. Consisting mainly of cod and other bottom fish, the Japanese vessel's catch was valued at $16,000 to $17,000.

The previous record payment by a foreign vessel for illegal fishing was on February 26, when the Soviet Union paid $250,000 in fines and settlement after the Coast Guard apprehended a Russian stern trawler 9.5 miles from Lighthouse Rock near the Semidi Islands.

Arctic Merit Badges
January 1974

Boy Scouts not familiar with Canada's Arctic would have trouble earning merit badges at Pelly Bay in the Northwest Territories. Sister Victori Servant, who organized a Scout troop at Pelly Bay four years ago, offers merit badges for igloo building, dog team training, skinning seals, hunting and fishing, lamp making and carving.

Karen Lee, The Frontiersman

January 1974
Cabbage king of the Matanuska Valley, Ray Rebarchek stands beside the 15 giant heads that fill his pickup truck. Largest shown here weighs 69 pounds. Rebarchek-grown cabbages, ranging from 54 to 60 pounds, were displayed last fall at exhibits in Florida, Maine, Pennsylvania and Ohio.

They're 'Champions' All:
26 Mushers Race 1,100 Grueling Miles in the Iditarod Trail Sled Dog Classic

June 1974

By definition of Nome's Mayor Robert Renshaw, who declared that everyone who finished the Iditarod Sled Dog Race from Anchorage to Nome was a "champion," 26 names have been added to the roster of "champion" mushers who have completed the grueling 1,100-mile endurance test.

Leading the parade of winners in the second running of the race was Carl Huntington of Galena, who finished in 20 days, 15 hours, 2 minutes and 7 seconds to win $12,000. Second was Warner Vent of Huslia, whose father, Bobbie Vent, finished in the same position last year.

Oldest musher to finish was Joel Kottke, 61, of Anchorage, who trailed the only two women entrants, Mary Shields and Lolly Medley, both of Fairbanks. Winning the lantern for last place was Red Olson of Fairbanks who reached Nome after 29 days, 6 hours, 36 minutes and 19 seconds on the trail.

Others who finished in order behind Huntington and Vent were Herbert Nayokpuk, Rudy Demoski, Dan Seavey, Ken Chase, Rayme Redington, Ron Aldrich, Joee Redington, Dick Mackey, Joe Redington Sr., Tom Mercer, Bud Smyth.

Rod Perry, Dave Olson, Reuben Seetot, Robert Ivan, Victor Kotongan, Dr. Terry Adkins, Tim White, Desi Kamerer, Clifton Jackson, Mary Shields, Lolly Medley, Joel Kottke and Red Olson. Although they had dropped from the race, Bill Vaudrin of Anchorage and The Rev. Bernie Willis of Gambell also drove their teams to the Nome finish line.

Worst perils of the trip for two mushers were in Nome and on the outskirts of the city. Finishing fourteenth, Rod Perry's team was struck by a taxi as it moved to the finish line at 3:30 a.m. on March 28. Perry hauled four dogs from under the cab, and none were injured.

Less lucky was Tim White of Taylor Falls, Minnesota, who finished twentieth. A snowmobiler struck White from behind, 18 miles from Nome; the musher sustained cuts that required medical care.

Gordon Fowler, Anchorage Daily Times

Flashing a winner's smile, Carl Huntington, 26, reaches the Nome finish line of the Iditarod Trail Sled Dog Race just 20 days, 15 hours, 2 minutes and 7 seconds after leaving Anchorage on March 2, 1974. Beating a starting field of 43 teams, the Galena musher collected $12,000 for his victory, in the 1,100-mile contest.

Power from Snettisham
March 1974

JUNEAU—Now furnishing one-half Juneau's electricity, the new Snettisham hydroelectric project needs "more operating time" to prove its reliability, cautions Alaska Electric Light and Power Company's vice-president, Franz Nagel. Inaugurated December 1, the project has cut diesel-generated power consumption to one-fourth its previous level and is ultimately slated to replace all diesel-generating facilities in the city.

AELP General Manager Bill Corbus, urging electrical conservation, warns Juneau residents against switching from oil to electricity for heating. The 42-mile transmission line between Snettisham and the Thane substation could fall victim to snowslides, high winds or other natural phenomena. Should the project fail, Juneau would revert to diesel-generated power.

Noting "we're only going to build as fast as the load builds," Nagel estimates the project will not see completion for 20 years.

Once a Land Bridge
July 1974

Cape Krusenstern, a two-million-acre portion of land, thought once to have formed the land bridge between Asia and Alaska, has been designated a National Historical landmark by the U.S. Department of the Interior. Of known archeological interest and the largest historical landmark in the country, Cape Krusenstern is under the jurisdiction of the National Park Service and is administered by the State Division of Parks. The designation protects the land and allows the state to administer guidelines for protection.

Women Eye High-Paying, Heavy-Duty Pipeline Jobs
June 1974

Female reluctance and male scepticism stand in the way, but some Alaskan women are on the move toward heavy construction jobs on the trans-Alaska pipeline.

Cara Peters, director of Better Jobs For Alaska Women, an organization designed to show women the availability of high-paying heavy-duty pipeline jobs, says, "We have argued for at least 800 women to be hired for line work."

Eight major labor unions to be involved in pipeline construction maintain they are willing to train and hire capable women, but are averse to creating special facilities for women employees.

Ms. Peters points out that women are unlikely to start immediately "flocking to the jobs" traditionally viewed as for-men-only.

One woman who was admitted to the Teamsters' truck driving school, only to be dismissed four days later on grounds of inability to handle the job, has vowed to fight the dismissal. Betty Wooley reports she was once asked why she didn't apply for a job cooking in the construction camps. Responded Mrs. Wooley, mother of six, "If I wanted to cook, I'd stay home."

TV for Eskimos . . .
Good News and Bad News
July 1974

There was good news and bad news in the report on the six-month experiment, Project Wales, that brought modern television to the remote Bering Sea Eskimo village, Wales, last year. The good news is that Wales residents like television and were sorry to see it leave the village when the experiment ended, according to University of Alaska, Anchorage, professors R.J. Madigan and W. Jack Peterson. They revealed their findings of villagers' experiences with television, their viewing habits and how television affected their lives in a 132-page report, *Television and Social Change on the Bering Strait*. The bad news is that some people, especially those relatively far removed from the village, felt that television would destroy the Eskimo culture and the autonomy of the village.

Other findings were that villagers preferred commercial to educational TV; most watched movies and no one watched a program titled "How to Study"; attendance at community meetings dropped during television-viewing times but when it was announced that television would be stopped until a scheduled Native land claims meeting was concluded, ". . . attendance at the meeting was high and business rapidly accomplished," researchers reported.

Harry R. Mitchell

A Toklat Grizzly Sets his Sight on the Park Road
July 1974

Follow the nose of this guidepost-loving Toklat grizzly and you'll head for Entrance Station of Mount McKinley National Park. The debonair bear was hugging the post at the Stony Hill parking area.

A Pensive Husky? Or a Tired Wolf?

Judy Johnson

July 1974

Pensive husky is the wrong description for this handsome animal. She is Kechika, a full-blooded wolf, one of three raised by Mr. and Mrs. Ed Johnson of Kechika River, British Columbia. The Johnsons obtained the wolves as pups with eyes still not opened. Kechika had injured her right paw and was resting on the Kechika River ice when this photo was taken.

Potato History
July 1974

Agricultural history was made in late April, when more than 100 tons of Matanuska Valley potatoes were shipped to Seattle and Portland markets. A surplus of Alaskan potatoes, the high price of spuds in the Pacific Northwest and a favorable backhaul rate from Sea-Land made the shipment feasible. Paul Hupper, Palmer wholesaler, who packaged the deal involving five van loads, each carrying 22 tons of potatoes, said the shipment marked the first time Alaskan farm produce was exported to the South 49. He said the Alaska product was "well accepted." Additional shipments of Alaska-grown potatoes to Outside markets are being planned.

Bristol Bay – Disaster Area
July 1974

Without a commercial fishing season for red salmon for the first time in 81 years, Bristol Bay has been declared a disaster area by Governor William A. Egan. The governor and Congressional delegation were urging in mid-May that President Nixon also declare the area a disaster area to qualify for federal aid.

Governor Egan advised President Nixon that the desperate plight of about 5,000 Bristol Bay residents is "a man-made disaster, brought on by federal diplomatic policies, that is every bit as damaging to the lives of people as many natural disasters are."

Following an International Marine Fisheries Conference conducted at King Salmon in late April, the governor urged Secretary of State Henry Kissinger to close to high-seas fishing three areas in the western Aleutians.

"Direct and proximate cause of this human distress is the total destruction by Japanese high-seas fleets of the Bristol Bay red salmon fishery," said the governor in his plea to the White House. He claimed that in two decades, the Japanese have taken more than 40 million salmon of Alaska origin.

A Native 'Saving' Spree
July 1974

Fears that receipt of cash payments to Alaska's Natives would result in spending sprees haven't materialized among Eskimos of Northwestern Alaska, according to Chuck Baker, manager of the Kotzebue Branch of Alaska National Bank of the North. Following issuance in March and April, of the checks, which averaged $180 per person, the Kotzebue bank reported 1,100 new accounts.

"Six hundred of those are savings accounts, and the majority came from land claims settlement checks," said Baker. "Our branches in Nome and Barrow report the same thing, except they have even more Native accounts than we do."

The Seas Consume a Wounded Ship

Blake McKinley, Kodiak Mirror

June 1974

Victim of a February collision with a deadhead which punched a hole in her hull, and winds which later drove her ashore, the FV COLLETTE is pounded by the sea at Spruce Cape near Kodiak. The 47-footer is owned by Lloyd Sharratt, who escaped in a skiff with three crewmen.

Profitable Farm Carved from Wilderness near Fairbanks
August 1974

Proving that the pioneering spirit is very much alive in Alaska, the Julian V. Fowler family of Mile 78, Richardson Highway, has been named National Farm Family of the Year by the Farmers Home Administration.

In announcing the winner, Secretary of Agriculture Earl L. Butz cited the Fowlers for their demonstration of ingenuity, integrity and independence in carving a profitable farm out of the wilderness 80 miles southeast of Fairbanks and 30 miles northwest of Delta Junction.

The Fowlers moved to Alaska from Nebraska in 1947. They cleared their homestead and began dairying in 1960. When a Fairbanks creamery on which they depended stopped operating, the Fowlers and their four children established their own processing plant and delivery service. The Fowler Dairy Farm now spreads over 360 acres, and includes about 95 head of stock, with 60 milking cows.

New Ferry Route
June 1974

Prince of Wales Island is likely to be Southeastern Alaska's newest tourist mecca with the state ferry *Chilkat* now making a regular run between Ketchikan and Hollis, near the head of the island's Kasaan Bay. Once on the island, travelers can drive to Klawock over the state-built and maintained 23-mile gravel road and from Klawock seven miles to Craig. (The latter stretch is being reconstructed this summer.) A road leading from Klawock to Thorne Bay now is maintained jointly by the U.S. Forest Service and Ketchikan Pulp Company and may be opened for public use this summer.

Although logging roads are scattered through the island, safety considerations may keep them closed to the public during logging operations. About 15 additional miles of road, starting about midpoint of the Hollis-Klawock road and leading to Hydaburg, will be built in connection with planned timber sales, according to Forest Service planners.

Ship Rises from Grave
August 1974

A ship come up from her grave was in Wrangell at the beginning of May, getting spruced up and readied for work again. The vessel is the 44-foot troller-halibut boat REBEL, from Port Protection. REBEL spent the past six months on the bottom off the north shore of Kupreanof Island. She was sunk by a freak wave, sending two Wrangell men, Leonard Angerman and Rob Rooney, and her owner, Ted Case, to shore in a small skiff. The trio spent 20 hours huddling by a warming fire before rescue came. REBEL was recently located and raised and looked—at least outwardly—hardly scarred from her half year beneath the water.

Seafood and Scrap... Wood for Chopsticks

JAMES R. MACKOVJAK

August 1974

Alaskan exports for the Orient were being loaded aboard three ships tied up at Seward's dock in late April. At left in aerial photo is the *AGELOS MICHAEL*, taking aboard scrap metal for Japan. At right is the *ZENLINGLORY*, being loaded with wood products to be converted into chopsticks in Korea. Smaller ship on face of dock is the *DONG BANG NO. 73*, carrying a load of seafood for Japanese gourmets.

1974

Building Boom for Anchorage, Fairbanks, Valdez

July 1974

Start of the largest privately financed construction project in history, building of the $4.5 billion trans-Alaska pipeline from Prudhoe Bay to Valdez, was heralded with this banner in the April 29 edition of the Anchorage Daily Times.

A single sentence began a new era for Alaska on April 29, 1974. Carrying an Anchorage dateline, an announcement by Alyeska Pipeline Service Company read: "Construction work began today on the trans-Alaska pipeline project."

Because it was so long in coming, the historic day on which 1,200 workers north of the Yukon River began work directly on the pipeline was unmarked by celebrations.

Setting the stage for the clear green light on the $4.5 billion project, largest privately financed undertaking in history, was the April signing of union agreements, issuance of a certificate of public convenience by the three-member Alaska Pipeline Commission, and granting of a pipeline right-of-way lease across state land by Commissioner of Natural Resources Charles F. Herbert. The Department of the Interior permit for crossing federal lands was issued on January 23, 1974.

Optimism gushing from the work start on the pipeline produced mid-May forecasts that Anchorage, Fairbanks and Valdez would set new building records this year.

The first phase of the project, construction of a 360-mile haul road from the Yukon River to Prudhoe Bay, was in full swing by mid-May. Bechtel, Inc., management contractor for the road and pipeline, estimated about 2,177 workers will be building road north of the Yukon. Although the road project isn't slated for completion until the spring of 1975, a push is under way to finish it by December. The peak 1974 work force for road-building, work at the Valdez terminal and pump stations is estimated by ALPS at about 9,100 workers. The 1975 total is expected to reach 14,200 workers, tapering back to 10,600 in 1976.

Fluor Alaska, Inc., was authorized on May 1 to proceed as general contractor on the Valdez marine terminal and pumping stations along the route. Work assigned to Fluor will cost about $1 billion.

Prepared by Bechtel, a "Summary Network Analysis Diagram" gives production goals through 1977, including pumping of 600,000 barrels of oil a day to Valdez by mid-1977. Between Milepost zero at Valdez and Milepost 795.43 at Prudhoe Bay there will be 20 construction camps. The project is divided into six sections, three south of the Yukon River and three to the north.

The magnitude of the task of stringing the 48-inch diameter pipe across Alaska is shown by figures released by ALPS. Thirty million cubic yards of gravel will be required to complete the haul road, which will include 17 bridge crossings over streams. The pipe will pass over a 4,800-foot pass above the Dietrich River in the Brooks Range. To prevent thawing of underlying permafrost, Dow Chemical Company has been given a purchase order for 49 million board feet of plastic foam insulation.

Pipeline fever has even spread to an accelerated search for additional oil and gas throughout the state. The April bulletin of the Division of Oil and Gas stated: "The number of active rigs in the state is a two-digit figure!.... It has been almost four years since activity has been so great.... The future appears brighter for the first time since 1970."

While the state keeps pressing for a lease sale in contested waters of Lower Cook Inlet, Shell Oil is advancing with plans for an offshore test south of Anchor Point and Standard Oil of California has applied for a permit to drill 12.5 miles west of Kasilof. Amoco is reported to have found oil in a test hole near Cold Bay on the Alaska Peninsula.

Evidence that Alaska's oil era will continue to expand far beyond completion of the trans-Alaska pipeline was given the legislative committee by John H. McKeever, a veteran geologist. He said that the "best overall estimate of Alaska's total oil potential comes to about 74 billion barrels." His estimate of the state's natural gas wealth added up to 423 trillion cubic feet.

ALPS photo by Steve McCutcheon

Men and machines at work on a segment of the 360-mile pipe-haul road north of the Yukon River. Extending to Prudhoe Bay, the road will be used to supply equipment for the north end of the 796-mile pipeline route. More than 2,000 men are expected to be working on the road project by midsummer.

Tusks vs. Pipeline
August 1974

A mammoth tusk could halt the massive machinery re-arranging terrain along the trans-Alaska pipeline route. Under a contract with Alyeska Pipeline Service Company, archeological teams from the University of Alaska at Fairbanks and Alaska Methodist University have authority to stop construction and remove archeological remains unearthed on the 796-mile pipeline corridor.

Six professional archeologists are on the line now, with more to come as pipeline work expands. More than 200 areas showing "traces of prehistoric occupation" were mapped in pre-construction studies, according to John Cook, head of the University of Alaska Anthropology Department, and many more finds are anticipated with deeper pipeline excavation.

Twenty new sites have been discovered this year. All artifacts and archeological remains will be placed in the University of Alaska museum.

Derby Scholarships
September 1974

Territorial Sportsmen, Inc., which sponsors the Golden North Salmon Derby at Juneau each year, in June awarded $20,000 in college scholarships to eight graduating seniors at the Juneau-Douglas High School. Each of the eight received $2,500 to be used in the pursuit of a career in the conservation field. Money for the scholarship fund is derived from the sale of salmon turned in during the annual salmon derby.

Living without Cash...
Food from Land, River
August 1974

The land and waters of the lower Yukon and Kuskokwim River drainages provided one and one-quarter pounds of food for thousands of Natives each day in January and February, 1974, according to a recent survey conducted by the Association of Village Council Presidents.

The AVCP conducted the survey to convince congress of the heavy dependence of Natives of the region on the land for subsistence. Food consumption calendars were mailed to 2,100 household heads in the AVCP region, and 1,125 were returned.

During the first two months of the year, the survey showed that 7,000 people harvested more than 534,000 pounds of food, most of it fish, but also including land and sea mammals and birds.

"Subsistence allows us to maintain and feed our families without cash," said Charles Kiariauak, who noted that $516,000 would have had to been spent to provide comparable food. Extended throughout 1974, the January and February consumption figures project to a total of five million pounds of food harvested from the land.

"Remember, if we do not take care of the land and waters, someone is going to have to come up with five million pounds of meat to replace what we collect from the land today," Kiariauak told "Tundra Drums," Bethel newspaper.

Man Overboard!
August 1974

"I'm glad to be alive," Don Sjogren, 49, recently told people he met on the streets of Wrangell. And he had a story to tell that proved his point. Sjogren was fishing in Sumner Strait with his gill-netter OVERCOMER when he noticed that the required red light on top of the 20-foot mast was out. The boat wasn't rolling much so he took a new bulb and climbed the aluminum mast. Then the boat began to roll violently and the mast broke, throwing Sjogren into the water.

"It was my first high dive ever, and my first swim in three years," he told listeners. He swam to the stern of the OVERCOMER, but without a life jacket and in the cold water he was losing his strength. He held on, but that was all. "There was just no way I could climb aboard alone," he said. "No way."

But a friend, George Lamm of the gill-netter KARIOCA was in the vicinity and saw Sjogren go overboard. Lamm worked his boat up to the OVERCOMER and Mrs. Lamm jumped aboard and passed Sjogren a line which he put around his chest to keep himself afloat. He had been in the water for 30 minutes by the time the Lamms helped him aboard. Then he continued to fish through the night.

"I just didn't feel like quitting. But I was awfully cold for awhile."

A Record High Budget
July 1974

Passage of an all-time high state budget of $462 million was among the last acts of the Eighth Alaska Legislature which ended a 96-day session on April 26. Nearly $110 million above the previous record budget enacted last year, the appropriation for fiscal year 1975 will deplete the state's dwindling general fund by about $210 million. The once billion-dollar North Slope fund will contain about $250 million when the next legislature meets.

Winning legislative approval, a record $189 million in bond issues will be presented to voters in the general election. Reserved for the primary election in August is a statewide vote on whether the capital should be moved from Juneau. All of the 40 seats in the House of Representatives and 14 of 20 seats in the State Senate will be filled in the November election.

New Life for Hyder
September 1974

A great increase in tourist and other traffic through the port of Hyder, at the head of Portland Canal, has prompted the United States Customs Service to station a customs officer there. For some years Hyder has had only a part-time agent. The town is connected by highway with Stewart, British Columbia, which in turn has a road link to the Canadian highway system. Hyder was a busy mining town in the 1920's but has fewer than 100 people today. Customs officials from Ketchikan, Anchorage and San Francisco visited Hyder in June to prepare for the full time office.

Mountain Tragedy: Flier May Have Died Because He Left the Crash Site
September 1974

Death is presumed to be the price paid by an Anchorage-based pilot for failing to stay with his plane after it crashed just below the 10,000-foot level on Mount Spurr on June 15.

The tragic sequence of events began with a flight from Anchorage to a mining operation on the west side of the Alaska Range. John Brooks, 25, crashed his modified Rockwell Thrush Commander high on the glaciered mountain about 9 a.m. The plane's emergency locator beacon was activated and by 11 a.m., the downed plane was sighted by Roger Mills of the Civil Air Patrol.

Brooks waved at Mills and military aircraft which circled the crash site. High winds prevented a landing by military helicopters and worsening weather prevented an air drop of survival gear later in the day.

A five-man Army rescue team was landed by helicopter on June 17, reaching the crash site after struggling for three hours through heavy snow. The rescuers found no sign of Brooks, only a note which indicated he believed he had a broken right wrist and had decided to "hike out." The injured pilot did not indicate the direction of his hike on the steep slopes. Fresh snow had wiped out all sign of his tracks. The Army team searched four hours without success. Later a civilian Mountain Rescue Group spent two days on Mount Spurr without finding a trace of Brooks. The search for Brooks was suspended on June 24 by the Rescue Coordination Center at Elmendorf Air Force Base in Anchorage.

The apparent tragedy resulting from Brooks's decision to hike out caused Public Safety Commissioner Pat Wellington to comment, "If he had stayed with the plane he would have been picked up with a minimum of harm to himself. In electing to walk out at such times, a pilot not only lessens the chance of being found but exposes himself to considerable danger in descending through areas where precipices and cliffs could give him considerable trouble."

JIM MARTIN, ANCHORAGE DAILY TIMES

Wrecked plane of John Brooks is shown just below 10,000-foot level on Mount Spurr, west of Anchorage. Brooks survived the crash on June 15 and left a note indicating he would "hike out." He was still missing in mid-July.

Women on the Job . . . They Like Prudhoe Bay
September 1974

With little fanfare or hostility, women have come to the marshy flatlands of Prudhoe Bay—and the feminine contingent at BP Alaska's Operations Center finds part-time life on a sea of tundra agreeable.

Dorothy McGonigle, field records assistant and BP's first woman employee at the site of the North Slope oil discoveries, declared herself "thrilled" when hired to head north in January 1974. After 6 months of working 12 hours a day for 8 days followed by a week's leave in Anchorage, Mrs. McGonigle maintains working at the edge of the Arctic Ocean is "fantastic."

A room steward at the center, Cathy Schmoyer, 25, feels "there's always something to learn" at the starting point of history's largest privately financed project, and has toured oil rigs. Working 10 hours a day for 2 weeks, followed by a week's vacation in Anchorage, Miss Schmoyer finds no problem with boredom.

Milo Stover, 29, also a room steward, recalls when she arrived at Prudhoe Bay in April 1974, one man remarked, "In 2 years, there won't be any women on the North Slope." Responded Mrs. Stover, "In 2 years, there'll be 10 women training for your job."

Animal-tangling Telegraph Line to Be Removed
July 1974

The old Canol telegraph line, a hazard to wild animals, is to be removed this summer. The Canadian government has approved a grant of $20,000 to hire six Teslin area residents and purchase necessary equipment for the job, which has long been urged by northerners concerned with the safety of wildlife in the Canol region.

The old World War II poles will be cut down and the wire rolled onto spools. During the three-month period from mid-June about 100 miles of the 280 miles of Canol road will be cleared; the remainder will have to wait on another grant in 1975. Animals as large as caribou have met death by becoming ensnarled in the wire.

Gold's Soaring Price
August 1974

Klondike gold seekers have an easy device for measuring the zooming value of gold. They recall that a gold nugget weighing slightly more than 72 ounces was found near Dawson City in 1898. Its value 76 years ago was $1,158. The same nugget would be worth at least $13,775 in the summer of 1974.

Dangerous Living by Kodiak Minister
August 1974

A Kodiak minister is an unintentional expert on living dangerously. Days after he found a strange object while beachcombing at Ouzinkie, the Rev. Vernon Eggebraaten, interim pastor at the Community Baptist Church in Kodiak, learned that his discovery wasn't a lamp or gas butane burner, but a deadly boat mine.

After hosting the device in his home for four days, Pastor Eggebraaten showed it to Leonard Mealor, a veteran of 22 years as a Navy bomb disposal expert. Mealor identified the strange object as a boat mine, probably from a Russian or Japanese battleship or submarine. Designed to be planted in sand or surf for exploding on contact with a boat, the mine was of unknown age, but its explosive power was undiminished. Within minutes after being properly identified, the boat mine was retrieved by state troopers for disposal, according to the "Kodiak Mirror."

A Weakness for Beef Dooms a Kodiak Bear
September 1974

A weakness for beef led to death for a Kodiak brown bear in May and set something of a speed record for a big game hunt. Learning that a big bear was killing cattle in the Anton Larsen Bay area, Mike Shockley, Kodiak charter boat operator, guide Martin Kasser and his hunter, Donald Risk of Pennsylvania, left Kodiak at 3 a.m. They returned to Kodiak at 8 a.m. with a nine and one-half foot bear that Risk shot at Anton Larsen Bay.

"We pulled into the bay, looked up on the hillside and there—about 50 feet away—was the bear," Shockley told the "Kodiak Mirror." "We watched him for awhile, then he walked down to the beach—about 30 feet away—and the hunter shot him. We skinned him out, put him aboard the boat and were back in town by 8 a.m."

No Threat to McKinley
October 1974

The man who has reached the summit of 20,320-foot Mount McKinley more times than any other human has no fears that Alaska's great peak is threatened by climbers.

Ray Genet, owner and operator of Genet Expeditions of Talkeetna, led four parties up Mount McKinley last summer. Of the 46 climbers involved, 40 reached the summit. Genet has scaled the South Peak 17 times.

"Unsightly garbage along the route can be eliminated by using shovels," said Genet. "The problem is one of poor housekeeping practices on the part of some climbers.

"Small expeditions on Mount McKinley are unwise, and as a rule the larger the expedition the better. There is no need to limit the number of qualified climbers on the mountain."

Genet argues that the more expeditions there are ascending and descending the mountain the easier it is to effect interchanges, allowing an ascending team with a sick climber to transfer him to a descending team. This practice, which was carried out last summer, improves the safety factor and doesn't upset climbing schedules, according to Genet.

A Record Knuckle Hop
October 1974

Setting new world records in the ear weight, drop the bomb and knuckle hop contests, 100 Eskimo and Indian athletes met in Fairbanks in late July to celebrate the 14th annual World Eskimo-Indian Olympics.

Those capturing top spots in the 3-day competition included: Olive Anderson, Fairbanks—fish cutting, one minute, 50 seconds; Billy Ahalik, Barrow—ear pulling; Elizabeth Long, Barrow—seal skinning, one minute, two seconds; Billy Killbear, Barter Island—muktuk eating; James Killbear, Barrow—knuckle hop, 88 feet, 10 inches; Johnny David, Minto—Indian stick pull; James Itta, Barrow—ear weight contest, 990 feet, 18 pounds; and Eva Kowunna, Kotzebue—blanket toss.

Honors for the dance contests went to the Barrow Eskimo dancers and the Minto Indian dancers.

In a special opening event, Native women out-pulled white men for the third consecutive year in a tug-of-war contest.

The Land Rush
September 1974

The Matanuska-Susitna Borough joined in the state's frantic land rush with an auction sale of 920 borough-owned acres in late June, nearly doubling its expected return. The borough had set a minimum bid total of $281,600 for 19 tracts ranging from 12 to 145 acres.

Before the sale, Borough Manager Wesley M. Howe had expected the auction might bring in as much as $400,000. When action ended for more than 100 bidders, the sale total was nearly $700,000. Appraised at $5,400, a 30-acre tract on Willow Creek was finally sold for $30,100. Another tract on the same creek was appraised at $4,000 and sold for $20,000.

On a Bank of the Yukon: Flaming Death for Two Historic Sternwheelers

WHITEHORSE STAR PHOTO

Flaming end of the *CASCA*, veteran Yukon River sternwheeler, which was destroyed by fire at Whitehorse on June 20. Visible at extreme right is the flaming upper deck of the *WHITEHORSE*, also destroyed at its resting place on the bank of the Yukon.

September 1974

A Viking's funeral was the fate of two historic Yukon sternwheelers, the WHITEHORSE and CASCA, which were destroyed by fire at Whitehorse on June 20. While many Yukoners wept, flames reduced the massive old vessels to tangled wreckage in a few hours. Three transient youths who had been sleeping on the boats were rescued, questioned and later released by the Royal Canadian Mounted Police. By early July, no cause of the fire had been determined.

The WHITEHORSE was launched in 1901 on the very spot on which she was consumed by flames. The CASCA was also built at the turn of the century, but was twice replaced. The traditional sternwheeler run from Whitehorse to Dawson City was phased out with completion of what is now the Klondike Highway road link and moving of the Territorial capital from Dawson City to Whitehorse.

Death of the two sternwheelers has reduced the 250-vessel fleet which once plied the Yukon to three now-idle ships. The SS KENO made the final run downriver to Dawson City where it is preserved as an historic site. The SS KLONDIKE has been established as an historic site at Whitehorse, and the Historic Sites Branch is responsible for the SS TUTSHI at Carcross.

WHITE PASS & YUKON ROUTE PHOTO

Reduced to ashes by a June 20 fire at Whitehorse, the sternwheelers WHITEHORSE and CASCA are shown side by side at a Yukon River stop in an earlier and happier era.

'I Could Hear My Skull Being Raked': Yukoner Survives Three-Round Bout with Grizzly
October 1974

"I could hear my own skull being raked like an animal rakes a rock with its teeth," recalled Richard Bennett of Whitehorse after surviving a three-round bout with a mother grizzly bear on the Klukshu River south of Haines Junction.

In an interview with the *Yukon News* following his mauling in late July, Bennett said he was standing in the river when he heard his dog bark and looked up to see an orange blur.

"I didn't think she'd keep coming, but she never stopped. We wrestled for awhile and she took a swipe at my head. I managed to get away from her but she worked her way around to the far shore and came at me again. She tried to pull me out by the shoulders through some spruce trees along the edge of the creek, but again I broke away.

"I dove under the water and held my breath, popping up for air every now and again. I wanted to give her a chance to just walk away. But she crawled out on a floating log jam and came at me for the last time. She was scooping her paws down, raking my back, although she didn't managed to get hold of me."

During his ordeal, he spotted three cubs on the opposite shore and realized the reason for the attack. When the bear finally left, Bennett swam 150 yards downstream and walked to friends who summoned a helicopter which took him to Whitehorse General Hospital.

Two hundred stitches were required to close cuts on the veteran Yukoner's skull. He also suffered lacerations on his arms and chest and a bite on his right hand.

"I got past the point of terror and started figuring out how to survive," recalled Bennett from his hospital bed. "The only thing I could think of was to get into a deep hole and hold my breath."

Nest Doomed, Eggs Safe
December 1974

All trees on federal land in Southeastern Alaska which have eagle nests in them are marked and protected from logging operations.

Last May a nest that had gone unmarked in a logging area was discovered—it was in an unusual location inland. By the time it was discovered blasting charges had been put in place nearby as part of the logging operation. Since such charges cannot be removed, it was decided that the eggs would be taken from the nest and incubated.

Herb Smith, of the local power company, volunteered to climb for the eggs with his pole equipment, but the tree proved too large. A nearby pole-sized hemlock was close enough so that Herb climbed it and crossed over limbs into the nest tree.

The excited eagles circled continuously while the nest was robbed, and Smith lowered the eggs in a bucket to U. S. Fish and Wildlife Service employees Bruce Conant and Andy Anderson.

The eggs were flown to Juneau and placed under a somewhat dubious bantam hen belonging to U. S. Fish and Wildlife Service biologist Jim King.

Radar and Reindeer
September 1974

The use of radar and radio signals for locating lost reindeer was among tricks taught 15 Eskimo reindeer herders at a recent six-day workshop conducted by the University of Alaska's Institute of Arctic Biology at its reindeer research station at Cantwell.

Topics of the first such workshop ever conducted in Alaska included range and herd management, feeds and feeding, marketing, diseases and veterinary practices. There were roping, dehorning and hide tanning demonstrations, and an aerial classroom showed the use of planes to find good range from the air. The herders were shown how radar can be used in bad weather to locate lost herds. Also demonstrated was the use of radio telemetry which involves picking up signals from a reindeer with a transmitter attached to its neck.

Dr. Jack R. Luick, chief scientist at the Cantwell station, announced recently that the National Institute of Health has granted $63,630 for adding an animal health care center and research laboratory to the Cantwell facility.

Now a $5 Billion Line?
October 1974

The price tag on the 789-mile trans-Alaska pipeline, long billed as the most costly nongovernment project in history, is expected to jump from the presently estimated $4.5 billion to more than $5 billion.

Acknowledging that it could not speak for Alyeska Pipeline Service Company, responsible for construction and operation of the line, Atlantic Richfield Company reported in early August that it now estimates completion of the system to a 2-million-barrel-per-day capacity "could exceed $5 billion." Rising costs of materials and labor were given as reasons for the anticipated increase.

It was in 1927 that Noel Wien flew his "Jenny" to Wiseman from Fairbanks, in what is believed the first flight above the Arctic Circle in Alaska. The pioneer pilot is shown turning his plane's prop with an assist from a Wiseman helper.

Noel Wien Day... From Jenny to Jet

October 1974

It was Noel Wien Day in Alaska on July 15, officially proclaimed by Governor William A. Egan, as Alaskans paid tribute to the retired chairman of the board of directors of the airline which bears his name.

It was on July 15, 1924, that Wien flew his open cockpit Hisso-Standard J-1 from Anchorage to Fairbanks. "I was flying about 200 feet at about 60 miles an hour," he recalled. "We didn't have any charts, no windsocks, weather reports or radio aides—just the Alaska Railroad tracks to navigate by." Wien left Anchorage at 3 a.m., arriving at Weeks Field in Fairbanks at 7:16 a.m.

During his years at the controls, the venerable aviator made the first flight across the Arctic Circle, first flight to Nome, first commercial flight to Barrow and return, first round trip between North America and Siberia, first flight from the lower 48 to Alaska via the interior route and the first commercial flight from Alaska to Seattle in 1935. A license issued to Wien in 1926 by the Federation Aeronautique Internationale is signed by Orville Wright.

Seated with his pilot son, Merrill, in the cockpit of a Wien Air Alaska Boeing 737 jetliner on a flight from Anchorage to Fairbanks, Noel Wien, right, recalls his first flight from Anchorage to Fairbanks on July 15, 1924, in a Hisso-Standard J-1. He made that first flight in a bit over 4 hours. The 50th anniversary flight between the state's largest cities was completed in 45 minutes.

One Bay, 18 Glaciers ... Where Else But in Alaska?

September 1974

"Where else do 18 glaciers flow into one bay?" asked Lowell Thomas Sr., in Juneau recently, referring to his choice of Alaska's Glacier Bay as one of the wonders of the world. Asked by the editors of "Reader's Digest" to do an article on the seven scenic wonders, Thomas also picked Grand Canyon, Yellowstone Park, Mammoth Caves, Victoria Falls in Rhodesia, Mount Everest in Tibet and Lake Baykal in Siberia. The article appeared in the July issue of the magazine. Thomas was in Juneau to observe the 60th anniversary of his first visit to Alaska and incidentally to visit his son, Lowell Jr., an Anchorage resident who was in Juneau for a special session of the Alaska Legislature in which he is a senator.

A sightseeing boat is dwarfed by Margerie Glacier in Glacier Bay National Monument. Margerie Glacier heads on the south slope of Mount Root and trends 21 miles to Tarr Inlet.

Trucks Roll to Prudhoe
November 1974

Trucks were rolling from the Yukon River to Prudhoe Bay in early October, as the 360-mile pipe-haul road was completed a bit ahead of schedule. Rated a major engineering achievement, the new road is limited to travel by pipeline contractors. Once the pipeline is completed and the Yukon is bridged, the route through the Brooks Range to the Arctic Ocean will become part of Alaska's secondary road system.

With more than 4,000 workers along the 789-mile pipeline route from Prudhoe Bay to Valdez in late September, there were rumbles about the number of nonresidents employed on the huge project. A preliminary survey conducted by the State Department of Labor showed a bare majority of pipeline workers were Alaska residents, with the exception of operating engineers, a majority of whom were nonresidents. For survey purposes, workers with more than a year in Alaska were classed as Alaskans.

Commenting on interviews with 399 pipeline workers, Governor William A. Egan said, "We don't have enough detail to draw hard-nosed conclusions. The evidence isn't there on the basis of figures given to me."

Points for Fishermen
October 1974

Eligibility of commercial fishermen to participate in commercial salmon fisheries throughout the state would be established by a point system recently proposed by the Limited Entry Commission—the agency established by Alaska's legislature to control numbers of fishermen in the impacted commercial fisheries of the state.

Under the complex plan, which in 1975 would govern all salmon seine and gill-net fisheries, except that of the Arctic-Yukon-Kuskokwim, fishermen must amass a total of 20 points out of a possible 40, to get into the most crowded fisheries.

However, if a fisherman is excluded, he could claim "significant economic hardship" and be further considered. Nonresidents and residents would be considered under the same plan.

Points awarded will favor fishermen who have consistently fished Alaskan salmon in recent years; anyone who did not fish salmon in 1972 or earlier cannot be considered for a permanent entry permit.

A maximum of three points would be awarded to a fisherman who fished during 1972; three more points would be awarded for fishing in 1971; while 1970 and 1969 would be worth two points each.

The plan would also award points for consistent participation in a fishery, with minimums varying from three weeks to eight weeks a season in different fisheries.

The most controversial proposal of the plan will likely be the "income dependence percentage" section. This is arrived at by dividing the gross value of the annual catch in one area by total income.

For a fisherman who received 70 percent of his income from fishing in 1972, a maximum of six points would be awarded. Fewer points will be awarded for various levels of dependence in 1971.

A Rare White Bald Eagle

October 1974

Latest star of Alaskan ornithologists is this rare white bald eagle which has been sighted frequently at Steamer Point on the northwest coast of Etolin Island, south of Wrangell.

Farthest North Hunters

October 1974

This scene is being duplicated by several million waterfowl hunters this fall. The Marvin Peter family of Barrow crouches in a blind waiting for the next flock. Located at the tip of Point Barrow, about six miles from the village, the blind is the farthest north shooting site in the United States. While Marvin Peter scans the Arctic Ocean, he gets backup support from his daughter, Daisy Mae, 17, at left, his wife, Carrie, and son, Lloyd, 10. The young hunter had shot his first two ducks just before this photo was taken last September.

At Mercy of Court

November 1974

Last year the Copper River Highway was passable to a point 72 miles north of Cordova. By late summer 1974, the highway was closed to traffic at Mile 35 shown here because a Sierra Club-initiated court order was interpreted to mean no repair or maintenance work could be done. A September ruling by the Ninth Circuit Court of Appeals in San Francisco authorizes maintenance work on the completed section of the highway. It was not known when the controversial road would be opened to the public beyond Mile 35.

1974

Captain Tuzroyluke, a Teen-age Crew, and a Whale...
September 1974

One of seven bowhead whales taken at Point Hope early this summer, this 50-footer was taken by Captain Seymour Tuzroyluke's crew, made up largely of teen-agers. Present to witness the hunt and butchering was U.S. Senator James Buckley of New York, who helped haul the animal to secure ice. The whale was lost for two days after being killed, when harpoons loosened and the whale sank in 25 fathoms of water. When drifting ice cleared the area, the huge animal was recovered.

A New Bishop
November 1974

With services conducted in English, Eskimo and Indian dialects, the Rt. Rev. David R. Cochran was consecrated as Alaska's fourth Episcopal Bishop in ceremonies conducted at the University of Alaska, Fairbanks, on August 28.

Consecrated by Bishop John Allin, presiding bishop of the Episcopal Church, Bishop Cochran succeeds the Rt. Rev. William J. Gordon, who retired. The new bishop was selected at a diocesan convention in Anchorage last April.

Baranof Hotel Fire
September 1974

An early morning fire June 20 on the seventh floor of Juneau's nine-story Baranof Hotel routed some 300 guests and caused one death and several injuries. The fire started mysteriously in boxes of furnishings in a corridor of the new seventh floor and gutted several rooms and the corridor where it broke out.

Mrs. Katherine Dummer, 49, of Bloomington, Minnesota, died of smoke inhalation after she apparently lost her way in the smoke-filled corridor. Her husband and daughter escaped, as did newscaster Lowell Thomas Sr., who was on the ninth floor. Among the 15 who sustained injuries, the most seriously hurt was State Senator John Rader of Anchorage who fell while escaping via a bedsheet rope. He suffered a broken leg and arm. Phil Zarro, hotel manager, sustained second degree burns.

The Alaska Legislature was in special session and 31 of the 60 members were registered at the hotel. The three top floors of the hotel were added last year and the fire was confined to the seventh floor, although there was smoke damage above. The lower six floors were virtually undamaged and were back in full operation before nightfall.

A $6,000 Nugget
October 1974

There's still gold in them thar creeks! Max Fuerstner of Whitehorse can show you a nugget weighing 20.5 ounces to prove it.

He and his partners, Bob Miller and Gary McCully, started sluicing operations in May on Livingstone Creek, about 50 miles northeast of Whitehorse, after taking a bulldozer and front-end loader into the property during March. They had

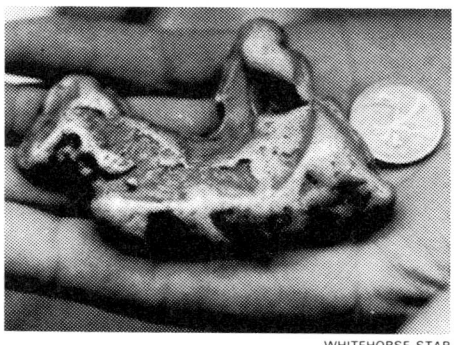

Dwarfing the Canadian quarter beside it, Max Fuerstner's big gold nugget is worth about 24,000 of the 25-cent pieces.

been finding coarse jewelry gold this summer and then on Sunday, July 21, Max let out a scream. He'd found the big, hollowed-out hunk of gold which nearly filled the palm of his hand.

His 11-year-old son carried it down to show the partners, who at first thought he had a rock or piece of wood in his hands.

At current gold prices, the nugget is valued at $3,500 minimum; but at nugget rates of $300 per ounce, more like $6,000. It's in the bank for safe keeping and Fuerstner, a former hotelman in Whitehorse, says he has no intention of selling it.

"It's something you give to your son, and your son gives to his son," he said.

The Wettest July... Alaska Highway Travelers Stranded
November 1974

It may be some small comfort to travelers who found themselves stranded along the Alaska Highway this past July to learn that it has now been recorded as the wettest July on record at the weather office. The hardest hit area was from Swift River to Muncho Lake, with two to three times the normal July amount of rainfall.

Muncho Lake with 7.19 inches of rain broke its previous July record of 4.95 inches, reported in 1944. Swift River had 4.02 inches compared with its previous July record of 3.77 in 1968. At Watson Lake, 5.01 inches of rain fell in July (275 percent of normal rainfall) and up at Beaver Creek, Milepost 1202 on the Alaska Highway (where no washouts occurred), 6.40 inches of rain beat the record set in 1972. Whitehorse had 2.05 inches, (175 percent of normal) but didn't break any records... and just to keep the visitors happy, Dawson City had only about half its normal rainfall and slightly above-normal temperatures.

A Photographer's Gruesome Death... Devoured by a Brown Bear in Unprovoked Attack
October 1974

Little suspecting that violent death was only hours away, Jay B. Reeves, 38, an amateur wildlife photographer and veteran Anchorage employee of the U.S. Postal Service, pitched his tent on the bank of Frosty Creek seven miles from Cold Bay on the afternoon of August 2.

The remains of his headless, partially devoured body were found a half-mile distant the next day. And within minutes after the gruesome discovery, an 8½-foot male brown bear that had killed and consumed Reeves in Izembek National Wildlife Refuge was shot from a helicopter by a federal biologist.

In rendering a verdict of accidental death on August 4, district magistrate Karl Heiker of Cold Bay said there was no evidence the attack on the unarmed visitor was provoked.

Heiker reported there was 60-knot winds with rain on the night of August 2. Reeves' tent was pitched very near the trail along Frosty Creek followed by salmon-seeking bears, according to Heiker. There is speculation that the bear, a 5-year-old, was attracted by the flapping tent and encountered Reeves, whose boots were found at the campsite, indicating he was attacked while sleeping.

Fishermen reported on August 3 that Reeves' tent was badly torn and there was no sign of him. The same day a brown bear that had become a nuisance in Cold Bay was tranquilized and flown across the bay by a Petty-Ray Geophysical helicopter which was based in Cold Bay for seismic exploration.

On the return flight to Cold Bay the helicopter crew was asked to look for Reeves. His remains were found in dense alders about one-half mile from Frosty Creek. The killer bear was sighted nearby as was Reeves' skull.

John Sarvis, a refuge biologist, shot the bear from the helicopter. Examination of the animal's stomach revealed bits of plastic, part of a pack of cigarettes and human bones.

Ed Bailey, a U.S. Fish and Wildlife Service biologist who formerly served as acting manager of Izembek National Wildlife Refuge, described the fatal incident as "bizarre." Bailey said he had never heard of a bear killing and eating a human, although there have been cases in which bears devoured humans who died from other causes.

With ample supplies of fish and berries in the refuge area, hunger was ruled out as a cause for the attack. Examination of the bear's head for rabies proved negative.

A Postal Service employee since 1961, Reeves had previously worked for the Alaska Railroad and Department of Fish and Game. An experienced woodsman, he had photographed wildlife in Mount McKinley National Park, on Kodiak Island and the Copper River Flats.

Reeves' death has led to speculation that a man lost near King Cove last April may also have been killed by a bear. Pat Wren, a newcomer to King Cove, decided to walk from King Cove to Belkofski, despite warnings that he was ill-equipped for the hazardous 16-mile journey. It is believed that Wren drowned or was killed by a brown bear. Magistrate Heiker issued a presumptive death decree for Wren in early July.

Logging in Alaska: Future Hinges on Outcome of Sierra Club Suit

December 1974

Continued growth of Alaska's logging industry in 1975 is heavily dependent on a complex trial which started in U.S. District Court in Anchorage early in October. The trial involved the U.S. Forest Service's sale in 1968 of 8.75 billion board feet of timber in the Admiralty Island, Port Houghton and Admiralty Island area.

Contested by the Sierra Club, the sale to Champion International, Inc. is the largest in Forest Service history. Whether it will be allowed and a $100 million pulp mill complex will be constructed at Berners Bay north of Juneau may not be known for months after U.S. District Court Judge Raymond Plummer renders his decision. The case was returned to Judge Plummer's court by the Ninth District Court of Appeals and is certain to return to the Appeals Court.

While the market for Alaska's pulp mill products remains steady, the market for lumber is depressed as a result of the inflation-caused housing slump.

"Inflation in Japan is worse than in the United States, and most of Alaska's lumber is exported to Japan, so you can imagine what has happened to our market," said an official of a major Alaskan lumber company.

Despite the depressed market, the logging industry continued expanding its activity range in Southcentral and Interior Alaska.

A new sawmill and chip plant complex was being constructed at Seward by Kenai Lumber Company, a subsidiary of Louisiana Pacific.

Southcentral Timber Company, a Japanese-owned firm, is transporting timber logged from Icy Bay around the Kenai Peninsula to a mill at Jakolof Bay opposite Homer for processing into cants. The firm is also logging in the Windy and Rocky Bay areas on the Kenai and buying cants from Interior mills.

The groundwork is now being laid for the biggest logging operations in Cook Inlet's history as Kodiak Lumber Mills, a Japanese-owned firm, prepares to log about 335 million board feet purchased from the U.S. Forest Service on Afognak Island. Camp and road work is scheduled for completion in 1975 and actual logging is expected to start late next year. The company has not yet decided on a location for its sawmill complex for the Afognak timber.

A subsidiary of Kodiak Lumber Mills also expects to start logging about 500 million board feet of state-owned beetle-damaged timber in the Trading Bay area by late 1975. A camp and roads are being constructed as well as a loading dock near Tyonek. The lumber will be processed into cants and chips for export to Japan.

Cut at Icy Bay near Yakutat, this bargeload of logs is headed for Jakolof Bay opposite Homer for processing into cants at the Southcentral Timber Company's mill.

New Alaska Home for Old Records
November 1974

With the completion of the new Alaska Records Center in Juneau late this year, many official records from earlier years will be returned from other depositories. These are records of some of the federal offices in Alaska between 1884 and 1913, when it was the District of Alaska, and from 1913 through 1958, when it was the Territory of Alaska. Most of these records were generated by the Office of the Governor and the Office of the Secretary of Alaska, but included are some U.S. District Court records from Southeastern Alaska and some from other agencies.

At the time of statehood, these records were transferred from Juneau to the Federal Archives and Records Center in Seattle for safekeeping and until Alaska could provide suitable space for them. After 1913, when the first Alaska Legislature met, a Territorial government was created, commencing with such offices as treasurer, attorney general and commissioner of education. The records of these purely Territorial departments and agencies, or such of them as have survived, have for the most part remained in Alaska and are in custody of the archives of the State of Alaska, a division of the Department of Administration.

Meanwhile, the state archives continue to grow each year and are in charge of Colleen Roguska, state archivist. They have been housed in the Public Safety Building in Juneau until the new facility is completed. The new building is scheduled for dedication on December 2 and Dr. James Rhoads, the national archivist, is expected to attend the ceremony and to personally return the historic documents.

"Having these documents back in Alaska will make it much easier for resident Alaska historians to research our early history under the United States," says archivist Roguska.

Alaskans Vote 3 to 2 to Move the Capital... Committee to Select Possible Sites
October 1974

ANCHORAGE—Alaska is going to have a new state capital, but its exact location won't be known until after the general election in November 1976. Solidly defeated in 1960 and 1962, the move-the-capital initiative came up again in the August 27 primary election and won the support of voters by a three-to-two margin. Unofficial returns, with absentee ballots and outlying precincts still uncounted, showed 40,083 "yes" and 27,932 "no" votes.

Despite a massive anti-move vote in Southeastern Alaska, the proposition was assured success by a four-to-one pro-move margin in Southcentral Alaska, which tallied more than half the state's votes. Fairbanks and Interior Alaska approved the move by a slim margin and the balloting in bush precincts was about evenly divided.

Next step in the process of moving the capital from Juneau, where it has been located since 1906, is appointment of a nine-member Capital Selection Committee by Governor William A. Egan. The committee will include one member from Northwest Alaska, two from Southeast, two from the Interior and three from Southcentral. The Commissioner of Natural Resources will complete the committee.

The initiative requires that the new capital be located west of 141 degrees west longitude, that it be on 100 square miles of land owned by the state or available for acquisition, and that it not be within 30 miles of either Anchorage or Fairbanks.

The Capital Selection Committee will choose not more than three possible capital sites and conduct public hearings throughout the state before March 1976. Alaskans will decide on the location in the 1976 general election. The new capital will be named by the state legislature.

The initiative approved by voters says, "The movement of the seat of government to the new capital city shall begin not later than October 1, 1980."

Seattle-based King Crabbers Forced to Back Down... 'Flagrant Challenge' Fails
October 1974

A group of Seattle-based king crab fishermen and processors were forced to back down last July, after they had formed a pseudo-official "Shellfish Conservation Institute," declared the State of Alaska's fishing regulations for the Bering Sea invalid, established their own regulations and went fishing.

Alaska's response to the challenge was to refuse to open the king crab season in the Bering Sea on July 1, as had been scheduled. The state ordered all king crab fishing pots out of the Bering Sea before it would allow any fishing. Four state vessels were sent to enforce the edict.

At the same time, Commissioner of Fish and Game James Brooks announced, "This flagrant challenge of authority neither justifies nor obscures the demonstrated intention of the parties involved to engage in unbridled exploitation of the king crab resource. The State of Alaska will not tolerate anarchy in this fishery or any other, and every possible legal action will be directed toward preserving our fishery resources against such piracy."

It took nearly a month to clear the Bering Sea of king crab pots. In late July Commissioner Brooks announced that the Bering Sea king crab season would finally open July 29. By August 1, there were 87 American king crab fishing vessels in the Bering Sea, with more expected.

In July, while the state waited for the Bering Sea to be cleared of king crab pots, the Alaska Department of Public Safety filed criminal charges against 13 captains of fishing vessels alleged to have illegally fished the Bering Sea north of Unimak Island.

A Four-Year University for Barrow this Fall
November 1974

A university at Barrow will open its doors this fall, a 4-year institution affiliated with Sitka's Sheldon Jackson College and Antioch-West Learning Communications, Inc., and funded by the North Slope Borough general fund.

Eben Hopson, mayor of the North Slope Borough, said the university will offer traditional curriculum and courses of special relevance to the North Slope Natives and will be "more or less locally controlled."

Where Now, Alaska?

This has been a year of tumultuous change. The oil pipeline is being built. The Native claims settlement is well along. . . . Now, what of the future? No one knows. Alaska can only bend to the winds of change and the whims of chance.

December 1974

There is no agreement on whether the massive changes sweeping through Alaska in 1974 will be for better or worse, but there is unanimous agreement that Alaska will never be the same.

The Most Reverend Joseph Ryan, Archbishop of Anchorage, touched on the electric mood when he wrote in a recent pastoral letter, "Alaska is immersed in a tumultuous transitional period."

A recent state report included this statement: "The most dramatic change in land ownership and land status in the nation's history is taking place now in Alaska."

Most graphic evidence of the change was completion on September 29 of the 360-mile road from the Yukon River to Prudhoe Bay on the Arctic Ocean.

Now rumbling with the movement of supply trucks engaged in construction of the trans-Alaska pipeline from Prudhoe Bay to Valdez, the $200 million road was built for the State of Alaska by Alyeska Pipeline Service Company. Involving workmen at 12 camps, the giant project was completed in just 154 days by more than 3,000 workers.

So important to the nation that it has been given top "defense priority" by the federal government, the $4.5 billion pipeline project is a major factor in the changes that are shaping Alaska's destiny.

The Year's Other Developments

In August voters approved relocation of the state's capital from Juneau to some undecided site, between Fairbanks and Anchorage.

Complying with the Alaska Native Claims Settlement Act, more than 200 villages were hurrying to complete selections of 22 million acres of land authorized by the 1971 act by the deadline, December 18, 1974. The remainder of the 40 million acres chosen by the Native corporations will be known by December 18, 1975.

Combining the 40 million acres to be selected by Alaska Natives, the 103 million acres to be acquired by the state and the slightly more than 83 million acres sought by the Department of the Interior for public interest lands such as parks, refuges and national forests, it is apparent that Alaska's land ownership maps are headed for mind-boggling changes.

The groundwork was laid in 1974 for invoking the state's new limited entry fishing law, an entirely new concept of management for the state's troubled fishery resources.

If '74 Was Hectic . . .

If 1974 was hectic, the coming year promises to be more so. Peak pipeline work force this year will be about 6,000; it will reach a project peak of 14,000 during 1975.

With 20 construction camps extending from Valdez to Prudhoe Bay, the pipeline is having the greatest impact on Valdez and such small highway communities as Delta Junction, Paxson and Glennallen.

Site of a billion-dollar tanker terminal, Valdez has seen its population more than triple in 1974, and Alyeska Pipeline Service Company is rushing to have quarters for 2,800 workers ready by the first of the year.

The pipeline's spin-off impact on booming Fairbanks and Anchorage is so great that new building projects make aerial photos obsolete after 24 hours. The City of Anchorage estimated its population at 79,000 on October 1, and the Greater Anchorage Area Borough figures there were 162,500 people living between Chugiak and Girdwood. Borough planners report 15,000 new residents in Greater Anchorage during 1974, and predict the borough population will be 175,000 by the end of 1975.

Next: A Natural Gas Pipeline?

A pending decision by the Federal Power Commission will determine whether Alaska's oil pipeline upheaval will be followed by a natural gas pipeline boom.

El Paso Alaska Company filed an application with the FPC in late September which calls for construction of a $6 billion project involving an 809-mile, 42-inch gas pipeline from Prudhoe Bay to Gravina Point near Cordova, a liquefaction plant, new marine terminal and a fleet of tankers. El Paso has indicated it would hope to utilize the camps built for the oil pipeline.

The FPC must decide between the El Paso application and an earlier one from Arctic Gas, which calls for construction of a gas pipeline from Prudhoe Bay down the Mackenzie Valley to the north-central United States. Estimated cost of the 2,500-mile project is $10 billion.

Hope that North Slope oil can ease the nation's energy crunch by 1977 is still strong, according to Charles Elder, vice-president of Alyeska Pipeline Service Company. He said on October 1, "Unless we run into serious material shortage problems, we still feel that our goal of a completed trans-Alaska oil pipeline and terminal by mid-1977 is attainable. We expect to be loading tankers at Valdez by that time."

This aerial photo of Alaska transportation history in the making shows a meeting of two bulldozers on September 29 to mark completion of gravel overlay on the 360-mile North Slope Road which links the Yukon River with Prudhoe Bay. Hard-hatted construction men gathered at the site 100 miles north of the Yukon River between the Coldfoot and Prospect Creek Camps to watch the last bit of gravel moved into place.

Index

Callison, Pat, I 87
Calvert School (correspondence), I 146
Calvin, Jack, II 118
Cameron, Mrs. G.I., I 31
Campau, Bob, I 97
Campbell, Lorne, I 94
Campbell, Norman, II 97
CAMPBELL, river ferry, II 12
Campbell, Scotty, I 105
Canada jay, II 8
CANNOCKO, barge, II 30
Cannon, Alvin, I 107
Canoe, II 32, 69, 159, 176
Canol Oil Project, I 42, 51, 60
Cantwell, I 107; II 194
CAPE CORAL, sloop, II 164
CAPE HENLOPEN, cutter, II 132, 164
Cape Krusenstern, II 190
CAPE ROMAIN, cutter, II 142
Capital punishment, I 18
Capital relocation, II 107, 197, 198
Caposseia, Raymond J., II 161
Carcross, I 161
Caribou, I 7, 8, 77, 123, 124, 137, 141, 148, 160, 162, 176, 194; II 97, 134, 183, 193
    hunting, I 67, 73, 95, 191; II 88, 91, 110, 111, 130, 151
    record, I 47
    "slaughter" of '71, II 166
Caribou (Cariboo) Trail, I 35
Carlanna Lake Dam, II 185
Carlo, Rose, I 29
Carlson, Ellery, I 4
Carlson, Evelyn, I 21
Carlson, Glen, I 178
Carlson, John, II 179
Carmack, George, I 158, 161; II 125
CARMACKS, river ferry, II 12
Carmichael, Fred, II 105
Carmichael, Jim, I 191
Carmody, M/M Maurice, II 54
Carpenter, Dan, I 143
Carr, Larry, II 127
Carr, Dr. R.W., I 88
Carrado, Victor, I 182
Carrighar, Sally, I 135
Carrol, Col. John E., I 145
Carrol, Capt. Robert, I 149
Carroll, Ward, II 4
Carson, A.R., II 122
Carson, C.M., I 17
Carson, Lawrence, I 18
Carter, Dr. A.R., I 13
Carter, Joe, I 121
Carter, Rev./Mrs. Orville E., II 140, 145
CASCA, river boat, I 6; II 30, 194
CASCADE, halibuter, I 76
Cascaden, Mrs. Blanche, I 58
Case, Ted, I 191
Cash, Joseph T., II 181
Casperson, John, I 75
Cassady, Mrs. Magdalene, II 81
Cassiar, area, I 2, 7, 126, 197; II 27
Castner's Cutthroats, I 35
Catron, M/M H.D., I 49
Cattle farms, I 4, 12, 42, 71, 85, 89, 140, 194; II 4, 27, 34, 60, 194
    dairyman of year, II 159
    rustling, I 47
Caves, George, I 33
CEDAR, cutter, I 53
Census, I 93; II 124
Centennial, II 41, 69, 79, 85, 86, 87, 124
    commemorative stamp, II 73, 86
Cesar, Sam, II 10
Cessnun, Pete, I 95
Chambers, Francis, II 104
Chambers, Jerome, I 77
Champion International, Inc., II 197. *See also* Champion Papers, Inc.; U.S. Plywood-Champion Papers, Inc.
Champion Papers, Inc., II 68, 79. *See also* Champion International, Inc.; U.S. Plywood-Champion Papers, Inc.
Chapple, Emery, I 153, 170, 179
Chapple, Emery Jr., II 132
Charles, Albert, I 179
CHARLES JOHN SEGHERS, Liberty ship, I 37
Charles, Nelson, I 18
Charles, Wade, II 6, 17
Charlie, Chief Alfred II 127
Charlie, Arthur, II 50
Charlie, Jane, II 145
Charlie, Lige/Susie, II 171
Charlie, Tagish, I 158
Charts/maps, I 20, 90, 200; II 66, 142, 144, 159
Chase, Ken, II 190
Chase, Dr. Will H., I 43, 103; II 33
Chatanika River, II 21
CHEBOTNYAGIN, Russian factory ship, II 46
Cheechakos, I 65
Chellis, Vince, I 163
Chena River, I 13; II 4, 74, 83, 154, 174
Chena River Recreational Area, II 81

CHENA, Santa Claus ship, II 32
Chency, L.K., II 103
Chenega, II 55
Chermak, Stan, I 108
Chernofski, I 11, 49
Chevigny, Hector, II 13
Chichagof Island, I 56, 119, 145, 159
Chickaloon, II 57
CHIEF, M.V., II 181
Chignik, II 17, 130
Chilkat Dancers, II 25, 109
CHILKAT, state ferry, II 27, 37, 191
Chilkoot Barracks, I 68
Chilkoot Pass, I 31; II 108
Chirikof Island, I 42, 71, 140; II 46
Chitina, I 103, 183
Choate, M/M Rufus & children, II 50
Christensen, Pete, I 19
Christensen, Sam, I 109
Christensen, Tony, I 47
Christenson, Helvig, I 110, 147
Christian, Chief, I 145
CHUCK-'N-NAN, fishing vessel, I 180
Chugach Electric Association, II 82, 112, 146
Chugach National Forest, I 16, 160; II 162
Chugach State Park, II 122
Chulik, Paul, I 179
Church, Donald, II 37
Church of the Holy Resurrection, Kodiak, II 100, 111, 175
Church, Zane D., I 146
Churches/missions, I 31, 35, 44, 77, 81, 93, 100, 116, 123, 180; II 10, 19, 20, 29, 57, 58, 60, 64, 166, 168, 196
    Cunningham, Father Tom, I 80, 118, 145, 169
    Duncan, Father William, I 33, 64, 173
    Gordon, Rt. Rev. William (Flying Bishop), I 82, 166; II 60, 196
    Russian Orthodox, I 19, 24, 33, 45, 58, 60; II 53, 65, 72, 83, 100, 111, 146, 165, 175
Circle Hot Springs, I 51, 134; II 64
CITY OF SEATTLE, S.S., I 143
Civilian Conservation Corps, I 12, 13, 16
CLARINDA, mail boat, I 63
Clark, M/M C.M., I 174, 175
Clark, Carl, I 131
Clark, Charles L., I 127
Clark, Don, II 21
Clark, M/M H.D., II 11
Clark, Dr. James D., II 150
Clark, Jerry, II 85
Clark, Dr. Joe, II 147
Clark, Kim, I 109
Clark, W.K., I 181
Clark, Gov. Walter E., II 31
Clarke, Barb, II 78
Clarke, Tom E., I 81
Claus, Robert, I 77
Clayton, Edward, I 2
Clear Lake Logging Co., II 176
Clegg, Dr. Sharon, II 152
Clements, Roy, II 37
Cleveland, Harry S., I 141
Cleveland, Rev. Thomas, I 166
CLIFFORD J. ROGERS, freighter, II 47
Climate, *see* Weather extremes
Cline, Clifton, II 56
Close, Victor, I 60
Cloud, Charles Martin, I 166
Coal, I 12, 42, 123, 175; II 47, 51, 66
    Healy River Coal Mine, I 101
    North Slope, II 107
COASTAL MONARCH, freighter, II 61
Cobb, Mack, I 86
Cochran, Bishop David R., II 196
Cochrane, Judge, O.D., I 38
Cold Bay, I 137; II 170, 196
Coldfoot, II 150
Coleman, Ann, I 156
Coleman, Herb, I 30
Coffin, John, II 173
Colkins, Virginia, I 89
COLLETTE, fishing vessel, II 191
Collier Carbon & Chemical Co., II 67, 78, 80, 111
Collins, Ernest B., I 146; II 39, 48
Collins, Grenold, I 9
Collins, H.B. Jr., I 186
Collins, R.H., I 139
Collins, Spencer, I 68
Colonists, I 29, 50, 182; II 50, 85. *See also* individuals; Matanuska
COLUMBIA, state ferry, II 179, 183
Columbus, J.A., I 159
Comklin, Dave, II 183
Commack, Jim, II 162
Communications Satellite Corp., II 98, 105, 107, 114
Communications, *see* Telephone; Television
Conant, Bruce, II 194
Conaway, Gerald, II 79
CONFIDENCE, cutter, II 135
Conkle, Bud, I 152
Conroy, E.L., I 150
Conservation, *see* Environmental concerns; Land

Constitutional Convention, II 129, 166
Conti, Judge Samuel, II 162
Conway, Mrs. Stella, II 139
Cook, Fred, I 107
Cook, Dr. Frederick, I 133
Cook Inlet Historical Society, II 188
Cook Inlet Native Corp., II 160, 187
Cook, John, II 192
Cook, Joseph, I 126
Cooke, Adam, II 150
Cooke, Gilbert Sr., I 112
Cooper, Dick, I 134
Cooper's Landing, I 182; II 64
Copper, II 21, 75, 90, 106
    Granby Consolidated Mining & Smelting Co., Granduc mine, I 160; II 181
    Kennecott Copper Corp., I 8, 11, 81; II 17, 54
    nugget, I 134
    SEREM of Alaska, Inc., II 130
Copper River, I 35, 81, 162; II 58, 110
Copper River & Northwestern Railroad, I 11, 14, 32, 81, 103, 150, 183; II 17, 58
Copper River Highway, I 103; II 17, 50, 58, 195
Coppuck, Jerry, II 160
Copstead, Elmer, I 42
Corbly, M/M Lewis, I 62
Corbus, Bill, II 190
Cordova, I 11, 13, 22, 26, 29, 32, 43, 56, 103, 130, 150, 154, 172, 193; II 17, 20, 33, 49, 90, 137, 141, 158, 160, 198
Cordova Airlines, I 143, 193; II 92
Cordova District Fishermen's Union, II 137, 158
Cordova Weekly Times, II 90
Corey, John, I 129
Corquin, Capt. A., I 116
Correspondence schooling, I 146; II 125
COTTAGE QUEEN, S.S., I 178
Couch, M/M Jim, II 8, 24
Council, I 76; II 42
Cousins, Harold, I 43
Coutu, Rita/Yvonne, II 43
Couture, William, I 165
Cowan, Harry, I 60
Cowan, Dr. Ian M., II 95
Cowan, Lee, I 102
Cox, Jack, II 148
Coyote, I 4, 5, 7, 13, 17, 60, 72, 87, 108, 138, 173; II 56, 96, 100
Crab fishery, I 37; II 38, 43, 46, 50, 59, 160, 186, 197
Craig, I 94, 182; II 39, 68, 80, 115, 191
Craig, Robert, I 64
Crammer, Dean, II 39
Crane, Lt. Leon, I 38
Cranston, Sen. Alan, II 177
CRASHES
    airplane, I 11, 36, 38, 48, 50, 51, 69, 71, 81, 92, 101, 109, 126, 130, 144, 149, 187, 190, 193; II 4, 14, 43, 56, 64, 73, 84, 87, 100, 107, 116, 138, 142, 145, 165, 193
    railroad, I 45
Crawford, Gary S., II 13
Crepeau, M/M Peter N., II 11
Crites, Donna, II 138
Croft, M/M Chancy & family, II 135
Cross, Bess (Queen Bess), I 46, 58
Cross, John, I 46, 148
Crosson Glacier, I 94
Crosson, Joe, I 94
Crosson, Joe E., I 188
Crow, Jerry, II 40
Crowther, George, II 27
Croxton, Loren, II 23, 91
Crumrine, Josephine, *see* Liddell, Mrs. Josephine
Crutcher, William, I 105
Cruz, Ernie, I 109
Cuddy, Dan, I 29
Culver, Mrs. U.M., II 18
Culver, Walter, I 15
Cunningham, Father Tom, I 80, 118, 145, 169
Curling, International Bonspiel, II 78
Curran, M/M Pete, I 175
Currie, M/M Archie, II 68
Curry, hotel/town, I 83; II 5
Curtis, Howard, I 47
Cushing, John/Martha/R.J., II 35
Cushing, Mrs. John, I 62
Cushman Street, Fairbanks, II 50
Cutler, Mrs. Thelma, II 126

D

D-2 "National interest" lands, II 178, 184, 186, 198
Dagley, Chuck, II 17
Dahl, Pete, I 35
Dahlager, Jules, I 6, 70
Daley, John, II 102
Dalquist, Tom, II 2
Dalton, George & George Jr./Richard/Thomas, I 145
Dams/hydroelectric projects, I 56, 130, 174; II 114, 185
    Rampart, I 196; II 78, 141

Snettisham, II 85, 110, 112, 149, 190
Danielson, Capt. Adolph, I 85
D'Aoust, Randy, II 176
Darnell, Rod, II 111
Daubenspeck, James, I 105
Dauchy, Jack, II 160
Daum, Jack, I 158
Davey, A.R., I 130
David, Johnny, II 194
Davidson, Art, II 76
Davies, Ralph, II 125
Davis, David, I 20
Davis, Judge Edward D., II 142
Davis, M/M Haddon, II 38
Davis, Jerome, II 77
Davis, Mrs. Pat, I 41
Davis, Perry, I 16
Davis, Rev. Samuel, I 116
Davis, Rod, I 119
Davis, Stanford/Clara J., I 144
Dawson, I 41, 77, 92, 94, 105, 107, 116, 117; II 12-3, 25, 112, 135, 185, 194
Dawson, Mrs. Mae & Richard, I 128
Dawson Patrol, II 120
Dawson, Wallace, II 106
Dawson, Wendell, II 91
Dean, Doug, II 77
Dean, Janet, II 78
Dean, Jeff, II 77
Dean, Tom, I 167
De Armond, Robert, II 168
Dedman, M/M George, II 11
Dedman, M/M Henry, II 11
Dee, Chester C., II 56
Deer, I 13, 20, 26, 41, 48, 95, 97, 98, 99, 116, 133, 194
    hunting, I 25, 43, 70, 73, 78, 115, 128, 136, 139, 155, 171, 188
    record, I 47
Defectors, I 186; II 60, 67
DeGruyter, Ferdinand, II 11
Dellenback, Rep. John, II 180
Delta High School, II 189
Delta Junction, II 67, 86, 122. *See also* Big Delta.
DeMay, Peter, II 187
Demidoff, Titus, I 6
Demientieff, Capt. Al, II 21
Demmert, Archie W., II 106
Demmert, Dennis, II 117
Demmert, Harold & family, II 106
Demmert, Larry, II 26
Demoski, Rudy, II 190
Demski, Rosemary, I 20
Dempster Highway, II 185
DENALI, S.S., I 53, 118
Denali, town, I 94
Denali Highway, I 163, 166, 188
Depner, Frank, II 154
DERBLAY, S.S., II 16
Deschout, Rev. Paul C., II 29
DeStacia, M/M Lyman, I 127
Dettinger, Bob, II 97
Devil's Thumb, I 64
Dew Line, I 180, 200; II 57, 80, 164
DeWitt, Charles, I 134
DeWitt, Forrest Sr. & Jonathon, II 123
DeWree, Frank P. & Diane, I 195
Dexter, Don, II 68
Diamond Lil, II 16
Dibbles, J.D., I 150
Dickerson, Marv, II 86
Dickerson, Milton/Ora, II 154
Dickey, Don, II 94
Dickinson, Mrs. George, II 10
Dietrick, Teddy, II 21
Digree, Sig/Betha, II 62
Dillingham, I 71, 72; II 171, 188
Dillon, George, II 11
Dimentieff, Michael, II 154
DiMeola, Dr. H.J., II 117
Dimond, Judge Anthony J., I 131; II 9
Dinkel, Dr. Don, II 133
Diomedes, *see* Big Diomede; Little Diomede
Di Rae, Peter, II 72
DIXIE, fishing vessel, I 110, 147
Dixon, Edna, I 38
Dixon, Sharon, II 161
Dobson, Thomas, I 127
Dodson, Jim, I 47
Dogs, I 2, 21, 50, 59, 80, 86, 98, 129, 141, 159, 179, 194; II 16, 130, 146, 150, 167, 188. *See also* Dog teams
    dog-power railway, I 10, 39
    fatal epidemic, I 119
    igloo, house, I 65, 128, 163
    killing/mauling, I 29, 32, 138; II 68
    rescues, I 15, 44, 66, 91
    starving, II 51
    vs. bear, I 26; II 2, 120
    vs. porcupine, I 163
Dog teams, I 24, 27, 51, 67, 74, 84, 93, 115, 118, 158, 171, 196; II 7, 48, 53, 63, 79, 88, 98. *See also* Sled-dog races
    Alaska to Maine, I 111

Index

attacked by moose, I 162; II 22
attacked by wolves, I 93
collisions, I 146, 156
frozen in ice, I 130
mail routes, I 57, 86, 117, 175; II 36, 64
Mounted Police patrol, II 105
Nome serum dash, I 117
reindeer drive, I 147
rescues, I 15, 19, 36, 51, 137; II 4, 64
weight-pulling, I 123, 173; II 120
Doheny, Larry, I 28
Dolan, Jimmy, I 70
Domke, Kim, II 134
Donahue, Phillip H., I 108
Donaldson, Vernon, I 139
DONBASS, Russian tanker, I 57
Doran, Harry, I 82
Dorman, Mrs. Doris, I 124
Dorman, Mrs. Max, I 13
Dorris, Capt. George C., I 50
Dosser, F.A., I 107
Douglas, I 142; II 72, 142
Douglas, Capt. Jack, I 185; II 2
Dow, Mrs. Russell, I 43
Downing, Mrs. Hazel, II 37
Downing, Richard A., II 21, 37
Doyle, Jim, II 2
Doyon Limited, II 187
Dozier, Robert, II 188
Drake, Mrs. Marie, I 148
Drew, M/M Dick, I 81
Ducks, I 60, 139; II 40, 110, 182, 195
Ducks Unlimited, II 176
Dufresne, Frank, I 12
Dulaney, Richard, II 117
Dumas, John, II 98
Dummer, Mrs. Katherine, II 196
Duncan, Father William, I 33, 64, 173
Dundas, M/M Frank & Dick, I 84
Dunker, Denise/Michael, II 138
Dunlop, Dick, I 133
Dunlop, Mrs. Florence, I 119
Dunlop, Richard, I 20
Durand, Victor, I 58
Durant, Stewart, I 181
Dutch Harbor, I 55; II 91, 150
Dye, Sgt. James W., I 112
Dyea, I 31; II 159
Dyson, M/M B.R., I 109

E

EAGLE LEADER, II 117
Eagle River-Homestead Schools, II 172
Eagle, town, I 112; II 16, 92
Eagles, I 97, 102, 105, 145; II 5, 181, 195
attack, II 107
bounty, I 4, 5, 14, 87
protection, I 96; II 99, 138, 194
Early, Dash, I 38
Earthquakes, II 44-46, 48, 52-58, 60, 62-64, 66, 71, 78, 86, 104, 162
Easley, George W., II 132
Eastman, Gordon, II 4
EBISU MARU, fishing vessel, II 189
Ebright, Dr. Donald, I 195
Eckis, Rollin, II 51
Eckols, Fran, I 154
Edenshaw, Charles, II 34
Edwards, Darrell, II 31
Edwards, G. Kent, II 94, 95, 148, 189
Edwards, John, II 76
Effler, Gene, I 148
Egan, Mrs. Neva, II 37, 63
Egan, William A., II 4, 10, 38-40, 52-4, 56, 60, 63, 72, 108, 127, 129, 131, 132, 134, 135, 137, 142-6, 150, 156, 158, 159, 162, 163, 166, 169, 177, 180, 183, 184, 187, 191, 195, 197
Eggebraaten, Rev. Vernon, II 193
Egowa, Arnold, I 136
Eichner, Ken, I 102, 112
Eide, Sterling, II 69
Eielson Air Force Base, I 136, 176; II 18, 42, 58
Eielson, Carl Ben, I 176, 194; II 92, 188
EIGHT BELLS, fishing vessel, I 49
Eisenminger, William, I 74
Ekemo, Mrs. Fena, I 109
Ekowanna, Perry, I 177
Elasanga, Frank, II 10
Elbert, Douglas, I 103
Elder, Charles, II 198
Elections, I 48, 63, 79, 81; II 14, 57, 72, 84, 92, 110, 113, 126-7, 129, 142, 147, 165-6, 183, 197
electoral college, II 168
Electric power, I 21, 157; II 82, 112. *See also* Dams/hydroelectric projects.
Elk, I 1, 16; II 69
Elkins, W.A., I 139
Elliott, Rodger, I 95
Ellis Airlines, I 42, 74, 91, 174
Ellis, Lee, I 77
Ellis, Robert (Bob), I 174
Ellsworth, M/M Babe, I 27, 46
Elmendorf Air Force Base (Field), I 81, 85, 132; II 9, 73, 84, 146, 165
Elmendorf, Capt. Hugh M., II 9
Elmore, Lt. Col. William S., II 132
El Paso Alaska Co., II 198. *See also* El Paso Natural Gas Co.
El Paso Natural Gas Co., II 166, 180, 189. *See also* El Paso Alaska Co.
Elrod, Charles, II 138
Elvey, Dr. C.T., I 182
Elvioyak, Annie, II 145
Elwell, Luke/Niska, I 52, 107, 189; II 2
Emery, E.J., II 50
Emmard, Allen W., I 88
Emmons, Don, I 64, 74
Employment/jobs, I 26, 56; II 97, 110, 114, 156, 187, 190, 192-3, 195, 198
government salaries, II 41, 47, 49, 70, 122
job racketeering, II 163
minimum wage, II 93
minorities, II 163
ENDEAVOR, fishing vessel, II 151
Engdahl, Dr. E.R., II 162
Engel, Father Emmett R./George, II 176
Enockson, Martin, I 74
Environmental concerns, II 79, 81, 106, 126, 131, 133, 146, 164, 174, 183
Copper River Highway, II 195
D-2 "national interest" lands, II 178, 184, 186, 198
Fairbanks auto ban, II 179
logging ban, II 162
North Slope cleanup, II 126, 127, 134
nuclear protest, II 67, 74, 111
oil pipeline, II 127, 134, 146, 156, 158, 169, 172, 184
pollution, II 78, 86, 91, 103, 111, 115, 117, 125, 189
Prince William Sound, II 137, 141
timber sale protest, II 118, 124, 136, 143, 197
wilderness, II 104, 108, 127, 130
wildlife protection, I 96, 99; II 15, 69, 99, 110, 121, 138, 139, 157, 159, 176, 182, 185, 188, 193, 194
Enzler, Warren, II 121
Erickson, Al, I 194
Erickson, Olaf, II 19
Erlam, Bob, II 168
Ernst, Rose, II 77
Eskimos, I 1, 2, 15, 21, 29, 54, 59, 60, 67, 77, 86, 96, 104, 106, 114, 120, 124, 129, 141-2, 149, 153, 159, 161, 165, 186, 196; II 2, 4, 9, 19, 21, 33, 40, 43, 51, 72, 95, 99, 102, 105, 124, 134, 136, 138, 142, 151, 153. *See also* individuals by name.
Anaktuvuk, II 66, 85, 91, 104
arts/crafts, I 23, 28, 36, 87, 141, 167, 169; II 23, 49, 163, 176
Barrow, I 46, 97, 133, 190; II 56, 57, 106
Bethel, II 163
food storage, I 156; II 36, 127, 168
games, I 191; II 128, 145, 162, 194
King, I 27, 57, 73; II 32, 42
Little Diomede, I 80, 118, 134; II 36
ordeals, I 44, 83, 122, 160; II 32, 42
Point Hope, I 61, 188; II 97, 111
polar bear, I 51, 99, 155, 162, 173; II 154
reindeer, I 22, 114; II 194
St. Lawrence, I 27, 36, 39, 115, 151, 157; II 1, 70, 72, 127, 143
Togiak, II 27, 103
Wales, II 94, 190
walrus/whale, I 42, 44, 45, 65, 146, 148, 154, 157, 158, 175; II 10, 19, 96, 128, 133, 196
whale festivals/muktuk, I 97, 133, 166; II 93, 106, 158
Eubank, C.C., I 16
Evans, Brock, II 104
Evans, Commander Griffith C., II 18
Evanson, Dave, II 107
EVELYN, vessel, I 78
Evenson, M/M Irvin, II 67
Everts, Clif, I 181
Evon, M/M Joseph & Timothy, II 95
Explorers, I 30, 45, 50, 66, 75, 114, 133, 155, 171, 176, 180, 194; II 33, 154

F

Faa, Mickey, II 36
Fader, Carroll, II 146
Faessler, Whitey, I 161
Fagerlie, M/M Ole, I 5
Fairbanks, I 12, 36-7, 48, 64, 67, 84, 101, 134, 155, 157, 181; II 16, 21, 43, 50, 57, 59, 74, 77, 85-6, 89, 91, 103, 116, 124, 127, 134, 136, 141-2, 145, 161-3, 166, 179, 198
aviation, I 44, 176; II 42, 51, 92, 188, 195
Chena River ice pool, I 13; II 4, 154, 174
flood, II 83
gold, I 82, 184, 193, 201; II 60, 175
honorary hostess, I 144; II 109
hydrants, I 171; II 13
ice shortage, I 43, 50
Nordale Hotel, I 144; II 153
sled-dog races/teams, I 1, 8, 51, 82, 88, 89, 110, 121, 172, 197; II 6, 9, 79
University of Alaska, I 14, 23, 56, 62, 92, 97, 105, 109, 145, 167, 171, 195-6; II 49, 72, 73, 75, 92, 96, 125-6, 128, 131, 133, 140-1, 144-6, 150, 155, 158, 163, 175, 192
weather extremes, I 68, 198; II 135, 136, 170
Fairbanks Exploration Co., I 8; II 77
Fairchild, Michael, II 163
FAIRMOUNT, II 101
Fairview Hotel, Fairbanks, II 74
Falk, Erling, II 7
Farley, John L., I 171
Farms/gardens, I 4, 13, 15, 29, 31, 36-7, 41, 46, 49, 64-5, 85, 96, 119, 127, 128, 136, 160, 167, 186, 188; II 23, 27, 107, 122, 168, 181. *See also* Cattle farms; Fur farms; Sheep farms.
cabbage, I 172, 181; II 106, 113, 189
corn, II 133
farm family of year, II 191
4-H Clubs, I 181, 188
potato, I 21; II 67, 191
Faro, Yukon Territory, II 95, 118
Farrier, II 138
Faulkner, Earl, I 17
Faulkner, William M., I 187
FAVORITE, U.S.S., II 185
Feathers, Col. E.D., II 2
Federal Office Building, Juneau, II 56
Feero, M/M John, II 11
Fejes, Claire, II 16
Felder, Jenny, II 145
Fenn, Bruce, II 92
Fenton, Lloyd, I 2
Ferguson, Archie, I 15, 49, 56, 58, 60, 76
Ferguson, Frank, II 166
Ferguson, Henry R., II 138
Ferguson, John, I 183
Ferguson, Monte, I 60
Ferguson, Reb, II 79
Fernandes, Arthur, II 141
Ferries, *see* Marine Highway System
Ferris, L.S., I 183
Fidalgo Island Packing Co., II 52, 59, 139
Field, Fred, I 141
Field, Maurice, I 147
Fields, Art, I 185
Fields, DeWitt, II 34
Filmore, Mrs. Paul, II 111
Filstrup, Scott, I 155
Fink, Tom, II 119
Fires, I 15, 21, 32, 33, 35, 95, 118, 172, 178, 188; II 43, 50, 56, 146
Cordova, II 49, 90
forest, II 97, 101, 162, 176, 181
Hoonah, I 40
hospitals, I 94, 107
hotels, I 31; II 74, 153, 160, 196
Ketchikan waterfront, I 183; II 59, 126
oil well, II 41, 110
St. Michael's Cathedral, II 65
salmon canneries, I 16, 61, 182; II 59
ships, I 51, 63, 72; II 142, 194
Skagway, I 31; II 113
Wrangell, I 115
Whittier, I 133
Fischer, Bob, II 100
Fischer, Clyde, II 169
Fish & Game Department (Alaska), II 23, 47, 54-6, 59, 60, 78, 89, 93, 95-6, 105, 111, 122, 126, 128, 130, 134, 139, 146, 166, 182, 184-5, 188
Fish & Wildlife Service (U.S.), I 53, 88, 91, 115, 119, 130, 138, 145, 148, 153-4, 159, 160, 162, 166, 168, 176, 187; II 18, 121, 194. *See also* individual agents.
Fish hatchery, I 148; II 146
Fish, Isabelle, I 45
Fish ladder, I 98; II 47, 128
Fish traps, I 6, 24, 26, 50, 63, 74, 79, 89, 104, 115
Fisher, Victor, II 95
Fisheries, commercial, I 23, 26, 29, 49, 67, 84-5, 91, 98, 100, 113, 123, 163, 167, 178, 180, 184; II 59, 73, 95, 98, 100, 106, 121, 123, 126, 139, 141, 172, 178. *See also* Fishing, sport; individual species.
cold storage, II 29
course of study, II 97, 133
earthquake damage, II 55
international tensions, I 84; II 38, 46, 54, 59, 81, 94, 102, 148, 175, 186, 189, 191
limited entry, II 89, 174, 195, 198
Fishing, sport, I 12, 23, 44, 82, 125, 170; II 2, 110. *See also* individual species.
Fishwheel, town, I 92
Fitzgerald, J.B., II 149, 161
Flat, I 6, 104
Flatt, Art, I 48
Fleck, Elmer, I 75
Fleck, Francis G., I 18
Fleharty, George, II 160, 182
Fleischer, Susan, II 188
Fletcher, Lt. Col. Joseph, I 120
FLICKA, troller, II 181
Floods, I 41, 49, 75, 85, 94, 143, 157, 162, 171; II 4, 19, 21, 26, 42, 83, 144, 157, 185
Florendo, Mrs. Nora Marks, II 163
Flores, Ralph, II 49
Fluor Alaska, Inc., II 192
Flynn, Rev. James A., II 36
Fohn-Hansen, Lydia, I 172
Folta, Judge George W., I 89, 91, 102, 125
Folta, Richard, I 102
Fonda, Skagway Bill, I 110
Food prices, I 76, 115, 119, 181; II 93, 186, 192
Foode, Jim, II 97
Football, I 97
Foote, Joan, II 77
Forbes, Ben, I 31
Forbes, Judge Vernon D., II 2
Ford, M/M Alva, I 132
Ford, Mrs. Annabel, I 175
Ford, Mrs. Hulda, I 171
Foreman, Ed, II 11
Forest industries. *See* Logging; Pulp/paper mills; Sawmills. *See also* Forests.
Forests, I 23; II 75, 99, 109, 162
Chugach National Forest, I 16, 160; II 162
fires, II 97, 101, 162, 176, 181
Tongass National Forest, I 16, 23, 79, 160, 200; II 51, 79, 117, 162
Forrest, Emil, II 13
Forsberg, Walter, II 15
Fort Good Hope, N.W.T., II 181
Fort Greely, II 152
Fort Jonathan M. Wainwright, II 18
Fort McPherson, II 120
Fort Norman, I 42, 51, 60
Fort Rae, N.W.T., II 110, 130
Fort Richardson, II 68, 81, 143, 158
Fort Simpson, II 130
Fort William H. Seward, II 10
Fort Yukon, I 85, 94, 157; II 51, 86
Foss, Carl, II 71
Foster, Grover, I 50
Foster, L.A., I 69
Foster, Mrs. Midge, I 188
Foster, Will, I 86
Fowler, Frank, II 11
Fowler, Howard, I 150
Fowler, M/M Julian V. & children, II 191
Fox, Kirk, II 149
Fox, Red, I 163
Foxes, I 1, 9, 10, 21, 26, 55, 78, 138; II 80
trapping, II 154
Frakes, Fred, I 190
FRAM, II 154
Frank, M/M John, II 64
Frank, M/M Sherwin & children, I 63
Frantz, Jack, II 103
Frazer Fishway, II 47
Fredericksen, Stan, I 161, 187, 196
Frederickson, Eric, I 87
Freericks, Jim, I 120
Freese, Dr. Leonard, II 67, 130
Freezer ships, II 52
Friedland, Steve, II 95
Friends of the Earth, II 134, 137, 156, 158
Fromme, Francis, II 104
Frostbite, II 29
Fuerstner, Max & son, II 196
FUKUYOSHY MARU, II 102
Fuller, Mark, I 113
Fur farms, I 5, 10, 12, 14, 26, 57
Fur seal, I 12, 19, 20, 37, 63, 71, 86, 103; II 73, 79, 89, 121. *See also* Hair seal.
international treaty, II 42
Furs/trapping, I 18, 36, 58, 63, 76, 95, 118, 138; II 85, 89, 150, 171. *See also* Fur farms; individual fur-bearing species; individual trappers by name.
longest trapline, II 103
parkas, I 36; II 80, 171
regulation, enforcement, I 9, 11, 17, 27, 53, 60
trapper death/injury, I 2, 20, 24, 30, 32, 35, 44, 68, 69, 86, 130, 149, 165, 189; II 12, 72

G

Gaier, Ralph H., I 127
Gakona Lodge, I 195
Gale, George & family, I 155
Gale, James E., I 114
Galena, I 49; II 40
Galla, Donna, II 154
Gallahorn, Mike, II 68
Gambell, I 36, 84; II 1, 40, 51, 53, 70, 133, 141, 143
Gann, Berk/Linda, I 112
Ganty, Prosper, I 144
Gardner, Douglas/Mike, I 177
Gardens, *see* Farms
GARLAND, M.V., I 127
Garrett, M/M Ralph & Michael, II 18
Gastineau Hotel, Juneau, II 154
Gates, Jeffery, II 50
Gatey, John Jr., II 104

Index

Gatz, Peter, II 10
Gavin, Shirley, II 188
Gay, Ward, II 2, 130
Gearhart, Owen C., I 191
Geese, I 60, 139; II 40, 74, 182
Geist, Otto William, I 171
Gellenbeck, Ben, I 31
Gelzer, Warner, II 85
General American Oil Co., II 101
Genet, Ray, II 76, 138, 194
Geographic names, *see* Alaska, state of; Board of Geographic Names
George, Chris, II 178
George, Corporal H., I 118
George, Milton, II 181
George, Robert, II 26
Georgia-Pacific Plywood Corp., I 186
Gerasim, Archimandrite, II 175
Getty Oil Co., I 105
Ghost ships, II 179, 181
Gibson, Comdr. Jack E., I 83
Gideon, Sister Mary, I 94
Giersdorf, Robert, II 82
Gilbertson, George, II 87
Gilchrist, Duncan, II 69
Gildersleve, R.G., I 122
Gillam, Harold, I 179
Gilliland, Dayton, I 149
Gillis, Dan, I 102
Girdwood, II 48
Gitkov, Capt. G. David, II 27
GJOA, sloop, I 45, 180
Gjosund, Mrs. Louis, I 119
Glacier Bay National Monument, I 200; II 80, 195
Glacier Bay (Silent City), I 131
GLACIER, icebreaker, II 86
GLACIER QUEEN, cruise ship, II 86
Glaciers, I 91, 94, 113, 190; II 39, 179
   Bering, II 73
   Eklutna, II 147
   Grand Pacific, II 56
   Knik (Lake George), II 40, 94, 110
   Mendenhall, I 64, 69, 108, 180
Glaser, Frank, I 83, 121, 122, 153
Glass, Clyde, I 20
Glavinovich, Carl, II 42
Gleason, Bishop Francis, I 145
Gleason, Henry, I 19; II 12
Glover, Art, I 92
Glowa, Patricia Ann, II 107
Glud, M/M Bob, II 5
Goat, domestic, I 90
Goat Mary, *see* Thompson, Mary
Goat, mountain, I 119, 120, 145
   hunting, I 30, 104, 139, 162; II 64
Goddard, A.J., I 185
Gold, I 14, 110, 111, 175; II 47, 51, 90, 95, 110, 175.
   See also individual miners, mines by name.
   Alaska-Juneau Gold Mining Co., I 3, 26; II 20, 56
   Diamond Lil, II 16
   dredges, I 74, 72, 101, 166, 184; II 77
   Fairbanks, I 82, 184, 193, 201; II 60, 175
   Fairbanks Exploration Co., I 8; II 77
   Hyder-Stewart, I 10
   Independence Mine, I 15, 20
   Klondike, I 30, 31, 87, 158, 161, 193; II 9, 19, 25, 77, 125, 175, 188
   Klondike Kate, I 62, 92, 169
   mining, prospecting, I 2, 7, 9, 56, 68, 79, 91, 94, 140, 170, 181, 193, 195; II 7, 26, 75, 111, 160
   Nome, I 51, 61, 184, 193; II 26, 42, 81, 101, 179
   nuggets, I 18, 21, 30, 92, 107, 179; II 42, 111, 188, 193, 196
   U.S. Smelting, Refining & Mining Co., I 184, 193; II 42, 147
   war closes mines, I 29, 52, 53
Golden North Hotel, Skagway, II 11
Goldstein, Charles, I 6, 28
Golf, II 81, 108
Golodoff, Benjamin, II 100
Gologergen, Tim, II 70
Gonnason, Warren C., II 90
Goodman, Don H., I 124
Goodnews Bay, I 9, 15, 68; II 51
Goodridge, Mrs. John & Cade/Wade, II 189
Gordon, M/M Dick, II 24
Gordon, Frank, I 100
Gordon, Mickey, II 162
Gordon, Rich, II 104
Gordon, Stanley, II 4
Gordon, Tom/Sophie, I 152
Gordon, Tommy, II 105
Gordon, W.D., I 116
Gordon, Bishop William, I 82, 166; II 60, 196
Gordon, Wolf, I 29
Gorison, Martin, I 120
Gorman, Mrs. Frank, I 95
Goshawk, II 181
Gould, Rev. P. Gordon, II 15
Government Hill School, Anchorage, II 44
Grabowski, Edwin T., II 100
Graham, Capt. Charles, I 64
Graham, David, I 49

Graham, Willis G., I 123
Grand Pacific Glacier, II 56
Granduc mine, I 160; II 181
Grant, Bishop A. Raymond, II 15
Grant, M/M Bob, I 147
Grant, Ted, II 138
Grasser, Al, I 83
Gratias, M/M Dave & Theresa, II 120
Gravel, Mike, II 114, 124, 137, 157, 177
Gray, Douglas, II 172
Gray, Gordon, I 153
Gray, Michael, I 108
Greeley, A.W., I 75
Green, Andrew, I 120
Green, Perry, II 171
Gregg, John, I 21
Gregorcheck, Frank, I 135
Gregory, Albro, II 110, 127, 164
Gregory, M/M Glenn, I 122
Gregory, Joseph Paul, II 138
Griffin, Glenn, I 161
Griffin, Walter, I 148
Griffiths, T.M., I 114
Grisko, Tony, I 35
Groceau, Paul, I 198
Gromtzeff, Julie, I 47
Gross, W.D., I 29, 138, 178
Grouse, II 61
Growden, James, II 53
Gruening, Ernest, I 37, 42, 81, 87, 176, 196; II 43, 73, 108
Gruening, Mrs. Ernest, I 42
Grussendorf, Mrs. Karen, II 139
Grutzner, Charles, II 117
Gubsen, Harlan, I 5
Guess, Gene, II 132, 166
Guides, I 192; II 31, 95, 111. *See also* individual names.
Guinn, John, II 163
Gulf Oil Corp., II 127, 156
Gully, Dora, II 187
Gunderson, Andy, I 60
Gunderson, M/M Emil, II 10
Gunderson, John, II 88
Gunderson, Reggie, I 109
Guthrie, Clare, I 88

H

Hackett, Capt. W.D., I 114
Haffner, Andy, I 94
Hager, Edwin, II 120
Haggland, Dr. P.B., I 37, 45
Hagmeier, M/M John, II 28
Hagmeier, Lee, II 28, 179
Hah, Kenneth, II 162
Haidahs, I 116; II 34, 117. *See also* individuals by name.
   basketry, II 176
   land settlement, I 200; II 105
Haines, I 69; II 10, 25, 113, 142, 144
Haines, Chris, II 77, 145
Haines, Marvin, I 130
HAINES MARU, II 81
Hair seal, I 4, 5, 16, 87, 114, 173; II 1, 17, 56, 138.
   See also Fur seal.
Halibut, I 100; II 50, 181
   commercial, I 75, 89, 136; II 20, 28, 59, 175, 177
   "Greenland halibut," II 96
   prices, I 10; II 111
   record, I 33; II 71, 126, 141, 183
   sport, I 86, 90, 97, 191; II 141, 145, 160
Hall, Byron W., I 153
Hall, Doc, II 62
Hall, George, II 99
Hall, John, II 104
Hall, L.R., II 22
Halle, Rolf, II 92
Halleran, William, II 154
Halvorsen, Henry, I 43
Hamilton, Chuck, II 49
Hammond, Jay, I 121
Hammond, Rear Adm. Robert E., II 121
Hand, W.E., II 13
Hanford, J.H., I 80
Hankins, Charles, II 39
Hanna, Dr. Dallas, II 52
Hansen, Bob, II 127, 151
Hansen, Julia Butler, II 107
Hansen, Mart, I 89, 130
Hansen, Paul, II 100
Hansen, Thorwald, I 99
Hansen, Vic, II 38
Hanson, Bert, II 93
Hanson, David, I 78
Hanson, Eric, I 67
Hanson, Hans, I 100
Hanson, Thorvig, I 94
Happle, Harry, I 43
Harder, Fayette, II 166
Hardin, George, II 162
Harding Icefield, II 93
Harding, Dr. J.K., II 174
Harding, President Warren G., I 68, 77, 148; II 64

Harkness, Mrs. Grace, II 145
Harned, Capt. Albert E., II 31
Harper, Fred, I 100
Harper, Johanna, II 145
Harrington, Keith, I 179
Harris, Mrs. Arthur J., I 127
Harris, Rip, I 83
Harris, Steve, II 78
Harrison, Robert, II 53
Harrison, William, II 93
Hart, Judge George L. Jr., II 158, 163, 169
Hartig, Robert, II 103, 168
Hartigan, William, II 36
Hartman, Cliff, II 125
Harvey, Kenneth, I 148
Haskin, Mrs. Ada, II 97
Haskins, Scotty, II 104
Hasselborg, Allen, I 130, 134
Hatch, Jesse, I 151
Hatley, Alexander, I 112
Hautala, William A., I 38
Havelock, John, II 132, 163, 168, 170, 172, 178
Havemeister, M/M Bob & sons, II 159
Hawkins, M/M Jim, II 16
Hayes, George, II 38
Hayes, James, II 21
Hays, Andy, I 66
Hayward, Del, II 162
HAZEL B., river boat, I 16; II 27
HAZEL H., fishing vessel, I 97
Hazelet, George C. & Calvin/Craig, II 46
Hazeletville, II 46
Headless Valley, I 58, 66; II 39
Healy, Capt. Mike, II 71
Healy River Coal Mine, I 101
Heath, Ken/Hazel, I 64
Heaven, M/M Foster C. & LeRoi, I 181
Hegger, Hans, I 68
Heidelberger, Mrs. Laure, II 135
Heiker, Karl, II 170, 196
Heinmiller, Carl, II 25, 109, 181
Heinrich, Paul, I 31
Heintzleman, B. Frank, I 144, 150, 156, 158
Hellaby, Deaconess Hilda A., II 121
Heller, Dr. Herbert Lyman, I 195
Heller, Olaf, I 37
Helmericks, Bud, I 198
Helms, Pacita, II 174
Hemen, M/M Denys, I 160
Hemming, James, II 91
Henault, Maj. Steven, II 138
Henderson, M/M Patsy, I 161
Hendrickson, John W., II 176
Hendrickson, Waino, II 178; II 168
Heney, Michael, II 20, 58
Henkins, Clancy, I 163
Henratty, Ed, I 66
Henri, Joseph R., II 132, 174
Henricks, Ray, II 142
Henry, Frank, I 160
Henry, Oscar, I 108
Henry, Corporal Royce, I 118
Herbert, Charles, II 132, 134, 137, 160, 170, 192
Herman, Saint, II 111, 175
Heron, M/M Jack, I 78
Herring, I 3, 60, 182
   roe, II 50, 80, 89, 115
Hershberger, Mike, II 176
Hess, Elvin, II 58
Hess, Brother John, I 144
Hetten, Edgar, II 7
Hibbard, Dr. Walter R. Jr., II 82
Hickel, Walter J., II 72-4, 79, 83-5, 90, 94, 98-9, 101, 105, 108, 111, 117, 119, 122, 125-9, 131-2, 134-5, 148
Hickel, Mrs. Walter J., II 72, 94, 148
Hight, Mrs. Betty, II 136
Highways, I 31, 43, 69, 78, 98, 151, 155, 191; II 7, 12, 25, 33, 86, 99, 125, 145, 156, 185, 187.
   See also Marine Highway System.
   Alaska (Alcan), I 1, 24, 31, 33, 35, 37, 43, 50, 57, 61, 75, 76, 85, 94, 99, 143, 159; II 47, 67, 86, 156, 196
   Anchorage-Seward, II 121
   Copper River, I 103; II 17, 50, 58, 195
   Craig-Klawock, II 115, 191
   Dawson-Tok, I 92, 105
   Denali, I 163, 166, 188
   Glenn, I 151; II 106, 144
   Hart, I 107, 108, 121
   Ice Bridge/Road, II 101, 111, 119, 187
   Richardson, I 65, 75, 85, 88, 98, 126, 145, 154, 169, 201
   Steese, I 7, 73, 162; II 21, 146
   Sterling, I 117, 182
   Stewart-Watson Lake, II 164
   Taylor, I 112; II 166
   Valdez Trail, I 183
   Winter Haul Road, II 104, 122, 192, 195, 198
Hill, Mrs. Lenaya, II 87
Hill, M/M Victor, II 33
Hilliard, Dr. J.K., II 174
Hilscher, Herb, I 88, 130
Hines, Bishop John E., II 60

Hirohito, Emperor of Japan, II 146
Hixon, Bill, I 30
Hobart, Jerry, II 7
Hockey, II 103, 150, 189
Hodge, Judge Walter F., II 16
Hodges, Ross (Tiger), II 189
Hodgson, Stuart, II 152
Hodson, Bruce, II 129
Hodson, Clell, II 37
Hoeman, Dr. Grace, II 147
Hoeman, J. Vin., II 85, 93, 147
Hoff, Mrs. George, I 48
Hofseth, Morris, II 170
Hofstad, Andrew Edward, II 109
Hofstad, Mrs. Kelly, II 109
Hogan, Kathleen Ann, II 109
Hogins, Carole, II 163
Holdsworth, Phil R., II 34, 40
Holen, Lee, II 37
Holikachaget, village, II 72
Hollis, I 91; II 115, 191
Holloway, Dorr, II 170
Holm, Norman, II 10
Holmberg, Sonny, II 142
Holmburg, Ollie, I 66
Holmes, E.H., I 183
Holmes, Jay, II 37
Holtner, Dean, I 59
Holy Cross, I 51, 39, 81, 144
Holzworth, John M., I 91, 134
Home Oil Co., II 118
Homer, I 4, 14, 22, 64, 119
Homesteads, I 4, 5, 16, 29, 31, 41, 46, 64, 83, 102, 136, 152, 167, 182, 191; II 23, 43, 167, 178, 188
Honey wagon, *see* Nome
Honsinger, Dr. Fred, II 98
Hood, Jim, I 66
Hoonah, I 40, 145; II 35, 174
Hooper Bay, I 31, 42, 61, 114, 147; II 2, 78
Hoopes, Fannie L., II 51
Hootch, I 14; II 171
Hope, Donald A., I 165
Hope, Ed, I 31
Hope, John, II 170
Hopson, Charlie, II 138
Hopson, Eben, II 197
Hopson, Patricia, I 190
Horchover, Dr. Robert, II 124
Horne, Fred, I 11
Hospitals, I 94; II 67, 72, 87, 94, 114, 143, 187, 189.
   See also Natives.
   mental, I 113; II 39, 63, 81
House, M/M Fred, I 113; II 4
House, Wayne, I 68
Housel, M/M Baslor, I 69
Housing, II 96, 114, 183. *See also* Natives.
Hovely, Otto, I 44
Howard, Frances Jean, II 108
Howe, Bob, II 104
Howe, Lloyd, I 80
Howe, Wesley M., II 194
Howell, Billy, I 19
Howkan, I 20
Howson, Roger, II 160
Hoylman, Robert L., II 13
Hubbard, Mrs. Charles, I 99
Hubbard, Percy, I 82
Hudson, Cliff/Glenn, I 116
Hudson, E.C., I 69
Hudson, Everett, I 88
Hudson, John, I 49
Hudson, Lou, I 25
Hudson, Mrs. Mary, I 64
Hudson's Bay Co., II 28
Huffaker, Merlin D., I 130
Hughes, Carroll, I 168
Hughes, Capt. Graham O., I 125
Hughes, M/M Roy C., I 153
Hukill, M/M David, II 11
Hulien, John, II 59
Huling, Clinton, II 169
Hult, Carl, I 12
Humble Oil & Refining Co., I 180, 190; II 40, 43, 61, 101, 105
Humes, Fred, I 33
Hungerbuhler, Emil, I 2
Hunt, H.L., II 108, 130
Hunter, Celia, II 21, 79, 104, 106, 183
Hunter, E.W., I 186
Hunting, I 13, 19, 20, 22, 60, 77, 86, 113, 128, 131, 139, 144, 151, 162, 168, 177; II 2, 13, 43, 47, 48, 74, 195. *See also* individual species.
   bow/arrow, I 185; II 9, 127, 129, 151, 189
   deaths, I 19, 24, 25, 113, 149, 155, 177; II 4, 37, 56, 184
   injuries, I 32, 67, 73, 77, 101, 104, 115, 128, 137, 151, 168, 187; II 38
   lost hunters, I 73, 85, 115; II 36
   regulation/enforcement, I 9, 19, 24, 26, 60, 87, 139, 195; II 20, 70, 95
Huntington, Carl, II 190
Huntington, Jenny, I 122
Huntington, Jim, II 162

Index

Huntington, Roger, II 162
Hupper, Paul, II 191
Huslia, I 127; II 51, 81
Hussey, C.E. (Jim), II 37
HY GENE, marine health lab, I 47
Hydaburg, I 86, 98, 105, 116, 125; II 2, 191
Hyder-Stewart, I 10, 91, 130, 150, 160; II 26, 72, 164, 181, 193
Hydroelectric projects, see Dams
Hylton, Roswell W., I 38

I

Ibach, Joe, I 99
Ice Bowl, Fairbanks, I 97
Ice bridge, II 119, 187
Ice fog, II 135
Ice islands, I 120, 200; II 2, 18, 138
Ice pools/lotteries, I 9, 13, 57; II 4, 91, 138, 154, 174
Ice Road, I 101, 111
Ice worms, I 93
Icebergs, I 50, 121, 187; II 109, 179
Iditarod, II 48, 173, 190
Igloolik, II 152
Igloos, I 65, 141; II 103, 124, 150, 158, 175. See also Natives.
Iklesik, Isaac, I 197
Iknokinok, Clifford, I 157
Independence Mine, I 15, 20
Iniskin Drilling Co., I 10, 19
Interior Airways, I 169; II 92
Inuvik, I 82; II 128, 145, 162, 168
Ioanin, George, II 184
Iron, II 75
  Pan American Petroleum Co., II 52
  U.S. Steel Corp., II 128
Iron chink (canning machine), I 167
Iron Curtain, I 80, 134; II 70
Iron Trail, see Copper River & Northwestern Railroad
Isaacson, Jack, I 6
Isaaksen, Anton, II 38
Isabell, James, II 150
Itjen, Martin, I 20, 37, 117; II 11, 85, 159
Itta, Brenda, II 166
Itta, James, II 194
Itta, Katherine, II 145
Ivan, Robert, II 190
Ivanoff, Paul, I 21
Iverson, Mrs. Doris, I 154
Iya, Cora, II 2
Izembek National Wildlife Range, II 15

J

Jackovich, Dolores, II 78
Jackson, Clarence, II 185
Jackson, Clifton, II 190
Jackson, Gerald A., II 109, 115
Jackson, Sen. Henry M., II 172, 177, 184
Jackson, Mansel/Ray, I 148
Jackson, Nathan, II 116
Jackson, Norman, II 181
Jackson, Mrs. Ora, I 21
Jackson, Dr. Sheldon, II 10
Jacobs, Duane, I 171
Jacobs, Gordon, II 125
Jacobs, Capt. William R., I 50
Jacobson, Carl, II 140
Jacobson, Dr. Jake, II 143
Jacobson, Les, II 59
Jade, I 167
Jager, Bill, I 149
Jails, I 114; II 7, 16, 69, 85, 179
James, Kelly, II 123
Janes, Mrs. Betty, I 31
Janes, Henry, II 85
Jangaard, Otto, II 126
Japan Gas Co., II 80
Japan/Japanese, I 24, 196; II 42, 101, 109, 134, 160
  Emperor's visit, II 146
  fisheries, I 118, 184; II 50, 52, 91
  fishery tensions, I 84; II 54, 102, 148, 175, 186, 189, 191
  forest industry, I 58, 141, 184; II 29, 75, 109, 197
  oil, gas, II 77, 80, 117, 146, 162
  World War II, I 32, 49, 51, 55, 57, 77, 90, 118, 130; II 49, 143
Japan Whaling Co., II 148
Japonski Island, I 54; II 90, 143
Jarvela, Gil, II 12
Jennings, Larry, II 166
Jensen, Franklin, II 13
Jensen, Louis, II 73
Jensen, R.D. (Chuck), II 116
Jesse Lee Home, II 32, 40, 57, 81
Jessen, E.F., II 89
Jessen's Weekly and *Morning Daily*, II 89
Jewell, Homer, I 9
Jim, Charlie Jr., II 140
Jim, Frankie, I 90

Jim, George, I 179
Jobe, Jack L., II 156
Jobs, see Employment.
Johanson, M/M Knut, I 173
Johanson, Lesa, I 199
Johansson, Sven, II 166, 199
John, Charlie, I 121
John, Johnnie, II 97
John, Walter, I 121
Johns, Greg Sr. & Jr., II 39
Johns, M/M Robert, II 178
Johnson, A.D., I 22
Johnson, Bob, I 179
Johnson, Chief, II 14
Johnson, Dick, I 64
Johnson, M/M Ed., II 190
Johnson, Capt. Elmer V., II 91
Johnson, Ernie, I 66
Johnson, Frank, I 68
Johnson, Frank (legislator), I 135
Johnson, Frank W./Minnie, II 1
Johnson, Franklin, I 108
Johnson, George B. Sr., II 106
Johnson, Harry, II 148
Johnson, Mrs. Herman, II 141
Johnson, Sgt. John, I 64
Johnson, Joseph W. Sr., II 106
Johnson, Capt. Knute, II 150
Johnson, Knute A., II 137
Johnson, Louis, I 58
Johnson, President Lyndon B., II 73
Johnson, Mabel, II 135
Johnson, Mrs. Mary, I 138; II 5
Johnson, Mrs. Myrtle, II 1
Johnson, Neal, II 24
Johnson, Capt. Richard L., I 190
Johnson, M/M Sam, II 25
Johnson, W. Howard, II 79, 97, 104, 115, 118
Johnson, Walter, I 185
Johnson, Warren, II 4
Johnson, Wayne, I 25
Johnson, William O., I 130
Johnston, Bruce, I 31
Johnston, Dave, II 76, 93, 138
Johnston, M/M Dick, I 31
Johnston, Mike, I 57
Johnston, Mrs. Ray, II 9
Johnston, Walker, II 182
Johnston, M/M William L., I 130
Joiner, Gene, I 99, 167
Jones Act, II 94, 135, 151, 179
Jones, Art, I 66
Jones, Chief Billy, II 81
Jones, Bob, I 95
Jones, Charles F./Etta E., I 51, 57, 77
Jones, Dr. Charles H., I 111
Jones, Charles J., I 177, 180, 189, 190
Jones, Charlie, I 146
Jones, Ed, I 69
Jones, Howard, I 67
Jones, Jarvis, II 177
Jones, Capt. Joyce & Jamie/Lore/Tammy, II 177
Jones, Stan, II 164
Jonz, Don, II 165
Jorgensen, Martin, I 66
Joseph, M/M Charles Sr., I 144
Joseph, Lillian, I 142
Josephson, Joe, II 127, 178
Josie, Edith, II 162
Joule, Tony, II 60
Joyce, Mary, II 63
JUDITH ANN, river boat, II 81
Judkins, Clifford, II 115
Juneau, I 32, 138; II 5, 16, 37, 39, 42, 47, 53, 63, 82, 94, 122, 126, 145, 152, 154, 161, 162, 195, 197
  Alaska-Juneau mine, I 3, 26; II 20, 56
  Baranof Hotel fire, II 196
  capital relocation, II 107, 197, 198
  Gravina airport, II 171, 179
  jet-plane crash, II 145
  legislature, I 46, 146, 150; II 48, 122, 193
  Mendenhall Glacier, I 64, 69, 108, 180
  museum, I 28, 37, 159; II 34, 63, 77, 97, 176
  pulp-mill project, I 126, 186; II 68, 79, 97, 109, 115, 118, 124, 136, 143, 197
  Snettisham power project, II 85, 110, 112, 149, 190
  sport fishing, I 103, 111, 153; II 141, 162, 192
Juneau Icefield, II 110
JUNEAU, U.S.S., I 52
Juneby, M/M William & son, I 64
Justesen, Betty, I 196

K

KINY, Juneau radio, I 50, 152
Kaasen, George/John, II 3
Kadake, Benjamin, I 100
Kadlutsiak, Josiah, II 152
Kadow, Kenneth, II 132
Kagak, David C., II 68
Kagueyak, Nick, I 82
Kahler, Erick, I 42
Kail, George, I 16

Kaiser, Paul D., II 132
Kaiser, Pi, I 154
Kakaruk, Paul, I 88
Kake, I 92, 100, 135; II 35, 85, 109, 115, 176
Kaleak, Joe, II 145, 162
Kalen, Barbara Dedman & Barbie, II 11
Kalentenko, Peter, II 60, 67
Kamerer, Desi, II 190
Kaminski, Henry, I 54
Kanari, M/M John, I 100
Kane, Gordon, II 149
Kannizi, Andrew, II 120
Kantishna, II 12, 41, 182, 193
Karakin, Evan, I 71
Karametros, John (the Turk), II 14
Karbbe, Capt. Otto, II 66
KARLUK, S.S., II 33
Karmatique, Bob, II 54
Karsten, M/M Heinie, I 43
Kasaan, I 15, 91, 116, 119; II 117, 143, 147
Kasak, Joe, II 145
Kashevaroff, Father Andrew P., I 19, 138
Kasko, Mrs. Jessie, II 72
Kasser, Martin, II 193
Katalla, I 42; II 71, 156
Kate's Needle, I 64
Katexac, Ramauld, II 42
Katmai National Monument, II 12, 14
Kavanaugh, Mrs. Ethel, II 110
Kay, Wendell, II 127, 129
Kayak, I 23
Kayvanuk, Frank, II 32
Keen, Master Sgt. Kenneth, II 58
Keenan, F.J., I 183
Keithahn, Edward L., I 37, 159; II 34, 40, 50
KELECO, tug, I 191
Keline, Jim, II 146
Keller, Mary, II 145
Kellogg, V. Louise, II 181
Kelly, C.G., I 137
Kelly, Maurice, I 83, 139, 141, 162
Kelly, Raymond, I 82
Kelly, Judge Raymond J., I 178
Kelly, Tom, II 108
Kempton, Mrs. G.O., II 18
Kenai, I 24, 66, 81, 88, 113; II 7, 77, 80, 93, 99, 100, 136, 146
Kenai Lumber Co., II 138, 197
Kenai National Moose Range, II 159, 182
Kenai Native Association, II 160
Kenai Peninsula, I 2, 86, 88, 110, 125, 156, 161, 166, 187, 193; II 55, 59, 78, 82, 85, 96, 97, 100, 112, 133, 147
  covered bridge, I 182
  moose, I 12, 85; II 18, 134, 159, 182
  oil/gas, I 177, 180, 189, 190; II 2, 4, 7, 19, 26, 38, 47, 77, 80, 99, 112, 153
Kendall, Everett A., I 161
Kendler, Mrs. Joe, I 119
Kennecott Copper Corp., I 8, 11, 81; II 17, 54, 130
Kennedy, Jim, I 50
Kennedy, Kay, I 159
Kerner, Mrs. Stephen, I 131
Kerr, Glenn, I 20
Kerr-McGee, I 143
Ketchikan, I 1, 3, 11, 19, 21-2, 30, 33, 35, 45, 46, 54, 57, 68, 70, 76, 80, 89, 98, 101, 123, 131, 135, 139, 145, 149, 188; II 14, 22, 32, 52, 62, 71, 100, 102, 114, 116, 123, 129, 135, 138, 139, 140, 141, 161, 163, 174, 176, 189
  Carlanna Dam burst, II 185
  fires, I 51, 72, 183; II 59, 126
  Ketchikan Pulp (& Paper) Co., I 79, 86, 95, 124, 126, 143, 188; II 48, 115, 185, 191
  Ketchikan Spruce Mills, I 19, 22; II 115
  rainfall, I 56, 97, 155
  sport fishing I 44, 77, 124, 128, 148, 153; II 31, 141, 146, 162, 181
KETCHIKAN MARU, II 81
KEV ALASKA, barge, II 19
Keyes, Edward, I 100, 105
Kiariauak, Charles, II 192
Kienzle, Mrs. Leona, I 76, 98
Kier, Louie, I 181
Kignak, Paul, II 57
Kilcher, Yule, II 93
Kilkenny, Cliff, I 114
Killbear, Billy, II 194
Killbear, James, II 145, 194
Killen, M/M Warren, I 147
Killigivuk, Jimmy, II 33
Kilmurray, Brendan, II 116
Kimbel, Ed, I 100
Kimball, Ross, I 134
Kimball, Thomas L., II 86, 188
Kinegak, Mrs. John, II 95
King, M/M George, I 121
King, Harley, II 9
King, Sgt./Mrs. Bill, I 156
King crab, see Crab fishery
King, M/M George, I 121
King Island, I 27, 57, 73, 77, 118; II 32, 42
King, Jim, I 153; II 194

King, Maurice, I 66
Kirk, Chuck, II 53
Kirkland, Fred, I 76
Kirkness, Walter, II 47, 54
Kirmse, Herman D., II 11
Kirsteatter, Mrs. Paul & Freddy, II 96
Kiska Island, I 26, 32, 55, 90
Kitchen, George, II 4
Kitimat, I 130, 143
Kitka, Herm, II 69
Kito, Richard, II 105
Kivalina, I 10; II 4, 158
Kivett, M/M Gene, I 140
Kiyukteluk, Stephen, I 191
Kjeksted, Paul, II 3
Kjera, Ed, II 154
Klaben, Helen, II 49
Klawock, I 92, 112; II 39, 115, 120, 191
Klein, Dave, II 166, 171
Kleinfeld, Dr. Judith, II 134
Klemm, Val, I 100
Klepser, Merritt, II 62
Klonas, George, I 63
Klondike, I 30, 31, 87, 158, 161, 180, 193; II 9, 19, 25, 77, 110, 112, 125, 175, 188
  Diamond Lil, II 16
  Klondike Kate, I 62, 92, 169
  Klondike Mines Railway, II 25
KLONDIKE, river boat, I 6; II 112, 117, 194
Klukwan, II 106, 116, 128
Knackstedt, Henry, I 128
Knapp, George, II 162
Kneeland, Bill, II 158
Knickerbocker, Floyd, I 128
Knight, Prof. Ado., II 41
Knudsen, Mrs. Emil, I 45
Knudson, M/M Howard, I 193
Knuutila, Tony, II 77
Kobuk area, I 15, 23, 30, 160; II 35, 54, 130
Kodiak, I 45, 62, 84; II 31, 39, 62, 64, 75, 151, 152, 170, 193
  Baranof Mansion, II 99, 113
  earthquake/tidal wave, II 44, 46
  fisheries, II 29, 43, 46, 54, 59, 81, 88, 95, 97, 100, 106, 123, 133, 153, 172, 181, 186, 191
  Katmai eruption, II 12
  Naval Station, I 14; II 13, 140, 151, 158
  Russian Orthodox Church, I 33; II 100, 111, 175
Kodiak Island, I 12, 15, 71, 80, 82, 137, 181; II 9, 34, 47, 55, 59, 60, 72, 102, 117, 152, 176, 193
KODIAK, Liberty ship, I 45
Kodiak Lumber Mills, II 197
Kodiak Mirror, newspaper, II 62, 100
Kodiak National Wildlife Refuge, II 176
Koe, Abe, II 120
Koenig, L.S., I 105
Kokoles, Nicholas, II 47
Kokrine, Effie, I 197; II 6, 17
Kolby, Christ, I 15
Komok, John, II 173
Konradt, Gus, I 30
Koonalook, Furst, I 177
Koons, Emmett, II 39
Koontz, Velma, II 157
Koppers Company, II 41
Korba, Jack, I 61
Korslien, Vern, II 162
Kotongan, Victor, II 190
Kottke, Joel, II 190
Kotula, Wayne/Nancy, II 62
Kotzebue, I 15, 122, 132, 160, 176, 193; II 21, 41, 42, 53, 86, 92, 102, 107, 135, 162, 187, 191
Kovach, Carl, I 138
Kowalke, Mrs. Alta, II 90
Kowunna, Eva, II 194
Koyuk, I 155
Kraft, Otto & Walter O., II 64
Krause, Joe, II 95, 124, 128, 154
Krautter, Raymond, I 82
Krepps, William, II 102
Kreta, Rt. Rev. Joseph, II 165
Krevie, Alvin, II 176
Kriska, Leo, I 122, 197; II 6
Kristovich, John, I 98
Kropf, Al, I 84
Kubley, M/M Wallace & Donnie/Karen/Larry, II 22
Kuchta, Al, II 145
Kuehl, L., I 50
Kuehn, Dan, II 165, 182
KUKUYOSKI MARU, II 102
Kulan, Al, II 72
Kulper, Dave, II 97
Kunkel, J.M., I 35
KUSKO, river boat, I 134
Kuskokwim area/river, I 2, 9, 15, 16, 20, 23, 24, 27, 68, 78, 85, 90, 94, 107, 134, 141, 171, 193; II 7, 27, 41, 42, 51, 72, 95, 157, 163, 170, 192
Kuskokwim National Wildlife Range, II 15
Kuysters, Wally, II 154
Kyle, Mrs. Burt, I 49

Index

L

LABRADOR, icebreaker, I 180
Ladd Air Force Base (Field), I 44, 50, 85, 105, 118, 179, 185; II 2, 18
Lafon, Mrs. Joseph, I 30
LaFon, L.A., I 18
La Fortune, Father Bellarmin, I 77
Lake George, II 40, 94, 110
Lake Minchumina, I 139
Lakinoff, Frank, I 77
Lamm, M/M George, II 193
Lampe, Maggie, I 190
Land, I 192
  D-2 "national interest," II 178, 184, 186, 198
  Delta Junction, II 122
  homestead/open to entry, I 5, 16, 83; II 23, 96, 126, 183, 188
  Matanuska-Susitna Borough auction, II 194
  Native claims (Settlement Act), I 174; II 72, 120, 124, 132, 141, 146, 148, 150, 160, 170, 185, 198
  Petersburg auction, II 156
  Tlinget-Haidah settlement, I 200; II 105
Land otter, I 10, 31, 138, 148; II 75
  trapping, I 58, 76; II 89
Lander, A., I 42
Landru, Mrs. Hortense (Jack), I 129; II 9
Landry, Richard, I 179
Landt, M/M Fred, I 170
Lane, Edmond, I 159
Lane, Ernest, I 98
Lang, Roger, II 105
Langford, T.A., I 127
Langton, Helen, II 153
Lanier, Verell, II 86
Lanni, Dave, I 170
LaPierre, Sgt. Everett, I 118
LARK, fishing vessel, I 107
Larsen, Sgt. Henry A., I 45, 63
Larsen, Holger, I 85, 87
Larsen, Nils, I 73
Larsen, Richard, I 109
Larson, Oscar, I 3, 70
Larson, Pete & James/Pete Jr., I 147
Lathrop, Austin E. (Cap), I 101
Lathrop, Dr./Mrs. Robert, I 176
Laufbaum, Graden, II 93
Laurin, Emil, I 62
Lawing, Nellie Neal (Alaska Nellie), I 37, 86, 125, 156, 161, 193
Lawrence, Gene, I 110
Lawrence, Maurice, I 105
Leach, M/M Frank, II 64
LEAD, ZINC
  Anvil Mining Corp., II 89, 95, 118
Leary, Mark, II 178
Leask, Kenneth, II 105
Leavitt, Luther, II 103
Lee, Ben, I 61
Legg, Roland E., I 150
Legislature, *see* Juneau
Leige, Clarence, I 163
Leinan, Clare, I 71
Lekanof, Anatoly, II 154
Lekanof, Flore, II 88
Leland, Joe, I 161
Lemmings, I 135
Lemmon, George, I 4
Lerdahl, Herman, II 63
LeRoux, Paul A., II 134
Leslie, George, I 68
Leutfer, Jack, I 194
Lewellen, Adm. Bafford E., I 21
Lewis, C.R., II 127
Lewis, Judge Eben H., II 169
Lewis, Fred, II 43
Lewis, Commander J.R., II 131
Lewis, Mrs. J.R., II 63
Lewis, M/M Jerry & Shawn, II 107
Lewis, Victor Alonzo, I 110
Liar award, I 83
LIBBY I, seiner, I 159
Libe, M/M Bert, I 70
Libraries, I 73, 153, 156; II 21. *See also* Alaska Historical Library & Museum.
Liddell, Mrs. Josephine Crumrine, II 16
Liddicoat, M/M E.J., II 11
Lie, Leif, II 152
Lien, M/M Charles, I 182
Lies, Elbert, I 57
Lifesaving awards, I 157, 171; II 9, 68, 106, 138, 142, 176
Lifkins, John, II 164
Lightfoot, Eugene L., I 155
Lighthouses, *see* U.S. Coast Guard
Lightning, I 154; II 98
Likins, J.H., I 59
Lilly, Joseph, I 7
Limited-entry fishing, II 89, 174, 195, 198
Linck, Alaska, I 46
Lincoln, Melville N., I 137
Lincoln, Rodney, I 141
Lindamood, Ruby D., I 69

Lindblom, Erik, II 42
Lindeberg, Jafet, II 42
Lindemuth, Al, I 59
Lindley-Liek Expedition, I 171
Lindquist, Mrs. Ernest, II 58
Lindsley, Roy, I 137
Ling, Carl, I 86
Lisbourne, Dan, II 47
Little Diomede Island, I 28, 80, 118, 134, 168, 169, 178, 186; II 4, 36, 95, 105, 162, 182
Littlefield, Evelyn, I 88
Lituya Bay, I 20; II 80
Livengood, I 29, 155, 188
Lloyd, Chet, I 41
Lloyd, Tom, I 133
Lockwood, M/M Howard & children, II 122, 132
Lofgren, Wayne, II 18
Lofstedt, Bud, II 4
Loftus, Ed, I 62
Loftus, J.B., I 14
Logging, I 21, 23, 58, 72, 113; II 29, 31, 51, 145, 162, 176, 191, 194, 197
Lombard, Dr. Roland, I 197; II 6, 17
Lomen, Alfred, II 3
Lomen, Alonzo, I 136
Lomen, Carl, I 135
Lomen Commercial Co., II 21, 135
London, Jack, I 116; II 9, 125
Long, Elizabeth, II 194
Long, CWO/Mrs. Robert F. & Dwight, II 12
Longenecker, M/M Harvey, II 130
Longley, Gary T., II 150
Loomis Armored Car Service, II 64
Loomis, Buck, I 109
Loomis, Lee, II 64
Lord, Roland, II 162
Lorentz, Mrs. Cindy, II 189
Losonsky, Mrs. Rose, I 172, 197; II 17
Lost River City, II 152
Lost River Mining Corp., II 152
Lotteries, *see* Ice pools
Louie, Mrs. Regina & Curtis, II 135
Loussac, Z.J., I 153
Lovelace, Mrs. Hazel, II 97
Low, Doug, II 68
Lowe, John, I 187
Lowell, Deputy Marshal Ted, I 134
Lowell, Mrs. Ted, I 45
Lown, Bud, I 73
Lubke, A.C., I 93
Luchterhand, Dennis, II 85
LUCINDA J., seiner, II 160
Luddington, Dan, I 93
Ludecke, Edward, II 39
Ludwigsen, Herman, I 95
Luick, Dr. Jack R., II 194
Luke, Howard, I 82
Lund, Mrs. Lawrence, I 48
Lunde, Peter, II 11
Lundgren, Carol, II 17
Lundgren, Janice, II 6
Lundstrom, Mrs. Martha, I 93
Lupro, Harry, II 62
Luttinger, Capt. J.R., II 2
Lutz, Andy, II 36
Lyman, M/M Dean & Lorna, II 107
LYNDA, crabber, II 150
Lynds, D.E. (Pete), II 96
Lynn, John, I 38
Lynx, I 21, 126, 131, 161, 163; II 47, 171
  trapping, I 122, 184
Lypa, Fred, II 68

M

Maas, Peter, I 20
MacDonald, Jack, I 87
MacDonald, John K., I 2
Machetanz, Fred, II 98
Machetanz, Mrs. Sara, I 101
MacInnes, Ann/Scott, II 6, 17, 82
MacInnes, Charles, I 156; II 17
MacInnes, Mrs. Kit, I 151; II 6, 17
Mack, Jack, I 130
MacKenzie, Angus, I 41
MacKenzie, Bob, I 123
MacKenzie, Douglas, II 64
Mackey, Dick, I 173, 190
Mackie, Capt. William, II 21
MacLennan, H.L., I 31
Maddison, Justice Harr, II 179
Madigan, R.J., II 190
Madsen, Alf, II 12
Mafia, II 117
Magnusia, Lawrence, I 128
Magoffin, James, I 82, 122, 169
Magoffin, James Jr., I 169
Magoffin, James S., I 92
Mahoney, Lt. Col. Dan, II 70
Mahoney, Joe, I 25
Mahoney, Margie, II 145

Mail, I 5, 10, 12, 23, 63, 64, 85, 113; II 18, 73, 143, 145, 156, 168
  1st air mail, II 188
  via dog team, I 57, 86, 117, 175; II 36, 64
MALASPINA, state ferry, II 39, 135, 142, 179
Malemute, Jimmy, I 197; II 6
Malinowski, Andrew, II 18
Manley Hot Springs, I 162; II 57
MANNING, cutter, II 12
Mantilla, Walter, II 16
Manton, Frank, II 11
Maps, *see* Charts
MARATHON
  Equinox, Fairbanks, II 163
  river boat, II 162
  Seward, I 166, 199; II 64
Marathon Oil Co., II 59, 77, 80, 108
Marble, I 26; II 79
Marchant, Pvt. Raymond, I 116
MARGARET ROSE, river boat, II 81
Marine Highway System, II 21, 27, 37, 39, 43, 50, 56, 90, 91, 94, 100, 129, 132, 135, 142, 151, 179, 183, 186, 191. *See also* individual ferries.
Marine Mammals Protection Act, II 157
MARIPOSA, S.S., II 53
Marks, M/M Magnus & Kristen, I 32
Marmoochka, Tony, I 42
Marshall, Ralph, II 64
Marshall, Thomas, II 146
Marsters, George, II 56
Marten, II 10, 58, 119, 138
  trapping, I 135; II 89
Martin, Roy, I 87
Marvin, Harvey, II 105
Marx, Ethel F., I 6
Marx, Mrs. William, I 6
MARY FOSS, tug, II 19
MASSET MAID, fishing vessel, II 142
Massey, Lt. Donald R., II 2
Mast, Capt. G.C., I 200
Matanuska River, II 144
MATANUSKA, state ferry, II 39, 129, 179
Matanuska Valley, I 12, 49, 85, 96, 102, 186; II 26-7, 144, 164, 191
  cabbage, I 172, 181; II 106, 113, 189
  colonists, I 2, 7, 10, 13, 14, 20, 36, 65, 160; II 67, 122, 159
  potato, I 21; II 67, 191
Mather, Casper, I 123; II 14
Mather, Rev. Paul, I 123
Mathiesen, Andy, II 160
Matney, M/M Arthur, I 29, 77
Matney, Harvey, I 29
Matson, M/M John, *see* Klondike Kate
Matthew, Dr. James, II 133
Matthews, Dr. Mildred, II 136
Matthews, Warren, II 143
Mattson, M/M Andrew G. & Laura, II 123
May, Bert, I 119
May, Fred, II 162
Mayfield, Mrs. Julie, I 93
Mayo, Alfred, II 6
Mayo Landing, II 30
Mayo, Patricia, I 47
McCall, Dr. John, I 140
McCann, Alfred, II 11
McCarthy, I 21
McCarthy, J. Ellsworth, I 161
McCay, Bert, I 114
McClelland, Albert, I 160
McComber, Alex, I 61
McConnell, Dee, II 140
McCord, Jack, I 42, 71, 82; II 47
McCormack, James, II 98
McCracken, Dr. Harold, II 72
McCrary, Mrs. Jesse, I 156
McCullough, M/M Arthur H., I 58
McCully, Gary, II 196
McCutcheon, Steve, II 32
McDonald, George W., I 37
McDonald, Terry, II 14
McDonnell, Mrs. Harry, II 25
McDougall, Roy, II 33
McGahan, Richard, II 86
McGilton, Fred, II 194
McGinnis, Dr. Frederick P., II 15, 55
McGlashan, Hugh, II 88
McGonagle, Charlie, II 133
McGonigle, Dorothy, II 193
McGowan, M/M Jim, II 84
McGown, Eva, I 144; II 109, 153
McGrath, I 85; II 9, 188
McHale, Bill, II 72
McIntyre, Dick, I 185
McIntyre, Father William, II 58
McIver, Wallace, I 76
McKay, Fred, I 48
McKechnie, Lloyd, I 168
McKee, Lynne, I 167
McKee, Pat, II 160
McKeever, John H., II 192
McKennan, Dr. Robert A., II 96

McKenny, Keith, II 162
McKenzie, A.E., I 23
McKenzie, Frank, I 195
McKillop, Bob, II 181
McKinley, Dr. Lee, II 72
McKinley, Ovid, II 188
McKinley Park Hotel, II 160
McKinnon, M/M Duncan & John/Mary, II 34
McLane, Homan, I 63
McLaughlin, Mark, II 85
McLean Arm, II 75
McLellam, Arthur, I 149
McLennan, Donald, I 36
McMahan, M/M Cleo, I 139
McNeil, Gary, II 154
McNeil, Ron, II 116
McQUESTEN, river ferry, II 12
McVeigh, Richard, II 86
Meade, Kirk, II 171
Mealor, Leonard, II 193
Meals, Andrew J. & John, II 46
Meals, Owen E., I 123; II 46
Medley, Lolly, II 190
Meier, Edwin & family, I 119
Mekiana, Homer, II 91
Melewotkuk, Florence, II 49
Menadelook, Walter, II 10
Mendenhall Glacier, I 64, 69, 108, 180
Mendenhall, Mrs. J.W., I 91
Mendenhall, Marie, I 102
Mentasta, II 106
Mercado, D.B., I 94
Mercer, Tom, II 190
Mercier, John, II 96
Mercury, II 90
  Red Devil Mine, II 51
Merley, Mrs. Esther, II 92
Merric, Inc., II 150
Merrill, Field, I 15; II 29, 58, 105, 166
Merrill, Russel Hyde, II 29
Merry, Wayne, II 76
Messerschmidt, Don, I 155
Messmer, Eugene, I 44
Metcalf, Frank, I 191
Metcalfe, M/M Vern & Peter, II 82
METEOR, M.V., II 142
Metlakatla, I 33, 42, 64, 88, 119, 152, 173; II 52, 130
Meyer, Uwe, II 120
Meyers, Larry, I 95
Meyers, Larry Jr., I 97
Meyers, Raymond, I 97
MICA
  British Columbia Mica Co., I 145
Mice, I 162
Middleton Island, II 71, 105
MIDGETT, cutter, II 189
Miklautsch, Thomas J., II 101
Miller, Bob, II 196
Miller, Dick, I 29
Miller, Dorothy, II 141
Miller, M/M Frank, I 43; II 146
Miller, Fritz, II 146
Miller House, I 43; II 146
Miller, Keith, II 72, 107, 108, 111, 113-5, 118, 122, 124, 127, 129, 132
Miller, Les, II 162
Miller, Mrs. Mary Bourne, I 170
Miller, Dr. Maynard, II 110
Miller, Neil, I 46
Miller, Ross, I 131
Miller, Sara, I 161
Millett, Isabelle, II 168
Milligan, Fred, I 117
Milligrock, Edmorris, II 95
Million Dollar Bridge, I 81; II 17, 58
Milotte, M/M Al, I 145
Minifie, John D., II 161
Mining/prospecting, I 1, 68, 126; II 26, 73, 82, 90, 162, 170. *See also* individual miners, mines by name; specific minerals.
Mink, I 1, 9, 10, 21, 58, 138; II 150
  trapping, I 76, 135, 177
Mintken, Elwood, II 104
Minto, I 50, 94; II 50, 106
Misconceptions about Alaska, I 5, 46, 88, 122, 200; II 28
Mishimae, Shiro, II 76
Mishko, Nicholas, II 46
Miskoff, Steve, I 48
Missions/missionaries, *see* Churches
Mitchell, Roy, I 131
Mobil Oil Co., II 43, 59, 80
Moe, Gene A., I 154
Moennekes, Frank, I 101
Moller, Freddie, I 36
Molner, George, II 172
Monagle, John, I 90
Mondale, Sen. Walter, II 177
MONROE, fish boat, II 109
Monsen, Capt. Al, I 69, 117
Montague Island, II 52, 138
Montgomery, Monty, II 50
Moore, Mrs. Bessie, I 52
Moore, Bill, I 150

Index

Moore, Cecil A., I 111
Moore, Mrs. Elwood, I 124
Moore, George, I 28
Moore, Howard & Robert, I 60
Moore, Dr./Mrs. Terris, I 92, 114, 126; II 49
Moose, I 10, 12, 19, 42, 87, 99, 131, 139, 156, 165, 174-5, 185, 194, 200; II 2, 62, 81, 91, 95, 134, 139, 148, 172, 185
  albino, I 145; II 104
  attacks, I 24, 44, 63, 95, 125, 128, 138, 160, 162, 174; II 18, 22, 32
  horns locked, I 19, 122
  hunting, I 18, 24, 26, 32, 64, 75, 85, 93, 101, 104, 129, 139, 151, 169; II 32, 37, 38, 74, 91, 99, 104, 111, 125, 151, 158
  Kenai National Moose Range, II 159, 182
  marauders, I 85, 112, 195; II 67
  on road, runway, track, I 19, 39, 53, 83, 122, 143, 145, 154, 157, 159; II 129, 134, 176
  records, I 90, 114, 149, 178; II 4, 129
More, Jerry, I 114
Morelain, Michael, II 82
Morgan, Beverly, I 47
Morgan, Dean, II 115
Morgan, Matt J., I 20
Morgan, Lt. Stanley, I 47
Morgan, Terrence, II 150
Morgan, William II, II 29
Mork, Betty/Marie, I 110
Morningside Hospital, I 113; II 81
Moros, Richard E., I 179
Morran, Myron, I 72
Morris, M/M Jack, I 62
Morris, M/M Lee & Mary, I 184
Morris, Ray, II 172
Morris, Raymond W., II 86
Morrison, George, II 113
Morrow, Justice William, II 151
Morton, Rogers C.B., II 137, 141, 146, 156, 158, 160, 169, 172, 178, 180, 184, 186, 187
Moses, Alfred & Abbott, I 52
Moses, Beattus, II 17
Moses, Carl E., II 88
Moses, Johnny, I 118
Moses, Little David, I 114, 149
Mosquitoes, I 78, 84, 89; II 73, 172
Mount Alyeska, II 92, 110, 134, 172
Mount Cleveland, I 41
Mount Crosson, I 94
Mount Dimond, II 9
Mount Edgecumbe School, II 14, 56, 107, 112, 145
Mount Hayes, I 30
Mount Kathryn, II 29
Mount Katmai, II 12
Mount McKinley, II 138. *See also* Mount McKinley National Park.
  climbing expeditions, I 66, 114, 133, 140, 171; II 76, 85, 94, 147, 160, 194
Mount McKinley National Park, I 15, 40, 44, 56, 62, 94, 163, 166, 171, 183, 188, 201; II 84, 94, 158, 160, 161, 181, 182, 190
MOUNT McKINLEY, S.S., I 4
Mount Old Katmai, II 12
Mount Pavlof, I 39; II 67
Mount Redoubt, II 67
Mount Sanford, II 138
Mount Spur, I 132, 141; II 193
Mount Tobert, I 132
Mount Trident, I 14
Mount Wickersham, II 9
Mountain climbing, I 30, 64, 154; II 138, 147.
  See also Mount McKinley.
Mozee, M/M Ben, I 39
MOZYR, Russian refueler, II 117
Mueller, Teddy, I 93
Muir, John, I 57; II 10, 56
Mukluks, I 167
Muktuk, I 133, 198; II 93, 106, 158
Mulcahy, William F., I 73
Mullin, Mike, I 109
Mulvihill, Carl E., II 25
Munz, Bill, I 47, 73, 132
Murdey, Dave, II 115
Murkowski, Frank, II 109, 115, 127, 129
Murphy, August, I 75
Murphy, Dale, II 126
Murphy, Jerry, I 98
Museums, I 134, 137; II 40, 150
  Alaska Historical, I 28, 37, 159; II 34
  Anchorage, II 98, 178, 188
  Lawing, Alaska Nellie, II 86, 156, 193
  Pullen House, I 68, 117
  Smith, Soapy, II 85, 159
  State of Alaska, I 63, 77, 97, 176
  University of Alaska, I 109, 145; II 72, 155, 163, 175
  Yukon Territory, I 149; II 13, 25, 86, 188
Musgrove, Gladys, II 72, 131
Mushrooms, II 18
Musk ox, I 8, 14, 137, 166; II 2, 15, 37, 97, 106, 122, 140
  qiviut, II 100, 131, 171
Muskrat, I 1, 9, 10, 21, 138
  trapping, I 35, 118; II 107, 171

N

NANA Corp., II 187
Nachand, Tom, I 25
Nadeau, Louis, I 30
Nagazuk, Grace, I 109
Nagel, Franz, II 190
Nahanni Valley, *see* Headless Valley
Nansen, Fridtjof, II 154
NANUK, schooner, I 176
NAOMI, vessel, I 163
Napaiskak, II 157
Napamute, II 170
NASUTLIN, stern-wheeler, I 116; II 12, 30
Nathan, Ben, II 2
Nation, Jimmy, I 186
National Audubon Society, II 74
National Guard, *see* Armories
National Oceanic & Atmospheric Administration, II 162
National Wildlife Federation, II 86, 188
Natives, I 2, 36-7, 39, 40, 50, 63, 110, 118, 119, 120, 121, 123, 135, 141-2, 161; II 4, 27, 74, 81, 92, 106, 162, 192. *See also* Aleuts; Eskimos; Haidahs; individuals by name; Tlingets; Tsimpsheans.
  arts/crafts, I 13, 16, 20, 23, 28, 36, 54, 64, 87, 105, 123, 141, 143, 159, 167, 169, 189; II 1, 14, 23, 25, 34, 49, 69, 73, 106, 109, 117, 123, 131, 134-5, 140, 147, 157, 163, 174, 176, 178, 188
  chiefs' conferences, II 43, 97
  festivals/games, I 97, 133, 166, 191; II 128, 145, 162, 194
  fishing, I 1, 24, 46, 92, 104
  health/hospitals, I 17, 39, 47, 73, 87, 107, 112, 120, 176; II 2, 9, 177
  housing/igloos, I 36, 57, 61, 63, 65, 73, 141, 142; II 34, 100, 141, 186
  land claims (Settlement Act), I 174, 200; II 72, 105, 120, 124, 132, 141, 146, 148, 150, 160, 170, 178, 184, 185, 186, 191, 198
  potlatch, I 16; II 116, 123
  regional corporations, II 160, 178, 187
  reservations, I 96, 98, 125, 200; II 128
  schools, I 2, 4, 106, 142, 143; II 56, 83, 107, 163, 197
Nava, Joe, II 188
Naval Research Laboratory, II 138, 146
Nayukpuk, Herbert, II 173, 190
Neakok, Sadie, II 164
Nearod, M/M Steve, I 68
Neary, Jim, II 21
Neiland, Ken, II 88
Neill, Fred, I 13
Neilson, Capt. Carl, I 118
Nelson, Bud, I 134
Nelson, Carl, I 163
Nelson, Carl, I 174
Nelson, Charles, I 36, 178
Nelson, Charles, II 105
Nelson, George, II 72
Nelson, James, II 37
Nelson, John, I 19
Nelson, L. Clair, II 124
Nelson, O.A., I 103
Nelson, M/M Paul & family, I 160
Nelson, M/M Robert C., II 91
Nelson, Urban C., I 119; II 96
Nenana, I 9, 13, 57, 77, 93, 148, 161; II 4, 19, 30, 50, 83, 90, 91, 122, 154, 174
NENANA, stern-wheeler, I 131, 155, 181
Nerysoo, Peter, II 120
Ness, Albert, I 128
Netro, M/M Joe & children, II 93
Nevada Bar, Fairbanks, II 141
New Archangel Dancers, II 139
New England Fish Co., II 59, 84, 139
New, Howard & Morley, II 37
Newhall, Rev./Mrs. Albert, II 57
Newman, Mrs. Dana, I 119
Nichols, Sgt./Mrs. Edwin, I 98
Nichols, Roy, I 35
Nicholson, Herbert, I 72
NICKEREI MARU, II 86
Nielsen, Stu, II 107
Niemi, William J., I 163
Nightingale, Joe, II 49
Nikiski, II 19, 38, 91, 103
Nikolski, I 127; II 170
Nillson, Marian, I 163
Nilsson, W. Don, II 67
Ningeulook, Ray H., II 141
Ninilchik, II 17, 141, 145
Nixon, President Richard, II 146
Noerenberg, Walter, II 115
Nolan, Danny, II 91
Nolan, James, II 94
Nome, I 10, 30, 44, 73, 83, 85, 115, 127, 147, 148; II 3, 14, 52, 55, 66, 85, 110, 127, 132, 147, 149, 152, 157, 164, 187
  Air Force base, I 108
  gold, I 51, 61, 184, 193; II 26, 42, 81, 101, 179
  honey wagon, I 124, 135
  Iditarod race, II 173, 190
  "Pupmobile" railway, I 10, 39
  serum dash, I 117
  storms, I 53, 62
Nome Nugget, II 110, 127, 164
Noongwook, Chester, II 36
Noorvik, II 47, 174
Nord, Pete, I 56
Nordale Hotel, Fairbanks, I 144; II 153
Nordale, Tony, II 153
Norman, Airman 1/c Martin, I 196
Norris, Danny, II 78
Norris, Earl, I 97
Norris, Natalie, II 6
North American Championship, *see* Sled-dog races
North Pole landing, I 120
NORTH SEA, crabber, II 100
NORTH SEA, S.S., I 64
North Slope, II 107, 121, 126, 189. *See also* Oil/gas.
  borough, II 153, 169, 197
  ice bridge/road, II 101, 111, 119, 187
  railroad plan, II 158, 172, 182
  winter haul road, II 104, 122, 192, 195, 198
North Star Borough, II 57
NORTH STAR, supply ship, I 2, 22, 123; II 2
NORTH STAR III, supply ship, II 36
Northern Consolidated Airlines, I 109, 129; II 14, 29, 92
Northern Cross Airlines, I 24
NORTHERN LIGHT, cutter, I 49
Northern Lights, I 58; II 93, 144
Northland Transportation Co., I 12, 18, 39, 64
Northrup, Mrs. Walt, II 141
Northwest Airlines, I 196; II 28
Northwest Passage, I 45, 63, 180
Northwest Reindeer Processing Co., II 78
Northwest Territories, I 42, 51; II 105, 110, 122-3, 128, 130, 152, 160, 168, 171, 175, 181, 189
NORTHWESTERN, dormitory ship, I 55
NORTHWIND, cutter, II 51
Norton, George, I 82
Norton, George, II 158
Notti, Emil, II 127
Novik, Kaare, II 59
Noyes, Dan, I 85
NUCLEAR
  power plant, II 152
  testing, II 67, 74, 95, 108, 111, 113, 150, 162, 183
Nugget Shop, Juneau, I 160; II 34, 37
Nulato, I 29
Nungak, Lloyd, II 40
Nunivak Island, I 21, 35, 166; II 2, 15, 21, 29, 37, 97, 100, 106, 122
Nusinginya, John, II 70
Nutter, William, I 5
Nyman, Fred, I 38

O

Oberg, M/M Clyde, II 164
O'Brien, Capt. Johnny, I 23
O'Brien, M.J., I 49
O'Connell, John, II 143
O'Conner, Diane, II 77
O'Connor, Jack, I 18
Octopus, I 10, 35
Odell, Mrs. Eden, II 62
Odeman, James, II 141
O'Donnell, M/M Pat, I 92, 96
ODUNA, freighter, II 66
Oglend, Oscar, II 142
Ohio Oil Co., I 177; II 4, 7
Ohlson, Col. Otto F., I 148, 181
Ohmer, Earl N., I 91, 155
Oil/gas, I 10, 19, 140, 168, 190; II 4, 7, 23, 33, 37, 41, 43, 51, 55, 62, 71, 85, 95, 110. *See also* Pipelines.
  Canol Project, I 42, 51, 60
  Cook Inlet, II 34, 35, 37, 38, 42, 52, 55, 59, 61, 66, 82, 93, 168, 169, 187, 192
  discovery wells, I 177, 180, 190; II 34, 35, 59, 112, 117
  1st millionaires, II 101
  leases/royalties, I 184; II 7, 10, 34, 40, 51, 55, 58, 61, 62, 66, 71, 103, 105, 108, 117, 124, 146, 163, 177, 187
  liquefied gas, II 77, 80, 153, 162, 172
  Navy Petroleum Reserve, I 90, 132; II 48, 57, 180
  North Slope, I 102, 132; II 48, 55, 58, 98, 101, 103, 105, 111, 134, 146, 169
  Oil & Gas Conservation Committee, II 112
  oil spills, II 86, 91, 103, 111, 117, 125, 189
  petrochemical, II 67, 80, 111
  Prudhoe Bay, II 91, 93, 108, 112, 117, 156
  refineries, I 42, 60; II 26, 38, 99, 105, 112
  Swanson River, I 177, 180, 189, 190; II 2, 19, 47
Okakok, Guy A., I 158, 173, 175, 187, 196, 198
Okeaha, Clair & Carl, II 42
O'Keefe, Dennis, I 74, 170
Okleasik, Isaac, II 173
Old-age assistance, I 19; II 72, 122, 174, 175, 188
Old Crow, I 23, 118; II 93, 105, 107, 127, 139, 168
Oldham, Kenneth, II 190
O'Leary, Charles, I 193
O'Leary, Christian, I 30
Olendorff, Mary, I 172
Olmstead, Mrs. Richard, II 23
Olrun, Daniel T. Sr., II 151
Olsen, Alex, II 10
Olsen, Dick, II 143
Olsen, Elmer, II 100
Olsen, Fred, II 163
Olsen, Mrs. Hilbert, I 47
Olsen, Marvin, II 183
Olsen, Willard, I 18
Olson, Dave, II 190
Olson, Douglas, II 10
Olson, George, I 29
Olson, Rev./Mrs. Gordon, II 140
Olson, Gus, I 35
Olson, Martie, I 27
Olson, Mrs. Ken, I 26
Olson, Mannie, I 52
Olson, Red, II 190
Olson, Sigurd, I 136
Olympic, Evon, II 89
O'Neill, Jack, I 21
ONONDAGA, cutter, I 53
Onstad, Judith, II 21
Oogevaseuk, Stanley & Alex, II 106
Oogruk, I 115, 167; II 152
Oomiak, I 73
Opheim, Edward Nikolia Sr., II 175
Ophir, I 85
Oppedal, Antone, I 107
Ordeals, I 6, 20, 33, 35, 38, 39, 44, 53, 59, 72, 83, 86, 87, 100, 104, 110, 120, 129, 137, 138, 140, 149, 161, 165, 168, 170, 175, 181, 190, 191; II 21, 28, 32-3, 36, 64, 76, 82, 84, 87, 116, 142, 149, 162, 170, 179, 184
ORLANDO, U.S.S., I 57
Orlov, Vladimir, II 139
Ornstein, Honora, *see* Diamond Lil
Orr, Arthur, I 108
Orr, Sharon, II 157
Orrick, Betty, I 154
Ortell, George, I 33
O'Shea, Jack II 35
Oskolkoff, Father Simeon, II 53
Ostlund, Doug, I 149
Ostrum, Charlie, II 37
Ott, Martin, II 43
Otter, *see* Land otter; Sea otter
Otto, Ray, I 50
OURINGONDY, scalloper, II 95
Ousterhout, Gerald, II 66
Overwik, Tom, I 149
Owens Brothers, loggers, I 58
Owens, J.E. & Patsy, I 26
Owls, I 86, 119; II 24
Oxereok, Danny, II 128
Oyster, I 3; II 12

P

Pacific Lighting (Service) Corp., II 153, 162, 172
Pacific Northern Airlines, I 78; II 7, 54, 98
Packard, Sy, I 144
Padersen, Mrs. Fred, I 6
Palm, John, I 67
Palmer, I 102, 114, 181, 195; II 61, 122, 169, 170, 176, 181
Palmer, Bob, II 174
Palmer, Capt. James A., II 121
Pamplona Rock, I 200
Pan American Airways, I 13, 17, 36, 39, 46, 50, 62, 65, 69, 72, 117, 123, 136, 195; II 14, 42
Pan American Petroleum Corp., II 34, 41, 52, 61, 66, 103
Paneak, Raymond, II 66
Paneak, Simon & Roosevelt, II 163
Paneok, Mrs. Nita & son, II 40
Parka squirrel, I 47, 201
Parkas, I 36; II 80, 171
Parker, Al, II 11
Parker, E.W., I 48, 52
Parker, M/M Fred B., II 9
Parker, Patrick, I 194
Parking garages, II 88
Parking meters, I 115, 150; II 88, 107, 133
  "anti-meter maid," II 168
Parks, George A., II 77
Parrish, Lance, II 77
Parsons, Fred, II 148
Parsons, Fred W., I 138
Parsons, Michael, II 129
Parsons Hotel, Anchorage, II 148
Pastall, Paul, I 168
PATHFINDER, survey vessel, I 200
PATRIOT, M.V., II 181
Patton, Edward L., II 127, 137, 153, 169, 180
Patty, Dr. Ernest N., I 195; II 29
Patty, Ernest N. Jr., I 71
Patty, Mrs. Kathryn Stanton, II 29

Index

Paul, Raymond, I 151
Paul, Sam Jr., II 62
PAVEL CHEVATNIAGIN, factory ship, II 59
Payne, Mrs. Eloise, II 187
Payne, Capt. Harold, II 142
Peacock, Jim, II 103
Peacock, Percy, I 7
Pearce, Walter H., I 95
PEARL, tug, I 63
Pearson, Alex, I 57
Pearson, Grant, I 50, 66, 171
Pearson, Joyce, II 141
Pease, M/M Francis, I 191
Peck, Cyrus E., I 174
Peck, Jack, II 92
Pecora, Dr. William, II 117, 128, 153
Pedersen, Einar, II 87
Pedersen, Lieutenant, II 3
Pederson, Mrs. Lena, II 146
Pedro, Felix, I 82, 201
Peirce, Walt, II 80
Pelican City, I 110, 147; II 35, 52
Penetuck, Edward, I 39
Penguins, I 194
PENNEY, J.C. CO.
    Anchorage, II 63, 88, 114, 160
    Fairbanks, II 83
Pennington, Dick, I 156
Pennington, Lloyd L., I 161
Pennock Island, I 189
Pensions, *see* Old-age assistance
Peratrovich, Mrs. Selina, II 176
Perela, La Raine, I 88
Perkins, Elmer, I 61
Permafrost, I 124; II 92, 125, 128, 137, 164, 179, 192
Perot, H. Ross, II 116
Perry, Rod, II 190
Perry, Starr H., I 69
Petajahn, Dr. Jack H., II 76
Pete, Frankie, II 178
Peter, M/M Marvin & Daisy Mae/Lloyd, II 195
Peter, Richard, II 41
Peters, Cara, II 190
Peters, M/M J.A., I 91
Petersburg, I 4, 12-4, 82, 155, 187, 194, 198; II 37, 43, 71
Petersburg Fisheries, II 71
Petersen, Raymond, II 98, 99
Peterson, M/M Arthur, II 134
Peterson, Charlie, II 178
Peterson, Charles, I 128
Peterson, M/M Charles, I 180
Peterson, Don, I 82
Peterson, Ernest, I 58
Peterson, John, I 138
Peterson, Obert, I 75
Peterson, Ray, I 128
Peterson, Mrs. T.A., I 6
Peterson, W. Jack, II 190
Petrich, Capt. J.H., I 63
Petticoat Gazette, newspaper, II 58, 71
Petticrew, Joe, I 62
Pettit, Bruce, II 6
Pfeuffer, Hans, I 44
Phelps, Al, II 89
Phillips, Brad, II 117, 127
Phillips, E.C. & Son, II 163
Phillips Petroleum, I 143; II 77, 80
Phillips, Vance, II 105
Philpott, Lon, I 79
Piamuit, I 32, 172
Pichler, Joe/Normal, I 83
Picton, Dr. John O., II 145
Pike, Allen, I 14
Pilferage, cargo, I 73, 129
Pinkerton, James G., I 184; II 62
Pinkham, Harry, II 2
Pinska, Martin, I 45, 77
PIONEER HOMES
    Fairbanks, II 81, 86
    Sitka, I 100, 105, 110, 173, 178; II 39, 48, 81, 86
PIONEER, river boat, I 134
Pioneers, I 65, 82, 83, 185; II 50. *See also* individuals by name; Pioneer Homes.
Pipelines, oil/gas, II 2, 4, 19, 74, 101, 103, 105, 107, 127, 144, 169, 170, 172, 174, 177
    Alyeska Pipeline Service Co., II 125, 127, 134, 137, 141, 150, 153, 156, 158, 163, 169, 180, 184, 187, 192, 194, 198
    Arctic Gas Pipeline Co., II 180, 189, 198
    El Paso Alaska Co., II 198
    El Paso Natural Gas Co., II 166, 180, 189
    Trans-Alaska Pipeline System, II 111, 112, 119, 124, 125
    wartime, I 36, 42, 45, 51, 60, 72
Piracy, I 6, 115; II 12
Pitts, Fred, I 170
PLANTS
    poison, I 106
    wild edible, I 120
Platinum, I 9, 15, 175; II 47, 51
Pleasant, Betsy, II 168
Plover, II 8

Plum, Grace, I 47
Plummer, Judge Raymond E., II 136, 148, 197
Poachers, I 9, 17; II 20
Point Hope, I 61, 159, 188; II 33, 47, 60, 97, 111, 125, 158, 196
Polet, Antonio & Alvin, I 127
Police, I 114, 164; II 88, 158
Poling, John, II 16
Pollack, Frank, I 38, 58
Pollock, Howard, II 72, 124, 127
Pollution, *see* Environmental concerns
POMARE, M.S., I 108
Pool, Bob, II 22
Population, I 14, 21, 24, 44, 60, 78, 106, 117, 124; II 15, 53, 55, 79, 85, 110, 111, 121, 124, 126, 140, 152, 182, 198
Porcupine, I 163; II 50
Porcupine River, I 118, 150
Port Althorp, II 16, 116
Port Chilkoot, II 25, 109, 113
Port Heiden, II 123, 156
Port Lions, I 54
Portage, II 48
Porter, Fred, II 94
Porter, Walter, II 25
Portman, William, II 104
Post, M/M Ely, I 26
Post, Rex, II 138
Post, Wiley, I 47, 94, 137; II 42, 56
Potlatch, I 16; II 116, 123
Potter, George, I 56
Potts, Fred, II 87
Powyouruk, Jerry, II 33
Pratt, Jack, I 16
Pribilof Islands, I 12, 19, 37, 44, 63, 71, 86, 103, 119; II 18, 42, 66, 73, 79, 89, 131
Price, Warren, II 138
PRINCE GEORGE, S.S. I 51, 72
PRINCE GEORGE, S.S. (new), I 102
Prince Rupert, I 40, 107, 108, 130; II 28, 90, 152
PRINCE RUPERT, S.S., I 64
PRINCESS KATHLEEN, S.S., I 125
PRINCESS LOUISE, S.S., II 39, 72
PRINCESS SOPHIA, S.S., I 125
Prisoners of war, I 51, 55, 57, 77
Proffokof, Alex, I 77
Prospect Creek, II 135, 136
Prospecting, *see* Mining
Prospector statue, I 110
Prudhoe Bay, II 125, 169, 193. *See also* Oil/gas.
    3,500-Mile sea haul, II 181
Providence Hospital, Anchorage, II 67, 72, 114, 187
PTARMIGAN
    Alaska bird, I 150
    hunting, I 27, 67, 122, 139
PUENTE HILLS, tanker, I 57
Pullen, Col. Daniel D., I 68
Pullen, Harriet (Ma), I 31, 68, 117; II 11
Pulp/paper, I 5; II 75
    mill, Ketchikan, I 79, 86, 95, 124, 126, 143; II 48
    mill project, Juneau, I 126, 186; II 68, 79, 97, 109, 115, 118, 124, 136, 143, 197
    mill, Sitka, I 79, 141, 159, 184, 196
Pure Oil Co., II 43
Pusey, Roy, I 152
Pushruk, Simon, II 157
Pusich, Michael & family, I 142
Putvin, William, I 97

Q

Queen Bess, *see* Cross, Bess
QUEEN OF PRINCE RUPERT, II 90
Quicksand, I 120
Quigley, Fannie, I 18, 41, 182, 193
Quigley, Joseph P., I 41, 193
Quinn, Capt. F.B., I 200
Quintal, Tim, II 77
Quirk, Mrs. Devon T., II 73

R

RCA Alaska Communications, II 108, 117, 126, 148, 182
Raatikainen, Kalle, I 147
Rabbits, I 113, 121; II 171
Radak, Tony, I 188
Rader, John, I 196
Ragel, Prof. Richard, I 92
Railroads, II 158, 172, 182
    Alaska, I 29, 45, 50, 72-3, 77-8, 83, 122, 124, 131, 146, 148, 158, 181; II 5, 64, 71, 111, 115, 136
    Alaska Central, I 77; II 29
    Copper River (Iron Trail), I 11, 14, 32, 81, 103, 150, 183; II 17, 58
    Klondike Mines, II 25
    Seward Peninsular (Pupmobile), I 10, 39
    White Pass & Yukon, I 31, 42, 72, 117, 161; II 13, 25, 47, 56, 58, 62, 87, 89, 113, 168
Rainbird, II 140
Ramos, Mrs. Elaine, II 163

Rampart Canyon, I 196; II 78, 141
Ramstead, Joe/Phillip, I 150
Randall, Norman, I 21
Randall, M/M R.E., I 103
Rapp, Albert/Ole, II 3
Rapuzzi, M/M George, II 11, 85, 159
Rapuzzi, Ma, II 11
Rasmuson, Elmer, II 170
Rasmuson, Mrs. Elmer, II 115
Rasmusson, Pilot Elmer, I 93
Ratcliffe, Capt. Chet, I 194
Rausch, Dr. Robert, II 134
Raven, I 165
Ray, Dr. Dixy Lee, II 183
Reams, Walt, II 73
Rearden, Jim, II 78
Rearick, Guy, II 148
Rebarchek, Ray, II 113, 189
REBECCA, tanker, II 91
REBEL, fishing vessel, II 191
Red Dragon Parish Hall, Cordova, II 20
Redington, Joe, II 17, 173, 190
Redington, Joe Sr., II 190
Redington, Ray, II 6
Redington, Rayme, II 190
Reed, A.S., I 178
Reed, Ed, I 60
Reeder, Mrs. LaVonne, I 96
Reese, Eldon, II 174
Reetz, Augie, II 95
Reeve Aleutian Airways, I 120, 137, 177; II 170
Reeve, Bob, I 41, 81, 101, 127, 177; II 99
Reeves, Jay B., II 196
Reeves, Tom, II 184
Regan, Bob, I 99
Reid, Rev. Robert H., I 93
Reifsteck, Ted, I 172
Reimnitz, M/M Rudi, II 75
Reindeer, I 6, 8, 9, 15, 17, 20, 22, 31, 35, 49, 62, 114, 119, 124, 147, 148; II 2, 29, 36, 74, 78, 98, 101, 143, 151, 194
Reinosky, Franklin, II 99
RELIANCE I, halibuter, I 75
Rengard, Sam, II 62
Rensch, Joe, II 162
Renshaw, Ray, I 11, 26
Renshaw, Robert, II 173, 190
Resoff, Pete, II 97
Resurrection River Road, II 86
Reynolds, Bert, II 2
Rhoads, James, II 197
Rhode, Clarence, I 26, 28, 91, 123, 130, 139, 145, 148, 160, 161, 187, 196
Rhode, Jack, I 187, 196
Ribar, Dr. Charles, II 115
Rice, Bill, I 127
Rice, Don, I 38
Rich, Bert, I 94
Rich, Paul, II 7
Richardson, Bud, I 109
Richardson, Fred, II 92
Richardson Highway (Valdez Trail), I 65, 75, 85, 83, 98, 126, 145, 154, 169, 183, 201
Richardson, Gen. Wilds P., I 201
Richfield Oil Corp., I 177, 180, 189, 190; II 7, 19, 33, 35, 37, 38, 41, 42, 51, 61. *See also* Atlantic Richfield Co.
Richter, Francis Liddicoat, II 11
Rigling, Mark, II 179
Rigsby, Walt, II 25
Rinear, Berman, I 83
Rinehart, Jimmie, II 144
Ringstad, George, I 168
Ripple Rock, I 152, 185
Risk, Donald, II 193
Ritchie, Al, I 60; II 21
Ritchie Transportation Co., II 21
Ritti, Commander, R.A., II 59
River boats, I 2, 6, 9, 16, 23, 29, 50, 90, 116, 131, 134, 155, 181, 185; II 9, 12, 13, 21, 27, 28, 30, 81, 112, 117, 162, 194. *See also* individual boats.
Rivers, Ralph J., II 14, 72
Rivers, Victor C., I 153
Riverside Mine, II 26
Robbins, Dale, I 178
Robbins, James S., I 26
Roberson, Ken, I 171
Robert, George, II 120
Roberts, Harold, I 112
Roberts, Mrs. James H., II 90
Roberts, Joe, I 54
Roberts, Kay, II 49
Roberts, Sandy, II 54
Robertson, Edward A., I 21
Robertson, Edwin A., I 21
Robinson, Fulton C., I 193
Robinson, Howard, I 102
Roden, Henry, I 146; II 48
Rogan, Ed & family, I 155
Rogers, Lawrence, I 51
Rogers, Morris T., I 164
Rogers, Will, I 47, 94, 137; II 42, 56
Roguska, Colleen, II 197

Roland, Dale, II 169
Rollins, Gen. Andrew P. Jr., II 187
Romig, Dr. H.G., I 29
Ronan, John, I 183
Rooney, Bob, II 191
Roosevelt, President Franklin D., I 41
Rorrison, L.P., I 99
Rose, Bob, I 113
Rose, Capt. George, I 185
Rose, Robby, II 68
Rosenberger, M/M Smokey & Gary/James, II 82
Rosenbush, Buck, I 93
Ross, Alec, I 20
Ross, Barbara, II 184
Ross, Beatrice, I 26
Ross, Capt. George, II 9
Ross, Gerald D., I 113
Rotman, Louis, I 136
Rottier, Jack, II 181
Rowe, Bishop Peter Trimble, I 123; II 20
Rowland, M/M David & children, II 135
Royal Canadian Air Force, II 130
Royal Canadian Mounted Police, I 57; II 105, 150
Royce, Dr. William F., II 5, 22
Ruby, I 29
Rudd, Olin, I 139
Rude, Dr. Joseph O. & Donald, I 168
Rude, Stanley & Orville, I 175
Rumohr, John, I 15, 44
Runge, Mary Ellen, I 123
Rungee, Fred, II 69
Rusing, E.J./Russell, I 136
Russell, James, I 127
Russell, M/M James H., I 170
Russell, John, II 85
Russell, John, II 179
Russia, I 23, 44, 80, 115, 134, 154, 168, 178, 182, 186; II 1, 2, 4, 38, 42, 46, 59, 60, 67, 70, 73, 75, 81, 85, 94, 105, 176, 189. *See also* Russian Alaska.
Russian Alaska, I 20, 24, 71, 75, 115, 138, 144, 150, 179, 189, 190, 200; II 5, 13, 23, 31, 34, 64, 65, 73, 89, 139, 165. *See also* Churches.
Rust, Clara, II 168
Ryan, Bill, II 129
Ryan, M/M Conrad, I 88
Ryan, Mrs. Irene, II 132
Ryan, Dr. James C., II 116
Ryan, Most Rev. Joseph, II 198
Ryan, Lillian, I 88
Ryan, Patrick, II 94

S

Saario, S.T. (Bud), II 59
Sackett, John, II 81, 97, 102
SACKETTS HARBOR, tanker, I 57, 157
Sageak, Morgan, II 145
Sager, Hubert, I 83
St. Ann's Hospital, Juneau, II 94, 143
St. Clair, M/M Jimmy, II 43
St. George Island, I 6, 119; II 18, 131
Saint Herman, II 111, 175
St. Joseph's Hospital, Fairbanks, II 94
St. Lawrence Island, I 27, 36, 39, 77, 84, 115, 151, 154, 157, 158, 170, 178, 186; II 1, 2, 36, 40, 49, 53, 84, 127, 133, 143, 158
St. Mary's, II 82, 157, 179
St. Mary's Mission School, II 64
St. Matthew Island, I 148
St. Michael's Cathedral, Sitka, II 65, 83, 111, 165
St. Paul Island, I 6, 119; II 18, 79, 131, 184
St. Regis Paper Co., II 68, 79
ST. ROCH, schooner, I 45, 63, 180
Saleen, Paul, I 155
Salmon, I 21; II 128
    caviar, II 52
    commercial, I 5, 11, 16, 61, 67, 84, 88, 182; II 26, 37, 47, 51, 61, 71, 84, 89, 191, 193
    limited entry, II 89, 174, 195, 198
    packs, I 88, 135, 171; II 2, 84, 139
    prices, I 13, 19, 95, 105
    record, commercial, I 13
    record, sport, I 168; II 140, 145, 184
    sport, I 103, 128, 154, 168, 175; II 31
    sport derbies, I 77, 111, 124, 153, 174; II 39, 126, 141, 145, 162, 181, 192
    stake net, I 23
    trap, I 26, 50, 63, 74, 79, 89
    trap piracy, I 6, 115
Salvation Army, II 111
Sam, Bergman, I 172, 197
Sam, Harry, I 104; II 32
Sampson, Steven, I 121
Sampson, Wilbur, II 6
Samuel, Joe, I 41
Samuelson, John, II 147
Sand dunes, II 35
Sand, gravel, I 175; II 47, 51
Sand Point, II 20
Sande, Ed, II 8
Sande, Wes, I 91
Sanders, Norman, I 194

Index

Sanders, Judge William H., II 85
Sands, Clarence M., I 20
Sandstrom-Anderson Construction Co., II 179
Sangris, Peter, II 154
Sarapushkin, Gregory, II 60, 67
Sarber, Hosea, I 15, 52, 65, 83
Sargent, Charles, II 115
Sarles, Father, II 57
SARSI, tug, II 154
Sarvela, Mrs. Myrth, I 170
Sarvis, John, II 196
Sassara, Charles, II 127
Sasseene, Tiny, I 63
Satellite earth station, II 98, 107, 126, 133
Sather, Martin, I 140
Satko, M/M Paul & family, I 29, 182
Sato, Kunio, II 49
Saunders, Jerry, I 95
Savage, Patrick, I 179
Savard, Ernest, I 58, 66
Savin, Alex, II 139
Savoonga, I 154, 158, 170, 178; II 53, 72, 127, 143
Savoy Bar building, Fairbanks, II 91
Sawmills, I 113; II 109, 197
 Ketchikan, I 19, 22; II 115
 Wrangell, I 58; II 53, 75
Sayers, Hallet, II 181
Scallops, II 88, 95, 98
Schaible, Dr. A.J., I 47
Schaller, George B., I 156
Schaub, Herb, I 63
Schlesinger, James, II 150
Schlossberg, Ben Jr., II 95
Schmaltz, Father Gerassim, I 60
Schmidt, Louis, I 58
Schmidtke, Clifford, I 64
Schmitt, Ron, II 160
Schmoyer, Cathy, II 193
Schneider, Speed, II 61
Schoenberger, pilot, I 72
Schofield, Mrs. Robert, I 107
Scholarship, II 77, 95, 192
Schomburg, Irvin, I 186
Schools, I 133, 146, 161, 193; II 10, 44, 47, 53, 83, 106, 114-6, 123-5, 151, 166, 169. *See also* Natives.
 unusual studies, II 97, 133, 146-7, 149, 152, 171
Schooner's Bend Bridge, I 182
Schrioch, Joan, II 168
Schuerch, Lorenz, II 102, 164
Schultz, John, II 173
Schwahn, M/M Art, I 98
Schwamm, M/M Tony, I 25, 121
SCHWATKA, river boat, II 9
Scotch Cap, I 59; II 50
Scott, Hugh, I 162
Scott, John D., I 9
Scott, Vallie, II 85
Scouten, Cal, II 141
Scud, Bernard, II 175
Sea elephant, I 15
Sea lion, I 178
Sea otter, I 75; II 5, 23, 67, 77, 85, 90, 136, 183
Sea turtle, I 39
Seal, *see* Fur seal; Hair seal
Sealaska Corp., II 187
Seaman, Betty, II 162
Searfus, Cathy, II 145
Searle, Fred, II 126
Seattle Post-Intelligencer, I 143
Seavey, Dan, II 173, 190
Secession, I 44; II 174
Secord, Jack, II 142
See, Mrs. Connie, I 174
See, Frank Jr., II 138
Seeds, Cyrus H., I 54, 73
Seemel, Bob, II 159
Seetot, Reuben, II 190
Seghers, Bishop Charles J., I 37
Seinfield, Dr. Edward, I 47
Selanoff, Norman, II 97
Selawik, II 171
Seldovia, I 88, 117; II 58
Selective Service, I 48; II 70
Selig, William, I 11
Selman, Guy, II 19
Semple, John, I 64
Seppala, Asle, II 3
Seppala, Leonhard, I 117, 129; II 3
Seppala, Sigurd, II 3
Seppilu, Mrs. Mary & children, II 53
SEREM of Alaska, Inc., II 130
Servant, Sister Victori, II 189
Service, Robert W., I 149, 154, 158, 172
Seveck, Asogook, I 159
Seward, I 117, 166, 199; II 29, 57, 58, 64, 71, 86, 95, 126, 145, 149, 162, 191
 earthquake, II 44, 46, 48
Seward, Bob, I 120
Seward Day, I 189; II 73
Seward, William H., II 73, 79
Seward's Success, II 133, 172
Seyfert, Ed, I 181
Shaeffer, William, II 145

Shakes, Chief, I 16; II 123, 157
Shakes Island, II 157
Shaktoolik, II 4
Shanly, John J., II 96
Shapley, Kathy, II 68
Shapsnikoff, Mrs. Anfesia, II 155
Shark, I 50, 91; II 22, 126, 141
Sharp, Frank, II 144
Sharp, Robert, II 182
Sharratt, Lloyd, II 191
Shavings, Edward, II 21
Shaw, George, II 12
Shawback, Harry, II 130
Sheep, Dall, I 166; II 59
 hunting, I 139, 147, 152, 162, 193; II 127
 record, I 134
Sheep farms, I 11, 16, 36, 49, 82, 184; II 50
Sheill, John, I 155
Sheldon, Charles A., II 19
Sheldon, Don, I 101; II 76
Sheldon Jackson College, II 145, 163, 197
Sheldon Jackson School, II 81, 83
Sheldon, Mrs. John, II 19
Sheldon, Nita, II 174
Sheldon, Robert (Bobby), I 183
Shellabarger, Leon, I 148
Shellabarger, Max, I 32, 127
Shell Oil Co., I 180, 190; II 26, 35, 38, 41, 42, 46, 101, 131, 169, 170, 192
Shemya Island, II 28, 152
Shepard, Mrs. Ted & George, I 159
Shepherd, Beatrice, I 120
Shepherd, Ed, I 99; II 85
Shepherd, Peter, I 173
Sherrod Elementary School, Palmer, II 169
Sherrod, Max, I 181; II 106, 113
Sherwood, Donald, II 126
Shewchuk, Ken, II 161
Shields, Mary, II 190
Shinn, Bob, II 87
Ships/shipping, I 4, 10, 12, 16, 18, 27, 39, 48, 83, 111, 127, 129; II 19, 39, 52, 135, 152, 191. *See also* individual ships; Shipwrecks.
 ghost ships, II 179, 181
 longest strike, II 145
Shipwrecks/small-boat casualties, I 2, 11, 24, 59, 64, 78, 97, 121, 125, 149, 170, 178, 191; II 13, 30, 37, 43, 66, 86, 102, 103, 150, 164, 179, 191. *See also* individual ships.
 fatalities, I 38, 49, 53, 57, 94, 110, 152, 155, 168, 175, 179, 185, 188; II 10, 53, 97, 100, 109, 132
 salvage, I 60, 62, 108
Shishmaref, II 117, 165, 191; II 141
Shockley, Mike, II 193
Short, L.C., II 30
Shough, Harry, I 73
Shrimp, II 81, 106, 133, 153
Shungnak, II 19
Shuster, Gentry W., I 64
Siberia, *see* Russia
Sidney, Robert L., II 128
Siems, Robert, II 169
Sierra Club, II 104, 118, 124, 127, 134, 136, 143, 146, 162, 195, 197
Silbak Premier Mines, II 26
Silcock, Burton W., II 178
Silver, II 30
 United Keno Silver Mines, II 57
Simienoff, Fred, I 38
Simmerville, Don, I 179
Simmett, Mrs. Rachel, II 194
Simmond, Thomas, I 158
Simon, Mrs. Sarah, I 153
Simons, Andrew A. (Andy), I 5; II 31
Simons, Dean, II 162
Simonsen, Mrs. Ruth, I 170
Simpson, Mrs. Belle, I 160; II 34, 37
Simpson, Earl, I 153
Simpson, Dr. Robert, II 37
Sims, Alyce, I 15
Sims, Bill, II 129
Sims, Dr. Foster R., I 104
Sinclair Oil Co., II 33, 55
Singer, Fritz, II 127
Sinn, Sgt. Walter, I 164, 176
Siple, M/M Greg, II 164
Sissons, Judge J.H., II 70
Sitka, I 44, 75, 82, 150, 170, 174, 182, 190; II 13, 14, 43, 62, 69, 71, 80, 82, 86, 145, 162, 183
 Japonski (John O'Connell Memorial) bridge, II 90, 143
 National Historical Park, II 165
 National Monument, II 147
 Naval Air Base, I 54
 New Archangel Dancers, II 139
 Pioneer Home, I 100, 105, 110, 173, 178; II 39, 48, 81, 86
 pulp mill, I 79, 141, 159, 184, 196
 St. Michael's Cathedral, II 65, 83, 111, 165
SITKA MARU, II 81
Sitkalidak Island, I 71, 82; II 47
Sjogren, Don, II 193

Skagway, I 20, 31, 184; II 11, 48, 56, 61, 74, 84, 87, 162
 Itjen, Martin/streetcar, I 20, 37, 117; II 159
 Pullen, Harriet (Ma), I 31, 68, 117
 Smith, Soapy, I 37, 117; II 85
 White Pass & Yukon Route Railroad, II 47, 62, 89, 113, 168
Skal, Ottokar, II 111
Skarland, Ivar, I 67
Skeen, E.G., I 193
Skelly Oil Co., II 80
Skiing, I 9, 199; II 3, 77, 88, 92, 110, 134, 145
Skolka, David, I 115
Skoog, Ronald, II 194
Skookum Jim (Klondike co-discoverer), I 158; II 19, 188
Skov, Louis/Nancy, I 188
Slater, Ben, I 163
Slater, M/M George, II 74
Sled-dog races, II 139, 141
 Anchorage/Alaska, I 97, 151, 197; II 6, 154, 188
 Fairbanks/North American, I 1, 8, 82, 88, 89, 110, 121, 172, 197; II 6, 9
 Iditarod, II 173, 190
 Nome-Candle, I 76, 117
 women's, I 129, 151, 172, 197; II 6
Slim, Frank, II 13
Slot machines, II 50, 89
Slwooka, Mrs. Joe, II 106
SMARAGD, scalloper, II 95
Smedley, Dr. Dennis, II 141
Smith, Alexander (Sandy), II 185
Smith, Alexander (White Horse), I 36
Smith, Alison, II 21
Smith, Aloysius, II 2
Smith, Barney, I 3
Smith, Bob, II 37
Smith, Edwin A., I 167
Smith, Eli A., I 76
Smith, Everett E., I 69
Smith, Frank & Roland, I 95
Smith, George, II 130
Smith, H.G., I 134
Smith, Herb, II 194
Smith, James, II 118, 125
Smith, John C., I 40
Smith, Rev. Kenneth, I 180
Smith, M/M Loren & family, I 82
Smith, Murray C., I 43
Smith, Norman, I 118
Smith, Dr./Mrs. R.C., I 198
Smith, Dr. Raymond L., II 82
Smith, Mrs. Robin, II 148
Smith, Richard, II 10
Smith, Soapy, I 37, 117; II 85, 159
Smith, Stan, II 14
Smith, Theron, I 196
Smith, Thomas S., I 55
Smithers, Carl, I 83
Smoke, Horace (Holy), I 104, 110, 121; II 32
Smoke, John, I 104
Smyth, Bud, II 190
Snag, Y.T., II 72
Snapp, Tom, II 89
Snepp, Lorenzo, I 74
Snettisham hydro project, II 85, 110, 112, 149, 190
Snider, Heinie, I 75
Snodgrass, Lawrence, I 112
Snow, C.R., I 94
Snowmobiles, I 134; II 7, 88, 91, 94, 98, 99, 100, 102, 103, 141, 143, 158, 164, 166, 170
 races, II 86, 102, 136, 141
 Wasilla Grand Prix, II 148
Snowshoes, II 30, 122; II 50, 124
Snyder, Dan, I 97; II 162
Soares, M/M Manual, I 173
Soderbaum, Fred, I 1
Soderberg, Pat, II 176
Sol Lines, Ltd., II 186
Soldin, M/M Hans, II 11
Soldotna, II 36, 162
Solinger, Paul, II 60
Solomon, Paul, II 60
Somerville, Ron, II 185
Sommerville, Bernard, I 187
SONYA, fishing vessel, I 62
Soule, Agnes, *see* Newhall, Rev./Mrs. Albert
Soule, Tommy, I 97
Sourdough starter, II 14
Sourdoughs, I 65, 158. *See also* individuals by name.
 Rendezvous, II 120, 139
Sours, Eugene/Freddie, I 160
Southcentral Timber Co., II 197
Southern California Gas Co., II 162
Southern Lights, II 144
Soviet Union, *see* Russia
Spahr, Charles E., II 156
SPAR, cutter, I 180
Sparks, Louis R., II 13
Sparks, M/M Vic, II 11
Sparks, M/M Winfield, II 11
Spaulding, Dale, II 40

SPEED QUEEN, fishing vessel, I 188
Speer, Otis H., I 27
Spencer, David L., II 15
Spring, Herbert, I 134
Sprowl, Lieut. Robert, I 81
Sputnik, I 182
Squires, R.L., I 14
Stahr, Rudolph, I 1
Stajeli, Lee/Bonnie, II 53
Stall, M/M Vern, I 141; II 18
Standal, John, I 9
Standard Oil Co. of California, I 190; II 2, 7, 19, 26, 35, 37, 38, 41, 43, 61, 98, 112, 187, 192
Standard Oil of Ohio, II 117, 126, 156
Stanley, Paul, I 141
Stansk, Joe, II 77
Starbuck, Stewart, I 109
Starr, Jim, I 69
State of Alaska, *see* Alaska
Statehood, I 48, 60, 63, 106, 138, 189
STATEN ISLAND, cutter, II 125
Steel, Robert, II 14
Steele, Mrs. Lee, II 74
Steelhead, I 75; II 5, 96
 record, II 132
Steers, Nancy, I 153
Steers, Vince, I 153
Stefansson, Vilhjalmur, II 33
Steffen, Ed, I 124
Steinbrecher, Robert/Marjorie, I 107
Stella, Marc, II 40
Stenberg, Marv, II 17
Stensland, John, I 89
Stensland, Tilden, I 46
Stepetin, Tikhon, II 88
Stephen, Walter M., II 156
Stephl, John L., I 143
Stepovich, M/M Michael, I 178, 179
Stern-wheelers, *see* River boats
Stevens, B. Dickerson, II 127
Stevens, Bud, II 103
Stevens, Gary, II 172
Stevens, John, II 130
Stevens, Ted, II 108, 117, 127, 129, 131, 156, 163, 177
Stevens Village, I 104
Stewart, Angus, II 13
Stewart, B.C., *see* Hyder-Stewart
Stewart, B.D., I 79
Stewart, George, II 168
Stewart, Capt. James, I 72
Stewart, Tom, II 109
Stewart-Watson Lake Highway, II 164
Stickman, Joe, I 172
Stickman, Walter, II 57
Stikine River, I 2, 16, 19, 60, 114; II 21, 27, 81, 141
Stikine Transportation Co., II 81
Stiley, William, II 37
Stimaker, Nelson, II 161
Stitt, Richard, II 115
Stockley, Clint, I 110
Stoecker, Bob, II 6, 17
Stokes, Dick, II 157
Stokes, Col. Robert C., I 119
Stolen, Ernie Jr., II 55
Stone, Dave, II 157
Storfold, Mrs. Marian, I 165
Storhavg, Rolf, II 87
STORIS, cutter, II 51, 59
Storrs, Dr. Henry G., II 29
Stover, Milo, II 193
Strand, Fred, II 31
Strandberg, Harold, II 94
Strauss, Ricky, II 95
Stretton, James/Sheila, I 170
Strode, Don, II 161
Strong, Benjamin F., II 88
Stubbs, Jesse, I 137
Stuck, Hudson, II 133
Studdert, Jeff, I 123; II 79
Sturgeon, I 163
Sturrock, Mike, II 138
Sullivan, Bud, I 184
Sullivan, George, II 94
Sung, Bruce, I 186
SURVEYOR, survey vessel, I 20
Susitna (Little) River, I 9; II 4, 144
Sutherland, Dan, I 146
Sutherland, Robert, I 137
Svendberg, Pete, I 78
Svendsen, Charles, I 155
Swans, II 74, 182
Swanson, Dale, II 146
Swanson, David P., II 41
Swanson, Margaret, II 30
Swanton, Harry, I 48, 49
Sweazey, M/M Manley, M 43, 138; II 55
SWEETBRIER, cutter, II 132, 164
Swift, Dan, II 79
Swift, W.H., II 124

Index

T

Tagg, Chris, II 25
Tagish River, II 68
Takotna, I 94
TAKU CHIEF, river boat, II 21
Taku Contractors, II 149
Taku Lodge, I 165
TAKU, state ferry, II 37, 39, 43, 56, 132, 179
Talbot, Bill, I 78
Talkeetna, I 101; II 5, 35, 65, 76, 98, 107, 126, 133, 194
Tamura, Mamie, I 49
TANA, river boat, I 2
TANANA, freighter, II 29
Tanana River, I 9, 13, 46, 50, 57, 77, 85, 90, 93, 131, 155, 162; II 7, 21, 27, 30, 90-1, 110, 154, 174
raft classic, II 122
TANANA, towboat, I 131; II 21
Taplin, Mrs. Sammye, II 138
Tassie, Capt. F.J., I 69
Taxation/government, I 14, 56, 79, 85, 89, 101, 196; II 48, 55, 59, 72, 117, 122, 147, 158, 160, 169, 174, 193
bond issues, II 21, 84, 129, 166, 183
elections, I 48, 63, 79, 81; II 14, 57, 72, 92, 110, 113, 126-7, 142, 147, 165, 168, 197
first Legislature, I 146; II 48
miscellaneous income, I 195; II 29, 51
oil leases/royalties, I 184; II 7, 10, 34, 40, 51, 55, 58, 61, 71, 103, 105, 108, 111, 117, 124, 153, 163, 168, 169, 177
old-age assistance, I 19; II 72, 122, 174, 175, 188
salaries, II 41, 47, 70
Taylor, Bill, I 133
Taylor, Chuck, II 154
Taylor Highway, I 112; II 166
Taylor, Ike P., I 112
Taylor, Marvin, II 168
Taylor, Sgt. S.J., II 2
Taylor, Stephen A., II 85
Taylor, Walter, II 85
Teeth, false, I 21, 54, 188
Tega, Charles, I 142
Telegraph Creek, I 2; II 27, 81
Telephone/telegraph, I 15, 47, 62, 123, 132, 162, 179, 185; II 18, 35, 57, 73, 97-9, 102, 107-8, 111, 117, 126, 133, 141, 148, 182, 183, 193
Television, I 139; II 114, 116, 133, 149, 163, 184, 190
Telgenhoff, Ted, II 126
Teller, I 6, 161, 176; II 150
Tennant, Mrs. Paula A., I 170
Tenneco Oil Co., II 105
Terwilliger, Fred, I 163
Tesoro-Alaskan Petroleum Corp., II 112, 117
Tessier, Virginia, II 154
Tetlin, I 93
Tetlin-Northway basin, II 35
Texota Oil Corp., I 168
Teya, William, II 120
Thayer, M/M Elton, I 140
Thecia, Sister, II 64
Theile, Ann Louise, I 32
Theodosius, Bishop, II 100, 111
Thibault, Rollie, II 171
Thibbert, Alfred M., I 25
Thibedeau, M/M Juel & children, I 138, 176
Thiele, George, I 138, 185
Thom, Mrs. Miriam, II 126
Thomas, Franklin R., I 108
Thomas, Jacob, I 115
Thomas, James, II 105
Thomas, Lowell Jr., II 195
Thomas, Lowell Sr., II 195, 196
Thomas, Paul, I 100
Thomas, Robert L. & Nancy, II 84
Thomas, Stanley, II 99
Thompson, Denny, II 129
Thompson, Edna, I 141
Thompson, Mary (Goat Mary), I 90
Thompson, Stan, II 7
Thompson, Stanley F., II 182
Thompson, Tom, I 115
Thorne Bay, II 191
Thorpe, Sven (Whitey), II 153
Ticket, Herman, I 49
Tidal waves, I 59; II 44, 45, 46
Tides, record high, I 82; II 32, 58
Tillotson, Candy/Judy, II 111
Tilson, Lloyd, I 130
Tim, Dan, II 182
Tin, I 7, 135
Lost River Mining Corp., II 152
Tisserand, Eldred, II 141
Titus, Fred, II 145
Titus, Virgil, I 197
Tiulana, Paul, II 157
Tjonveit, Thor, II 87
Tlingets, I 16, 75, 92, 107, 119, 135, 138, 159, 168, 174, 179, 189, 200; II 5, 14, 69, 81, 105-6, 109, 115, 117, 123, 135, 147, 163, 174, 178, 182, 185. *See also* individuals by name.
land settlement, I 200; II 105
shelling of Angoon, II 185
Toayak, Enoch, I 93
Todd, Albert, II 75
Togiak, II 27, 103
Tok, I 88, 92, 105, 112; II 83, 107, 144
Tokeen, I 26; II 79
Tokeina, John, II 51
Toksook, Bay, II 100
Tolbert, J.W., I 59
Tolmie, Jack, I 126
Tom, Frank, II 140
Tom, Chief/Mrs. Peter, I 168, 179
Tongass Island, I 136, 143
Tongass National Forest, I 16, 23, 79, 160, 200; II 51, 79, 117, 162
Tony, M/M Paul & Karen/Paul Jr./Peter, II 26
Tony, Tony, II 42
Tootkaylook, Mrs. Katie, II 100
Torgerson, Mae, II 32
Tornberg, Bruce & Kurt, II 149
Torres, Al, I 115
Tourism, *see* Travel
Totem poles, I 16, 20, 105, 123, 143, 189; II 14, 73, 109, 117, 123, 135, 140, 147
restoration, I 16; II 147, 157
Townsend, Harry, I 134
Townsend, Constable Warren, II 105
Traffic fatalities, II 7
Trafton, William, I 179
Trans-Alaska Pipeline System, II 111, 112, 119, 124, 125. *See also* Alyeska Pipeline Service Co.
Trapping, *see* Furs
Travel/tourism, I 12, 45, 46, 94, 102, 105, 173; II 12, 27, 39, 158, 164, 182. *See also* individual companies.
restrictions, I 31, 35, 45, 57, 76, 99
Traxler, Glen & Eugene, II 87
Trefzger, Hardy, I 90, 150
Tremarello, Ann, II 92, 126
Tremblay, Raymond H., II 9
Trent, Mrs. Marcie, II 163
Trepte, Mike, I 96
Triber, Casey, I 107
Trimble, Roderick, I 12
Trindle, J.R., I 1
Triplett, Woody, I 25
Tritt, Allen, II 64
Trondsen, Capt. Christian, I 53
Trout, I 3, 13, 44, 52, 102, 107, 130
Truck transportation, I 67, 85, 88; II 104, 113, 144, 187, 195
Truelson, George, II 91
Trueman, Imo, I 149
Truestead, Tom, II 87
Tsimpsheans, I 42, 64, 123, 200. *See also* individuals by name.
Tuberculosis, I 87, 106; II 177
Tucker, Mrs. Minnie, II 92, 127, 142
Tuna, II 163
Tunguk, Edwin, II 157
Tununak, II 29
Turcotte, Lawson P., I 95, 124
Turenne, William, I 25
Turnagain Heights, Anchorage, II 45, 78
TUSTUMENA, state ferry, II 39, 100
TUTSHI, river boat, II 194
Tuttle, Harold, II 31
Tuzroyluk, Thomas, I 93
Tuzroyluke, Seymour, II 196
Twitchell, A.H., I 94
Tyler, E.L., I 181
Tyonek, I 95, 123, 132; II 54, 71, 80, 146

U

U-V Industries, II 179
Udall, Stewart L., II 69
Uglowook, Doris, II 2
Uglowowook, Don Harry, II 51
Ulah, Mrs. Mamie, I 149
Ulmer, Joe, I 43, 55
Umnak Island, I 11, 16, 55, 89, 184
Unalakleet, II 47, 69, 168
Unalaska Island, I 13, 36, 49; II 50, 57, 72, 150, 184
Unimak Island, II 50, 150
Union Oil Co., I 177; II 4, 7, 59, 67, 93, 114, 118
Union Marathon Oil Co., II 66
Union-Texas Petroleum Co., II 43
United Keno Silver Mines, II 57
U.S. Air Force, I 112, 137, 162; II 28. *See also* individual bases; U.S. Army.
U.S. Army/Air Force, I 36, 39, 41, 42, 46, 55, 85, 111, 135; II 10, 18, 144. *See also* individual bases; U.S. Air Force.
Corps of Engineers, I 196; II 62, 64, 81, 85, 141
U.S. Coast & Geodetic Survey, I 1, 20, 75, 90, 200
U.S. Coast Guard, I 75, 180; II 36, 50, 59, 60, 101, 121, 135, 142, 144, 158, 164, 177, 181, 186, 189. *See also* individual cutters.
Bering Sea patrol, II 51
lights, lighthouses, II 31, 98, 100, 110
U.S. Fish & Wildlife Service, *see* Fish & Wildlife Service
U.S. Forest Service, I 79, 159, 162; II 31, 51, 68, 79, 97, 118, 124, 136, 138, 143, 162, 197. *See also* Forests.
U.S. Geological Survey, I 79; II 52, 73, 170
U.S. Immigration & Naturalization Service, II 156
U.S. Navy, I 14, 36, 42, 54, 55, 74, 76, 151, 157, 176; II 18, 140, 158, 185
Petroleum Reserve #4, I 90, 132; II 48, 57, 180
U.S. Plywood-Champion Papers, Inc., II 97, 109, 115, 118, 124, 136, 143. *See also* Champion International, Inc.; Champion Papers, Inc.
U.S. Smelting, Refining & Mining Co., I 184, 193; II 42, 147
U.S. Steel Corp., II 128
University of Alaska, I 56, 92, 97, 167, 195-6; II 49, 73, 75, 96, 125-6, 131, 133, 140-1, 144-6, 150, 158, 192
attendance, I 14, 23, 62, 105, 171; II 92, 128
Museum, I 109, 145; II 72, 155, 163, 175
Unuk River/Valley, I 4, 12, 29, 31, 63, 70, 77, 84
Uranium, I 102; II 31, 75, 90
Urie, Sol, II 64, 73
Urquhart, Robert, II 91
Utech, Mike, I 127

V

VI, halibut boat, II 177
Valdez, I 65, 105, 120, 123, 183; II 61, 63, 92, 126, 134, 145
earthquake, tidal wave, II 44, 46, 53
pipeline terminus, II 105, 107, 111, 112, 134, 137, 146, 172, 180, 198
Valentine, M/M Bill, I 163
Valley of 10,000 Smokes, I 50; II 12
Van Bibber, M/M Alex, II 104
Vandalism, I 112; II 75
Van Der Laan, Hans, II 147
Vandermar, Marjorie, I 155
Van Duren, Mrs. W.L., *see* Klondike Kate
Vaneltsi, Abe, II 120
Van Enkevort, Marianne, II 145
Vania, John, II 90
Van Kirk, Guy/Lloyd, I 24
Vantrease, Jack, I 129
Van Wyhe, George, II 110
Vaudrin, Bill, II 190
VELVET, seiner, II 158
Venes, Lillian, II 145
Venetie, II 64
Vent, Bobby, II 173, 190
Vent, Warner, II 6, 17, 190
Vesper, H.G., II 7, 38
Veteran bonus, I 56, 79
VICTORIA, S.S., I 23, 56, 85, 141
Vierick, Leslie, I 140
Viet Nam War, II 73, 84, 116
VIKING QUEEN, scalloper, II 95
Villesvik, Phyllis, I 168
Vincent, Capt. Donald, I 138
Vincent, Leon S., I 42, 47
VIRGINIA CITY, R.V., II 81
Vissers, Joe, II 154
Vittrekwa, Fred/Jim/William, II 120
VIVIAN JUNE, fishing vessel, I 62
Vodicka, Maj. Robert, II 41
Vogel, M/M Oscar & Mary, I 96; II 186
Vogler, Joe, II 174
Volcanoes/eruptions, I 1, 39, 41, 50, 88, 132, 141; II 12, 14, 50, 67
Vollmer, Adella, I 6
von der Heydt, Judge James A., II 168, 189
Vroman, Robert, II 103

W

W.H. BERG, tanker, II 19
WACHUSETT, cutter, II 51
Wacker, Eugene, I 79, 98
Wackowitz, Fred, II 7
Wade, Hugh, I 173; II 72
Wade, Mrs. Katherine, II 57
Wagner, Darrold & Nancy May, I 10
Wagner, Paul, I 27
Wagner, Russ, II 160
Wakefield, Howard, II 29
Wainwright, I 51; II 96
Walatka, John, I 17
Walatka, Mark, II 145
Wales, I 21, 60, 67, 94, 128, 190
Walker, M/M D.C., I 66, 81
Walker, Earl, I 112
Wallace, Amos, I 189; II 63, 73
WALLACE LANGLEY, stern-wheeler, I 2
Wallen, Jane, II 117
Waller, Charles, I 140
Waller, Ed, I 38
Walrus, I 115, 134, 158, 160, 196; II 51, 72, 105, 127
hunting, I 44-5, 84, 146, 148, 154, 158; II 10, 70, 96, 128, 133
Sea Mammals Protective Act, II 157
Walunga, Willis, I 157
Wanamaker, James, II 145
War games, II 79
Warber, Paul, I 85
Ward Cove Packing Co., II 139
Ward, Edward L., I 193
Ward, Joseph J., II 11
Ward, Rev. R.C.W., II 86
Ward, Robert, II 127, 129
Wardlow, M/M Clyde, II 22
Waselie, Laurence, I 149
Washburn, M/M Bradford, I 30, 66, 94, 114
Washington-Alaska Military Cable & Telegraph System, II 73, 141
Wasilla, I 20, 73, 75, 83; II 148
Wassilie, M/M Simeon & children, I 161
Wassillie, Accenia, I 39
Wassillie, Nick & Elia, I 130
Water supplies, I 56, 68, 104, 137, 142, 148, 171; II 13, 69, 70, 88, 102, 140, 152, 172, 185
Waters, William C., II 21
Watkins, Les, I 95
Watson, Craig, II 164
Watson, John, II 62
Watson, M/M Willard A., II 20
Watt, Mrs. Mary Etoline, II 34
Watts, James, I 26
Watts, Murray, II 152
Waverick, Paul, I 13
Waybum, Dr. Edgar, II 156
Weather extremes, I 7, 39, 53, 62, 65-6, 68, 97, 105, 116, 118, 127, 129, 154, 161, 198; II 42, 52, 62, 98, 100, 102, 109, 112, 114, 135, 152, 170, 196
record cold, II 72, 136
Weaver, Capt. F.R., I 149
Webb, Herman, I 13
Webb, Mrs. J.W., I 178
Weber, O.L., I 12
Weber, Terry, II 145
Weeden, Robert B., II 79, 104, 118
Weisz, Wilbert, II 136
Weitzel, Chris, I 69
WELCOME, fishing vessel, I 49
Welfare, II 38, 84, 101, 110, 111, 146
Wellbaum, E.W., II 169
Wellington, Pat, II 193
Wells, Charles Merle, II 100
Wells, Lt. Lewis, I 149
Wells, Ray, II 50
Wells, Mrs. Ward W., II 18
Welsh, M/M Dewey, II 4
Welsh, Mrs. Jennie, I 175
Welty, Charles, I 122
Wentland, Debbie, II 176
Werner, M/M Joseph, II 63
Werner, Karen, II 63
Wescott, Bob, II 6
Wescott, Libby, I 197; II 6
West, Earl, I 133
West, George, II 106
Westcott, Lt. Commander Richard N., II 135
Western Airlines, II 98, 187
Western Frontier Oil & Refining Co., II 99
Westlake, Larry, I 197
WESTWARD, halibuter, II 183
Wetche, Fred & Fred Jr., I 110, 147
Whales, I 11, 25, 57, 76, 102, 113, 122, 127, 159, 163, 180; II 80, 82, 126, 141, 142, 160, 178
commercial whaling, I 27, 118; II 8, 69, 80
hunting, sport/subsistence, I 7, 42, 65, 84, 175 198; II 19, 40, 106, 125, 157, 158, 196
Native festivals, I 97, 133, 166; II 158
Sea Mammals Protective Act, II 157
Whaley, Frank, I 47, 73, 159, 178
Whaley, Frank B., I 178
Wharton, Francis, I 188
Wheeler, Mrs. Ida, I 173
Whipple, Tim, II 77
WHISTLER, M.V., II 97
Whistling swan, II 182
White, Al, I 183
White Alice network, II 18, 102, 108
White, M/M Ferris L. & Ferris Jr./Matthew, I 50
White, Frank, I 139
White, Harold, II 68
White, Dr. Leslie A., I 17
White, Mrs. Morrie, I 75
White Pass & Yukon Railroad, I 31, 42, 72, 117, 161; II 13, 20, 25, 47, 56, 58, 62, 87, 89, 113
mercy train, II 168
White, Dr./Mrs. Robert & David, II 132
White, Deputy Marshal Sam, I 54
White, Sam O., I 7, 24, 177
White, Shirley, II 162
White, Tim, II 190
Whitehorse, I 42, 45, 69, 72, 107, 149, 158, 186; II 9, 12-3, 28, 36, 42, 86, 88, 94-5, 98, 106, 112, 117, 120, 125, 128, 133, 139, 141, 145, 168, 179, 188, 194, 196
WHITEHORSE, river boat, II 30, 194
Whitehorse Star, II 88, 98, 168
Whiteout, II 58

Index

Whitmarsh, Vern, **I** 18
Whitney-Fidalgo Seafoods, **II** 150
Whitt, Earrie, **I** 197
Whittaker, Jim, **II** 76
Whittier, **I** 45, 133; **II** 41, 44, 74, 149, 183
Wholecheese, Mrs. Eleanor & son, **II** 40
Wichman, Dr. George, **II** 76
Wickersham House, **II** 94
Wickersham, Judge James, **I** 116; **II** 9, 16, 50
WICKERSHAM, M.V., state ferry, **II** 94, 132, 135, 151, 179, 183, 186
Wickstrom, Alf/Ingvas, **I** 49
Wickstrom, M/M Carl, **II** 26
Wieber, M/M R.L. & sons, **I** 194
Wiedemann, Sgt./Mrs. Stefan J., **I** 190
Wien Alaska Airlines (Air Alaska), **I** 23, 38, 60, 120, 158, 173, 193; **II** 42, 51, 53, 56, 92, 195
Wien, Fritz, **II** 51
Wien, Merrill, **II** 195
Wien, Noel, **I** 173; **II** 51, 99, 195
Wien, Ralph, **II** 95
Wien, M/M Robert P. & Robert, **II** 95
Wien, Sig, **I** 62; **II** 51
Wiesner, Fritz W., **I** 64
Wigg, George, **II** 162
Wilderness, *see* Environmental concerns
Wilderness Society, **II** 104, 134, 156, 158
Wilke, Jim, **II** 145
Wilkins, Sir George Hubert, **I** 176, 194
Willard, Rev./Mrs. Eugene S. & daughter, **II** 10
Williams, Art, **I** 128
Williams, Bob/Dave, **II** 141
Williams, David J. Sr., **II** 174
Williams, Frank, **II** 47
Williams, George C., **I** 119
Williams, Glenn, **I** 109, 145
Williams, James A., **II** 90
Williams, Jeff, **I** 112
Williams, Ken, **I** 122
Williams, M/M L.B., **I** 73, 96
Williams, Lew, **I** 94, 124, 157
Williams, Maxcine, **I** 106
Williams, Mike, **I** 19; **II** 12
Williams, Pete, **I** 90
Williams, Ralph B., **II** 2

Williams, M/M William C. & Edna May, **I** 32
Willis, Rev. Bernie, **II** 190
Willmarth, Dick, **II** 173
Willoughby, Professor, **I** 131
Wilson, Dr./Mrs. A.N., **I** 91, 130
Wilson, Dr. Charles R., **II** 93
Wilson, George W., **I** 89
Wilson, Harry H., **I** 148
Wilson, Jack, **II** 87
Wilson, Capt. John, **I** 159
Wilson, Leonard H., **I** 171
Wilson, Mary Al, **II** 181
Wilson, Wayne, **II** 128
Windsor Hotel, Cordova, **I** 172; **II** 160
Wine patent, **II** 176
Wingren, Paul, **II** 71
WINONA, cutter, **II** 181
Winter Haul Road, **II** 104, 122, 192, 195, 198
Wiseman, **I** 21, 128, 148, 173; **II** 51, 195
Witchcraft, **I** 172
Wohlforth, Eric, **II** 132, 137, 138
Wolf, **I** 1, 12, 18, 21, 23, 28, 31, 43, 56, 65, 67, 84, 101, 108, 138, 153, 160, 176, 198; **II** 22, 26, 181, 188, 190
  airborne hunting, **I** 25, 27, 46-7, 50, 72, 93, 109, 116, 121, 132, 139, 141
  attacks/stalking, **I** 9, 15, 20, 30, 31, 42, 47, 61, 77, 90, 93, 129, 144, 177; **II** 107, 143, 146
  bounties, **I** 4, 14, 17, 56, 60, 87, 173; **II** 56, 100, 118, 126, 182
  hunting/trapping, **I** 5, 7, 14-5, 20, 22, 24, 29, 30, 36, 38, 52, 61, 68-70, 72, 100, 112, 177; **II** 21, 171
Wolfe, Al, **I** 47
Wolverine, **I** 19, 72, 100, 112, 122, 159, 173; **II** 29, 56, 89, 100, 171
Wood, Andy, **I** 126
Wood, Ginny, **II** 77, 79, 183
Wood, Commander Harold L. & Timothy, **I** 180
Wood, Joe, **I** 41, 46
Wood, Morton, **I** 140
Wood, M/M Robert, **I** 59
Wood, Ron, **II** 87
Wood stove, **II** 186
Woodman, Isaac, **II** 61

Woods, M/M Charles, **I** 173
Woods, Fred, **I** 24
Woodworking, **II** 33
Wooldridge, Glen, **II** 125
Wooley, Betty, **II** 190
Woolford, Ray, **I** 73, 122, 141
Wooten, Ralph, **I** 77
Workman, Harper, **I** 173
World War II, **I** 14, 19, 25, 26, 29, 32, 35, 36, 37, 38, 39, 41, 48, 54, 57, 68, 90, 130
  Aleut evacuees, **I** 30, 37, 39, 44, 45
  Battle of Attu, **I** 118; **II** 49, 143
  Canol Oil Project, **I** 42, 51, 60
  civilian casualties, **I** 38, 51
  Dutch Harbor bombing, **I** 55
  Navy ships lost, **I** 76
  planes for Russia, **I** 44
  prisoners of war, **I** 51, 55, 57, 77
  travel restrictions, **I** 31, 35, 45, 46, 57
  veteran bonus, **I** 56, 79
Worrell, Billy, **II** 52
Woslyng, Bev, **II** 116
Wrangell, **I** 2, 16, 19, 58, 80, 88, 115, 142, 154; **II** 27, 34, 53, 71, 75, 81, 112, 123, 125, 126, 141, 146, 154, 157, 162, 193
Wrangell Institute, **I** 142
Wrangell Lumber Co., **II** 75
WRANGELL MARU, **II** 75, 81
Wren, Pat, **II** 196
Wright, Alfred E., **I** 69
Wright, Annie, **I** 109
Wright, Gareth, **I** 97, 197
Wright, Laura, **II** 80
Wright, Mrs. Vera, **I** 197
Wybrew, Bert, **II** 138

Y

Yackwan, Jack, **II** 182
Yakataga, **I** 42, 92, 143; **II** 71, 72
Yakutat, **I** 111, 200; **II** 1, 163
Yates, Charles, **I** 48
Yellowknife, **I** 61; **II** 107, 130, 154, 181, 187
Yevtushenko, Yevgeny, **II** 75

Yoinkovich, Villey, **I** 42
York, Joe, **II** 52
Yost, Randolph, **II** 52
Young, Don, **II** 165
Young, M/M Lyman, **I** 188
Young, Paul, **I** 69
Young, Dr. S. Hall, **II** 10
Yuk dialect, **II** 124
Yukon Consolidated Gold Corp. Ltd., **I** 87
YUKON HEALTH, stern-wheeler, **I** 181
Yukon River, **I** 1, 6, 7, 20, 41, 49, 85, 90, 94, 116, 131, 134, 155, 165, 185; **II** 7, 9, 12, 21, 27-8, 30, 72, 157, 162
YUKON, S.S. **I** 53, 57
YUKON, stern-wheeler, **II** 30
Yukon stove, **II** 186
YUKON, tanker, **II** 103
Yukon Territory, **I** 33, 65, 79, 107, 117-8, 134, 144, 161, 180; **II** 28, 30, 91, 95, 104, 118, 138, 147, 149, 161, 183, 185, 193, 196
  Canol Oil Project, **I** 42, 51, 60
  Klondike, **I** 30, 62, 87, 92, 158, 169; **II** 16, 19, 25, 77, 110, 112, 125, 175, 188
  Service, Robert W., **I** 149, 158, 172
YUKON, towboat, **I** 131; **II** 21
Yutana Barge Lines, **II** 21
YUTANA, river boat, **I** 134

Z

Zager, Melody A., **II** 167
Zarro, Phil, **II** 196
Zeigler, Tex, **I** 83
Zeusler, Adm. F.A., **II** 36
Ziegler, A.H., **I** 126
Ziegler, Eustace Paul, **I** 150
Ziemer, Gil, **II** 47
Zimmerman, Tony, **I** 52
Zinkowitz, Fritz, **I** 168
Zunker, Terry, **II** 104
Zuvon, Al, **II** 141

FROM TERRITORIAL DAYS TO STATEHOOD...

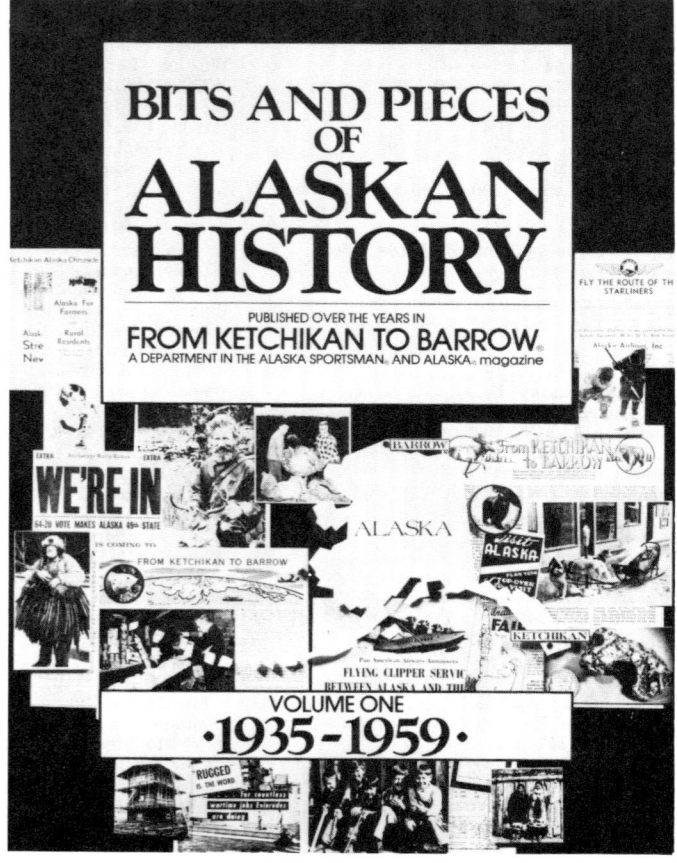

...FROM KETCHIKAN TO BARROW®...
Don't miss a bit of it! If you don't already have a copy of *Bits and Pieces of Alaskan History,* Volume I, get yours today. From the first issue of *The ALASKA SPORTSMAN®* in 1935, *From Ketchikan to Barrow®* has been one of the most popular features in the magazine. Get all the news of that first quarter century in Volume I, covering 1935 to 1959. Pick up your copy where you purchased Volume II, or write direct to Alaska Northwest Publishing, Box 4-EEE, Anchorage, Alaska 99509. It's $14.95 too, and please include $1 for postage and handling when ordering direct.